# Europ
# MUSEUM
# Guide

# 97 98

**Publisher**
Museum Media Publishers

**Editorial director**
A.B. van der Lans

**Cover design & lay-out**
Marc Heymans

**Print**
Drukkerij Dröge

**Binding**
In Otabind by Binderij Hexspoor

Museum Media Publishers
Stationsstraat 28
P.O. Box 154
5260 AD  Vught
The Netherlands
Telephone  +31 73 684 03 13
Telefax      +31 73 656 96 34
Internet     http://www.museumguide.com
e-mail       museumguide@tip.nl

*Although this guide has been compiled with the greatest care and attention, Museum Media Publishers cannot accept responsibility for the consequences of any error or inaccuracy appearing in the European Museum Guide.*

**MUSEUM MEDIA PUBLISHERS**

We are proud to present the European Museum Guide '97|'98. This Guide is special: it describes both the permanent collections and the temporary exhibitions of museums in twelve European countries.

Details are conveniently listed according to country.
The entry for each country begins with a map showing the cities where the museums are situated. The information regarding each museum follows under the names of the cities, arranged in alphabetical order.

If you are interested in a particular exhibition, we suggest you contact the museum to verify, as details may change at short notice.

Museum Media Publishers operates independently and guarantees the editorial neutrality of the European Museum Guide.

We wish you plenty of enjoyment with the European Museum Guide, and we hope it puts you on the track of interesting museum visits.


Museum Media Publishers

*A.B. van der Lans*
*Editorial director*

# CONTENTS　3

# Graz

## ALTE GALERIE DES STEIERMÄRKISCHEN LANDESMUSEUMS JOANNEUM
Neutorgasse 45  8010 Graz  Director: Gottfried Biedermann
☎ +43 316 80174770  🖷 +43 316 80174847
Open: Tuesday-Friday 10.00-17.00  Saturday, Sunday 10.00-13.00
Closed: Monday

**COLLECTION**

**The Middle Ages**  The collection focuses on Styrian art and includes the 'Procession Cross', 'Madonna of Admont', 'Reicheneck Epitaph Picture', pietàs from Admont, 'Madonna with Corona', 'Votive Tablet of St. Lambrecht', 'Martyrdom of Thomas Becket' and the 'Small and Large Miraculous Altar of Mariazell'.
**Renaissance, Mannerism and Baroque**  Dutch and Flemish masters: Herri met de Bles, Jan and Pieter Brueghel, Hendrik de Clerck, Josse de Momper, Bartholomäus Spranger, Cornelis de Vos and Philips Wouwerman.

Pieter Brueghel the
Younger (1564-1638)
*The fairground,*
*detail*
© Landesmuseum
Joanneum, Abteilung
Alte Galerie, Graz

**Italian masters:**  Sofonisba Anguissola, Luca Cambiaso, Giacomo Francesco Cipper, Dosso and Battista Dossi, Teodoro Ghisi, Giambologna, Giovanni Pietro de Pomis and Rosa da Tivoli.
**German and Austrian masters:**   Lucas and Hans Cranach, Franz Christoph Janneck, Veit Königer, Franz Anton Maulbertsch, Johann Georg Platzer, Johann Michael Rottmayr, Kremser Schmidt, Johann Heinrich Schönfeld, Josef Thaddäus Stammel, Paul Troger and Hans Adam Weissenkircher.

**EXHIBITIONS**

No exhibitions planned.

## Graz

**LANDESMUSEUM JOANNEUM, BILD- UND TONARCHIV**
Sackstraße 17/II  8010 Graz  Director: Armgard Schiffer-Ekhart
☎ +43 316 830335  🖷 +43 316 844797
Open: Monday Tuesday Thursday 08.00-16.00  Wednesday Friday 08.00-13.00
Closed: Saturday and Sunday

COLLECTION

**Photography**  The main themes of this collection are (local) art, architecture and landscape. The archive contains more than half a million negatives and 60 000 positives, as well as 50 000 slides on various subjects. The earliest photographs date back to 1840. Documentations of cultural manifestations and political events are present, and various material on the history of photography.
**Sound recordings**  The collection includes gramophone records, tapes, cassettes and CD's; for the most part the recordings cover regional events and persons.
**Moving images**  Though small (150 films), the film collection contains a number of productions which are of great local importance, such as documentation of a prisoner-of-war camp in Styria in 1914-1915 and films of the reconstruction of Graz between the world wars. There is also a video collection consisting mainly of recordings from local television.

EXHIBITION
11·10·97-11·11·97

[JOANNEUM ECKSAAL, NEUTORGASSE 45, GRAZ]
*Berique & Sebastianutti*   *5 Photographers, 4 Generations, 3 Continents*

## Innsbruck

**TIROLER VOLKSKUNSTMUSEUM**
Universitätsstraße 2  6020 Innsbruck  Director: Hans Gschnitzer
☎ +43 512 584302  🖷 +43 512 582682
Open: Monday-Saturday 09.00-17.00  Sunday 09.00-12.00

COLLECTION

**Arts and crafts, popular art**  The museum is situated in an old monastery building next to the Court Church (Hofkirche) that includes the tomb monument of Emperor Maximilian I.
The Tyrol Museum of Popular Art houses a large collection of popular arts and crafts representing everyday life and customs in the German and Romance speaking regions of Tirol from the close of the Middle Ages to present times.
The most memorable parts of the permanent exhibition are the Gothic, Renaissance and Baroque parlours that illustrate the lifestyles of the aristocrats, the middle-class and the peasants. Other exhibits include rustic furniture with rich carving and colourful painting, models of old Tyrol farmhouses, original costumes from the valleys and an impressive collection of cribs.

EXHIBITION
06·06·97-Sep 97

*Gardens and Parks*   Since the late 1970s, historical gardens and parks have come to be appreciated as part of Western Europe's cultural heritage. This exhibition is intended to make local people and foreign visitors aware of this cultural heritage and to point to hidden paradises in the Alps.

# Linz

**NEUE GALERIE DER STADT LINZ/WOLFGANG-GURLITT-MUSEUM**
Blütenstraße 15  4040 Linz  Director: Peter Baum
☎ +43 732 70703600  📠 +43 732 236190
Open: Monday-Saturday 10.00-18.00  Thursday 10.00-22.00
During summer Saturday 10.00-13.00
Closed: Sunday

**COLLECTION**

The New Gallery in the city of Linz is one of the most important museums of modern and contemporary art in Austria. The museum possesses a collection of 1170 paintings, sculptures and objects, nearly 8000 drawings, watercolours and works of graphic art, as well as a catalogue and poster collection.

Oskar Kokoschka
(1886-1980)
*Linz (Landscape around Linz), 1955*
© Neue Galerie der Stadt Linz

The collection also includes 600 original pen drawings of the artist Kubin, who died in 1959. This 'Kubin Cabinett' is the third largest collection of his works in the world.
In the Central European Art Collection a special emphasis has been placed on the landscape paintings of the 19th century, as well as the German and Austrian Expressionists.
The most important works of the collection include paintings by Liebermann, Corinth, Thöny, Kokoschka, Klimt, Schiele, Hofer, Mueller, Pechstein, Kolig, and Nolde, among others.
The Gallery's collection also includes works of Informal and Pop Art, Concrete Art, and Geometrical Abstraction. In addition, Austrian contemporary art and examples of international avant-garde art are represented, with works by many prominent artists.

**EXHIBITIONS**

until 18·05·97    **Markus Prachensky**  *On the 65th Birthday of the Artist*

until 25·05·97    **Maconde and Mapico Masks**

22·05·97-29·05·97    **Association of Friends of the New Linz Gallery**  *Avramidis, Appel, Damisch, Scheibl, Lüpertz and others*

05·06·97-14·09·97    **Hermann Nitsch**  *Retrospective*

25·09·97-02·11·97    **Osamu Nakajima & Joshitatsu Yanaguihara**  *Sculptures*

# Salzburg

**RESIDENZGALERIE SALZBURG**
Residenzplatz 1  5010 Salzburg  Director: Roswitha Juffinger
☎ +43 662 840451  📠 +43 662 840451-16
Open: Daily 10.00-17.00

**COLLECTION**    The current collection of Old Masters continues the tradition of the

Episcopal art collection in the historical setting of the Residence Palace. It was founded in 1789, but was short-lived due to political causes. In 1923 the Residenzgalerie Salzburg was newly founded in the form of a county gallery. 41 paintings of the Austrian collection of Count Rudolf Czernin were purchased by the county of Salzburg in 1980. In 1994 the 70th painting of this collection was bought, meaning that the main bulk of the Czernin collection is now in the Residenzgalerie. In addition, 28 of the best paintings from the Schönborn-Buchheim Collection have been on loan to the museum since 1956.

The main focus of the Residenzgalerie Salzburg is the exhibition of Austrian and German painters, together with a range of Italian, Flemish, Dutch and French masters offering a good selection of European painting of the 16th, 17th and 18th centuries. Austrian 19th-century landscape works provide a better understanding of a famous period in Austrian painting. Special attention is devoted to the fact that Salzburg played a significant role as a meeting point for many painters of the Romantic period.

**EXHIBITIONS**

until 02/07/97 | ***Copper Rust and Shield Louse***   Masters of the Residenzgalerie Salzburg and their Working Methods

20·07·97-24·09·97 | ***Dream Images of the Orient***   *Austrian Painters of the Orient in the 19th Century*

30·10·97-28·02·98 | ***Heavenly Messengers - Devilish Fellows***   *Selected 18th-Century Portrayals of Angels*

## Salzburg

**RUPERTINUM**
**Wiener-Philharmoniker-Gasse 9  5010 Salzburg  Director: Otto Breicha**
**☎ +43 662 80422541   🖷 +43 662 80422542**
**Open: Tuesday-Sunday 10.00-17.00  Wednesday 10.00-21.00; during summer exhibitions: Tuesday-Sunday 09.00-17.00  Wednesday 09.00-17.00**
**Closed: Monday**

**COLLECTION**

The focus of the collection (paintings, sculptures, works on paper, mainly graphics) concentrates on the European art of the turn of the century (Kollwitz, Barlach, Kubin, Dix) down to the Austrian avantgarde (Arnulf Rainer, Günter Brus, Ch.L. Attersee). The 'Österreichische Fotogalerie' is in possession of stocks of over 10 000 works in the field of contemporary Austrian photography.

An intensive range of changing and special exhibitions focuses on artists and tendencies of European contemporary and recent art developments. Two floors, a sculpture hall on the ground floor and the 'studio' continuously present special exhibitions, the first floor of the house is dedicated to the presentation of its own collection stocks.

**EXHIBITIONS**

08·05·97-06·07·97 | ***Christo & Jeanne Claude***   *Models and Collages for Project Works 1969-1995*

15·05·97-15·06·97 | ***Rössing Prize 1997***   *Presentation of the Prizewinner*

18·07·97-19·10·97 | ***Wilhelm Thöny (1888-1949)***   *Pictures and Works on Paper from Private Collections*

04·09·97-19·10·97 | ***Peter Krawagna***   *New Works*

09·10·97-23·11·97 | ***The Hellmut Czerny Donation***   The Presentation of the Hellmut

Czerny Donation, featuring work by Rudi Stanzel, Michael Kienzer, Werner Reiterer and others.

20·10·97-30·11·97   ***Creative Workshop and Presentation of the Work***   *Still-life Today - Demonstrating a Feeling for Life*

30·10·97-Jan 98   ***John Heartfield***   *Title Page Designs for the Arbeiter Illustrierten Zeitung/Volksillustrierte and Orginal Photomontages, Berlin 1930-1938*

11·12·97-Feb 98   ***Christian Rohlfs***   *Tempera Works*

## Wien · Vienna

**GEMÄLDEGALERIE DER AKADEMIE DER BILDENDEN KÜNSTE**
Schillerplatz 3  1010 Wien  Director: Renate Trnek
☎ +43 1 58816225  🖷 +43 1 5863346
Open: Tuesday, Thursday, Friday 10.00-14.00
Wednesday 10.00-13.00 / 15.00-18.00  Saturday, Sunday 09.00-13.00
Closed: Monday and 1 Jan, 1 May, 1, 2 Nov, 24, 25 Dec, 31 Dec, Good Friday, Easter Sunday, Whit Sunday, Corpus Christi

COLLECTION

**Old Masters**   Part of this collection is formed by the works of 14th to 18th-century Italian masters, including Botticelli, Titian, Testa, Giordano, Tiepolo and Guardi. A number of Spanish and French artists from the same period are also represented, among which Murillo, Subleyras and Hubert Robert. The main core of the collection, however, consists of works from Northern European painting schools, including Early Netherlandish and German paintings such as Bosch's 'Last Judgement' and Baldung Grien's 'Rest on the Flight'. A large part of the collection is made up of 17th-century Dutch paintings: Rembrandt's 'Portrait of a Young Woman' and Pieter de Hoogh's 'Family Group in a Courtyard' are just two examples. Works by Jacob van Ruisdael, Asselijn, Both and Berchem are also on display.

Hieronymus Bosch
*The last Judgement,*
*tryptich detail*
© *Gemäldegalerie*
*der Akademie der*
*bildenden Künste,*
*Wien*

**19th Century**   The academic tradition of the gallery is expressed through its 18th and 19th-century collection, consisting primarily of works by Austrian artists, such as Meytens, Brand, Wutky, Quadal, Waldmüller, Füger and Führich.

EXHIBITIONS

No exhibitions planned

## Wien - Vienna

### GRAPHISCHE SAMMLUNG ALBERTINA
Augustinerstrasse 1  1010 Wien  Director: Konrad Oberhuber
☎ +43 1 53483  📠 +43 1 5337697
Internet http://www2.telecom.at/albertina
Open: Monday-Thursday 10.00-16.00  Friday-Sunday 10.00-13.00

**COLLECTION**

Situated in the centre of Vienna, the Albertina Collection is one of the most important collections of prints and drawings in the world. The most valuable treasures are shown in changing exhibitions, sometimes in combination with loans from all over the world. 50 000 drawings and approximately 1.5 million prints represent the cultural heritage of our past, constantly enriched with works by contemporary artists.

Wilhelm Thöny
*New York, 1933*
*Aquarel*
© Graphische
Sammlung Albertina,
Wien

At the Albertina, visitors can view a great number of masterpieces by Raphael, Dürer, Rembrandt and Rubens, as well as drawings from other European artists spanning the centuries.
Since 1920, the collection has comprised the former collection of Duke Albert of Saxe-Teschen and his wife the Archduchess Mary-Christine and the collection of the former imperial library. Together they represent one of the largest collections of prints in the world, with materials dating back to the beginning of printmaking in the 15th century. Special collections are Architectural Drawings, Posters, Miniatures and Illustrated Books.

**EXHIBITIONS**

| | |
|---|---|
| 06·05·97-15·07·97 | *Ludwig Attersee* |
| 06·05·97-15·07·97 | *Hildegard Joos* |
| 06·05·97-15·07·97 | *Masterpieces of the Albertina Museum*   Originals and Facsimiles |
| 16·09·97-Nov 97 | *German Drawings from the Time of Goethe* |
| Dec 97-Jan 98 | *Acquisitions of the Austrian Ludwig Foundation for the Albertina, Part II* |
| Dec 97-Jan 98 | *Expressionist Graphics in the Albertina* |

## Wien - Vienna

### ÖSTERREICHISCHE GALERIE BELVEDERE
### AUSTRIAN GALLERY BELVEDERE
Prinz Eugenstraße 27  1030 Wien  Director: Gerbert Frodl
☎ +43 1 795570  📠 +43 1 7984337
Open: Tuesday-Sunday 10.00-17.00
Closed: Monday and 1 Jan, 1 May, 1 Nov, 24, 25 Dec

**COLLECTION**

The Austrian Gallery Belvedere provides a broad survey of Austrian art. In the two Baroque castles of the Belvedere complex, the former summer residence of the famous Austrian General Prince Eugen of Savoy, a great many of the major works produced by Austrian artists over the last nine centuries are on display. After the general renovation of the Belvedere castle most parts of the permanent collection are already reopened to the public.

Egon Schiele
(1890-1918)
*Four Trees, 1917*
© Österreichische
Galerie Belvedere,
Wien

The collection 'Art around 1900' presents major works of Austrian art at the turn of the century and places them in the context of the development of international art (Gustav Klimt, Egon Schiele, Oskar Kokoschka, Vincent van Gogh a.o.). The main art currents of 19th century art are shown in the section 'Historicism-Realism-Impressionism' with words of Hans Makart, Carl Schuch, Claude Monet, Auguste Renoir, a.o. The collection of 'Classicism-Romanticism' and 'Biedermeier' (C.D. Friedrich, F.G. Waldmüller a.o.) will be reopened in June 1997. Medieval art with emphasis on late Gothic in Austria is on a new display in the Orangery. In the Lower Belvedère Baroque art is shown in historically preserved rooms like the Hall of Grotesques, the Marble Gallery and the Cabinet of Gold, Austrian Baroque painting and sculpture is represented by G.R. Donner, F.X. Messerschmidt and Paul Troger.

**EXHIBITIONS**
until 15·06·97 | *Rudolf Hoflehner*

until 22·06·97 | *Georg Eisler*

25·06·97-31·08·97 | *Henry Koerner 1915-1991*

19·09·97-26·10·97 | *Conrad Laib*

# Wien - Vienna

**KUNSTFORUM BANK AUSTRIA**
Freyung 8  1010 Wien  Director: Klaus Albrecht Schröder
☎+43 1 71191 5730  🖷 +43 1 71191 5747
Open: Daily 10.00-18.00  Wednesday 10.00-21.00

**COLLECTION** | No permanent collection.

**EXHIBITIONS**
until 01·06·97 | *William Turner*   This is the first Turner retrospective in Austria, organised in collaboration with the Tate Gallery, focusing on landscapes, seascapes and history themes.

12·06·97-24·08·97 | *The Froehlich Collection*   This is one of the outstanding collections of German and American art of the last decades. Some 150 works include contributions by Beuys, Judd, Richter and Warhol, to name just a few.

05·09·97-07·12·97    ***Art and Madness***    An exhibition on the art of the mentally ill and its effect on 20th-century art, exemplified in some 200 oil paintings, drawings and sculptures ranging from Paul Klee and Max Ernst through Wölfli and Dubuffet to Arnulf Rainer.

# Wien - Vienna

## KUNSTHAUSWIEN
Untere Weißgerberstraße 13   1030 Wien   Director: Joram Harel
☎ +43 1 7120495   🖷 +43 1 7120496
Open: Daily 10.00-19.00

COLLECTION    The Hundertwasser collection of the KunstHausWien provides a retrospective of works by the painter, architect and ecologist, Friedensreich Hundertwasser (born Vienna, 1928). Early works, watercolours, oils and recent mixed media paintings are exhibited. His graphics include the Rotaprint portfolio of 1951, Japanese woodcuts, etchings, lithographs and silk screens.
The tapestries, based on works by Hundertwasser, were made by weavers in Mexico and Vienna. 'Pissing Boy with Sky-Scraper' was handwoven by the artist in 1952.
Hundertwasser's concern for architecture is manifested in a collection of scale models such as the 'Hundertwasserhaus' in Vienna and 'In the Meadow Hills', which demonstrates the 'Pit houses' and 'Eye-Slit houses', the 'St. Barbara Church' in Bärnbach, Styria, the 'Incinerator Spittelau' in Vienna, and the Day-Care Centre in Frankfurt.

EXHIBITIONS
until 24·08·97    ***Schmidt-Rottluff***   *Paintings, Drawings, Watercolours, Etchings, Woodcuts, Sculpture*    This is the most comprehensive presentation of German Expressionist artist Karl Schmidt-Rottluff ever exhibited, with approximately 200 of his works, including examples of his later period.

11·09·97-25·01·98    ***Herb Ritts***   *Works*    The first full-scale retrospective of this pre-eminent American photographer features more than 230 of Ritts' photographs, ranging from intimate portraits to ten-foot murals.

# Wien - Vienna

## KUNSTHISTORISCHES MUSEUM
Maria Theresien Platz   1010 Wien   Director: Wilfried Seipel
☎ +43 1 52524404   🖷 +43 1 5232770   Internet http://museum.kem.ac.at
Open: Tuesday-Sunday 10.00-18.00   Thursday 10.00-21.00
Closed: Monday

COLLECTION    Many of the treasures of the collections of the Kunsthistorisches Museum were assembled by members of the Habsburg Imperial Family, enthusiastic patrons and collectors over many centuries. The exhibits range from ancient Egyptian, Greek and Roman art to Medieval art and Renaissance and Baroque collections. On show are paintings, sculptures, tapestries, goldsmith work, jewellery, musical instruments, carriages, sleighs, armour and other items. The museum is divided into eight collections, some of which are housed in the Hofburg and in Schönbrunn Palace. On display in the Schönbrunn Palace are the collection of Ancient Egyptian art, the Greek and Roman exhibits, the decorative-art sculptures, the historical musical instruments, the arms and armour, the historical carriages and the coins and medals, as well as the picture gallery, which includes many paintings by Pieter Brueghel the Elder, Dürer, Titian and Rubens. The highlights of the Treasury are the Austrian imperial crown and the insignia and coronation robes of the Holy Roman Empire.

*Central Hall*
Gottfried Semper,
Karl Hasenauer,
1871-1891
© *Kunsthistorisches*
*Museum Wien, Wien*

**EXHIBITIONS**

[KUNSTHISTORISCHES MUSEUM, ROOM VIII]

until 25·05·97

***Vittoria Colonna*** *Michelangelo's Muse*   In continuation of the exhibition cycle on famous women of the Italian Renaissance, the Art History Museum presents the poetess Vittoria Colonna. Her close relationship to Michelangelo is expressed in letters, sonnets and, above all, in the drawings he made for her.

Aug 97-Oct 97

***Gold from Mexico***

Autumn 97

***The Pharaohs' Gold***

Nov 97-Feb 98

***Jan Brueghel***

[PALAIS HARRACH]

06·05·97-27·05·97

***Orient & Occident***

26·05·97-29·09·97

***Henry Moore***   Moore was often called the 'Michelangelo of the 20th century'. Apart from the aesthetic judgement inherent in this statement, it also refers to the artist's ability to create within his figures vital aspects of our century's view of humanity.

29·06·97-21·09·97

***Capriccio***   Capriccio - i.e., humour, inspiration and imagination - comprises some 120 paintings from Arcimboldo to Turner and almost 130 prints and drawings from Callot and Castiglione to Tiepolo and Goya.

Oct 97 onwards

***Karl Rössing***

[KÜNSTLERHAUS]

Sep 97-Jan 98

***Treasures from the Land of the Bible***

[NEUE BURG]

07·09·97-19·10·97

***South German-Austrian Violin Construction***

# Wien - Vienna

**MUSEUM MODERNER KUNST STIFTUNG LUDWIG WIEN**
**20er Haus  Schweizer Garten  1030 Wien  Director: Lóránd Hegyi**
**☎ +43 1 7996900  ⛁ +43 1 7996901**
**Open: Tuesday-Sunday 10.00-18.00**
**Closed: Monday**

**COLLECTION**

The 20er Haus at the Schweizergarten, a pavilion building originally constructed for the world exhibition in Brussels in 1958, is one of two buildings occupied by the Museum moderner Kunst Stiftung Ludwig Wien. On the first floor of 20er Haus, large alternating exhibitions are presented. The museum's international collection, which was expanded in 1991, is exhibited on the second floor, and features Concept Art, Minimal Art and Land Art from approximately 1950 to the present. Along with work by Joseph Beuys, works by artists such as Peter Halley, Mario Merz, Richard Serra, Sol Le Witt, Jannis Kounellius, Donald Judd, Lawrence Weiner, Hanne Darboven, Bertrand Lavier and Günther Förg can be seen. The Austrian avant-garde is represented by Franz West, Heimo Zobernig, Hartmut Skerbisch, Gerwald Rockenschaub and others. In the sculpture garden, works by Henry Moore, Fritz Wotruba, Alberto Giacometti and others are on display.

*20er Haus Schweizer Garten with a sculpture of Henry Moore in front © Museum Moderner Kunst, Wien*

**EXHIBITIONS**

until 15·06·97

***Valie Export: Split: Reality***   Born 1940 in Linz (Austria) Valie Export has been an eminent exponent of media-art in Europe since the sixties. Photography, video and film became at the same time the means to work with and the context of Export's interest in visual and textual oeuvre. This retrospective will present a selection of Valis Export's media art since 1968.

04·07·97-31·08·97

***East-Middle-West***   The exhibition will feature a representative selection of American art after 1945 from the collection of the Denver Art Museum. Apart from the works of wellknown artists of Abstract Expressionism (such as Robert Motherwell), Pop Art, Minimal Art and Concept Art, as well as current examples of artists from the West, the show will focus on Midwestern art.

12·09·97-02·11·97

***Manfred Wakolbinger***   The Austrian sculptor Manfred Wakolbinger will present about 60 new works - sculptures dangling from the ceiling and photographies depict the topics of balance and motion.

15·11·97-13·01·98

***Haim Steinbach***   Haim Steinbach's first comprehensive show in Vienna will mainly feature a selection of his 'Shelves'. The American artist positions various objects of everyday use in puristic arrangements on consoles. Steinbach draws an analogy between the communicative function of these objects and words and language.

## Wien - Vienna

### MUSEUM MODERNER KUNST STIFTUNG LUDWIG WIEN
Palais Liechtenstein  Fürstengasse 1  1090 Wien  Director: Lóránd Hegyi
☎ +43 1 3176900  🖷 +43 1 3176901
Open: Tuesday-Sunday 10.00-18.00
Closed: Monday

**COLLECTION**

The Palais Liechtenstein has been used as an exhibition space by the Museum moderner Kunst Stiftung Ludwig Wien since 1979. Formerly housing the Liechtenstein Galerie, it was added to accommodate growth in the museum's collection when parts of the important Ludwig Collection were brought from Aachen to Vienna and the Hahn Collection of Cologne was acquired. The building is used for the display of a cross-section of 20th-century international art. Special rooms are dedicated to various art movements including Expressionism, Cubism, Futurism, Constructivism, Surrealism, Nouveau Realism, Vienna Actionism, Pop Art and Photorealism. International painting of the 80s and 90s is also exhibited.

**EXHIBITIONS**

until 08·06·97

*Nahum Tevet*   Nahum Tevet, one of the most renowned Israeli installation artists, will show a selection of his works covering a period of the past 30 years. His complex installations and objects made from simple pieces of furniture such as stools, tables and easels feature various allusions to developments of Modernism.

27·06·97-31·08·97

*Jiri Georg Dokoupil*   The oeuvre of Jiri Dokoupil (born 1954 in what is today the Czech Republic) will be presented in a comprehensive retrospective including about 150 paintings, sculptures and water colours. The exhibition will show works from the time of the legendary 'Müllheim Freedom', as well as his famous 'Soot Pictures' and the recent lyrical-meditative series of 'Green Paintings'.

11·09·97-02·11·97

*Alois Mosbacher*   Approximately 100 paintings, drawings, and sculptures by the Austrian artist (born 1954) will be shown in the museum, grouped in the various exhibition rooms by motifs (such as sunflowers) or formal phenomena.

## Wien - Vienna

### MUSEUM FÜR VÖLKERKUNDE
Neue Hofburg  Heldenplatz  1014 Wien  Director: Peter Kann
☎ +43 1 534300  🖷 +43 1 5355320
Open: Wednesday-Monday 10.00-16.00
Closed: Tuesday

**COLLECTION**

The Museum for Ethnography possesses a collection of about 250 000 ethnographical and archaeological objects from Asia, Africa, Oceania-Australia and America. The most outstanding and oldest collection consists of the 'Mexican Treasures', including the unique Quetzal feather headdress, the only featherwork shield with a figural image, and the feather fan of the Aztec culture. The museum's collection also includes a part of James Cook's famous collection of 18th-century objects from Polynesia and Northwest Coast Indians, an outstanding collection of Benin-Bronzes (West-Africa), the collection of K.A.Freiherr von Hügel (1830-1836) from India, Southeast Asia and China, and a collection acquired by the frigate 'Novara' during the circumnavigation of the globe between 1857 and 1859.
The collection was significantly broadened by contributions during the second half of the 19th century of objects from South Africa,

New Guinea, Southeast Asia, Japan, New Zealand, the Caucasus and Siberia. More than 14 000 objects, primarily from India and other Asian cultures, were collected during the world tour of Archduke Franz Ferdinand during 1892 and 1893.

*Female figure; amulet, ivory carved,* Tonga-Islands, Polynesia; Collection James Cook
© *Museum für Völkerkunde Wien*

**EXHIBITIONS**
until 01·06·97

*Shining South Seas*   The world of the Micronesian Islands

Nov 97-Mar 98

*Bhutan - A Kingdom in Balance*   Major exhibition on Bhutan with loans from Bhutan, including objects of high artistic and symbolic value, which have till now never been shown outside Bhutan; and loans from important European collections - private and museums.

## Wien · Vienna

**ÖSTERREICHISCHES MUSEUM FÜR VOLKSKUNDE**
**Laudongasse 15-19  1080 Wien  Directors: Mr. Beitl, Mr. Grieshofer**
☎ +43 1 4068905  ⊠ +43 1 4085342
**Open: Tuesday-Friday 09.00-17.00  Saturday 09.00-12.00  Sunday 09.00-13.00**
**Closed: Monday**

**COLLECTION**

The Austrian Folklore Museum, founded in 1895 and located in the Palais Schönborn in the Josefstadt quarter of Vienna, houses a diverse collection of items reflecting the cultures of Austria and its neighbours. The building has been renovated and the permanent collection redesigned to give an overview of traditional folklife through the medium of the museum's folk art collection.

Mechanical World Theater, Wien c.1850
© *Österreichisches Museum für Volkskunde, Wien*

The exhibitions depict people in their relationship to nature and the environment, show them striving for economic survival, and offer insights into the prevailing social order. The selection and arrangement of the exhibits, as well as the design of the displays, aims to help visitors appreciate the objects in their real-life contexts.

Objects from the 17th to the 19th century give the visitor a picture of everyday life and everyday needs, vernacular architecture, work and religious faith, poverty and rural pride.
Special emphasis is placed on the folk art of countries that were once part of the Austro-Hungarian Empire, but the museum also possesses an extensive collection of objects from Alpine regions.

**EXHIBITIONS**

until 29·06·97 | *Pictures from Galicia*   *Original Picture Drafts from the 'Crown Prince Work' 1898*

04·05·97-14·09·97 | *The Bagpipes in Europe*

20·06·97-14·09·97 | *Tool Transformations*   *Sculptures by Franz Russ*

26·10·97-29·03·98 | *With Baggage and Bags*   *The Cultural History of Carrying Baggage*

30·12·97-01·02·98 | *Christmas Exhibition 97/98*

## Wien · Vienna

**WIENER SECESSION**
Friedrichstraße 12  1010 Wien  Director: Ms. Hillebrandt
☎ +43 1 5875307  🖷 +43 1 587530734
Internet; http://www.to.or.at/secession
Open: Tuesday-Friday 10.00-18.00  Saturday and Sunday 10.00-16.00
Closed: Monday

**COLLECTION** | **Gustav Klimt**   The Beethoven Frieze  This frieze was created for the XIVth Secession exhibition in 1902. The monumental wall painting is one of the most significant works of this Art Nouveau painter. Since its restoration it has once again been on display at the Secession building since 1986.

**EXHIBITIONS**

until 25·05·97 | *James Coleman*   *Audio-Visual Installation*

until 25·05·97 | *Thomas Reinhold*   *Paintings*

04·06·97-13·07·97 | *It's a Better World*   *Actual Art from Moscow*

23·07·97-14·09·97 | *Zoe Leonard*   *Photography and Objects*

23·07·97-14·09·97 | *X2*

24·09·97-09·11·97 | *Nobuyoshi Araki*   *Photography*

19·11·97-Jan 97 | *Group Exhibition*

## Antwerpen - Antwerp

### ETNOGRAFISCH MUSEUM
Suikerrui 19  2000 Antwerpen  Director: Jan Alphen
☎ +32 3 2320882  📠 +32 3 2270871
Open: Tuesday-Sunday 10.00-16.45
Closed: Monday and 1, 2 Jan, 1 May, Ascension Day, 1, 2 Nov, 25, 26 Dec

**COLLECTION**

The Ethnographic Museum is one of the newest museums of the City of Antwerp. It focuses on objects of the peoples of Africa, Asia, the Americas and Oceania. The objects are displayed by topic and describe the spiritual and social world of various tribes and cultures.

*'Uli', Malanggan-figure*
*Oceania, Melanesia,*
*New-Ireland*
*© Etnografisch*
*museum, Antwerpen*

The different collections contain a total of nearly 25 000 items, of which some 2500 are permanently displayed. Highlights include: sculptures and masks from Africa and Oceania, feathery ornaments from South America, pre-Columbian ceramics, paintings and sculpture from India and Tibet, prints and lacquered works from

China and Japan and a collection of textiles of particular importance.

**EXHIBITION**
21·11·97-29·03·98

***Shamanism in Tuva and the Altai Region*** Organised in co-operation with the Tuvan Museum of Regional Studies 'Aldan Maadyr' in Kyzyl, Tuva Siberia, this exhibition consists of approximately 200 objects varying from bronze shaman mirrors and amulets, steles with petroglyphs, horse harnesses and ritual objects of prehistoric times, to modern shaman costumes, drums and amulets.

## Antwerpen - Antwerp

**KONINKLIJK MUSEUM VOOR SCHONE KUNSTEN**
Leopold de Waelplaats  2000 Antwerpen  Director a.i.: Erik Vandamme
☎ +32 3 2387809  📠 +32 3 2480810
Internet: http://www.dma.be/kultuur/kmska
Open: Tuesday-Sunday 10.00-17.00
Closed: Monday and 1, 2 Jan, 1 May, Ascension Day, 25 Dec

**COLLECTION**

**Old Masters**  The museum contains a fine collection of Old Masters. It provides an interesting survey of South Netherlandish art dating from the 14th to the 18th century. Masterpieces by Jan van Eyck, Rogier van der Weyden and Hans Memling are witnesses of the artistic flowering in the 15th-century Burgundian Netherlands. Paintings by Quinten Metsys, Frans Floris, the Brueghel family, Peter Paul Rubens, Jacob Jordaens and Anthony van Dijck illustrate the prominent role of Antwerp as a leading art centre in West-Europe during the 16th and 17th century. The museum owns 21 paintings and oilsketches by Rubens.
The collection also includes work by French, Italian, German and Dutch artists. Highlights are, to name but a few, the 'Orsini-quadritych' by Simone Martini, 'Madonna surrounded by angels' by Jean Fouquet, Titiano's 'Jacopo Pesaro' and the famous 'Portrait of Stephanus Geraerdts' by Frans Hals.

James Ensor
(1860-1949)
*The intrigue, 1890*
© Koninklijk Museum
voor Schone Kunsten,
Antwerpen

**Modern Art**  The collection of Modern Masters shows the Belgian art production covering the 19th century until the present. The museum, till the end of the 19th century strongly tied to the Antwerp Royal Academy of Fine Arts, contains many works by local academic artists. Besides those 'avant-garde' artists, followers of Realism, Impressionism and Post-Impressionism, are represented with various paintings. World famous is the rich collection of paintings and drawings by James Ensor. The 20th-century art collection contains representative works from the different currents ranging from Futurism to Neo-Realism. Of special interest are the Flemish Expressionists, and the Belgian Surrealists René Magritte and Paul Delvaux. Also a small number of foreign modern artists is represented such as Appel, Breitner, Chagall, David, Degas, Fontana, Modigliani, Rodin, Willink and Zadkine.

## Antwerpen - Antwerp

### MUSEUM MAYER VAN DEN BERGH
Lange Gasthuisstraat 19  2000 Antwerpen  Director: Hans Nieuwdorp
☎ +32 3 2324237  ⛶ +32 3 2319387
Open: Tuesday-Sunday 10.00-17.00
Closed: Monday and 1, 2 Jan, 1 May, Ascension Day, 1, 2 Nov, 25, 26 Dec

**COLLECTION**

The museum contains the former collection of Fritz Mayer van den Bergh, who died in 1901. Its core consists of Western European paintings and sculptures, ranging from the 6th to the 18th century, with particular emphasis on Medieval art from the 14th to early 16th century. The collection includes examples of all genres of painting and of various schools. There are works by Pieter Brueghel the Elder: the famous 'Dulle Griet' and the 'Twelve Proverbs'. Works by Pieter Brueghel the Younger and Jan Brueghel are also exhibited. Flemish painting of the 15th and 16th century is on show as well, with some unique Dutch works such as the 'Antwerp-Baltimore' panels (c. 1400).

*The 'Birth of Christ' and 'St.Christopher', Netherlands c. 1400 Two panels from the 'Antwerp-Baltimore' polyptich © Museum Mayer van den Bergh, Antwerpen*

Medieval sculptures are well-represented in the museum, with works in marble, alabaster and polychromed wood of the Gothic period are on display. The sculpture section contains works such as the monumental group of 'Christ and St. John' (c. 1300) and carved altar-pieces from Brabant as well as French 14th-century ivory sculptures and work by Jean de Liège.
The museum has a wide range of Medieval decorative art, in the form of enamels, tapestries, furniture, silver and ceramics, in addition to selected examples from the smaller collections of drawings, textiles, plaquettes, numismatics, miniatures and manuscripts.

**EXHIBITIONS**    No exhibitions planned.

## Antwerpen - Antwerp

### NATIONAAL SCHEEPVAARTMUSEUM - NATIONAL MARITIME MUSEUM
Steenplein 1  2000 Antwerpen 1  Director: W. Johnson
☎ +32 3 2320850  ⛶ +32 3 2271338
Open: Tuesday-Sunday 10.00-16.45
Closed: Monday and 1, 2 Jan, 1 May, Ascension Day, 1, 2 Nov,  25, 26 Dec

COLLECTION
The National Maritime Museum is the only museum of its kind in Belgium and is located in 'Het Steen', an old castle on the Schelde. The collection is displayed in 12 halls, each devoted to a different aspect of the shipping trade. It is didactically arranged and accompanied by captions in 4 languages. Model ships, paintings and ships' instruments help trace the history of shipping. The museum owns a unique collection of maritime paintings behind glass. Antique harbour equipment, ships and cranes are displayed in the department of maritime industry and harbour archaeology alongside 'Het Steen'. The highlights of this department are the barge 'Lauranda' and the steam-tugboat 'Amical'.

EXHIBITION
until 30·09·97
**Rika Loyens & Leon Ost**   Maritime Art   Rika Loyens and Leon Ost are both employed at municipal museums. Loyens' specialties include pastel techniques, figure drawings and watercolours. Ost's specialties include painting, graphic art and the restoration of paintings.

# Antwerpen - Antwerp

**OPENLUCHTMUSEUM VOOR BEELDHOUWKUNST MIDDELHEIM**
**OPEN AIR MUSEUM OF SCULPTURE MIDDELHEIM**
Middelheimlaan 61  2020 Antwerpen  Director: Menno Meewis
☎ +32 3 8271534  🖷 +32 3 8252835
Open: Daily  Oct-Mar 10.00-17.00; Apr and Sep 10.00-19.00; May and Aug 10.00-20.00; Jun, Jul 10.00-21.00

COLLECTION
In the summer of 1950, the late Burgomaster Lode Craeybeckx first suggested the idea of an international open-air sculpture exhibition at Middelheim Park. After deciding to permanently exhibit sculptures in the park, the Antwerp City Council founded the Open Air Museum of Sculpture Middelheim. Today, after more than 40 years of collecting, the historical sculpture collection endeavours to offer a broad international view of the development of modern sculpture.
In 1993 a rejuvenation programme was launched. The museum now spans the entire park, and acquisitions are no longer made just to fill historical gaps. On the occasion of Antwerp being named Cultural Capital of Europe for 1993, the permanent collection was enriched with works by Deacon, Genzken, Kirkeby, Klingelhöller, Lohaus, Mullican, Munoz, Panamarenko, Schütte and Vermeiren. These were exhibited in Lower Middelheim, where the Biennials used to be held, and which is now reserved for contemporary sculpture. Between 1994 and 1996 the museum acquired Guillaume Bijl's 'Roman Street', Luciano Fabro's 'Bathers', Henk Visch's 'Telling no Lies' and Tony Cragg's 'Envelope'.

EXHIBITIONS
18·01·97-onwards
**Wide White Space Gallery in the Braem Pavillion**   Loan from the Antwerp Wide White Space Gallery with works by Carl André, Joseph Beuys, Marcel Broodthaers, Christo, Hugo Heyrman, Bernd Lohaus, Richard Long, Panamarenko, Lawrence Weiner a.o.

24·05·97-17·08·97
**Anthony Caro (1924, New Malden)**   An important survey of Anthony Caro's monumental work from the 60th till now. Most of the sculptures come from the United States and will be shown for the first time in Europe.

06·09·97-16·11·97
**Wim Delvoye**   New works by this Belgian artist.

Spring 98
**Franz West**

## Antwerpen - Antwerp

### MUSEUM PLANTIN-MORETUS
Vrijdagmarkt 22  2000 Antwerpen  Director: F. de Nave
☎ +32 3 2330294  ⅲ +32 3 2262516
Open: Tuesday-Sunday 10.00-16.45
Closed: Monday

**COLLECTION**

The Plantin-Moretus Museum is the only one of its kind. It traces its origins back to the leading printer of the second half of the 16th century, Christopher Plantin (Saint-Avertin, Tours c. 1520 - Antwerp 1589). In 1576 he installed his famous Golden Compasses on the Vrijdagmarkt, which was to remain the 'Officina Plantiniana' for the rest of his life. Plantin's descendants and successors, the Moretus family, kept the firm in the forefront of the printers' trade for almost three centuries and the Golden Compasses remained their home.

Today, the Plantin Moretus Museum is a harmonious combination of stately patrician dwelling and authentic business. The rooms, with their priceless works of art, tapestries, gilded leather, paintings (including 18 by Rubens), clocks, ceramics and porcelain still exude the atmosphere of refined luxury which the Moretus family imparted to their home.

The original workshops of the 'Officina Plantiniana' give the museum its unique personality. The type foundry, workshop, with the two oldest presses in the world (from c. 1600), type store, corrector's room, bookshop and office of the master of the house are still intact and preserved as they were in the 16th and 17th centuries.

The collections brought together here in their original historical setting are imposing and of considerable importance as the fruits of three hundred years of typographic work and art collecting.

*Interior of the © Museum Plantin-Moretus Antwerpen*

**EXHIBITIONS**

until 29·06·97

***Abraham Ortelius***   Antwerp cartographer Abraham Ortelius (1527-1598) is considered the founder of the modern atlas. His 'Theatrum Orbis Terrarum' was published in different languages and reprinted several times. The texts of the maps were printed by various Antwerp printers, among whom Christophe Plantin.

19·09·97-21·12·97

***Justus Lipsius and the Plantin House***   This exhibition celebrates the 450th anniversary of the birth of Flemish humanist Justus Lipsius (1547-1606). It includes a variety of the philosopher's publications, an extensive selection of correspondence, and hand-written preparatory notes and corrections to the printed editions.

## Antwerpen - Antwerp

### RUBENSHUIS
Wapper 9-11  2000 Antwerpen  Director: Paul Huvenne
☎ +32 3 2324747  📠 +32 3 2319387
Open: Tuesday-Sunday 10.00-17.00
Closed: Monday and 1, 2 Jan, 1 May, Ascension Day, 1, 2 Nov, 25, 26 Dec

COLLECTION

**The Rubens House**  Antwerp is renowned as the city of Sir Peter Paul Rubens. In 1610, one year after his marriage to Isabella Brant, Rubens bought an estate in the Wapper where he had his house and studio built. The imposing portico separating the inner court from the garden and pavilion was depicted many times in his paintings and were undoubtedly built from his own designs.
**The collection**  The collection includes several works by Rubens and focuses on Rubens' own collection, his studio, his work as a humanist and diplomat, his family and his daily life in Antwerp. The historical garden was one of the winning projects of the European Community in 1993.

EXHIBITIONS

No exhibitions planned.

## Antwerpen - Antwerp

### STEDELIJK PRENTENKABINET
Vrijdagmarkt 22-23  2000 Antwerpen  Director: F. de Nave
☎ +32 3 2322455  📠 +32 3 2262516
Open: Daily 10.00-16.00  Exhibitions: Daily 10.00 - 16.45
Closed: Saturday and Sunday  Exhibitions: Monday

COLLECTION

The collection of drawings and engravings in the Municipal Print Room originated in the private collection of Max Rooses (1838-1914), the first director of the Museum Plantin-Moretus. The collection was systematically enlarged, and now contains 45 000 antique and modern prints, 2 240 drawings by Old Masters and 20 000 modern drawings, 1 200 antique and modern print books, copper plates, woodblocks, etc. The library contains about 14 000 volumes on graphic arts.

Maarten de Vos
*Africa*
© *Stedelijk*
*Prentenkabinet,*
*Antwerpen*

EXHIBITIONS
May 97

*Acquisitions Municipal Printroom 1995-1997*

10·10·97-16·11·97

*Frans Dille Award 1997*  *Award to Promote the Graphic Arts*
Works by this year's laureates are on display.

## Brugge · Bruges

### ARENTSHUIS (THE BRANGWYN MUSEUM)
Dijver 16  8000 Brugge  Director: V. Vermeersch
☎ +32 50 448711  🖷 +32 50 448778
Open: Wednesday-Monday Apr-Sep 09.30-17.00;
Oct-Mar 09.30-12.30 / 14.00-17.00
Closed: Tuesday

**COLLECTION**

The Brangwyn museum or Arenthuis was originally purchased by the City of Bruges at the beginning of this century and has since evolved into a museum with two very different permanent collections.

**Frank Brangwyn**   The collection of the Pre-Modernist all-round artist Frank Brangwyn includes 40 easel paintings, 500 etchings (preferred by the author for city views and travel impressions) and examples of his interior and decorative art demonstrating both the Art Nouveau and Art Deco movements.

**Lace 'At Its Best'**  The lace collection contains lace from the 16th to the 20th century with three sections dedicated to needlepoint lace, bobbin lace (more common in Flanders) and some remarkable examples of 'mixed lace'.

**EXHIBITION**
10·09·97-16·11·97

*Lace in Europe*

## Brugge · Bruges

### GROENINGE MUSEUM
Dijver 12  8000 Brugge  Director: V. Vermeersch
☎ +32 50 448711  🖷 +32 50 448778
Open: Wednesday-Monday Apr-Sep 09.30-17.00;
Oct-Mar 09.30-12.30 / 14.00-17.00
Closed: Tuesday

**COLLECTION**

The Groeninge Museum is a traditional Fine Art museum that collects and displays work purely on the basis of its quality.

Illustration of 6
centuries of art
© *Groeninge*
*Museum, Brugge*

**Flemish Primitives 15th century**   The 'Gallery of the Flemish Primitives' contains 30 works from the 15th and the beginning of the 16th century painted by masters from the Southern Netherlands who include Jan van Eyck, Rogier van der Weyden, Petrus Christus, Hugo van der Goes, Hans Memling, Gerard David and Hieronymus Bosch.

**Southern Netherlands 16th century**  The collection from the Southern Netherlands in the 16th century includes Jan van Hemessen, Cornelis van Cleve, Adriaan Key and Pieter Brueghel the Younger, with particular focus on Jan Provoost and Lanceloot Blondeel.

**Bruges**  Painting in the second half of the 16th century in Bruges is represented by Pieter Pourbus and the 17th century by Jacob van Oost.

**Modern Art**  The aim of this collection is to build a historically founded and comprehensive survey of modern Belgian art with the accent on the 'most original moments' and limited to the most important artists.

Other collections include: Flemish and Dutch history and cabinet pieces from the 17th and 18th centuries, Jan Garemijn, Bruges Classicists, Romanticism and Realism, Symbolism, and landscape painting in the 19th century.

**EXHIBITIONS**  No details available.

## Brugge - Bruges

**GRUUTHUSE MUSEUM**
Dijver 17  8000 Brugge  Director: V. Vermeersch
☎ +32 50 448711  🖷 +32 50 448778
Open: Wednesday-Monday Apr-Sep 09.30-17.00;
Oct-Mar 09.30-12.30 / 14.00-17.00
Closed: Tuesday

**COLLECTION**  The municipal Gruuthuse Museum is located in a local 15th-century patrician palace of the same name.

The sculpture department includes works in stone, wood and alabaster and carvings in ivory. One of the most important works in the museum is the fired polychrome earthenware bust of Charles V.

The museum's furniture is mostly 17th and 18th-century local Baroque, with the exception of a number of Gothic items.

Silver and non-precious metalwork is well represented. The silver collection features religious and secular artefacts and an important collection of 16th to 19th-century 'guild silver'.

The monumental 15th-century fireplace in the Gruuthuse kitchen is used to display the collection of copper, pewter, bronze and iron work. Other metalwork includes ecclesiastical objects and secular artefacts such as snuffboxes.

The large collection of ceramics offers a fairly comprehensive survey of all historical types and centres of production.

Tapestries are the main attraction in the textile collection.

The numismatic collection features clocks and mechanical objects and instruments of punishment as well as coins. The collection of early musical instruments is permanently on display.

**EXHIBITIONS**  No exhibitions planned.

## Brugge - Bruges

**MEMLING MUSEUM**
Mariastraat 38  8000 Brugge  Director: V. Vermeersch
☎ +32 50 448711  🖷 +32 50 448778
Open: Thursday-Tuesday Apr-Sep 09.30-17.00;
Oct-Mar 09.30-12.30 / 14.00-17.00
Closed: Wednesday

**COLLECTION**  **Hans Memling**  The heart of the collection is based on six masterpieces by Hans Memling, the Medieval Bruges painter. The museum is housed in the Bruges 12th-century hospital.

**Hospital wards** Are temporarily closed.

**The church** The church is part of the hospital and the 'Memling panels' were moved there in 1985. The church was chosen for their permanent exhibition as four of the panels were originally designed for the church and it is spacious enough to house all the panels together. The only other work in this area is the statue of Cornelius.

**The pharmacy** In 1971 the hospital chemists were rehoused so that the 17th-century pharmacy, established in a part of the old monastery, could became part of the museum. Much of the pharmacy inventory and attributes from the 17th and 18th century are on exhibit.

**EXHIBITIONS** No exhibitions planned

## Bruxelles - Brussels

**BRUSSELS MUSEUM OF MUSICAL INSTRUMENTS**
17, Petit-Sablon 1000 Bruxelles Director: Malou Haine
☎ +32 2 5113595 🖷 +32 2 5128575
Open: Tuesday-Saturday 09.30-16.45
Closed: Sunday and Monday

**COLLECTION** The Brussels Museum of Musical Instruments has its origin in the collection of ancient and ethnic instruments of François-Joseph Fétis (1784-1871), the first director of the Brussels Conservatoire, and in a collection of Hindu instruments presented in 1876 by King Leopold II. The instrument maker and organ expert Victor-Charles Mahillon (1841-1924) became the museum's first director in 1877. He was responsible for a rapid growth of the collection (up to 3300 pieces in 1924) and for its international reputation as a research centre. The collection of over 7000 instruments remains one of the largest in the world today. Only about 10% is on permanent display, but it is hoped that the museum will be housed in new accommodation before the end of the century. The exhibition is divided into four main topics: wind instruments from the 16th to the 19th century, keyboard instruments, stringed instruments and European folk instruments.

**EXHIBITIONS** No details available.

## Bruxelles - Brussels

**PALAIS DES BEAUX-ARTS PALEIS VOOR SCHONE KUNSTEN**
23, Rue Ravenstein 1000 Bruxelles Director: Piet Coessens
☎ +32 2 5078468 🖷 +32 2 5110589
Open: Tuesday-Sunday 10.00-17.00
Closed: Monday

**COLLECTION** No permanent collection.

**EXHIBITIONS**

until 25-05-97

*The Art of Collecting 20th Century Art from Dutch Museums*
Major exhibition of international modern art marking the Dutch Presidency of the European Union. The work of fourteen Dutch artists (e.g. Mondrian, Van Dongen, Charley Toorop, René Daniels) is set off against work by contemporary or stylistically-related artists from other countries.

until 25-05-97

*Esko Männikkö* Colour photographs of North-Finnish people and landscapes by young artist Esko Männikkö.

| 05·06· 97-17·08·97 | ***Alberto Burri***   First major retrospective of the Italian artist Alberto Burri (1915-1995), whose work has been of great importance and influence to Land Art, Arte Povera and Pop. |

05·06· 97-17·08·97   ***Alberto Burri***   First major retrospective of the Italian artist Alberto Burri (1915-1995), whose work has been of great importance and influence to Land Art, Arte Povera and Pop.

05·09·97-28·09·97   ***Prix de la Jeune Peinture Belge***   *Rijksacademie Amsterdam 1986-1996*

24·10·97-04·01·98   ***Paribas Bank Collection***   17th century paintings and tapestries and work by Magritte, Ensor, Permeke etc..

## Bruxelles - Brussels

**MUSEUM VAN HET KONINKLIJK BELGISCH INSTITUUT VOOR NATUURWETENSCHAPPEN**
29, Rue Vautier  1040 Bruxelles  Director: Daniel Cahen
☎ +32 2 6274211   +32 2 6464432
Open: Tuesday-Saturday 09.30-16.45  Sunday 09.30-18.00
Closed: Monday and 25 Dec, 1 Jan and election days

COLLECTION

**Palaeontology**   The highlight of the museum's collection is a group of 29 iguanodons, the largest single dinosaur discovery ever made. They were found in a colliery in the border village of Bernissart in 1878 and are now displayed together with animated models of other dinosaurs in a splendid Victorian hall. A wide diorama portrays the sea that covered what is now Belgium during the Cretaceous and Jurassic periods. Strolling along the bottom of the 'sea' you meet unique skeletons of mosasaurs and turtles. The evolution of vertebrate animals and of man is also portrayed.
**Mineralogy**   This exhibition provides a systematic survey of minerals, explaining characteristics such as growth, forms, optical qualities, mechanical features, density, magnetism and radioactivity. A separate section deals with mineralisations of Belgian stone and clay quarries, both still functioning or closed down.
**Zoology**   This systematic display of all terrestrial mammal families is of great scientific and educational value. Some of the more familiar groups such as primates, predators and hoofed animals are displayed separately. The collection of cavicorns is one of the most comprehensive in the world.
The marine mammals collection is very large and includes recent whale skeletons, seals, walruses. Penguins and polar bears can be seen in two dioramas of the North and South Poles. The shell and insect halls contain a unique collection of unicellular animals, sponges, corals, anemones, worms, molluscs and arthropods. Other exhibits include a 'living' termite hill and dangerous insects. The Belgian fauna is illustrated in a fine series of dioramas.

EXHIBITIONS

No details available.

## Bruxelles - Brussels

**MUSÉES ROYAUX D'ART ET D'HISTOIRE
KONINKLIJKE MUSEA VOOR KUNST EN GESCHIEDENIS**
10, Parc du Cinquantenaire  1000 Bruxelles  Curator: Francis van Noten
☎ +32 2 7417211   +32 2 7337735
Open: Tuesday-Friday 09.30-17.00
Saturday, Sunday and public holidays 10.00-17.00
Closed: Monday and 1 Jan, 1 May, 1, 11 Nov and 25 Dec

COLLECTION

**Ancient Art**   The collection of Ancient Art focuses on the Egyptian, Mesopotamian, Greek and Roman civilisations and includes such objects as the Lady of Brussels, the relief of Queen Tiy married to Amenhotep III, vases, Etruscan works, portraits, mosaics from

Aparnea-Syria, jewels, earthenware and painted ceramics.

**Non-European Civilisations**   This department houses collections from India and Southeast Asia, China, America, Polynesia and Micronesia and includes the bronze statue of Siva Nataraja, bark clothes (tapa), Coptic textiles from Egyptian excavations and statues, and painted vessels and jewels from the pre-Columbian civilisations of the Incas, Mayas and Aztecs.

**National Archaeology**   The Prehistory room reconstructs the life of man using didactic boards and models. The Gallo-Roman room explores the development of handicrafts (ceramic crockery, glasswork, bronze and silver vessels). Eight reconstructed tombs allow insight into the Merovingian civilisation.

**European Decorative Arts**   This collection includes sculptures, furniture, ceramics, altar pieces, tapestries, copperware, pewter and silver.

The museum is to open six new rooms dedicated to 20th-century Belgian decorative art, from Art Nouveau to the present day.

Charles van der
Stappen, 1897
*The mysterious
sphinx*
© Musées Royaux
d'Art et d'Histoire,
Bruxelles

**EXHIBITIONS**

until 18·05·97

*Yemen*   An exhibition of photographs by Claire Eykerman ('Cheyk') showing the architecture in the cities of the Sanas, Shibam, El Hajjara and others which together determine the image of this ancient British colony.

until 26·10·97

*The Gallo-Romans in Belgium*   This exhibition is especially intended for the blind and visually handicapped. Under the supervision of a guide, the visitors will be allowed to touch the items on display. These include bronze and glass objects, fibulae, coins and pottery.

12·09·97-Feb 98

*The Belgian Excavations at Lehun in Jordan*   Photographs, maps and models offer an impression of the Belgian contribution to the archaeological research at the ancient site of Lehun. The finds from this village of the late Bronze Age include a Mameluke mosque and Ottoman houses.

## Bruxelles - Brussels

### MUSÉES ROYAUX DES BEAUX-ARTS DE BELGIQUE
3, Rue de la Régence  1000 Bruxelles  Director: Eliane de Wilde
☎ +32 2 5083333  🖷 +32 2 5083232
Internet http://www.fine-arts-museum.be
Open: Tuesday-Sunday 10.00-17.00  Wednesday 10.00-21.00
Closed: Monday and 1 May

**COLLECTION**   The Royal Museums of Fine Arts of Belgium, consisting of the

Museum of Ancient Art and the Museum of Modern Art, comprise
the country's largest museum complex.

The Museum of Ancient Art displays paintings and sculpture from
the 15th to the 19th centuries. Works by Brueghel the Elder and his
sons are dislayed alongside sketches and altar pieces by Rubens and
works by other outstanding painters from the southern Low
Countries. Foreign artists are also richly represented, with notable
work from Neo-Classicism to Post-Impressionism displayed on the
ground floor.

The Museum of Modern Art, established in 1984, presents 20th-
century art from Fauvism to Conceptual Art. Highlights are the
Delvaux and Magritte Rooms; the collection of work by Rik
Wouters, Spilliaert and Marcel Broodthaers; the exhibit of Flemish
Expressionism; and the Cobra exhibit. Major figures such as Chagall,
Dali, Miro, Ernst, Moore, Bacon, Zadkine, Long, Negal and Nam
June Paik are featured. The museum also shows the works of
contemporary artists.

Paul Delvaux
*The Spitzner
museum, 1943*
in the exhibition
`Paul Delvaux'
*Musées Royaux des
Beaux-Arts de
Belgique*
© Foundation Paul
Delvaux, St-Idesbald,
Belgium

**EXHIBITIONS**

until 27·07·97        ***Paul Delvaux***   This exhibition celebrates the 100th anniversary of
the birth of Belgian artist Paul Delvaux. Delvaux, influenced
especially by De Chirico and the Surrealists, created a universe
somewhere between dreams and reality where striking images are
often juxtaposed in totally unexpected ways.

06·03·98-28·06·98    ***René Magritte (1898-1967)***   To commemorate the centenary of the
birth of this master of surrealism, the Royal Museums of Fine Arts of
Belgium are organising a prestige exhibition in honour of René
Magritte.

## Charleroi

**MUSÉE DES BEAUX-ARTS**
Hôtel de Ville  Place Charles II  6000 Charleroi  Director: C. Lemal-Mengeot
☎ +32 71 230294   📠 +32 71 317005
Open: Tuesday-Saturday 09.00-17.00
Closed: Sunday and Monday

**COLLECTION**      The Fine Arts Museum of Charleroi is located on the second floor of
the Town Hall, which was constructed in 1936. The museum's
permanent collection includes Walloon paintings from the 19th and
20th century, representative of a range of styles including Neo-
Classicism, Realism, Neo-Impressionism, Surrealism, and constructed
and abstract art.

The foundation of the collections is the work of F.-J. Navez. Navez
was a pupil and emulator of the Neo-Classical painter David. The
works of a leading painter of the Social Realist style, Constantin

Meunier, are representative of artists who stressed the importance of social values.

A variety of other Walloon movements are included, but the majority of the collection consists of six works by René Magritte, by important local representatives of Surrealism, and by Surrealist Paul Delvaux.

**EXHIBITIONS**

until 07·06·97 — *International Triennial of Young Talent*

17·06·97-16·08·97 — *New Acquisitions*

20·09·97-08·11·97 — ***The Painter Arsène Detry (1897-1981)*** *Retrospective* This exhibition celebrates the 100th anniversary of the birth of this

# Charleroi

**MUSÉE DE LA PHOTOGRAPHIE**
11, Avenue Paul Pastur 6032 Charleroi (Mont-sur-Marchienne)
Director: Georges Vercheval
☎ +32 71 435810  📠 +32 71 364645
Open: Tuesday-Sunday 10.00-18.00
Closed: Monday

**COLLECTION**

The permanent collection of the museum comprises fine photographic images starting with the very beginnings of photography and continuing up to the present day. Photogenic drawing, daguerreotypes, salt prints, albumen prints and autochromes are all employed to show the technology and aesthetics of photography. Included are the pioneers, such as Poitevin, Fenton, Du Camp and Baldus; pictorialists such as Misonne, Dubreuil and Marissiaux; and the 'moderns' such as Kertesz, Florence Henri and Ueda, as well as Sander, Arbus, Dieter Appelt, Klein and others.

The museum also possesses a rich collection of original cameras covering all periods, as well as modern facsimiles of the box cameras used by Niépce, Daguerre and Talbot. There are explanatory displays, and displays of a variety of cameras ranging from huge wooden cameras up to the contemporary reflex camera, including models from Voigtlander, Ernemann, Leica, Rollei, Kodak, Agfa, Polaroid and other manufacturers.

There is also a learning area area where the visitor can experience the mysteries of light and the darkroom, review the history of cameras and images up to their use in newspaper, or see a turn-of-the century laboratory and reconstructed portrait studion.

**Archives of Wallonia** Housed in the museum but independent of it, the foundation 'Archives de Wallonie' records the region's past, bringing together images relating to daily life, work and local customs, and offering an ambitious series of documentary programmes.

**Library - Documentation Centre** The museum also includes a library with 3 000 books, supplemented by photography magazines and documentary files on individual photographers.

**EXHIBITIONS**

until 31·08·97 — *Derision and Reason*

05·09·97-21·11·97 — *Gustave Marissiaux*

05·09·97-21·11·97 — *Paul Den Hollander* *Botanical Voyage*

05·09·97-21·11·97 — *Cameras from the Collection*

28·11·97 onwards — *12th National Open Photography Prize*

# Deurle

## MUSEUM DHONDT-DHAENENS
Museumlaan 14  9831 Deurle  Director: Frank Benijts
☎ +32 9 2825123  📠 +32 9 2810853
Open: Wednesday-Friday 14.00-17.00/18.00  Saturday, Sunday and
public holidays 10.00-12.00 / 14.00-17.00/18.00
Closed: Monday and Tuesday

COLLECTION

The Dhondt-Dhaenens Museum, which was founded in 1968, owns
an extensive collection of paintings by internationally known
painters such as G. and L. De Smet, J. Ensor, C. Permeke, A. Servaes,
A. Van Den Abeele, F. Van Den Berghe, G. Van De Woestijne and
many others.
The works of art were collected by Jules and Irma Dhondt-Dhaenens
and the museum has now become a cultural meeting place.
Regular exhibitions are organised by contemporary artists from
both Belgium and abroad.

EXHIBITIONS

until 19·05·97

*Jacques Charlier (B) & Ray Grayson (GB)*

25·05·97-29·06·97

*Klaas Kloosterboer (NL), Peter Zimmermann (G), Walter Obholzer
(A) & Adrian Schiess (G)*

06·07·97-05·10·97

*Exhibition of Architects*  Paul Robbrecht (B) & Hilde Daem (B)
*Artist*  Craigie Horsfield (GB)

12·10·97-07·12·97

*Günter Umberg (D)*

# Gent - Ghent

## MUSEUM VAN HEDENDAAGSE KUNST
Citadelpark  9000 Gent  Director: Jan Hoet
☎ +32 9 2211703  📠 +32 9 2217109
Open: Tuesday-Sunday 09.30-17.00
Monday

COLLECTION

The Museum of Contemporary Art in Ghent focuses on national and
international art movements from the Second World War to the
present. The museum's collection was enlarged by a substantial
inheritance from the Museum of Fine Arts - including works by
Magritte, Delvaux, Bacon and Poliakoff - and is continually enriched
by loans from private collectors, the state and the Friends of the
Museum.
The collection includes work by the Cobra group (P. Alechinsky, K.
Appel, Corneille, A. Jorn and Lucebert) and Belgian Lyrical and
Geometrical Abstract painters such as A. Mortier, A. Cortier, G.
Bertrand and A. Bonnet. Pop Art and French Nouveau Realism are
represented by the likes of Warhol, Christo, Arman and Villeglé. Pop
Art's counterpart in Belgium, New Figuration, with its everyday
reality, is best seen in the work of R. Raveel and R. De Keyzer.
Works by D. Judd, S. Lewitt, C. Andre, D. Flavin and B. Nauman
illustrate Minimal Art, while the work of artists such as J. Kosuth, D.
Huebler and L. Weiner clarify conceptual Art. Arte Povera and Land
Art are represented by the work of M. Merz, J. Kounellis, L. Fabro,
R. Long and B. Flannagan. The museum also owns an important
selection of works by such artists as Beuys, Marcel Broodthaers,
Panamarenko, M. Buthe and Royden Rabinowitch. Recent
developments in art are captured in specific works by artists such as
I. Kabakov, Th. Schütte, D. Hammons, M. Kelly, R. Gober, C. Noland
and H. Steinbach. The latest crop of Belgian artists such as J.

Vercruysse, Th. De Cordier, L. Tuymans and M. François are also included in the collection.

**EXHIBITIONS** No details available

## Gent - Ghent

**MIAT (MUSEUM FOR INDUSTRIAL ARCHAEOLOGY AND TEXTILES)**
Minnemeers 9  9000 Gent  Director: René De Herdt
☎ +32 9 2235969  📠 +32 9 2330739
Open: Tuesday-Sunday 09.30-17.00
Closed: Monday

**COLLECTION**

The MIAT is a young, developing museum, which aims at illustrating and evoking the evolution of industrial society. This is realised in a former cotton mill in the centre of Ghent.
Besides the first permanent exhibition, 'Our Industrial Past 1750-1900', the public may visit the exhibition on 'Child Labour from about 1800 up to 1914'.
There is also a project for the last three years of primary school: 'From Raw Material to Clothing'.
In collaboration with the Taptoe Theatre and the Museum of Scientific History, attention will be paid to 'Two Ghent Gents': Lieven Bauwens and Leo Baekeland.

**EXHIBITION**
12-09-97-28-12-97

***Worker or Matron, Domestic Slave or Mistress***  *The History of Women's Life in the 19th and 20th Century*

## Gent - Ghent

**MUSEUM VOOR SCHONE KUNSTEN  MUSEUM OF FINE ARTS**
Citadelpark  9000 Gent  Curator: Robert Hoozee
☎ +32 9 2221703  📠 +32 9 2217109
Internet http://www.artsite.be/MSKG/parisbrussels.htm
Open: Tuesday-Sunday 09.30-17.00
Closed: Monday

**COLLECTION**

The collection of the Ghent Museum of Fine Arts consists of mainly Flemish art from the 14th century to the present. In the hall there are a series of Brussels tapestries from the 17th century, depicting the story of Darius, and an 18th-century series depicting the Glorification of the Gods. The first room contains a 13th-century French 'Sedes Sapientiae' and 15th-century paintings from the schools of Hugo van der Goes and the Master of Flemalle.

Edouard Manet
*The balcony,*
*c. 1868-1869*
in the exhibition
'Paris-Bruxelles/
Bruxelles-Paris'
Collection: © Musée
d'Orsay, Paris

Among the other 15th-century works are 'Madonna with the Carnation', attributed to Rogier van der Weyden, a Spanish 'Adoration of the Magi' and 'The Coronation of Maria', part of a polyptych by Puccio di Simone. The museum also has 'The Bearing of the Cross' and 'St.Jerome at Prayer' two important paintings by Hieronymus Bosch. One room has 14th-century bas reliefs from Italy and the Nottingham school. The 16th century is represented by Mostaert's 'Village Feast', Gheeraert Hoorenbaut's 'Triptych of St. Anne with the portraits of the donors, Lieven van Pottelsberghe and his wife and 'Calvary' by Heemskerk. There are large 17th-century works by Jacob Jordaens, Gaspard de Crayer and Peter-Paul Rubens ('Stigmata of St. Frances of Assisi), as well as 'The Village Lawyer' by Pieter Brueghel the Younger, 'The Scourging of Christ' by Rubens, 'Jupiter and Antiope' by Van Dyck, landscapes by Roelant Savery, seascapes and animal paintings by Snyders, still lifes by Cornelis Gysbrecht, portraits by Frans Hals and works by Nicholas Maes, Jan van Goyen, Tintoretto and others.

The collection of Belgian and foreign art from the 19th and 20th century includes Impressionist work by Emile Claus, 'Village Fair' by Gustave de Smet, 'Young Peasant Woman' by Gustave van der Woestyne, 'The Poet E. Verhaeren Reading to his Friends' by Theo van Rijsselberghe and 'Old Woman with Masks' and charcoal drawings by James Ensor. Foreign artists include Rodin, Kokoschka, Courbet, Daumier and others. Several contemporary streams are represented, such as Cobra, Pop Art and Minimal Art.

**EXHIBITION**
06·09·97-14·12·97

***Paris-Brussels / Brussels-Paris 1848-1914*** *The Artistic Dialogue between France and Belgium from Realism to Art Nouveau*
This exhibition illustrates the interchanges between progressive artists in France and Belgium during the second half of the 19th century, and will demonstrate how French Realism and Impressionism were received in Belgium and how, in turn, Belgian Symbolism and Art Nouveau were admired in French artistic circles.

# Gent - Ghent

## MUSEUM VOOR SIERKUNST EN VORMGEVING
Jan Breydelstraat 5  9000 Gent  Director: Lieven Daenens
☎ +32 9 2256676  📠 +32 9 2244522
Open: Tuesday-Sunday 09.30-17.00
Closed: Monday

**COLLECTION**

The Museum of Decorative Arts, established in 1903, contains 17th and 18th century furniture displayed in the Hotel de Coninck (built 1755). Its main highlight is the original dining room with a wooden chandelier made by the Ghent sculptor Jan Allaert.

Philippe Wolfers
*Coffee and tea silver service, c.1900*
© *Museum voor Sierkunst en Vormgeving, Gent*

There are also 18th-century paintings, silk wall coverings, more than twenty 18th-century chandeliers and portraits, including one of the

French King Louis XVIII which is placed amidst a collection of French furniture.

The Art Nouveau exhibit contains artefacts by Belgian and other artists. Art Deco and Interbellum styles are represented by Albert van Huffel, Le Corbusier and others. Belgian and Italian designers predominate in furniture, glassware and pottery from the 60s, 70s and 80s. Work by leading Post-Modernists is also on display, including furniture, glassware, pottery, a collection of jewellery made by leading Belgian designers and Belgian carpets and upholstery materials.

**EXHIBITIONS**

until 24·05·97

**Design and Identity**   *Aspects of European Design (Italy and Germany)*

until 24·05·97

**The Other Vessel**   *New International Directions*   An exhibition of works by 17 European ceramic artists.

20·06·97-17·08·97

**Lacquerwork from East Asia**   *Burma, Sumatra and Thailand*

12·09·97-23·11·97

**Art Nouveau**   *From the Museum Collection*

12·12·97-Jan 98

**The Henry van de Velde / Vizo Awards 1997**   An exhibition of the prizes awarded for the categories of Career, Young Talent, Company and Best Product.

## Liège - Luik

**MUSÉE D'ANSEMBOURG**
114, Rue Feronstrée  4000 Liège  Directors: A. Chevalier and M.-C. Gueury
☎ +32 41 219402
Open: Tuesday-Sunday 13.00-18.00  also on 21 Jul
Closed: Monday and 1 Jan, 1, 8 May, 1, 2, 11, 15 Nov, 24-26, 31 Dec

**COLLECTION**

The collection of decorative arts is housed in an 18th-century mansion built in transitional Louis XIV-XV style for the 'haute bourgeoisie'. Much of the original decor has been preserved, including mythological motifs in stucco and elegant woodwork and wainscotting. Chandeliers, porcelain, tapestries, tiles from Delft and Liège and furniture in the styles Louis XIV, Liège Regency, Louis XV and Louis XVI can all be seen in their original setting. The house is listed as one of Liège's historical monuments.

**EXHIBITIONS**

No details available.

## Morlanwelz

**MUSÉE ROYAL DE MARIEMONT**
7140 Morlanwelz-Mariemont
Director: Patrice Dartevelle
☎ +32 64 212193  🖷 +32 64 262924
Open: Tuesday-Sunday 10.00-18.00
Closed: Monday (except holidays) and 1 Jan, 25 Dec

**COLLECTION**

The museum is situated in a park, conceived as an English garden, with lawns and centuries-old trees encompassing monumental sculptures and castle ruins. The architectural structure of glass, steel and concrete is reminiscent of Le Corbusier. Classical civilisations (Egypt, Greece and Rome) and Chinese art are displayed side by side with European decorative arts, local archaeology and history. In both the Classical world and Eastern Asia, cultural evolution can be defined by ceramics and bronzes. Egypt adds granite and alabaster, Greece the whiteness of marble, Rome the magnificent display of colour of the Pompeian frescoes. China completes the pattern with its lacquer, enamel and jade.

*Winged Eros*
From the neck area of a tunic
Small fragment of tapestry, c. 5th-6th C.
in the exhibition 'Egyptian Coptic Textiles of the Nile'
© *Musée Royal de Mariemont, Morlanwelz*

Neolithic artefacts, Gallo-Roman vases and coins, and Merovingian jewellery illustrate the Archaeology of Hainaut. The gallery devoted to the History of Mariemont depicts the old royal domain and its successive castles, the industrial revolution and the flourishing of the Centre-region.
The Tournai Porcelain collection bears witness to the aristocratic refinement of the Age of Enlightenment. The collection of precious books in the library contains thousands of antique and modern volumes, including incunabula, bookbindings and bibliophile editions. This enables regular exhibitions with renewed themes.

**EXHIBITION**
25·04·97-28·09·97

***Egyptian Coptic Textiles of the Nile***   These Coptic textiles were discovered at Egyptian burial sites dating to the late Roman, early Byzantine and early Islamic periods. This exhibition features more than 100 pieces, including 10 complete tunics and many fragments that were decorative elements of the tunics.

## Namur - Namen

**MUSÉE DES ARTS ANCIENS DU NAMUROIS**
24, Rue de Fer  5000 Namur  Director: Jacques Toussaint
☎ +32 81 220065  📠 +32 81 227251
Open: Tuesday-Sunday 10.00-18.00 (17.00 between 1 Nov and Easter)
Closed: Monday and 25 Dec-1 Jan

**COLLECTION**

The museum is housed in the 18th-century Gaiffier d'Hestroy Mansion, a listed monument. Noteworthy objects in the main building of this patrician residence, which has been renovated to accommodate the museum, are a Gothic kitchen chimney decorated with plantain leaves and an Empire double staircase with Ionic columns.
The museum's collection of Medieval and Renaissance art includes numerous wood and stone sculptures, religious paintings (Henri Blès) stained-glass windows, gold and silver objects, glassware and embroidery.

**EXHIBITIONS**
24·05·97-14·09·97

***The Namur Glassmaking Heritage***   This exhibition presents glass from Namur, the birthplace of European crystal manufacture, a tradition which developed in Namur between 1753 and 1867. Different types of glass and crystal from the 19th and 20th century are also on display.

09·11·97-31·12·97 | ***Aegedius Gaspard Pierard*** *A Cabinet-Maker from Bouvignes*

## Oostende - Ostend

### PMMK - MUSEUM VOOR MODERNE KUNST
Romestraat 11  8400 Oostende  Director: Willy van den Bussche
☎ +32 59 508118  📠 +32 59 805626
Open: Tuesday-Sunday 10.00-18.00
Closed: Monday

**COLLECTION**

The PMMK collection provides a survey of Modern art in Belgium, starting from the origins of Modern art through to works of the present day. The collection can be chronologically divided into three parts: the oldest part, represented chiefly by Expressionism; the following part, from around the time of the Second World War and shortly thereafter; and Contemporary art.

Bram Bogart:
*retrospective*
*17-06/24-09-95*
© PMMK - Museum
voor Moderne Kunst,
Oostende

The exhibition policy is international. Belgian art, and especially the most contemporary Belgian art, is constantly being confronted by developments abroad. The museum also strives to promote Belgian art abroad and to display special exhibitions centred around various themes and historical periods.

**EXHIBITIONS**

| until 01·06·97 | *Riera i Arago* |
| until 01·06·97 | *Barcello* |
| 14·06·97-05·10·97 | *Emiel Claus* |
| 14·06·97-05·10·97 | *Antoon De Clerck* |
| 18·10·97-30·11·97 | *Mc Dermott & McGough* |
| 18·10·97-30·11·97 | *Wouter Deruytter* |
| 18·10·97-30·11·97 | *Angh Duong* |
| 20·12·97-01·03·98 | *The Collection of Stephane Janssen* |

## Tervuren

**KONINKLIJK MUSEUM VOOR MIDDEN-AFRIKA**
Leuvensesteenweg 13  3080 Tervuren
Director: Dirk Thijs van den Audenaerde
☎ +32 2 7695211  📠 +32 2 7695638
Open: Tuesday-Friday 10.00-17.00  Saturday, Sunday and public holidays
10.00-18.00  Special opening times during the exhibition.
Closed: Monday and 25 Dec, 1 Jan

**COLLECTION**

A collection of sculptures, masks, utensils and musical instruments illustrates the wealth of African traditional culture and its artistic expression, and allows the visitor to view all aspects of the African continent.

© Koninklijk Museum
voor Midden-Afrika,
Tervuren

There is a Geology & Mineralogy room for those interested in minerals, rocks, the development of the earth's crust, erosion, weathering and vulcanism. A great variety of insects, fishes, amphibians, reptiles, birds and mammals are shown in a reconstruction of their natural environment. The museum also provides a historical account of the explorations of Central Africa and of the work of the Belgians in the former Belgian Congo, now Zaire. Those who wish to go further back in time may view the evolution of the material cultures from the Palaeolithic up to the Iron Age.

**EXHIBITIONS**

Summer 97

***Tervuren and the World Exhibition of 1897***   1997 marks the centenary of the 'Exposition Bruxelles-Tervuren', an event which shook the municipality of Tervuren out of its lethargy. Set in the framework of Tervuren's history, the exhibition will visualise the events surrounding and following the successful Colonial Exhibition.

18·09·97-30·03·98

***Zimbabwe***   An exhibition on the renowned stone architecture of Great Zimbabwe, Khami, Danangombe and Natale, numerous cultural and artistic aspects of Zimbabwe, the material cultures of the different peoples, traditional music and contemporary art.

Calai

Cherbourg

Honfleur

CAEN

ROUEN

St. Germa
en-La

St-Lô

Brest

St-Brieux

Alençon

Chartre

Quimper

RENNES

Laval

Sceaux

Vannes

Le Mans

Angers

Tours

Bl

NANTES

La Roche-
sur-Yon

Châteauro

Niort

POITIERS

La Rochelle

CORSE

Bastia

LIMOGES

Ajaccio

Angoulème

Périgueux

BORDEAUX

Agen

Mt-de-Marsan

Montauba

Auc

Bayonne

TOULOUSE

Pau

Tarbes

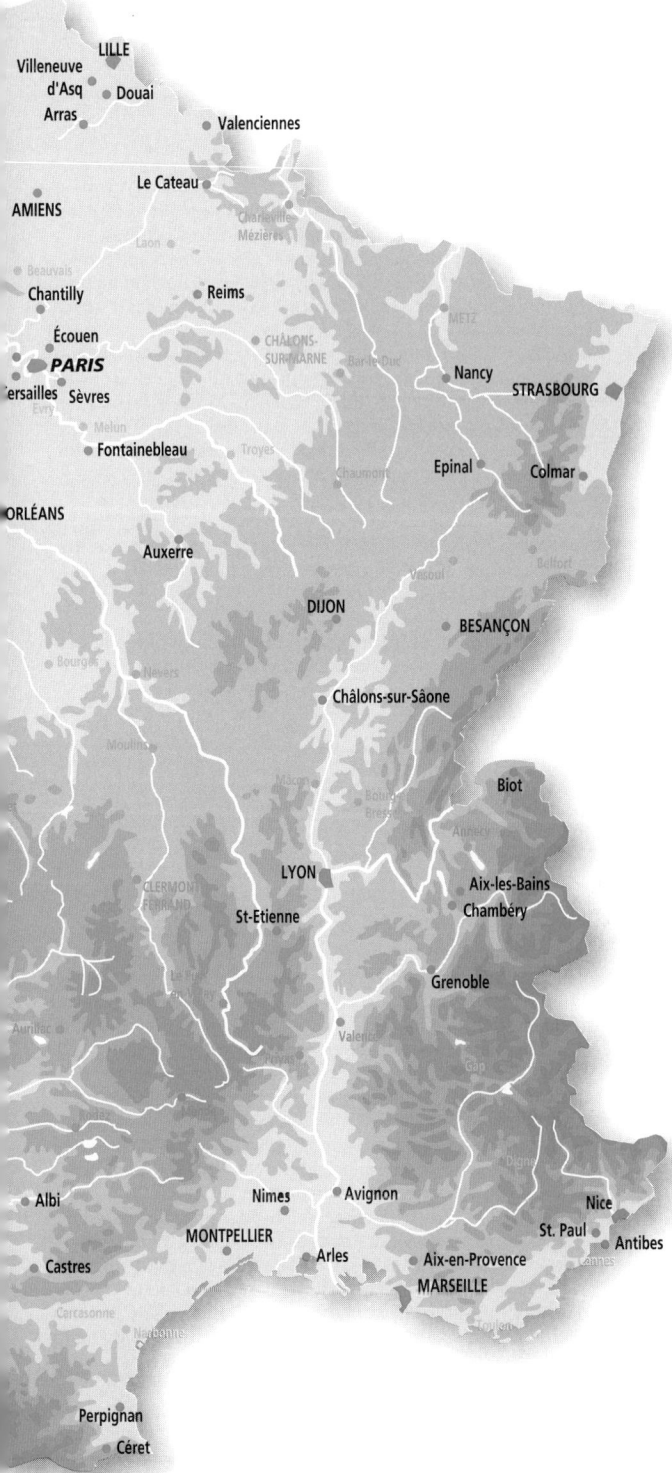

LILLE
Villeneuve d'Asq
Douai
Arras
Valenciennes
Le Cateau
AMIENS
Chantilly
Reims
Écouen
PARIS
ersailles Sèvres
Fontainebleau
ORLÉANS
Auxerre
DIJON
BESANÇON
Châlons-sur-Sâone
Biot
LYON
Aix-les-Bains
St-Etienne
Chambéry
Grenoble
Nancy
STRASBOURG
Epinal
Colmar
Albi
Nimes
Avignon
Nice
MONTPELLIER
St. Paul
Antibes
Castres
Arles
Aix-en-Provence
MARSEILLE
Perpignan
Céret

# Agen

## MUSÉE DES BEAUX-ARTS
Place du Docteur Pierre-Esquirol  47916 Agen Cédex 9  Curator: Y. Lintz
☎ +33 5 53694723  📠 +33 5 53662561
Open: Wednesday-Monday May-Sep 11.00-18.00 Thursday 11.00-20.00;
Oct-Apr 11.00-17.00
Closed: Tuesday

COLLECTION

**Archaeology, Painting, Decorative Art**   The museum of Agen has a collection of archaeological material ranging from prehistory to the Middle Ages, with the emphasis on Celtic and Roman times. Noteworthy is the famous collection of Celtic helmets and arms. Many of the finds will be restored by 1996. From the Roman period is the famous Hellenistic sculpture the 'Venus of the Mas d'Agenais' (1st century A.D.).
The museum's most important paintings are by Goya, Maella and Lucas. There is a fine collection of French paintings, including works by Philippe de Champaigne, Pierre Subleyras, Greuze, Jean-Baptiste Oudry, Corot, Sisley and others.
The museum's decorative arts include French, Italian and Spanish crockery and a collection of glass paperweights.

EXHIBITIONS
31·05·97-30·06·97

*A Poet and a Traveller*   Activity dominates this performance thanks to a combination of words, materials and a theatrical representation of specific situations.

13·06·97-Nov 97

*Goya*   A rediscovery of Goya through the paintings of the museum in combination with the prodigious Spanish collections.

# Aix-en-Provence

## MUSÉE GRANET
Place Saint Jean de Malte  13100 Aix-en-Provence  Director: Denis Coutagne
☎ +33 4 42381470  📠 +33 4 42268455
Open: Wednesday-Monday 10.00-12.00 / 14.00-18.00
Closed: Tuesday

COLLECTION

The Priory of the Knights of Malta, built in 1675, now houses the museum's collection of archaeological finds and art from the 14th to the 20th century. Celto-Ligurian sculptures (3rd to 2nd century B.C.) from the sanctuary of Entremont in Sales, including groups of armed warriors, death masks and bas reliefs, are displayed in the section devoted to the archaeology of Arles in the museum's basement. Everyday life in the Roman city Aquae Sextiae has been reconstructed here. There are also Celtic heads, perhaps sculpted models of real ones that the Celts kept as oracles. The collection also contains Greek and Egyptian finds, including the statue of a Gallic Warrior (200 B.C.) from the school of Pergamon, as well as a 5th-century Christian sarcophagus sculpted in Arles.
**The collection of French paintings** on the first floor begins with primitive works from Avignon such as two panels of the 'Triptyque de la reine Sanche' (1340-1345) by Matteo Giovanetti de Viterbe. There are also 16th and 17th-century works attributed to Carpassin and Le Nain. 18th-century paintings include 'Madame de Gueidan en Flore' by Largillière; 'Portrait de jeune garçon' by David; 'Jupiter et Thétis' and 'Portrait de Granet' by Ingres; 'L'Oriental assis sur un roche' by Géricault; 'Étude de paysage d'Ile-de-France, fin du jour' by Corot (1874); and a collection of works by the Neo-Classical Aix artist Granet (1775-1849) and other artists from Provence including Cézanne.
**The Flemish and Dutch schools** are represented by Frans Hals,

Joos van Cleve, 'Portrait of the artist Rickaert' by Van Dyck and two portraits by Rubens. There are early Italian paintings by Luca Signorelli, Albani, Pietro da Cortone, Luca Giordano and Rosalba Carriera. There are more modern works by Matisse, Masson, Prassinos, Vasarely and others, and sculptures by Puget, Laurana, Houdon and d'Angers.

**EXHIBITIONS**

until 15·06·97

**Devotion**  *Masterpieces of Religious Art, 12th-17th Century, from the Museum's Collections*

Jul 97 onwards

**Regards from Cézanne**

## Aix-les-Bains

**MUSÉE FAURE**
**10, Boulevard des Côtes  73100 Aix-les-Bains  Director: Françoise Guichon**
**☎ +33 4 79610657   📠 +33 4 79882748**
**Open: Daily 09.30-12.00 / 13.30-18.00  Saturday, Sunday 14.00-19.00**

**COLLECTION**

The museum contains the collection bequeathed to the city by Dr. Faure which, together with other donations, is presently housed in the mansion 'Les Chimères'. The attractively displayed works include two pastels and two bronzes of ballet dancers by Degas, and a Rodin collection of 13 watercolours and 28 sculptures in bronze and plaster, among which are 'Faunesse debout', 'Frère et soeur', 'Les Sirènes' and 'Amour et Psyche'. There are landscapes by Corot and Jongkind and Impressionist paintings by Pisarro, Renoir, Sisley, Cézanne and Boudin. The 20th century is represented by Vuillard, Bonnard, Maillol and others.

**EXHIBITIONS**

until 23·05·97

**Joël Negr**  *Sculptures*

30·05·97-30·06·97

**Joe Downing**  *Paintings*

07·07·97-28·09·97

**Paintings of Lake Bourget**  *Paintings of the 19th Century*

10·10·97-14·12·97

**Alfred Boucher**  *Sculptures*   This 19th-century sculptor was a friend of Rodin.

## Albi

**MUSÉE TOULOUSE-LAUTREC**
**Palais de la Berbie  81003 Albi  Director: Danièle Devynck**
**☎ +33 5 63494870   📠 +33 5 63494888**
**Open: Wednesday-Monday Apr-Jun 10.00-12.00 / 14.00-18.00;**
**Jun-Oct 9.00-12.00 / 14.00-18.00;  Oct-Apr 10.00-12.00 / 14.00-17.00**
**Closed: Tuesday**

**COLLECTION**

The museum owns an exceptional collection of works by Henri de Toulouse-Lautrec (b. Albi 1864), spanning his career and covering his preferred subjects: horses, the theatre, brothels, cafe-concerts, and portraits.
Also on view are works by Bonnard, Vuillard, Valadon, and Sérusier among others. The first half of the 20th century and the Paris school are represented by Rouault, Utrillo, De Vlaminck, Dufy and Matisse, etc.

**EXHIBITION**

29·06·97-29·09·97

**Paul Belmondo (1898-1982)**   This exhibition presents bronze busts, medals, monumental sculptures as well as watercolours and red ochre drawings of the female body by the portraitist Belmondo, whose works reflect the classical tradition of the Paris School of Fine Arts.

# Alençon

**MUSÉE DES BEAUX-ARTS ET DE LA DENTELLE**
12, Rue Charles Aveline  61000 Alençon  Director: Aude Pessey-Lux
☎ +33 2 33324007  📠 +33 2 33265166
Open: Tuesday-Sunday 10.00-12.00 / 14.00-18.00
Closed: Monday

**COLLECTION**

The Museum of Fine Arts and Lace has a joint collection of paintings and lace works on display in a specially renovated (1981) section of a 17th-century Jesuit College.
The painting collection includes drawings, prints and paintings from the 15th to the 19th century, with particular emphasis on French and Dutch painters of the 17th century (Champaigne, Jouvenet Macs, Ryckaert) and 19th-century French painting (Boudin, Courbet, Fantin-Latour, Legros, Lacombe).
The major attraction is the unique collection of lace created with various techniques (needle, bobbin, machine) from most of the European schools: Bruges, Brussels, Chantilly, Malines, Milan, Le Puy, Valenciennes, Venice, etc. A highlight of this panorama of lace from the 12th century to the present is the display of Point d'Alençon, the unique lace of Alençon.
A collection of Cambodian objects and artefacts provides an unexpected finale to the exhibits on display.

© Musée des Beaux-
Arts et de la
Dentelle, Alençon

**EXHIBITIONS**

15·06·97-21·09·97

*Jean-Jacques François Monanteuil (1785-1860)*  Retrospective
This unknown painter in the neoclassical style lived in Alençon for more than 20 years and pursued his career in Le Mans in collaboration with Girodet. The exhibition reunites drawings, prints and paintings from France and abroad.

18·10·97-18·01·98

*Goya - Lacombe*  ...To Each His Own Caprices  The 19th century is well represented in the museum's print collection. This exhibition compares 80 engraving plates made by Goya (1746-1828) with those of the contemporary artist Bernard Lacombe, which they inspired.

# Amiens

**MUSÉE DE PICARDIE**
48, Rue de la Republique  80000 Amiens  Director: Mathieu Pinette
☎ +33 3 22913644  📠 +33 3 22925188
Open: Tuesday-Sunday 10.00-12.30 / 14.00-18.00
Closed: Monday and 1 Jan, 1 May, 14 Jul, 1 Nov, 25 Dec

**COLLECTION**

**The Paintings**  The collection of works from the 15th to 20th century includes the Puy d'Amiens from the Cathedral, 'Portrait of a

Man' by El Greco, 'The Miracle of Saint Donat d'Arezzo' by Ribera, 'Portrait of the Pastor Langelius' by Frans Hals and a self-portrait by Quentin de la Tour. The 18th century is represented by Chardin, Fragonard, Hubert Robert, Guardi, Tiepolo, Subleyras, Vien, Regnault and the series 'Hunting in Foreign Lands' painted for Louis XV's 'Petits Apartements' at Versailles. There are also French landscapes mainly from the Barbizon School (Isabey, Diaz, Millet, Courbet, Corot, Th. Rousseau and Daubigny) and 20th-century paintings by Vuillard, Masson, Manessier, Hélion, Jorn, Dubuffet, Fautrier and Picabia.

**The Medieval Collection** This section displays enamels, ivories, objets d'art, sculptures, lapidary work, statues and religious architecture from Picardy in the 12th century and at the end of the Gothic period.

*Carchesium*
*© Musée de Picardie,*
*Amiens*

**The Archaeological Collections** The collection contains tools from Palaeolithic sites in Saint-Acheul and Cagny-la-Garenne, weapons and objects from the Bronze Age, and vestiges of a Roman forum, thermal baths and other items from the Gallo-Roman period.

**EXHIBITIONS**
until 01·06·97

*Homages* *Famous Men, Heroes and Common People.* This exhibition deals with the question of paying homage to famous or fictious people in modern and contemporary art. Works by: Adami, Arroyo, Baselitz, Cucchi, Del Re, Dimitrijevic, Dubuffet, Giacometti, Immendorf, Kiefer, Lupertz, Matisse, Penck, Picasso, Saura and Warhol.

28·06·97-02·11·97

*Antique Glass* This exhibition is based on the important collections of the Musée de Picardie (over 400 pieces) completed with pieces from the British Museum and museums from Périgueux and Rouen.

Dec 97-Mar 98

*100 Drawings from the Museé de Picardie* *French Drawings from the 18th and 19th Centuries* All the masters of the 18th and 19th centuries of the collections of drawings of the Museé de Picardie will been shown for the first time. Works from Boucher, La Tour, Greuze, Fragonard, Prud'hon, David, Boilly, Delacroix, Millet and Gauguin.

## Angers

**MUSÉE DES BEAUX-ARTS**
10, Rue du Musée 49100 Angers Director: Patrick Le Nouëne
☎ +33 2 41886465 📠 +33 2 41860638
Open: Tuesday-Sunday Jun-Sep 09.00-18.30; Oct-May 10.00-12.00 / 14.00-18.00
Closed: Monday

**COLLECTION** The museum's first-floor displays include a remarkable selection of art objects from the medieval and Renaissance periods (ivories, enamels, goldsmiths' crafts, furniture).

The great galleries, built in the middle of the 19th century, house the painting collection. The Livois collection, acquired in 1799, is the nucleus from which the collection has grown. This connoisseur had assembled a fine collection of 18th-century French paintings, as well as an outstanding ensemble of works by 17th-century Dutch and Flemish painters.

Medieval works include fine examples from Italy and a rare Swiss panel.

17th-century examples include paintings by Jordaens, Teniers, Poslenburgh, and Van Thulden of the Northern School, and French artists Mignard, Champaigne and Corneille. The Italian 'Allegory of Simulation' of the Florentine Filippo Lippi is one of the masterpieces of the museum.

The French 18th-century painting collection is particularly rich, with masterpieces by Watteau, Chardin, Boucher, Fragonard and other significant works by artists such as Hubert Robert Oudry and Greuze.

The collection of 19th-century paintings, comprised largely of portraits and landscapes, including Ingres' 'Paolo et Francesca' and Jongkind's 'L'Estacade', reveals the evolution of French art during the first half of the century, from Neo-classicism to Romanticism.

**EXHIBITIONS**

until 08·06·97

*The Painter Alexis Mérodack-Jeaneau (1873-1919)*   This well-travelled and original artist had contact with Matisse, Manguin and others. He and Rodin were among the founders of the International Union of Fine Arts and Letters. New acquisitions and works from the collection are displayed.

until 08·06·97

*Sébastien Leysner*   *A German Sculptor in Anjou*   The artist was born in Würzburg in 1728, studied in Paris and finally settled in Angers in 1758. He was sculptor, decorator and restorer. The collection of drawings and terracotta models helps to recall his forgotten work.

04·07·97-19·10·97

*François Morellet*   *An Amateur Artist*

# Angoulême

**MUSÉE DES BEAUX-ARTS**
1, Rue Friedland  16000 Angoulême  Director: Monique Bussac
☎ +33 5 45950769  🖷 +33 5 45959826
Open: Daily 12.00-18.00  Saturday, Sunday 14.00-18.00
Closed: Public holidays

**COLLECTION**

The Museum of Fine Arts presents a wide collection, spanning 500 000 years of Charente prehistory from the first human habitation to the Casque d'Agris, including a masterpiece of Celtic goldwork from the 4th century B.C., precious stones from medieval Charente, 16th to 20th-century paintings from the French and foreign schools, painting and sculpture from Charente, an extensive collection of art from Eastern and Central Africa, New Caledonia, New Guinea and the Marquise Islands, ceramics from Charente, Rouen, Moustiers and Marseilles and a collection of weapons from the 15th to the 19th century.

**EXHIBITIONS**

until 31·08·97

*Armand Vergeaud (1876-1949)*   *A Painter's Itinerary*   Photographic studies, drawings, paintings and prints allow one to follow the painter's itinerary of artistic creation between tradition and modernity.

| until Sep 97 | ***In André Juillard's Footsteps***   *The Museum Revisited*   The exhibition is organised in a number of themes, such as nature, nymphs, tortured bodies, which distinguish Juillard as a significant artist. |
| 01·10·97-05·01·98 | ***When Charente was under the Sea***   A geological exhibition, in collaboration with the University of Poiters, for those interested in the stories the stones have to tell. |

## Antibes

**MUSÉE PICASSO**
**Château Grimaldi  06600 Antibes  Curator: Maurice Fréchuret**
**☎ +33 4 92905420  📠 +33 4 92905421**
**Open: Tuesday-Sunday  Jun-Sep 10.00-18.00**
**Oct-May 10.00-12.00 / 14.00-18.00**
**Closed: Monday and public holidays**

**COLLECTION**

**Picasso**   During his stay at the Château Grimaldi in 1946, Picasso produced numerous works which he then donated to the museum. Since then, this initial collection has been considerably enriched and includes ceramics, engravings, sculptures and paintings. The materials Picasso used clearly reflect the hardships of the post-war period, but at the same time Picasso captures the joy of living in a newly liberated country in the images he created.
**Modern Art**   The collection includes works from artists belonging to the main movement of 20th-century art: Adami, Alechinsky, Arman, Atlan, Bioulès, Boisrand, César, Combas, Dezeuze, Di Rosa brothers, Equipo Crónica, Ernst, Erro, Gleizes, Hartung, Klein, Magnelli, Messagier, Picabia, Pignon, Raysse, Saura, Spoerri and Viallat.

**EXHIBITIONS**

| until 15·06·97 | *Pierrick Sorin* |
| 28·06·97-30·09·97 | *Black Sun (in the context of the large exhibition The Azure Coast and Modern Art 1918-1958)* |
| 30·10·97-04·01·98 | *Tal Coat* |
| mid Jan 98-Mar 98 | *Jessica Stockholder* |

## Arles

**MUSÉE RÉATTU**
**10, Rue du Grand-Prieuré  13200 Arles  Director: Alain Charron**
**☎ +33 4 90493758  📠 +33 4 90493697**
**Open: Daily 09.30-12.30 / 14.00-19.00**

**COLLECTION**

The museum is housed in the Priory of St. Gilles, built in the 15th to 16th century and bought by the Arles painter Jacques Réattu (1760-1833). Réattu's own works on display include 'Autoportrait', 'La Mort de Tatius', 'La Vision de Jacob', 'La Mort d'Alcibiade' and 'Le Peintre et sa famille au parapluie rouge'. Among the works by his contemporaries are 'Le Peintre et sa famille' and 'Atelier de couturières à Arles' by Antoine Raspal, 'Autoportrait' by Simon Vouet, 'Nature morte à l'aiguière' and 'Jeune Femme au miroir' by Meiffren Compte. There are three Flemish tapestries from the 17th century, 18th and 19th-century paintings from the school of Provence and contemporary works from Arles, including 'Les Alpilles'(1970) by Prassinos and a polyptych 'N.E.W.S.' (1987) by

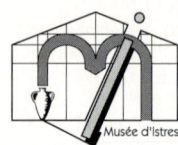

Pierre Mercier. In 1972 Pablo Picasso donated 57 of his drawings to the museum, and his widow Jacqueline later donated a portrait of his mother, Maria Picasso Lopez, from 1923. There is also a statue by Picasso of a woman with a violin. The museum has a photography collection with works by Nadar, Vigneau, Man Ray, Weston, Cecil Beaton, Cartier-Bresson, Gisèle Freund and many others.

**EXHIBITIONS**

Jul 97-Aug 97

***International Encounters with Photography***

15·09·97-15·12·97

***Jacques Réattu*** *Drawings*   A total of 100 drawings, most of which have never been exhibited to the public.

## Arras

**MUSÉE DES BEAUX-ARTS ANCIENNE ABBAYE SAINT-VAAST**
22, Rue Paul-Doumer 62000 Arras Director: Mrs. Notter
☎ +33 3 27712643 📠 +33 3 21231926
Open: Wednesday-Monday
Apr-Sep 10.00-12.00 / 14.00-17.30 Sunday 10.00-12.00 / 15.00-17.30;
Oct-Mar 10.00-12.00 / 14.00-17.00 Sunday 10.00-12.00 / 15.00-17.00
Closed: Tuesday

**COLLECTION**

The museum is located in the centre of the Benedictine Abbey of Saint-Vaast. The ground floor houses an archaeological section and a collection of Medieval sculpture. The most important of the medieval works are funerary sculptures, among which are the tombstone of Bishop Frumauld (late 12th century), several engraved tombstones, wall stelae and the tomb of Guille Lefrançois from 1446. There are also capitals in Tournai stone from the 12th-century cathedral, 13th-century baptismal fonts and a maquette of the city in 1716. In the Alabaster Hall is a 14th-century marble sculpture of the Virgin and Child from Gosnay, a 14th-century St.John the Baptist in English alabaster and the marble funerary mask of a young woman from the early 14th century. There is also a room with wood sculptures from the 12th, 15th and 16th centuries. Also featured are a series of 6 paintings of the Muses by Baglioni, Flemish and Dutch works by Brueghel, Maes and Rubens, French decorative and religious art and paintings by Delacroix, Dutilleux and Corot.

**EXHIBITION**

Nov 97-Dec 97

***Oceania*** *Curious People, Navigators and Scientists*   The exhibition is comprised of objects from museums in Boulogne-sur-Mer, Dunkerque, Lille and Saint-Omer which were collected as far back as the end of the 18th century.

## Auxerre

**ABBAYE SAINT GERMAIN**
2bis, Place Saint Germain  89000 Auxerre  Director: Micheline Durand
☎ +33 86510974  🖷 +33 86427050
Open: Wednesday-Monday Jun-Oct 10.00-18.30
Nov-May 10.00-12.00 / 14.00-17.30
Closed: Tuesday and 1 Jan, 1, 8, May, 1,11 Nov, 25 Dec

**COLLECTION**

The Benedictine abbey of Saint-Germain encompasses 15 centuries of Auxerre history. Overlooking the Yonne River, it includes a crypt containing the tomb of St. Germain, from the time of Charlemagne in the 9th century, adorned by highly-regarded frescoes The original monastery buildings still exist and have been restored. They are now used to house the permanent collections and for special exhibitions. On the grounds are a number of notable sites, including the church (13th century), the cellar (14th century), and the scriptorium and chapter house (12th century). The monks' old dormitory (17th century), has been converted into exhibition space for the local archaeological collections, which consist of prehistoric objects and reconstructions, and artefacts dating to the Gallo-Roman era, including sculptures, tombstones, and murals.

**EXHIBITIONS**

| | |
|---|---|
| until 26·05·97 | ***Marie-Christine Poulenc***   *Photographs* |
| 07·06·97-15·09·97 | ***Yapa, Aboriginal Australian Painters***   *Contemporary Art* |
| Jul 97-Aug 97 | ***New Acquisitions of the Art Library***   *Contemporary Art* |
| Oct 97-Dec 97 | ***Martine Lafon & Florence Mercier***   *Painting, Sculpture* |
| 03·10·97-01·12·97 | ***Janine Niepce, France 1947-1993***   *Photographs* |
| 02·11·97-01·12·97 | ***Gallo-Roman Murals*** |

## Avignon

**MUSÉE DU PETIT PALAIS**
Place du Palais des Papes  84000 Avignon  Director: Esther Moench-Scherer
☎ +33 4 90864458  🖷 +33 4 90821872
Open: Wednesday-Monday Sep-Jun 09.30-12.00 / 14.00-18.00;
Jul-Aug 10.20-18.00
Closed: Tuesday

Vittor Carpaccio
*Holy conversation*
© *Musée du Petit Palais, Avignon*

**COLLECTION**

After many vicissitudes, the collection of paintings acquired by the Marquis Gian Pietro Campana (part of which was bought by Napoleon III in the 19th century) was re-united and came to rest in the 'Petit Palais' in 1976. The collection consists of 300 Italian

Primitive paintings. The works of Botticelli, Carpaccio and Giovanni di Paolo are surrounded by Medieval sculptures and rare examples of the Avignon School of Painting (Enguerrand Quarton, Josse Lieferinxe) on loan from the Calvet Museum.

EXHIBITIONS | No details available.

## Bayonne

**MUSÉE BONNAT**
5, Rue Jacques Laffitte  64100 Bayonne  Director: Vincent Ducourat
☎ +33 5 59590852  ⊞ +33 5 59595326
Open: Wednesday-Monday 15 Jun-10 Sep 10.00-12.00 / 15.00-19.00
Friday 15.00-21.00; 11 Sep-14 Jun 13.00-19.00  Friday 15.00-21.00
Saturday-Sunday 10.00-12.00 / 15.00-19.00
Closed: Tuesday and public holidays

COLLECTION | Louis Bonnat, an academician and painter of many official and society portraits, also collected paintings and over 2 000 drawings which he left to his native city. The museum has since acquired other collections and donations. An archaeological section contains Greek and Roman sculptures, bronze and terracotta statuettes, Phoenician glass and Egyptian amulets. There are 16th-century ivory sculptures, early Spanish paintings including a 15th-century Adoration of the Magi from Valencia, Brussels tapestries, 15 works by Rubens, two portraits by Van Dyck, and works by Murillo, Goya ('Self-Portrait'), Ribera and El Greco. Among the English portraits are Bonaparte by Thomas Phillips and Col. Tarleton by Reynolds. Bonnat also collected sketches by David and several studies and paintings by Ingres, including 'La Bagneuse à mi-corps'. On the first floor there are animal sculptures by Barye and Romantic paintings by Vernet, Corot, Courbet, Delacroix, de Chavannes and Géricault, as well as a portrait by Degas of Léon Bonnat Jr. A room is devoted to the works of Bonnat and a gallery contains his society portraits.

EXHIBITIONS

Summer 97 | ***Henri Zo (1873-1933)*** *The Bullfights*   The museum presents paintings by this student of Léon Bonnat

Autumn 97 | ***Auguste Durst (1842-1930)*** *A 'Barnyard Painter'*   Work by another student of Léon Bonnat

Dec 97-Mar 98 | ***Italian Art 1861-1911***   An exhibition of 100 Italian works in the framework of the cultural agreements between France and Italy.

## Besançon

**MUSÉE DES BEAUX-ARTS ET D'ARCHÉOLOGIE**
1, Place de la Révolution 25000 Besançon  Director: Françoise Soulier-François
☎ +33 3 81823989  ⊞ +33 3 81818109
Open: Wednesday-Monday 09.30-12.00 / 14.00-18.00
Closed: Tuesday

COLLECTION | The Museum of Fine Arts and Archaeology occupies a former grain market adapted to serve as a museum by Miquel, a follower of LeCorbusier. The museum's varied collections include archaeological finds (local, Egyptian, Greek and Roman), Medieval art, paintings ranging from the primitive to the 20th-century, ceramics, sculpture, and objets d'art. Some of the highlights of the collection are a sculpted bull with 3 horns, a number of Egyptian sarcophagi and paintings by such famous masters as Tintoretto, Cranach, Rubens, Boucher, Courbet, Renoir, Bonnard, Matisse and Marquet.

View of the Interior
© Musée des Beaux-
Arts, Besançon

## Biot

**MUSÉE NATIONAL FERNAND LÉGER**
Chemin du Val de Pome  06410 Biot  Curator: Brigitte Hedel-Samson
☎ +33 4 92915030  📠 +33 4 92915031
Open: Wednesday-Monday Summer 10.00-18.00;
Winter 10.00-12.30 / 14.00-17.30
Closed: Tuesday

**COLLECTION**    The museum has been specially designed to display the 348 works
by Léger. There are paintings, tapestries, ceramics and mosaics,
including one that is reflected in a mirror, arranged in chronological
order. Some of the early works are 'Portrait de l'oncle', 'Le Jardin de
ma mère' (1905) and 'Toits de Paris' (1912). The study 'La Femme en
bleu' is in Cubist style. Paintings from his 'mechanical' period
include 'La Joconde aux clés' (1930) and 'L'Avion dans le ciel'.
Among the other works on display are 'Les Belles Cyclistes',
'Les Loisirs' and 'La Grande Parade sur fond rouge' (1953).

## Bordeaux

**MUSÉE DES BEAUX-ARTS**
20, Cours d'Albret  33000 Bordeaux  Director: Francis Ribemont
☎ +33 5 56101749  📠 +33 5 56449816
Open: Wednesday-Monday 10.00-18.00
Closed: Tuesday

COLLECTION

The museum is housed in the Palais Rohan, built in the late 18th century by Prince Archbishop Mériadeck de Rohan, a part of which is the Town Hall of Bordeaux. Its collection of paintings from the Quattrocento and the Renaissance include 'Magdalen' and 'Tarquin and Lucretia' by Titian, 'Virgin and Child with St. Jerome and St. Augustine' by Perugino, 'Holy Family and Donor' by Veronese, 'The Four Ages of Man' by Lionello Spada, 'Embarkation of the Galley Slaves' and 'Galley Slaves' Arrival at the Genua Prison' by Alessandro Magnasco, 'Portrait of a Senator' by Lavinia and 'The Ecstasy of St. Anthony of Padua' by Murillo.
The Flemish paintings include 'The Martyrdom of St. George' by Rubens, 'Magdalen' by Van Dyck, 'Wedding Dance' by Jan Brueghel de Velours and paintings by Pieter van Mol, Gerard Seghers, Otto Venius, Joos de Momper, Frans Snyders and Jan Silberechts. The Dutch school is represented by Salomon and Jacob Ruysdael, Cornelis Verbeck, Claes Molenaer, 'The Lute Player' by Terbrugghen, 'Wheat Field' and 'Lute Player' by Van Goyen, still lifes by David Heem and 'Man with his hand on his heart' by Frans Hals. French portraits include the 'Duc d'Orléans, frère de Louis XIV' by Pierre Mignard, 'La Marquise du Châtelet' by Marianne Loir and 'Joueuse de mandoline' by Grimou. Among the English portraits are 'Baron Rockeby' by Reynolds and 'Mrs Arden' by Gilbert Stuart. Among the paintings from the Romantic period are 'La Grèce expirant sur les ruines de Misselonghi' by Delacroix, 'l'Incendie du steamer l'Austria' by Isabey, 'Le Bain de Diane' by Corot, 'Les Fraises' by Renoir and eight paintings and other works by the Bordeaux artist Odilon Redon. There is an original plaster work by Rodin. Two other Bordeaux artists are Albert Marquet (1875-1947), represented by 'Portrait de mes parents', 'Nu fauve', 'Le port de Bordeaux' and other works, and André Lhote (1885-1962), a Neo-Cubist whose works include 'Baigneuses' and 'Paysage méridional'. There are also works by Braque, Kokoschka and Matisse.

EXHIBITIONS
23·05·97-29·08·97

*Rosa Bonheur*

16·04·98-30·06·98

*Goya*

## Bordeaux

**CAPCMUSÉE D'ART CONTEMPORAIN**
7, Rue Ferrère  33000 Bordeaux  Director: Jean-Louis Froment
☎ +33 5 56008150  📠 +33 5 56441207
Internet http://www.mairie-bordeaux.fr
Open: Tuesday-Sunday 12.00-18.00  Wednesday 12.00-22.00
Closed: Monday and 1 May, 25 Dec and 1 Jan

COLLECTION

The collection, which the museum has been building since the beginning of the '80s, includes representatives of the major international movements from the end of the '60s and the beginning of the '70s, Minimal art, Conceptual art, Land art, Arte Povera, Support Surface, the Nouvelle Figuration artists from the 1980s and the Post-Minimalists. The collection is periodically enriched with new works acquired from current exhibitions, keeping the museum in touch with the latest developments in contemporary art.

At the present time, the museum's collection includes some 500 works of reference by 50 international artists.

**EXHIBITIONS**
until 25·05·97

***The Collection Unveiled***   Nine chapters reveal how the museum's collection developed: shapes, attitudes and concepts (1); painting and deconstruction (2); renewal of pictorial language (3); the return to the painting and to the figure (4/5); photography (6/7); signs, objects, diversions, fictions and organic architecture (8/9).

Jun 97-Sep 97

***Richard Baquié***   This French artist's work can be approached according to three criteria: the displacement of meaning, the almost systematic use of words or phrases, and the effectiveness of strong images.

Jun 97-Sep 97

***Jack Pierson***   This American artist develops work from photographs and sculpture with the characteristically intimate touch of the Boston photographic school.

Oct 97-Dec 97

***Niele Toroni***   Niele Toroni honoured our request to employ the delicate touch of his brush to the monumental architecture of the main nave of the Entrepôt.

Oct 97-Dec 97

***Tony Oursler***   A taste of this artist's dramatic world, in powerful plastic shapes, which is characterised by the use of extremely efficient video systems.

## Bordeaux

**MUSÉE DES ARTS DÉCORATIFS**
Hôtel de Lalande  39, Rue Bouffard  33000 Bordeaux  Director: J. du Pasquier
☎ +33 5 56007250  📠 +33 5 56816967
Open: Wednesday-Monday 14.00-18.00
Closed: Tuesday and public holidays

**COLLECTION**

The museum occupies the Hôtel de Lalande, built in 1780 by the Bordeaux architect Étienne Laclotte. The museum's collections of furniture, miniature paintings, metalwork, ceramics, porcelain and glass, locks, keys and weapons, mainly from the 18th century, are displayed in the panelled rooms of the ground floor and the floor above.

© Musée des Arts
Décoratifs, Bordeaux

There is a collection of French Venetian style glass from the 16th to 18th century, an important collection of French 18th-century faience, a 12th-century gilded and enamelled copper cross and a 13th-century gemellion. The stairway to the first floor has a fine Bordeaux wrought-iron bannister.

**EXHIBITION**
Nov 97-Mar 98

***50 Years of Creative Glass Art***   95 masterpieces of glasswork,

comprising Art Nouveau and Art Deco from the collections of the
Museum of Decorative Arts in Paris.

The furniture includes a divan and chairs in Louis XV style, a
Louis XVI spinet and Chinese vases. Among the paintings are
landscapes, portraits and 500 miniatures, most of them by the
Bordeaux artist Dagoty. There is a bronze statue of Louis XV on
horseback, a bust of Montesquieu by Jean-Baptiste Lemoyne and a
bust of 'Young America' from the house of the first American
consul in Bordeaux. Silver and goldwork includes teapots, cof-
feepots and sugar bowls.

## Caen

**MUSÉE DES BEAUX-ARTS  MUSEUM OF FINE ARTS**
Le Château  14000 Caen  Director: Alain Tapié
☎ +33 2 31852863  📠 +33 2 31791647
Open: Wednesday-Monday 10.00-18.00
Closed: Tuesday and public holidays

COLLECTION

The Museum of Fine Arts of Caen is known for its large collection of
paintings, and in particular for its 16th and 17th-century Italian,
French and Dutch collection, which is considered to be one of the
finest in France. This includes works by Le Pérugin, Véronèse,
Le Guerchin, Tiepolo, Poussin, Philippe de Champaigne and Rubens,
among others.

The museum also possesses a fine collection of paintings relating to
Normandy during the 19th century, and a modern and
contemporary collection based on themes of light and space, by
artists such as Gleizes, Villon, Joan Mitchell, Vieira da Silva, Tobey,
Olivier Debré and Rebeyrolles.

In addition, the museum has a highly-regarded collection of more
than 50 000 prints, including works by Dürer, Callot, Rembrandt,
Tiepolo and Piranese. The printroom regularly presents exhibitions
of works from the collection, as well as exhibitions of modern and
contemporary artists. There is also a public library of art numbering
some 20 000 books.

EXHIBITION
until 26·05·97

*Engravings*   Jacques Deschamps, Monique Frydman, Maurice
Maillard, Charles Marq and Nadjia Mehadji.

## Caen

**MUSÉE DE NORMANDIE**
Logis des Gouverneurs, Château  14000 Caen  Director: Jean-Jacques Bertaux
☎ +33 2 31860624  📠 +33 2 31852794
Open: Apr-Sep Wednesday-Friday 10.00-12.30 / 13.30-18.00
Saturday-Monday and public holidays 9.30-12.30 / 14.00-18.00;
Oct-Mar Wednesday-Monday 9.30-12.30 / 14.00-18.00
Closed: Tuesday

COLLECTION

Founded in Caen in 1946 on the initiative of G.H. Rivière, the
Museum of Normandy aims, through archaeological and
ethnographical collections, to show the cultural evolution of man
within the historical boundaries of Normandy from its very
beginnings up to the present day.

The Museum of Normandy collected the first of its ethnographical
specimens during investigations undertaken in collaboration with
the National Museum of Folk Arts and Traditions. These and other
collections were significantly enriched when the museum acquired
the collections of the Normandy Antiquarian Society in 1984.

The museum's Archaeological Service organises systemic excavations
on the original religious sites in the city of Caen whenever urban
development projects are undertaken.

The museum has established a conservation workshop particularly suited to the restoration of metallic objects and ceramics. After the establishment of the workshop, a survey of the entire museum collection was undertaken, which revealed that it was just as important to restore the ethnographical items as it was to maintain the archaeological collections.

In the mid-80s the permanent exhibition was completely renovated. It is now divided along three principal themes: settlement, techniques, and religious beliefs. These themes are explored in the three sections of the museum: 'From Prehistory to the Vikings', 'Man and the Land', and 'Man and Materials'.

**EXHIBITIONS**

30·05·97-01·09·97

*Archaeology of the Black Sea*  *Crimea during the age of the Great Invasions, IV-VIII centuries*  Recent archaeological finds have shed light on the migrations of Eastern peoples to Western Europe during the first millennium A.D. Gold and silver ornaments are on display, crafted by the artisans of the Steppes.

Jun 97-Oct 97

*Cows and People*  This exhibition illustrates the evolution of cattle breeding over the past three centuries from traditional practices to modern techniques. It explains the organization of agricultural space, management of the herd and selection of animals.

# Calais

## MUSÉE DES BEAUX ARTS ET DE LA DENTELLE
**25, Rue Richelieu  62100 Calais  Curator: Annette Haudiquet**
**☎ +33 3 21464840  📠 +33 3 21464847**
**Open: Wednesday-Monday 10.00-12.00 / 14.00-17.30**
**Closed: Tuesday and public holidays**

**COLLECTION**

**The 19th-Century Sculpture Gallery**  The sculpture collection of the Fine Arts Museum in Calais is based on studies and maquettes realised by the sculptor Auguste Rodin for the 'Monument to the Citizens of Calais'. The works of other 19th-century French sculptors are represented, as well as works marking the transition from the 19th to the 20th century, and contemporary sculptures.

**The Painting Gallery**  The collection includes Flemish and Dutch paintings from the 15th and 16th century, Italian paintings and French paintings, including a 16th-century nude in the form of a Memento Mori and works with maritime subject matter.

**Lace**  Calais has been a centre of industrial lace since the mid-19th century. The museum has a collection of about 300 000 pieces from Calais and other important lace centres which includes hand-crafted as well as industrial products. There are also designer dresses illustrating the use of lace, a collection of looms, tools, plans and maquettes of tulle factories.

**Contemporary Art**  The museum has acquired works by Jean Dubuffet, Andy Warhol and Pablo Picasso, amongst others, and displays works by regional artists.

**EXHIBITIONS**

until 08·06·97

*State of Places, State of Things*  *Photographs by Valérie Belin, Olivier Mériel and Nancy Wilson-Pajuc of a Museum in Creation: The Lace and Fashion Museum of Calais*  Three photographers have been invited to make a record of the museum and its collections before the transformation. This exhibition is also part of the preparations to launch the architectural competition for the Lace Museum.

28·06·97-28·09·97

*Carmen Perrin*  *Sculpture*  Carmen Perrin is a native Bolivian artist whose work has been shown at several important museums. Recent works are presented, including large and small sculptures and a construction specially made for this exhibition.

18·10·97-end Dec 97    *Lace and Lingerie*   This exhibition traces the history of Calais lace as it has been used in lingerie from the beginning of this century to the present. Contemporary collections and older pieces are presented.

early 1998    ***English 19th-Century Watercolours from the Public Collections of Kent and Nord-Pas-de-Calais***   16 drawings are shown, mostly landscapes but also genre scenes and portraits, by famous and lesser known artists such as Richard Parkes Bonington, Peter de Wint, Thomas Rowlandson and others.

## Castres

**MUSÉE GOYA**
Hôtel de Ville  81100 Castres  Curator: Jean Louis Augé
☎ +33 5 63715858  📠 +33 5 63715999
Open: Tuesday-Sunday 09.00-12.00 / 14.00-17.00
Closed: Monday

COLLECTION    The museum's Spanish paintings, displayed in the former bishop's palace built in 1666, were collected by Marcel Briguiboul (1837-1892), a local painter. The four paintings by Goya are 'Self-Portrait Wearing Spectacles', 'Portrait of Francisco del Maza', 'Portrait of Mathias Allué' and the 'Junta of the Philippines' (c. 1814) There is also a series of his engravings. The paintings are displayed in a room containing works by Domingo and father and son Lucas, Hispano-Moorish faience, pharmaceutical vases from the 15th century and Flemish tapestries. The États diocésains room contains a 16th-century Flemish tapestry and paintings from the Dutch, French and Italian schools, as well as a portrait of Lord Ligonier by Saura and a helmet which belonged to George II of England. One room is devoted to archaeological finds in the area of Castres and Celtic and Cathar objects. The Spanish works date from the 14th century to the present, including works by Borassa, Juan Rexach (panels from a retable), Luis de Morales ('Adoration of the Magi'), Velásquez and Osona, and 20th-century works by Bueno, Mateo-Hernandez and Picasso (drawing).

EXHIBITIONS
17·05·97-22·06·97    *Luis Penaranda*   Poetic Illustration

05·07·97-05·10·97    ***French and Spanish Painters***  From Delacroix to Manet   This exhibition presents 56 canvases and 70 drawings, watercolours and lithographs by Millet, Dauzats, Daumier and other French artists who went to Spain between 1830 and 1874 for political, economic and aesthetic reasons.

## Céret

**MUSÉE D'ART MODERNE**
8, Boulevard Maréchal Joffre  66400 Céret  Director: Joséphine Matamoros
☎ +33 4 68872776  📠 +33 4 68873192
Open: Wednesday-Monday Jul-Sep 10.00-19.00; Oct-Jun 10.00-18.00;
May-Sep open daily
Closed: Oct-Apr Tuesday and 1 Jan, 1 May, 1 Nov, 25 Dec

COLLECTION    The collection has been built up with gifts from artists who have stayed in Ceret since the beginning of the century, in particularly Picasso and Matisse, who contributed 53 works and 14 drawings respectively.

**20th Century Historical Art**   These schools are represented by the works of Brune, Chagall, Cocteau, Coutaud, Dalí, Dufy, Apelles Fenosa, Grjs, Gargallo, Haviland, Herbin, Hugué, Jacob, Kisling, Krémègne, Lhote, Maillol, André Marchand, Jean Marchand, Marquet, Masson, Matisse, Miró, Picasso, Pignon, St. Saëns, Survage.
**Contemporary Art**   The museum has significant works by Arnaudiès, Ben, Bertrand, Bordarier, Brossa, Capdeville, Dolla, Eulry, Fauchier, Fischer, Fourquet, Jaccard, Jude, Martin, Messager, Rebeyrolle, Rossell, Tàpies, Viallat, Vila.
The collection is completed by works of New Realism, including works by Arman, Bellegarde, Bertini and Gérard Deschamps.
In years to come the museum will complete the collection of 20th-century Historical Art and will build up collections consistent with contemporary art by encouraging artists to think and work around the area.

**EXHIBITIONS**

May 97

*25 Years of Contemporary Art from the Collection of Yves Michaud*

29·06·97-31·08·97

*Picasso*   *Drawings and Collages in Céret 1911-1913*   This exhibition presents 60 drawings and collages produced by Picasso in Céret, where he was joined by Braque and others and helped to start the museum.

## Chalon-sur-Saône

**MUSÉE NICÉPHORE NIÉPCE**
**28, Quai des Messageries  71100 Chalon-sur-Saône  Director: Paul Jay**
☎ +33 3 85484198   +33 3 85486320
**Open: Wednesday-Monday 14.30-17.30**
**Closed: Tuesday**

**COLLECTION**

The museum focuses on the history of photography and is most renowned for the original equipment used by Joseph Nicéphore Niépce, who invented photography in May 1816. The route through the museum starts with the first heliographs, the first photo-landscape, the first photo-engraving, calotypes and the paper printing processes. One notable item acquired by the museum is the 'Pencil of Nature' by William Henry Fox Talbot published in six parts between 1844 and 1846. The museum also acquired the collection of calotypes from M. Le Prévost d'Iray containing works by Stephane Geoffray, Julien Vallou de Villeneuve and Louis Adolphe Humbert de Molard, three names regularly associated with the origins of photography and the calotype.
Photographs are on display from a complete range of photographers, from the very first to the very latest, and on a wide range of support mediums including wood, canvas, photographic enamel and porcelain. The collection of photographic equipment ranges from the Camera Obscura to Hasselblad's lunar camera, from the 3D table to the 3D camera, from the daguerreotype camera to the Number I Kodak camera and from Niépce's first camera to ferrotyping.

**EXHIBITIONS**

until 19·05·97

*Shaken but not Stirred*   28 photographs from European academies represent young photographic art of Europe.

13·06·97-end Autumn 97

*The Red Eye*   *Dominique Pasqualini*   In this exhibition a creator is given carte blanche.

end Autumn 97

*The Little Bird of Light*   The Gaudin brothers, three important figures in the history of photography.

end Autumn 97

*The 1997 Niépce Prize*   *Awarded by the Gens d'Images*

# Chambéry

**MUSÉE DES BEAUX-ARTS**
Place du Palais-de-Justice  73000 Chambéry  Director: Armand Amann
☎ +33 4 79337503  🖷 +33 4 79750779
Open: Wednesday-Monday 10.00-12.00 / 14.00-18.00
Closed: Tuesday and public holidays

COLLECTION

The museum is situated in the former grain market opposite the Palais de Justice. Thanks to the Daille and Garrod donations, the museum has a collection of works ranging from the 14th to 20th century. The earliest work is the 'Retable de la Trinité' (1396) by Bartolo di Fredi. 15th-century works include the 'Passion Triptych' (c. 1440) attributed to Domenico di Michelino and 'Portrait of a Young Man' by Paolo Uccello. Among the 16th-century artists are Jan van Dornicke, Anton von Worms, Joos van Cleve, Bassano and Naldini. The 17th century is represented by, among others, Nicolaes Moyaert, Abraham Storck, Luca Giordano and Claudio Francesco Beaumont, and the 18th-century Neo-Classicists by Langlois and Isabey.

EXHIBITIONS

21·06·97-20·09·97

***From Landscape to Landscape***   Various landscapes are presented from the collections of the museums and different museums in the Rhône Alps region.

21·06·97-20·09·97

***Marcel Giraud***   This 20th-century artist from Savoy produced landscapes, still-lifes, portraits and ceramics.

Autumn 97

***10th Anniversary of the 'Artothèque'***   The Artothèque of Chambery presents a representative selection of contemporary prints reflecting the artistic expression of the Western world from 1960 to the present.

Winter 97

***Nicole Lombard***   The work of a local artist who was given a chance to exhibit her works in the framework of the museum's carte blanche scheme.

# Chantilly

**MUSÉE CONDÉ**
Château de Chantilly  60631 Chantilly  Director: Amélie Lefébure
☎ +33 3 44626261  🖷 +33 3 44626262
Open: Mar-Oct Wednesday-Monday 10.00-18.00; Nov-Feb
Tuesday-Friday 10.30-12.45 / 14.00-17.00  Saturday and Sunday 10.30-17.00
Closed: Tuesday

COLLECTION

The collection of the Musée Condé is housed in Chantilly Castle, parts of which date back to the 14th century. Its last private owner, the Duke d'Aumale, bequeathed the castle and its extensive art collection to the French Institute and restored the building to its present condition.
**Manuscripts, books, and archives**   The collection includes approximately 800 manuscripts, books and book bindings.
**European paintings**   European paintings from the 14th to the 19th century are displayed in the Great Gallery. The wide-ranging collection includes representative works of the Italian, Northern, and French Schools, as well as examples of French Orientalism.
**Furnishings**   Fine examples of furniture, oriental porcelain, and Chantilly lace are on display in the museum.
**Sculpture**   Sculpture in the classical style, commissioned by the Duke d'Aumale, is on display alongside other works of sculpture pre-dating the French Revolution.

**Building and grounds**   In addition to the castle itself, the surrounding grounds include a park, commissioned in 1666 and designed by Le Nôtre and his nephew Gittard, a pond, five thatched cottages dating from 1774, an English garden, and an 18th-century Jeu de Paume (tennis court) which is used for concerts and other events.

**EXHIBITIONS**

until 29·05·97

*Raphaël and his Circle*   *Italian Drawings of the Musée Condé*
Fifty-two drawings by Raphaël and his circle (Giulio Romano, Polidoro de Caravaggio, Girolamo Genga).

Sep 97-Jan 98

*Pierre-Paul Prud'hon (1758-1823)*   *Drawings and Paintings*
The Musée Condé presents twenty-six drawings of Prud'hon and four paintings in the style of Prud'hon, belonging to the collections of Chantilly.

Sep 97-Jan 98

*A Prince and His Architects*   The Reconstruction of Chantilly in the 19th Century

## Chartres

**MUSÉE DES BEAUX-ARTS**
29, Cloître Notre-Dame  28000 Chartres  Director: Naithe Valles-Bled
☎ +33 2 37364139  🖷 +33 2 37234199
Open: Wednesday-Monday Apr-Oct 10.00-18.00;
Nov-Mar 10.00-12.00 / 14.00-17.00
Closed: Tuesday and 1 Jan, 1 May, 11 Nov, 25 Dec

**COLLECTION**

The collections include paintings from the 16th to the 19th century, an extensive series of Medieval polychrome woodcarvings, 16th and 18th-century tapestries, enamel work, harpsichords and spinets dating from the 17th and 18th centuries. A number of paintings by Vlaminck and a collection on French overseas territories are also on display. In addition to the collections, the architecture of the museum itself includes an 18th-century hall with a horseshoe-shaped staircase, an 18th-century chapel and a room in Italian fashion which is used for the annual 'Mai du Clavecin' (spring concerts).

Chaim Soutine
*The steps of Chartres, 1933*
© Musée des Beaux-Arts, Chartres

**EXHIBITIONS**

30·05·97-29·09·97

*10 Years of Restoration of the Chartres Museum*

16·10·97-05·01·98

*Remembrances of Madeleine Castaing*   Photographs by Claire Flanders

# Cherbourg

## MUSÉE THOMAS HENRY
Rue Vastel  50100 Cherbourg  Director: Jean-Luc Dufresne
☎ +33 2 33230223  📠 +33 2 33230227
Open: Tuesday-Sunday 9.00-12.00 / 14.00-18.00
Closed: Monday

**COLLECTION**

The Thomas Henry Museum owns 300 paintings and sculptures from the 15th to the 19th century, with masterpieces from the Italian, French and Northern schools. These include a famous Fra Angelico, Romantic sculptures by Le Veel, numerous portraits and sketches by J.F. Millet and a superb collection of works by Guillaume Fouace.

Fra Angelico
(1387-1455)
*The conversion of
St.Augustine*
© Musée Thomas
Henry, Cherbourg

**EXHIBITIONS**

06·06·97-12·10·97

**Henri Hayden (1883-1970)**  *Retrospective*   Henri Hayden was a first-generation Cubist who went back to studying nature, finding a unique style. His landscapes were praised by his friend Samuel Beckett.

15·11·97-15·01·98

**Painting in Jersey**  *A Selection of Painters from Jersey*

# Colmar

## MUSÉE D'UNTERLINDEN
1, Rue d'Unterlinden  68000 Colmar  Curator: Sylvie Lecoq-Ramond
☎ +33 3 89201550  📠 +33 3 89412622
Open: Wednesday-Monday Apr-Oct 09.00-16.00;
Nov-Mar 09.00-12.00 / 14.00-17.00
Closed: Tuesday, 1 Jan, 1 May, 1 Nov, 25 Dec

**COLLECTION**

The museum is housed in what was once a Dominican convent dating from the 13th century, dedicated to St. John the Baptist. It contains fine examples of Rhenish art from the late medieval and Renaissance period. The Issenheim altarpiece, composed of sculptures by Nicolas Haguenau (c. 1490) and paintings by Grünewald (c. 1512-1516), is the masterpiece of the collection. The basement and ground floor contain the following sections: archaeology, the minor arts, decorative and popular arts from Alsace and contemporary art. Works by artists ranging from Lucas Cranach and Holbein the Elder to Bonnard, Picasso and Bazaine have been added to the Unterlinden Museum's collection.

**EXHIBITIONS**

until 01·06·97

**The Carnation Period**  *The Technique of the Primitives*

14·06·97-14·09·97

**Tal-Coat**

18·10·97-15·02·98

**Outside the Walls**  *The Fifties*

## Dijon

**MUSÉE ARCHÉOLOGIQUE DE DIJON**
5, Rue Docteur Maret  21000 Dijon  Curator: Monique Jannet
☎ +33 3 80308854  🖷 +33 3 80745299
Open: Wednesday-Monday Jun-Sep 09.30-18.00;
Oct-May 09.00-12.00 / 14.00-18.00
Closed: Tuesday and public holidays

COLLECTION

The museum occupies the so-called 'dormitory of the Benedictines', dating from the 13th century, of the Abbey of Saint-Bénigne and another smaller 11th-century room. Its collection ranges from prehistoric times to the Middle Ages. The exhibit begins with monumental Gallo-Roman sculpture, including funerary figures of a wine merchant, butcher and Saône boatman. There is a collection of votive figures in wood, bronze and stone from the source of the Seine, including two rare anatomical examples, and a bronze figure of the goddess Sequana standing on a beaked boat.
Medieval and Renaissance stone sculpture includes the Bust of Christ (c. 1400) by Claus Sluter, two Romanesque tympana from the old Saint-Benigne church, the Head of Christ by Claus de Werve and two 12th-century capitals.
The prehistoric collection includes artefacts confirming the presence of Neanderthal man on the Côte-d'Or, such as a reconstructed skull fragment (70 000 years old), silex knives and arrowheads. There is a Paleolithic fragment of a laurel-leaf solutrean implement (c. 18 000 years old), a Merovingian gold bracelet and other funerary articles.

© Musée
Archéologique
Dijon

EXHIBITIONS

18·06·97-25·06·97

***The Children's Workshop***   Under the direction of three supervisors, the children - varying in age from 8 to 12 - discover the museum's collections and the practice of various techniques: drawing, painting, modelling, sculpture. This exhibition displays what the children have created in the past year.

10·10·97-12·01·98

***The Birth of Art in Europe***   This exhibition does not hope to provide knowledge but to cause emotions. Cave-wall art (paintings and engravings), the common heritage of humanity, lies at the origin of the great history of man. 'The Birth of Art in Europe', conceived by prehistorians from Spain, France, Italy and Portugal, is essentially an exhibition of photographs.

## Dijon

**MUSÉE DES BEAUX-ARTS**
Palais des Etats de Bourgogne  21000 Dijon  Director: Emmanuel Starcky
☎ +33 3 80745270  🖷 +33 3 80745344
Open: Wednesday-Monday 10.00-18.00
Closed: Tuesday except 14 Jul

COLLECTION

Housed in the medieval palace of the Dukes of Burgundy, which served as the seat of regional political power almost continuously from the 15th to the 18th century, the Dijon Museum of Fine Arts has one of the largest and finest collections in France. Relics of the Burgundian dynasty itself include the tombs of Philippe le Hardi and Jean Sans Peur, several altarpieces from the neighbouring necropolis, Chartreuse de Champmol, and a series of paintings from the Flemish School, including the 'Adoration of the Shepherds' by the Master of Flémalle.

Remnants of the Medieval era include the Chapter House, the Philippe le Bon Tower and the Ducal Palace kitchen.

One of the oldest institutions of its kind in France, the museum was originally intended to serve educational purposes and was formally associated with the School of Drawing in 1766. At that time, the museum consisted of two rooms decorated in lavish 18th-century style, both of which can still be visited today. In the 'Salle des Statues', sculptures and copies from ancient originals produced by 18th-century art students are on display, while the 'Salon Condé' exhibits 18th-century paintings, sculpture and furniture, as well as some Louis XVI wood panelling.

Donations, bequests and loans have steadily enriched the museum over the years, permitting a number of extensive and varied collections to be created, including medieval weapons, Swiss and Rhenish Old Masters (unique in France), paintings from the Northern and Italian Schools, drawings and prints, French Renaissance art from the School of Fontainbleu, etc.

The 19th century is represented by James Tissot, Eugène Boudin and Edouard Manet, as well as local sculptors such as François Rude and his pupil Emmanuel Fremiet.

---

# B I B R A C T E

## Visit the site of Bibracte, a Gallic town on Mont Beuvray (Burgundy, France) and its museum of Celtic civilization.

Bibracte is the name used by Julius Caesar to refer to the Gallic town situated on Mont Beuvray. It was the economic, political and religious center of the Ædui, a powerful Gallic tribe.

In the museum of Celtic civilization and on the site itself, European and local archeology are on show by side and complement each other.

The site is open throughout the year.

In 1997, the museum is open from 15th march to 16th november.

Guided tours are organized on request.

Special activities are available for children (heritage classes, excavation school).

For further information, call : 33 (0) 3 85 86 52 35.

CENTRE
ARCHEOLOGIQUE EUROPEEN
DU MONT BEUVRAY

F - 58 370 GLUX-EN-GLENNE - Tél. : 03 86 78 69 00 - Fax : 03 86 78 65 70
E-mail : Diffusion@beuvray.galeode.fr

The collection of contemporary art has been enlarged by a series of donations from Pierre and Kathleen Granville, including works by Lapicque, Messay Bertbolle, Vieira da Silva and others.

Alfons Mucha
*Seated woman*
in the exhibition
'Prague 1900-1938'
*Collection: © Galerie*
*Nationale de Prague*

## EXHIBITIONS

14·06·97-13·10·97

**Prague 1900-1938**  *Secret Capital of the Avant-Garde*   Prague was a centre of modern art during the first half of the 20th century. This exhibition of more than 200 works combines painting, sculpture, photography, applied arts and architecture by artists such as Mucha, Kupka, Preisler, Rodin, Munch, Sima, Styrsky and Toyen.

20·12·97-Mar 98

**Hans Hartung   Drawings**

20·12·97-Mar 98

**Egyptian Masks from the Roman Period**

# Dijon

## LE CONSORTIUM
16, Rue Quentin  21000 Dijon  Directors: Douroux & Gautherot
☎ +33 3 80307523  📠 +33 3 80305974
Open: Tuesday-Saturday 14.30-18.30
Closed: Sunday and Monday

### COLLECTION

The collection of Le Consortium recalls the art centre's past exhibition activities, consisting of almost 150 works, predominantly from the 1980s. Largely comprised of new geometric works (Armleder, Mosset, Federle, Diao, Parrino, etc.), the painting section also includes more 'conceptual' canvasses by artists such as Kawara, Zaugg, G. Merz and others.
The sculpture collection is characterised by large pieces, including works by Graham, Genzken, Stockholder and Knoebel. Lavier, Burkhard and DiBenedetto are especially well represented in the collection.
The international range of the collection is notable (from McCollum to Ruthenbeck and from Vermeiren to Nordman), as is the particularly good representation of recent French art, including works by Boltarski, Morellet, Verjux, Messager, Vieille and Rutault. Labels such as minimal, conceptual, post-modern and especially expressionist and decorative are not applicable; the collection is nevertheless testimony to contemporary artistic approaches.
Exhibits organised by Le Consortium take place at the principal exhibition space as well as at l'Usine, a secondary exhibition space.

EXHIBITIONS

until 21·06·97

04·07·97-Sep 97

until 21·06·97

04·07·97-Sep 97

[LE CONSORTIUM]

*Pierre Huyghe*

*Liam Gillick*

[LE CONSORTIUM, USINE 37, RUE DE LONGVIC]

*Angela Bulloch*

*Peter Halley*

## Dijon

### MUSÉE MAGNIN
4, Rue des Bons Enfants  21000 Dijon  Director: Emmanuel Starcky
☎ +33 3 80671110  📠 +33 3 80664375
Open: Tuesday-Sunday Jun-Sep 10.00-18.00; Oct-May 10.00-12.00 / 14.00-18.00
Closed: Monday and 25 Dec, 1 Jan

COLLECTION

A visit to the Magnin Museum is a visit to the home of two extraordinary collectors. The museum, located in the heart of Dijon, houses the collection of over 2000 paintings, drawings and art objects assembled by Jeanne and Maurice Magnin at the turn of the century. The collection is displayed in their 17th-century mansion, the Hôtel Lantin, which was bequeathed to the state in 1937. In addition to the collection, the furnishings assembled by the Magnins are on display. While the collection includes some important works, the Magnins rarely made expensive acquisitions and thus much of the collection is comprised of paintings and drawings by minor masters.

The collectors continuously sought out rare works, and the museum's rooms, taken together, present a brief history of painting. Northern European artists are especially well represented, including works by Lastman (Rembrandt's master), Bijlert, Janssens, Van der Helst, Lairesse, Van Bloemen and Mengs. The collection also includes a large number of paintings by relatively unknown Italian painters from Venice, Rome and Lombardy.
The major painters of the French school are represented, including Sébastien Bourdon, Laurent de La Hyre, Eustache Le Sueur, Jean-Baptiste de Champaigne, and others. The collection extends to the 19th century, with works by David, Girodet, Isabey, and Delaroche. Drawing and tracings, which are too fragile to be permanently displayed, are exhibited on a rotating basis. The Magnins also purchased furniture and original or unusual objects including a combined desk and chest of drawers by Carel, a double-sided lady's desk, and many faience pieces.

EXHIBITIONS

No exhibitions planned.

## Douai

### MUSÉE DE LA CHARTREUSE
130, Rue des Chartreux  59500 Douai  Curator: Françoise Baligand
☎ +33 3 27871782  📠 +33 3 27990981
Open: Monday-Saturday 10.00-12.00 / 14.00-17.00
Sunday 10.00-12.00 / 15.00-18.00
Closed: Tuesday and bank holidays

COLLECTION

The Musée de la Chartreuse consists of a town hall and a Carthusian convent dating from the 16th and 17th century, where visitors can view the former cloister and refectory.
The collection itself includes works from the Northern Schools

dating from the 15th, 16th and 17th century. One example is the impressive Anchin's Polyptych by the Flemish artist, Jean Bellegambe, which is exhibited in the Carthusian refectory. Dutch works include paintings by the Master of Manna, Van Scorel, Saenredam, Van Ruisdael and Balthazar van der Ast.

From the Italian Schools of the Renaissance Period and the 17th century come works by Maestro di Desco Da Parto, Cavaliero d'Arpino, Vasari, Veronese, Carrache and the sculpture of Jean de Bologne. The masterpiece entitled 'The Denial of Saint Peter' by Pensionante de Saraceni is the only work belonging to a French public collection.

The French Schools of the 18th and 19th century include masters such as Chardin, Nattier, Lebrun, Corot, Isabey and Boudin. Impressionism is represented by works of Sisley, Pissaro and Renoir. The Modern Art collection boasts paintings by Cross, Maurice Denis and Bonnard. The Musée de la Chartreuse is one of the few French museums owning the relief map of a town. The map representing the town of Douai was commissioned by Louis XIV in 1709.

Veronese
*Portrait of a Venetian woman*
© Musée de la Chartreuse, Douai

**EXHIBITIONS**

until 30·06·97

**Douai and Its Fortifications**   This exhibition shows the history of Douai's fortifications from the 11th century up until the 19th century, when the French government authorised their destruction.

04·12·97-01·03·98

**St. Barbara**  *Iconography, Artwork and History*   An exhibit of paintings, sculptures, engravings, tapestries and majolica presenting the story of St. Barbara, who became the patroness of coal miners in the 18th century after gunpowder started to be used in the mines.

Spring 98

**The Tradition of Beer-Making in the North of France**

# Écouen

**MUSÉE NATIONAL DE LA RENAISSANCE**
Château d'Écouen  95440 Écouen  Director: Hervé Oursel
☎ +33 1 34383850  🖷 +33 1 34383878
Open: Wednesday-Monday 09.45-12.30 / 14.00-17.15
Closed: Tuesday

**COLLECTION**

The National Renaissance Museum occupies one of France's most beautiful 16th-century châteaux. Spectacularly overlooking the Plaine-de-France, this lavish residence was built between 1538 and 1555 for Anne de Montmorency, High Constable of France. Some of the most famous artists of the era were engaged, and the château epitomises French architecture towards the middle of the

16th century, including innovations such as the portico on the south wing built to house Michelangelo's 'Slaves', which had been given to the High Constable by King Henri II. The château has retained much of its original painted décor, including a dozen monumental fireplaces reflecting the influence of King Francis I's gallery in Fontainebleau, and it remains a unique example of mid-16th-century French decorative painting.

Chateau d'Ecouen;
South wing: to the
right, portico of the
slaves
*Musée National de la
Renaissance, Ecouen*
© RMN

This setting serves to display one of the most important collections of artwork of the period, illustrating the extraordinary luxury and refinement of the European Renaissance. It includes tapestries, furniture, painted enamels, sculpture, arms and armour, leather wall hangings, goldsmith's work, glasswork, ceramics and stained glass. Notable amongst these treasures are the automaton-cum-clock once know as 'Charles V's Nef', and 'The Story of David and Bathsheba', a 245-foot long tapestry of silk and silver threads. The château is surrounded by 42 acres of park and woodland accessible to museum visitors.

**EXHIBITIONS**
14·05·97-01·09·97

***From the Légion d'Honneur to the National Renaissance Museum***
Using drawings, prints, photographs and other documentary material, this exhibition focusses on the physical transformations of the château of Écouen between 1791 and 1977.

24·09·97-12·01·98

***Bernard Palissy and the Saint-Porchaire Ceramics***    Recent research has shown that Bernard Palissy created at least some of the mysterious 16th-century Saint-Porchaire ceramicware. Some 100 exhibits will be on show, from France, Europe and the United States.

## Epinal

**MUSEÉ DÉPARTEMENTAL D'ART ANCIEN ET CONTEMPORAIN**
1, Place Lagarde  88000 Epinal  Curator: Bernard Huin
☎ +33 3 29822033  📠 +33 3 29820163
Open: Wednesday-Monday Apr-Sep 10.00-12.00 / 14.00-18.00;
Oct-Mar 10.00-12.00 / 14.00-17.00
Closed: Tuesday and 1 Jan, 1 May, 1 Nov, 25 Dec

**COLLECTION**

The museum's collection includes archaeological finds from prehistoric times and the Iron Age, the Celtic and Gallo-Roman period and the medieval period. Small objects and statues illustrate Gallo-Roman religious practice and the beginnings of Christianity. There are also household objects and coins on display. The sculpture and furniture rooms contain illuminations, tapestries, sculptures and other items from the Renaissance and the 17th and 18th centuries.

The museum's ethnographic collection includes handicrafts, signs, farming tools and other objects that provide a survey of traditional rural life. The print collection has a wide variety of prints from France and other countries. There is also a collection of 17th and 18th-century paintings from Italy, France, Flanders, Germany and the Netherlands, containing works by Fragonard, Boucher and others. The museum's collection of contemporary art includes minimal art, Arte Povera and Pop Art by Andy Warhol and others.

## EXHIBITIONS

| 09·05·97-20·06·97 | ***Ephemeral Sanctuary*** *Ceramics by Thiébaut Chagué and Adewuyi Kehinde Ken* |
|---|---|
| 27·06·97-15·09·97 | ***Centenary of the Painter Louis Français*** |
| 15·10·97-end Dec 97 | ***Works by Women Plastic Artists from the Camille Foundation*** |
| Jan 98-Mar 98 | ***The Archaeologist and the Watercolourist*** *From the Expedition to Egypt (1798-1802) to the Excavations of the Department of the Vosges (1818-1824)* *This exhibition is a homage to Prosper Jollois and Charles Pensée.* |
| Apr 98-Jun 98 | ***Pictures of Epinal*** |

# Fontainebleau

## MUSEE NATIONAL DU CHÂTEAU DE FONTAINEBLEAU

Château de Fontainebleau  77300 Fontainebleau  Director: Amaury Lefébure
☎ +33 1 60715070  📠 +33 1 60715071
Open: Wednesday-Monday Nov-May 09.30-12.30 / 14.00-17.00;
Jun 09.30-17.00; Jul-Aug 09.30-18.00; Sep-Oct 09.30-17.00
Closed: Tuesday and 1 Jan, 1 May, 25 Dec

COLLECTION

**Eight centuries of art and history** The epithet of 'House of the centuries, true residence of Kings' given to the Château de Fontainebleau by Napoleon reflects the memory of more than 700 years of sovereigns in France, from the enthronement of Louis VII in 1137 to the fall of the Second Empire in 1870. Much of the interior appearance of the Château as it appears today is due to Napoleon Bonaparte.

**Napoleon I Museum** The Napoleon I Museum is devoted to the Emperor and his family. The decision to create this museum was taken in 1979 when Prince Napoleon, his wife the Princess and Countess de Witt made an arrangement with the state involving the donation and transfer of a part of the imperial family's collections. The museum is located in the Louis XV wing, constructed between 1738 and 1774, and divided thematically between the rooms of the first and ground floors. The themes include: Napoleon, Emperor of the French and King of Italy; the splendour surrounding imperial power; everyday life in the palaces and on campaigns; the tireless worker; Empress Marie-Louise; the birth of his son 'the Little King'. There are also several rooms each depicting one of the members of the Bonaparte family.

**The Chinese Museum** The Chinese collections of Empress Eugénie are exceptional due to both their origin and their sheer number. The Napoleon III salons that house these pieces have been restored. Almost 400 objects were seized as war trophies from the Chinese Emperors' Summer Palace in 1860, mainly jades, porcelains, silks, candelabra, vases, perfume burners in enamelwork and a great 'stupa' in gilded copper decorated with turquoises.

**Apartments, Courts, Gardens and the Park** The Château has many other places of interest, including the Private Apartments situated on the ground floor below the Great Apartments, the various courts, gardens and lakes as well as The Great Border, The Great Park and The Grand Canal.

Exterior view of the main façade and Cour d'honneur *Musée Nationale du Château de Fontainebleau,* Fontainebleau © RMN - Gérard Blot

**EXHIBITION**
Autumn 97

***Books for Exile***   This exhibition in the Diane Gallery of the Château de Fontainbleau contains books from the library of Napoleon I during his exile to Elba. It includes historical essays, ancient and modern classics, novels, the philosophy of the Enlightenment and scientific works.

# Grenoble

**MUSÉE DE GRENOBLE**
5, Place de Lavalette  38000 Grenoble  Director: Serge Lemoine
☎ +33 4 76634444  📠 +33 4 76634410
Open: Thursday-Monday 11.00-19.00  Wednesday 11.00-22.00
Closed: Tuesday and 1 Jan, 1 May, 25 Dec

**COLLECTION**

The Musée de Grenoble houses a fine collection with a remarkable range of Old Masters and many modern and contemporary works. The collection includes many Flemish, Dutch, Italian, Spanish and French artists from the 16th to the 18th century. Highlights are 'Saint Jérôme' by Georges de la Tour, 'Saint Grégoire' by Rubens, 'L'adoration des bergers' by Francisco de Zurbarán and 'Roger délivrant Angélique' by Delacroix. The 19th century is also well represented, but the museum's main strength is its 20th-century collection, with works by Matisse, Marquet, Derain, Vlaminck, Van Dongen, Picasso, Matisse, Léger, Bonnard and leading figures of Surrealism including Magritte, Tanguy, Miró and Max Ernst. The various trends in geometric or informal abstract art are represented by artists such as Van Doesburg, Kupka, Arp, Bill Lohse, Gorin and Soulages. In the contemporary art collection, a great diversity of themes are explored, with works by Sol LeWitt, Kenneth Noland, Ellsworth Kelly, Carl André, Imi Knoebel, François Morellet, Niele Toroni, Allan MacCollum, Christian Boltanski and Bertrand Lavier, among others.

**EXHIBITIONS**
until 25·05·97

***Signac and the Liberation of Colour***   *From Matisse to Mondrian*

Summer 97

During the summer months, there will be a presentation on the reorganisation of the museum's permanent collections.

## Honfleur

**MUSÉE EUGÈNE BOUDIN**
Place Erik-Satie  14602 Honfleur Cedex  Director: Anne-Marie Bergeret
☎ +33 2 31895400  ☴ +33 2 31891876
Open: Wednesday-Monday 15 Mar-30 Sep 10.00-12.00 / 14.00-18.00;
1 Oct-14 Mar 14.30-17.00  Saturday-Sunday 10.00-12.00 / 14.30-17.00
Closed: Tuesday and 1 May, 14 Jul, 25 Dec and 1 Jan-15 Feb

COLLECTION

The museum was officially founded as a municipal museum in 1868 by two painters and natural sons of Honfleur, Louis-Alexandre Dubourg and Eugène Boudin. Renamed the 'Eugène Boudin Museum' on the occasion of significant expansion in 1974, the museum was further enlarged by the addition of a neighbouring building in 1988. Today, the museum offers 1200 sq.m. of permanent exhibition space on six different levels.

**The Désirée-Louveau Hall**  An extensive ethnographic collection including costumes, accessories, lace, furniture, dolls and headgear from various regions of Normandy.

**The Katia-Granoff Hall**  Works by contemporary artists who have lived or worked in Honfleur and Normandy: Vallotton, Dufy, Marquet, Friesz, Ozenfant, Villon, de Belay, Souverbie, Cappiello, Lagar, Grau-Sala, Oudot and the painters of the Rouen School.

**The Chapel**  Temporary exhibitions (2-3 times a year) devoted to artists who have worked in Normandy or to ethnographic and historic themes. When no temporary exhibitions are planned, the Chapel is used to display works kept in reserve.

**The Eugène Boudin Hall**  19th-century painters, including Jongkind, Huet, Isabey, Cals, Courbet, Dupré, Pécrus, Hamelin, Dubourg, Boudin, Monet, Gagnery, Lebourg, Georges-Michel, etc. The Hambourg-Rachet Donation. Works by Boudin, Dubourg, Cals, Saint-Delis, Gernez, Carrière, Gen-Paul and André Hambourg.

**The Hall of Drawings**  Some hundred drawings classified according to theme and artist. New drawings are selected for exhibition each year.

EXHIBITIONS

10-05-97-30-06-97

*Louis Garneray*  A Painter and Sailor  (1783-1857)

05-07-97-06-10-97

*The Cow*  The cow is the theme of this exhibition of paintings from the second half of the 19th century. They depict cows, country scenes and animated landscapes.

25-10-97-end Mar 98

*Headdresses, Costumes and Objects from 19th-Century Normandy*
A selection of objects bequeathed to the museum by Marie-Thérèse and Marcel Legrand.

## Lille

**MUSÉE DES BEAUX-ARTS**
Place de la République  59000 Lille  Director: Arnauld Brejon de Lavergnée
☎ +33 3 20570184  ☴ +33 3 20546948
Open: Wednesday-Monday 12.00-18.00
Closed: Tuesday and public holidays

COLLECTION

[DUE TO RENOVATION THE MUSEUM IS CLOSED UNTIL JUNE 1997]
The museum has extensive collections of art objects from the Middle Ages and Renaissance, sculpture and paintings. The oldest piece is an ivory from Saint-Omer from c. 1100, 'Vieillard de l'Apocalypse'. The Censer of Lille, made of brass decorated with figures, dates from about 1120. From the north of France are a fragment of a Christ figure from 1170, a 14th-century ivory diptych, an alabaster figure of the Virgin nursing the Christ Child and a wax

head by Duquesnoy. There are 15th-century works by Dirk Bouts, Jean Bellegambe and Dirck Vellert. The museum also has 'Herod's Feast', a major work by Donatello in marble. Other rooms contain tapestries from Brussels, Ghent and Tournai, ivories, goldwork, enamels, manuscripts and liturgical objects. There is an archaeological collection with Egyptian, Greek and Roman artefacts and bronze statuettes of Mercury and Mars, found in a Gallic sanctuary in Lille.

The paintings begin with Flemish works from the 16th to 18th century by Uytewael, Van Heemskerk, Floris, Jordaens, Rubens ('Descent from the Cross' 'Martyrdom of St. Catherine', 'Maria Magdalena' and other works) and Van Dyck (including 'Crucifixion' and 'Portrait of Maria de'Medici'). Among the French painters are Philippe de Champaigne, Jean Restout and Quentin de La Tour. There are drawings by, among others, Raphael, Michelangelo, Titian, Ingres, Delacroix and Matisse.

French Romantic and Naturalist paintings include 'Médée' by Delacroix, 'Course de chevaux barbes à Rome' by Géricault, 'L'Après-midi à Ornans' by Courbet, and works by Corot, Rousseau, de Chavannes, Fantin-Latour, Gustave Moreau, Amaury-Duval, Bonnat and others. The Impressionist paintings begin with Boudin's 'Le Port de Camaret par ciel d'orage', followed by 'La Seine à Port-Marley' by Sisley, 'Jeune femme au chapeau noir' by Renoir and works by Monet, Vuillard, Van Gogh and others, and marble statues by Rodin. There are Dutch paintings by Jan van Goyen, Frans Hals, Van Ruysdael and Peter de Hoogh, Italian works by Tintoretto, Bassano Veronese and Guardi and Spanish works by Goya and Ribera.

**EXHIBITION**

Jun 97-Aug 97

***From Raphael to Guardi*** *Italian Paintings from the Palais des Beaux-Arts.*

## Limoges

**MUSÉE NATIONAL ADRIEN DUBOUCHÉ**
Place Winston Churchill  87000 Limoges  Director: Chantal Meslin
☎ +33 5 55330850  ⃞ 33 5 55330855
Open: Wednesday-Monday Sep-Jun 10.00-12.30 / 14.00-17.45;
Jul-Aug 10.00-17.45
Closed: Tuesday

**COLLECTION**

The permanent collection contains more than 12 000 items of porcelain, earthenware, stoneware, pottery and glass.
The pottery section displays works from as far back as the 7th century B.C., proving that pottery is undoubtedly one of the oldest crafts practised by man. This section also features Graeco-Roman, Medieval and 19th-century terracotta works.

Interior view:
central hallway
*Musée Nationale
Adrien Dubouché,
Limoges*
© RMN

Faience is produced by steeping modelled clay in a bath of enamel with a tin base. First developed in the Middle East during medieval times, this technique later spread across Europe. The collection includes outstanding examples of faience from various countries. Made from clay with a high silica content, stoneware was developed in China. In use in Germany since the Middle Ages, it was only used in France on a large scale during the 19th century by such artists as Delaherche, Chaplet and Decoeur.
Porcelain is made from a mixture of quartz, felspar and kaolin. When fired at 1400 C, the material becomes white, hard and translucent. The museum owns an astonishing collection of Chinese porcelain and an unrivalled collection of Limoges porcelain from around 1771 right up to the present. The museum also houses a collection of 16th to 19th-century European glassware.

**EXHIBITION**
Summer 97

*Jean Jaques Prolongeau (1917-1995)*   Ceramist Artist Limousin

## Limoges

**FRAC LIMOUSIN**
Impasse de Charentes  87100 Limoges  Director: Frédéric Paul
☎ +33 5 55770898  📠 +33 5 55779070
Open: Tuesday-Friday 12.00-19.00  Saturday 14.00-19.00
Closed: Sunday, Monday and public holidays

**COLLECTION**

The 'Fonds Régional d'Art Contemporain' (FRAC) has the largest collection of contemporary art in the Limousin region. The sculpture collection features works by Duprat, Toni Grand, Monnier, Muñoz, Séchas, Schütte and Whiteread. The museum also focuses on the various ways in which artists use photography: as a document (work by Acconci, Bas Jan Ader, Burden, Cohen, Dimitrijevic, Huebler, Matta-Clark, Wegman); in its relationship to text (Aballéa, Calle, Kruger, Messager, Mogarra) and as a substitute for sculpture (Culbert, Cumming, Raetz, Webb). The FRAC collection also includes work by the French Supports-Surfaces movement of the late 60s and early 70s.
One-man exhibitions alternate with displays culled from the museum's collection, supplemented by loans from private collectors.

**EXHIBITIONS**
13·05·97-14·06·97

*Collection, Part II*

26·06·97-31·10·97

*William Wegman*   This retrospective exhibition presents more than 200 of Wegman's drawings from the late 1960s to the present day.

07·11·97-03·01·98

*Collection, Part III*

## Lyon

**MUSÉE DES BEAUX-ARTS**
20, Place des Terreaux  69001 Lyon  Director: Philippe Durey
☎ +33 4 78280766  📠 +33 4 78281245
Open: Wednesday-Sunday 10:30-18.00
Closed: Monday and Tuesday

**COLLECTION**

Founded in 1801 and located in the former Benedictine Abbey of the Dames de Saint-Pierre, which was built in 1659, the Museum of Fine Arts houses a collection which includes paintings of the French, Flemish, Dutch, Italian and Spanish Schools, and has sections devoted to local painters, Impressionists, and modern art. There are also displays of ancient, medieval and modern sculpture; French, Italian Oriental and Hispano-Moorish ceramics; and drawings, prints and furniture. The museum has an Islamic collection and a numismatic collection.

28·05·97-17·08·97

***Campaigning for Modern Art***   *Homage to René Déroudille*
The 80 works presented in this exhibition are a salute to the campaign led by this Lyon art critic from 1945 to 1990 on behalf of modern art and to expand the museum's collections (work by Gleizes, Léger, Dubuffet, Villon, Picasso and others).

16·10·97-11·01·98

***Barye***   *Claws and Teeth*   Barye (1795-1875) was a renowned French sculptor of animals, specialising in fights between wild beasts. 90 sculptures in stone, plaster, wax and bronze and 50 watercolours are on loan from the Louvre and various public collections in France.

Mar 98-May 98

***Renovation Phase V***   New reception areas, restored Baroque refectory, conference room, tearoom, bookshop, 7 rooms of 19th-century paintings, large sculptures from the 19th and 20th centuries and large paintings.

## Lyon

**MUSÉE DES ARTS DÉCORATIFS**
**30, Rue de la Charité  69002 Lyon  Director: Guy Blazy**
☎ **+33 4 78371505  ⓕ +33 4 72402512**
**Open: Tuesday-Sunday 10.00-12.00 / 14.00-17.30**
**Closed: Monday and public holidays**

COLLECTION

The Decorative Arts Museum was opened to the public in 1925 and is designed to complement the neighbouring Textile Museum. The museum is housed in the Hôtel Lacroix Laval and displays the use of textiles and tapestries in a 17th and 18th century interior setting. This is one of France's rare 'ambiance' museums with the objects and furniture fitting in perfectly with the décor of a typical town mansion of the classical age. Visitors will also enjoy discovering fine collections of pottery, old watches and clocks, jewellery, enamels and furniture.

EXHIBITIONS

No exhibitions planned.

## Lyon

**MUSÉE DES TISSUS**
**34, Rue de la Charité  69002 Lyon  Director: Guy Blazy**
☎ **+33 4 78371505  ⓕ +33 4 72402512**
**Open: Tuesday-Sunday 10.00-17.30**
**Closed: Monday and public holidays**

COLLECTION

The Textile Museum is closely associated with the history of silk and is housed in the 18th-century Hotel de Villeroy. The collections are divided into two categories, Eastern and Western. The visitor can trace the development of weaving and textile décor, with a special focus given to the Lyon silk industry between the 17th and 20th centuries and to the various uses of the silk produced in Lyon, from high-quality interior decoration to 18th-century costumes through to 20th-century haute couture.

EXHIBITIONS
23·05·97-31·08·97

***Lyon Silk from the 18th to the 20th Century***   The Textile Museum presents 150 pieces of silk from its collection. These textiles, most of which have never been shown publicly, illustrate the many facets of Lyon silk from the 18th to the 20th century.

Nov 97-Jan 98 ***Olivier Lapidus and the Lyon Silk Industry*** Olivier Lapidus, recipient of the 33rd Golden Thimble for Haute Couture, has given the museum 60 samples and 120 accessories from the winning collection, created in close collaboration with Lyon silk makers.

## Marseille

### MUSÉE DES BEAUX-ARTS
Palais Longchamp  13004 Marseille  Director: Marie-Paul Vial
☎ +33 4 91622117   ▤ +33 4 91847372
Open: Tuesday-Sunday Oct-May 10.00-17.00  Jun-Sep 11.00-18.00
Closed: Monday

COLLECTION

The museum is housed in a wing of the Palais Longchamp, built by Espérandieu in 1870. The collection includes two 19th-century works by Puvis de Chavannes: 'Marseille colonie grecque' and 'Marseille porte de l'Orient' and earlier views of Marseille by Michel Serre (1658-1733), one depicting the plague of 1720-1723.
The ground floor contains 15th to 17th-century paintings from the Flemish, Dutch, Italian and German schools, and French works mainly from Provence. Among them are a 'Crucifixion' in the style of Van der Weyden, 'Virgin and Child with donors' by the Master of the Death of the Virgin, two anonymous German panels, 'Noah Building the Ark' by Bassano, 'Gypsy Camp' by Jean de Venne, 'Adoration of the Shepherds' and 'Boar Hunt' by Rubens, 'Village Wedding' by Annibal Carrache, 'The Tears of St. Peter' by Zurbarán, and works by Joos van Cleve, Pieter Brueghel the Elder, Teniers, Snyder, and Ruysdael. Provençal works include 'The Ecstasy of St.Catherine' by Barthélemy Chasse, 'Samson and Delilah' by Louis Finson and 'Virgin and Child' by Nicolas Mignard.
Two rooms are devoted to the works of the Marseille artist Pierre Puget (1671-1745). Among his paintings are 'St. Cécile' and 'The Baptism of Constantine'. His sculptures include 'Perseus and Andromeda' and 'Immaculate Conception'. There are also works by Vannini and Tiepolo, 18th-century paintings of the port of Marseille by Joseph Vernet, and busts and lithographs by Daumier (1808-1897), including 'Don Quixote and Sancho Panza'.

EXHIBITIONS

until 27·07·97 ***Rodin*** *The Inner Voice*  The exhibition presents Rodin's Meditation, part of the Monument to Victor Hugo and representing the Inner Voice, along with other sculptures by Rodin and photographs by photographers who worked with him.

Autumn 1997 ***New Acquisitions***  The works acquired during the past five years include a very rare landscape by Nicolas Mignard and a totally unknown painting by Pierre Puget, The Miracle of Soriano, both from the 17th century.

## Marseille

### MUSÉE CANTINI D'ART MODERNE ET CONTEMPORAIN
19, Rue Grignan  13006 Marseille  Curator: Nicolas Cendo
☎ +33 4 91547775   ▤ +33 4 91550301
Open: Tuesday-Sunday Oct-May 10.00-17.00  Jun-Sep 11.00-18.00
Closed: Monday and public holidays

COLLECTION

The museum is housed in the Hôtel Montgrand, which was bequeathed to the city together with the collections by Jules Cantini. It contains Modern and contemporary art from the beginning of the 20th century up to the present. Among the important earlier works are 'Arcades à l'Estaque' by Dufy; 'Le Tramway' by Vuillard; 'A tire-d'aile by Braque; 'Les Lutteurs' by Kandinsky; 'Self-Portrait' by Bacon; and works by Miró, Dubuffet, Chabaud, Kupka and others. Later works include 'Colère de violon' by Alechinsky; 'Le Verre vert' by Honegger; 'Pretextat' by Picabia; an untitled work by Sam Francis from 1971; 'Peinture' by Yves Klein; 'Ritva dans un fauteuil' by Saura; 'La Fête à Seillans' and other works by Max Ernst; and 'King of the Zulus' by J-M. Basquiat. There are sculptures by Arp, 'Genèse' and 'Ptolémée III'; Christo, 'Empaquetage'; and works by Gonzalez, Brauner, Pons and others. The photography collection includes work by Clergue, Giordan, Mulher Pohle, Pham Viet-Si, Martine Franck, Ralph Gibson and others as well as photographs of Marseille taken in the period 1930 to 1935.

**EXHIBITIONS**

May 97-Jul 97

***Oskar Schlemmer (1888 - 1943)*** This exhibition presents 140 of the artist's prolific works over a 30-year period, including paintings, sculptures, drawings, watercolours, figurines and films of his choreography. He is best known for his influence on the Bauhaus.

Aug 97-05·10·97

***Collective Antifascist Painting, 1961*** Painted by a group of artists in connection with a manifesto proclaiming Algeria's right to rebel, this very large work was seized by the authorities in Milan and the organizers of the first exhibition were prosecuted.

24·10·97-18·01·98

***Charles Camoin (1879-1965) retrospective.*** *The influence of Cézanne and Fauvism* The artist's personal style and sensitivity are illustrated by about 100 paintings and 60 drawings, accompanied by books, catalogues, photographs and correspondence with his teacher, Cézanne, as well as with Matisse, Marquet, Bonnard and others.

# Montauban

**MUSÉE INGRES**
19, Rue de l'Hôtel-de-Ville  82000 Montauban  Director: Georges Vigne
☎ +33 5 63221292  📠 +33 5 63221353
Open: Tuesday-Saturday 10.00-12.00 / 14.00-18.00
Closed: Monday, Sunday morning

**COLLECTION**

The museum is housed in the 12th-century episcopal palace which became the Town Hall of Montauban after the French Revolution. In 1843, a legacy from Baron and former Mayor Vialètes Mortarieu formed the basis for the museum's collection. Subsequently, by means of an initial donation in 1851 and a legacy in 1867, Ingres considerably enriched the museum of his native city with collections of antiquities and Classical paintings as well as more than 4 000 drawings and 20 paintings from his own hand, numerous personal belongings (including the famous violin), and his entire collection of documentation, including engravings, photographs, calques and copies.
In addition to the great Montauban artist, a general survey of painting in France and other countries since the 14th century is provided. The collection features works by renowned artists from Daddi to Delacroix, including Masolino, Lesueur, Mignard, Boucher and David. A hall devoted to the sculpture of Bourdelle provides the link with the 20th century, represented by Olivier Debre, Zao Wou-Ki, Vieira da Silva and others.

**EXHIBITIONS**

until begin Jul 97

***The Apotheosis of Homer*** *Sketches by Ingres, no. 17* A collection of sketches for the painting in the Louvre (1827) among the 300 kept at Montauban.

| | |
|---|---|
| begin Jun 97-end Sep 97 | ***From Heaven to Earth***   This exhibition presents the works of psychic artists who were guided by celestial voices, including Victor Hugo and Augustin Lesage, and artists who were fascinated by the heavens. |
| mid Jul 97-begin Nov 97 | ***The Golden Age (Third Stage)***   *Sketches by Ingres, no 18* Following the exhibitions of drawings from the Montauban and Lyon collections, preparatory studies are presented for the murals of 1840 and the Cambridge paintings of 1862. |
| begin Nov 97-end Jan 98 | ***The Watercolours of Bourdelle at the Ingres Museum***   The museum presents its collection of Bourdelle's watercolours and ink on paper, which have remained mostly unpublished until now. |

## Montpellier

**MUSÉE FABRE**
**39, Boulevard Bonne Nouvelle  34000 Montpellier  Curator: Michel Hilaire**
☎ +33 4 67148300  🖷 +33 4 67660920
**Open: Tuesday-Friday 09.30-17.30  Saturday, Sunday 09.30-17.00**
**Closed: Monday**

COLLECTION   The museum's collection, housed in a former Jesuit College and the adjacent Hôtel de Massilian where Molière once performed, is based on the donations of François-Xavier Fabre, Antoine Valedau and Alfred Bruyas, a friend of Delacroix and Courbet. The basement houses works by Rubens, Brueghel, Teniers, Ruysdael, Jan Steen, Albert Cuyp, M. van de Velde, Van Goyen and Gérard Dou. There is a display of ceramics and faience from Montpellier in the former kitchen. Fabre's collection includes 'Infant Samuel in Prayer' by Joshua Reynolds, 'Virgin and Child with St. John' by Botticelli, 'The Mystic Marriage of St. Catherine' by Paolo Veronese, 'St.Agatha' and the 'Angel Gabriel' by Zurbarán, English landscapes by Richard Parkes Bonington, 'Fontenelle' and 'Louis XIV' by Rigaud, portraits by the Montpellier artist Sébastien Bourdon, 18th-century sculptures by Pajou, Roland, d'Antoine and Houdon, including his 'Voltaire' in terracotta, portraits by Fabre of the Countess of Albany, Alfieri, Canova and Allen Smith, and a self-portrait.
The Bruyas collection contains portraits of Bruyas by Delacroix, Courbet, Glaize and Tassaert, 'St. Jerome in the Desert' by Vincent (1777), 'Portrait of Dr Leroy' by David, 'Solitude paysage franccomtois' and 'Bonjour Monsieur Courbet' by Courbet, 'The Tempest' by Isabey, 'Portrait of Lord Byron' and sketches by Géricault, 'Stratonice ou la maladie d'Antiochus' and studies by Ingres, 'Matinée' and other works by Corot, and works by Cabanel, Degas, Berthe Morisot and Monet.

EXHIBITIONS
May 97   ***Claude Viallat***

Summer 97   ***Geer van Velde***

## Nancy

**MUSÉE DES BEAUX-ARTS**
**3, Place Stanislas  5400 Nancy  Curator: Béatrice Salmon**
☎ +33 83376501  🖷 +33 83853076
**Open: Wednesday-Monday 10.30-18.00**
**Closed: Monday morning, Tuesday**

COLLECTION   The museum occupies one of four pavilions built by the architect Héré in 1755. The exhibit opens with Cubist and Post-Cubist sculptures by Arp, Duchamp-Villon, Henri Laurens and Zadkine ('Vénus accroupie'). Among the 19th and 20th-century French paintings are 'Portrait of Zélie' by Courbet, 'Autumn' by Manet, 'Sunset at Étretat' by Monet, 'Portrait of Germaine Survage' by Modigliani, and works by Suzanne Valadon, Matisse, Utrillo, Vlaminck, Vuillard and others. A section is devoted to decorative art by the Maison Daum from 1878 to the present.

The first floor contains early Italian, Flemish, Dutch and Spanish works, including 'The Tomb of Christ' by Tintoretto, 'The Annunciation' by Caravaggio, 'The Cumaean Sibyl' by Pietro da Cortana, 'Transfiguration' by Rubens, 'The Baptism of Christ' by Ribera and works by Perugino, Palmerucci, Stetter, Van Goyen and others.

Among the French paintings are Claude Lorrain's 'Pastoral Landscape'(1635), Philippe de Champaigne's 'Charity' and Boucher's 'Aurora and Cephalus'. The graphics collection contains drawings by the Nancy artist Grandville, 'La Bataille de Nancy' by Delacroix, and works by Isabey, Friant, Ingres and others.

**EXHIBITIONS**     No details available.

## Nantes

**MUSÉE DES BEAUX ARTS**
10, Rue Georges Clemenceau  44000 Nantes  Director: Jean Aubert
☎ +33 2 40416565  🖷 +33 2 40416790
Open: Wednesday-Monday 10.00-18.00  Friday 10.00-21.00
Sunday 11.00-18.00
Closed: Tuesday

**COLLECTION**     Established in 1801 by consular decree, the restored Museum of Fine Arts presents a chronology of western painting from 13th-century Italy up to the present day. Each period is represented by works of art of exceptional quality, displayed in galleries surrounding a large central courtyard.

**Old Masters**   Less than ten years after its foundation, the museum's collection was enriched when the city of Nantes purchased the private collection of François Cacault which included, among other works, three masterpieces by Georges de La Tour. In the period following this acquisition, the museum focused primarily on acquiring contemporary art. As a result, it made important purchases including 'Portrait of Madame de Senonnes' by Ingres, 'The Winnowers' by Courbet and 'The Kaïd' by Delacroix.

**Modern Art**   Donations from the 'société des Amis du Musée', created in 1911, have permitted continuous expansion of the collection by acquisition. For example, works by Monet, Signac and Dufy were first exhibited at the museum and then later acquired by the society. The Modern Art section also contains works by Sonia Delaunay, Max Ernst, Marc Chagall, Jean Hélion and Pablo Picasso. There is, in addition, an entire room devoted to Vassily Kandinsky.

**Contemporary Art**   The works of numerous contemporary artists, including Pierre Soulages, François Morellet, Martin Barré, Claude Viallat, Toni Grand and Rosemarie Trockel are on display in the museum to provide an impression of contemporary art trends. The museum's focus on contemporary art has been further underscored by the creation of 'La Salle Blanche' (The White Room), where the work of younger artists is on display.

**EXHIBITIONS**

until 19·05·97    *Sarkis*

end May 97-mid Sep 97    *James Reilly*   This British artist, born in Pays de Galles in 1956, represents the figurative tradition of Pop Art, but his subject matter is exclusively the human family.

| | |
|---|---|
| 20·06·97-15·09·97 | ***Faces of the 17th Century*** *French Portraits during the Reign of Louis XIV* |
| Summer 97 | ***Ricardo Lanzarini*** |
| Summer 97 | ***Claude Parmiggianni*** |
| Autumn 97 | ***Camille Bryen*** |
| Autumn 97 | ***The Museum Factory*** *Presentation of the Modern Art Collections* |
| Nov 97-end Jan 98 | ***Jessica Stockholder*** Born in Vancouver and living in New York, this artist assembles monumental, many-coloured constructions containing an element of painting. A new work will be created for this exhibition. |
| end Jan 98-May 98 | ***Kandinsky*** |

## Nice

### MUSÉE ARCHEOLOGIQUE DE CIMIEZ ET SITÉ ARCHEOLOGIQUE
160, Avenue des Arènes 06000 Nice Director: Danièle Mouchot
☎ +33 4 93815957 📠 +33 4 93810800
Open: Oct-Mar Tuesday-Sunday 10.00-13.00 / 14.00-17.00 Apr-Sep
Tuesday-Sunday 10.00-12.00 / 14.00-18.00
Closed: Monday and certain public holidays and 17-30 Nov

COLLECTION

The museum, inaugurated in January 1989, exhibits glassware, ceramic and bronze objects, jewellery and documents - discovered during excavations - from Cemenelum and the Alpes Maritimae province, together with Greek and Italic ceramic vases from the 5th to the 2nd century B.C. Artefacts, inscriptions, scale models and plans are thematically arranged with explanatory notes in a contemporary setting on two levels. The archaeological site includes three complete Roman thermal complexes dating from the 2nd to the 3rd century A.D. and a Paleochristian cathedral and baptistry from the 5th century A.D.

EXHIBITION
Jul 97-Sep 97

***Photographies of archaeological sites of the Near East***

## Nice

### MUSÉE DES BEAUX-ARTS
33, Avenue des Baumettes 06000 Nice Directors: B. Debrabandère / J. Forneris
☎ +33 4 93445072 📠 +33 4 93976707
Open: Tuesday-Sunday May-Sep 10.00-12.00 / 15.00-18.00;
Oct-Apr 10.00-12.00 / 14.00-17.00
Closed Monday

COLLECTION

The 17th-century collection is mainly Italian and includes works by artists including Tassi, Cozza, Guarino, Keil.
The Vanloo dynasty, Natoire, Hubert Robert, Fragonard and Vien (France), Zuccarelli, Creti, Trevisani and Batoni (Italy) form the core of the 18th-century section.
19th and early 20th-century (French) art is well represented from Neo-classicism to Impressionism and beyond. There are works by Besnard, Benjamin Constant, Cabanel, Carolus-Duran, Flameng, Dinet, Degas, Boudin, Monet, Sisley, Guillaumin, Ziem, Bonnard,

Vuillard and Van Dongen, ceramics by Picasso and the glass works of Maurice Marinot.

The museum also houses the collections of Jules Chéret, J.B. Carpeaux, Bastien-Lepage, Marie Bashkirtseff and Marcellin Desboutin.

The Raoul Dufy collection and the Symbolist works of Gustav Adolf Mossa are now exhibited at 77 and 59 quai des Etats-Unis at Galerie-Musée Dufy and Galerie-Musée Mossa.

**EXHIBITIONS**
until 28·07·97

***Nicaise de Keyser*** *The Great Masters of Painting* The redescovery of four huge canvases, painted by Nicaise de Keyser (1813-1887) for the famous art dealer Ernest Gambart (1814-1902). An interrogation on the ideology of the glorification of painting.

28·06·97-26·10·97

***Dufy, the Art of Fashion and the Art of Landscape on the Côte d'Azur*** Focus on the inventive textile projects by Dufy for Paul Poiret and Bianchini-Férier. The Riviera from Vence to Menton seen by Dufy in his mature years.

## Nice

**MUSÉE MATISSE**
**164, Avenue des Arènes de Cimiez  06000 Nice  Curator: Xavier Girard**
☎ **+33 4 93534053   ▤ +33 4 93530022**
**Open: Wednesday-Monday Oct-Mar 10.00-17.00; Apr-Sep 10.00-18.00**
**Closed: Tuesday**

**COLLECTION**

The museum's permanent collection is composed of works donated by the painter and his heirs supplemented with works on permanent loan from the State. The artist lived in Nice from 1917 to 1954.

Entrance hall, new
section of the
museum
© *Musée Matisse*
*Nice*

The collection includes 68 oil paintings and paper collages, 236 drawings, 218 engravings, 57 sculptures, 14 illustrated books, 95 photographs, as well as 187 objects from Matisse's personal collection of silk screen prints, tapestries, ceramics, stained glass windows and documents. The comprehensive nature of the collection provides an insight into Matisse's creativity, sensitivity and tireless labour.

Included here are works from all periods of Matisse's career, from his very 'first' painting, 'Nature morte aux livres' (1890) to the paper collages of 1952: 'Nu bleu IV', 'La Vague' and 'Fleurs et Fruits'. The museum also boasts masterpieces from the artist's Neo-Impressionist and Fauve periods: 'Jeune Femme à l'ombrelle' (1904) and 'Portrait of Madame Matisse' (1905), as well as an ensemble of Matisse's best-known works: 'Interieur à l'harmonium' (1890), 'Tempête à Nice' (1919), 'Fenêtre à Tahiti' (1935-1936), 'Nu au fauteuil plante verte' (1936-1937), and 'Nymphe dans la fôret' (1935-1943).

The Vence period, displayed in the familiar context of the artist's furniture and personal belongings, is represented with 'Liseuse à la table jaune' (1944), 'Fauteuil rocaille' (1946), 'Nature morte aux grenades' (1947).

**EXHIBITIONS**

27·06·97-20·10·97

*La Côte d'Azur and Modern Times*   This exhibition, a collaboration among more than 20 institutions, presents different aspects of artistic creation along the Côte d'Azur between 1918 and 1958. Painting, sculpture, decorative arts, architecture, music, dance, literature, photography and cinema are all featured.

31·10·97-10·01·98   *A Contemporary Editor of the Artist's Book*   *The Picaron Editions*

# Nice

**MUSEUM OF MODERN AND CONTEMPORARY ART**
Promenade des Arts  06300 Nice  Director: Gilbert Perlein
☎ +33 4 93626162  ☎ +33 4 93130901
Open: Wednesday-Monday 11.00-18.00  Friday 11.00-22.00
Closed: Tuesday and 1 Jan, Easter Sunday, 1 May, 25 Dec

**COLLECTION**

The collection contains works by all major artists of the New Realism movement: Arman, César, Martial Raysse, Yves Klein, Niki de Saint-Phalle, Tinguely, Rotella, Deschamps, Villeglé, Raymond Hains, Christo, etc. Each of these artists is represented by at least two works from various periods. Works donated by M. and Mme. Moquay made it possible to create an Yves Klein Room and install the 'Wall of Fire' on the terraces.
American Pop Art is well represented by artists as Andy Warhol, Robert Rauschenberg, Tom Wesselman, Roy Lichtenstein, Claes Oldenburg and James Rosenquist.
Works of the most recent New York abstract school, by artists as Morris Louis, Olitski, Larry Poons and Kenneth Noland are also part of the collection.
The museum also exhibits an important collection of Minimalist art, including works by Viallat, Pagès, Dolla, Flexner, Bioulès and Cane. Works by Groupe 70 artists such as Charvolen, Chacallis, Miguel and Maccaferri are set off against works by Sol Lewitt, Richard Serra and others.

Sculpture by
Jonathan Borofsky
*'Man with Briefcase',*
*1988-89*
© Musée d'Art
Moderne et d'Art
Contemporain, Nice

Artists related to these movements, such as Bernar Venet, Gilli, Malaval, Sosno, Verdet and many others are also featured. A special place is reserved for Ben, a tireless driving force, and other artists connected with Fluxus, such as Filliou, Manzoni, Serge III, etc. A number of works by young artists complete the collection, justifying the double title of the Museum of Modern and Contemporary Art.

## Nîmes

**CARRÉ D'ART-MUSÉE D'ART CONTEMPORAIN**
Place de la Maison Carrée  30000 Nîmes  Director: Guy Tosatto
☎ +33 4 66763570  📠 +33 4 66763585 Internet: http://www.mns.fr/carreart/
Open: Tuesday-Sunday 10.00-18.00
Closed: Monday

**COLLECTION**

The permanent collection is comprised of about three hundred
sculptures, paintings, photographs and works on paper of mainly
European art from 1960 to the present day. Important streams of
contemporary art originating from the Mediterranean countries are
represented, such as the Nouveaux-Réalistes, Arte Povera and
Support-Surface. Work from outstanding personalities can also be
found, for instance J.P. Bertrand, C. Boltanski, B. Lavier, R. Long,
J. Munoz, S. Polke, G. Richter, T. Schütte and S. Solano. A selection
of American art is on display with work from R. Artschwager,
D. Flavin and J. Schnabel.

## Orléans

**MUSÉE DES BEAUX-ARTS**
1, Rue Fernand Rabier  45000 Orléans  Curator: Eric Moinet
☎ +33 2 38533922  ⊠ +33 2 38792008
Open: Wednesday-Monday 10.00-12.00 / 14.00-18.00
Closed: Tuesday and 1 Jan, 1 and 8 May, 1 Nov, 25 Dec

COLLECTION

The Museum of Fine Arts occupies a relatively new five-floor building. The collection ranges from the 16th to 20th century, with an emphasis on 17th and 18th-century French painting. Among the foreign paintings are 'Portrait of a Venetian' by Tintoretto, 'Holy Family' by Correggio, 'St. Thomas, Apostle' (1602) by Velásquez and works by Lambert Doomer, Van Goyen, and Ruysdael. The French paintings begin with 16th and 17th-century works including 'Four Evangelists' by Martin Fréminet, 'St. Carlo Borromeo' by Philippe de Champaigne and 'Triumph of St. Ignatius' by Vignon. Later works include Le Nain, 'Bacchus et Ariane'; Baugin, 'Christ mort'; and portraits by Nonotte, Subleyras, Perroneau, Boucher and others. There are early 19th-century works by Scherrer ('Entrée de Jeanne d'Arc)', Etty, Glaize, Courbet ('La Vague') and Boudin, and later works by Gauguin, ('Fête Gloanec'), Sérusier ('Tricoteuse au bas rouge'), Rouault ('Le Député'), Soutine ('La Raie'), Kupka ('En forme de bulbe'), and Dufy. The section dedicated to Max Jacob contains a portrait of him from 1928 by Picasso. The sculptures include works by Pilon, Houdon, Rodin ('L'Ombre'), Maillol ('Figure centrale des trois Nymphes'), Zadkine ('Le Compositeur') and Gaudier-Brzeska. There is also a collection of 5 000 drawings and 35 000 prints.

EXHIBITIONS

until Aug 97

*Collection of Architectural Models*

May 97-Jun 97

*Drawings by Aignan-Thomas Desfriches 1715-1800*

Jun 97-Sep 97

***The Time of Passion***  *Paintings, Drawings and Romantic Sculpture from the Orleans Museum*

Nov 97-Jan 98

*Michel Leiris  Friendship*

## Paris

**ARC-MUSÉE D'ART MODERNE DE LA VILLE DE PARIS**
11, Avenue du Président Wilson  75116 Paris  Director: Suzanne Pagé
☎ +33 1 53674000  ⊠ +33 1 47233598
Open: Tuesday-Friday 10.00-17.30 Saturday, Sunday 10.00-18.45
Closed: Monday

COLLECTION

Inaugurated in 1961, the Museum of Modern Art of the City of Paris is located in the left wing of the Palais de Tokyo, designed by the architects Dondel, Aubert, Viard and Dastugue for the International Exposition of 1938. The museum owns a large part of its distinctively Parisian image to the generosity of numerous donors, as well as artists from Matisse to Boltanski.
Since 1988 the museum has dedicated itself primarily to specifically European art, an identity which is affirmed in its acquisition and exhibition policies. The priority of the current purchasing policy is to compile a coherent and representative collection of contemporary works from the 1960s to the present. The programme of 'historic' exhibitions alternates between presentations of the work of major figures such as Fautrier, Kupka, Van Dongen, Manzoni, Lissitzky, Giacometti, Sima, Pougny and Derain, and critiques of the European scene organised by the departments of historic and contemporary art ('20th-Century Art in Belgium, Flanders and the Walloon

Region', 'German Expressionism 1905-1914', 'Holland in the 20th Century', etc.)

The ARC provides up-to-date information on current national and international artistic events and developments and supports young talent and innovative artistic research. The museum organises regular complementary events (cinema programmes, readings, contemporary music and jazz concerts, discussions).

**EXHIBITIONS** | No details available.

## Paris

### MUSÉE NATIONAL DES ARTS ET TRADITIONS POPULAIRES
6, Avenue du Mahatma Gandhi  75116 Paris  Director: Michel Colardelle
☎ +33 1 44176000  ⌨ +33 1 44176060
Open: Wednesday-Monday 09.45-17.15
Closed: Tuesday and 1 Jan, 1 May, 25 Dec

**COLLECTION** | The collection of the Museum of Folk Art and Tradition is a testimonial honouring French peasant and craft culture. Dating from the Middle Ages to contemporary times, the works primarily concern aspects of rural life (crafts and occupations) and of social life (festivities, celebratory art, customs and beliefs).

Glass case:
Engagement and
marriage costums
*Musée National des
Arts et Traditions
Populaires, Paris*
© RMN - G.Blot

The museum also houses a documentary and research studies centre, including a book and record library, text and photography archives and an iconography department. In addition, the museum includes two exhibit halls: reconstructions of past times can be visited in the cultural gallery of the museum, while the study gallery offers a more systematic approach to various themes.

**EXHIBITION**
04·11·97-20·04·98 | *Street Musicians of Paris*

## Paris

### MUSÉE DES ARTS DÉCORATIFS
107, Rue de Rivoli  75001 Paris  Curator: Pierre Arizzoli-Clémentel
☎ +33 1 44555750  ⌨ +33 1 44555784
Open: Tuesday-Friday 11.00-18.00  Wednesday 11.00-22.00
Saturday, Sunday 10.00-18.00
Closed: Monday

*Due to renovation works certain parts of the permanent collections are closed. Sep 97 reopening of Middle Ages and Renaissance exhibits as well as the first part of the 19th century collection. 98 reopening of all the permanent display areas with the exception of the 20th Century which will follow in 1999.*

**COLLECTION**

The Decorative Arts Museum was created through the initiative of the Central Union of Decorative Arts in the 19th century and has been housed in a wing of the Louvre Palace and the Marsan pavilion since 1905. It also englobes the Nissim de Camondo museum, and the museums of Publicity, Fashion and Textiles. The museum's collections are very rich and form a reconstitution of the stages of the `art of living' from the Middle Ages up to present day. Some 220 000 works are milestones in the collection: from ceramics to glassware, silverware to jewellery, from furniture to wallpapers and drawings, not forgetting toys and posters. And a large number of these pieces were realized by such reputed creators as Lalique, Vever, Gallé, Majorelle, Riesener, Jacob, Oudry among others.

**EXHIBITIONS**

until 31·08·97

***Saint Cloud Porcelain***   A selection from the museum's Decorative Arts collection, consisting of some 400 pieces of Saint Cloud porcelain dating from the firm's establishment around 1693 up until its closure in 1766.

07·10·97-28·12·97

***Chinese Cloisonné Enamel***   The exhibition features some 200 Chinese Cloisonné enamels from the 15th century up to the present, including a donation from D. David Weill in 1923. It also includes French 19th-century imitations of the models from the Far East.

## Paris

**MUSÉE NATIONAL DES ARTS ASIATIQUES - GUIMET**
6 and 19, Place d'Iéna  75116 Paris  Director: Jean-François Jarrige
☎ +33 1 47236165  🖷 +33 1 47205750
Open: Wednesday-Monday 09.45-18.00
Closed: Tuesday  The museum on nr. 6 will be closed for renovation until beginning of 1999

**COLLECTION**

The Guimet Museum is one of the largest museums of Asian art in the world. During the renovation of number 6 the original collections of Guimet are for viewing in the nearby superb neo-baroque mansion that encloses a Japanese garden.

View of the exterior,
place d'Iéna
*Musée National des
Arts Asiatiques-
Guimet, Paris*
© RMN

The galleries tell the Chinese and Japanese religious history from the 4th to the 19th century. In 1876 Emile Guimet brought from Japan this unique collection that depicts all types of divinities regarded by the various Schools and Sects of the selected ones. If the majority among Buddhists practises Jôdo, the Imperial family's devotion is the Tendai, the nobility's the Shingon and the samurais' the Zen.

On display are paintings and sculptures of Buddhas and Saints, serene or fierce gods, historical Masters, and the largest Mandala in the western museums. Plus some exceptional images of kamis, divinities of prebuddhic religion, the Shinto.

**EXHIBITIONS**　No details available.

# Paris

## MUSÉE CARNAVALET
23, Rue de Sévigné  75003 Paris  Curator: Jean Marc Léri
☎ +33 1 42722113  📠 +33 1 42720161
Open: Tuesday-Sunday 10.00-17.40
Closed: Monday and public holidays

**COLLECTION**　Although several wings of the hotel Carnavalet are currently undergoing restoration, visitors still have access to the archaeological rooms; the Café Militaire and the reception room of the hotel d'Uzès; and portions of the Louis XV and Louis XVI period rooms, where most of the Bouvier and Debray collections are on display.

The great staircase, with its mural paintings by Brunetti, and the drawing room of the engraver Demarteau, whose paintings were executed in 1765 by Boucher, Fragonard and Huet, are especially impressive. Noteworthy in the hotel Le Peletier are the Room of Mirrors, the souvenir collection of the Royal family at the Temple, the gouaches by Le Sueur, the cradle of the Imperial Prince, and works by Jean Beraud depicting Paris during the 'Belle Epoque'. Also noteworthy are the restored settings, including the private room of the Café de Paris, in the Art Nouveau style; Fouguet's jewellery shop by Mucha; and the Art Deco ballroom of the hotel de Wendel.

**EXHIBITIONS**

30·04·97-27·07·97　*Nureyev*　This exhibition presents the artist's collections, souvenirs of his artistic career (costumes, posters, photographs, choreography), personal souvenirs (furniture, paintings, etchings) and remnants of his collections (costumes from the East and the Far East, kilims, precious shawls).

Autumn 97-Winter 97　***The Paris of the Sun King***　Centering on Israel Silvestre and Abraham Bosse, the exhibition shows Paris at the time of Louis XIV as depicted in the etchings of the Musée Carnavalet: crafts, fashion, historical persons.

# Paris

## COGNACQ-JAY MUSEUM
8, Rue Elzévir  75003 Paris  Director: Pascal de Lavaissière
☎ +33 1 40270721  📠 +33 1 40278944
Open: Tuesday-Sunday 10.00-17.40
Closed: Monday and public holidays

**COLLECTION**　During the course of his long life, the businessman, philanthropist and collector Ernest Cognacq (1839-1928) managed to assemble an impressive painting collection.

To accommodate his treasures he built his own museum on the boulevard des Capucines, which was opened in 1929. In 1986 the museum was transferred to the 16th-century Hôtel Donon, which provides a rare example of the Philibert de L'Orme's style as applied to a modestly proportioned mansion. It was restored by the City of Paris and the garden, which stretches as far as the rue Payenne, has been reinstated.

The house comprises some 20 cabinets, galleries, salons, a spacious loft used for temporary exhibitions, and a research library. The aim is to recreate a museum which appears lived in.

The eclectic collection reflects Cognacq's wide range of interests. While paintings predominate, the display also includes wood panelling, tapestries, china figures (Meissen), terracotta busts, furniture (Louis V, Louis XVI), porcelain (Sèvres), marbles (Houdon, Falconet) and precious objects made of gold, enamel and ivory. There are also drawings by Boucher, Fragonard, Watteau, Ingres and many more. The painting collection, including a wealth of portraits, comprises mostly 18th-century works by a range of renowned French artists: Watteau, Chardin, Fragonard, Greuze, Quentin de la Tour and Robert. Other European artists are also represented, such as Rembrandt, Ruysdael, Canaletto, Guardi, Tiepolo and Reynolds.

**EXHIBITIONS** | No exhibitions planned

# Paris

## GALERIES NATIONALES DU GRAND PALAIS
3, Avenue du Général Eisenhower  75008 Paris  Director: Gaïta le Boissetier
☎ +33 1 44131730  📠 +33 1 45635433
Open: Thursday-Monday 10.00-19.00 Wednesday 10.00-22.00
Closed: Tuesday

**COLLECTION** | No permanent collection.

**EXHIBITIONS**

| until 26·05·97 | *Angkor and 10 Centuries of Khmer Art* |
| until 12·07·97 | *Paris-Brussels / Brussels-Paris*  Realism, Impressionism, Symbolism, Art Nouveau 1848-1914 |
| 15·10·97-05·01·98 | *The Iberians* |
| 26·09·97-12·01·98 | *Prud'hon* |
| 08·10·97-05·01·98 | *Georges de la Tour* |
| mid Mar 98-end Jun 98 | *The Arts under Philippe Le Bel* |
| 09·04·98-20·07·98 | *Delacroix*  The Final Years |

# Paris

## MUSÉE JACQUEMART-ANDRÉ
158 Boulevard Haussman  75008 Paris  Director: Axelle Givaudan
☎ +33 1 42890491  📠 : +33 1 42250923
Open: Daily 10.00-18.00

**COLLECTION** | The lifelong devotion of Edouard André and his wife, Nélie Jacquemart, to art resulted in a collection rich in signatures and records of the past.

Major 18th-century French School painters in the collection include Fragonard ('Tête de Vieillard'), Boucher ('Le Sommeil de Vénus'), Chardin ('L'Allégorie des sciences'), Nattier ('La Marquise d'Antin'), Vigée-Lebrun and others.

Paintings by great Dutch and Flemish masters include Rembrandt ('The Disciples of Emmaus'), Franz Hals, Ruysdael and Van Dyck.

Italian Renaissance painting and sculpture includes Bellini ('Virgin

View of the interior
© Musée Jacquemart-
André, Paris

and Child'), Uccello ('St. George Defeating the Dragon'), Tiepolo, Botticelli ('Virgin and Child'), Mantegna (Ecce Homo) and Della Robbia.
Finally, the collection features outstanding furniture (chests by Joseph, Reisner), and carpets and tapestries from leading workshops (Beauvais, Savonnerie).

**EXHIBITIONS**    No details available.

# Paris

**GALERIE NATIONALE DU JEU DE PAUME**
Place de la Concorde  75001 Paris  Director: Daniel Abadie
☎ +33 1 47031250  🖷 +33 1 47031251
Open: Tuesday 12.00-21.30 Wednesday-Friday 12.00-19.00
Saturday, Sunday 10.00-19.00
Closed: Monday

**COLLECTION**    No permanent collection.

**EXHIBITIONS**

until 18·05·97    **Bernard Moninot**    This exhibition presents developments in the artist's work from 1981 to 1996. Moninot continues the tradition of work over transparencies begun in Duchamp's 'Grand Verre'.

until 18·05·97    **Jaume Plensa**    Recent work (1991-1996) of the Spanish sculptor is on display. Plensa's work can be described as a meditation on materials.

10·06·97-19·10·97    **César**  *Restrospective*    This retrospective shows the best of César's polymorphic work, upon which his reputation as one of the most important sculptors of the century is based. The focus is on his revolutionary intuition.

13·11·97-04·01·98    **Emil Schumacher**  *Retrospective*    Emil Schumacher is an essential figure of German art, linking Informal Abstraction and Expressionism.

## Paris

**MUSÉE DU LOUVRE**
75058 Paris Cédex 01   Director: Pierre Rosenberg
☎ +33 (0)1 40205050   ✒ +33 (0)1 40205442
Internet: http://www.louvre.fr/
General information for visitors: ☎ +33 (0)1 40205151 (answering machine)
Reception desk: ☎ +33 (0)1 40205317
Reservation for groups bringing their own guide: Tel: 01 40205760
Reservation for groups requiring a museum guide: Tel: 01 40205177
Main entrance: Pyramid.  Minitel 3615 Louvre
Entrance for groups and visitors with free access: Passage Richelieu.
Open: Entrance Pyramid: Wednesday-Monday 09.00-18.00  Evening opening
hours on Monday (short tour) and Wednesday (entire museum) till 21.45.
The Hall Napoleon (under the Pyramid): 09.00-22.00  Temporary exhibitions
Hall Napoléon: 10.00-21.45 Closing of the galleries starts 30 minutes
before closing of the museum.
Closed: Tuesday and certain public holidays.

**COLLECTION**

The Musée du Louvre is one of the most comprehensive museums in
the world. Its collections present western art from the Middle Ages
to the mid-19th century and the antique civilisations that have
preceded and influenced this art. They are divided into seven
departments: Oriental Antiquities; Egyptian Antiquities; Greek,
Etruscan and Roman Antiquities; Paintings; Sculptures; Objets d'Art;
Prints and Drawings. In addition to these departments, the museum
presents a section devoted to the history of the Louvre, including
the medieval moats erected by Philippe Auguste in 1190.
Various publications are available to the visitors to help them
discover the museum and its works: an orientation handbook (free
of charge, in seven languages), an audioguide (in six languages),
printed guides (to propose different routes), information leaflets in
the galleries...

Louvre-Richelieu
Wing, view of the
Pyramid
© Musée du Louvre,
Paris

The museum also offers guided tours (in French and English) and
workshops and organises annually several temporary exhibitions, as
well as series of lectures, films, readings and concerts in its
Auditorium.

**EXHIBITIONS**

[HALL NAPOLÉON]

until 21·07·97

***Sponsors by the Thousands***  *A Century of Donations by the Friends
of the Louvre*   The spirit of the 'Société des Amis du Louvre' has
been clear from the start: the task was artistic (to purchase works
for the museum), but also patriotic (to enable the Louvre to be a
competitive with foreign museums).

24·10·97-19·01·98

***Augustin Pajou, Sculptor of the King (1730-1809)***   The exhibition,
which includes some 85 sculptures (marble statues, bas-reliefs,
portraits, terracotta's) and 50 drawings, will evoke all aspects of the

personality of an artist who, as a sculptor, is considered to dominate the second half of the 18th century due to his numerous talents.

[RICHELIEU WING]

until 23·06·97

***A Challenge to Good Taste,*** *18th-Century Masterpieces from the Sèvres Porcelain Factory* To avoid heaviness and the trivial, and to give light, subtlety, novelty and variety. Those were the orders given by the first artistic director of the factory around 1750. Personal property of the King since 1759, this factory played a major role in the evolution of style in the 18th century.

03·10·97-05·01·98

***A Mission in Persia,*** *Centenary of the French Archaeological Delegation* To take place at the same time that the new galleries of Iranian antiquities are to be inaugurated, the exhibition, composed mainly of drawings, watercolours, prints, ancient photographs and some archaeological objects, will provide a historical context for the works of art found during this institution's excavations in the period 1897-1912.

[SULLY WING]

until 21·07·97

***Drawings from the Dezallier d'Argenville Collection*** The exhibition comprises approximately 60 drawings from this 18th-century collector who, being a scholar and encyclopedist, collector and art historian, musician and amateur artist, traveller and author of scientific and artistic studies, is considered a representative of the intellectual elite of the century of Enlightment.

03·10·97-05·01·98

***Engravers from the Netherlands in the 15th and 16th Century*** A fine selection of a hundred line-engravings (burin prints and etchings) based on the rarity of the works (unique, engraving known in a few copies only, or engraving not described before) and the beauty of their printing and preservation.

**Paris museum pass**

Valid for 1, 3 or 5 days, the "carte musées monuments" gives wait-free admission to see the permanent collections of 70 museums and sights in and around Paris.

On sale at museums and monuments, Tourist information Bureau (Carrousel du Louvre), metro stations, the Paris Tourist Office.

Information: interMusées 25 rue du Renard F - 75004 Paris. Tel: 1 44 78 45 81. Fax: 1 44 78 12 23.

## Paris

**MUSÉE DE LA MARINE**
Palais de Chaillot  Place du Trocadéro  75116 Paris  Director: François Bellec
☎ +33 1 45533170  📠 +33 1 47274967
Open: Wednesday-Monday 10.00-18.00
Closed: Tuesday and 1 May

COLLECTION

The Musée de la Marine is housed in the Palais de Chaillot, opposite the Eiffel Tower and the Champ de Mars. Its long glass-roofed main gallery retraces the history of the French Navy, beginning in the 17th century.
The Musée de la Marine contains an important collection of original scale models of warships dating from the 17th century and

onwards, including large-scale models. The collections include models of famous ships from the last years of sailing ships and inventions by French engineers from the early years of steam - the archetypes for contemporary naval fleets. These models, along with those of merchantmen, make the Musée de la Marine the guardian of three centuries of naval construction.

A depository for prestigious paintings from the Louvre, the Musée de la Marine exhibits numerous works from various French schools. Among dozens of figureheads, caryatids and atlantes, the museum contains the original sculptures of the galley Réale which sing the praises of the Sun King.

**EXHIBITIONS**

mid Jun 97-mid Nov 97    *Antarctica Winter in Spitzberg*   This exhibition, in the framework of the French Polar Year, is a photographic account of the last mission of Dr. Jean-Louis Etienne to Spitzberg. It recalls the history of French polar expeditions, comparing the conditions, boats and materials of yesterday and today.

mid Oct 97    *Books about the Sea*   An exhibition dedicated to writers about the sea. Including presentation of the Neptunia Prize.

## Paris

**MUSÉE DE LA MODE ET DU TEXTILE**
Union centrale des Arts décoratifs  Palais du Louvre
107 Rue de Rivoli  75001 Paris  Curator: Pierre Arizzoli-Clémentel
☎ +33 1 44555750  🖷 +33 1 44555947
Open: Tuesday-Friday 11.00-18.00  Wednesday 11.00-22.00
Saturday, Sunday 10.00-18.00
Closed: Monday

**COLLECTION**    These collections combine those of the Union Centrale des Arts Décoratifs with those of the Union Française des Arts du Costume, in all 20 000 costumes, and 35 000 accessories dating from the XVIIth century to the present day. The collection also includes 21 000 examples of fabric.

Important pieces by XXth century Haute Couture designers complete the collection: with work by Madeleine Vionnet (who bequeathed her personal archives) to Paul Poiret, the Callot Sisters, Lanvin, Schiaparelli, Mainbocher, Chanel, Dior, Courrèges, Paco Rabanne, Guy Laroche or designers such as Michèle Rosier, Elisabeth de Senneville, Guy Paulin.

The textiles collection includes a remarkable array of silks, printed cloth, lace, decorative braid and embroideries, including part of the embroiderers' Bataille and Rebé archives, or again the little known collection of Rodier fabrics (1859-1910).

**EXHIBITIONS**    No details available.

## Paris

**MUSÉE MARMOTTAN**
2, Rue Louis-Boilly  75016 Paris  Director: Arnaud d'Hauterives
☎ +33 1 42240702  🖷 +33 1 40506584
Open: Tuesday-Sunday 10.00-17.30
Closed: Monday

**COLLECTION**    The collection assembled by Jules Marmottan, founder of the Mines de Bruay and Treasury Paymaster in the Gironde Region, reflects a particular interest in the German, Flemish and Italian Primitives. In contrast, his son Paul concentrated on the history and art of the Napoleonic period, acquiring paintings, sculptures and Empire furniture created most often for the Emperor and his family, including bronzes by Thomire, settees by Georges Jacob and paintings by Carle Vernet and Louis Boilly.

A collection was also donated by Henri Duhem (born 1860), containing paintings, pastels and sculptures by Boudin, Carrière, Corot, Gauguin, Guillaumin, Monet, Pissarro, Renoir, Rodin, Lebourg and Le Sidaner.

The donation made by Madame Donop. de Monchy includes works by Monet, Pissarro, Renoir and Sisley collected by her father, Geroges de Bellio, doctor and friend to the Impressionist painters. Michel Monet, second son of Claude Monet and Camille Doncieux, bequeathed to the museum an important collection of paintings which he had inherited from his father. This not only contained eighty oils, four pastels and three drawings by Monet, but also works by the painter's friends, including Boudin, Caillebotte, Guillaumin, Jongkind, Manet, Morisot, Pissarro, Renoir and Rodin. The Daniel Wildenstein donation consists of his father's extraordinary collection of 228 illuminated miniatures taken over the centuries from French, Italian, German, English, Flemish and Dutch antiphonaries, missals and books of hours.

**EXHIBITIONS**   No details available.

## Paris

**MUSÉE NATIONAL DU MOYEN AGE  THERMES DE CLUNY**
6, Place Paul-Painlevé  75005 Paris  Director: Viviane Huchard
☎ +33 1 53737800  📠 +33 1 46345175
Open: Wednesday-Monday 09.15-17.45
Closed: Tuesday

**COLLECTION**   **Medieval Art**  The National Museum of the Middle Ages, founded in 1843 by the French state, combines two edifices: the ruins of the Gallo-Roman baths and the Hotel of the Abbots of Cluny, housing a substantial collection of Medieval art assembled by Alexandre Du Sommerard. This ranges through sculpture, stained glass, tapestries, textiles, furniture, caskets, metalwork and paintings. The museum is situated in the heart of the Latin Quarter near the Sorbonne.

View of the courtyard of the Hôtel de Cluny
*Musée National du Moyen Age Thermes de Cluny*
© RMN - Gérard Blot

The Paris residence of the Abbots of Cluny was reconstructed by Jacques d'Amboise. The U-shaped building enclosing an inner courtyard was surrounded by a stone wall and overlooked a garden on the north side. The well-preserved inner lay-out of the Hotel has been maintained. The chapel has a vaulted ceiling in the Flamboyant Gothic style.

According to tradition, the Gallo-Roman baths consisted of three large rooms, one for hot steam baths, another for tepid baths and the frigidarium for cold-water baths, with additional common and service rooms. The greater part of these ruins still remain, including the 15-metre high vaulted cold room.

The museum's varied collection evokes all aspects of medieval life and activities. The tapestries, including the magnificent series of the 'Lady and the Unicorn', and stained glass windows conjure up the colourful decoration of Medieval buildings.

**EXHIBITION**
28·05·97-08·09·97

*Insignia and Souvenirs of Medieval Pilgrims*   The exhibition contains lead and tin brooches and other objects mostly discovered in the 20th century during dredging of the Seine. The insignia, worn on hats, capes or other clothing from the 11th to the 16th century, bear religious or profane images.

## Paris

**MUSÉUM NATIONAL D'HISTOIRE NATURELLE**
36, Rue Geoffroy Saint-Hilaire  75005 Paris  Director: Henry de Lumley
☎ +33 1 40793000  ▦ +33 1 40793855
Open: Wednesday-Monday  10.00-18.00  Thursday 10.00-22.00
Closed: Tuesday

**COLLECTION**

Established in 1635, the Royal Garden of Medicinal Plants, which became the Museum of Natural History in 1793, is today still devoted to the conservation and enrichment of collections in the field of the natural and human sciences, basic and applied research, education and the dissemination of knowledge to the general public.

The collection contains meteorites, giant crystals, butterflies, dinosaur skeletons, plants and a herbarium, stuffed animals, shells and prehistoric and cultural objects from all over the world, as well as an arboretum, greenhouses and parks with animal figures. It is one of the three largest in the world which are capable of displaying the biodiversity of our planet.

The museum's staff of 1800 geologists, palaeontologists, mineralogists, botanists, zoologists, entomologists, physiologists, chemists, biologists, ethnologists, gardeners, animal trainers and administrators work in 26 research laboratories and service centres towards a better understanding of the history of life, the mechanisms of evolution, the origin of man and his relationship to nature.

**EXHIBITION**
until 05·01·98

*Life between the Sky and the Sea*     The introduction to this multi-disciplinary approach to island life, "What is an island?", explains phenomena unique to islands. The main themes, "isolation" and "ties", show that an island is basically isolated but subject to changes from outside. The fourth and fifth parts examine the effects of accessibility on unique island flora, fauna and societies.

## Paris

**MUSÉE NATIONAL DE L'ORANGERIE**
Jardin des Tuileries  75001 Paris  Director: Pierre Georgel
☎ +33 1 42974816  ▦ +33 1 42613082
Open: Wednesday Monday 09.45-17.00
Closed: Tuesday

**COLLECTION**

Installed in an old orangery in 1852, the Musée de l'Orangerie des Tuileries is devoted entirely to the presentation of two collections of pictures. The first is Claude Monet's 'Water Lilies', which were painted in the period from 1918 until the artist's death in 1926. Here one may view this collection in a presentation designed by the artist himself. The second is the Jean Walter and Paul Guillaume

Collection, which consists of 143 pictures dating from the Impressionist period until 1930. Examples of artists included in this collection are: Renoir (24 works), Cézanne (14 works), Matisse (11 works), Rousseau (9 works), Derain (28 works), Picasso (12 works), Soutine (22 works) and Utrillo (10 works). The collection was compiled with no particular regard for systematics and is above all a reflection of the taste and preferences of its creators. It represents fifty years of artistic creation in Paris.

*Musée National de l'Orangerie, Paris*
*© RMN - P.Bernard*

**EXHIBITIONS** | No exhibitions planned.

# Paris

## MUSÉE D'ORSAY
1, Rue de Bellechasse  75007 Paris  Director: Henri Loyrette
☎ +33 1 40494814  📠 +33 1 45485660  Internet http://www.musee-orsay.fr
Open: Tuesday, Wednesday, Friday, Saturday 10.00-18.00  Sunday 09.00-18.00
Thursday 10.00-21.45  18 Jun-20 Sep Museum opens at 09.00
Closed: Monday

**COLLECTION** | A splendid turn-of-the-century edifice on the banks of the Seine, the Gare d'Orsay originally served as the major rail terminus for the Southwest of France. Classified as a national monument in the 1970s, the arching iron and glass structure of this defunct railway station has since been transformed into an important art museum. The museum houses a magnificent collection of thousands of diverse works of 19th-century (1818-1914) art, including numerous representatives of Impressionism, Realism, Post-Impressionism and Art Nouveau, in some 80 galleries on three exhibition floors. Masterpieces on display on the ground floor include Ingres' 'LaSource', Millet's 'L'Angelus', Whistler's 'Mother', Manet's 'l'Olympia', as well as works from the Barbizon School and other early Impressionists.
On the top floor, more Impressionist works are exhibited, including Manet's 'le Dejeuner sur l'herbe', Renoir's 'le Moulin de la Galette', Degas' 'l'Absinthe', Van Gogh's 'Self Portrait', as well as works by Sisley, Pissarro, Cézanne, Seurat, Gaugin (including a new acquisition, 'Portrait au Christ Jaune') and the Pont-Aven School. The middle floor is devoted to Symbolism, Naturalism and Art Nouveau, along with sculptures by Rodin, Pompon and Maillol.

**EXHIBITIONS**
until 18·05·97 | ***Auguste Préault (1809-1879)*** *Romantic Sculptor*  A contemporary of Barye, Rude and David d'Angers, Préault's work has been forgotten except for three masterpieces: 'The Slaughter', 'Ophelia' and 'Christ'.

until 18·05·97 | ***Théophile Gautier*** *Liberated Critic*  This exhibition investigates

Exterior view of the musée d'Orsay, façade section on the bank of the Seine © Photo RMN-M. Bellot

what Gautier called "the beauty in art". His career as a critic influenced such painters as Delacroix, Courbet and Monet.

until 13·07·97

***Emile Verhaeren*** *An Imaginary Museum* The visionary universe of the poet is expressed in a dialogue with his painter and sculptor friends. This relationship between text and works evokes Verhaeren's involvement with Ensor, Seurat, Rodin, Redon and others.

10·06·97-31·08·97

***Eugène Cuvelier (1837-1900)*** *Photographer of the Woods of Fontainebleau*

10·06·97-31·08·97

***Photography in Sèvres during the Second Empire*** An exhibition featuring Louis Robert.

10·06·97-31·08·97

***Scenes of the Polish Ghetto, 1914-1918*** *The Berlewi Donation*

06·10·97-04·01·98

***Jean-Paul Laurens (1838-1921)***

## Paris

**MUSÉE DU PETIT PALAIS**
Avenue Winston Churchill  75008 Paris  Director: Thérèse Burollet
☎ +33 1 42651273  📠 +33 1 42652460
Open: Tuesday-Sunday 10.00-17.40 Thursday 10.00-20.00
Closed: Monday

COLLECTION

The Petit Palais exhibits a general survey of Western art from antiquity to 1925. The art of the Renaissance and the Northern schools (including stained glass, ceramics, and the work of French and German clockmakers from the 16th and 17th century) occupies a prominent place.
The Italian Renaissance is represented by an important collection of majolica, furniture, and paintings by Mantegna and Botticelli.
Works by 17th-century Flemish and Dutch masters include paintings by Jordaens, Rubens, Rembrandt, Téniers, Metsu, Van Goyen, Ruysdael and Hobbema. A collection of 18th-century paintings, sculpture and other works of art is also on display.
Romantic painting is represented by the work of Chassériau and Delacroix, while artists of the Realist school include Millet, H.Daumier and Gustave Courbet. Landscape painting from the second half of the 19th century highlights the development of French art from the Romantic period (Huet and Isabey) through Impressionism (Monet, Pissarro, Sisley and Guillaumin), the modified Realism of Corot, and the more vivid Realism of Rousseau, Harpignies and Breton.

The collection contains impressionist portraits by Cézanne, Monet, Pissarro, Renoir, Cassatt, Morisot and Toulouse-Lautrec, as well as sculptures by Carpeaux, Dalou, Carriès and other artists.

**EXHIBITIONS**
until 22·06·97

***Forerunners of Europe***   1500 objects from France, Germany, Belgium and Luxembourg trace the history of the Franks from their origins through the Roman times up to the Frankish kingdom under Childeric and Clovis. Objects found in Merovingian tombs give an idea of everyday life.

08·11·97-15·02·98

***Marianne and Germania***   *A Century of Franco-German Passions 1789-1889*

# Paris

## CENTRE NATIONAL DE LA PHOTOGRAPHIE
Hôtel Salomon de Rothschild
**11, Rue Berryer  75008 Paris  Director: Régis Durand**
☎ +33 1 53761232   ⊠ +33 1 53761233
**Open: Wednesday-Monday 12.00-19.00**
**Closed: Tuesday**

**COLLECTION**

No permanent collection.

**EXHIBITIONS**
until 05·05·97

***Hannah Collins***   *Hotel of Being, Works 1986-1996*   An overview of the artist's work, conceived as a series of nine 'rooms' based on such themes as unpopulated landscapes, deserted places, everyday things and their use or non-use, classical or unconventional still lifes, etc.

Hannah Collins
*Courtesy of the artist*
*'Bed', 1993*
in the exhibition
'Hotel of Being',
works 1986-1996
© *Centre National de*
*la Photographie,*
*Paris*

14·05·97-11·08·97

***Anthony Hernandez***   *Landscapes for the Homeless*   The photographs of Anthony Hernandez, depicting the dull traces of vacated places, testify to the conditions of homeless people in Los Angeles, and to a 'failure' in American culture.

14·05·97-11·08·97

***Carl de Keyzer***   *Historical Pictures*   Magnum Photographer Carl de Keyzer has most recently photographed scenes representing demonstrations of political, cultural and social power. De Keyzer focuses especially on how power presents itself to the public.

14·05·97-11·08·97

***Pascal Convert***   *'Live' (A Video Programme)*   Pascal Convert's images show the unseen element of television news — trembling cameramen facing the violence of events and war reporters committing themselves to the story despite their fear.

10·09·97-14·11·97

***Thomas Ruff***   *Works 1979-1996*   This retrospective shows the various series through which Thomas Ruff's work has developed over the last 18 years: interiors, portraits, homes, stars, stereoscopic views, photomontage, and retouching.

26·11·97-26·01·98   ***Anna and Bernhard Blume***   The Blumes use photography to convey expressionism and humour, and to show the absurd features of things through chaotic imagery. In their world, everything seems to be animated with spirit and creative energy.

04·02·98-13·04·98   ***Eugene Richards***   *Retrospective*   Considered one of America's most important photo-reporters, Eugene Richards is a radically committed, critical, and demanding observer of America's social problems and the decay and contradictions in American society.

## Paris

### MUSÉE PICASSO
**5, Rue de Thorigny  75003 Paris  Director: Gérard Regnier**
☎ +33 1 42712521  📠 +33 1 48047546
**Open: Wednesday-Monday Apr-Sep 09.30-18.00  Oct-Mar 09.30-17.30**
**Closed: Tuesday**

COLLECTION

The museum's collection consists primarily of works by Picasso, including 203 paintings, 158 sculptures, 16 papiers collés, 29 tableaux-reliefs, 88 ceramic pieces, over 3 000 drawings and prints, sketchbooks, illustrated books and manuscripts.
A chronological visit to the museum begins with the Blue Period 'Self-Portrait' which marks the arrival of the artist in Paris in 1901. It is followed by 'Celestina' (1904), 'Three Figures Under a Tree' (1907) and the 'Demoiselles d'Avignon'. The Cubist Period is expressed by the bronze 'Head of Fernande' (1909) and the 'Still Life with Chair Caning' from 1912, along with a series of constructions and collages. Works from Picasso's so-called Classical Period, such as 'Portrait of Olga' (1917), 'Pipes of Pan' (1923) and numerous drawings, are followed by those of the Surrealist Period: 'The Kiss' (1925) and 'The Crucifixion' (1930). The sculpture collections are dominated by the complete series of monumental 'Heads' made at Boisgeloup in 1931. Austere still-lifes from the war years and ceramics and sculptures from the Vallauris Period at the beginning of the 50s are also displayed. Finally, works can be viewed from the last decade of Picasso's life, such as 'Seated Old Man' (1970-1971). Because of their fragility, drawings and prints are exhibited on a rotating basis as a complement to the permanent collection.

*Exhibition room*
*© Musée Picasso,*
*Paris*

The museum also displays Picasso's personal collection of some fifty works by artists he admired (Renoir, Cézanne, Rousseau) and his friends (Braque, Matisse, Miró).
The mansion in which the museum is housed was built between 1656 and 1659 by Pierre Aubert, Lord of Fontenay. The classic courtyard and garden arrangement were designed by Jean Boullier.

Acquired by the City of Paris in 1964 after an eventful history with various occupants and functions, the mansion was given the status of Historical Monument in 1968 and restored.

EXHIBITION
until 09·06·97

***The Black Mirror. Picasso, Photographic Sources***   This exhibition compares paintings and drawings from the period 1900-1917 with unpublished photographs kept by the artist in his personal files.

## Paris

### CENTRE NATIONAL D'ART ET CULTURE GEORGES POMPIDOU
**19, Rue Beaubourg  75004 Paris  Director: François Barré**
**☎ +33 1 44781233   ⊠ +33 1 444781216**
**Open: Wednesday-Monday 12.00-22.00  Saturday, Sunday 10.00-22.00**
**Closed: Tuesday**

COLLECTION

The brightly painted 'inside-out' architecture of the Centre National d'Art et Culture Georges Pompidou was designed by the English architect Richard Rogers and the Italian architect Renzo Piano in 1977. The centre is comprised of a number of galleries and exhibition spaces including the Musée National d'Art Moderne, the Galerie d'Art graphique, the Galerie du Musée, the Galerie Photo, the Grande Galerie, the Galerie Nord, the Galerie Sud, and the Forum. The museum's collection covers the period from 1904 to the present day. The collection contains works by the Fauves with the emphasis on Matisse. The schools of Cubism, Dadaism and Surrealism are well represented with works by such artists as Picasso, Braque, Duchamp, Picabia, Man Ray, Ernst, Magritte and Dali. Other works of interest featured in the collection are mobiles by Calder, sculptures by Giacometti and works by Kandinsky, Klee, Mondrian, Pollock, Miró, Bacon and Rothko among others.

EXHIBITIONS

until 12·05·97    *Prints*

until 19·05·97    *The Seven Deadly Sins: Gluttony*

until 09·06·97    *Martial Raysse*

until 15·06·97    *Identical, Not Identical*   *An Exhibition of Prints*

until 29·09·97    *Made in France 1947-1997*   *50 Years of French Creations*

28·05·97-30·06·97    *The Seven Deadly Sins: Greed*

29·05·97-29·09·97    *Fernand Léger*

18·06·97-04·08·97    *Jean-Jacques Rullier*

25·06·97-29·09·97    *The Art of the Engineer*   *Builder, Entrepreneur, Inventor*

09·07·97-11·08·97    *The Seven Deadly Sins: Lust*

04·08·97-29·09·97    *The Seven Deadly Sins: Pride*

20·08·97-29·09·97    *Didier Trenet*

10·12·97-09·03·98    *Bruce Nauman*

## Paris

**MUSÉE RODIN**
77, Rue de Varenne  75007 Paris  Director: Jacques Vilain
☎ +33 1 44186110  ☏ +33 1 45511752
Open: Tuesday-Sunday Oct-Mar 09.30-16.45  Apr-Sep 09.30-17.45
Closed: Monday and 1 May

COLLECTION

The museum contains many original works, including bronze and marble sculptures and drawings, by the Late Romantic sculptor Auguste Rodin (1840-1917). It is housed in the Hôtel Biron, a mansion built c. 1730 for the Duke of Biron, later used as a convent and purchased by the State in 1901. The building was used from 1907 as a studio by Rodin, whose secretary Rainer Maria Rilke also lived there from 1908 to 1909. It was agreed that Rodin would bequeath his collection to the State.

Rodin made many sculptures of prominent literary and musical figures. He sculpted busts of Mahler, Carrier-Belleuse, Lady Sackville-West, Victor Hugo and Balzac. 'The Age of Bronze' was done after studying Michelangelo's work in Italy. Other works on display include 'The Kiss', 'The Hand of God', 'Orpheus', 'Eve' 'Young mother and her dying daughter', 'The Good Genius', 'Eternal Spring' and a sculpture of the artist's father. There are models for the 'Gates of Hell', a bronze museum door commissioned but never completed which served as inspiration for several independent sculptures, including the 'Three Shadows'. Among the bronzes and marbles displayed in the gardens are 'The Thinker', 'The Burghers of Calais' and 'Balzac'. Many studies and models are displayed, as well as paintings from Rodin's collection by Renoir, Monet and Van Gogh.

EXHIBITION
until 15·06·97

***Towards The Bronze Age. Rodin in Belgium***   This exhibition contains 24 busts made of terracotta, plaster, marble and bronze and other sculptures done by Rodin during his six years in Belgium (1871-1877), of which The Bronze Age is the most personal. There are also drawings, previously unknown paintings and caricatures and old photographs.

## Paris

**LA CITÉ DES SCIENCES ET DE L'INDUSTRIE**
30, Avenue Corentin-Cariou  75930 Paris Cédex 19  Director: Gérard Théry
☎ +33 1 40057000  ☏ +33 1 40058237
Open: Tuesday-Sunday 10.00-18.00
Closed: Monday

COLLECTION

Twenty minutes from the heart of Paris, La Cité des Sciences et de l'Industrie is one of the world's largest cultural centres aimed at popularising science and promoting understanding of the world in which we live.

Opened in 1986, La Cité is situated within the 55 hectare Parc de la Villette, in northeast Paris in a striking building converted from the city's old slaughterhouse. It is now one of the most popular attractions in Paris, along with the Eiffel Tower, the Louvre and Centre Pompidou. La Cité receives over 5 million visitors annually. Unlike more traditional museums or places of learning, La Cité is very much a 'hands on' experience with fully interactive exhibitions and participatory attractions providing fun and knowledge for all groups.

'Explora' is the core permanent exhibition area in the Cité, and new temporary exhibitions are opened throughout the year, many of which are now translated into English. As well as exhibitions, attractions ranging from a full-scale hunting submarine and

*Cité des Sciences et de l'Industrie, Paris*
© Arnand Legrain

planetarium to the 'Géode' omnimax theatre, and the 'Cinaxe' simulator theatre can be seen. There is also the highly popular 'Cité des Enfants', a children's science village devoted to entertaining and educating children aged from 3 to 12 years.

**EXHIBITIONS**

until end Jun 97 | **Engineers of the Sky**   *L'ONERA, 50 Years of Aeronautical and Space Engineering*

until Apr 98 | **Electricity**   *An Exhibition for Children from 5 to 12*   This exhibition shows how electricity is produced, how electrical circuits work at home, in cities and in factories, and what kinds of electricity are present in nature.

end Jun 97 onwards | **The Large Greenhouse**   This is an exhibition on the biological and physiological mechanisms of plants and the new technologies for raising vegetables, fruits and ornamental plants.

## Pau

**MUSÉE NATIONAL DU CHÂTEAU DE PAU**
64000 Pau  Director: Paul Nironneau
☎ +33 5 59823800   📠 +33 5 59823818
Open: Daily 09.30-11.45 / 14.00-17.15

**COLLECTION** | The town of Pau grew up around a medieval fortress, later transformed into a Renaissance chateau by the kings of Navarre. In the 19th century Louis Philippe and Napoleon III commissioned architects to do considerable work on the chateau and the result is an example of the furnishings of the years 1830 to 1860. The furnishings were supplied by purveyors to the crown. The interior is a good example of the style of decoration common under the July monarchy. The tapestry collection is one of the most valuable in France: the tapestries were selected from the royal furniture repository to complement the interior decorations of the Chateau. Most of the hangings represent mythological scenes or portray aristocratic life and help to recreate the special atmosphere of the chateau.

**EXHIBITIONS**

until 15-06-97 | **At the Palace Tables**   The exhibition is dedicated to the arts of the table at the Château de Pau under Louis-Philippe and Napoleon III.

until Jun 97 | **Restoration of the Château Park**   This is a presentation of the restoration project for the Château Park, which lasted 15 years.

15-10-97-mid Feb 98 | **Jacques-Charles Derrey**   The exhibition presents 150 paintings, drawings, engravings and book illustrations by Jacques Derrey (1907-1975), painter, decorator, engraver, theoretician and art teacher, along with his mostly unpublished writings.

## Périgueux

**MUSÉE DU PÉRIGORD**
22, Cours Tourny  24000 Périgueux  Curator: Véronique Merlin-Anglade
☎ +33 5 53064070  ☎ +33 5 53064071
Open: Wednesday-Monday Apr-Sep 10.00-12.00 / 14.00-18.00;
Oct-Mar 10.00-12.00 / 14.00-17.00
Closed: Tuesday

**COLLECTION**

Built on the site of an Augustinian monastery, the Musée de Périgord has an exceptional collection of prehistoric relics, as well as sculptures and Gallo-Roman mosaics. Many of the artefacts were recovered from excavations in the Périgord region, an area rich in prehistoric remains.

**EXHIBITIONS**

until 16·06·97

*Marcel Loth*  Paintings

Jul 97-Nov 97

*19th-Century Physics Collection*

Dec 97-Feb 98

*Homage to Robert Filliou*

Mar 98-Jun 98

*Emile Vergeaud*  Paintings

## Perpignan

**MUSÉE HYACINTHE RIGAUD**
16, Rue de l'Ange  66000 Perpignan  Director: Marie Claude Valairon
☎ +33 4 68354340  ☎ +33 4 68663280
Open: Wednesday-Monday 15 Jun-14 Sep 09.30-12.00 / 14.30-19.00
15 Sep-14 Jun 09.00-12.00 / 14.00-18.00
Closed: Tuesday and public holidays

**COLLECTION**

The museum has been moved to the Hotel de Lazerme, a 17th century mansion which can be considered one of the most beautiful dwellings in Perpignan.
The collection, ranging from 13th-century masters to contemporary art, includes Hispano-Moresque ceramics, Catalan Primitives and portraits by Hyacinthe Rigaud.
Amongst the well-known artists represented are Maillol, Dufy, Alechinsky, Brueghel, Bram van Velde, Calder, Clavé, Greuze, Géricault, Ingres, Krasno, Marie Laurencin, Appel, Saint Aubin and Picasso. The museum also exhibits a collection of 211 paintings by 211 contemporary artists.

**EXHIBITIONS**

until 31·05·97

*Pierre Daura (1886-1974)*  This Catalonian painter (inventor of the logo and co-founder of the 'Cercle et Carré' movement) developed his career in France during the 1930s and later in the United States.

14·06·97-27·07·97

*The Sculptor Gabriel Farail in the Museum's Collection.*

01·08·97-end 97

*Daura and the Rousillon Painters of the First Half of the 20th Century*  This exhibition takes a closer look at the artistic life of Rousillon during this century.

## Reims

**MUSÉE DES BEAUX-ARTS**
8, Rue Chanzy  51100 Reims  Director: Véronique Alemany-Dessaint
☎ +33 3 26472844  📠 +33 3 26868775
Open: Wednesday-Monday 10.00-12.00 / 14.00-18.00
Closed: Tuesday and 1 May, 14 Jul, 1 and 11 Nov, 25 Dec

COLLECTION

Founded in 1794, the museum is currently one of the ten largest provincial museums in France.
On the ground floor, a remarkable collection of ceramics from 19th and 20th-century French and European potteries is on display, as well as a number late-19th and early-20th-century sculptures.
The first floor has a unique series of religious paintings executed between 1460 and the mid-1500s.
Thirteen 16th-century portraits by Lucas Cranach the Elder and his son, Lucas Cranach the Younger, as well as two by Barthel Bruyn, have been given a special place in the museum. The 17th century is represented by a collection of Flemish, Dutch and French paintings, while an assortment of 18th-century art objects and furniture recreates the intimate ambience of that epoch.
The following section traces developments from the dawn of the 19th century (Neo-Classicism with David's 'Marat') to the 20th century (Dufy, Matisse, Puy, Vuillard, Bonnard). Landscapes have a privileged place, beginning with a comprehensive collection of Corots and continuing with the Barbizon School (T. Rousseau, Diaz, Millet, Dupré, Chintreuil, Daubigny). Works by Boudin, Jongking, Monet, Mauffra, Moret, Sisley and Pissarro are also on display.
A remarkable series of visionary paintings by the Czech artist Sima completes the collection.

EXHIBITIONS

15·07·97-15·11·97 | *Collection 'Le Legs Lundy'*   *100 Pictures of the 19th Century*

Dec 97-Jan 98 | *Victor & Dana Roman*   *Pictures and Objects*

## Rennes

**MUSÉE DES BEAUX-ARTS**
20, Quai Emile Zola  35000 Rennes  Director: Laurent Salomé
☎ +33 2 99285585  📠 +33 2 99285599
Open: Wednesday-Monday 10.00-12.00 / 14.00-18.00
Closed: Tuesday

COLLECTION

The museum's collection offers a comprehensive overview of the visual arts from the 14th to the 20th century. The Renaissance gallery includes masterpieces by Veronese ('Perseus and Andromeda') and Heemskerck. The section on the 17th century includes Ruben's 'Tiger Hunt', works by Guercino, Champaigne, Le Brun and the world-famous Nouveau-Né by Georges de La Tour. Two of Chardin's still- lifes dominate the 18th-century selection. Corot, Sisley, Gauguin and Caillebotte are some of the more modern artists whose works are on display, together with several Pont-Aven masterpieces, paintings by Picasso, Kupka and Tanguy, and sculptures by Magnelli and Richier. There is a rotating display of drawings by Leonardo, Botticelli, Dürer and Rembrandt. Finally, the archaeology department focuses on Egyptian, Greek and Roman archaeology.

EXHIBITION

May 97-Sep 97 | *Caravaggio in Rennes*   An exhibition about 'The Cardsharps' (on loan from the Kimbell Museum of Art, Fort Worth).

## Centre Culturel Abbaye de Daoulas - France

A great event from April to September:
**"The Mayas in the Land of Copán"**: splendid
items from this enigmatic civilization like stone altars, jade
jewellery, coloured ceramics...
Presented for the first time in Europe !

*Un grand événement d'avril à septembre :*
*"**Les Mayas au pays de Copán**" : de splendides*
*pièces appartenant à cette civilisation énigmatique*
*tels des autels en pierre, des bijoux en jade,*
*des céramiques colorées...*
*Présentés pour la première fois en Europe !*

And from December 97 to Spring 98
**"Traditionnal Arts from China"**

*Et de décembre 97 au printemps 98*
*"Arts Traditionnels Chinois"*

---

**BP 34 - 29460 DAOULAS - FRANCE**
**Tél. 00 33 2 98 25 84 39 / Fax. 00 33 2 98 25 89 25**

## Rouen

**MUSÉE DES BEAUX-ARTS**
Square Verdrel  76000 Rouen  Director: Claude Petry
☎ +33 2 35712840  🖷 +33 2 35154323
Open: Wednesday-Monday 10.00-18.00
Closed: Tuesday and public holidays

COLLECTION | The museum has a collection of paintings and sculpture from the 16th to the 20th century. The sculpture garden has works by Etex, ('Le Tombeau de Géricault'), Leroux, ('Le Fruit'), Bourdelle and Grun. The early paintings include a polyptych by Perugino from c.1500, 'Christ ending the Plague' by Veronese, an anonymous Spanish 'Adoration of the Magi', Caravaggio's 'Flagellation of Christ', 'The Good Samaritan' by Luca Giordano and works by Guerchin, David and Metsys. The collection contains a Brussels tapestry from 1525 and a series of 30 Russian icons from the 16th to the 19th century. Among the Spanish works are 'Democritus' by Velásquez and 'Zachariah' by Ribera. French paintings include 'The Storm' by Poussin and 'God Creating the Universe' by Philippe de Champaigne. There are also works by Rubens, Jan Steen and Ter Borch. French paintings include portraits by Watteau, 'Blanchisseuses' by Fragonard, 'Portrait of Delacroix' by the Rouen painter Géricault, 'Portrait of Gachot' by Millet, 'Chrysanthemums' by Renoir and nine paintings by Monet. There are also collections of Rouen faience, silver, jewellery and oriental works of art.

until 20·11·97

**Joan Mitchell (1926-1992)** For the first time, an anthology is shown of the pastels which accompanied the artist's paintings throughout her life.

17·09·97-15·11·97

**Romanian Icons** *Treasures of the Bucharest Museum* 30 Romanian icons are presented from the 16th, 17th and 18th centuries.

17·09·97-15·12·97

**The Dufy Collection of the Havre Museum of Fine Arts** Paintings by Dufy can be viewed during the Jacques-Emile Blanche exhibition.

15·10·97-15·01·98

**Jacques-Emile Blanche (1861-1942)** *Painted Memoirs* This first large retrospective of 80 works recalls the artist's relationships with writers, musicians, artists and salons. He was an unknown decorator and a painter of landscapes and still-lifes.

## Saint-Etienne

**MUSÉE D'ART MODERNE**
La Terrasse  42000 Saint-Etienne  Director: Bernard Ceysson
☎ +33 4 77795252  +33 4 77795250
Open: Daily 10.00-18.00
Closed: 1 Jan, 1 May, 1 Nov, 25 Dec

COLLECTION

The museum's collection of modern art includes works by such artists as Chabaud, Delaunay, Exter, Gleizes, Hélion, Kandinsky, Koudriachov, Kupka, Magnelli, Matisse, Monet, Rodin and Severini. It features four paintings by Picasso and two major works by Léger, as well as a large selection of paintings and Dada objects from Surrealists such as Arp, Victor Brauner, Duchamp, Ernst, Masson, Miro, Picabia, Schwitters and Tanguy.
Other artistic movements are also represented here, including works by Bissière, Dubuffet, Fautrier, Hartung, Manessier, Soulages and Bram van Velde and sculptures by Germaine Richier, Jacobsen, etc. The trends and movements marking the 60s and 70s, such as Pop Art and New Realism, are particularly well-represented and include works by Arman, César, Dine, Hains, Klein, Lichtenstein, Oldenburg, Spoerri, Villeglé, Warhol and Wesselmann. Minimal Art objects can also be admired, among which works by Andre, Cane, Fabro, Flavin, Grand, Judd, LeWitt, Merz, Morris, Noland, Pagès, Saytour, Stella, Viallat and Zorio. Finally, the museum also has a collection of works by German artists, including Baselitz, Lüpertz, Penck, Richter, etc.

EXHIBITIONS
23·05·97-07·09·97

*Pivovarov*

27·06·97-07·09·97

**Erik Dietman** *A 'Classical Sculptor'* Along with some older pieces by Erik Dietman, recent monumental works will be shown which use the materials and techniques of classical sculpture to confound order and meaning.

19·09·97-23·11·97

*Jochen Gerz*

## Saint-Germain-en-Laye

**MUSÉE DES ANTIQUITÉS NATIONALES**
Château de Saint-Germain-en-Laye  78103 Saint-Germain-en-Laye
☎ +33 1 34515365  +33 1 34517393
Open: Wednesday-Monday 09.00-17.15
Closed: Tuesday

COLLECTION

The Museum of National Antiquities is housed in a castle built by Louis VI in the 12th century. Rebuilt three times, and enlarged by Louis XIV, it owes its present aspect to Millet, who restored it in the 19th century. Today the museum shows archaeological collections from the first man-made tools up to the 9th century. They have since grown with the discovery of many rare objects and masterpieces during archaeological excavations in the 19th and 20th centuries. The museum includes sections devoted to the Palaeolithic, Neolithic and Bronze Ages, the Celts, the Gallo-Romans, the Merovingians, and comparative archaeology.

*Clasps used by Greeks and Romans* Jovy-le-Comte, Val d'Oise, c. 550 A.D. © Musée des Antiquités Nationales, Saint-Germain-en-Laye

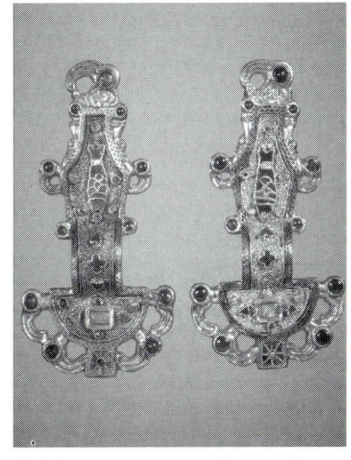

EXHIBITIONS

until 29·06·97

***Merovingian Treasures from Ile de France***   This exhibition presents a selection of precious objects found at burial sites of the Merovingians (5th century - 8th century), including jewels, silver and gold buckles, vessels and gravestones. The famous treasure of the Saint-Denis basilica is also on display.

until 29·06·97

***Gregory of Tours (538-594)***   This exhibition focuses on Gregory of Tours, who wrote the 'Ten Books of Histories', which has served as the primary source of information about Gaul and the Frankish kings in the 6th century.

# Saint-Paul

## FONDATION MAEGHT
**06570 Saint-Paul  Director: Jean Louis Prat**
☎ +33 4 93328163  📠 +33 4 93325322
**Open: Daily Oct-Jun 10.00-12.30 / 14.30-18.00; Jul-Sep 10.00-19.00**

COLLECTION

Located in a lush, verdant setting, the Marguerite and Aimé Maeght Foundation is an outstanding example of a private foundation functioning as a museum in Europe. Its architectural design was specially conceived to exhibit contemporary and modern art in all its aspects. Painters and sculptors worked in direct collaboration with Catalan architect Josep-Lluis Sert to create works of art, often monumental in scale, that were incorporated into the building's design and blended into the surrounding nature. The Giacometti Court, the Miró Labyrinth enlivened with sculptures and ceramics, mosaic murals by Chagall and Tal-Coat, stained glass by Miró, Braque and Ubac, and a fountain by Pol Bury are some examples. The Maeght Foundation owns one of Europe's most important collections of 20th-century painting, sculpture, drawing and graphic work. Works by such prominent artists as Arp, Bonnard, Braque, Calder, Chagall, Dubuffet, Giacometti, Gonzalez, Hartung, Kandinsky, Lam, Léger, Miró, Tal-Coat, Ubac, Bram and Geer van Velde are displayed alongside works of Bazaine, Bury, Chillida, Sam Francis, Hantai, Kelly, Matta, Mitchell, Palazuelo, Riopelle, Soulages, Steinberg Tapies and other notable artists representing the young generation, including Adami, Alechinsky, Arroyo, Cane, Erró, Klapheck, Madden, Moninot, Monory, Oppenheim, Récalcati, Rouan, Stampfli, Szafran, Gasiorowsky and Viallat.

**EXHIBITION**
02·07·97-19·10·97

*Sculpture by Painters*    This exhibition presents 20th-century sculpture as undertaken by painters. These artists were innovative, offering different solutions and an unfamiliar approach. Works are also shown by painters such as Daumier, Degas, Modigliani and many others who produced significant sculpture as autonomous work.

## Sceaux

**MUSÉE DE L'ILE DE FRANCE**
Chateau de Sceaux   92330 Sceaux   Director: Jean-Georges Lavit
☎ +33 1 46610671   ☷ +33 1 46610088
Open: Wednesday-Monday Apr-Sep 10.00-18.00   Oct-Mar 10.00-17.00
Closed: Tuesday

**COLLECTION**

The Ile-de-France Museum is housed in a chateau built by the second Duke and Duchess of Trévise and restored by the current owner of the building, the Department of Hauts-de-Seine. It has served as a museum since 1937. In addition to exhibits dealing with the history of the property surrounding the chateau, and a documentation center on the ground floor focusing on the history of Ile-de-France, the museum includes a variety of artistic exhibits.

*© Musée de l'ile de France*
*Chateau de Sceaux*

Paintings and furniture provide insight into life in the royal and princely residences of Ile-de-France. Landscapes by artists including Michel, Dunouy, Lépine, Huet, Lepère, Utrillo, le Sidaner, Foujita, and others depict Ile-de-France from the 17th to the 20th century. Ceramics on display include a unique collection of objects manufactured in Sceaux. The museum collection also includes contemporary artworks. Graphic works, engravings and old photographs are on display throughout the chateaux.

**EXHIBITIONS**

No exhibitions planned.

## Sèvres

**MUSÉE NATIONAL DE CÉRAMIQUE**
Place de la Manufacture  92310 Sèvres  Curator: Antoinette Hallé
☎ +33 1 41140420  🖷 +33 1 45346788
Open: Wednesday-Monday 10.00-17.00
Closed: Tuesday

**COLLECTION**

The museum's collection is devoted exclusively to ceramics. Although founded by Alexandre Brongniart, the director of the Sèvres Porcelain Manufacturing Company from 1800 to 1847, the collection is by no means limited to ceramics from this company. The collections present a panoramic view of all that has been accomplished in the field of ceramics and include Oriental ceramics, European glazed ceramics, pottery, Islamic ceramics, Spanish Muslim ceramics, Italian and European ceramics and 16th to 18th-century tin-glazed wares and porcelains. A selection of contemporary ceramics is displayed in the entrance hall and is changed at frequent intervals.

**EXHIBITION**
25·09·97-05·01·98

*Japanese Stoneware*   1000 Years of Japanese Tradition: The Ceramics of Bizen

## Strasbourg

**MUSEÉ ALSACIEN**
23, Quai St-Nicolas  67000 Strasbourg  Curator: Malou Schneider
☎ +33 3 88525033  🖷 +33 3 88525009
Open: Tuesday-Saturday 10.00-12.00 / 13.30-18.00  Sunday 10.00-17.00
Closed: Monday

**COLLECTION**

The museum of folk art is located in a group of old Strasbourg houses. The region's traditions are recorded in its decorative painted furniture, ceramics, toys and colour prints, both sacred and profane. Reconstructions of farmhouse interiors from the Rhine delta, the vineyards and the Vosges mountain valleys represent the different types of Alsatian habitats. Traditional workshops have also been reconstructed, including those of a blacksmith and a carpenter.

*Faience pan, 17th century*
*© Musée Alsacien, Strasbourg*

**EXHIBITION**
06·12·97-08·03·98

*Shawls from Alsace*

## Strasbourg

### MUSÉE ARCHÉOLOGIQUE
Palais Rohan  2, Place du Château  67000 Strasbourg  Curator: B. Schnitzler
☎ +33 3 88525000  📠 +33 3 88525009
Open: Wednesday-Monday 10.00-12.00 / 13.30-18.00 Sunday 10.00-17.00
Closed: Tuesday

**COLLECTION**

Located on the lower floor of the Rohan palace, the Archaeological Museum - one of the most important in France because of the size of its collections - invites you to discover several thousand of years of history of the Alsace from 600 000 B.C. to 800 A.C.

*Funeral Stela*
*1st century A.D.*
*© Musée*
*Archéologique,*
*Strasbourg*

The paleolithic mammouth hunters, the first agriculturers of the neolithic era, the necropolis of the Bronze and Iron ages, the everyday life of the gallo-romans and the richness of the merovingian civilisation in Alsace.

**EXHIBITION**
until 02·11·97

*Niedernai A princely necropolis from the 5th to the 7th century A.D.*

## Strasbourg

### MUSÉE DES ARTS DÉCORATIFS
Palais Rohan  2, Place du Château  67000 Strasbourg  Curator: Etienne Martin
☎ +33 3 88525000  📠 +33 3 88525009
Open: Wednesday-Monday 10.00-12.00 / 13.30-18.00 Sunday 10.00-17.00
Closed: Tuesday

*Palais Rohan, Salle*
*des Evêques*
*Photographer:*
*A.Schaffner*
*© Musée des Arts*
*Décoratifs,*
*Strasbourg*

**COLLECTION**

Located on the main floor of the Rohan palace, the former residence of the bishop princes built between 1731 and 1742, this museum is composed of two sections: the sumptuous apartments of the cardinals on the one hand, and the collections of Strasbourg decorative arts covering the period from 1681 to the middle of the nineteenth century on the other hand (world renown Hannong ceramics, furniture, sculpture and paintings, clockmaking, wrought iron, pewter ware, gold and silver ware). The museum also houses the famous toy collection from the Tomi Ungerer Donation.

**EXHIBITION**
18·10·97-04·01·98

***Olympe Aguado, photographer*** *A Noble Amateur (1827-1894)*
[ROBERT HEITZ GALLERY - PALAIS ROHAN - 2 PLACE DU CHÂTEAU]

## Strasbourg

### MUSÉE DES BEAUX-ARTS
**Palais Rohan  2, Place du Château  67000 Strasbourg  Curator: Jean-Louis Faure**
☎ +33 3 88525000  📠 +33 3 88525009
**Open: Wednesday-Monday 10.00-12.00 / 13.30-18.00 Sunday 10.00-17.00**
**Closed: Tuesday**

**COLLECTION**

At the Museum of Fine Art located on the first floor of the Rohan Palace, the european painting collections from the Middle Ages to 1870: the Italian and Flemish Primitives (with amongst others, works of Giotto and Memling); Renaissance and Mannerism, (Botticelli Raphael, Veronese, Lucas de Leyde, el Greco); Baroque, Realism and

Raffaello Sanzio dit
Raphaël (1483-1520)
*Portrait of La
Fornarine, c. 1520*
© Musée des Beaux-
Arts, Strasbourg

Classicism in the seventeenth and eighteenth centuries (Rubens, Van Dyck, Dutch landscape and still-life paintings, Vouet, Philippe de Champaigne, Largillière, Boucher, Canaletto, Tiepolo, Ribera, Goya); works of the nineteenth century (Corot, Courbet).

**EXHIBITION**
mid May 97-mid Sep 97

***Kaufman/Sclagcter Donation***    [ANCIENNE DOUANE GALLERY, LA RUE DU VIEUX-MARCHÉ-AUX-POISSONS]

## Strasbourg

### MUSÉE DE L'OEUVRE NOTRE-DAME
**3, Place du Château  67000 Strasbourg  Curator: Cécile Dupeux**
☎ +33 3 88525000  📠 +33 3 88525009
**Open: Wednesday-Monday 10.00-12.00 / 13.30-18.00 Sunday 10.00-17.00**
**Closed: Tuesday**

**COLLECTION**

Located since 1939 in buildings that were initially used by the administration of the cathedral masons, this museum shows the evolution of the arts in Strasbourg and in the regions of the upper Rhine between the eleventh and the seventeenth centuries: masterpieces of medieval sculpture from the Strasbourg cathedral, major works from the Rhenish fifteenth century (for instance works of Conrad Witz and Nicolas Gerhaert van Leyden), collections of stained-glass windows, tapestry, gold or silver ware and furniture, a still-life collection of Sebastien Stoskopff.

Nicolas de Leyde
*Bust of pensive man,*
*c. 1467*
Photographer:
Zvardon
© *Musée de l'Oeuvre*
*Notre Dame,*
*Strasbourg*

**EXHIBITION**
until 15·06·97          ***Sebastien Stoskopff*** *Master of the Still Life (1597-1657)*

## Toulouse

**MUSÉE DES AUGUSTINS**
**21, Rue de Metz  31000 Toulouse  Director: Alain Daguerre de Hureaux**
☎ +33 5 61222182   🖷 +33 5 61223469
**Open: Wednesday-Monday Summer 10.00-18.00; Winter 10.00-17.00**
**Closed: Tuesday**

COLLECTION

The museum, situated in a 14th-century Augustinian monastery, is one of the oldest museums in France. The Gothic sculptures include a marble effigies, a 14th-century Virgin and Child and monumental figures of apostles and saints.
Religious paintings from the 14th to 18th century from several European schools are displayed in the nave of the church, including works by Murillo, Van Dyck, Jan Jansen, Charles de La Fosse, Rubens and anonymous 14th-century French artists. The church also contains 16th-century terracotta statues from the Saint-Sernin cloister and a German Baroque organ.
The Neo-Gothic ship contains Romanesque sculpture, with a capital from Saint-Sernin illustrating the 'War of Angels', and capitals from the cloisters of the Daurade and St. Etienne. There are also early Christian sarcophagi.
The first floor houses a collection of Italian, Flemish and Dutch paintings mainly from the 17th to 19th century. These include works by Matteo Rosselli, Valentin, Fontebasso, Guido Reni and works by Francken, De Momper, Rombouts, Van Goyen, Van de Velde and others. There are Medieval portraits of 'Capitouis', those allowed the privilege of having their portraits painted, and portraits of other prominent persons of Toulouse. The Romantic period is represented by 'Muley Abd-ar-Rahman, sultan du Maroc, sortant de son palais de Meknès' (1845) by Delacroix, 'L'Etoile du matin' by Corot, 'Le Ruisseau au puits noir' by Courbet. There are also works by Toulouse-Lautrec, Berthe Morisot, Vuillard, Utrillo, Rodin and Maillol.

## Toulouse

**MUSÉE PAUL DUPUY**
13, Rue de la Pleau 31000 Toulouse Director: Jean Penent
☎ +33 5 61222175
Open: Wednesday-Monday Oct-May 10.00-17.00; Jun-Sep 10.00-18.00
Closed: Tuesday and public holidays

COLLECTION

Paul Dupuy (1867-1944) bought and restored the former 'Hôtel de Besson' in order to house his collections and, during his lifetime, to establish a museum there bearing his name. The Musée Paul Dupuy was considerably enlarged after 1949 as a result of the efforts of its first curator, Robert Mesuret, and is now in the care of the city. It was expanded following a redistribution of the city collections and after renovations taking place from 1980 until 1985, and now houses extensive collections ranging from the Middle Ages to 1939. The department of prints and drawings contains a rich collection of works by artists from Toulouse and the Languedoc. The department of applied arts is divided into several sections: ivories (including the famous 'cor de Roland'), enamels, silver, ceramics (mainly from Toulouse, Bordeaux, Montpellier, Marseille, Moustiers, Nevers and Strasbourg), glass, wrought iron, textiles (ranging from the 14th-century antependium from the Cordeliers church to 18th and 19th-century costumes), furniture (dressers from the Toulouse area and 17th-century medicine cabinets from a Jesuit pharmacy), and wood carving. Besides the world-famous Gélis collection of timepieces, the museum also contains an interesting collection of weaponry, musical instruments, and a large collection of magic lanterns and vintage cameras. There are also sections on weights and measures, numismatics, and seals.

EXHIBITIONS

until 07·07·97

**The Major Engraved Portraits of François de Troy** In connection with the François de Trois exhibition, portraits of the artist are presented which were engraved by well-known contemporaries such as Edelinck, Daullé and others.

until 07·07·97

**François de Troy (1645-1730)** Drawings and Paintings The works of this portrait artist, who belonged to a family of Toulouse artists, are on loan from museums in France and other countries.

Sep 97-Nov 97

**Alexandre Roubtzoff (1884-1949)** Painter of Light The exhibition presents the part of the artist's paintings and drawings which is dedicated to the Islamic world, North Africa and Tunisia.

## Tours

**MUSÉE DES BEAUX-ARTS**
18, Place François Sicard 37000 Tours Director: Jacques Nicourt
☎ +33 2 47056873 ⓕ +33 2 47216936
Open: Wednesday-Monday 09.00-12.45 / 14.00-18.00
Closed: Tuesday and 1 Jan, 1 May, 14 Jul, 1 and 11 Nov, 25 Dec

COLLECTION

The Tours Museum of Fine Arts is housed in a former archiepiscopal palace set in a delightful French garden. Its renowned collections are displayed throughout sumptuously furnished rooms which reflect the atmosphere of 18th-century palace life.

**Diana Gallery**   This former synod room, painted in false marble after the original colours, owes its name to the statue of Diana by Jean-Antoine Houdon (1740-1828). Other works on exhibit were submitted by aspiring artists to the Royal Academy of Painting and Sculpture during the 18th century.

**Louis XV Reception Hall**   The paintings of François Boucher and a magnificent commode signed by Jean Demoulin (1715-1798) form a good illustration of the combination of sensitivity, refinement and libertinage which characterised the age of Louis XV.

**Mantegna Gallery**   The two panels painted between 1456 and 1460 for the San Zeno church in Verona by Andrea Mantegna (1431-1506), one of the major artists of the Northern Italian Renaissance, are considered to be the most significant works of art in the museum.

**Delacroix and Orientalism**   Delacroix' 'The Arab Comedians or Buffoons' reflects the impact made on the artist by the intense light, bright colours and picturesque scenes of the East.

**Around Impressionism**   Degas, Monet, Henri Martin. This diverse assortment of Impressionist works includes Degas' masterly study of Mantegna's Crucifixion.

**20th Century**   Alexander Calder   Several works by Alexander Calder (1898-1976) are on display, including a watercolour and a tapestry as well as mobiles.

**Rembrandt Gallery**   The small 'Flight to Egypt' which is on display, a youthful work monogrammed and dated 1627, marks the beginning of a more introspective phase in the artist's career.

**Rubens Gallery**   The fresh colours and fluid transparency of 'Ex Voto of the Virgin presenting the Child to the Donor', painted in 1615, reflect the stimulating influence which Peter Paul Rubens (1577-1640) had on his times.

**EXHIBITIONS**
16·05·97-31·08·97

*Freemasonry*   On the 150th anniversary of the Démophiles Lodge, the exhibition investigates the identity and the historical role of the masonic movement. Collections are on loan from several European museums, libraries and masonic museums.

01·10·97-15·12·97

*The legend of St. Martin in the XIX century*   In celebration of the year of St. Martin, this exhibition presents a selection of XIX Century hagiographic paintings and drawings, most of which were commissioned by the State for the churches of Paris and the provinces.

# Valenciennes

**MUSÉE DES BEAUX-ARTS**
Boulevard Watteau  59300 Valenciennes  Director: Patrick Ramade
☎ +33 3 27225720  📠 +33 3 27225722
Open: Wednesday-Monday 10.00-12.00 / 14.00-18.00
Closed: Tuesday

**COLLECTION**

With renovation and expansion now completed, the museum's collection can be viewed in its new galleries and spaces for the first time.

The Fine Arts Collection, initially based on works of art seized from religious communities and aristocratic families during the French Revolution, was gradually enlarged during the 19th and 20th centuries through purchases, gifts and legacies.

The Flemish School is particularly well represented, with well-known religious paintings and altar pieces from Valenciennes churches by artists such as Rubens (whose tríptych, 'The Martyrdom of

St. Stephen', is a famous example of the Baroque style), Abraham Janssens (including his masterpiece, 'Christ on the Cross'), Jordaens, Van Dyck and Pourbus.

French painting is represented primarily by the works of Antoine Watteau, a native of Valenciennes, including his 'Portrait of Antoine Pater' and 'La Vraie Gaieté'.

The collection of 19th-century sculpture is highlighted by an extensive exhibition of the work of Jean-Baptiste Carpeaux (150 sculptures, 50 paintings and more than 2 000 drawings).

The Archaeological Collection has been assembled on the basis of finds made during the course of construction and excavation in the area. This eclectic collection features miniature masks from the Celtic period, Gallo-Roman wall paintings and Merovingian ornaments, as well as recumbent figures and funeral paintings from the Middle Ages.

**EXHIBITION**
16·05·97-19·10·97

***Archaeological Treasures of the North of France***    The exhibition comprises a selection from the collections of various European museums and brings together major archaeological finds dating from Gallo-Roman and Merovingian times. At the same time, it recounts the history of archaeological research.

# Versailles

**CHÂTEAU DE VERSAILLES ET DE TRIANON**
78000 Versailles  Director: Jean-Pierre Babelon
☎ +33 1 30847400  🖷 +33 1 30847648
Open: Tuesday-Sunday  May-Sep  Chateau 09.00-18.30  Grand Trianon and Petit Trianon 10.00-18.30; Oct-Apr  Chateau 09.00-17.30  Grand Trianon and Petit Trianon Tuesday to Friday 10.00-12.30  Saturday and Sunday 10.00-17.30
Closed: Monday, public holidays and for official ceremonies

**COLLECTION**

The Château and Gardens of Versailles are some of the finest examples of French 17th-century art in existence. King Louis XIII's former hunting lodge was transformed and enlarged by his son Louis XIV and new apartments were added during the reigns of Louis XV and Louis XVI. Versailles was abandoned by the royal family and court within days of the outbreak of the French Revolution. In 1837, King Louis-Philippe opened the Château museum which was to be devoted to glorious events in the history of France.

The Château's interior features numerous works of art; highlights include the Hercules Drawing Room which serves as an anteroom to the Kings State Apartment and houses Veronese's 'The Meal at the House of Simon'. The other drawing rooms are decorated with 17th-century mythological scenes, marble panelling, antiques and works of art such as Bernini's bust of Louis XIV. In Mansart's Hall of Mirrors, the ceiling by Le Brun evokes the wars of Louis XIV. The Queen's Bedchamber looks just as it did during Marie-Antoinette's reign and features brocade and Tours silk furniture. The private apartments include the Kings Bedchamber, the Clock Cabinet with its astronomical clock by Passement and Caffieri, the Private Cabinet featuring a medal cabinet by Gaudreaux, secretaires by Oeben and Riesener and candelabra of the American War of Independence by Thomire. The Royal Opera and the Royal Chapel by Gabriel and Mansart respectively are elaborately decorated, the former with trompe l'oeil paintings and the latter with carved scenes from the Old and New Testaments. On the ground floor, the Princes' Apartments have been restored and redecorated with 18th-century furniture. The Château's wings house a collection of 17th to 19th-century paintings of French historical subjects. The Grand Trianon (by Mansart) is decorated with mythological paintings commissioned by Louis XIV, as well as Napoleonic furniture. The Small Trianon (by Gabriel) is surrounded by an English garden. The gardens surrounding the Château were designed by Le Nótre and feature perspective avenues, marble statues, the Orangery and fountains.

**EXHIBITIONS**

until 13·07·97

*From Joseph Vivien to Jacques-Emile Blanche*   *4 Centuries of Pastels in Versailles*

Oct 97

*Louis de Silvestra*   *An 18th Century French Painter at the Court of Dresden*

# Villeneuve d'Ascq

**MUSÉE D'ART MODERNE**
1, Allée du Musée  59650 Villeneuve d'Ascq  Curator: Joëlle Pijaudier
☎ +33 3 20196868  🖷 +33 3 20196899
Open: Wednesday-Monday 10.00-18.00
Closed Tuesday

**COLLECTION**

The Musée d'Art Moderne is housed in a building designed by French architect Roland Simounet. The core of its collection is a donation from Mr. and Mrs. Masurel, which includes representative works by most of the major Pre-Avant-Garde artists who lived in France during the first half of the 20th century. The permanent collection includes a group of Cubist reference works by Georges Braque, Henri Laurens and Pablo Picasso. It also includes the third largest collection of Fernand Léger; the finest collection of Amedeo Modigliani in France; and important pieces by André Derain, Paul Klee, André Masson, Joan Miro, and Georges Rouault.

**EXHIBITION**

02·02·97-14·07·97

*Outsider Art*   *Aracine Collection*   'Outsider art' refers to works by people working outside the usual training and distribution channels. Started in 1982, the Aracine collection comprises paintings, sculptures, assemblies and other objects, by both French and foreign artists, which bear witness to an inexhaustible technical inventiveness.

Bremerhaven

BREMEN

HANNOVER

Osnabrück

Münster • • Bielefeld

• Haltern

Duisburg Essen • Dortmund Paderborn

Mönchengladbach

Wuppertal

DÜSSELDORF Kassel •

Leverkusen

• Köln (Cologne)

Aachen

*BONN* Göttingen •

WIESBADEN Frankfurt

Trier • MAINZ Darmstadt Würzb

Ludwigshafen

SAARBRÜCKEN • Mannheim

• Karlsruhe

Baden Baden STUTTGART

Esslingen •

Ulm •

• Freiburg

• Weil am Rhein

# Aachen

**LUDWIG FORUM FÜR INTERNATIONALE KUNST**
Jülicher Straße 97-109  52070 Aachen  Director: Wolfgang Becker
☎ +49 241 18070  🖷 +49 241 1807101
Internet http://heimat.de/ludwigforum
Open: Tuesday, Thursday 10.00-17.00  Wednesday, Friday 10.00-20.00
Saturday, Sunday 11.00-17.00
Closed: Monday

COLLECTION | The Ludwig Forum for International Art is a showcase for the presentation and confrontation of various forms of contemporary art. The sunken 'quadrum' in the middle of the main hall is the heart of the forum, from which the 'lighthouse', the galleries, the upper floors, the performance space, workshops, ateliers, garden, library and bookshop are all accessible. Rotating exhibitions are complemented with a range of performing arts including music, dance, performance art and film.

EXHIBITIONS
until 15·06·97 | *Art in Rumania Today*   *Visual and Performing Arts from Bucharest* This exhibition presents works from the Ludwig collection, works created in the past years by Rumanian artists-in-residence in Aachen and newly selected works by artists and groups from Bucharest.

27·06·97-07·09·97 | *Günther Grass*  *Drawings, Paintings and Sculptures*   The latest purchases of Peter Ludwig in 1996. This exhibition on the occasion of the 70th birthday of the famous writer is complemented by a series of events in which the Volkshochschule, the Public Library and the Newspaper Museum will also participate.

25·07·97-14·09·97 | *Art in Aachen*   An exhibition of works, selected by a jury and presented by the Federal Association of Visual Artists in Aachen (established in 1996).

26·09·97-16·11·97 | *Johannes Gruetzke*  *A Theatrical Presentation, Paintings*   One of the founders of the 'Neue Schule der Prächtigkeit' in Berlin, his works display an aggressive, caricature-like realism which gives Gruetzke a special place among his sexagenarian German colleagues.

Autumn 97 | *Music Box*   Following its premiere in the Ludwig Forum, this Euregional performing/visual arts project will 'tour' through the five provinces of the Euregion. Dance, theatre, music, sound, visual art and sculpture - but no text.

Winter 97/98 | *Cuba & North-Rhine Westphalia*   *An Exchange*   A major event in the Ludwig Forum calendar for 1997. Exhibitions, a performing arts programme and exchange of artists-in-residence, in co-operation with the Ludwig Foundation and the Ministry of Culture in Düsseldorf.

Dec 97-Feb 98 | *Love, Sadness and Time*  *The Murken Collection, Aachen* A travelling exhibition, the premiere of which will take place in the Ludwig Forum.

# Aachen

**SUERMONDT LUDWIG MUSEUM**
Wilhelmstraße 18  52070 Aachen  Director: Ulrich Schneider
☎ +49 241 479800  🖷 +49 241 37075
Open: Tuesday-Friday 11.00-19.00  Wednesday 11.00-21.00
Saturday, Sunday 11.00-17.00
Closed: Monday

**COLLECTION**

**Sculpture and Paintings**   The museum is especially renowned for its Medieval wooden sculptures. Masterpieces in painting from Germany, the Netherlands and Flanders dating from the 15th to the 17th century give an insight into the different iconographical approaches of these periods, especially the 17th century. Included are works from the Northern Netherlands, with its profane iconography, and the Southern Netherlands, with its ideas of the counter-reformation. Furthermore, the collection provides an interesting selection of Spanish and Italian painters. Important works illustrate the different historical developments and cover the period up to the 19th and 20th century.

Willem Claesz Heda
(1594-1678)
*Still-life, 1640*
© Suermondt-
Ludwig-Museum,
Aachen

**Glass paintings**   Another highlight of the collection is the assemblage of glass windows from the 14th to the 20th century.
**Prints and drawings**   The Print Room, with its 15 000 European prints and drawings, provides an excellent opportunity to study these works. Included are works such as the four series by Goya, the Carceri by Piranesi, and works by Dürer and Rembrandt.
**Applied Arts and Textiles**   Precious courtly and sacred objects from the Renaissance to the Baroque periods, and over 200 examples of textiles, are housed in the museum.

**EXHIBITIONS**

[MAIN EXHIBITION HALL]

until 08·06·97

***Enzo Cucchi***   *Più vicini alla Luce*

05·07·97-05·10·97

***Sebastian Stoskopff***   *European Master of Baroque Still Lives*

25·10·97-07·12·97

***Albert Renger-Patzsch - Rudolf Schwarz***   *The Buildings of Rudolf Schwarz in Aachen*   On occasion of the 100th birthday of both artists.

18·12·97-Feb 98

***Friedrich Gräsel***   *Sculptures*

[STUDIO]

until 01·06·97

***Lotte Jacobi 1896-1990***   *Photojournalist and Portraitphotographer*

14·06·97-10·08·97

***Ralf Kreuels***   *Between Magic and Realism*   *Photographies from the Ruhr area*

24·08·97-24·10·97

***Heiner Hoffman***   *Architecture - Imaginations*

08·11·97-Jan 98

***Chargesheimer***   *Vintage Prints 1958-1961*

[GRAPHIC DEPARTMENT]

until 22·06·97

***Franz-Josef Weidenhaupt***   *Cut-Objects and Cubes*

18·09·97-16·11·97

***Luisa Schatzmann***   *Remembering is Future*

27·11·97-Jan 98

***Mediaeval Antiphonar Sheets***

## Baden-Baden

**STAATLICHE KUNSTHALLE BADEN-BADEN**
Lichtentaler Allee 8a  76530 Baden-Baden  Director: Jochen Poetter
☎ +49 7221 23250  ⅛ +49 7221 38590
Open: Tuesday-Sunday 11.00-18.00  Wednesday 11.00-20.00
Closed: Monday

**COLLECTION**

No permanent collection.

**EXHIBITIONS**

until 25·05·97
***Urban Legends 'London'***    Looking into the young scene of London

14·06·97-14·09·97
***Photography in the 20th Century***   From the collection of Kunsthaus Zürich

14·06·97-14·09·97
***...Just Below My Skin...***  *Interacting Performance Programme*
Changing exhibitions of contemporary art. Performances, Jazz- and Pop concerts, MTV Clips, readings and lectures.

18·09·97-21·09·97
***New Pop Festival***   Various concerts and performance programme

04·10·97-16·11·97
***Water Colours of the Romantic Movement***

04·10·97-16·11·97
***Sol LeWitt '100 cubes'***

06·12·97-01·03·98
***Impressionism & Symbolism***   *Paintings from the turn of the century from Poland*

## Berlin

**ALTE NATIONALGALERIE**
Bodestraße 1-3  10178 Berlin  Director: Peter-Klaus Schuster
☎ +49 30 20905802  ⅛ +49 30 20905801
Open: Tuesday-Sunday 09.00-17.00
Closed: Monday and 24, 25 and 31 Dec, 1 Jan, 1 May,
Tuesday after Easter and Whitsun

**COLLECTION**

The museum building, designed by Friedrich August Stüler of the Schinkel School (1867-1876), houses examples of paintings and plastic arts from the 19th century.

Adolph von Menzel

(1815-1905)

*The balcony window,*
*1845*

© *Alte National*
*Galerie, Berlin*

The large canvases by Adolph von Menzel provide interesting insights into court life and industrial activity under Frederick II, while the world of the Prussian Army is depicted in the works of court painter Franz Krüger.

The life of the poor is the province of portrait painter and social observer Max Lieberman.

French painting from the same period is represented by the predecessors of Impressionism (Barbizon School), Rousseau, Corot and Gustave Courbet as well as a splendid collection of Impressionist paintings, including works by Eduard Manet, Claude Monet, August Renoir, Camille Pissarro and Paul Cézanne.

Examples of German Idealism include impressive paintings by German expatriates in Rome: Hans von Marées, Anselm Feuerbach and Arnold Böcklin.

The plastic arts are represented by notable works by Johann Gottfried Schadow and Christian Daniel Rauch, as well as important sculptures by Hildebrand, Rodin, Maillol and Degas.

**EXHIBITIONS**

until 11·05·97    *Adolph Menzel 1815-1905*    *The Labyrinth of Reality*

until 20·05·97    *Christen Koebke*    *A Painter from Denmark's Golden Age*

# Berlin

## ANTIKENSAMMLUNG
**Kupfergraben  10178 Berlin  Director: Wolf-Dieter Heilmeyer**
☎ +49 30 20905202  📠 +49 30 20905201/5204
**Open: Tuesday-Sunday 09.00-17.00**
**Closed: Monday and 24, 25 and 31 Dec, 1 Jan, 1 May,**
**Tuesday after Easter and Whitsun**

**COLLECTION**

The collection of ancient art is a part of the Pergamonmuseum. The museum was built between 1910 and 1930 according to the plans of Alfred Messel and finished by Ludwig Hoffmann. The display of ancient architectural remains, like the Pergamonaltar, made the museum world famous. The big central Hall houses the reconstruction of the west side of the Pergamonaltar in its original dimensions and the 2,30 m high frieze with the battle between olympic gods and giants. The big marble altar was erected during the reign of King Eumenes II (165-156 BC) and excavated by Carl Humann and Alexander Conze (1878-1886).

The Pergamon Altar:
*Giant from the Artemisgroup (east frieze)*
© Antikensammlung, Berlin

The other halls and rooms houses remains of excavations in many sites in Asia minor, like Milet, Priene, Magnesia.

The collection of Greek and Roman sculpture includes in the main floor masterworks of the archaic, classical, hellenistic and Roman period, like the 'Berliner Göttin', the Hera of Cheramyes, the seatted goddess of Tarantum, a good selection of gravestones and Roman copies of Greek sculptures.

The first floor includes masterpieces of Roman portrait art. The Green Head of Julius Caesar and the marble portrait of Cleopatra represent the high level of the collection. The collection contains also an important quantity of Greek and Roman mosaics.

**EXHIBITION**
28·02·97 onwards

*The Telephos Frieze on the Pergamon Altar*   *The Freshly Restored Exhibit*

# Berlin

## BAUHAUS-ARCHIV / MUSEUM FÜR GESTALTUNG
Klingelhöferstraße 14  10785 Berlin  Director: Peter Hahn
☎ +49 30 2540020  ⛶ +49 30 25400210
Open: Wednesday-Monday 10.00-17.00
Closed: Tuesday

**COLLECTION**

The Bauhaus, now more than three quarters of a century old, was founded in 1919 in Weimar by Walter Gropius. Although it was a rather small school for architecture and applied arts and was soon suppressed by the Nazis, it became well-known throughout the world, mainly as a result of the design it pioneered. Many teachers of the Bauhaus achieved fame: Wassily Kandinsky, Paul Klee, Oscar Schlemmer and Lyonel Feininger for instance. The teaching strategies developed at the Bauhaus - especially by Johannes Itten, Josef Albers and Laszlo Moholy-Nagy - were adopted internationally. The Bauhaus Architecture is viewed as part of the International Style.

*© Bauhaus Archiv/Museum für Gestaltung, Berlin*

The attention which the Bauhaus has continued to attract is due to the achievements during the brief fourteen years of its existence between 1919 and 1933, the year in which the Bauhaus was closed down by the Nazis. The Bauhaus Archive focuses on that period. The museum devotes its energies to collecting, examining and presenting all kinds of information that is related to the Bauhaus. The museum contains architectural models, designs, paintings, drawings, works of applied art and industrial products as well as materials related to the teaching. In addition, works from the Bauhaus workshops such as furniture, ceramics, woven materials, metal objects, prints, typographical studies, sculptures, photographs and theatre designs are exhibited. Examples of architecture by Walter Gropius, Hannes Meyer and Ludwig Mies van der Rohe as well as works of art by the Bauhaus Masters are also on display.

**EXHIBITIONS**
until 31·05·97

*Ulrich Bauss*   *Sculptures in Concrete*

until Dec 97

*The Bauhaus*   *Weimar Dessau Berlin 1919-1933*

| | |
|---|---|
| 13·05·97-20·07·97 | **Home and Workspace** The Work Association Housing Estate in Breslau 1929 |
| 05·08·97-05·10·97 | **Velten Articles** Ceramics of the 1920s from the Velten-Vordamm Earthenware Factory |
| 24·10·97-23·11·97 | **New Swedish Design** Industrial and Graphic Design |

## Berlin

**BERLINISCHE GALERIE**
**MUSEUM FÜR MODERNE KUNST PHOTOGRAPHIE UND ARCHITEKTUR**
Martin-Gropius-Bau Stresemannstraße 110  10963 Berlin  Director: J. Merkert
☎ +49 30 254860  📠 +49 30 25486345
Open: Tuesday-Sunday 10.00-20.00
Closed: Monday and Apr - Aug '97

COLLECTION

The museum features paintings, drawings, sculpture, photography, architecture, and artistic archives of Berlin artists from the late 19th and 20th centuries. The collection of visual arts focuses on the painters of the Berlin Secession, Expressionist painters and the Dada collection. Important artists of the 20s included in the collection are Otto Dix, George Grosz, Rudolf Schlichter, Christian Schad, and the Russian artists Naum Gabo and Iwan Puni. Featured post-war artists include Werner Heldt, Alexander Camaro and Hans Uhlmann. Georg Baselitz, Eugen Schönebeck and K.H. Hödicke are representative of the 60s. There is also a substantial collection of contemporary Berlin artists. The photography collection focuses primarily on art photography and features works by Heinrich Zille, Erich Salomon, El Lissitzky, Laszlo Moholy-Nagy, and numerous contemporary photographers, including many from the ex-GDR. The architectural collection consists of material concerning the history of architecture and urban development, particularly after the Second World War. There is a very large collection of 'art and construction', including the estate of the 'Puhl und Wagner' factory for mosaics and glass. The museum's archives include the estates of the gallery Ferdinand Möller, and those from artists such as Hannah Höch, Raoul Hausmann, Naum Gabo, George Rickey, and others.

EXHIBITIONS

| | |
|---|---|
| Oct 97-Nov 97 | **Henry Ries** On his 80th Birthday |
| 16·09·97-23·11·97 | **Jeanne Mammen** Retrospective |
| 04·09·97-03·11·97 | **Correspondences Berlin-Edinburgh** |

## Berlin

**BRÜCKE-MUSEUM**
Bussardsteig 9  14195 Berlin-Dahlem  Director: Magdalena Moeller
☎ +49 30 8312029  📠 +49 30 8315961
Internet: http://www.dhm.de/museen/bruecke
Open: Wednesday-Monday 11.00-17.00
Closed: Tuesday

COLLECTION

The museum is devoted exclusively to the 'Brücke' group of artists. The building, designed by Werner Düttmann, and situated in the leafy suburb of Grünewald, consists of four rooms grouped around a small central courtyard and a graphic cabinet in the basement. It was opened in 1967.
The 'Brücke' group was active between 1905 and 1913. Central members of the group included Karl Schmidt-Rottluff and Erich

Heckel (the two initiators of the museum), Ernst Ludwig Kirchner and Fritz Bleyl. Among other artists who belonged to the group for shorter or longer periods were Emil Nolde, Max Pechstein, Otto Meuller and Kees van Dongen. Their subjective-expressive approach to painting, with its strong colours and terse forms, laid the foundations of Expressionism.

The work of Heckel and Schmidt-Rottluff is strongly represented, along with Nolde and Pechstein (with several important works), Herbig, Kerschbaumer, Gramatté, Kaus and Roeder. In addition to paintings, the collection includes prints, watercolours, drawings, sculptures and glass windows by various artists. Other documents and publications of the group are also on display.

**EXHIBITIONS**

until 14·09·97 — *Painters of 'Die Brücke'*

17·05·97-20·07·97 — *Ernst Ludwig Kirchner*  Photographs

26·07·97-14·09·97 — *Max Klaus*  Graphic Reproductions

28·09·97-04·01·98 — *The Blue Rider*

Spring 98 — *Ernst Ludwig Kirchner*  Watercolours and Drawings

# Berlin

**DEUTSCHES HISTORISCHES MUSEUM GMBH**
Zeughaus  Unter den Linden 2  10117 Berlin  Director: Christoph Stölzl
☎ +49 30 215020  📠 +49 30 21502402  Internet: http://www.dhm.de
Open: Thursday-Tuesday 10.00-18.00
Closed: Wednesday

**COLLECTION**

Founded in 1987, the Deutsches Historisches Museum was originally to have been given a new building; in 1990, however, the holdings of the dissolved Museum für Deutsche Geschichte were transferred to the Deutsches Historisches Museum, and the combined collection was ultimately accommodated in the Zeughaus.

The Zeughaus is one of the most beautiful Baroque buildings in Northern Germany. However, extensive remodelling is needed to turn it into a modern museum. Renovation, including an estimated 10 000 square meters of exhibition space divided over three storeys, will be completed in 2000.

A committee of noted German historians and museum specialists have developed the concept of the museum, which centres on enlightenment and communication. The permanent display will contain artefacts and documents from the 9th century to the present, depicting political, social and economic aspects of Germany's history within a European context.

The museum's varied holdings include the well-known Zeughaus collection of military paraphernalia relating to Brandenburg-Prussian history, as well as many posters and documents associated with the history of the labour movement.

The museum also boasts more than two million illustrations relating to German history from 1933 to the present.

**EXHIBITIONS**

16·05·97-12·08·97 — *Wolfsburg/Eisenhüttenstadt*  Two New Towns in the Post-1945 New Beginning

27·06·97-25·11·97 — *Bohemia and Dictatorship in the GDR*  Groups, Conflicts, Districts

03·10·97-09·12·97 — *Klaus Fußmann*  Landscape Pictures from the New Federal States

| | |
|---|---|
| 24·10·97-06·01·98 | ***Feelings of Affinity***  *Scandinavia and Germany 1800-1914* |
| 18·12·97-03·03·98 | ***The Lion and the Cock or the Sun and the Frogs***  *Visual Propaganda in Dutch and French Graphic Reproductions 1672-1714* |
| 06·03·98-26·05·98 | ***Tsingtau***  *A Chapter of German Colonial History in China 1897-1914* |
| 20·03·98-onwards | ***Myths of the Nations*** |
| | [PHOTO GALLERY] |
| 17·07·97-02·09·97 | ***Photographs by Orgel-Köhne*** |
| 04·09·97-23·09·97 | ***Clicks***  *Photographs by Simone Kornfeld from the Collection of the German Historical Museum* |

## Berlin

**GEMÄLDEGALERIE**
**Berlin-Dahlem: Arnimallee 23/27, 1495 Berlin**
**Open: Tuesday-Friday 09.00-17.00, Saturday-Sunday 10.00-17.00**
**Berlin-Mitte: Bodemuseum, Museuminsel, entrance Monbijoubrücke,**
**10178 Berlin**
**Open: Tuesday-Sunday 09.00-17.00**
       **[In 1998, second or third quarter, both museums will be moved**
       **to the Berlin Tiergarten]**
**Stauffenbergstraße 40  10785 Berlin  Director: Jan Kelch**
**☎ +49 30 2666  📠 +49 30 2662103**
**Open: Tuesday-Sunday 09.00-17.00**
**Closed: Monday and 24, 25 and 31 Dec, 1 Jan, 1 May,**
**Tuesday after Easter and Whitsun**

COLLECTION

The Gemäldegalerie in Dahlem, which occupies two floors in the right wing and one in the left wing of the old part of the museum, houses a major collection of European paintings from the 13th to the 18th centuries.
A second collection can be viewed in the Pinacotheca in the Bodemuseum on the Museum Island.
Both collections will be moved to the Kulturforum in the Berlin Zoo in 1998.

*Rembrandt
Harmensz. van Rijn
(1606-1669)*
***The man with the
golden helm, c.1650-
1655***
*Photographer: J.P.
Anders
© Gemäldegalerie,
Berlin*

**The ground floor:**  Works from all schools of painting up to the end of the 16th century, including paintings by Glatz (Bohemian School), Hieronymus Holzschuhers and Jakob Muffels (German Renaissance), Albrecht Dürer, Hans Holbein, Albrecht Altdorfer (the Master of the Danube School) and Lucas Cranach the Elder.

One section of the gallery is dedicated to Dutch painting, with renowned works by artists such as Van Eyck, the Master of Flemalle and his pupil Rogier van der Weyden, Pieter Brueghel and Hieronymus Bosch.

The section feauturing French painting includes works by J. Fouquet (15th century) and 18th-century artists such as A. Pesne and Chardin.

Italian Painting (13th-16th century) is represented by Giotto and Botticelli (Florentine School), Mantegna (Early Renaissance), Raphael and Titian.

**The upper floor:** Flemish and Dutch painting (17th century), including works by Van Dyck, Rubens, Vermeer, Pieter de Hoogh, Van Goyen, Ruysdael, Jan Steen, Frans Hals and Rembrandt and his school.

Examples of French and Italian painting from the 17th and 18th century include works by George de la Tour and the masters of Italian Baroque, Caravaggio and Annibale Carracci. The Venetian Schools are represented by Tiepolo, Canaletto and Guardi. Works by the classic French landscape painters, Poussin and Claude Lorrain, are also on display.

**EXHIBITION**
until 25·05·97

***Masters of the Sea, Masters of Art*** *Dutch Seascapes in the 17th Century*

# Berlin

**KUNSTGEWERBEMUSEUM**
Matthäikirchplatz 10785 Berlin Director: Barbara Mundt
☎ +49 30 2662902 ⊠ +49 30 2662947
Open: Tuesday-Friday 09.00-17.00 Saturday-Sunday 10.00-17.00
Closed: Monday and 24, 25 and 31 Dec, 1 Jan, 1 May,
Tuesday after Easter and Whitsun

**COLLECTION**

Housed on three exhibition floors in a new building designed by Rolf Gutbrod, the museum offers an excellent survey of arts and crafts from the Middle Ages to the Modern Industrial Era.

Works from the Middle Ages are displayed on the ground floor. The treasure from the Dionysius Cloister at Enger/Herford (Westphalia), with its valuable Purse Reliquary (Bursenreliquiar) set with precious stones (second half of the 8th century), is on view right next to the entrance. In the centre of the hall, the Dome Reliquary (Cologne, ca. 1175/80) from the famous Guelph Treasure is exhibited. Designed in the form of a Byzantine church, the Reliquary was intended to preserve the head of St. Gregory of Nazianz, which was brought from Constantinople in 1173. The portable Altar of Eilbertus dates from the same era, while the golden Guelph Cross (11th century) is said to originate in Northern Italy.

In the other rooms on the ground floor are on display: important collections of Italian Majolica (14th-17th century), Venetian glass (mainly 16th-17th century), French furniture and enamels, the Treasure of the city council of Lüneburg (Late Gothic and Renaissance) as well as work by the goldsmiths of Nuremberg.

The upper floor shows items from cabinets of curiosity made of ivory, amber, rock cristal, semiprecious stones, highly finished by the work of gold- and silversmiths (16th and 17th century), clocks, watches and measuring instruments. Also Dutch and German fayence, Chinese and German porcelain and a Chinese cabinet. Other exhibits on this floor include a timbered mirror cabinet in rococo style, furniture by the Roentgen family as well as arts and crafts of the art nouveau and art deco period.

The lower floor houses a collection of 20th century international design objects.

Meistermarke J.B.
*Tureen and bowl,*
*18th century*
© *Kunstgewerbemu-*
*seum, Berlin*

**EXHIBITIONS**

| | |
|---|---|
| May 97-29·06·97 | *Shellfish and Snails* |
| Jul 97-Sep 97 | *Porcelain Brands* |
| 22·08·97-05·10·97 | *Walked All Over*   Historical Wooden Floors |
| 01·09·97-20·12·97 | *Contemporary Jewellery*   Germany and Scandinavia |
| Oct 97-Dec 97 | *Prussian Portraits*   Miniature Art by Leonhard Posch |
| Autumn 97 | *The Dowry of Princesses* |

## Berlin

**NEUE GESELLSCHAFT FÜR BILDENDE KUNST**
Oranienstraße 25  10999 Berlin  Director: Leonie Baumann
☎ +49 30 6153031  🖷 +49 30 6152290
Open: Daily 12.00-18.30

**COLLECTION**   No permanent collection.

**EXHIBITIONS**

until 01·06·97   ***The Work Factor***   *On the History and Future of Work*   A multi-media exhibition comprising objects, photography, performances and events.

07·06·97-13·07·97   ***Dorothy Iannone   Works 1966-1989***   An exhibition featuring paintings, objects and video.

19·07·97-24·08·97   ***Art and the Computer***

30·08·97-12·10·97   ***Timm Ulrichs***   *The Detecting Glance*

29·11·97-Jan 98   ***Interrupted Career***   Mark Morrisroe (1959-1989)

[HAUS AM KLEISTPARK, GRÜNEWALDSTR. 6-7]

11·10·97-16·11·97   ***In the Wrong Body: Transsexual People in Germany***   Photographs by Daniel Fuchs

[PARTLY IN THE KUNSTAMT KREUZBERG/BETHANIEN]

18·10·79-23·11·97   ***Contemporary British Photography***

# Berlin

## NEUE NATIONALGALERIE
Potsdamer Straße 50  10785 Berlin  Director: Dietrich Honisch
☎ +49 30 2662651  📠 +49 30 2624715
Open: Tuesday-Friday 09.00-17.00  Saturday-Sunday 10.00-17.00
Closed: Monday and 24, 25 and 31 Dec, 1 Jan, 1 May,
Tuesday after Easter and Whitsun

**COLLECTION**

The museum, housed in a glass and steel building designed by Mies van der Rohe (1968), exhibits a varied collection of 20th-century painting and plastic arts, including important works by European exponents of Classic Modern art and a selection of American art from the 60s and 70s.

Beginning with the pioneers of Expressionism (Gaugin, Munch, Hodler), the collection continues with an impressive array of works by the Brücke artists (Kirchner, Schmidt-Rottluff, Heckel, Otto Müller). Works by L. Corinth, O. Kokoschka, W. Lehmbruck and Ernst Barlach are also on display.

Edvard Munch
(1863-1944)
*Harry Graf Kessler,*
*1906*
© Neue National
Galerie, Berlin

French Cubism is represented by Picasso and Juan Gris, Classic Modern art by the Bauhaus painters (Schlemmer and Kandinsky), George Grosz, Paul Klee and the Surrealist Max Ernst.

Highlights of the contemporary art collection include works by the Zero Group and Nouveau Réalisme artists as well as American Colour Painting.

Important sculptures on display in the central part of the gallery and on the terrace include 'Die Wäscherin' by Renoir, 'Köpfe und Schwänze' by Calder and Gerhard Marcks' graceful 'Maja'.

**EXHIBITION**
09·10·97-04·01·98

*Exile and Emigrants 1933-1948*

# Berlin

## MUSEUM FÜR OSTASIATISCHE KUNST
Lansstraße 8  14195 Berlin  Director: Willibald Veit
☎ +49 30 8301382  📠 +49 30 8315972
Open: Tuesday-Friday 09.00-17.00 Saturday, Sunday 10.00-17.00
Closed: Monday and 24, 25 and 31 Dec, 1 Jan, 1 May, Tuesday after Easter and Whitsun

**COLLECTION**

The collection of the Museum of East Asian Art comprises Chinese, Japanese and Korean fine and decorative arts as wel as archaeology from 3000 BC to the present.
Highlights include Chinese and Japanese paintings and Japanese woodblock prints.

*Wang Hui*
*(1632-1717)*
*Study amid trees*
*near a stream, China*
*Qing-dynasty dated*
*1680*
*© Museum für*
*Ostasiatische Kunst,*
*Berlin*

**EXHIBITIONS**

until 25·05·97 | ***Masterpieces of Japanese Woodcut Art, Part III***

30·05·97-20·07·97 | ***Haiga and Haiku*** *Sketches and Short Poems by Takebe Sôchô (1716-1814) from the Shôzaburô Masuda Collection, Tokyo*

12·06·97-02·11·97 | ***The White Gold of the Far East*** *The Porcelain Bridge between East-Asia and Europe in the 17th and 18th Century*

24·07·97-21·09·97 | ***Andô Hiroshige (1797-1858)*** *Coloured Woodcuts from the Museum Collection*

15·08·97-26·10·97 | ***Nurimono*** *Contemporary Japanese Lacquerwork*

26·09·97-30·11·97 | ***Inrô*** *Japanese Medicine Boxes from a Private Collection*

26·09·97-30·11·97 | ***Robes in Japanese Woodcuts***

# Berlin

**SKULPTURENSAMMLUNG**
1. Arnimallee 23-27  14195 Berlin  Director: Arne Effenberger
☎ +49 30 8301252  📠 +49 30 8316384
Open: Tuesday-Friday 09.00-17.00  Saturday, Sunday 10.00-17.00
Closed: Monday and 24, 25 and 31 Dec, 1 Jan, 1 May,
Tuesday after Easter and Whitsun
2. Bodestraße 1-3, 10178 Berlin, in Bodemuseum, entrance Monbijoubrücke
☎ +49 30 20905601/02  📠 +49 30 20905602
Open: Tuesday-Sunday 09.00-17.00
Closed: Monday and 24, 25 and 31 Dec, 1 Jan, 1 May,
Tuesday after Easter and Whitsun

**COLLECTION**

The collection includes masterworks of Byzantine and European sculpture from the 3rd to the 19th century. Excellent examples from the early Christian and Byzantine periods include the great ivory Berlin Pyxis (a 4th-century ciborium for consecrated wafers) and the stone and glass mosaic of Christ the Merciful from the 12th century. The section of German statues from the Middle Ages mainly features statues from Swabia and High Rhineland: outstanding wood carvings, such as the 'Schutzmantelmaria' from Ravensburg, the Christ and St. John's group and the Madonna of Dangolsheim. The four Evangelists and the Singing Angels represent two highlights of the work by Tilman Riemenschneider.
A life-size Maria as the queen of heaven (14th century) represents the French Gothic style.

*Titman Riemensch-
neider*
**God the Father with
the body of Christ,** c.
*1515*
© Skulpturensamm-
lung, Berlin

The Italian Renaissance section features important sculptures of the Quattrocento: the graceful Madonna Pazzi by Donatello, the terracotta Marias by Luca and Andrea della Robbia, small bronzes by Giovanni da Bologna.
The Baroque and Rococo section contains statues by the 18th-century German master Martin Zürns as well as work by Feuchtmayr.
Another part of the collection is exhibited at the Bodemuseum on the Museum Island in the centre of Berlin.

**EXHIBITIONS**     No exhibitions planned.

## Berlin

**DEUTSCHES TECHNIKMUSEUM BERLIN**
**GERMAN MUSEUM OF TECHNOLOGY BERLIN**
Trebbiner Straße 9  10963 Berlin  Director: Günther Gottmann
☎ +49 30 254840  📠 +49 30 25484175
Open: Tuesday-Friday 09.00-17.30  Saturday, Sunday 10.00-18.00
Closed: Monday

**COLLECTION**     The German Museum of Technology Berlin is housed on the site of the former Anhalter railway station in Berlin-Kreuzberg. It continues a tradition of large technical museums in Berlin, the exhibits of many of which were destroyed during the Second World War. The museum's aim is to interpret the world as a complex interactive system as opposed to exhibiting isolated technical objects. Showing the interrelationship of technology, science, history, art, nature and its influence on people's everyday life is the museum's main objective. The 14 departments provide a unique insight into man's technical accomplishments. On view are exhibitions (at present on 14 000 m$^2$.) on aviation, road transport, railways, manufacturing techniques and household appliances, telecommunications, computer and automation technology, textiles, paper and printing technology, navigation and hydraulic engineering, scientific instruments, film and photo technology and power engineering. The museum is surrounded by a park including such exhibits as windmills, solar technology, a forge and a historical brewery. Numerous historical machines and models are explained and shown in operation. Visitors can take part in printing, weaving, dipping their own paper, grinding corn and much more.
**The science centre SPECTRUM** (separate entrance: Möckernstraße 26) is the interactive department of the museum where the visitor can experience science for himself - by getting his hands on one of the 220 exhibits.

High speed
locomotive V200 on
the turntable in front
of the locomotive
shed
© Deutsches
Technikmuseum
Berlin, Berlin

**EXHIBITIONS**

until 15·05·97

*The History of the Berlin Gas Service*

20·06·97-end 97

*Arbours on Wheels*   This special exhibition presents an extensive collection of caravans, focusing on their history, highlighting their importance within the economy, and providing insights into the lifestyle and culture of holidays.

end Nov 97-end Feb 98

*Scent*   This is a comprehensive exhibition on perfume, including advertising, marketing, and interactive presentations to sniff and sample.

end Mar 98-Summer 98

*Peter Behrens and Household Technology*   This is an exhibition of the most attractive and interesting exhibits and documents collected in the comprehensive AEG Archive.

# Berlin

## MUSEUM FÜR VÖLKERKUNDE
Lansstraße 8  14195 Berlin  Director: Klaus Helfrich
☎ +49 30 8301226  📠 +49 30 8315972
Open: Tuesday-Friday 09.00-17.00  Saturday, Sunday 10.00-17.00
Closed: Monday and 24, 25 and 31 Dec, 1 Jan, 1 May,
Tuesday after Easter and Whitsun

**COLLECTION**

The museum features an important collection from countries all over the world.
**Central and South America:**   Tomb (steles) and stone sculptures from Cozumalhuapa (Guatemala) and objects from the Maya culture. Important objects of sacred and profane plastic art from the Aztecs (sacrificial blood dish).
**Pre-Inca period:**   Colourfully patterned textiles and anthropo-morphic ceramics from Peru. The golden room features splendid ornamental and cult objects from the 7th century B.C. up to the 11th century A.D.
**The Pacific:**   Objects from collections which have been assembled since the end of the 18th century (partially from the expeditions of James Cook) include wooden sculptures and painted masks from New Guinea. Also on display are the Southern Pacific Boat and the wonderful garment of red and ochre coloured feathers of the King of Hawaii.
**Africa, South and East Asia:**   Terracotta statues from Ife (Nigeria), bronze works and painted wooden sculptures from the former kingdom of Benin belong to the more interesting part of the collection.

*Double boat
(reconstruction)*
Tonga Islands
© *Museum für
Völkerkunde, Berlin*

**EXHIBITIONS**    [MUSEUM FOR THE BLIND]

until further notice    ***Pre-Columbian Stone Sculptures from America***

[JUNIOR MUSEUM]

until Nov 97    ***Masks and Disguises***    *A Small Exhibition of Masks from all Parts of the World*

Nov 97 onwards    ***Japanese Bath Sculptures***

[SPECIAL EXHIBITION HALL]

06·06·97-30·11·97    ***The Treasure in the Sea***    *Raising the 'San Diego' near Manila*

## Bielefeld

**KUNSTHALLE BIELEFELD (RICHARD-KASELOWSKY-HAUS)**
Artur-Ladebeck-Straße 5  33602 Bielefeld  Director: Jutta Hülsewig-Johnen
☎ +49 521 512479  📠 +49 521 513429
Internet http://www.uni-bielefeld.de/kunsthalle/
Open: Tuesday-Sunday 11.00-18.00; Wednesday 11.00-21.00;
Saturday 10.00-18.00
Closed: Monday

**COLLECTION**    **Art of the 20th Century**    The Kunsthalle Bielefeld, which opened to the public in 1968, is the only building in Germany designed by the American architect Philip Johnson. The museum houses a rich collection of 20th-century art, especially strong in Expressionism. The collection includes works by painters associated with 'Die Brücke' and 'the Bauhaus', and Cubist sculptures. The museum's collection also includes paintings by Max Beckmann, and contemporary German and American works.

**EXHIBITIONS**
15·05·97-03·08·97    ***Not Vital***    *Totem and Taboo*    20 sculptures and several drawings on a life-and-death theme by this highly unusual New York-based Swiss sculptor.

15·05·97-03·08·97    ***African Masks from the Barbier-Mueller Collection***    *The Second Face*    Some 200 masterpieces from many different African cultures, culled from the collection which was begun in 1918.

17·08·97-05·10·97    ***Robert Longo***    *The Magellan Project*    366 black & white drawings created in 1996 as a sort of personal calendar, dealing with our entire visual culture.

17·08·97-16·11·97    ***New Collection III***    *Classics of the 20th Century*    Famous and less well-known major works created between 1910 and 1990, on loan from European and American museums and private collections.

19·10·97-04·01·98    **Peter August Böckstiegel**   Böckstiegel (1899-1951) was the most important Expressionist of the East Westphalia-Lippe region. The Kunsthalle Bielefeld owns many of his works.

30·11·97-25·01·99    **Jonathan Lasker**   More than 40 pictures by the prominent American painter of the 80s and 90s. The works date from between 1975 and the present.

## Bonn

**BONNER KUNSTVEREIN**
August-Macke-Platz/Hochstadenring 22   53119 Bonn   Director: Annelie Pohlen
☎ +49 228 693936   🖷 +49 228 695589
Open: Tuesday-Sunday 11.00-17.00   Thursday 11.00-19.00
Closed: Monday

**COLLECTION**

**Artothek im Bonner Kunstverein**   Founded in 1987, the main objective of the 'Artothek im Bonner Kunstverein' is to provide art for loan. Totalling c. 1000 works of art, the collection consists of comtemporary art stemming from the 60s until the present day. It includes the artists Joseph Beuys, Sigmar Polke, Felix Droese and Rosemarie Trockel, but consists largely of works from various younger artists. Because of frequent transport to private users, the collection focuses on works on paper which can be protected by frames.

Kogler, Peter;
*exhibition 1996*
© Bonner
Kunstverein, Bonn

**EXHIBITIONS**

until 25·05·97    **Graw Böckler**   *Generation 'Uscha'*

until 25·05·97    **Tamara Grčić**   *Duchamps Urenkel VI*   In her installations, the German artist gives supposed familiar reality a second reality. The sensual qualities of the banal-real objects acquire an unexpected, seductive presence.

until-29·06·97    **Jochen Lempert**   *Symmetry and Body Build Genetical Resources and Other Photoinstallations*   The artist and biologist includes in an extensive number of photographic work his scientific research of the relationship between human and animal.

03·06·97-06·07·97    **Nana Petzet**   *Duchamps Urenkel VII*   A curious world of objects founded on the cycle of things and the attempt of the individual to give the supposed waste a new reality.

15·07·97-07·09·97    **Bon Direct 3**   The smallest common denominator to reflect positions in the world of contemporary art. Invited artists include: Renate Brandt (photography), Detlef Beer (painting), Manuel Franke (sculpture, installation), Valentina Pavlova (painting, installation).

23·09·97-02·11·97   **_Böttcherstrasse Kunstpreis 1997_**   Presenting the work of 10 young artists for the prize founded in 1954 to support young undiscovered artists.

23·09·97-02·11·97   **_Peter Mertes Stipendium '97_**   Young artists from the Rhineland have been selected by an impartial expert jury for this stipend funded by Peter Mertes.

10·11·97-Jan 98   **_Mediation_**   Two Bonn institutes aim to fuse a theoretical approach to the theme of space with practical student training into an exhibition framework.

## Bonn

**KUNST- UND AUSSTELLUNGSHALLE
DER BUNDESREPUBLIK DEUTSCHLAND**
Friedrich-Ebert-Allee 4   53113 Bonn   Director: Wenzel Jacob
☎ +49 228 9171200   ▤ +49 228 9171209   Internet http://www.kah-bonn.de
Open: Tuesday-Sunday 10.00-19.00
Closed: Monday

**COLLECTION**   No permanent collection.

© Kunst und Ausstel-
lungshalle der
Bundesrepublik
Deutschland, Bonn

**EXHIBITIONS**

until Autumn 97   **_Future Garden Part 1_**   _The Endangered Meadows of Europe_ 'Future Garden' is an exhibition project by the American environmental artists Helen Mayer Harrison and Newton Harrison, who have been active in this field for 25 years.

08·05·97-24·08·97   **_German Photography_**   _The Impact of a Medium, 1870-1970_ This exhibition features 300 works by 150 photographers from the fields of architecture, art, photo-journalism, fashion, design and advertising, and offers a representative survey of developments up to 1970.

13·06·97-19·10·97   **_Sigmar Polke_**   _The Three Lies of Painting_   Comprising 180 works from all the artist's creative periods and genres from 1962 to the present day, this exhibition offers the first comprehensive insight into the diverse work of one of Germany's most important contemporary artists.

10·10·97-11·01·98   **_Kunsthalle Bremen in Bonn_**   _500 Years of Masterpieces_   170 paintings and sculptures, and more than 200 engravings from the Kunsthalle are featured, including works by Van Goyen, Rembrandt, Dürer, Delacroix, Beckmann, Moderson-Becker, Nam June Paik and John Cage.

19·12·97-19·04·98   **_Arctic - Antarctic_**   This exhibition depicts the conquest of the North and South Poles, the people of the arctic region, and artistic visions of icy wastelands.

27·03·98-25·01·99  **Gene Worlds**  This exhibition invites the visitor to learn about and ponder science, its technologies and fields of application. Fascinating genetic discoveries and their importance for both our real world and our imagination are displayed in the context of cultural history.

01·05·98-23·08·98  **The Iberians**  This exhibition gives the first detailed insight into the little-known civilisation of the Iberians, one of the original peoples of Spain, and includes stone sculptures, painted ceramics, jewellery and gold handicrafts.

## Bonn

**KUNSTMUSEUM BONN**
Friedrich-Ebert-Allee 2  53113 Bonn  Director: Dieter Ronte
☎ +49 228 776212  📠 +49 228 776220
Open: Tuesday-Sunday 10.00-18.00
Closed: Monday

COLLECTION  **20th-Century Art**  The core of the museum's collection consists of a representative survey of German art since 1945, with an emphasis on works by August Macke and the Rhenish Expressionists. The museum began its systematic collecting activities after the Second World War with the work of August Macke, who lived in Bonn from 1900 onwards. The collection was extended with works by the Rhenish Expressionists, H. Campendonk, H. Thuar and the young Max Ernst, whose pictures were shown at an exhibition in Bonn (1913) organised by Macke.
As a result of the museum's acquisition policy, its holding of German art since 1945 is significant and thus receives pride of place in the museum. Works on view include those by young German artists which the Kunstmuseum collected and exhibited in its early days. When some of these artists gained a world-wide reputation, such as Beuys and his pupils at the Academy of Düsseldorf, the museum changed its collecting strategy and began to concentrate on the work of individual artists, such as Richter, Polke, Knoebel, Palermo, Ruthenbeck, Rückriem and Droese.
One of the museum's greatest acquisitions is the extensive collection of Beuys' 'Multiples' of 1965-1986. Neo-Expressionist figurative painting is represented by the work of Kiefer, Baselitz and Penck. Thanks to Ingrid Oppenheim, the museum owns an important stock of international art videos on view to the public at the Video Centre Ingrid Oppenheim. Finally the Kunstmuseum's holdings include a collection of international graphic art of the 20th century.

EXHIBITIONS

until 19·05·97  **Giuseppe Penone**  *The Veins of the Stone*

until 08·06·97  **Drawing Today I**  *Sivia Bächli, Camill Leberer, Nanne Meyer*

until 28·09·97  **François Morellet**  *Rokokolossal: Neon Installation*

01·05·97-30·04·98  **P.O. Box**  The P.O. Boxes have been arranged by C. Dahlhausen, W. Haypeter, A. Kuhlmann, M. Noël, V. Pavlova, H. Pawelzik and I. Wegmann.

31·05·97-24·08·97  **Body and Soul**  *U. Rosenbach, K. Sieverding, R. Bonvie, K. v. Bruch, J. Klauke*  An exhibition of works by artists who, using cameras and video cameras, are in permanent search of their own identity.

Jun 97-Aug 97  **Art in Nature: Holland**  *H. and N. Harrison*  A green heart in the middle of the Amsterdam/Rotterdam/Utrecht triangle, on the subject of art, culture, bio-diversity, lifestyle and the future.

| | |
|---|---|
| 06·06·97-07·09·97 | ***Multiple Identity***  *Works of Art 1975-95 from the Whitney Museum of American Art*    Some 80 installations, objects, paintings, drawings and photographs convey how American art can be regarded as a unity, as a multiple identity. |
| 05·09·97-09·11·97 | ***August Macke and the Rhenish Expressionists*** |
| 24·09·97-26·10·97 | ***Tinka Von Hasselbach*** |
| 25·09·97-16·11·97 | ***Oswaldo Romber***  *Bypass* |
| 21·11·97-18·01·98 | ***Arnulf Rainer***  *Etchings* |
| 04·12·97-Feb 98 | ***Andy Warhol***  *Last Supper*   Warhol, having always shown a great interest in art-historical works, depicted the subject 'Last Supper' by Leonardo. |

## Bonn

**RHEINISHES LANDESMUSEUM BONN**
**Colmanstraße 14-16  53115 Bonn  Director: Hartwig Lüdtke**
**☎ +49 228 72941  ⛶ +49 228 7294299**
**Open: Tuesday-Friday 09.00-17.00  Wednesday 09.00-20.00**
**Saturday and Sunday 10.00-17.00**
**Closed: Monday**

**COLLECTION**

The Rheinisches Landesmuseum Bonn, founded in 1820, is one of the oldest museums in Germany. It houses a fine collection of art, applied art and cultural assets from the Rhineland. The region's historical and cultural development is presented from the Stone Age up to the present. One of its most famous objects is the only skull of a Neanderthal man ever discovered. Neanderthal people lived near Düsseldorf about 50 000 years ago.
There are additional exhibits on the culture of the Celts, the Roman period, the Franconian period, art and applied art of the Middle Ages, Renaissance, Baroque, Rococo, and Classicism. Objects by noted artists, including paintings, sculpture, glass, furniture, earthenware, gold and photography, are presented within the period rooms.

**EXHIBITIONS**

| | |
|---|---|
| until 08·06·97 | ***Glass Painting of the 20th Century***  *Walther Benner* |
| 15·05·97-24·08·97 | ***..and they left Germany***   A documentation of all photographers who were forced to flee Germany after the National Socialists came to power, or who left for other reasons. |
| 26·06·97-10·08·97 | ***Sitting***  *120 Masterpieces from the Vitra Design Museum*  Miniature chairs to the scale of 1:6, together with originals from the 70s and 80s, imaginatively question classical assumptions. |
| 20·08·97-12·10·97 | ***The Total Healing Method of Prof. Pilzbarth***   Prof. Pilzbarth represents an unusual addition to the ranks of 19th-century scholars. In this exhibition the visitor experiences a convincing swindle. |
| 09·10·97-31·12·97 | ***The House Laughs for Silver***  *The Lanx of Bizerta and Roman Table Silver*   A range of Roman table silver, including the richly decorated bowl from Tunis, gives a picture of how wealthy Romans dined. |
| 15·10·97-31·12·97 | ***Coin Propaganda***  *War and Peace* |
| 06·11·97-31·12·97 | ***Jupp Darchinger***  *The Bonn Republic*   Some 300 photographs by |

Darchinger document the history of the Federal Republic from the end of the war to the present day.

23·10·97-31·12·97 | *New Excavations in the Rhineland*

## Braunschweig

**HERZOG ANTON ULRICH MUSEUM**
Museumstraße 1  38100 Braunschweig  Director: Jochen Luckhardt
☎ +49 531 4842400  🖷 +49 531 4842408
Open: Tuesday-Sunday 10.00-17.00  Wednesday 10.00-20.00
Closed: Monday

**COLLECTION**

The collections are largely based on a ducal Baroque collection.
**Old Masters**  300 paintings are exhibited from the 1 200 Flemish, Dutch, Italian, German and French paintings from between 1500 and 1800 in the collection. Highlights include a self-portrait by Giorgione, 'Judith with the Head of Holofernes' by Rubens, a late family portrait by Rembrandt, and 'Young Lady with a Glass of Wine' and 'Two Gentlemen' by J. Vermeer van Delft.
**Arts and Crafts**  The collection includes bronze statuettes and ivory carvings mainly from the 16th and 17th century, early clocks, fine furniture, an important collection of Venetian and Flemish lace and 16th and 17th-century Limoges enamels.
**Oriental Arts**  Some exquisite examples of oriental art, mainly lacquer work, are on display.
**Antiquities**  The collection includes exhibits from Ancient Egypt, Greek vases and Roman portrait busts and sculptures.
**Drawings and Prints**  The comprehensive collection, dating from the late Middle Ages to the Modern movement, includes almost 10 000 drawings, 100 000 prints and over 1000 sumptuously illustrated books from the Baroque period.
**Middle Ages**  The Medieval collection is displayed in Burg Dankwarderode, the restored palace of Duke Henry the Lion. Among the objects exhibited are some valuable liturgical works including altars, altar fragments, altar utensils, liturgical books and chasubles.

**EXHIBITIONS**
05·06·97-17·08·97

*Dialogue with the Old Masters*  *Prague Cabinet Painting around 1700*  This exhibition presents — for the first time — a survey of baroque Prague cabinet painting around 1700. Historic and genre painting, landscapes, still lifes and gallery paintings reflect the strong influence of the Flemish masters. Works by Bys, Hartmann, Angermayer, Hirschely and others are featured.

18·09·97-18·01·98

*Fürstenberg Chinaware*  To commemorate the 250th anniversary of the manufacture of Fürstenberg chinaware, the museum presents an exhibition focused in particular on tableware and vases of the late rococo period from 1760 to 1770. Works by Witsch and Albert are highlighted.

Apr 98 - Jun 98 | *Duke Heinrich Julius and Prague around 1600*

## Bremen

**FOCKE-MUSEUM BREMER LANDESMUSEUM**
**FÜR KUNST UND KULTURGESCHICHTE**
Schwachhauser Heerstraße 240  28213 Bremen  Director: Jörn Christiansen
☎ +49 421 3613575  🖷 +49 421 3613903
Open: Tuesday-Sunday 10.00-18.00
Closed: Monday

COLLECTION

The Focke-Museum came into existence following a merger between the Historical Museum of Bremen, which was founded by Johann Focke at the turn of the century, and the Bremen Museum of Arts and Crafts. Today, the Bremen State Museum displays collections which cover the economical, political and cultural aspects of the history of both the city and the state of Bremen.

The collections, which range from the prehistoric to the most recent times, emphasise the history of this Hanseactic city, the history of shipping and overseas trade, and middle-class culture. The latter is represented by important collections of silver plate, china and glass. Objects of traditional applied art are supplemented with contemporary products and specimens of modern design.

Relics of peasant life and labour can be viewed in the various rural buildings which can be found on the museum grounds. One of these in particular, a farmhouse, illustrates the changes in village life that occurred as a result of industrialisation in the Bremen area.

EXHIBITIONS

No details available.

## Bremen

**ÜBERSEE-MUSEUM BREMEN**
Bahnhofsplatz 13  28195 Bremen  Director: Viola König
☎ +49 421 3619176  📠 +49 421 3619291
Internet http://www.bremen.de/info/uebersee
Open: Tuesday-Sunday 10.00-18.00
Closed: Monday and 24, 25 and 31 Dec

COLLECTION

The South Seas Collection  includes boats, houses and masks, and dioramas featuring this region's unique flora and fauna.

The Asian Collection  includes a Rajasthani village illustrating the Indian agricultural economy, caste system, and art. A rubber plantation shows the problems and opportunities associated with aid to developing countries. Other displays include a Japanese garden, an exhibit on Shamanism, a traditional Chinese house and Indonesian musical instruments.

The American Collection  includes exhibits of pipes, clothing, masks and basketry. Visitors can learn about the various Indian tribes. An exhibition of Pre-Columbian gold and Andean objects is opened in the summer of 1995.

Topics covered in the African Collection include Ancient Egypt, nomadism, the ecology of the Sahara Desert and the Sahel Crisis. Visitors can view a model of a farmstead, and dioramas of savanna animals. Since June 1995 a collection of African art and musical instruments is on display.

The origins and development of the universe, the earth and life on earth are explained using interactive models, photographs, and fossil and mineral displays. Included are a model of a cell, a weather satellite station, a dinosaur skeleton, and an electron microscope.

EXHIBITIONS

until 13·07·97

*Huichun - Chinese Medicine*   *Historical Objects and Illustrations*

Sep 97

*Manus*   *Art and Life of an Island in the South Pacific*

15·11·997-26·01·98

*The Best Nature Photographies of the Year 1994*

01·02·98-29·03·98

*Images of Power*   *Balinese Paintings Made for Margaret Mead and Gregory Bateson*

## Chemnitz

**STÄDTISCHE KUNSTSAMMLUNGEN CHEMNITZ / CITY ART GALLERY**
Theaterplatz 1  09111 Chemnitz  Director: Ingrid Mössinger
☎ +49 371 4884424  🖷 +49 371 4884499
Open: Tuesday-Sunday 11.00-17.00
Closed: Monday

COLLECTION

The Städtische Kunstsammlungen Chemnitz, founded in 1920, presently contains the following sections, which together hold about 80 000 exhibits: painting and sculpture, prints and textiles and applied art.

There are a large number of paintings and drawings by Karl Schmidt-Rottluff (one of the founders of the 'Brücke' group), who was born in Rottluff, a suburb of Chemnitz. Dresden Romanticism is represented by the painters C.D. Friedrich, C.G. Carus, J. Chr. Clausen-Dahl, G.F. Kersting and L. Richter. Among the German Impressionist paintings are works by R. Sterl, M. Liebermann, M. Slevogt and L. Corinth. There are also Expressionist paintings, Western European works from the Lühl Collection, art from the GDR and sculptures by Rodin, Lehmbruck, Barlach, Maillol and many others.

The large collection of textiles and applied art (Coptic fabrics, industrial design, furniture by H. v.d. Velde, historical posters, fine crafts and more) is one of the most important in Germany. The print collection contains over 20 000 works on paper by A. Dürer, M. Wohlgemut, Rembrandt, various Romanticists, K. Kollwitz, E. Munch, various Expressionists and many others. Parts of these collections are displayed in changing exhibitions.

EXHIBITIONS

until 06·07·97

*Wolfgang Mattheuer on his 70th Birthday*    Graphic Reproductions from the Koch Collection

Jul 97-Aug 97

*Richard Anuszkiewicz*   *Paintings and Painted Constructions: American Op-Art.*

Sep 97-Nov 97

*20 Years of Clara Mosch*

02·11·97-04·01·97

*Jan Dibbets*   *Perspective Corrections*

02·11·97-04·01·97

*Rembrandt van Rijn*   *Original Etchings 1629-1659*   Works from the collections of the Vienna Künstlerhauses and the Municipal Collections of Chemnitz.

## Darmstadt

**HESSISCHES LANDESMUSEUM DARMSTADT**
Friedensplatz 1  64283 Darmstadt  Director: Sybille Ebert-Schifferer
☎ +49 6151 165703  🖷 +49 6151 28942
Internet http://www.darmstadt.gmd.de/Museum/HLMD/index.html
Open: Tuesday-Saturday 10.00-17.00  Wednesday 10.00-17.00 /19.00-21.00
Sunday 11.00-17.00
Closed: Monday

COLLECTION

The Hessian Regional Museum possesses a comprehensive section of Medieval mural paintings. Among the paintings from 1550 to 1800 are works by Pieter Brueghel, Domenichino and Rubens. The 19th-century collection includes works by Arnold Böcklin, Liebermann, Slevogt, Corinth and Darmstadt painters such as Schilbach and Lucas. The 20th century is represented by Feininger, Dix, Kirchner, Duchamp and others. The contemporary art section, with some 300 works includes 'Informal' and Pop Art, as well as works by

Gerhard Richter, Arnulf Rainer and Sigmar Polke and German paintings from the 80s. The Hessische Landesmuseum, with its 'Beuys Block', owns the largest work complex by Joseph Beuys (270 works from the years 1949-1972).

The graphics collection illustrates the development of lithography and the art of drawing from the Late Middle Ages to the present day. It contains works by Italian, French and Dutch artists from the 16th to the 18th century and a collection of posters from about 1900 onwards. There is a collection of glass paintings from the 9th century to the present.

Works from the Carolingian era, a crucifixion group by Tilman Riemenschneider and Baroque sculptures by Zürn and Zamels are among the museum's sculptures. The Hübsch collection contains Medieval goldwork, carved ivory and enamel work. There are also goblets, hollow glassware and armour from the royal cabinet, archaeological finds from the Early Stone Age to Merovingian-Frankish times and provincial Roman objects.

The natural science sections contain a survey of the animal kingdom, rare specimens and a paleontology and mineralogy display.

**EXHIBITIONS**

until 01·06·97

***L'Art Gourmand***   *Still Lifes for the Eye, Cuisine and Gourmets from Aertsen to Van Gogh*   An exhibition of food still lifes, ranging from the 16th to the 20th century.

Apr 97-Jun 97

***Antonio Canaletto***   *Drawings and Etchings*

## Darmstadt

**SCHLOßMUSEUM DARMSTADT E.V.**
Residenzschloß  Marktplatz 15  64283 Darmstadt  Director: Volker Illgen
☎ +49 6151 24035
Open: Monday-Thursday 10.00-13.00 / 14.00-17.00
Saturday, Sunday 10.00-13.00
Closed: Friday

**COLLECTION**

Founded in 1924 by Grand Duke Ernst Ludwig of Hesse, the museum covers the history of the former state, later Grand Duchy, of Hesse. Destruction by bombing in 1944 and dispersal to former East Germany has reduced the collection somewhat, though it remains representative.

There are over 20 rooms displaying pictures, artefacts, etc. relating to the social history of Darmstadt and surroundings. Parts of Landgrave Ernst Ludwig's carpentry workshop, the hunting diary of Ludwig VIII and militaria of Landgrave Ludwig XI are also on display.

The paintings include a large collection of local 18th and 19th-century artists and other masters such as Ziesenis, Winterhalter and Wilhelm Schadow. There are also 18th and 19th-century decorations, clothing and pre-1914 uniforms, including those of famous figures such as Bismarck and Moltke. Historic carriages, sedan chairs and riding gear, etc. from the House of Hesse are also exhibited. Central exhibit is the Madonna of the Bürgermeister of Basle, Jacob Meyer, painted by Hans Holbein the Younger in 1625 - one of the greatest German paintings, on the threshold between Gothic art and the Renaissance.

**EXHIBITIONS**

No exhibitions planned.

## Dortmund

**MUSEUM AM OSTWALL**
Ostwall 7  44122 Dortmund  Director: Ingo Bartsch
☎ +49 231 5023247  📠 +49 231 5025244
Open: Tuesday-Sunday 10.00-17.00
Closed: Monday

**COLLECTION**

The pivot of the collection is formed by German Expressionism. In addition to works of the renowned 'Brücke' and 'Blauer Reiter' artists' groups, many associated German artists are also featured, including a considerable collection of works by August Macke and Alexej Jawlensky. Post-war European art is also strongly represented, with Geometric, Kinetic and Concrete art from such artists as Brüning, Mack, Götz, Uecker, Graeser and Spagnulo. There is a wide-ranging collection of sculpture, both from the pre-war period (including works by Lehmbruck, Archipenko, H. Blumenthal, Maillol) and from the post-war era (including works by Moore, Calder, Arp, Chadwick, Melotti, Wotruba and Pistoletto). Also on view is a representive selection from the major Cremer Collection consisting of diverse European works from the 50s to the 70s.

Karl Schmidt-Rotluff
*Early spring, 1911*
*Museum am Ostwall,*
*Dortmund*
© Jürgen Spiler

The museum also reserves a special space for important artists of the Fluxus and Happening movements (Beuys, Brecht, Filliou and Païk, among others), having exhibited these works permanently since 1972 and finally acquiring them from the Feelisch Collection in 1988. Since 1995, art regularly purchased by the Dörken Foundation for the Museum am Ostwall can be seen as well (Bury, Emde, Linnenbrink). The Bernhard Hoetger estate with its Expressionist architectonic maquettes and sculptures also belongs to the museum. The Graphics Collection focuses on Expressionism and international post-war drawings and prints.

**EXHIBITIONS**

until 15·06·97

*Heinze-Günter Prager*   The renowned sculptor of steel presents a series of new works, conceived, in part, specifically in relation to the space and dimensions of the Museum am Ostwall.

until 22·06·97

*Otto Mueller*   In comparison to other Expressionists, this 'Brücke' artist has been somewhat overlooked. Mueller's work bears witness to the harmony between the human individual and nature.

29·06·97 - onwards

*Masterpieces from the Collection of the Museum am Ostwall*
Major works from the permanent collection are on view from the end of June. New acquisitions in the realm of color field painting are especially noteworthy.

14·09·97-09·11·97

*Ian Hamilton Finlay*   71-year old Ian Hamilton may be considered one of Great Britain's important artists. This exhibition pays tribute to his life's work, presenting new large-scale intallations and making accessible to a broader public the works he did for the 'Wild Hawthorn Press'.

21·11·97-11·01·98   ***Inge Prokot***   This Cologne-based artist shows a series from her so-called 'Encyclopaedic Painting', in which she justaposes well-known images from art history with significant text quotations.

## Dresden

**ALBERTINUM  STAATLICHE KUNSTSAMMLUNGEN DRESDEN**
Brühlsche Terrasse 01067  Dresden
☎ +49 351 4914619   📠 +49 351 4914616
Open: Friday-Wednesday 10.00-18.00
Closed: Thursday

COLLECTION

[GEMÄLDEGALERIE NEUE MEISTER]

 Dresden's collection of 'Neue Meister' (artworks from the start of the bourgeois epoch in the 19th century through to the present day) has been accommodated in the rebuilt Albertinum since 1965, but its origins extend back to an annual financial donation instituted in 1843. A large number of works were either destroyed in the Second World War or expropriated shortly after and taken to Russia. New acquisitions have, however, partly made up for these losses.
The collection begins with German Romanticism and bourgeois Realism, including works from Böcklin, Thoma, Menzel, Uhde, Spitzweg, Friedrich, and the largest collection of the works of F. von Rayski. German and French Impressionism are also featured. German Expressionism forms a further focus, along with some remaining examples of the collection of 'Contemporary Socialist Art' from GDR days. One of the major works of the collection is Grundig's triptych 'The Thousand Year Reich', a prophetic anti-war work painted before the Second World War, now fittingly exhibited together with Otto Dix's 'War Triptych'.

[GRÜNES GEWÖLBE]

Between 1723 and 1729, King August the Strong converted the strong-rooms of the Dresden Schloß into a public treasure-chamber museum. Here he exhibited his outstanding collection of jewellery, goldsmiths' work, ivory and stone carvings, and bronze statuettes. Following the destruction of the Schloß in the Second World War, about half the original collection has been on view in four large halls of the Albertinum since 1974 and still forms the largest and more important treasure-chamber collection in Europe. It includes works of the Middle Ages, Renaissance, early Baroque and the reign of August the Strong himself. Particularly worthy of mention in the collection, which is one of the oldest museums for applied arts, are the ivory and ebony carvings of Balthasar Permoser and the goblets and jewelled works of Johann Melchior Dinglinger.

[MÜNZKABINETT]

The Coin-Cabinet has a universal collection of about 280 000 objects of Europeam importance. There are coins and medals of all times and countries, also decorations, banknotes, historical bonds, coin- and medal-dies, deals and many technical elements of the saxon mint.

[SKULPTURENSAMMLUNG ]

The Sculpture Collection, that includes about 15 000 originals from over five millenniums, is divided into two main sections: the collection of art from the ancient world and the collection of European post-ancient sculptures dating from the Late Middle Ages to the present day.

The main works in the collection of art of the ancient world are marble sculptures, mainly valuable Roman replicas of Greek masterpieces from the Classical period to Hellenism. The pieces include 'Athena Lemnia' after Phidias, an ancient copy of Myron's 'Head of Athena', the three female statues from Herculaneum, the 'Head of Diadumenos', a statue of a Victor after Polyklet, 'Reclining Hercules' after Lysipp, 'Wine-pouring Satyr' after Praxiteles and the unique preserved copy of a Maenad by Skopas which is only otherwise mentioned in literature. There are also Greek originals such as funeral and votive reliefs and many precious examples of Greek, Etruscan and Roman ceramics, terracottas and bronzes.

The second part of the collection includes pieces from German, Italian, French and Dutch masters from the Middle Ages to the present day, notably the four smaller bronzes by Giambologna and sculptures by Adrian de Vries and Permoser. Sculptures from famous 19th and 20th-century artists, such as Schadow, Rauch, Degas, Rodin, Maillol, Meunier, Rosso, Lehmbruck, Kirchner, Kolbe and Glöckner are exhibited together with paintings from the Modern Masters Picture Gallery.

**EXHIBITIONS**

| | |
|---|---|
| until 29·06·97 | ***Ernst Ferdinand Oehme*** |
| until Feb 98 | ***The Medals of the Saxon States*** |
| 07·05·97-13·07·97 | ***Treasures from German Private Collections***   *Early Meissener Porcelain* |
| 27·05·97-Aug 97 | ***Gerda Lepke***   *About te Ancient World*   Exhibition in the Antiquity-hall |
| 13·07·97-28·09·97 | ***Conrad Felixmüller*** |
| 16·08·97-19·10·97 | ***Van Eyck, Brueghel, Rembrandt***   *Three Centuries of Dutch Drawings* |
| 12·10·97-04·01·98 | ***'Brücke' and 'Blauer Reiter'***   Works from the Collection Etta und Ott Stangl |
| 19·10·97-07·12·97 | ***Birkas, Elgin, Maning*** |
| 14·12·97-Feb 98 | ***4 x 1 in Albertinum*** |

# Dresden

**GEMÄLDEGALERIE ALTE MEISTER -
STAATLICHE KUNSTSAMMLUNGEN DRESDEN**
Semperbau am Zwinger 01067 Dresden  Director: Harald Marx
☎ +49 351 4914620  ⊥ +49 351 4914694
Open: Tuesday-Sunday 10.00-18.00
Closed: Monday

**COLLECTION**   The Dresden Old Masters Picture Gallery has a collection of works by Italian Renaissance masters, including Raphael's 'Sistine Madonna', Giorgione's 'Sleeping Venus', Titian's 'The Tribute Money' and Correggio's 'Holy Night', as well as paintings from the Italian Baroque.

There are 17th-century Flemish and Dutch paintings by Rubens, Van Dyck and Jordaens, Rembrandt and his school, Jan Vermeer van Delft and the so-called Dutch 'minor masters'. This Gallery, created as the result of the passion for collecting of two Saxon Electors and Kings of Poland in the first half of the 18th century, also contains works by Spanish, French and German artists.

*Interior view: view of the Sixtina*
*© Gemäldegalerie Alte Meister, Dresden*

Some paintings were part of the 'Kunstkammer' (Art Chamber), founded as early as 1560 and considerably enlarged from the middle of the 17th century onwards. In 1707 the best paintings were removed from the 'Kunstkammer' and displayed separately in a room in the palace. They were eventually moved into the Great Hall and adjacent rooms, thus creating the first Dresden Picture Gallery within the Palace.

**EXHIBITIONS** | No exhibitions planned.

## Dresden

**PORZELLANSAMMLUNG -**
**STAATLICHE KUNSTSAMMLUNGEN DRESDEN**
Zwinger Entrance 'Glockenspielpavillon' 01067 Dresden  Director: U. Pietsch
☎ +49 351 4914627  📠 +49 351 4914629
Open: Friday-Wednesday 10.00-18.00
Closed: Thursday

**COLLECTION** | The Dresden Porcelain Collection was established by Augustus the Strong, King of Poland and Elector of Saxony, during a period of

*Exhibition in the curved gallery*
*© Porzellan-sammlung, Dresden*

about fifteen years from 1715 and 1730. The nucleus of the collection still consists of Chinese and Japanese porcelain acquired

during this period, and of Meissen porcelain manufactured for the king's porcelain palace known as the Japanese Palace.
During the 19th century, following a long period of stagnation, the collection was expanded to include European porcelain (especially from Germany and Austria) of the 18th and 19th century. Since 1900, the Far Eastern collection has been enlarged with the addition of Chinese tomb figures from the Tang period, Chinese stoneware in the style of the Song period and Ming porcelain. The Meissen collection has been similarly enlarged with the addition of figures and tableware from the mid-18th century.

**EXHIBITIONS**   No exhibitions planned.

## Duisburg

**WILHELM LEHMBRUCK MUSEUM DUISBURG - EUROPEAN CENTER OF MODERN SCULPTURE**
Friedrich-Wilhelm-Straße 40  47049 Duisburg  Director: C. Brockhaus
☎ +49 203 2832630  📠 +49 203 2833892
Open: Tuesday-Saturday 11.00-17.00  Sunday 10.00-18.00
Closed: Monday

**COLLECTION**   **20th-century art**   The collection features Wilhelm Lehmbruck's oeuvre, together with sculpture, painting, graphic art by other artists. Set in a wooded park in the heart of the city, the museum displays over 300 sculptures, 80 paintings and 100 works of graphic art by over 200 artists from 20 countries. Noteworthy are the sculpture garden and park.
The core of the collection consists of Wilhelm Lehmbruck's oeuvre beginning with his early works created at the Düsseldorf Art Academy (1901-1908) and masterpieces from his Paris time (1910-1914), such as the 'Standing Female Figure' (1910), which was inspired by Maillol and established Lehmbruck's worldwide fame. Lehmbruck's drawings and graphic works reveal his ideas at their purest, while his paintings also show his expressionistic nature.
Building on Lehmbruck's oeuvre is the collection of 20th-century international sculpture and object art, from Expressionist works by Barlach and Kollwitz to masterpieces of Cubism and Constructivism by Archipenko, Duchamp-Villon, Laurens, and others. Surrealism informs Picasso's and Arp's biomorphic shapes and the objets trouvés in Dali's and Ernst's works exemplify a whimsical and poetic approach to materials.
Following classical modern art is the steel sculpturing executed in many styles and techniques since 1945. Object art, Photo-Realism and Serial Art of the Zero evolved during the 1950s and 1960s. Finally there are works by Bill, Heerich, Le Witt, Judd, and Beuys, who, inspired by Lehmbruck, carried on his life work into the present.The collection of German paintings from the first half of the 20th century reviews artistic development from Expressionism to Bauhaus-oriented art, Surrealism and Informel.
The varied graphic collection concentrates on drawings, prints, and photographs by 20th-century sculptors represented in the permanent collection.

**EXHIBITIONS**   [MAIN EXHIBITION ROOM]

until 15·06·97   ***INTER ACT!***   *Key Works of Interactive Art*

29·06·97-27·07·97   ***Constantin Brancusi***   *The Photographic Work*

17·08·97-14·09·97   ***The Photography Collection of the Wilhelm Lehmbruck Museum***

27·09·97-26·10·97   ***Heinz-Günter Prager***   *Borobodur*

09·11·97-25·01·98      *100 Years of 'Sculpture and Photography'*

[STUDIO]

until 25·05·97        *Max Couper*   The Plot

29·11·97-14·01·98     *Homage to Erwin Heerich on his 75th Birthday*

# Düsseldorf

**KUNSTMUSEUM DÜSSELDORF IM EHRENHOF**
Ehrenhof 5  40479 Düsseldorf  Director: Hans Albert Peters
☎ +49 211 8992460  ⛁ +49 211 8929046
Open: Tuesday-Sunday 11.00-18.00 and Easter Monday, Whit Monday
Closed: Monday and Easter Sunday, 1 May, Whit Sunday

COLLECTION

**Old Masters**  The Gallery of Old Masters shows magnificent examples of Dutch and Flemish painting of the 16th and 17th century and French and Italian painting of the 18th century. The highlights among the old masters are 'Venus and Adonis' and the 'Assumption of the Virgin' by Peter Paul Rubens. The 19th century is represented by paintings of the famous 'Düsseldorf School'.
**Sculpture**  The sculpture collection focuses on the Medieval and Baroque eras, including numerous Southern German Late Gothic sculptures.
**20th Century**  The 20th century is represented by works of Expressionism, Neue Sachlichkeit and Constructivism. A particularly important ensemble consists of the Academy artists of Düsseldorf, including Otto Pankok and Joseph Beuys.
**Glass**  The Kunstmuseum features one of the leading glass collections of Europe. It shows a complete documentation of the development of glass-making from luxury glass of Pre-Roman times to the main trends of Art Nouveau and contemporary studio glass.
**Prints and Drawings**  With some 80 000 paper works from the 15th century up to the present, the collection of prints and drawings is one of the largest of its kind in the Federal Republic.
**Arts and Crafts**  The collection of arts and crafts features tapestry, furniture, old household implements and a large collection of ancient Iranian and Islamic crafts. The textile collection represents almost all textile techniques from the majority of European and Eastern countries. The 20th century is represented by an extensive collection of industrial design and applied arts.

EXHIBITIONS
until mid 97        *The 7th Year*   Children's Pictures

until 01·06·97      *Balance - Length x Width x Depth x Duration*   23 Years of the Rinke Class

until 03·08·97      *Eye-Witnesses*   Paper Works of the 1980s and 1990s from the Hanck Collection

| | |
|---|---|
| 19·10·97-15·02·98 | *New Glass*   *1960s to 1990s* |
| 10·10·97-11·01·98 | *1967/68*   *Design and Everyday Culture between Consumption and Conflict* |
| | [IN THE KUNSTHALLE] |
| 06·12·97-01·02·98 | *The Alpha and Omega of the Landscape*   *Andreas and Oswald Achenbach* |

## Düsseldorf

**KUNSTHALLE DÜSSELDORF**
**Grabbeplatz 4  40200 Düsseldorf  Director: Jürgen Harten**
☎ **+49 211 8996241** 🖷 **+49 211 8929168**
**Open: Tuesday-Sunday 11.00-18.00**
**Closed: Monday**

**COLLECTION**   No permanent collection.

**EXHIBITIONS**

| | |
|---|---|
| until 20·07·97 | *Ich Narr des Glücks*   An exhibition for the Bicentenary of Heinrich Heine (borm 1797 in Düsseldorf - died 1856 in Paris). A glance into the famous German poet's epoch, as echoed in the paintings and sculptures of the German and French romanticism. |
| 09·08·97-21·09·97 | *Imi Knoebel*   An exhibition of early and new works of the Düsseldorf artist. |
| 03·10·97-10·11·97 | *Marcel Broodthaers*   *Cinema*   An exhibition about the filmproduction and the film-collection of Marcel Broodthaers |
| 06·12·97-06·02·98 | *Andreas & Oswald Aschenbach*   *Retrospective with 130 paintings and drawings* |

## Düsseldorf

**KUNSTSAMMLUNG NORDRHEIN-WESTFALEN**
**Grabbeplatz 5  40102 Düsseldorf  Director: Armin Zweite**
☎ **+49 211 83810** 🖷 **+49 211 8381202**
**Open: Tuesday-Sunday 10.00-18.00  Friday 10.00-20.00**
**Closed: Monday**

**COLLECTION**   The Kunstsammlung Nordrhein-Westfalen was established in 1960 when the regional government of North Rhine-Westphalia acquired a collection of 88 paintings and drawings by Paul Klee from the American private collector David Thompson, of Pittsburgh, and exhibited them in Schloss Jägerhof in Düsseldorf. The Klee collection was the basis for the establishment of the Stiftung Kunstsammlung Nordrhein-Westfalen in 1961.
Virtually all the significant artists, movements and streams of 20th century painting are represented in the museum. The collection is comprised mainly of works of art produced before 1945, commencing with those many movements and streams at the beginning of the century which represented a drastic break with the traditional notion of art. Included in those movements are Fauvism, Expressionism and 'Der Blaue Reiter', Cubism and its many ramifications, and 'Pittura Metafisica'. By the 20s and 30s, Dadaism and Surrealism were pre-eminent at one extreme, while Constructivism, Bauhaus and De Stijl dominated at the other. The museum's collection of works produced after 1945 ranges from Abstract Expressionism in the USA and Europe through Pop Art and Colour Field Painting.

© Kunstsammlung
Nordrhein-Westfalen
Düsseldorf

**EXHIBITIONS**

until 24·08·97

*Moved Unmoved*   *Perception of Movement in the Pictorial Arts*

17·05·97-10·08·97

*Barnett Newman*   *Sculptures, Paintings, Graphics*   This first large presentation of Newman's work for 25 years focuses on his sculptural work, relating its formal elements to his works on paper and canvas and showing its enormous influence on Western art past and present.

06·09·97-30·11·97

*Max Beckmann*   '*The Night*'   This exhibition centres on 'The Night', Beckmann's major work created in 1918/19 which interweaves current political events with his own horrific war experiences. It marked Beckmann's break with Impressionism and the inception of a new phase. Also included are other of his related works.

21·03·98-14·06·98

*The Blue Four*   *Feininger, Jawlensky, Kandinsky, Klee*

## Essen

**MUSEUM FOLKWANG ESSEN**
Goethestraße 41  45128 Essen  Director: Georg-W. Költzsch
☎ +49 201 888484  ⌨ +49 201 888450
Open: Tuesday-Sunday 10.00-18.00  Thursday 10.00-21.00
Closed: Monday  Due to renovation, the ancient part of the building-including the collection of the 19th and the 20th century-will be closed until 1998.

**COLLECTION**

The Folkwang Museum has an excellent collection of paintings, plastic arts, drawings, graphics (c. 25 000 pieces) and photography (c. 20 000 pieces) of the 19th and 20th century.
The collection features German Romanticists (Carus, Clausen Dahl, C.D. Friedrich, Hackert, Koch, Morgenstern) and Realists of the 19th century (Böcklin, Feuerbach, Leibl, Marées, Trübner, Thoma), in addition to French Realists (Corot, Courbet, Daumier, Delacroix) and Impressionists (Cézanne, Gauguin, Van Gogh, Manet, Monet, Pissarro, Renoir, Signac, Sisley). Also strongly represented are the French Cubists (Braque, Delaunay, Gris, Léger, Picasso) and Surrealists (Dalí, Ernst, Miró, Magritte, Tanguy). The painters of the 'Brücke' (Heckel, Kirchner, Mueller, Nolde, Pechstein, Schmidt_Rottluff) and of the 'Blaue Reiter' (Kandinsky, Macke, Marc) and artists connected with ideas of those groups (Modersohn-Becker, Rohlfs), Bauhaus artists (Feininger, Klee, Maholy-Nagy, Molzahn, Schlemmer), all represent the variety of German Expressionism and of 20th-century art.

**EXHIBITIONS**

11·05·97-06·07·97

*Ansgar Nierhoff*   *Sculptures and Drawings*

15·05·97-15·06·97

*Karl Heinz Adler*   *Objects and Graphic Works*

| | |
|---|---|
| 22·06·97-03·08·97 | **"World Art Grows Under The Italian Sky"**  *Italian Drawings of the Romantic by Ludwig and Ferdinand Deurer* |
| 03·08·97-14·09·97 | **Patrick Tosani**  *Colour Photographs* |
| 10·08·97-21·09·97 | **Antique Art from the 13th to 18th Century**  *Paintings, Sculptures, Handicrafts from the Collection of the Museum Folkwang* |
| 28·09·97-16·11·97 | **Lotte Errell**  *Journalist of the 1930s* |
| 12·10·97-04·01·98 | **Border Crossings and Infidelities**  *Sculptures by Famous Painters, from Degas to Gerhard Richter* |
| 23·11·97-11·01·98 | **Tony Cragg**  *Drawings* |
| | [ZECHE ZOLLVEREIN] |
| Sep 97-Nov 97 | **Norske Profiler**  *Contemporary Art from Norway* |

## Esslingen

**GALERIE DER STADT ESSLINGEN**
Villa Merkel  Pulverwiesen  7300 Esslingen  Director: R. Damsch-Wiehager
☎ +49 711 35122461  ✇ +49 711 35122903
Open: Wednesday-Sunday 11.00-18.00  Tuesday 11.00-20.00
Closed: Monday

COLLECTION

Villa Merkel was built in the year 1873 for the Esslingen industrialist Oskar Merkel. The building was designed by the Stuttgart architect Otto Tafel.

The graphic collection of the city of Esslingen am Neckar was founded in the year 1957 by the Mayor of that time. Ever since, the collection has been enlarged continuously. In the year 1979, 1 300 works were registered in the first catalogue. In 1991 the second catalogue was published, featuring 1 940 items. By now the collection consists of about 2 800 works. The collection is entirely devoted to art of the 20th century. The emphasis lies on German Expressionism, French art of the 'École de Paris', contemporary European art and artists whose biographies are linked with Esslingen. The latter include high-quality works by Volker Böhringer, Adolf Fleischmann and Rolf Nesch. The foundation of the International Triennial of Photography at Esslingen in 1989 provided an occasion to enlarge the collection of selected examples of contemporary photography.

Villa Merkel is a municipal gallery with changing exhibitions of contemporary art. Besides the Triennial of Photography a small series of the international Zero-movement was initiated.

EXHIBITIONS

| | |
|---|---|
| | [VILLA MERKEL] |
| 25·05·97-20·07·97 | **Heimo Zobernig (Vienna)** |
| 25·07·97-07·09·97 | **Esslingen Artists' Society** |
| 21·09·97-30·11·97 | **ZERO in Paris 1960. And Today**  An exhibition featuring Arman, Hains, Klein, Spoerri, Tinguely and artists from their circle (Aubertin, Bury, César, Dufrêne, Leblanc, Megert, Morellet, Saint Phalle, Soto, Villeglé, Verheyen). |
| 05·12·97-18·01·98 | **Esslingen Artists' Society** |
| | [BAHNWÄRTERHAUS] |
| 25·05·97-29·06·97 | **Beate Jacob (Esslingen) and Tamara Khundadze (Georgia)** |

| | |
|---|---|
| 04·07·97-24·08·97 | *Hauke Harder (Kiel) and Stephan Ullmann (Cologne)* |
| 21·09·97-30·11·97 | *Martin Gostner (Innsbruck)* |
| 07·12·97-18·01·98 | *Eva Maria Reiner (Stuttgart)* |

## Frankfurt am Main

**DEUTSCHES ARCHITEKTUR-MUSEUM**
Schaumainkai 43  60596 Frankfurt am Main  Director: Wilfried Wang
☎ +49 69 21238844  🖷 +49 69 21237721
Open: Tuesday, Thursday-Sunday 10.00-17.00  Wednesday 10.00-20.00
Closed: Monday

COLLECTION

The Architecture Museum, which opened in 1984, serves not only as an exhibition space and a discussion forum for German and international architecture and urban planning, but also as a repository for historically important architectural sketches, plans and models. Since the opening of the museum, some 80 exhibitions have taken place. The building, designed by Ungers, is meant to be more than a museum building — it is intended to illustrate the very essence of architecture. The collection currently includes 110 000 plans and drawings and 400 models, primarily of 20th-century buildings. In addition, the museum houses a libarary of more than 10 000 volumes on architectural history and theory since 1800, and numerous architectural monographs and periodicals of the 20th century. The museum's first permanent exhibition utilises scale models to depict the history of architecture and housing from the oldest known Stone Age hut to the urban dwellings of New York. A second, more comprehensive exhibition is currently in development.

EXHIBITIONS

| | |
|---|---|
| until 25·05·97 | *Architecture in the 20th Century: Ireland* |
| until 25·05·97 | *Work Exhibition at the 2nd International Urban Planning Discourse* |
| 14·06·97-24·08·97 | *FORUM in the German Architecture Museum* |
| 13·09·97-23·11·97 | *Architecture in the 20th Century: Portugal* |
| 13·12·97-22·02·98 | *Power and Monument* *Modern Architecture in Germany 1900-2000* |

## Frankfurt am Main

**MUSEUM FÜR KUNSTHANDWERK**
Schaumainkai 17  60594 Frankfurt am Main  Director: Arnulf Herbst
☎ +49 69 21234037  🖷 +49 69 21230703
Open: Tuesday-Sunday 10.00-17.00  Wednesday 10.00-20.00
Closed: Monday

COLLECTION

The municipal Museum of Decorative Art of the City of Frankfurt has been in existence since 1877. Its collection of over 30 000 objects from all areas of the applied arts is assembled in five departments. The European Department covers the Middle Ages to the present, as does the collection of book-art and graphics. The Near Eastern Department presents Islamic arts and crafts of the 9th to the 19th century. Art and applied art from China and Japan are to be found in the Department for Eastern Asia. In 1988 the Icon Museum of the City of Frankfurt, founded on Dr Schmidt-Voigt's generous gift and housed in the nearby Deutschordenshaus, was incorporated as a fifth department. One of the main aims of the museum lies in the demonstration of relationships and influences between western and eastern cultures.

All of the collections have found an appropriate setting in the museum's new building designed by the New York architect Richard Meier and constructed between 1982 and 1985.

**EXHIBITIONS**

until 15·06·97

*Brave Old World*   *Book Art and Graphics from the 17th to 19th Century*   A selection of artwork in books and graphics culled from the museum's own collection. The focus is on landscape and nature, ranging from sweeping vistas to ornamental decoration.

03·07·97-31·08·97

*A Leased Inheritance*   *Young Chinese Artists*   On the occasion of the takeover of Hong Kong by the People's Republic of China, the museum is showing work by young Chinese artists.

## Frankfurt am Main

**MUSEUM FÜR MODERNE KUNST**
**Domstraße 10  60311 Frankfurt am Main  Director: J.C. Ammann**
☎ **+49 69 21230447  📠 +49 69 21237882**
**Open: Tuesday-Sunday 10.00-17.00  Wednesday 10.00-20.00**
**Closed: Monday**

**COLLECTION**

The MMK is entirely devoted to contemporary art. The heart of its collection is formed by a group of 84 works dating from the 60s. The collection includes works by Chamberlain, de Maria, Johns, Judd, Lichtenstein, Oldenburg, Rauschenberg, Rosenquist, Segal and Warhol, as well as Bacon, Klein, Palermo, Rainer, Richter, Ruthenbeck and Walter.
From the mid-80s onwards this stock has been supplemented with contemporary art works.
Approximately every six months there is a 'Change of Scene' at the museum, which involves six to eight rooms being refitted.

**EXHIBITIONS**

27·06·97-15·01·98

*Change of Scene XII*   The new Change of Scene selection features the following artists: Rei Naito (drawings), Vija Celmins (works 1964-1996), Inge Rambo (photography), Stefan Exler (new workgroup), Cecilia Edefalk (paintings, new workgroup), Katharina Fritsch ('Table Company'), August Sander (photography), Hilla and Bernd Becher (expanded workgroup), Martin Honert ('Childrens' Crusade', 1985-1987), Jochen Flinzer & Alighiero Boetti ('All the Wonders of the World') and Albert Oehlen (linocuts).

[KARMELITENKLOSTER]

until 17·08·97

*Rei Nato*   *Spatial Installation*

## Frankfurt am Main

**PORTIKUS FRANKFURT AM MAIN**
**Schöne Aussicht 2  60311 Frankfurt  Director: Kasper König**
☎ **+49 69 60500830  📠 +49 69 60500831**
**Open: Tuesday-Sunday 11.00 18.00  Wednesday 11.00-20.00**
**Closed: Monday**

**COLLECTION**

No permanent collection.

**EXHIBITIONS**

until 08·06·97

*Steve McQueen*

19·06·97-10·08·97

*Matthew Barney*

## Frankfurt am Main

### SCHIRN KUNSTHALLE
Römerberg  60311 Frankfurt am Main  Director: Hellmut Seemann
☎ +49 69 2998820  🖷 +49 69 29989240
Open: Tuesday-Sunday 10.00-19.00  Wednesday, Thursday 10.00-22.00
Closed: Monday

| COLLECTION | No permanent collection. |
| --- | --- |

**EXHIBITIONS**

until 01·06·97  *Collection of the Aargauer Kunsthaus, Aarau, Switzerland*

until 29·06·97  *Zoran Music*  *Retrospective*

10·06·97-06·07·97  *Georg Heck*  *100th Anniversary Exhibition*

10·06·97-06·07·97  *Pietro Donzelli*  *In the Light of Loneliness*  *In co-operation with
the Kunstmuseum Wolfsburg.*

13·09·97-02·11·97  *Hans Hofmann*  *In co-operation with the Lenbachhaus, Munich.*

27·09·97-30·11·97  *Fernando Pessoa*  *Classical Modern Art in Portugal 1910-1940*
*Portugal is the major theme of the 1997 Frankfurt International
Book Fair.*

28·11·97-01·03·98  *Between Heaven and Earth*  *Moscow icons and illuminated
manuscripts from the 14th to the 16th century.*

18·05·98-18·09·98  *1848  En Route to Freedom*  *The German Revolution of 1848.*

## Frankfurt am Main

### STÄDELSCHES KUNSTINSTITUT UND STÄDTISCHE GALERIE
Holbeinstraße 2  60598 Frankfurt am Main  Director: Herbert Beck
☎ +49 69 6050980  🖷 +49 69 610163
Open: Tuesday-Sunday 10.00-17.00  Wednesday 10.00-20.00
Closed: Monday

COLLECTION

Founded in 1815 by the Frankfurt merchant Johann Friedrich Städel, the museum was originally conceived as both collection and art college, and is now the city's major art gallery. The museum building itself was seriously damaged during the war and was first restored in 1966, with an extension added in 1990. The museum's collections span almost all European schools from the 14th to 20th century and it continues to acquire contemporary works.
There are a number of particularly strong collections. German Renaissance painting is represented by fine works from Cranach, Dürer, Altdörfer, both Holbeins, Baldung and anonymous masters. There is an outstanding collection of early and later Flemish and Dutch Renaissance works, including Jan van Eyck's 'Lucca Madonna' and paintings by Campin, Van der Weyden, Van der Goes, Bosch and Memling; this is augmented by works from the Dutch Golden Age from Rembrandt, Vermeer, Rubens, Van Ruysdael, Hobbema, Brouwer, Steen, Hals and Kalff. Italian schools are also strongly represented, both of the Renaissance (Fra Angelico, Botticelli, Pontormo, Tintoretto, among others) and of the 18th century (Tiepolo). French painting of the 18th and 19th century is exemplified by such artists as Watteau, Chardin, Corot, Delacroix, Courbet, Monet, Renoir, Manet, Degas and Cézanne. German painting comes to the fore again in the 19th and 20th-century departments, with Böcklin and Feuerbach followed by a large collection of German Expressionists, including Beckmann, Nolde and Kirchner. The museum also has a major graphic collection.

## Freiburg im Breisgau

**AUGUSTINERMUSEUM**
Augustinerplatz  79098 Freiburg i. Br.  Director: Saskia Durian-Ress
☎ +49 761 2012531  🖷 +49 761 2012597
Open: Tuesday-Friday 09.30-17.00  Saturday, Sunday 10.30-17.00
Closed: Monday

**COLLECTION**

The Augustiner Museum is located in the centre of Freiburg's Old Town in a former monastery for Augustinian monks. The setting is ideal for the display of the municipal art collection, which includes art and craft from many eras, with a focus on the art of the Upper Rhine region. The highlight of the museum is an extensive collection of Medieval stone and wooden sculptures, glass and panel paintings, tapestries, and gold and silver utensils. Many original ornamental sculptures from Freiburg Cathedral are also on display.

There are exhibits of goldsmiths' work dating back more than a thousand years, embroidered and knitted textiles from the High and Late Middle Ages, paintings by late Medieval masters, and unique specimens of book illumination. The Augustiner Museum also has a collection of Baroque sculptures, an extensive collection of historic furniture and interiors, a collection of glassware and a picture gallery of Baden paintings of the 19th century.

**EXHIBITIONS**

05·06·97-31·07·97 **Crystal Polishing in the Breisgau Region in the Early Modern Times**
[UNIVERSITY LIBRARY, WERTHMANNSPLATZ]  The craft of crystal polishing reached its peak in the Breisgau region in the 16th and 17th century. Elaborately cut crystals were manufactured here, as well as liturgical items, goblets, bowls and candelabra.

27·11·97-Jan 98 **Francisco de Goya**  *Prints*  Famous among other things for his series of etchings 'Caprichos', the Spaniard de Goya can be considered one of the great masters of occidental art. This exhibition is notable for its completeness and the excellent quality of the prints.

Dec 97-Jan 98 **Johann Christian Wentzinger (1719-1797)**  *On the 200th Anniversary of the Sculptor's Death*  [WENTZINGER HAUS, MÜNSTERPLATZ]  Considered the most eminent artist of the region in the late Baroque and Rococo era, Wentzinger was commissioned with a most ambitious task in 1757, one which was to become his major oeuvre: the paintings and sculptures for the collegiate church of St. Gallen.

## Goslar

### MÖNCHEHAUS-MUSEUM FÜR MODERNE KUNST
Mönchestraße 3  3380 Goslar  Director: Th.K.Peter Schenning
☎ +49 5321 29570  📠 +49 5321 42199
Open: Tuesday-Saturday 10.00-13.00 / 15.00-17.00  Sunday 10.00-13.00
Closed: Monday

COLLECTION

The 'Mönchehaus' was built in 1528 and is one of the oldest buildings in the centre of Goslar. The first floor contains the 'Apostelzimmer', an historical best room with one of the last existing plaster floors.
The permanent display in the museum and the sculpture garden consists of paintings, environment works and sculptures, in particular by recipients of the Kaiserring: Henry Moore, Max Ernst, Alexander Calder, Victor Vasarely, Joseph Beuys, Richard Serra, Max Bill, Günther Uecker, Willem de Kooning, Eduardo Chillida, Georg Baselitz, Christo, Gerhard Richter, Mario Merz, Anselm Kiefer, Nam June Paik, Rebecca Horn, Roman Opalka and Bernd & Hilla Becher. Work by young artists is also on display, especially those who have won the Kaiserring Grant.

EXHIBITIONS

03-05-97-07-09-97
*Heinz Mack*   A major exhibition in the entire museum building, featuring pictures and objects.

14-09-97-end Jan 98
*Art for Goslar   An Art Association Collects For Its Town*

10-10-97-end Jan 98
*The Kaiserring Scholarship 1997*

18-10-97-end Jan 98
*Franz Gertsch   Winner of the Kaiserring Scholarship of the Town of Goslar 1997*

## Göttingen

### STÄDTISCHE MUSEUM GÖTTINGEN
Ritterplan 7/8  37073 Göttingen  Director: Jens-Uwe Brinkmann
☎ +49 551 4002843  📠 +49 551 4002059
Open: Tuesday-Friday 10.00-17.00  Saturday, Sunday 10.00-13.00
Closed: Monday

COLLECTION

The museum's collection of religious art presents a survey of the development of sculpture from the 12th century to the late Middle Ages, the Renaissance Age and the Baroque Age, up to the late 18th century.

© Städtisches
Museum Göttingen

The oldest objects date from the Paleolithic period. There are also objects on display from the Neolithic period up to the Bronze Age. These give an impression of the development of human culture in the Göttingen region. The history of the city of Göttingen is

represented from the Merowingian period up to the end of the
Second World War: beginning with a document from 953 first
mentioning a village called 'Gutingi', up to models, pictures,
photographs and everyday items from the 19th century.
Finally, objects from the departments of the 'Georgia Augusta',
along with photographs, give a brief view of the development of
Göttingen University, starting from its foundation in 1737. The
culture and history of the city can also be viewed through some
special collections of art and craft objects from Jewish culture and
history, and collections on the history of literature and publishing.

**EXHIBITIONS**

| | |
|---|---|
| 25·05·97-06·07·97 | **Compassion and Rebirth in Tibetan Art**   *Thangkas from the Tibet House in New Delhi* |
| 13·07·97-31·08·97 | **In Memoriam Kurt Mannig**   *Paintings and Drawings* |
| 27·07·97-31·08·97 | **Jutta Keul**   *Paintings and Sculptures* |
| 21·09·97-09·11·97 | **250 Years Freemasonry in Göttingen** |
| 30·11·97-18·01·98 | **Erhard Joseph**   *Paintings* |
| 29·08·98-03·05·98 | **Torun**   *The development of the City in the 19th century* |

# Haltern

## WESTFÄLISCHES RÖMERMUSEUM
Weseler Straße 100  45721 Haltern  Director: Rudolf Asskamp
☎ +49 2364 93760  📠 +49 2364 937630
Open: Tuesday-Friday 09.00-17.00  Saturday, Sunday 10.00-18.00
Closed: Monday

**COLLECTION**
This new museum, opened in 1993, displays old and new finds from
the Haltern camps and other military installations established by the
Romans along the Lippe River during the initial stages of their war
against Free Germany from 12 B.C. to 16 A.D. The front of the
building runs parallel to the partly reconstructed defences of the
camp. Upon entering the museum across the Roman V-shaped ditch
and rampart, the visitor is thus placed in the centre of Rome's
easternmost outpost in the conquered German lands.
The exterior of the building is topped with fourteen skylights in the
form of legionnaires' tents. The interior is one large exhibition hall
flooded with light. More than 800 objects of daily life and soldiers'
equipment, such as weapons, articles of clothing, tools of carpenters
and metal workers, pottery, glass, coins and medical instruments are
on display.

**EXHIBITIONS**
No exhibitions planned.

# Hamburg

## HAMBURGER KUNSTHALLE
Glockengießerwall  20095 Hamburg  Director: Uwe M. Schneede
☎ +49 40 24862612  📠 +49 40 24862482
Open: Tuesday-Sunday 10.00-18.00  Thursday 10.00-21.00
Closed: Monday

**COLLECTION**
**Medieval Art**  The collection begins with art from the Middle Ages
and includes one of the greatest and most moving paintings in
North German Gothic art, the Grabow Altar ('Petri-Altar') of 1379 by
Master Bertram. The twenty-four plates contain naive and lively

scenes from the Old and New Testament. An interesting comparison can be made between this polyptych and the 'Thomas-Altar' by Master Franke, also in the collection.

**Dutch 17th-Century Painting**   Dutch 17th-century painting is represented by an early Rembrandt work ('Simeon in the Temple'), land and seascapes by Averkamp, Van Goyen, S. and J. Ruisdael, Van de Velde and genre paintings by Jan Steen and P. de Hoogh.

**German Painting of the 19th Century**   A particularly strong feature of the Kunsthalle, this part of the collection is centred around the works of the Romantic painters Caspar David Friedrich ('Das Eismeer', 'Wanderer über dem Nebelmeer') and Philipp Otto Runge ('Die Hülsenbeckschen Kinder', 'Der Morgen'), which together highlight the movement toward subjectivity in painting. The Kunsthalle also has works by Feuerbach, Von Marées and Böcklin. Additional highlights include the Menzel Room and the famous 'Drei Frauen in der Kirche' by the Realist Wilhelm Leibl.

**The Kunsthalle collection**   contains groups of works by Max Liebermann ('Die Netzflickerinnen'), Lovis Corinth and Edvard Munch ('Madonna'). The Classical Modernists are dominated by Max Beckmann and Oskar Kokoschka, together with artists from the 'Brücke' and 'Blauer Reiter' groups (Ernst Ludwig Kirchner, Emil Nolde, Franz Marc). 'Der Goldfisch' by Paul Klee also belongs in this context.

**Contemporary art**   is featured in temporary room exhibitions of individual artists' work. One such room is devoted over a longer term to works by Joseph Beuys.

**EXHIBITIONS**

| | |
|---|---|
| 24·02·97 onwards | *International Art since 1960* |
| until 20·07·97 | *Menzel*   The Soldiers of Frederick the Great |
| 09·05·97-27·07·97 | *Johann Christoph Erhard*   The Rediscoverd Romantic |
| 22·08·97-19·10·97 | *The Hamburg Artists Club of 1897*   On Its 100th Anniversary |
| 07·11·97-25·01·98 | *Max Liebermann*   The Realist   From the early 1870s onwards, Liebermann's unusually realistic portrayals of working people were famous and controversial. Some 80 paintings and 40 drawings illustrate his development up to the turn of the century. |
| 23·01·98-05·04·98 | *Lyonel Feininger*   Retrospective of the Drawings |

# Hamburg

**MUSEUM FÜR KUNST UND GEWERBE HAMBURG**
Steintorplatz 1   20099 Hamburg   Director: Wilhelm Hornbostel
☎ +49 40 24862732   🖷 +49 40 24862834
Open: Tuesday-Sunday 10.00-18.00   Thursday 10.00-21.00   Easter Monday, Whit Monday, 25 , 26 Dec and public holidays 10.00-18.00
Closed: Monday and 1 May, 24 Dec, 31 Dec, 1 Jan

**COLLECTION**

**Applied Arts from the Middle Ages to Historism**   The collection provides a fine survey of European arts and crafts. It includes sculptures, bronzes, articles of gold, ivory, glass, ceramics, tapestries, scientific instruments, majolica, faience, porcelain, period rooms, and musical instruments.

**Art Nouveau**   The museum possesses one of the most important collections of Art Nouveau, acquired at the 1900 World Fair in Paris and representing a broad cross-section of the Art Nouveau trends.

**Modern Applied Art and Industrial Design**   This section includes works in the French Art Deco style, German Expressionist graphics and sculpture, Bauhaus and De Stijl furniture, ceramics and studio pottery of the 20 and 30s, Kinetic objects and modern industrial design.

**East Asia and the Islamic World**   Covering the period from antiquity to the Ming and Quing dynasties, the Chinese collection contains ceramics, jade, bronzes and paintings. The collection of Japanese art shows swordguards, woodcut prints and books. The Islamic collection consists of textiles, wall tiles, ceramics, glass, bronzes and the art of books.

**Ancient Art**   The Ancient Art section includes Egyptian reliefs, bronzes, faience and painted mummy portraits, as well as Etruscan bronzes, vases and sculpture. Ancient Greece is represented by ceramics, bronzes, terracottas, sculpture, glass and jewellery. Ancient Rome is represented by a marble portrait collection, glass, and bronzes.

**Graphic Design and Photography**  The graphic design collection includes ornamental engravings and a famous poster collection.The development of photography from its beginnings to the present is documented in a collection which includes daguerreotypes, other early techniques, and photos exemplifying the pictorialism characteristic of the turn of the century.

## EXHIBITIONS

| | |
|---|---|
| until 25·05·97 | *René Lalique*  Perfume Bottles  [Modern Department] |
| until 06·08·97 | *From South to North*  Photographic Work by Sabine Korth [Photography Forum] |
| 25·04·97 onwards | *Original - Photography - History*  From the Daguerreotype to the Vintage Print  [Photographic Collection] |
| 04·05·97-29·06·97 | *Uwe Loesch*  Graphic Design  [Exhibition Room, 2nd floor] |
| 16·05·97-13·07·97 | *Japanese Lacquer Art of the Present*  [Asian Department] |
| 16·05·97-20·07·97 | *Alphonse Mucha*  Triumph of the Jugendstil |
| 23·05·97-13·07·97 | *The Secrets of the Pharaohs*  Ancient Egypt in Lego Blocks [Forum K] |
| 06·06·97-17·08·97 | *The Anne Wolf Class and Hartwig Ulrich 65th Birthday*  [Modern Department, "Contemporaries" Series] |
| Sep 97-Oct 97 | *Frauke Hänke & Klaus Kienle*  Rubbergraphy  [Photography Forum] |
| Sep 97-Nov 97 | *Seven German Goldsmiths*  [Modern Department] |
| 05·09·97-02·11·97 | *On the 100th Anniversary of the Death of Johannes Brahms* [Historical Department] |
| 12·09·97-02·11·97 | *Viewing a Century*  Martin Haller - Architect of Hamburg Town Hall (as part of the Hamburg Architecture Summer) |
| 12·09·97-02·11·97 | *Ten Years of Painting*  An Exhibition by Guest Teachers  [Exhibition Room, 2nd floor] |
| Nov 97-Dec 97 | *Annual Northern German Craftwork Fair* |
| Nov 97-Jan 98 | *Gerhard Vormwald*  [Photography Forum] |
| 12·12·97-15·02·98 | *Porcelain of the 18th Century*  [Porcelain Department] |

# Hamburg

## HAMBURGISCHES MUSEUM FÜR VÖLKERKUNDE
Rothenbaumchaussee 64  20148 Hamburg  Director: Wulf Köpke
☎ +49 40 44195524  📠 +49 40 44195242
Open: Tuesday-Sunday 10.00-18.00  Thursday 10.00-21.00
Closed: Monday

COLLECTION

The museum's seven main departments house around 350 000 objects and 300 000 historical-ethnographical photographs.
The museum's highlights include the famous 'Chamber of Gold' which houses Central and South American gold treasures, the bronze and ivory works of the kingdom of Benin, and the largest collection of Siberian artefacts outside Russia.
The museum also houses artefacts from the Near East, Middle East and Southern and Eastern Asia. The peoples and cultures of Oceania have always occupied a prominent position within the collection, and the Maori meeting house and the display of Oceanic religious objects are sure to leave a lasting impression. The building's Art Nouveau lobby and the lecture hall with its original fixtures are equally impressive.

EXHIBITIONS
until 31·08·97

*Indians of the Plains and Prairies*

until 31·08·97

*Red Cloud, Blue Horse*    *Photographs of Sioux Indians*

# Hannover

## HISTORISCHES MUSEUM
Pferdestraße 6  30159 Hannover  Director: Waldemar R. Röhrbein
☎ +49 511 1682352  📠 +49 511 1685003
Open: Tuesday 10.00-20.00  Wednesday-Friday 10.00-16.00
Saturday, Sunday 10.00-18.00
Closed: Monday

COLLECTION

The Museum of History, which was founded in 1903, lost its building and a quarter of its collection during the war. It subsequently moved into its new accommodation in the old part of the town, in which the remnants of the Medieval town wall are integrated.
The collection consists of three departments.
The central and largest department offers the visitor a chronological tour through the civic history of the City of Hannover from the Middle Ages up to the present. Medieval archaeological finds, town plans, models, paintings, graphics, photos, posters, porcelain, Hannover silver, household effects, furnished rooms and garments between 1760 and 1960 illustrate the development, the changes, the political and everyday life of the town. Handicraft tools, industrial products, vehicles and children's toys complete the picture.
The presentation of the union between Great Britain and Hannover from 1714 until 1837 is the largest section of the department of State History. Here, among other items, are displayed portraits of Guelph dukes, electors and kings, garments, banners, the rare garment of a mint apprentice, coins, relics of the mining industry in the Harz and Deister regions and military equipment. Also featured are the coaches from the Hannoverian royal stables, including the Gilded State Coach, built in London around 1783, and the Perchhigh Phaeton.
The development of country life and labour between the 17th century and the beginning of the 19th century are presented in the third department. There are a number of farmhouse models, a reconstructed fireplace, a farmhouse parlour from the middle of the

© Historisches Museum Hannover, Hannover

17th century, Fritz Mackensen's painting 'Church Service on the Moorland', country garments, a combine harvester and a threshing machine.

**EXHIBITIONS**

until 16·06·97

***Old Hannoverian Security Papers*** This exhibition of mining shares, security papers and stock certificates from the 18th century to the Second World War traces the economic history of Lower Saxony.

14·05·97-19·10·97

***At 17*** *Youth in Hannover from 1900 to the Present* 'At 17' examines 20th-century youth, with attention focused on themes such as social authority, fashion and style, a room of one's own, youth protest, escape from reality, love and sex, and music.

14·10·97-14·12·97

***Ornate Handicrafts*** This exhibition presents an exquisite choice of needlework, showing different techniques used during the period 1820 to 1920.

10·11·97-10·02·98

***200 Years of the Natural History Society***

05·03·98-30·07·98

***Jewish Culture, Jewish Destiny*** *On the 60th Anniversary of the Pogrom Night*

## Hannover

**NIEDERSÄCHSISCHES LANDESMUSEUM HANNOVER**
Willy-Brandt-Allee 5  30169 Hannover  Director: Heide Grape-Albers
☎ +49 511 98075  📠 +49 511 9807640
Open: Tuesday-Sunday 10.00-17.00  Thursday 10.00-19.00
Closed: Monday. Due to renovation the main building of the museum is closed up to 1998.

**COLLECTION**

**Art Gallery** The Niedersächsische Landesgalerie exhibits paintings and sculptures dating from the Middle Ages to the 20th century, including works by Cranach, Riemenschneider, Botticelli, Rubens, Rembrandt, Poussin, Tiepolo, Caspar David Friedrich, Carl Spitzweg, Monet, Max Liebermann, Max Slevogt and Lovis Corinth and an important collection of drawings and prints.
**Natural Science** The collections of the Natural Science Department represent the biology and geology of Northern Europe, with special reference to Lower Saxony. Exhibitions on ecology aim to promote a better understanding of the natural environment.
**Aquarium** The Aquarium displays fish, amphibians, reptiles and insects in realistic reconstructions of their natural habitats.
**Prehistory** In the Department of Archaeology the most important archaeological finds from Lower Saxony are on display, illustrating the history of this county from Palaeolithic up to the Middle Ages. In the newly created 'Kindermuseum' children can explore

prehistoric time with the help of realistic models made by children and activities like grinding corn or working stone tools.

**Ethnology** The permanent exhibition of the Department of Ethnology includes collections from Oceania, Asia, Africa and the Americas, and a special reflection on themes covering Ethnomedicine, Ethnobotany and Natural Philosophy

© Niedersächsisches
Landesmuseum
Hannover
*Hannover*

**EXHIBITIONS**

[FORUM LANDESMUSEUM, AM MARKTE 8 (OPPOSITE CHURCH) HANNOVER]

20·06·97 onwards

***Max Liebermann, Max Slevogt, Lovis Corinth*** *Paintings* The similarities as well as the artistic differences between these three major artistic personalities are revealed in this selection from the collection of the Lower Saxony State Gallery.

20·06·97-24·08·97

***Max Liebermann, Max Slevogt, Lovis Corinth*** *Drawings* A selection from the Department of Prints and Drawings of the Lower Saxony State Gallery. Many of these masterly works have never been displayed to the public before.

28·11·97-01·03·98

***Masterpieces on Visit to the State Gallery III*** *Max Slevogt* To complete and to throw new light on the State Gallery's own collection, at least one important masterpiece from another museum will be included in this exhibition devoted to Max Slevogt.

[HISTORISCHES MUSEUM, PFERDESTRAßE 6, HANNOVER]

10·11·97-10·02·98

***200 Years of the Society of Natural History*** *A Trip through the History of Hannover and of Natural Philosophy* Founded by citizens of Hannover in 1797, the society has collected works of art up to the 20th century. This society and two others initiated the 'Provinzial Museum Hannover', now Lower Saxony State Museum, where the extensive collection is housed.

# Hannover

## SPRENGEL MUSEUM HANNOVER
Kurt-Schwitters-Platz 30169 Hannover  Director: Ulrich Krempel
☎ +49 511 1683875  🖷 +49 511 1685093
Open: Tuesday 10.00-22.00  Wednesday-Sunday 10.00-18.00
Closed: Monday

**COLLECTION**

Situated by the Maschsee, the large lake near the centre of Hannover, the Sprengel Museum houses major collections of classic modern and contemporary art. The museum was created in response to a donation to the city of more than 300 modern works by the industrialist Bernhard Sprengel in 1969. The museum building itself is notable: completed in two phases, in 1979 and 1992, it provides an optimal setting and protection for the collections while opening up to its surroundings. The architecture

itself easily vies for attention with many of the exhibited works.
The classic modern section has outstanding exhibits of German
Expressionism (works from the 'Brücke' and 'Blaue Reiter' groups,
Nolde, Beckmann and Kokoschka), French Cubism (Picasso, Léger,
Laurens), 'Neue Sachlichkeit', Surrealism, Constructivism and
excellent Kurt Schwitters and Paul Klee collections, together with
sculpture by Arp, Barlach, Lehmbruck and Moore, among others.
The contemporary collection is similarly constructed around
particular artists, rather than taking an encyclopaedic approach.
In addition to large quantities of excellent German art, other
collections focus on the 'Ecole de Paris', work complexes by
Baumeister, Nay and Schumacher, décollages by Rotella and Hains,
Minimal Art by Judd, LeWitt, Rückriem and Sandback, and
Conceptual Art by Barry, Kosuth, Sonnier, Tuttle, Walther and
Weiner. A major graphic collection completes the overview of
20th-century art.

**EXHIBITIONS**

until 18·05·97    *Bogomir Ecker*

until 22·06·97    *Albert Renger-Patzsch   Retrospective on the 100th Anniversary of
his Birth    An exhibition in collaboration with the Albert Renger-
Patzsch Archive, Cologne.*

01·06·97-24·08·97    *Felix Gonzalez-Torres*

27·08·97-16·11·97    *Art in Context   Project: Artist's Museum (3) Emil Schumacher*

07·09·97-30·11·97    *Conrad Felixmüller   The Dresden Years 1910-1934*

14·12·97-22·02·98    *International "Spectrum" Prize for Photography, Awarded by the
Lower Saxony Foundation   Thomas Struth*

[GRAPHICS ROOM]

until 25·05·97    *Peter Brüning   Works on Paper*

01·10·97-18·01·98    *Henri Toulouse-Lautrec   An exhibition of prints from the collection
of the Sprengel Museum.*

## Karlsruhe

**BADISCHES LANDESMUSEUM KARLSRUHE**
Schloß 76131 Karlsruhe  Director: Harald Siebenmorgen
☎ +49 721 9266542  🖷 +49 721 9266549
Internet http://www.Karlsruhe.De/Kultur
Open: Tuesday-Sunday 10.00-17.00  Wednesday 10.00-20.00
Closed: Monday

**COLLECTION**    The 'Grossherzoglich Badische Altertümersammlung', the 'Museum
of Industry', founded in 1860, and part of the Grand Duke's
personal collections are now the nucleus of the Badisches
Landesmuseum Karlsruhe, founded in 1919. It is owned by the State
of Baden-Württemburg.
Prehistory, Egyptian art, Greek, Roman and Oriental antiquities,
sculptures and decorative art of the Middle Ages, the Renaissance
and the Baroque period are on display in the former residence of
the margraves, later the Grand Dukes of Baden. In addition to these
collections there are state and hunting weapons, coins, medals and
the 'Turkish Booty' of the margrave Ludwig Wilhelm von Baden.
European decorative art from Art Nouveau to Art Deco, arts, crafts
and 20th-century design have been put on show in the 'Museum
beim Markt', situated between the castle and Karlsruhe's
marketplace.

Alfons Mucha
*Bust of 'Nature'.*
*Bronze, c. 1899*
© *Badisches*
*Landesmuseum*
*Karlsruhe*
*Karlsruhe*

An overall picture of the production of the Majolika-Factory Karlsruhe, founded in 1900 and still producing, can be seen in the 'Museum in der Majolika-Manufactur'.
There are branch museums in Hirsau, Staufen, Osterburken and Bruchsal with an interesting collection of mechanical musical instruments in the Bruchsal castle.

## EXHIBITIONS

until 01·06·97

**Paul Speck**    *A Swiss Ceramist and Sculptor in Karlsruhe*

21·06·97-07·09·97

**New Building in the 20s**    *Gropius, Schwitters and the Dammerstock Settlement in Karlsruhe*    The design and construction of Karlsruhe-Dammerstock, which is considered one of the most progressive settlement achievements of the 1920s in Germany, was supervised by Walter Gropius. The graphic designer of the exhibition which was held at the time of its opening was Kurt Schwitters.

31·05·97-14·09·97

**Germany's Longing for Italy in the 20th Century**
The exhibition discusses the social background of the longing for Italy during Germany's 'Economic Miracle' (1950s), in which everyone tried to visit Italy, to hear Italian songs, eat Italian food, and bring the Italian way of life to the cold north.

22·06·97-14·09·97

**Stefan Szczesny**    *Ceramics*

27·09·97-23·11·97

**Janna Syvänoja**    *Working in Paper*

29·11·97-07·12·97

**Arts and Crafts** *Christmas Market*

28·02·98-Jul 98

**The Revolution of the German Democrats in Baden 1849-1849**
Men and women from Baden were the first to struggle for democracy in Germany. The exhibition will commemorate the highly important years of the first democratic revolution in Germany in 1848/49.

# Karlsruhe

**STAATLICHE KUNSTHALLE KARLSRUHE**
Hans Thoma-Straße 2-6   76133 Karlsruhe   Director: Horst Vey
☎ +49 721 9263370   🖷 +49 721 9266788
Open: Tuesday-Friday 10.00-17.00   Saturday, Sunday 10.00-18.00
Closed: Monday and 24, 31 Dec and Carnival (Tuesday)

COLLECTION   |   The origins of the Staatliche Kunsthalle collection in Karlsruhe can be traced back to the art collection of the margraves, later to become Grand Dukes of Baden. Margrave Christopher I (1474-1515) commissioned Hans Baldung Grien in 1511 to paint a devotional image of him and his family praying to St. Ann, Mary and Christ. He was also responsible for the acquisition of important works of Old German Masters including Baldung's 'The Adoration of the Christ Child', Lucas Cranach the Elder's 'Madonna with Child' and 'The Judgement of Paris' and a collection of Flemish masters of the 17th century.

Margrave Karoline Luise (1723-1783) was largely responsible for the acquisition of the Dutch masters of the 17th century and French contemporary painters, together with the notable acquisitions of Rembrandt's sombre self-portrait and the four still lifes by Chardin. Acquisitions during the 19th century include the Hans Thoma collection which he donated himself while he was Director of the Kunsthalle and the panels 'Christ Carrying the Cross' and 'Christ on the Cross between Mary and John' by Grünewald.

The collection is further complemented by works from French and German masters, European sculpture from the 19th and 20th century, outstanding Italian painting from the 15th to 18th centuries, and German and French drawings and graphic art.

**EXHIBITIONS**

| until 01·06·97 | ***Edda Renouf***  *Retrospective* |
| until Autumn 97 | ***Paper Art*** |
| 07·06·97-mid Aug 97 | ***Paco Knöller*** |

## Kassel

**GEMÄLDEGALERIE ALTE MEISTER UND ANTIKENSAMMLUNG**
Schloß Wilhelmshöhe  34131 Kassel  Director: Hans Ottomeyer
☎ +49 561 93777   +49 561 9377666
Open: Tuesday-Sunday 10.00-17.00
Closed: Monday

**COLLECTION**

GEMÄLDEGALERIE ALTE MEISTER IS CLOSED FOR RENOVATION UNTIL 1999.

The Old Master paintings will be exhibited in the 'Neue Galerie' (Kassel) and in the 'Hessisches Landesmuseum' (Kassel).
The collection of classical antiquities is one of the major collection of this type in Germany, containing exhibits from the Neolithic to the late Roman period. Two particular highlights are the marble sculptures of the 'Kassel Apollo' and 'Kassel Muse', with vessels, figurines, jewellery and objects of terracotta, stone and bronze also on display.

**EXHIBITION**

| until 25·05·97 | ***Carthage***  *The Excavations by the Archaeological Institute of the University of Hamburg since 1986* |

## Kassel

**HESSISSCHES LANDESMUSEUM**
Brüder-Grimm-Platz 5  34117 Kassel  Director: Hans Ottomeyer
☎ +49 561 78460   +49 561 14551
Open: Tuesday-Sunday 10.00-17.00
Closed: Monday

**COLLECTION**

**Pre-History and Early History**   Relics of the Palaeolithic, Mesolithic and Neolithic Ages, and also the richly furnished grave of a woman from Molzbach and other relics of the Bronze Age.
**Crafts and Sculpture**   Objects from the Middle Ages, the

Renaissance 'Kunstkammer' with silver vessels, objects of ivory, amber, mountain crystal. Goblets, faience pottery and collection of glasses are on show, together with medieval sculptures and a princely alabaster chamber.

**German Wallpaper Museum**   Several hundred exhibits illustrate the history of wallpaper from its beginnings through Renaissance and Baroque up to modern times in this unique collection.

**EXHIBITIONS**

May 97 onwards

*Dürer - Tizian - Poussin*   Some 40 German, Italian, French and Spanish masterpieces from the collection of the Kasseler Gemäldegalerie.

May 97 onwards

*Small Renaissance and Baroque Bronzes*   *From the Landgrave Collection.*

## Kassel

**NEUE GALERIE STAATLICHE UND STÄDTISCHE KUNSTSAMMLUNGEN**
Schöne Aussicht 1  34117 Kassel  Director: Hans Ottomeyer
☎ +49 561 709630  ⛶ +49 561 7096345
Open: Tuesday-Sunday 10.00-17.00
Closed: Monday

**COLLECTION**

The New Gallery is close to the city centre, above the Karlsaue Park. It has a permanent exhibition of European paintings and sculpture from 1750 to the present day, and also features temporary exhibitions, mostly of 20th-century art.
There is an extensive collection of works from the period when the Kassel Academy of Painting was established around 1777/78, featuring J.H. Tischbein, F.A. Tischbein and J.A. Nahl.
19th-century works range from the Biedermeier era through Classicism, Romanticism to Realism and Naturalism. Corinth's 'Lake Walchen' is a highlight of Impressionism. The collection progresses further through Modern Classic (Kirchner, Ernst) to the Informal movement and the 'Documenta' artists, including Beuys, Christo, Baselitz, Oldenburg and Richter.

**EXHIBITIONS**

12·12·96 onwards

*Rubens - Rembrandt - Hals*   *Dutch Masterpieces of the Kasseler Gemäldegalerie on show in the Neue Galerie*

07·06·97-05·10·97

*Olav Christopher Jenssen*   *Paintings and Graphics*

Jun 97-Oct 97

*Joseph Beuys   7000 Oaks*   An exhibition on the reality of a social sculpture: idea, reality, perspectives.

## Kiel

**KUNSTHALLE ZU KIEL**
Düsternbrooker Weg 1  24105 Kiel  Director: Hans-Werner Schmidt
☎ +49 431 5973751  ⛶ +49 431 5973754
Open: Tuesday-Sunday 10.30-18.00  Wednesday 10.30-20.00
Closed: Monday

**COLLECTION**

A collection of Schleswig-Holstein art from the 17th to the 20th century is represented by artists such as Ovens, Blunck, Jessen, Wrage, Feddersen and Olde. The 19th and early 20th- century gallery features works by Kersting, Dahl, Schwind, Feuerbach, Rodin, Rohlfs, Krøyer, Trübner, Liebermann, Corinth and Slevogt, and especially by the Russian painters (Aiwasoffski, Kramskoi, Lewitan, Repin, Schischkin and others).

The collection possesses fine examples of German Expressionism including paintings by Emil Nolde, sculptures by Ernst Barlach and works of the 'Brücke' artists Kirchner, Heckel, Schmidt-Rottluff and Pechstein, as well as works representative of New Objectivity and Magical Realism. Current acquisitions focus on art produced since 1945, such as works of the Informel, CoBrA and SPUR groups, Constructive Art, and works exhibiting realistic tendencies. The gallery contains important paintings, sculptures and objects by contemporary artists such as Richter, Paik, Kubota, Ruthenbeck, Kirkeby, Baselitz, Polke and Knoebel.
The graphic collection includes more than 30 000 drawings, watercolours and prints from the 16th century to the 20th century, primarily by Dutch, German, Italian and French artists, and international contemporary graphic artworks

**EXHIBITIONS**

until 15·06·97    ***Max Pechstein***   *Paintings*

22·06·97-03·08·97    ***Olav Christopher Jenssen***   *Radio*

09·08·97-21·09·97    ***Gustav Kluge***   *Watercolours and Sculptures*

30·11·97-11·08·98    ***David Lynch***   *Paintings, Drawings, Photography*

## Köln - Cologne

**MUSEUM FÜR ANGEWANDTE KUNST / MUSEUM OF APPLIED ARTS**
An der Rechtschule  50667 Köln  Director: Brigitte Tietzel
☎ +49 221 2213860  🖷 +49 221 2213885
Internet: http://www.artworks.de/museenkoeln
Open: Tuesday-Friday 11.00-17.00  Saturday, Sunday 12.00-17.00
Closed: Monday

**COLLECTION**    The Museum of Applied Arts is one of the four major museums for arts and crafts in Germany. The items on display include fashions and jewellery, as well as objects of everyday use.
The full range of applied arts from the last 1000 years is on display on three floors, starting with contemporary design, moving back through the 60s and 50s to the Art Deco of the 30s and 40s and on to the Bauhaus and Werkbund styles. Specific aspects are shown in separate departments, e.g. the fashion collection, modern ceramics, textiles, furniture, sculpture, weapons, metals, as well as ceramic and glass art. There is also a graphic collection.

**EXHIBITIONS**

16·05·97-03·08·97    ***Rudolf Schwarz***   *Inhabited Images*

27·06·97-14·09·97    ***From the Tables of Farmers and Princes***   *European Cutlery from Six Centuries*

01·08·97-05·10·97    ***Ernst Riegel***   *Goldsmith between Historicism and Working Union*

17·10·97-07·12·97    ***Friedrich Becker***   *Kinetic Jewellery and Objects*

## Köln - Cologne

**JOSEF-HAUBRICH-KUNSTHALLE**
Josef-Haubrich-Hof  50676 Köln  Director: Mia M. Storch
☎ +49 221 2212335  🖷 +49 221 2214552
Internet: http//www.artworks.de/museenkoeln
Open: Tuesday-Sunday 10.00-17.00 during exhibitions
Closed: Monday

**COLLECTION**

No permanent collection.

**EXHIBITIONS**
until 25·05·97

*Keith Haring*   *The Graphic Work*

15·09·97-23·09·97

*Antiquarian Days*

21·11·97-08·03·98

*Female Power and Male Domination*   *Gender Relationships in Cultural Comparison*   Relationships between the sexes as revealed by anthropological, historical and archaeological studies and by European and non-European art, creating perspectives on our own customs.

# Köln · Cologne

**MUSEUM LUDWIG**
Bischofsgartenstraße 1  50667 Köln  Director: Marc Scheps
☎ +49 221 2212382  🖷 +49 221 2214114
Internet http://www.artworks.de/museenkoeln.
Open: Tuesday 10.00-20.00  Wednesday-Friday 10.00-18.00
Saturday, Sunday 11.00-18.00
Closed: Monday

**COLLECTION**

Cologne's most recent museum contains works of art of the 20th century. It includes paintings and sculptures, found objects and 'environments', a collection of graphic art, as well as one of the largest sections of photography of Germany.
The collection, which initially consisted of key works of German Expressionism, was considerably enlarged in the 50s and 60s, thus forming the basis of the Modern Section of the 'Wallraf-Richartz' Museum.
More than 300 objects d'art of the Ludwig Collection were handed over to the municipality in 1976 under the name Ludwig Donation. As a result of the opening of the new museum, Cologne now has a complete survey of modern art at its disposal, a great part of which has been devoted to contemporary artists. Cubism, the works of the 'Brücke' and of Expressionism, Italian Futurism and Russian Avant-Garde illustrate the beginning of the 20th century with excellent examples.
European art of the 20s is present in works of Pittura Metafisica, Bauhaus, Constructivism, New Objectivity and Surrealism. The evolution of the works of Picasso over six decades can be followed. New Realism and British and American Pop-Art form the strong features of the museum. The flowering of German art from the end of the 60s up to the present day is amply documented. Other important expressions of art, situated between Minimal Art, Colour Field Painting and Individual Mythology complete the portrait of the last two decades.

Jasper Johns
*Map of the world*
*1967-71*
in the exhibition
'Retrospective'
*Museum Ludwig,*
*Köln*
© *VG Bild-Kunst,*
*Bonn '96*

## Köln - Cologne

**MUSEUM FÜR OSTASIATISCHE KUNST  MUSEUM OF EAST ASIAN ART**
Universitätsstraße 100  50674 Köln  Director: Adele Schlombs
☎ +49 221 9405180  📠 +49 221 407290
Internet: http://www.artworks.de/museenkoeln
Open: Tuesday-Sunday 11.00-17.00  Thursday 11.00-20.00
Closed: Monday

**COLLECTION**

Germany's oldest museum of Far Eastern Art was moved to a modern building in 1977 by Kunio Mayekawa (1905-86), a student of Le Corbusier. The Japanese garden within the premises was designed by the contemporary artist Masayuki Nagare (born 1923).

*Horse and groom, bronze*
China, Eastern Han-Dynasty, 2-3 Century AD
© *Museum für Ostasiatische Kunst, Köln*

The museum displays works of Chinese, Japanese and Korean art, from the Neolithic period to modern times. The Chinese ritual bronzes of the Shang dynasty (13th-11th century B.C.) are as renowned as the museum's vast collection of Buddhist art consisting of exquisitely sculpted stone, wood and lacquer images, delicately painted cult images and powerful Zen-related impressions of human beings and nature.

The collection of Chinese ceramics is especially well represented in the celadon range. The three-coloured tomb figurines together with other vessels are fine examples porcelain from the Tang dynasty (610-907) and later. The collection of Korean ceramics is one of the best in continental Europe. Chinese literati paintings, decorative hanging scrolls and folding screens from Japan as well as the profane, colourful Ukiyo-e prints introduce the visitor to the everyday life of times long past. New on display are early Chinese

Buddhist and Daoist sculptures (8th-12th century) and the collection of Chinese furniture.

The museum also presents spectacular highlights from the collection of Chinese art of Peter ( †) and Irene Ludwig, such as the bronze horse with groom from the Eastern Han-dynasty (height of the horse 118 cm; fig. X). The pieces are excellently preserved. Originally they served as funerary gifts to a highranking Chinese official.

**EXHIBITION**
20/09/97-07/12/97    *Masterpieces of Japanese Woodcuts: The Otto Riese Collection*

# Köln - Cologne

**RAUTENSTRAUCH-JOEST-MUSEUM  MUSEUM OF ETHNOLOGY**
Ubierring 45  50678 Köln  Director: Gisela Völger
☎ +49 221 3369413  🖷 +49 221 3369410
Internet: http://www.artworks.de/museenkoeln
Open: Tuesday-Friday 10.00-16.00  Saturday, Sunday 11.00-16.00
Closed: Monday

**COLLECTION**
The museum collection includes approximately 65 000 objects from Melanesia, Polynesia, Micronesia and Australia, Africa south of the Sahara, Ancient Egypt, Southeast Asia, and North and South America. Additional highlights of the collection include textiles and documents from the Ottoman Empire. The collections are complemented by an important historical photographic archive and an excellent reference library. A primary focus of the museum's work is the scientific research of its collection. With its exhibitions, special programmes and publications, all stressing cross-cultural comparisons, the museum also fosters understanding and respect for 'foreign', non-European cultures and lifestyles. The concept for the new building now in the planning stage envisions the museum even more as a meeting place between members of the various cultures that are a vital presence in and around the city of Cologne.

**EXHIBITIONS**
until 27·07·97    *African Art*   The Arman Collection (in collaboration with the Musée d'Arts Africains, Océaniens, Amérindes, Marseille)   The Franco-American sculptor Arman has amassed a major collection of African sculptures and masks, chiefly from central Africa. This is the first major show of the collection.

until 19·10·97    *Art-icles from South-East Asia*   Paintings and Objects   17 artists from Java portray the world of work in their country. Their paintings show daily working life in both traditional and new fields of work.

16·12·97-17·05·98    *Treasures from the Golden Age of East Java*   Terracotta Art of the Majapahit Realm   Some 30 terracotta reliefs, on show for the first time, are augmented by many other artworks and artefacts from the Majapahit Realm of the 13th-16th centuries.

# Köln - Cologne

**RÖMISCH-GERMANISCHES MUSEUM**
Roncalliplatz 4  50667 Köln  Director: Hansgerd Hellenkemper
☎ +49 221 2214090  🖷 +49 221 2214030
Internet: http//www.artworks.de/museenkoeln
Open: Tuesday-Friday 10.00-16.00  Saturday, Sunday 11.00-16.00
Closed: Monday

**COLLECTION**
The Romano-Germanic Museum in Cologne is built upon the remains of a Roman civic villa and the medieval Imperial Palace, and includes a world famous floor mosaic, preserved on its original site,

that has been incorporated into the museum's exhibition rooms. The archaelogical heritage of the city is on display, ranging from the prehistoric to the medieval, with documentation of ancient Roman Cologne of particular note. There are also displays from the Stone Age, the Bronze Age and the Iron Age, tracing history from 100 000 B.C. up to the 1st century B.C., and including clay vessels of superb quality, finds from the graves of free Germanic tribes from the time of the Roman Empire, and artefacts revealing traces of Frankish settlement in Cologne. Exhibits focusing on Roman times include mosaics and wall decorations, jewellery and ceramics. There are also exhibits of everyday life in Roman times.

**EXHIBITIONS**

until Jun 97 | *Medieval Household Goods from the Stolkgasse in Cologne*

23·05·97-14·09·97 | *Death on the Rhine*  *Burials in Early Cologne*

# Köln · Cologne

**WALLRAF-RICHARTZ-MUSEUM**
**Bischofsgartenstraße 1  50667 Köln  Director: Rainer Budde**
**☎ +49 221 2212372  ⊠ +49 221 2212629**
**Internet http://www.artthing.de/museenkoeln**
**Open: Tuesday 10.00-20.00  Wednesday-Friday 10.00-18.00**
**Saturday, Sunday 11.00-18.00**
**Closed: Monday**

**COLLECTION**

The Wallraf-Richartz Museum is one of Germany's oldest museum foundations. The picture gallery is renowned for its three major collections.
**Medieval Art**  The Medieval department houses a unique range of panel paintings from the Cologne School and works from other regions. Together they provide an almost unbroken survey of panel painting from 1300 to 1550. The collection is augmented by a group of free-standing altar pieces. Later Gothic traditions and the new approaches of the early 16th century are seen emerging in numerous Dutch panel paintings and works by Old German Masters such as Dürer.
**16th to 18th century**  The museum's extensive collection of 16th to 18th-century Dutch and Flemish paintings include some of the best works of the Golden Age of the 17th century. The Rubens collection is especially fine and the Rembrandt self-portrait represents a high point in his late work. Great examples of Mediterranean art are also on display, including works by the Italian Paris Bordone, the French artist Claude Gellée and the great Spanish artists of the early Golden Age.
**19th century**  The comprehensive 19th-century collection opens with Romantic and Realist paintings and one of Germanies finest Leibel collections. German Impressionism is represented by Liebermann and Slevogt. The French paintings include works by the Realist Courbet, Renoir (the early portrait of the Sisleys), Monet, Sisley, Degas, Manet and Cézanne. The collection is completed by Symbolist paintings by Ensor and Munch, together with works by Van Gogh, Gauguin and Bonnard that take us beyond Impressionism towards the art of our own century.

**EXHIBITIONS**

20·06·97-14·09·97 | *L'Art Gourmand*  *Still Lifes for the Eye, Cuisine and Gourmets from Aertsen to Van Gogh*

06·09·97-30·11·97 | *Pointillism*  *A Theory becomes Art*

mid Jan 98-end Mar 98 | *Caspar Scheuren*  *Rhine Series*

# Leipzig

## MUSEUM DER BILDENDEN KÜNSTE LEIPZIG - MUSEUM OF FINE ARTS
Dimitroffplatz 1  04107 Leipzig  Director: Herwig Guratzsch
☎ +49 341 2169920  ✸ +49 341 286529
Open: Tuesday and Thursday-Sunday 09.00-17.00  Wednesday 13.00-21.30
Closed: Monday

**COLLECTION**

The museum's total holdings number 2 700 paintings from the late Middle- Ages to the present, 750 sculptures and more than 55 000 drawings and prints.

The permanent display includes Old German and Early Dutch and Flemish masterpieces, such as the renowned 'Liebeszauber' (Love Spell) by a Lower Rhine master from the late 15th century, paintings by Rogier van der Weyden, Lucas Cranach the Elder and Hans Baldung Grien, and outstanding Dutch 17th-century paintings by Frans Hals, Jan van Goyen and many others.

The museum's representative collection of German painting from the 20th century includes works by Anton Graff, Caspar David Friedrich, Wilhelm Leibl, Arnold Böcklin, Max Liebermann, Lovis Corinth, Max Klinger, Oskar Kokoschka and Max Beckmann. The graphic collection bears witness to the development of the graphic arts in Europe from the early days to the present. Highlights of the collection include works by Martin Schongauer and Lucas Cranach the Elder, as well as Italian Baroque drawings by Gianlorenzo Bernini and Salvator Rosa. There is also an unusually wide representation of Dutch 19th-century drawings.

**EXHIBITIONS**

08·05·97-13·07·97
*Paul Klee  Southern Journeys: Paintings and Drawings*  The exhibition features some 90 works from international public and private collections and focuses on Klee's interest in the Mediterranean and the Orient, and in nature in general.

19·06·97-03·08·97
*Cranach Rediscovered  Paintings of the Late Medieval Periods*  An exhibition of some 40 paintings.

02·10·97-31·12·97
*Art and Artists in Leipzig 1945-1995*  An exhibition of some 250 paintings and drawings.

06·11·97-14·12·97
*Second Art Award of the Leipzig Daily*  One artist is featured.

# Leverkusen

## STÄDTISCHES MUSEUM LEVERKUSEN SCHLOß MORSBROICH
Gustav-Heinemann-Straße 80  51377 Leverkusen  Director: Rolf Wedewer
☎ +49 214 56007  ✸ +49 214 56000
Open: Tuesday 11.00-21.00  Wednesday-Sunday 11.00-17.00
Closed: Monday

**COLLECTION**

This Late Baroque castle has been home to a museum for contemporary art since 1951. The sculpture park with its old trees is an extra point of interest to visitors from home and abroad. The international collection of the museum consists of paintings, sculptures, objects and important works on paper. All main post-war styles are represented.
Besides regular display of all collections, between eight and twelve temporary exhibitions are held every year. These present interna-tionally renowned artists or illuminate cultural-historical connections on the basis of various themes.

© Städt. Museum
Schloss Morsbroich
Leverkusen

### EXHIBITIONS

until 29·06·97 — *Dieter Goltzsche* Works on Paper

10·05·97-06·07·97 — *Location Germany*

02·09·97-02·11·97 — *On the Path to Natural Perception*

14·10·97-Jan 98 — *Bernd Zimmer* Works on Paper 1977-1997

11·11·97-Jan 98 — *The Bauhaus in the East*

## Lübeck

**OVERBECK-GESELLSCHAFT (SOCIETY FOR CONTEMPORARY ART)**
Königstraße 11 23552 Lübeck Director: Roswitha Siewert
☎ +49 451 74760 📠 +49 451 74760
Open: Tuesday-Sunday Apr-Sep 10.00-16.30 Oct-Mar 10.00-16.00
Closed: Monday

**COLLECTION** | No permanent collection.

**EXHIBITIONS**

11·05·97-15·06·97 — *Aldo Rossi* Architecture

13·07·97-17·08·97 — *Young Art International '97*

07·09·97-19·10·97 — *Georg Baselitz*

09·11·97-07·12·97 — *Leni Hoffmann*

## Ludwigshafen

**WILHELM-HACK-MUSEUM**
Berliner Straße 23 67059 Ludwigshafen Director: Bernhard Holeczek
☎ +49 621 5043411 📠 +49 621 5043780
Open: Tuesday 10.00-20.00 Wednesday-Sunday 10.00-17.30
Closed: Monday

**COLLECTION** | The collection endowed by Wilhelm Hack forms the core of the museum collection. One of the museum frontages is covered by a large work of art by Jóan Miró.
The museum's collection consists of three sections. The first comprises Franconian-Roman crafts form the period of the great migrations (3rd-8th century A.D.), in particular burial objects found at a burial site near Gondorf on the Moselle.
The second division contains panels and sculptures as well as crafts

and illuminations from medieval times, in particular from the area around the Rhine. This part of the collection covers a period from about 1150 to 1600.

The exhibits in this section are grouped in three major catagories: 1. Works of metal and ivory from the 12th to the 14th century. 2. Sculptures from the late Romanesque period until the Renaissance. 3. Glass paintings and illuminations, including a rare book from the end of the 13th century and panels from Late Gothic times and the German and Dutch Renaissance.

A special place in the collection of sculptures, which is dominated by madonnas, is the Madonna of Cologne dating from 1290, the 'rue shrub Madonna'.

The largest and most significant portion of Hack's endowment contains works from the period between 1910 and 1930. The collection includes objects by Mondrian, Van Doesburg, Malevitch, El Lissitzky, Kandinsky, Picasso, Delaunay and Schwitters.

In the 50s and 60s Hacks started collecting works of Abstract Expressionism. These include works by Jackson Pollock, Sam Francis, Manolo Millares, the artists in the Cobra Group, Karel Appel, Asger Jorn and Jean Dubuffet.

This collection is supplemented by works from the municipal collection representing German Expressionism, with important works by Kirchner and Beckmann and art from the post-war era. Today the focus of the museum's new acquisitions is on contemperary art, especially Constructivism and Concrete art.

| **EXHIBITIONS** | |
|---|---|
| until 29·06·97 | **Auguste Herbin**   *Retrospective* |
| 15·05·97-20·07·97 | **Rolf Nolden**   *Sculpture Installations* |
| 12·07·97-17·08·97 | **'The Anchor' Artists Group**   *Theme: The Elements* |
| 31·07·97-28·09·97 | **Jean-Michel Frouin**   *L'Infini du Paysage: A Cycle of Landscape Paintings* |
| 30·08·97-26·10·97 | **Hans Arp** |
| 09·10·97-07·12·97 | **Günther Meck**   *Paintings* |
| 08·11·97-17·01·98 | **Victor Vasarely**   *Retrospective* |
| 18·12·97-20·02·98 | **Siegfried Assfalg**   *Wood Prints: Constructive Concrete* |

# Mainz

## GUTENBERG-MUSEUM MAINZ
Liebfrauenplatz 5  55116 Mainz  Director: Eva Hanebutt-Benz
☎ +49 6131 122640  📠 +49 6131 123488
Open: Tuesday-Saturday 10.00-18.00  Sunday 10.00-13.00
Closed: Monday

**COLLECTION**

The Gutenberg Museum was founded in 1900 in honour of the famous inhabitant of Mainz. A video about Gutenberg, in several languages, is shown every morning in the entrance hall.

Downstairs in the workshop area there is a replica of the original Gutenberg printing office, a printing workshop, typesetting machines and electronic printing presses. Demonstrations of typesetting and printing are given daily.

The first floor of the museum houses early prints from Mainz, 16th to 19th-century books, examples of 19th-century graphic techniques and printing presses.

The upper floor is occupied by early printed books and 16th, 17th and 18th-century books. The display also details the various illustration techniques such as woodcut, engraving, etching and mezzotint. A late 18th-century printing shop has been set up along with examples of 17th to 19th-century newspapers. The adjacent section dealing with the 19th century focuses on the progress that the industrial revolution brought about in the printing trade. Lithography, steel engraving and cross-grain wood engraving are explained with the help of tools and presses.

In the mezzanine, an exhibition explains how books were made before Gutenberg invented his printing process, what his process entails and what the impact of his invention was. The final exhibit in the mezzanine traces the development of bookbinding.

The second floor exhibition traces the history of writing and early alphabets. The East Asian collection of polychrome woodcuts and examples of printing reveals that printing with separate blocks for separate characters was used in Asia before Gutenberg. The works of William Morris displayed in the Art Nouveau section had an enormous influence on the development of book printing in the late 19th and early 20th century. The rest of this section is devoted to Art Nouveau book art from England and Germany, book plates (ex-libris) and early 20th-century posters.

The printer of the Gutenberg-Museum demonstrating printing in the 15th century
© Gutenberg-Museum, Mainz

The mezzanine above this section contains the book art of the 20th century, a history of paper, artist's books, children's books, paper theatres, and a selection of the most beautiful German books of the year.

## EXHIBITIONS

09·05·97-29·06·97    **Miniature Books**

21·05·97-03·08·97    **Bülent Erkmen - Around Art and Culture**    *Works 1980-1996*

28·08·97-31·12·97    **'Look, there he is...'**  *'Struwwelpeter' Books from the Heinz Maibach Collection, Limburg*

18·09·97-09·11·97    **Finnland - 500 Years on the Map of Europe**    *Reproductions*

20·11·97-30·12·97    **Orient and Occident - Linked Signs**  *Wolfgang Heuwinkel & Nja Mahdaoi*

## Mainz

**LANDESMUSEUM MAINZ**
**Große Bleiche 49-51 D-55116 Mainz Director: Gisela Fiedler-Bender**
☎ +49 6131 28570 📠 +49 6131 285757
**Open: Tuesday 10.00-20.00 Wednesday-Sunday 10.00-17.00**
**Closed: Monday**

**COLLECTION**

The diverse collection of the Landesmuseum Mainz ranges from objects showing the existence of human habitation in the Mainz area as far back as 300 000 B.C., to artworks from the 1990s. Objects demonstrating Roman influence along the Rhine are on display, as are objects in the Prince Johann Georg Collection from Rome, Greece and Egypt. There are works from the early Middle Ages (450-900 A.D.) and both religious and secular works from the 14th and 15th centuries. The museum possesses a variety of Renaissance and Baroque works by German, French and Italian painters and sculptors, and 17th-century Dutch masterpieces by P. Brueghel the Elder, J. Jordaens, J. van Goyen and S. van Ruysdael. Porcelain and pottery from factories in Mainz and elsewhere in Germany are also on display. The 19th and 20th-century collection includes significant Art Nouveau (Jugendstil) objects produced in France, Germany, Austria and Bohemia. There is also a vast collection of watercolours, drawings and prints, and a notable collection of Judaica. The history of the city of Mainz is chronicled in exhibits which include models, pictures, coins, medals, documents and tools, as well as photographs from both before and after the Second World War.

**EXHIBITIONS**

until 11·05·97    **Peter Vogel**   *Cybernetic Objects*

15·06·97-17·08·97    **Hans Arp (1886-1966)**   Purchased by the state of Rhineland-Palatinate

29·06·97-24·08·97    **Johann Peter Melchior (1747-1825)**   On the occasion of his 250th Birthday - Porcelain Figures

Jul-Aug 97    **Ludwig Wilding**   On the occasion of his 70th Birthday

16·11·97-feb 98    **Oskar Moll (1875-1947)**   *Paintings and Watercolours*

# Mannheim

**REIß-MUSEUM**
Zeughaus C5  68159 Mannheim  Director: Karin von Welck
☎ +49 621 2933150/51  📠 +49 621 2933099
Internet http://www.mannheim.de.reiss-museum/index.html
Open: Tuesday-Sunday 10.00-17.00  Thursday 12.00-17.00
Closed: Monday

**COLLECTION**

**Museum for Archaeology and Ethnology**   The archaeological collections comprise objects from the Stone Age up to modern times, the highlights being Roman tombstones and finds dating from the Ancient Greek and Roman epochs.
The ethnological collections are particularly known for their African and Asian exhibits. Among the most attractive sights are the reconstruction of a Tuareg tent, the famous Begin collection and a Japanese tea house, where tea ceremonies are performed occasionally.
**Museum for Art, City and Theatre History**   Well-known are the porcelain, faience and furniture collections. The local history section shows the development of the city of Mannheim through four centuries. Numerous exhibits like prints, maps, town models or early bicycles such as the Draisine give a good impression of how people lived in Mannheim. The permanent exhibition 'Religion, the Court and the Bourgeoisie - Mannheim in the 18th century' gives a good insight into life at the court of the Elector Palatine.
Based on the important archives of the Mannheim National Theatre, the theatre collection documents the history of the theatre in Mannheim. Among its greatest treasures are a set model dating from the time of the theatrical manager Dalberg and its library with

the promptbook for the original performance of Schiller's 'Robbers'.
**Museum for Natural History** The beginnings of the Natural History collections go back to the time of the Elector Palatine Karl Theodor and his famous 'Naturalienkabinett'.
The permanent exhibition 'Life in the Ice Age' gives a good idea of life in that important period of the history of life on our planet.

**EXHIBITIONS**

| | |
|---|---|
| until 08·06·97 | *The Hats of Adele List* |
| until 22·06·97 | *Noah's Ark*   *Animals in the Antiquity* |
| 15·06·97-14·09·97 | *Correspondences* |
| 28·06·97-14·09·97 | *Garden-Furniture from the Art Nouveau* |
| 26·07·97-19·10·97 | *Confidants of the Gods*   *Comments on the Cultural History of Horses* |
| Dec 97-Easter 98 | *The Big 'Winter-Exhibition' in the Reiss-Museums* |
| 27·02·98-May 98 | *With Fury and Eagerness*   *Caricatures of the Revolution 1848-1849* |

## Mönchengladbach

**SCHLOß RHEYDT**
Schloßstraße 508  41238 Mönchengladbach  Director: Carsten Sternberg
☎ +49 2166 928900  🖷 +49 2166 9289049
Open: Tuesday-Saturday 14.00-20.00  Sunday 11.00-20.00
Closed: Monday

**COLLECTION**

Schloss Rheydt is a castle originally dating back to the 12th century, which houses the municipal museum of the town of Mönchengladbach in North Rhine-Westphalia. Parts of the current structure date back to the 15th century. Extensive restorations have been undertaken in recent years and today the manor house, with some of the original furnishings, as well as the grounds, the gatehouse, the keep, the ramparts and bastions are integral parts of the museum. The museum has an extensive collection pertaining to local history, with some objects dating back to Roman and prehistoric times. It has also built a collection devoted to the arts and decorative crafts of the Renaissance and installed displays depicting the technological history of the area, which has been a major centre for the manufacture of textiles.
The municipal history department has organised the displays at the Schloss Rheydt according to several basic themes: history of settlement, tracing the history of the community; personalities, focusing on the men and women of the community who have distinguished themselves; visual artists of Mönchengladbach; and industrial and social development, focusing especially on 19th and 20th-century developments and including 5 looms in working order. In the cellar vaults of the manor house there is a display devoted to the architectural history of Schloss Rheydt. The bastion, which is currently being renovated, will house archaeological displays when the work is completed.

**EXHIBITIONS**

| | |
|---|---|
| until 15·06·97 | *Pomp and Splendour from China*   Silky Robes from the Court of the Last Emperor   Collection Timmermann, Cologne |
| until 29·06·97 | *Anatolian Kelims*   Famous and rare Türkish woven carpets |
| 06·07·97-26·10·97 | *Max Röder* |

| | |
|---|---|
| Oct 97-Dec 97 | *Giottos Message* |
| 06-12-97-Jan 98 | *Santa Claus likes Polished Shoes*   Exhibition of the history and the evolution of shoes |
| Mar 98-May 98 | *Collection Köster*   Most famous European ceramics private collection |

## Mönchengladbach

**STÄDTISCHES MUSEUM ABTEIBERG**
Abteistraße 27  41061 Mönchengladbach  Director: Veit Loers
☎ +49 2161 252631  🖷 +49 2161 252659
Open: Tuesday-Sunday 10.00-18.00
Closed: Monday

COLLECTION   The museum was founded in 1904; in 1922 a donation from Walter Kaesbach transformed it into a collection of contemporary art based on German Expressionism. In 1982 the new building by the architect Hans Hollein was opened. Nowadays it is chiefly a collection of international contemporary art from 1960 up to the present. The specialisations include Pop Art, Minimal Art, Concrete Art and Radical Painting. Works by Joseph Beuys, Marcel Broodthaers, Ulrich Rückriem, Richard Serra, Gerhard Richter, Sigmar Polke, Lawrence Weiner, Palermo, Dorothee von Windheim, Günter Umberg, Joseph Marioni, Roni Horn etc. are on display. The collection includes a large number of site-specific works and installations.
The museum also owns a 20th-century collection of prints and drawings.

EXHIBITIONS

| | |
|---|---|
| 04-05-97-27-07-97 | *Lucio Fontana   Il Disegno* - Drawings and Projects |
| 07-09-97-23-11-97 | *In the Realm of Phantoms*   Photographs and Apparations (1870-1990) |
| 07-12-97-01-02-98 | *Ars Viva*   Art and New Media |

## München - Munich

**ALTE PINAKOTHEK**
Barer Straße 27  80799 München  Director: J.G. Prinz Von Hohenzollern
☎ +49 89 23805215  🖷 +49 89 23805221
Closed for renovations until spring 1998

COLLECTION   **Old Masters**  The Alte Pinakothek is one of the largest and most beautiful painting galleries in the world. It was commissioned by King Ludwig I, designed by the architect Leo von Klenze and built between 1826 and 1836. The collection unites previous galleries of various branches of the Wittelsbach family. King Ludwig added a considerable collection of Old German, Old Dutch and Italian paintings, which form the most important sections of the gallery, together with the Flemish, Dutch and French Baroque paintings. The 'Four Evangelists' by Dürer, the Columba Altar by Rogier van der Weyden, Raphael's 'Holy Family Canigiani', 60 paintings by Rubens and numerous pictures by Rembrandt, as well as excellent work from Poussin and Lorrain are part of the 800 paintings on permanent display.
The Alte Pinakothek and Neue Pinakothek, the State Gallery of Modern Art, the Schack Gallery and its 15 branches throughout Bavaria are all part of the Bavarian National Painting Collection.

Dürer, Albrecht
*The four Apostles*
© Alte Pinakothek,
München

Between 1994 and spring 1998 the Alte Pinakothek will be closed due to renovations. During that period 300 of the masterpieces will be exhibited at the Neue Pinakothek.

## München - Munich

**STAATLICHE ANTIKENSAMMLUNGEN UND GLYPTOTHEK**
Königsplatz  München  Director: Raimund Wünsche
☎ +49 89 598359 (Antikensammlungen) +49 89 286100 (Glyptothek)
🖷 +49 89 5503851
**Open: Antikensammlungen: Tuesday-Sunday 10.00-16.30**
**Wednesday 12.00-20.30**
**Glyptothek: Tuesday-Sunday 10.00-16.30  Thursday 12.00-20.30**
**Closed: Monday**

**COLLECTION**

[ANTIKENSAMMLUNGEN]
In building the Antikensammlungen, the architect Georg Friedrich Ziebland was inspired by Roman podium temples. The museum's monumental façade forms the south front of the classical Königsplatz. The museum posses a collection of antiquities ranging from the 14th century B.C. to the 4th century A.D.
In the collection are painted Attic black and red-figured vases by some of the best practioners of this art, including Exekias, Andokides and Euphronios. Among these works is the famous cup depicting Dionysos, the god of wine and ecstasy, making a voyage across the sea. Another vase depicts the poetess Sappho, celebrated for her love poems.
There is also an outstanding collection of terracotta statuettes from Tanagra and Myrina. The colourfully painted figurines, showing the beauty and elegance of Greek women, offer a glimpse of everyday life in ancient times.
The basement houses the collection of goldsmiths' work, including a Hellenistic burial wreath from Armento and a superb diadem of a Greek lady from the Black Sea. These pieces and others reveal another aspect of the artistry of ancient times. The collection of Roman silverware provides evidence of the high standard of metalworking as well as the luxurious lifestyle of the time.
On the upper floor of the museum, the world of the Etruscans, known best through their graves, is presented. A carriage found at Castel San Mariano, used by an Etruscan lady for her wedding and then for her last journey, is on display in the staircase. The function of many other object remains a mystery, however.

**EXHIBITIONS**

No details available.

COLLECTION

[GLYPTOTHEK]
The Glyptothek was built as a museum between 1816 and 1830 by the renowned architect Leo von Klenze. The museum houses a collection of antique sculpture, covering all periods of ancient Greece and Rome.
The 'Munich Kouros' and the 'Apollo of Tenea' are fine examples of the Archaic period. Other highlights of the collection are the two groups of figures originating from the pediments of the Temple of Aphaia on the Greek island of Aegina. They were discovered by British and German scholars in 1811. The sculptures date from around 500 B.C. and were made of marble from the island of Paros. Each group represents a battle between Greek and Trojan heroes. Also on display are works by Classical Greek artists such as Polycletes' 'Diadumenos' and the 'Eirene' of Kephisodot. There are busts of Plato, Euripides and Homer, and a collection of portraits representing famous Roman emperors and citizens.

EXHIBITIONS

No details available.

## München - Munich

**HAUS DER KUNST**
Prinzregentenstraße 1  80538 München  Director: Christoph Vitali
☎ +49 89 211270  🖷 +49 89 21127157
Open: Tuesday-Friday 10.00-22.00  Saturday-Monday 10.00-18.00

COLLECTION

No permanent collection.

EXHIBITIONS

until 20·07·97

*Carl Philipp Fohr*    *Drawings of the Romantism*

08·05·97-20·07·97

*Michail Wrubel*    *The Russian Symbolist*

08·05·97-20·07·97

*Frantisek Kupka & Otto Gutfreund*

End Jul 97-Oct 97

*München 1997*

01·08·97-12·10·97

*Deep Storage*

08·09·97-09·11·97

*From Füsli to Menzel*    *Drawings and Watercolours of the Winterstein Collection*

17·10·97-20·01·98

*Ellsworth Kelly*

24·10·97-20·01·98

*Jullao Sarmento - Joel Shapiro*

## München - Munich

**KUNSTHALLE DER HYPO-KULTURSTIFTUNG**
Theatinerstraße 15  80333 München  Director: Peter A. Ade
☎ +49 89 224412  🖷 +49 89 29160981
Open: Daily 10.00-18.00  Thursday 10.00-21.00

COLLECTION

No permanent collection.

EXHIBITIONS

until 29·06·97

*Alberto Giacometti (1901-1966)*    Alberto Giacometti was one of the major figures of Surrealist sculpture. This show presents 60 sculptures from the Fondation Maeght in St. Paul-de-Vence and other important objects from European museums and collections.

11·07·97-14·09·97    **Markus Lüpertz**    Markus Lüpertz was born in 1941 and now serves as director of the Academy of Fine Arts in Düsseldorf. He is one of the most prominent painters in Germany.

26·09·97-11·01·98    **Cobra**    The 'Cobra' group was founded in Paris in 1948, and consisted of Asger Jorn from Copenhagen, Corneille and Alechnisky from Brussels and Karel Appel and Constant from Amsterdam. The exhibition includes 130 works from museums in Belgium, the Netherlands and Denmark.

29·01·98-12·04·98    **Carl Rottmann (1797-1850)**    **Romantic Paintings**

## München - Munich

**STÄDTISCHE GALERIE IM LENBACHHAUS -
KUNSTBAU LENBACHHAUS**
Luisenstraße 33  80333 München  Director: Helmut Friedel
☎ +49 89 23332000  🖷 +49 89 23332003
Internet http://www.muenchen.de/lenbachhaus
Open: Tuesday-Sunday 10.00-18.00
Closed: Monday

COLLECTION

At the peak of his career, the highly successful portrait painter Franz von Lenbach (1836-1904) commissioned the architect Gabriel von Seidl to construct his residence in Munich. This architectural 'Gesamtkunstwerk' was later purchased by the City of Munich, which opened the Städtische Galerie im Lenbachhaus to the public in 1929. The original collection featured works by artists of the 19th and early 20th-century Munich school.
This collection has since been expanded and presently includes works by Jawlensky, Kandinsky, Klee, Macke, Marc, Münter and others who worked in Munich before the First World War. The Alfred Kubin archive was purchased from the Hamburg collector Kurt Otte.
In recent years the museum has acquired contemporary works of art, including works by Arakawa, Joseph Beuys, Oyvind Fahlström, Michael Heizer, Asger Jorn, Anselm Kiefer, Hermann Nitsch, A.R. Penck, Sigmar Polke, Arnulf Rainer, Sean Scully and the artists' group Spur.

© Lenbachhaus,
München

EXHIBITIONS

[LENBACHHAUS]

until 29·06·97    **Albert Bloch (1882-1961)**    *Retrospective*    This exhibition presents approximately 50 paintings and 30 watercolours of Albert Bloch, the only American artist associated with the Blue Rider school. His early Expressionist works show the influences of Kandinsky, Marc, Klee and Chagall.

16·07·97-26·10·97    **Paula Modersohn-Becker (1876-1907)**    Paula Modersohn-Becker was the most important member of the Worpswede circle of painters. This exhibition traces the path from early realism to monumental paintings based on stylised, geometric forms.

26·11·97-01·02·98　　***Christian Schad (1894-1982)***　This exhibition focuses on Schad's figurative works of the 1920s in a style known as 'Neue Sachlichkeit' (New Objectivity). Earlier Dadaist 'Schadographs' are also included.

[KUNSTBAU]

until 29·06·97　　***Hans Hofmann (1880-1966)***　*Magnum Opus*　The late work of Hans Hofmann presented in this exhibition is especially characterised by bold bands of colour and formal calligraphic structures. Hofmann's work had a major impact on Pollock, Still, Warhol and Stella.

23·07·97-05·10·97　　***Harald Klingelhöller (born 1954)***　Harald Klingelhöller's sculptures are concerned with language. He explores relationships between plastic and linguistic forms. This exhibition comprises the works from the last ten years.

29·10·97-11·01·98　　***Gerhard Richter (born 1932)***　*The 'Atlas' and Its Pictures*　This exhibition is devoted to Gerhard Richter's 'Atlas' complex. It features about 40 to 50 paintings, and traces the main lines of development in the artist's thinking.

## München - Munich

**NEUE PINAKOTHEK**
Barer Straße 29　80799 München　Director: J.G. Prinz Von Hohenzollern
☎ +49 89 23805195　📠 +49 89 23805221
Open: Wednesday-Sunday 10.00-17.00　Tuesday and Thursday 10.00-20.00
Closed: Monday

COLLECTION

Manet, Edouard
*The rowing boat*
© Neue Pinakothek,
München

**19th Century Paintings**　The Neue Pinakothek, a gallery for contemporary art, was commissioned by King Ludwig I and built between 1846 and 1853 opposite the Alte Pinakothek.

The museum was destroyed during the Second World War; since its renovation in 1981 is has featured German painting of the 19th century, as well as internationally important works of art from between 1800 and 1900, from Classicism up to Jugendstil. It includes major works by David, Goya, Turner, Courbet, Manet, Monet and Van Gogh. Paintings by the Nazarenes, C.D. Friedrich, Menzel, Spitzweg, Waldmüller, Marées, Feuerbach and Leibl are also on display.
During the renovation of the Alte Pinakothek, 300 paintings of the Old Masters are on display in the Neue Pinakothek.

EXHIBITION
until 06·07·97　　***Claude-Joseph Vernet (1714-1789)***

## München - Munich

### PRÄHISTORISCHE STAATSSAMMLUNG
Lerchenfeldstraße 2  80538 München  Director: Ludwig Wamser
☎ +49 89 293911  ⊟ +49 89 225238
Internet http://www.stmukwk.bayern.de/kunst/museen/praehist.html
Open: Tuesday-Sunday 09.00-16.00  Thursday 09.00-20.00
Closed: Monday

COLLECTION

The Prehistoric collection of the Bavarian State dates back to 1885, but it first received its own modern museum premises in 1977. The contents of the collection tell the story of Bavarian settlement, from the earliest finds of the Palaeolithic era (120 000 B.C.) on through prehistory into the Middle Ages (16th century). The main topics of the museum are the Stone Age and the Bronze Age, the Urnfield culture and the Iron Age with the Hallstatt era, the La Tène era and the Oppidum Manching. The Roman era and the Middle Ages are also represented with many objects. Opposite the entrance, the museum has a hall devoted to special exhibitions for which a separate admission is charged. The permanent exhibition is arranged in chronological order; the large historical timescale in each of the rooms lists the particular era shown in the room and links it with contemporary events in other parts of the world.

EXHIBITIONS

15·05·97-21·09·97     ***Mappot***   *Jewish Traditions from Alsace to Bohemia*

Oct 97-Jan 98     ***Culinaria Romana***

## München - Munich

### DIE NEUE SAMMLUNG
### STAATLICHES MUSEUM FÜR ANGEWANDTE KUNST
Prinzregentenstraße 3  80538 München  Director: Florian Hufnagl
☎ +49 89 227844  ⊟ +49 89 220282
Open: (only during special exhibitions) Tuesday-Sunday 10.00-17.00
Closed: Monday

COLLECTION

With a unique collection of almost 40 000 products and artefacts documenting the history of industrial design, graphic design and crafts, 'Die Neue Sammlung' is one of the leading international museums of 20th-century applied art - and the largest museum of industrial design in the world. The inspiration for the establishment of this institution came from the German 'Werkbund' movement in Munich in 1907. From 1912 onwards a collection of 'modern-day model artefacts' was gradually built up.
The traditional areas of the arts and crafts are represented by a comprehensive collection of everyday objects. In addition, the museum devotes much of the available space to mass produced products of modern industrial design. The graphic design section covers the range from posters, packaging and book design to photography. Over the last decade the museum has also built up a number of specialised collections. These cover areas such as the automobile, sports equipment, secondary architecture and the field of system development.

EXHIBITIONS

until 01·06·97     ***Jan Eisenloeffel***   *At the Beginning of Modern Design*
Known all over Europe for his utensils in silver, copper and brass, this Dutch artist (1876-1957) was an important Dutch designer as well as a pioneer of modern design.

| | |
|---|---|
| 27·06·97-07·09·97 | ***Photographing Architecture***  *Horst Schäfer*   Unusual visual angles, powerful graphic effects, alienating black-and-white contrasts, and intensive play of light and shadow characterise the work of this photographer. |
| Oct 97-Jan 98 | ***Plastics & Design***   This exhibition gives a comprehensive survey of the history of design in plastics, the 'magic material' of the 20th century, from the earliest plastic objects to the latest recycling designs. |

## München · Munich

### SCHACK-GALERIE
Prinzregentenstraße 9  80538 München  Director: J.G. Prinz Von Hohenzollern
☎ +49 89 23805224  ⌷ +49 89 23805221
Open: Wednesday-Monday 10.00-17.00
Closed: Tuesday

COLLECTION — **19th Century Paintings**   This is the former private collection of Count Adolf Friedrich von Schack. The collection consists of 274 paintings, 181 of which are constantly on display in a wing of the former Prussian Consulate on the Prinsregentenstraße.
Several paintings by Anselm von Feuerbach, Arnold Böcklin and Moritz von Schwind are the main features of the collection.

EXHIBITIONS — No exhibitions planned.

## München · Munich

### STAATSGALERIE MODERNER KUNST
Prinzregentenstraße 1  80538 München  Director: J.G. Prinz Von Hohenzollern
☎ +49 89 21127137  ⌷ +49 89 23805227
Open: Tuesday-Sunday 10.00-17.00  Thursday 10.00-20.00
Closed: Monday

COLLECTION — **Classical Modern Contemporary Art**   The Staatsgalerie Moderner Kunst has been built up since the Second World War. Its collection consists of works from the Classical Modern period ranging up to contemporary art. Thanks to gifts and works given in loan it became possible to focus on new trends, such as Surrealism. The best-known works include 'Struggling Forms' by Franz Marc, 'Dreamlike Improvisation' by Kandinsky, 'Full Moon' by Paul Klee, the paintings by Kirchner, a large collection of paintings by Max Beckmann, works of American Abstract Expressionism and Joseph Beuys' monumental work 'The End of the 20th Century'.

EXHIBITIONS — No exhibitions planned.

## München · Munich

### VILLA STUCK
Prinzregentenstraße 60  81675 München  Director: Jo-Anne Birnie Danzker
☎ +49 89 4555510  ⌷ +49 89 4555124  Internet http://www.muenchen.de
Open: Tuesday-Sunday 10.00-17.00  Thursday 10.00-21.00
Closed: Monday

COLLECTION — Not only is the Villa Stuck an important historical monument and a work of art itself, but its dramatic history reflects that of the city of Munich: the heady days of turn-of-the-century Munich as the City of Art, the dark days of the Second World War, the first post-war exhibitions of formerly banned artists such as Max Beckmann in the

Villa Stuck, the gallery's emergence as a centre for major private galleries, and the gallery's conversion to a private and then to a public museum. Eyewitness accounts of these events have been recorded by a television team in an oral history project entitled 'Memory Bank - Villa Stuck'. Excerpts from these interviews will be on view daily.

**EXHIBITIONS**

until 29·06·97 | **Pippilotti Rist & Samir**   *The Social Life of Roses or Why I'm Never Sad*   Video installations

17·07·97-19·10·97 | **Villa Stuck**   Anniversary exhibition

31·07·97-26·10·97 | **Grete Stern**   *Photographs*

20·11·97-Jan 98 | **Robert Wilson**   *Installations*

# Münster

**WESTFÄLISCHES LANDESMUSEUM FÜR KUNST UND KULTURGESCHICHTE**
Domplatz 10  48143 Münster  Director: Klaus Bußmann
☎ +49 251 590701  🖷 +49 251 5907210
Open: Tuesday-Sunday 10.00-18.00
Closed: Monday and 1 May, 24, 31 Dec, 1 Jan

**COLLECTION**

The collection of the Westphalian State Museum of Art and Cultural History consists of artworks and objects ranging from the Middle Ages up to the contemporary era.

August Macke
(1887-1914)
*Terrace of the country house in St.Germain, 1914*
Watercolour
© Westfälisches Landesmuseum für Kunst und Kulturgeschichte, Münster

**Old Masters**   In this section the focus is on sacred Westphalian art from the Romanic up to the Late Gothic period. Highlights are the 'Soester Antependium' (c. 1170), the 'Unnaer Marienklage' (c. 1380) and the 'Halderner Altar' by the Master of Schöppingen (c. 1440). The main pieces from the Renaissance period are the works by the Brabender family of artists (sculptures), by Tom Ring (paintings) and by Dutch paintings from the 17th century.
**Modern Art**   The Modern Art department, mainly consisting of paintings and sculptures, shows highlights of New Objectivity, Art Informel and Constructivism (Albers, Schumacher, Serra) In this field the museum is internationally oriented.
**Special Collections**   These include a large graphic collection: graphic art from the 16th to the 20th century, documentary graphics as part of the history of Germany and Westphalia in particular and portraits. In addition, the museum has a coin cabinet and a section with architectural designs focusing on the Baroque period in Westphalia (J.C. Schlaun).

[BRANCH OFFICES OF THE LANDESMUSEUM]

**Schloß Cappenberg:** Art and Culture from Baroque to the Jugenstil
Paintings and decorative art from the 18th century (silver, porcelain,
furniture) to the Jugenstil, including works from Rincklake, Carus,
Blechen and Pankok.
**Die Westfälische Galerie im Kloster Bentlage** the Westfalian
Gallery in Kloster Bentlage near Rheine documents the
development of Modern Art in Westfalia from 1900 on till the 50s,
including works from the Westfalian expressionists as Morgner,
Böckstiegel, Viegener, Rohlfs, Mense und Macke.

**EXHIBITIONS**
until 26·05·97

*The Unconditional Look/View* Paintings, photography and
drawings of a private collection. An exhibition of the Westphalian
Kunstverein Münster.

08·-6·97-17·08·97

*Artists in the Mirror of a Collection* Graphic arts by painters,
sculptors and copper engravers from the Porträtarchiv
Diepenbroick.

22·06·97-28·09·97

*Sculpture Projects in Münster 1997* In summer 1997 the 'Sculpture
Projects' will again take place in Münster. Münster has twice before
hosted this international exhibition, in 1997 and 1987.

26·10·97-04·01·98

*August Macke* *Watercolours* This extensive exhibition of the
famous German expressionist shows a representative overall view of
August Macke's watercolour paintings, also including some still
unknown works.

## Nürnberg - Nuremberg

**GERMANISCHES NATIONALMUSEUM**
Kartäusergasse 1  90402 Nürnberg  Director: Ulrich Großmann
☎ +49 911 13310  📠 +49 911 1331200
Open: Tuesday-Sunday 10.00-17.00  Wednesday 10.00-21.00  6 Jan, Easter
Monday, Whit Monday 10.00-17.00
Closed: Monday and 1 Jan, Shrove Tuesday, Good Friday, 1 May, 24, 25
and 31 Dec

**COLLECTION**

Founded in 1852, the Germanisches Nationalmuseum today houses
about 1.2 million objects relating to the artistic and cultural history
of German-speaking Central Europe between prehistoric times and
the present day. The permanent exhibitions display some 20 000
objects including prehistoric and early historic artefacts, paintings
and stained glass, sculpture, decorative arts and design, toys and
doll houses, historical musical and scientific instruments, historical
weapons and hunting gear, collections devoted to the healing arts,
the crafts and guilds, and folk arts.

View of the new
main entrance with
pillars of the Street
of Human Rights
© *Germanisches*
*Nationalmuseum,*
*Nürnberg*

The museum's study collections and research facilities include a department of prints and drawings and a cabinet of coins and medals, historical archives, and a fine art archive of papers left by artists and art historians. There is also a vast research library.

The core of the museum complex is a 14th-century Carthusian monastery with its church, cloisters, monks' houses and refectory. A recently opened wing provides modern facilities for special exhibitions, conferences, concerts and conservation workshops. Of particular note is the environmental installation, 'Way of Human Rights', by Israeli artist Dani Karavan, displayed in front of the new entrance.

**EXHIBITIONS**

until 08·06·97

**800 Years of European Cutlery** *Of Rustic Boards and Royal Banquets* An exhibition of cutlery from the Middle Ages to the 20th century, with more than 700 examples. Diverse forms and materials are included in this show: wood and iron alongside silver, amber, and mother-of-pearl.

15·05·97-07·09·97

**Art in Leipzig since 1945** 250 significant works of painting and drawing from Leipzig since 1945 permit a reassessment of the city's internationally renowned school of painting. Attention is drawn to the relationship between visual artists and others in the intellectual community.

29·05·97-01·06·97

**Blackwhiteblack** *22nd Leipzig Graphic Exchange* This annual event presents the current work of Saxon artists and invited international guests in order to promote interest in original printed graphics. This year, approximately 50 artists are participating.

26·06·97-24·08·97

**Valuables** An exhibition of the goldsmiths and silversmiths of the Akademie der Bildenden Künste (academy of fine arts) in Nuremberg.

Jul 97 onwards

**Art and Culture in the 2nd Half of the 20th Century** *A New Section of the Permanent Collection* The steadily expanding collection of post-1945 works will be installed in recently renovated gallery space. Works range from abstraction and the actionistic tendencies of the 60s and 70s to object-art and installation-art.

09·10·97-01·03·98

**The Best Awaits in Heaven** *German Painting from the Age of Dürer and the Renaissance* For the first time, the museum displays its entire collection of 16th-century paintings and carved altars with painted wings. Artists represented include Hans Holbein the Elder, Dürer, Grien, Altdorfer and Cranach.

06·11·97-01·02·98

**Horst Janssen** *The Portrait* This exhibition, arranged with the artist before his death, presents around 400 portraits, including many self-portraits. Woodcuts, monotypes, etchings, drawings, watercolours, collages and lithographs are all included.

# Nürnberg · Nuremberg

**KUNSTHALLE NÜRNBERG**
Lorenzer Straße 32  90402 Nürnberg  Director: Lucius Grisebach
☎ +49 911 2312853  🖷 +49 911 2313721
Open: Tuesday-Sunday 10.00-17.00 Wednesday 10.00-20.00
Closed: Monday and 1 May, 24, 25 and 31 Dec

**COLLECTION**

The collection is comprised of c. 1500 works of international art dating from the late 50s up to the present and including works by Richard Lindner, Jiri Kolar, Richard Long and Ulrich Rückriem, as well as by younger artists such as Stephan Balkenhol, Guillaume Bijl, Ange Leccia and Thomas Ruff.

**EXHIBITIONS**

08·05·97-22·06·97  **Rémy Zaugg**   In Swiss painter Rémy Zaugg's career, he has emphasised a systematic and logically consistent analysis of tableau painting. The Nuremberg exhibition shows early works addressing these issues, as well as very recent works.

10·07·97-24·08·97  **Unlimited**   *RENTA Gruppe Nürnberg's Art Project 1997*  'Unlimited' documents new initiatives by young artists working on the borderline dividing architecture/design, music, fashion and film.

02·10·97-07·12·97  **Arte Povera**   *Works and Documents from the Goetz Collection* This exhibition focuses on the Arte Povera movement, a movement which developed in the late 1960s, characterised by the use of such elements as soil, twigs, wax, lead, fire, smoke and electricity.

18·12·97-25·01·98  **Der Kreis**   *A Nuremberg Artists' Group, 1947-1997*   Established in 1947, 'Der Kreis' has, since its founding, been the most important association of artists on the Nuremberg art scene. Kunsthalle Nürnberg has organised this exhibition to celebrate the group's 50th anniversary.

## Paderborn

**WESTFÄLISCHES MUSEUM FÜR ARCHÄOLOGIE - MUSEUM IN DER KAISERPFALZ**
Am Ikenberg  33098 Paderborn  Director: Matthias Wemhoff
☎ +49 5251 10510  ⅎ +49 5251 281892
Open: Tuesday-Sunday 10.00-18.00
Closed: Monday

**COLLECTION**   The Archaeological Museum is housed in the rooms of the rebuilt Ottonian Palace which was discovered during excavation in the years 1964-1970. Since parts of the excavated foundations and remaining walls stood several metres high, it was decided to reconstruct the dimensions and character of the 11th-century edifice.

St. Bartholomee
Chapel
*Chapel of the
Ottonian Palace,
consecrated in 1017*
© *Museum in der
Kaiserpfalz,
Paderborn*

In front of the rebuilt palace are the walls of Charlemagne's first palace in Saxony, 'Karlsburg', built in 776. In 799 Charlemagne received Pope Leo III in Paderborn; in the course of these talks the emperor's coronation in Rome was planned. The exhibition gives a full inventory of what the palace contained: coins, ornaments, fragments of precious glassware, remains of Carolingian murals, roof and ornamental tiles, floor materials, fragments of pillars, metal objects and especially pottery.

**EXHIBITIONS**   No exhibitions planned.

## Regensburg

**MUSEUM OSTDEUTSCHE GALERIE**
Dr.-Johann-Maier-Straße 5  93049 Regensburg  Director: Lutz Tittel
☎ +49 941 2971418  📠 +49 941 2971433
Open: Tuesday-Sunday 10.00-16.00
Closed: Monday

**COLLECTION**

The museum is dedicated to the collection and exhibition of paintings, graphics and sculptures by 19th and 20th-century artists from the former East German provinces, as well artists from Eastern and Southeastern Europe. But the museum also presents a representative sample of other German art. Work of artists from East Prussia, Pomerania, Silesia, Bohemia, Moravia, the Baltic Provinces and Transylvania, rooted in the development of European art, are featured.

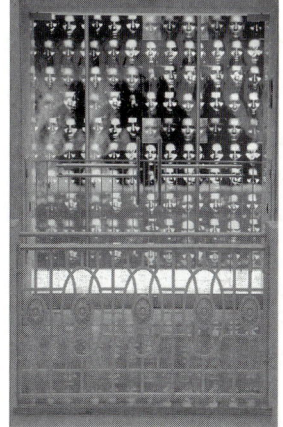

Katharina Sieverding
*Continental Nucleus,*
*XXXV, 1993*
© Museum
Ostdeutsche Galerie,
Regensburg

19th-century art is represented by Menzel, Gaertner, Von Max, Grützner, Von Werner, members of the Düsseldorf School, the Berlin Secessionism, Impressionism and Expressionism. The 20th century is represented by works of the Abstract and Constructive art movements, Realist tendencies appearing after the First World War, and art of the 30s, including works by Kokoschka, Feininger, Schlemmer, Molzahn, Sintenis, and sculptures by Käthe Kollwitz. There are also important contemporary works, and a sizeable collection of prints, drawings, portfolios and illustrated books.

**EXHIBITIONS**

01·06·97-13·07·97

*Lotte Jacobi (1896-1990)*  *Berlin-New York*  One of the most famous photographers of her time, Jacobi lived in Berlin, travelled to Russia, and later worked in London and New York. The exhibition includes more than 70 photographs.

20·07·97-07·09·97

*Gudrun Wassermann*  A follow-up to a 1995 exhibition entitled 'Not Light, Nor Yet Dark', this exhibition shows subsequent works characterised by the use of natural light supplemented by a variety of special techniques.

16·11·97-04·01·98

*Ulrich Behl*  Behl works with the effects of light on paper-covered objects and geometric structures. Problems of light, reflection and the visual angle are also central in his graphic works.

Jan 98-Feb 98

*Janosch*  One of the most famous German illustrators, Janosch has published more than 200 children's books since 1960. This exhibition presents original sketches as well as oil paintings and graphic art for adults.

| | |
|---|---|
| Mar 98-Apr 98 | **Rolf Cavael**  *Retrospective*   Cavael was one of the most outstanding Informal painters in Germany in the 1950s. He founded the 'Zen' group in Munich, based on concepts of Zen Buddhism. |

# Saarbrücken

## SAARLAND MUSEUM
**Bismarckstraße 11-19  66111 Saarbrücken  Curator: Ernst-Gerhard Güse**
☎ +49 681 99640  ⌕ +49 681 66393
**Open: Tuesday-Sunday 10.00-18.00  Wednesday 12.00-20.00**
**Closed: Monday**

COLLECTION

**Modern Collection**  The Saarland Museum, in its present-day conception, was established in 1950 by Rudolf Bornschein. The museum is known for a collection of 19th and especially 20th-century paintings and sculptures, as well as a sculpture park. The styles represented range from Impressionism to Contemporary art, including works by Max Beckmann and Alexander Archipenko. Focal points of the collection are its examples of Expressionism and Art Informel.

Franz Marc
*The little blue horse,*
*1912*
Saarland Museum,
Saarbrücken
© Stiftung Saarland
Kulturbesitz

**Graphic Collection**  The 'Graphisches Kabinett' includes drawings and prints by Manet, Ensor, Kubin, and Beuys, among others, and forms a complement to the collection of paintings.
**Antique Collection**  The 'Alte Sammlung' presents fine art from Saarland, Lorraine and Luxembourg dating from the 12th to the 19th century. Included are a large number of paintings, sculptures, china, silversmith and goldsmith works, coins and furniture. The High Medieval sculptures from Lorraine are especially noteworthy, as are the 17th and 18th-century landscape paintings which include representative works of the Frankenthal School by Huysmans, Savery and Lorrain.
**State Gallery**  The 'Landesgalerie' presents works by 20th-century artists from the region.

EXHIBITIONS
until 01·06·97

**Oskar Holweck**  *Day After Day*   Oskar Holweck is one of the best-known artists of Saarland; his work carries on the traditions of Bauhaus. The exhibition comprises some 60 drawings from the 1950s which together resemble a diary.

22·06·97-31·08·97

**Monika von Boch**  *The Nature of the Abstract*   The exhibition includes not only the photographer's major works but also a number of unknown ones.

15·09·97-14·11·97

**Till Neu**  *The St. Donat Project*   Till Neu's new paintings have been inspired by the deserted church of St. Donat in Haute Provence and remind the spectator of icons.

| | |
|---|---|
| 28·09·97-23·11·97 | **Drawings from Tuscany** *The Age of Michelangelo* This unique exhibition is the second part of a project that started in 1966 with 'The Early Renaissance in Italy'. It comprises some 100 drawings by great masters, among which works by Leonardo, Michelangelo and Vasari. Many of the most famous collections from all over the world have agreed to lend some of their beautiful drawings to this exhibition. |
| 07·12·97-Feb 98 | **Thomas Wojciechowicz** *Works on Paper* An exhibition in co-operation with Museum St. Wendel which includes drawings and other works on paper by the sculptor and wooden sculptures. |
| 15·12·97-13·02·98 | **Heinrich Zille** *Berlin Milieu* On the occasion of Zille's 140th anniversary, the Saarland Museum will show drawings by this 'master of the Berlin backyards' from its own graphic collection. |
| 01·03·98-19·04·98 | **Young Art** |

## Schwerin

**STAATLICHES MUSEUM SCHWERIN-KUNSTSAMMLUNGEN, SCHLÖSSER UND GÄRTEN**
Alter Garten 3  19055 Schwerin  Director: Kornelia von Berswordt-Wallrabe
☎ +49 385 5924027  🖷 +49 385 563090
Internet  http://www.museum-schwerin.de/
Open: Art Collection: Tuesday 10.00-20.00  Wednesday-Sunday 10.00-17.00
Castles (Schwerin, Ludwigslust, Güstrow) 15 Apr-14 Oct Tuesday-Sunday and
Easter 10.00-18.00 15 Oct-14 Apr Tuesday-Sunday 10.00-17.00
Closed: Monday

COLLECTION

The State Museum Schwerin, the national art museum of Mecklenburg-Vorpommern, exhibits extensive collections from the Middle Ages to contemporary art in the Gallery in Schwerin and in three former residences of the Mecklenburg dynasty, the castles Schwerin, Ludwigslust and Güstrow. The collection, started in the 18th century, contains 550 paintings and 4 000 graphics from the 'Golden Age' of Dutch and Flemish painting. Nearly all the painters, including Brueghel, Rubens, Rembrandt, Hals and Mieris, are represented by more than one work. There are 34 paintings and 56 sketches by the 18th-century French Court artist Jean Baptiste Oudry.

Schwerin has a large collection of porcelain by Meissen and other European manufacturers. The residence-castles are highlights of historic North German architecture.

Wilhelm Lehmbruck
(1881-1919)
*Head of pensive
man, 1913-1914*
© Staatliches
Museum Schwerin,
Schwerin

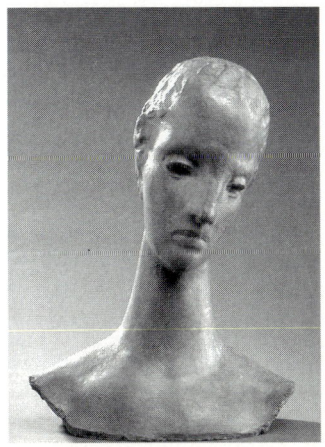

until 19·05·97　　　*Sonja Rolfs*　*Caspar-David-Friedrich-Prizewinner*

01·06·97-13·07·97　　*Georges Vantongerloo*

20·07·97-31·08·97　　*Positions of Contemporary Photography*

07·09·97-23·11·97　　*Paul Holz (1883-1938)*　One of the most important German drawers of the 20th century. Schwerin has the biggest public collection of Holz's works, first presentation of the whole collection (70 drawings, 12 graphics)

07·12·97-15·01·98　　*Georg Friedrich Kersting*　Kersting (1785-1847) is an important artist of the German Romantism. On the occasion of the 150th anniversary of Kersting's death, an exhibition of more than 100 works, among them less known works from the 30s and 40s.

01·02·98-13·04·98　　*Dutch Graphic Art of the 16th and 17th Century*

[NEUE GALLERY]

until 01·06·97　　　*Rainer Splitt*　Shows color in its material aspects, realises pouring and dipping colors.

[SCHLOß GÜSTROW]

10·08·97-12·10·97　　*Triennale of Arts and Crafts from North Germany*　Artists from North Germany and guests from Hamburg, Niedersachsen, Bremen and Poland show their latest works in glass, ceramics, textile and jewellery.


# Stuttgart

**GALERIE DER STADT STUTTGART**
Schloßplatz 2  70173 Stuttgart  Director: Johann-Karl Schmidt
☎ +49 711 2162188  ▤ +49 711 2167820
Open: Tuesday-Sunday 11.00-18.00  Wednesday 11.00-20.00
Closed: Monday

COLLECTION

**19th Century**　The collection of 19th-century paintings was founded in 1924 and now includes works by Philipp Friedrich Hetsch, Johan Baptist, Seele and other artists of Swabian Classicism. Together with the works of the School of Open-Air Painting from the turn of the century by Hermann Pleuer, Otto Reiniger and Christian Landenberger, they form the historical section of the museum's collection.

**Modern Art**　The Galerie der Stadt Stuttgart houses the largest and most famous public collection of works by the Realist, Expressionist and Dadaist Otto Dix. His work paralleled the German Old Masters in holding up a mirror to the troubled times of Germany and the German people during the First and Second World Wars and the intervening period. One of his major works, the 'Großstadt', is central to the Stuttgart collection.

**Abstract art**　is represented by works from Adolf Hoelzel and his students Oskar Schlemmer and Willi Baumeister. Hoelzel was the first to step beyond representational images at the beginning of the century. A collection of more than 300 paintings and drawings from Fritz Winter, a protagonist of non-figurative art after 1945, was given to the museum and is now on display.

**Contemporary Art**　The permanently displayed collection of paintings, sculptures and installations from the 60s up to the present day includes work by Diter Roth, Walter Stöhrer, Horst Antes, Dieter Krieg, Joseph Kosuth, Markus Lüpertz, Michael Buthe and Felix Droese.

**EXHIBITIONS**

05·06·97-24·08·97 | *Peter Chevalier*

17·06·97-24·08·97 | *Les Levine*

04·09·97-30·12·97 | *Man Ray*

Jan 98-mid Apr 98 | *Alessandro Mendini*

## Stuttgart

**STAATSGALERIE STUTTGART**
Konrad-Adenauer-Straße 30-32  70173 Stuttgart  Director: Christian von Holst
☎ +49 711 2124050  ℻ +49 711 2124068
Open: Tuesday-Sunday 10.00-17.00  Tuesday and Thursday 10.00-20.00
Closed: Monday

**COLLECTION**

Built in the neoclassical style of the early 19th century, the original building, the 'Alte Staatsgalerie', accommodates works from the 14th to the 19th century, as well as the museum's Graphics Collection, with its copious stock of drawings, watercolours, collages, original prints, illustrated books, posters and photographs.

*© Staatsgalerie Stuttgart Architects: James Stirling, Michael Wilford and Associates, Stuttgart*

Originating from the collection of the Duchy of Württemberg, the museum's outstanding paintings by Old Masters - Jerg Ratgeb, Canaletto, Memling and Rembrandt are just four examples - set the themes of the individual departments. The 19th-century department contains, besides its special collection of works of 'Swabian Classicism', exemplary works of the most important art movements of the time, from the Pre-Raphaelites to the Symbolists, from the Romantics to the Impressionists.
Adjoining the old museum on the gallery level is the 'Neue Staatsgalerie', the extension designed by James Stirling. This new museum building is dedicated to art of the 20th century. Since the end of the Second World War, the main points of emphasis of the collection have been Classic Modernism and contemporary painting and sculpture. The museum's concentration on significant groups of works from various movements ('Les Fauves', 'Die Brücke', 'Der Blaue Reiter' and Cubism), and on outstanding groups by individual artist including Picasso, Beckmann, Schlemmer, Beuys and Kiefer, accounts for the high international prestige which the Staatsgalerie Stuttgart enjoys today.

**EXHIBITIONS**

until 25·05·97 | **Eugène Cuvelier**  *The Legend of the Forest*

17·05·97-14·09·97 | **Tension**  *The Diagonal as a Structural Element*   A journey through 500 years of art on paper

| | |
|---|---|
| 31·05·97-07·09·97 | *Mapplethorpe* |
| Summer 97 | *Art Games*   Fluxus Boxes from the Sohm Archives |
| 12·07·97-28·09·97 | *Hanne Darboven*   Children of this World |
| 27·09·97-11·01·98 | *Johann Heinrich Füssli*   Paradise Lost |
| 09·10·97-23·11·97 | *Ars Viva 97/98 - New Media*   An exhibition of the winners of the art promotion award of the 'Kulturkreis der deutschen Wirtschaft im Bundesverband der Deutschen Industrie e.V.' |
| 18·10·97-25·01·98 | *Alligorical Cycles in the Graphic Art of the Mannerists* |

## Trier

**RHEINISCHES LANDESMUSEUM TRIER**
**Weimarer Allee 1  54290 Trier  Director: Hans-Peter Kuhnen**
☎ **+49 651 97740**  ✉ **+49 651 9774222**
**Open: Tuesday-Friday 09.30-17.00  Saturday, Sunday and public holidays 10.30-17.00**
**Closed: Monday except Easter Monday  Good Friday**

**COLLECTION**

This museum, the largest in Trier, spans the period from prehistory to early modern times, extensively displaying the civilisation, settlement, religion and art of the first four centuries A.D. Burial monuments illustrate life and commerce along the Moselle.
The 'Landesmuseum' houses about 200 colourful floor mosaics. The collection contains early imperial glassware, terra cotta and bronze figurines, and an abundance of household pottery and terra sigillata vessels from over 70 local pottery makers. Roman glassmaking is represented by cups, flasks, bowls and the 'diatret' vessel from Niederemmel.
There are also about 40 000 coins of Trier mintage, the largest collection in Western Germany, and weapons, jewellery, glassware, necklaces, fibulae, gold discs and harnesses from the Frankisch period. The Middle Ages and early modern times are represented by Romanesque and Gothic sculpture and architecture and ceramics from the Rhine-Moselle area.

*Polydus, victorious charioteer*
Mosaic detail, 250 AD; discovered in Trier
© *Rheinisches Landesmuseum Trier, Trier*

**EXHIBITIONS**
until 16·11·97

*Roman Mosaics*   After several years of restoration work, the museum now presents a major selection of these colourful Roman floor decorations in the new Mosaic Gallery.

| | |
|---|---|
| 16·02·97 onwards | **Carolingian Coins**   This exhibition features a recently discovered, and extremely rare, gold coin of Charlemagne (768-814) together with other fine coins of the period. |
| until further notice | **Roman Viticulture**   A range of stone reliefs, mosaics and wine ceramics illustrating the advanced level of Roman viticulture on the Moselle, which began in the 1st century A.D. |

## Ulm

**ULMER MUSEUM**
Marktplatz 9  89073 Ulm  Director: Brigitte Reinhardt
☎ +49 731 1614300   ⌨ +49 731 1611626
Open: Tuesday-Sunday 11.00-17.00  Thursday 11.00-20.00
Closed: Monday

**COLLECTION**

Since its establishment on 1924 the concept of the Ulm Museum has been to give equal attention to the cultivation and collection of both ancient and modern art. The core of the Ancient Art section is a unique collection of Late Gothic paintings and sculptures from Ulm and Upper Swabia. Excellent examples of regional arts and crafts can be seen, in particular goldsmith's work and Ulm cupboards and cabinets.

Hans Multscher
*Maria and child,*
*1455-60, alder wood*
© Ulmer museum,
Ulm

The Museum also has a Prehistoric section devoted to the history of archaeology and modern archaeological methods, together with natural science. The 32 000 year-old animal/man sculpture is the oldest in Central Europe.

The 'Weickmannianum' is unique; a collection of exotic rarities collected in the 17th century by Christoph Weickmann. It is one of the oldest collections in Germany.

The Kurt Fried Collection  This collection of contemporary art was donated by Kurt Fried in 1987. The collection includes paintings, graphic art, sculptures and other objects. It boasts excellent examples of all important post-war trends.

**EXHIBITIONS**
until-15·06·97

**William N. Copley (1919-1996).**   First retrospective after his death. Eroticism and sex are central subjects, which Copley brings up with wit and irony.

29·06·97-07·09·97

**Schopper - Schiffer - Donaufisher**   With many original exhibits - models, photos, productions - the exhibition gives a vivid description of the Ulmer shipping-history, it's guild and traditional festivals.

| | |
|---|---|
| 07·09·97-16·11·97 | **Hans Multscher**    He was one of the leading german sculptors of the 15th century. The exhibition shows wooden and stone sculptures. It documents the immense effect to the following generations of artists. |
| 21·09·97-09·11·97 | **The Deschler Collection**    This exhibition shows about 150 watercolours and drawings of the 20th century in the Ulmer Museum, as well as works of young artists from East-Europe in the Stadthaus Ulm. |
| 23·11·97-25·01·98 | **Otl Aicher**    In the field of the visual communications Otl Aicher is one of the most significant personalities of the century. The exhibitions shows the estate of his works. |
| 07·12·97-18·01·98 | **Ulmer Art**    A view in the actual work of the artists of the region Ulm/Neu-Ulm and Alb-Donau-Kreis. Paintings, sculptures and objects. |
| 14·12·97-22·02·98 | **Historical Tin-Plate Toys**    From 1850 to 1930 tin-plate toys were produced. Models of ships, cars, trains and steam-engines are on display. |

## Weil am Rhein

**VITRA DESIGN MUSEUM**
**Charles-Eames-Straße 1  79576 Weil am Rhein  Director: A. von Vegesack**
☎ **+49 7621 702200  🖷 +49 7621 77493**
**Open: Tuesday-Friday 14.00-18.00  Saturday, Sunday and public holidays**
**11.00-17.00**
**Closed: Monday**

**COLLECTION**

The Vitra Design Museum has one of the foremost collections of modern furniture design in the world. Over 1800 objects document major periods and styles, from early industrial production and the bent-wood furniture of the 19th century to Pop Art designs and the post-industrial furniture sculpture of the 80s and 90s. The highlight of the collection is the estate of Charles and Ray Eames, which was acquired in 1988. Other points of interest are Functionalist steel-tube furniture from the 20s and 30s, Gerrit Rietveld, key Scandinavian designs (1930-1960), Alvar Aalto, American furniture designers from the Shakers to Robert Venturi, Italian design from the 50s to the present day, George Nelson, Verner Panton and Jean Prouvé. The museum also houses an extensive archive which includes the estates of Anton Lorenz and George Nelson.

Vitra Design Museum
© Photographer:
Thomas Dix
Weil am Rhein

**EXHIBITIONS**
until 25·09·97

**Castiglioni!**  *Retrospective*  Archille Castiglioni is one of the last great designers whose oeuvre has decisively influenced international design.

| | |
|---|---|
| Sep 97-Jan 98 | *The World of Charles & Ray Eames* |
| Jan 98- Jun 98 | *Childrens Furniture - Between Cot and TV    Do we want Safe Containment or Age-Oriented Encouragement?*    Western history of children's education will be exemplified by children's furniture and compared to African, Asian and Latinamerican cultures. |

## Weimar

**KUNSTSAMMLUNGEN ZU WEIMAR**
Burgplatz 4  99423 Weimar  Director: Rolf Bothe
☎ +49 3643 546130  🖷 +49 3643 546101
Open: Tuesday-Sunday 10.00-18.00; Winter 10.00-16.30
Closed: Monday

**COLLECTION**

[SCHLOßMUSEUM, BURGPLATZ 4]

The Weimar Collection, housed in the early 18th to mid 19th-century Schloß Weimar complex, is one of the major collections of the former GDR. The Cranach Gallery contains more than 20 works by the artist along with works by Dürer. Another major focus is formed by Dutch and Flemish painting of the 16th to 18th century, featuring artists such as Honthorst, Van der Helst, Ruysdael and Van Ostade. Other important collections feature Russian icons, mainly from the Moscow and Novgorod Schools; a small selection of Italian Renaissance painting with works by Ribera, Tiepolo, Tintoretto and Veronese, among others; and a large collection of Classical, Romantic and Realist German painting from the period 1750-1850. The Weimar School is represented by artists such as Brendel, Hagen, Buchholz, Von Hoffmann and Beckmann, together with single works by Böcklin, Liebermann, Monet and Rodin. Contemporary art is chiefly represented by artists of the former GDR, with proponents of the Dresden, Leipzig and Berlin Schools. Many Schloß interiors are also on display, including the 'Dichterzimmer' which commemorates the famous poets of Weimar.

[ROKOKO MUSEUM, SCHLOß BELVEDERE]

Belvedere Castle, originally dating from 1724 and later enlarged, is in the south of the city within a spacious landscape garden. In the late 18th century - in Goethe's time - Belvedere was an important cultural meeting point. The current collection in the Rococo Museum is focused on items of German and European faience and porcelain, including many exhibits from Meissen, Berlin and Vienna, and from Thuringian factories. There is also a collection of glass from the 16th to 19th century, while portraits, landscape paintings, furniture and other craft objects show the style of courtly life in the 18th century.

[BAUHAUS MUSEUM, THEATERPLATZ]

With more than 500 exhibits, the Bauhaus Museum provides an overview of the development of art and art schools in Weimar between 1900 and 1930. It concentrates on the State Bauhaus Weimar from 1919 to 1925 and its global influence.
The work of Belgian artist Henry van de Velde is shown as a major precursor to the later developments. Teaching methods and goals of the school are illustrated by works from Itten, Gropius, Feininger, Kandinsky, Klee, Schlemmer and Moholy-Nagy, augmented by works by pupils and 'Young Masters'. Later Bauhaus phases in Dessau and Berlin are also covered.

**EXHIBITIONS**

[SCHLOßMUSEUM]

until 19·05·97

*The Other Bauhaus*  *Otto Bartning and the State Bauhaus Weimar 1926-1930*

| 15·06·97-31·08·97 | **Colours of the Light** *Paul Signac and the Genesis of the Modern* from Matisse to Mondrian |
|---|---|
| 22·06·97-31·08·97 | **Focus on the Time of Goethe I** *Drawings from the Time of Goethe* A selection of works from a major German private collection. |
| 08·10·97-09·11·97 | **Norbert W. Hinterberger** *New Works in Weimar* A range of installations and stagings in various rooms of the museum. |
| Nov 97-Jan 98 | **Focus on the Time of Goethe II** *Drawings from the Time of Goethe* A selection of works from the Weimar collection |
| | [SCHLOß BELVEDERE] |
| 19·07·97-26·10·97 | **The Karl-Peter Röhl Foundation Weimar** |
| | [BAUHAUS MUSEUM] |
| until 06·07·97 | **New Discoveries from the Early Bauhaus** *Margit Téry-Adler and Friends* |

# Wolfsburg

**KUNSTMUSEUM WOLFSBURG**
Porschestraße 53 D-38440 Wolfsburg  Director: Gijs van Tuyl
☎ +49 5361 26690  🖷 +49 5361 266911
Open: Tuesday 11.00-20.00  Wednesday-Sunday 11.00-18.00
Closed: Monday

**COLLECTION**

© Kunstmuseum
Wolfsburg
*Wolfsburg*

The Kunstmuseum's temporary exhibitions are devoted to the art of the 20th century, while the permanent collection features works beginning with Minimal Art, Conceptual Art and Arte Povera.

The collection is not designed to achieve total coverage of contemporary trends, but to record key positions within contemporary art. Artists represented included such established figures as Andre, Araki, Artschwager, Brouwn, Cragg, Daniels, Dibbets, Fischli/Weiss, Gilbert & George, Harold, Horn, Immendorff, Kiefer, Koons, Kounellis, McCollum, Merz, Nauman, Nam June Paik, Panamarenko, Warhol and Welling, as well as representatives of the younger generation such as Andreas Gursky, Paul Graham, Gary Hume and Wolfgang Tillmans.

**EXHIBITIONS**
until 19·05·97

**Pietro Donzelli** *The Light of Solitude* 120 photographs from the prolific output of Pietro Donzelli, whose major work was produced in the immediate post-war period and in the 1950s and 60s.

24·05·97-14·09·97

**Bruce Nauman** This exhibition focuses on Bruce Nauman's work in film and video, from his early shorts in the mid-1960s to the large-scale video installations of the 1990s.

# GERMANY

11·10·97–04·01·98 | **Frantisek Kupka**   This Czech artist charted an indep[...] abstraction. Approximately 60 of his oil paintings and 4[...] paper from 1901 until the 1950s are included in this exhib[...]

11·10·97–04·01·98 | **Josef Sudek**   A selection of approximately 130 works from th[...] extensive output of this photographer (born Kolín, 1896, died Prague, 1976).

end Nov 97–early Jan 98 | **Jeff Koons**   *Celebrations*   A selection of 17 sculptures — mostly large painted steel works — and 13 paintings from Koon's recent output, all based on motifs from the world of toys, fairgrounds and party decorations.

07·02·98–26·04·98 | **Peter Fischli & David Weiss**   *In a Restless World*   This is the first comprehensive survey of the work of these two Swiss artists. Their leitmotif is the beauty of everyday, often banal things. The exhibition includes sculptures, videos and photographs.

ndent path to
0 works on
tion.

STORNOWAY

KIRKWALL

LERWICK

INVERNESS

ABERDEEN

DUNDEE

STIRLING
GLENROTHES
Kirkcaldy
**EDINBURGH**
GLASGOW
New Bridge
NEWTOWN
ST BOSWELLS

S C O T L A N D

MORPETH

DUMFRIES

NEWCASTLE UPON TYNE

DURHAM

NORTHERN
IRELAND
**BELFAST**

CARLISLE

Grasmere

MIDDLESBOROUGH

SCARBOROUGH

Douglas

York

Blackpool
BEVERLEY

PRESTON
Leeds
WAKEFIELD
Hull

LIVERPOOL
MANCHESTER
LINCOLN

Holyhead
MATLOCK

Wrexham
Derby
NOTTINGHAM
NORWICH

SHREWSBURY
STAFFORD

BIRMINGHAM
Leicester
E N G L A N D

LLANDRINDOD
WELLS
WARWICK
Coventry
NORTHAMPTON
CAMBRIDGE

CARMARTHEN
Cheltenham
WORCESTER
BEDFORD

W A L E S
Newport
HERTFORD
CHELMSFORD

SWANSEA
BRISTOL
OXFORD
**LONDON**

**CARDIFF**
Bath
READING
MAIDSTONE

Southampton
Southend on Sea

EXETER
Bournemouth
CHICHESTER

DORCHESTER
Brighton

TRURO

St Ives

## Aberdeen

**ABERDEEN ART GALLERY**
Schoolhill  Aberdeen Scotland AB10 1FQ  Director: A. Hidalgo
☎ +44 1224 646333  📠 +44 1224 632133
Open: Daily 10.00-17.00  Thursday 10.00-20.00
Sunday 14.00-17.00

**COLLECTION**

Aberdeen Art Gallery houses an important art collection ranging from 18th-century portraits by Raeburn, Hogarth, Ramsay and Reynolds to powerful 20th-century works by Paul Nash, Ben Nicholson and Francis Bacon. The collection also includes paintings by Impressionists such as Monet, Pissaro, Sisley and Bonnard. Other permanent displays feature a significant collection of Scottish silver and other decorative arts. The Gallery seeks where possible to provide a platform for new and emerging artists and hosts an active programme of special exhibitions throughout the year.

**EXHIBITIONS**

03·05·97-25·05·97 **Aberdeen Artists' Society Annual Exhibition**  This major 'open' exhibition, now in its 63rd year, features painting, sculpture, textiles, ceramics, video, printmaking and photography.

31·05·97-26·07·97 **Fishing and Farming**  *Paintings from the Permanent Collection.*

07·06·97-02·08·97 **Hats, Headwear and Millinery**  *Hats from the Collections.*

13·09·97-04·10·97 **Sara Radstone**  *Ceramics*

04·10·97-08·11·97 **Fotofeis**  *International Festival of Photography in Scotland.*

15·11·97-10·01·98 **Camden Town**  Paintings from the collection featuring work by Walter Sickert, Augustus John and Spencer Gore.

22·11·97-13·12·97 **Gray's Former Students**  Work by former students of Gray's School of Art, Aberdeen.

## Bath

**HOLBURNE MUSEUM AND CRAFTS STUDY CENTRE**
Great Pulteney Street  Bath Avon BA2 4DB  Curator: Barly Roscoe
☎ +44 1225 466669  📠 +44 1225 333121
Open: Monday-Saturday 11.00-17.00  Sunday 14.30-17.30
Closed: Mid Dec to Mid Feb and Mondays Nov to Easter

**COLLECTION**

The Holburne Museum, Bath, is a successful combination of ancient and modern. The collection of decorative and fine art which it

*J.M.W.Turner*
*(1775-1851)*
*Pembroke Castle,*
*Watercolour*
*© Holburne Museum,*
*Bath*

contains was made by Sir William Holburne (1793-1874) and includes superb English and continental silver, porcelain, Italian majolica and bronzes, together with glass, furniture, miniatures and old master paintings. Since his time the collection has been added to by gifts and bequests, particularly of 18th century portraits by Gainsborough, Stubbs and Ramsey.

Fine examples of work by British 20th-century artist-craftsmen are also on view. This collection and archive was formed by the Crafts Study Centre, mainly from donations, and embraces printed and woven textiles, pottery, furniture and calligraphy as well as reference books, documents, photographs and craftsmen's working notes. In addition there is a selection of work by contemporary artist-craftspeople on long term loan from the Crafts Council collection.

**EXHIBITIONS**

until 13·06·97

***Lady in Waiting to Queen Victoria***   *Watercolours by Charlotte, Viscountess Canning (1817-1861)*   Charlotte was the daughter of Lord Stuart de Rothesay of Highcliffe, Hampshire and married Charles, 2nd Viscount Canning, in 1835. The exhibition focuses on the landscapes she painted during her years serving Queen Victoria.

until 13·06·97

***Dancing at Almack's***   *The Watercolours of Charlotte Augusta Sneyd (1800-1882)*   Charlotte Augusta Sneyd, daughter of a Regency landowner, compiled a careful key to her portraits, which include several notable Regency figures. Her later paintings of Victorian interiors, portraits and landscapes are also on display.

05·07·97-28·09·97

***John Downton (1906-1991)***   *Temperas and Drawings*
An exhibition toured by the Trustees of the John Downton Trust.

11·10·97-14·12·97

***British Folk Art Collection***   An exhibition toured by the Peter Moores Foundation.

# Belfast

**ULSTER MUSEUM**
Botanic Gardens  Belfast BT9 5AB  N. Ireland  Director: Post vacant
☎ +44 1232 383000  🖷 +44 1232 383003
Open: Monday-Friday 10.00-17.00  Saturday 13.00-17.00  Sunday 14.00-17.00
Closed: Phone to check Christmas an New Year closures

**COLLECTION**

The Ulster Museum possesses diverse collections of scientific, historic and artistic materials. The permanent gallery displays show a range of works from the collections. The Fine Art displays are changed on a regular basis.

Its Irish archaeological collections date from around 7000 B.C. until the late 17th century. The non-Irish collections feature notable holdings of Pacific Island and Australasian materials, specimens from North American Indian, African, and Egyptian cultures, and some 95 percent of the world's authenticated material from Spanish Armada ships which foundered off the coast of Ireland.

The Fine Art holdings cover a wide spectrum of works, encompassing a representative collection of Irish painting and sculpture from the late 17th century to the present day, as well as 20th-century British art. There are also small collections of contemporary international art and British and continental 'Old Master' paintings. In its collection of applied art are important examples of Irish ceramics, silver and glass, as well as modern European ceramics and glass, costumes and textiles, and jewellery.

Scientific displays include exhibits on botany and zoology, displays of minerals and gemstones, and a popular dinosaur gallery featuring a skeleton of 'Anatosaurus annectens'. The museum also possesses large collections of preserved plants and animals of great scientific importance. The Local History collections reflect the political and industrial history of Ulster from about 1600. The main galleries are devoted to the political and social history of Ulster and the origins of the city of Belfast.

**EXHIBITIONS**

until 22·06·97

**W.J. Leech**   Retrospective exhibition of one of the oustanding Irish artists of his generation.

until 21·09·97

**Travelling through Time**   Using transport-related artefacts from the Museum's Ethnography collection, this exhibition illustrates mehods of travel used by peoples of different societies throughout the ages.

until 16·11·97

**British and Irish Paintings**   · Selection of paintings from the Museum's own Fine Art collections.

until 11·01·98

**The 18th Century on Paper**   Selection of prints, drawings and watercolours from the Museum's own Fine Art collections.

09·05·97-31·08·97

**Dinosaurs: A New Generation**   Major exhibition of stunningly realistic robotic dinosaurs, focusing on family life and growing up in the world of dinosaurs.

16·05·97-31·08·97

**The Narrow Road to the Deep North**   Recent photographs of the north of Ireland by Belfast-born photographer David Gepp.

27·06·97-15·03·98

**A Century of Applied Art 1850-1950**   Selection of pieces from the Museum's own Applied Art collections.

10·10·97-16·11·97

**RUA Exhibition**   Annual exhibition of works by members of the Royal Ulster Academy of Arts.

28·11·97-19·04·98

**Paul Henry**   Selection of works by Irish artist.

03·04·98-30·08·98

**Up in Arms!** The 1798 Rebellion in Ireland   Major, bicentenary exhibition commemorating the 1798 rebellion and events in Ulster and Ireland from 1775 to 1830.

## Birmingham

**THE BARBER INSTITUTE OF FINE ARTS**
**The University of Birmingham  Edgbaston  Birmingham B15 2TS**
**Director: R. Verdi**
☎ **+44 121 4147333**  📠 **+44 121 4143370**
**Open: Monday-Saturday 10.00-17.00  Sunday 14.00-17.00**

**COLLECTION**

The Barber Institute of Fine Arts was founded in 1932 'for the study and encouragement of art and music' and has since grown to become one of the finest small picture galleries in the world.

Nirholas Poussin
*Tancred and Erminia*
© *The Barber*
*Institute of Fine Arts,*
*Birmingham*

Located at the East Gate of the University of Birmingham, it houses an outstanding collection of Old Master and Modern paintings, drawings and sculpture, and a magnificent Art Deco concert hall. The collections include major works by Bellini, Poussin, Rubens, Gainsborough and Turner, and also Rossetti, Whistler, Monet, Degas, Renoir and Magritte. Other important exhibits include Roman and Byzantine coins, illuminated manuscripts, rare books and objets d'art.

**EXHIBITIONS**

No exhibitions planned.

## Birmingham

**BIRMINGHAM MUSEUM AND ART GALLERY AND THE GAS HALL**
Chamberlain Square  Birmingham B3 3DH  Director: Evelyn A. Silber
☎ +44 121 2352834  ℻ +44 121 2356227
Open: Daily 10.00-17.00  Friday 10.30-17.00  Sunday 12.30-17.00
Closed: 25-27 Dec and 1 Jan

**COLLECTION**

Covers fine and applied art, from middle ages to present, archaeology, ethnography, local history and natural sciences. Highlights of the collection are 18th and 19th century English watercolours, paintings, sculpture, stained glass and drawings by the Pre-Raphaelites. A select Old Master selection includes works by S. Martini, G. Bellini, P. Giovanni, O. Gentileschi, C. Dolci, Canaletto, Reynolds, Gainsborough, Turner, Degas, Pissarro, Sisley, Renoir. The applied art collection is especially strong in silver and metalwork, jewellery, stained glass and ceramics. The work of W. de Morgan, William Morris & Co. and the Arts and Crafts Movement are well represented.
There are innovative displays of ethnographic material in Gallery 33.

Dante Gabriel
Rossetti
*Proserpine*
© Birmingham
Museum and Art
Gallery and the Gas
hall

**EXHIBITIONS**

[MUSEUM AND ART GALLERY]

05·06·97-11·07·97

***Roots of the Future, Ethnic Diversity in the Making of Britain***
Although not a complete record of immigration to Britain, the exhibition illustrates how immigrants have made, and are making, valuable and positive contributions to British life.

10·07·97-28·09·97

***Home from Home***   This exhibition explores the lives of Mirpuris both in Birmingham and in Pakistan, today and since the first settlers arrived in the 1940s.

13·09·97-30·11·97

***Print in Focus, Part 1***   Part 1, Durer to Millais, considers 16th and

17th-century masters of engraving and etching, well-known 18th-century exponents of mezzotint alongside work by Hogarth. Gainsborough, Rowlandson and Pianesi, and the invention of lithography.

14·12·97-01·03·98    **Print in Focus, Part 2**    Part 2, Whistler to Hockney and Beyond, looks at the most recent resurgence of printmaking by such artists as Eduardo Paolozzi, Krishna Reddy, Jim Dine, David Hockney, Paola Rego and Elaine Kowalsky.

12·11·97-01·02·98    **Anwar Shemza (1928-1985)**    Shemza had already established himself as an artist in Pakisatn when he emigrated to Britain in the 1950s. He then abandoned past achievements and sought a new direction and language through abstract art.

[GAS HALL]

until 02·06·97    **Star Trek, The Exhibition**    The exhibition celebrates an enduring media icon with original props, costumes, models and artwork, as well as material from Paramount's Los Angeles studio.

28·06·97-31·08·97    **Favourite Things!**    The man and woman in the streets of Birmingham have been given unprecedented access to our wide-ranging collections to choose their own favourites to show.

29·10·97-11·01·98    **Walter Langley**    After moving to Newlyn in 1881, Langley was the first painter to depict the lives of the Cornish fishing community, a subject which had affinities with his own working-class background.

## Bournemouth

**RUSSELL-COTES ART GALLERY AND MUSEUM**
East Cliff   Bournemouth BH1 3AA   Director: Simon Olding
☎ +44 1202 451800   📠 +44 1202 451851
Open: Tuesday-Sunday 10.00-17.00
Closed: Monday

COLLECTION

Built in 1894, East Cliff Hall was originally the home of Sir Merton and Lady Annie Russell-Cotes. Richly decorated with stained glass, stencilwork and elaborate woodwork, the house formed the perfect setting for the many works of art which they brought home from extensive world travels. Bournemouth Council opened Russell-Cotes to the public in 1922, following the donation of the house, its collections and the later Art Galleries.

Tim Harrisson
*'Horizon',*
*Cumberland Slate,*
*1995*
© *Russell-Cotes Art*
*Gallery and Museum,*
*Bournemouth*

The museum's collection consists of an impressive assortment of Victorian and Edwardian paintings, complemented by sculpture, decorative art and furniture, as well as a modern art collection.

Furthermore, important commissions of contemporary craft and sculpture are sited in the Display Space, Art Galleries and Garden.

# Brighton

**BRIGHTON MUSEUM & ART GALLERY**
Church Street  Brighton BN1 1UE  Director: Jessica Rutherford
☎ +44 1273 603005  📠 +44 1273 608202
Open: Thursday-Monday 10.00-17.00  Sunday 14.00-17.00
Closed: Wednesday and Good Friday, 25, 26 Dec, 1 Jan

**COLLECTION**

The Brighton Museum & Art Gallery possesses rich collections of both local and national importance, included Art Nouveau and Art Deco works ranging from Gallé to Clarice Cliff, non-Western items from textiles to masks, and archaeological artefacts from flint axes to silver coins. There is also a fashion gallery and a toy cabinet, and the museum has exhibits of fine art. From time to time, the museum presents temporary exhibitions and conducts special events.

**EXHIBITIONS**

until 29·06·97 | ***Les Sixties***   *Great Britain and France 1962-1973, The Utopian Years* The exhibition looks at the explosion of art and popular culture in Britain and France in the 60s, assembling artworks and objects that convey the excitement and spirit of the time.

12·07·97-24·08·97 | ***Regency Cartoons 1785-1830***   This exhibition examines the satirical portrayal of King George IV, his unlawful marriage to Mrs. Fitzherbert, his relationship with his estranged wife Caroline, Princess of Wales, and with his daughter Charlotte.

12·07·97-24·08·97 | ***Private Eye Times***   This exhibition is both a celebration and an examination of Private Eye, the most successful of satirical magazines in Britain for more than 30 years.

06·09·97-19·10·97 | ***Animals in Art***   This exhibition will show how companion animals, such as cats, dogs, horses and birds of prey used for hunting, have been portrayed by distinguished artists throughout the centuries.

01·11·97-30·11·97 | ***Lure***   *New Paintings and Other Works by Suzanne Hutchinson and Nicholas Martin*   Vibrant pastels and oil paintings by Hutchinson are shown alongside large figure and landscape composite pictures by Martin.

13·12·97-25·01·98 | ***Krishna***   *The Divine Lover*   An exhibition comprising some 120 miniatures of Krishna from the most important schools of Indian paintings of the 16th to the 19th century, to coincide with the 50th anniversary of Indian Independence.

21·02·98-22·03·98 | ***The Sussex Open***   An open-submission exhibition for all artists living and working in Sussex, it features works by the Sussex Watercolour Society.

# Bristol

**CITY MUSEUM AND ART GALLERY**
Queen's Road  Bristol BS8 1RL  Director: H. McGowan
☎ +44 117 9223571  📠 +44 117 9222047
Open: Daily 10.00-17.00

**COLLECTION**

The City Museum and Art Gallery houses an outstanding collection that can be divided into 6 main categories: decorative art, fine art, Eastern art and culture, archaeology and history, geology and natural history. The collection of decorative art encompasses European ceramics, glass, textiles, metalwork and furniture dating from the 17th century to the present. The fine art collection includes French 16th to 20th-century paintings, a number of charming Victorian paintings and works by the Bristol School. The collection of Eastern art is internationally significant and displays Chinese art, Japanese ceramics, carved ivories, metal sword fittings, Far Eastern lacquerware and the arts of the Indian subcontinent, Asia and the Islamic countries. Archaeological material from the Bristol area and from many parts of the world is displayed in the museum. The Egyptian Gallery contains exhibits illustrating ancient Egyptian beliefs about death and the afterlife and includes a display detailing the scientific unwrapping of a 21st-Dynasty mummy. The Bristol area is of special geological interest and the museum has a major collection of fossils and a mineral gallery. These are displayed in such a way that they help explain how the earth was formed and how species evolved through geological time.

**EXHIBITIONS**

[EXHIBITION GALLERY] (SOLAGLAS)

until 26·10·97

**Cabot 500** *From Bristol to the Sea*   18th and 19th-century paintings of the Avon Gorge and the fauna, flora and geology of the gorge, taken from the museum's collections.

Nov 97-Jan 98

**A Respectable Trade**   An exhibition on the slave trade in Bristol, including costumes and more from the film. Based on museum and archive material.

Feb 98-Mar 98

**Robert Lenkiewicz**   Large canvasses by this internationally known artist.

[FRONT HALL]

15·05·97-27·05·97

**Cabot 500**   Schools Fashion Show

30·05·97-29·06·97

**Cabot 500**   *The Italian Community in Bristol Now*   Cabot himself was an Italian. This exhibition shows the results of a photographic project with the Anglo-Italian Circle.

11·07·97-17·08·97

**Cabot 500**   *Avon Crafts Guild and Bristol Savages*   A combined exhibition of their work, with a modern interpretation of medieval crafts and views of the Avon Gorge today.

25·08·97-14·09·97

**50 Years of Twinning**   *Hannover Twinning Project*   A display about the Twinning Association and its links with Hannover and Bordeaux.

19·09·97-26·10·97

**Cabot 500**   *Schools Displays*   Work by Bristol children on Cabot-related themes.

# Cambridge

**CAMBRIDGE UNIVERSITY MUSEUM OF ARCHAEOLOGY AND ANTHROPOLOGY**
Downing Street  Cambridge CB2 3DZ  Director: D.W. Phillipson
☎ +44 1223 333511  📠 +44 1223 333503
Internet http://www.cam.ac.uk/CambArea/Museums/AAM/
Open: Monday-Friday 14.00-16.00  Saturday 10.00-12.30
Closed: Sunday

**COLLECTION**

Although primarily a University institution devoted to teaching and research, the museum's galleries contain much to interest the non-specialist visitor. The Archaeology Gallery surveys world history from the origins of mankind to the rise of literate civilisation. The Anthropology Gallery surveys cultures from all continents. Some subject areas, among which Oceanian anthropology and American and European archaeology, are particularly comprehensive.

**EXHIBITIONS**

until Spring 98

*Metal in Africa*   The exhibition illustrates some of the ways in which gold, copper, iron and other metals have contributed to Africa's various cultures from c. 4000 B.C. to the present time. It shows how metal objects may be tools, weapons, ornaments or symbols of wealth/authority, and how the same item may serve more than one of these functions, emphasising that sophisticated expertise in metal-working has existed for a very long time in many parts of the continent.

Spring 98 onwards

*The Torres Strait.*

# Cambridge

**FITZWILLIAM MUSEUM**
Trumpington Street  Cambridge CB2 1RB  Director: S.S. Jervis
☎ +44 1223 332900  📠 +44 1223 332923
Open: Tuesday-Saturday 10.00-17.00  Sunday 14.15-17.00
Closed: Monday (except Easter Monday, Spring and Summer Bank Holidays)
Good Friday, May Day Bank Holiday, 24 Dec-1 Jan

**COLLECTION**

The museum possesses rich collections of Egyptian objects, Greek and Roman art, antiquities from Mesopotamia and the kingdoms of Ur, Babylon, Assyria, Persia, and Arabia, as well as sculpture, bronzes, glass, jewellery, gems, grave furnishings and applied art covering the period from the Paleolithic to early Christian eras.

© Fitzwilliam
Museum
Cambridge

The applied arts include international ceramics, notably early European pottery; majolica; Korean, Chinese and Japanese porcelain and pottery; glass; armour; choice silver; furniture; notable English clocks; sculpture; textiles and fans.
There are important collections of Greek, Roman, and Medieval coins, additional collections of engraved gems and cameos, and fine Italian and foreign medals.
The museum's varied collection of paintings includes Italian paintings from the 15th century onwards, examples of the Dutch and Flemish schools, representative works of the French school, Impressionist and Post-Impressionist paintings and works by English artists including Hogarth, Reynolds, Gainsborough, Turner, Stubbs and Constable. There are also numerous English watercolours, miniatures, drawings and prints.
The museum also possesses a library containing fine illuminated, literary and music manuscripts, and fine printed books.

## EXHIBITIONS

until 26·05·97
**Gerhart Frankl**   Frankl's main oeuvre reveals a love of Alpine landscapes, but he also made a series of paintings based on photographs of concentration camps.

until 29·06·97
**Shakespeare and the 18th Century**   This exhibition examines the interpretation of Shakespeare by 18th-century artists including Romney, Blake and Barry, and includes satirical caricatures by James Gillray.

until 01·09·97
**Samplers**   An array of samplers from the museum's collections, including 17th to 20th-century English, German, Dutch and Spanish work.

06·05·97-31·08·97
**Mexican Prints from the Collection of Reba and Dave Williams** The Fitzwilliam hosts the first showing of this major exhibition of 20th-century Mexican printmaking. Highlighted are works by Rivera, Orozco, Siqueiros and Tamayo.

13·05·97-15·06·97
**Masterpieces of Japanese Printmaking Part II**   This show presents the best of Japanese printmaking, including works of Harunobu, Kiyonaga, Utamaro, Hokusai, Hiroshige, Kuniyoshi, Kunisada, and a newly acquired print by Okumura Masanobu.

24·06·97-28·09·97
**A Gardener's Roses**   This exhibition illustrates the variety of ways in which roses have been depicted by European painters from the 17th to the 19th century.

## Cardiff

**NATIONAL MUSEUM OF WALES**
Cathays Park  Cardiff CF1 3NP  Director: Colin Ford
☎ +44 1222 397951  📠 +44 1222 373219
Open: Tuesday-Saturday 10.00-17.00  Sunday 14.30-17.00
Closed: Monday, except public holidays

COLLECTION
The National Museum of Wales includes exhibitions on Natural History as well as Fine Art.
'The Evolution of Wales' gallery is a major interdisciplinary exhibition tracing the development of Wales from its earliest geological origins up to the end of the last great Ice Age, when the present landscape was moulded. The exhibition actually 'begins' with the origins of the universe, the solar system, the Earth and life on Earth, and introduces the concepts of plate tectonics and continental drift, up to the point in time when that piece of the Earth's crust which is now called Wales was located at latitude 50 south of the equator. It continues up through the age of dinosaurs to the emergence of man.
'The Natural History of Wales' is a new exhibition which illustrates the marine and woodland environments of modern Wales.
Six new art galleries display the museum's internationally acclaimed collection of fine art. The Davies Collection of French Impressionist art is especially noteworthy. Other galleries show Welsh, British and European paintings, as well as an impressive collection of sculpture and ceramics.

EXHIBITION
until 22·02·98
**Images of Botany**   An exhibition which investigates art in the service of science using the museum's stunning collections of Botanical illustrations.

# Cheltenham

## CHELTENHAM ART GALLERY & MUSEUM
Clarence Street  Cheltenham GL50 3JT  Director: George Breeze
☎ +44 1242 237431  ☒ +44 1242 262334
Open: Monday-Saturday 10.00-17.20
Closed: Sunday and public holidays

**COLLECTION**

Cheltenham Art Gallery & Museum possesses an internationally significant collection related to the Arts and Crafts Movement: that period at the turn of the century inspired by William Morris. Particularly strong in furniture, the collection also includes silver, textiles and paintings, much of which has a Cotswold connection. Cheltenham is the most complete Regency town in Britain and the museum houses a wide range of objects associated with its history. There is also a gallery devoted to one of the town's famous sons, Edward Wilson, who died with Captain Scott on their way back from the South Pole in 1912.

*Arts and Crafts interior, showing furniture and metalwork designed by Ernest Gimson and Ernest Barnsley dating from 1905-1930*
*© Cheltenham Art Gallery & Museum, Cheltenham*

Many other fascinating collections are on view, with the notable collection of Dutch and Flemish paintings, donated by the Baron de Ferrieres in 1898, of particular interest. A fine collection of oriental ceramics has been assembled from the many pieces brought back to Cheltenham by retiring civil servants who had served in the Far East. There are additional displays of archaeological treasures from the Cotswolds and a series of historical galleries depicting life from the Middle Ages to the 20th century.

**EXHIBITIONS**

until 31·05·97  ***Tsuguni Ota, Woodcuts and Carvings***

07·06·97-30·08·97  ***Sophie Ryder: Sculptures, Prints, Collages***

06·09·97-18·10·97  ***Cheltenham Fellows (Cheltenham School of Art), 1967-1997***

22·11·97-10·01·98  ***Art Pottery***

17·01·98-01·03·98  ***Nigel Temple: Collages and Constructions***

# Chichester

## PALLANT HOUSE GALLERY
9 North Pallant  Chichester West Sussex PO19 ITJ  Curator: David Coke
☎ +44 1243 774557  ☒ +44 1243 536038
Open: Tuesday-Saturday 10.00-17.15
Closed: Sunday, Monday and bank holidays

**COLLECTION**

The museum displays a collection of works by 20th-century artists, displayed in an 18th-century setting. There are works by Henry Moore, Graham Sutherland, Paul Nash, John Piper, Ivor Hitchens,

Barbara Hepworth, Ben Nicholson and many other British Masters as well as Europeans including Klee, Cézanne, Picasso, Severini, Léger and others.

**EXHIBITIONS**
until-21·06·97

***The Art of Drawing***  The collection of Colin St. John Wilson, controversial architect of the new British Library, is particular strong in drawings. Some are shown here adjacent to the finished paintings by Sickert, Coldstream, Bomberg and Caulfield. Others by Creffield and de Francia impress by their sheer scale and virtuosity. A third group, including Giacometti, Gill, Kitaj and Andrews show the medium in all its diverse aspects.

01·07·97-19·07·97

***Artist in Residence***

05·08·97-11·10·97

***The Sidney Burney 1934 Collection***  The exhibition includes intimate works by Paul Nash, Tristram Hillier, Augustus John, Vanessa Bell, Duncan Grant, Edward Wadsworth, Barbara Hepworth, Alan Durst and others.

28·10·97-03·01·98

***The Shell Art Collection***  Original paintings for many of the famous Shell posters (as well as the posters themselves) by Sutherland, Piper, Nash and Nicholson.

# Coventry

**HERBERT ART GALLERY & MUSEUM**
Jordan Well  Coventry CV1 5QP  Director: Peter Pinnell
☎ +44 1203 832385  ▥ +44 1203 832410
Open: Monday-Saturday 10.00-17.30  Sunday 14.00-17.00

**COLLECTION**

**20th-Century Art**  The collection features the work of numerous British artists.
**Graham Sutherland**  The gallery is one minute from Coventry Cathedral and contains the Iliffe Collection of over 150 of Sutherland's studies for the 75-foot high tapestry which forms the centrepiece of this showpiece of Modernism.
**Topographical Art**  The collection covering the period from 1650 to 1980 includes many paintings, watercolours, prints and drawings, mostly of Coventry, as well as of Warwick and Kenilworth Castles.
**Other Art Collections**  Additional collections include British Figure Drawings, 1875-1975; British Watercolours, 1775-1980; Local Artist David Gee (1793-1872); Paintings of Lady Godiva; and Luca Giordano's immense 'Bacchus and Ariadne'.
**Natural History**  The museum possesses approximately 250 000 specimens, including large and extensive insect collections spanning most insect orders, as well as a moderately-sized collection of stuffed birds and animals, bird's eggs and fossils.
**Social History**  These collections are comprised principally of Stevengraphs, silk ribbons and Coventry-made clocks and watches. There are also examples of objects manufactured in the city over the past 1000 years.
**Archaeology**  There is an excellent collection of Medieval artefacts, particularly rich in ceramics, metals and leather objects.

**EXHIBITIONS**
until 01·06·97

***Heart of England Biennial 2***  *Sculptures, Drawings, Prints*
A selection of work by artists who were born, live or work in Coventry and his vicinity.

17·05·97-14·06·97

***Free to Move***  An innovative project in which children can learn techniques making mobiles with professional craftspeople in residence in galleries across the country.

| | |
|---|---|
| 14·06·97-31·08·97 | ***Kaleidoscope*** An interactive exhibition which explores how colour is created, how we communicate through colour and the impact of colour on our lives. |
| 21·06·97-08·09·97 | ***Kaleidoscope*** Further exploration of colour. This space will also be used for Play and Holiday Activities, dates to be confirmed. |
| 03·09·97-19·10·97 | ***TBC*** |
| 29·10·97-14·12·97 | ***Frank Bowling*** Influenced by Weight and Bacon at one point and Johns and Rivers at another, Bowling's art can be described as a search for identity. |
| 25·10·97-07·12·97 | ***Animals in Art*** Works by Gainsborough, Degas, Hockney, Frink, Picasso and Constable among others will illustrate how companion animals have been represented in art throughout the centuries. |
| 01·11·97-11·01·98 | ***Chinese Children's Art*** A vibrant and charming exhibition of paintings by children from the Jilin Province of China which convey with humour and poetry the beauty of the life and traditions around them. |

## Derby

**DERBY MUSEUM & ART GALLERY**
The Strand  Derby DE1 1BS  Director: David Fraser
☎ +44 1332 255587  ⅈ +44 1332 255804
Open: Monday 11.00-17.00  Tuesday-Saturday 10.00-17.00
Sunday and public holidays 14.00-17.00

| | |
|---|---|
| COLLECTION | The Derby Museum & Art Gallery possesses a diverse collection of art, art objects, and historical displays. Featured in the collection are paintings by the 18th- century Derby artist Joseph Wright (1734-1797), including portraits, landscapes, and scenes depicting scientific and industrial activity. Also featured are examples of fine Derby porcelain ranging from the middle of the 18th century to the present. There are also local military regimental collections on display. Natural history exhibits depict the geology and wildlife of Derbyshire. Additional exhibits present local archaeology and history. |
| **EXHIBITIONS** | |
| until 25·05·97 | ***Denby Stonewares*** Denby Pottery is a leading and long-established Derbyshire manufacturer of stoneware products. This exhibition features stonewares made between 1809 and 1958. |
| until 25·05·97 | ***Derby Sketching Club*** *110 Years* To celebrate the 110th anniversary of the Derby Sketching Club, the gallery presents the work of its past and current members. |
| until 25·05·97 | ***Emmanuel Cooper*** Emmanuel Cooper was born and brought up within a Derbyshire mining community. His influence in the world of British ceramics has been incomparable. |
| 21·06·97-28·09·97 | ***Joseph Wright Bicentenary Exhibition*** The gallery presents a major exhibition of paintings and drawings by Joseph Wright of Derby (1734-1797). |

## Derby

**PICKFORD'S HOUSE MUSEUM**
41 Friar Gate  Derby DE1 1DA  Directors: Diane Moss & Elizabeth Spencer
☎ +44 1332 255363  🖷 +44 1332 255804
Open: Monday 11.00-17.00  Tuesday-Saturday 10.00-17.00
Sunday and public holidays 14.00-17.00

COLLECTION

Built in 1770 by the architect Joseph Pickford as his family home and work premises, the museum contains displays concerning domestic life in the 18th and early 19th century. Period room settings include a dining room, morning room, drawing room, kitchen, Georgian bedroom and a servant's bedroom. There are additional displays of costumes and textiles from the museum's permanent collection, and the Frank Bradley collection of toy theatres.

EXHIBITIONS

until 04·01·98
***The Art of 18th-Century Dress***   As part of the Joseph Wright bicentenary celebrations, this exhibition looks at costume as depicted in his work, accompanied by original 18th-century items from our own collections.

03·05·97-13·07·97
***Silent Companions and the Trials of Fashion***   With life-size cut-out figures, Andrew Brownfoot explores the dark, the ridiculous and the impractical results of fashion and clothing throughout history.

15·11·97-11·01·98
***Nature's Rich Tapestry***   *The Needlepoint Designs of Margaret Murton*   This inspiring and excitingly colourful exhibition by one of the country's leading needlepoint designers combines ready-made works, kits and paintings on wood.

## Dorchester

**DORSET COUNTY MUSEUM**
High West Street  Dorchester Dorset DT1 1XA  Director: Richard de Peyer
☎ +44 1305 262735  🖷 +44 1305 257499
Open: Monday-Friday 10.00-17.00  Jul and Aug Sunday 10.00-17.00
Closed: Saturday and Sunday

COLLECTION

The Dorset County Museum displays the principal county collections of archaeology, natural history and fossil geology, substantial local and rural history galleries and the world's major collection of manuscripts by Thomas Hardy. There is also a reconstruction of Thomas Hardy's study from Max Gate, Dorchester.

EXHIBITIONS

02·05·97-19·06·97
***Sandra Spencer***   *Photographs*   Portland Naval Base prior to its closure.

12·05·97-23·06·97
***George Dannatt***   Important paintings and bronzes from the St. Ives School.

30·06·97-25·08·97
***Elisabeth Frink***   Paintings and bronzes by one of Britain's leading artists whose work attracted international acclaim.

01·09·97-22·09·97
***Dorset Craft Guild***   The work of Dorset's leading craftsmen and women.

29·09·97-17·11·97
***Work of the Dorchester Camera Club***

24·11·97-Jan 98
***Howard Phipps***   Contemporary engravings of landscapes, people and places.

## Durham

**THE BOWES MUSEUM**
Barnard Castle  Durham DL12 8NP  Curator: Elizabeth Conran
☎ +44 1833 690606  🖷 +44 1833 367163
Open: Daily 10.00-17.30 Sunday 14.00-17.00; Oct, Mar, Apr 10.00-17.00
Sunday 14.00-17.00; Nov-Feb 10.00-16.00 Sunday 14.00-16.00

COLLECTION

The Bowes Museum was founded by John Bowes and his wife Josephine in the second half of the 19th century.
The chateau-like building was designed in Second Empire style by a Parisian architect and stands in 20 acres of gardens and parkland surrounded by countryside.
The founders were assiduous collectors of Fine and Decorative Arts of Western Europe, mainly in the time between 1850 and 1874.
The collection of about 1400 paintings covers most European schools and includes works by Sassetta, Primaticcio, Tiepolo, Canaletto, El Greco, Goya, Borgoña, Carreño de Miranda, Champaigne, Boucher, Vernet, Robert, Courbet, Van Heemskerck, Vinckeboons, De Vlieger and Snyders.
The many European and English ceramics are broad in range, taking in majolica, faience, delftware, stoneware etc. and porcelain from numerous well-known factories, such as Sèvres and Meissen. There is also a small collection of Oriental porcelain.
Sculptures, wood-carvings, silverware, glass and ivories form part of the collection as well. In addition, there are examples of tapestry, textiles, needlework and costumes together with dolls, doll's houses and toys. The vaults of the museum contain Prehistoric, Roman, Medieval and Modern archaeological finds of the region and items pertaining to the social history of Teesdale.

EXHIBITIONS

end May 97-mid Jul 97  *Royal Shakespeare Company Exhibition*

Jul 97-Aug 97  *Birds and Plants on the Royal Estates in Scotland*  *James Alder*
Exhibition of paintings made at the Castle of Mey and at Balmoral

Sep 97  *Tom McGuinness*  *Retrospective*  Paintings by one of County Durham's leading artists, based on his experiences as a coal miner.

## Edinburgh

**NATIONAL GALLERY OF SCOTLAND**
The Mound  Edinburgh EH2 2EL  Director: Timothy Clifford
☎ +44 131 5568921  🖷 +44 131 2200917
Open: Monday-Saturday 10.00-17.00  Sunday 14.00-17.00

COLLECTION

The National Gallery of Scotland houses an outstanding collection of paintings, drawings and prints by renowned masters from the Renaissance to Post-Impressionism, and includes works by Velasquez, El Greco, Rembrandt, Vermeer, Turner, Constable, Monet and Van Gogh.

EXHIBITIONS

until 08·06·97  [NATIONAL GALLERY OF SCOTLAND, THE MOUND, EDINBURGH]
*Cassiano dal Pozzo's Paper Museum*  *Drawings from the Royal Collection*  This exhibition of striking images, assembled in Rome by collector and connoisseur Cassiano dal Pozzo (1588-1657), reflects the encyclopaedic range of interests of dal Pozzo, one of the leading thinkers of his age.

13·06·97-21·09·97  [NATIONAL GALLERY OF SCOTLAND, THE MOUND, EDINBURGH]
*Sir Denis Mahon Collection*  Sir Denis Mahon's impressive

collection of 17th and 18th-century Italian paintings includes masterpieces by Guercino, Guido Reni, Domenichino and Annibale Carracci and superb pictures by Luca Giordano, Pietro da Cortona and Johann Liss.

Reaburn, Sir Henry
*Reverend Robert Walker (1755-1808) Skating on Duddingston Loch*
*c. 1795*
in the exhibition 'Reaburn'
© National Gallery of Scotland, Edinburgh

01·08·97-05·10·97

[ROYAL SCOTTISH ACADEMY, PRINCES STREET, EDINBURGH]
***Raeburn*** Sir Henry Raeburn is Scotland's most famous painter. This is the first full exhibition of his work since 1956, and includes between 60 and 70 masterpieces from collections throughout the world.

John Singer Sargent (1856- 1925)
*Lady Agnew of Lochnaw*
in the exhibition 'The portrait of a lady: Sargent and Lady Agnew'
© Scottish National Portrait Gallery, Edinburgh

08·08·97-19·10·97

[NATIONAL GALLERY OF SCOTLAND, THE MOUND, EDINBURGH]
***The Portrait of a Lady*** *Sargent and Lady Agnew*
This exhibition focuses on one of the world's most beautiful female portraits, 'Lady Agnew of Lochnaw' by John Singer Sargent. The exhibition explores Sargent's development as a portrait painter and Lady Agnew's background and lifestyle.

# Edinburgh

## ROYAL MUSEUM OF SCOTLAND (NATIONAL MUSEUMS OF SCOTLAND)
Chambers Street  Edinburgh EH1 1JF  Director: Mark Jones
☎ +44 131 2474106  ⊒≣ +44 131 2474308  Internet: http://www.nms.ac.uk
Open: Monday, Wednesday-Saturday 10.00-17.00 Tuesday 10.00-20.00 Sunday 12.00-17.00

COLLECTION | The National Museums of Scotland present the art, culture, and technology of Scotland to the world, as well as presenting the world to Scotland. In particular, the Royal Museum of Scotland houses a wide variety of international collections covering the decorative arts; science, technology and working life; geology; and natural history. These collections are displayed in the elegant surroundings of one of the finest examples of Victorian architecture, designed by Captain Francis Fowke. Permanent galleries include 'European Art: 1200-1800', 'Western Decorative Art: 1850-2000', 'Twentieth Century Jewellery', 'World in Our Hands', 'Bird Biology', 'Within the Middle East', 'Art and Industry since 1850' and 'The Ivy Wu Gallery: China, Japan and Korea'.

**EXHIBITIONS**

until 08·06·97

*Objects of Our Time - Crafts in the 90's*    An exhibition celebrating the Silver Jubilee of the Crafts Council in Great Britain, featuring new work by fifty craftspeople at the forefront of British comtemporary applied arts.

until 20·07·97

*Khalili Collection of Japanese lacquerware*    A display of Japanese lacquerware from the collection of Dr Khalili in the temporary exhibition area of the recently-opened Ivy Wu Gallery of Chinese, Japanese and Korean art and culture.

03·05·97-29·06·97

*Beauty and the Banknote*    An exhibition from the British Museum in London which explores the scope and significance of images of women on paper money.

18·05·97-13·07·97

*Scottish Potters Association*    A display of work by contemporary Scottish potters.

26·07·97-19·10·97

*Colours of Africa*    This exhibition will coincide with the 'Africa and Scotland 1997' project which is being staged all over Edinburgh. African textiles which have never been seen by the public will be on display.

08·08·97-02·11·97

*Precious Cargo - Scots and the China Trade*    An exhibition examining the rich and exciting story of trade between Europe and East Asia, through India and South East Asia, told through Chinese trade paintings from the 17th to early 20th centuries and trade objects such as ivory, silver, porcelain, lacquer screens and furniture.

Dec 97-Jun 98

*Art and Empire - Treasures from Assyria*    A spectacular exhibition of around 250 pieces of Assyrian art from the British Museum.

# Edinburgh

**SCOTTISH NATIONAL PORTRAIT GALLERY**
1 Queen Street  Edinburgh EH2 1JD  Curator: Duncan Thomson
☎ +44 131 5568921  📠 +44 131 2267649
Open: Monday-Saturday 10.00-17.00  Sunday 14.00-17.00

**COLLECTION**

The Scottish National Portrait Gallery was founded in 1882 to illustrate Scottish history by means of authentic portraits. The collection policy has been broadened over the years to include topographical views of Scotland, contemporary depictions of historical events and portraits that are notable landmarks in the history of Scottish portrait painting. The Gallery also now contains a constantly updated Reference Archive and Social History Index, as well as the Scottish National Photography collection.
Most of the best known figures of Scottish history are represented, including Mary, Queen of Scots, Bonnie Prince Charlie and Robert Burns. Contemporaries include the dress designer Jean Muir, the novelist Muriel Spark and the footballer Danny McGrain.

The distinctive Neo-Gothic building, specifically designed for its current function by Sir Rowand Anderson, is remarkable in its own right. The entrance hall contains a painted frieze showing a progression of the most celebrated Scottish men and women from ancient times to the end of the 19th century. Above are murals illustrating Scottish battles for independence.

**EXHIBITIONS**

until 01·06·97

***Signs and Wonders***  *Photographs by Owen Logan*   This exhibition explores the history of evangelical Christianity in Nigeria. The photographs, taken in Calabar, Southern Nigeria, depict the continuing struggle between the traditional cosmology and that of Christianity.

until 01·06·97

***John Kobal***  *Photographic Portrait Award 1996*   This exhibition features outstanding entries in Britain's leading portrait competition. The award, established in 1993 to encourage aspiring portrait photographers, honours the memory of the renowned authority on cinema and Hollywood portrait photography.

19·06·97-31·08·97

***The Face of Denmark***   Approximately 70 portraits by Danish artists will be on display, including works dating back to 1754, by such painters as Jens Juel and Christen Købke and sculptor Bertel Thorwaldsen.

11·09·97-16·11·97

***Women in White***  *Photographs by Lady Hawarden*   An exhibition of 42 photographs by one of the very few woman photographers from the 1860s. Her photographs, primarily of her daughters, reveal the interior lives and private experience of 19th-century women.

11·09·97-16·11·97

***Eve Arnold***  *In Retrospect*   'In Retrospect' celebrates the work of one of the great Magnum photographers. Eve Arnold has photographed many of the major figures and events of the latter half of the 20th century.

05·12·97-22·02·98

***Stanley Cursiter***   Stanley Cursiter (1887-1976) produced a notable group of avant-garde paintings of street life just before the First World War as well as fine landscape paintings of the rugged cliffs of Orkney.

## Edinburgh

**SCOTTISH NATIONAL GALLERY OF MODERN ART**
**Belford Road  Edinburgh EH4 3DR  Curator: Richard Calvocoressi**
☎ +44 131 5568921  🖷 +44 131 3324939
**Open: Monday-Saturday 10.00-17.00  Sunday 14.00-17.00**

**COLLECTION**

The Scottish National Gallery of Modern Art possesses Scotland's finest collection of 20th-century painting, sculpture and graphic art. The collection includes works by Picasso, Matisse, Magritte, Moore, Baselitz, Davie, Freud, Bellany, Campbell and Wiszniewski.

**EXHIBITIONS**

May 97-Jul 97

***Picasso***  *Works from the Collection and Works on Loan*   The museum's complete Picasso collection is displayed, alongside four loans. Of note are a recently acquired 1913 collage, a portrait of Lee Miller (1937), and a portrait of the artist's mistress, Dora Maar.

end May 97-mid Jul 97

***Botanical Paintings from the Sherwood Collection***   To celebrate the arrival of spring, approximately 35 botanical paintings and drawings from the collection of Shirley Sherwood are on display. Featured artists include Rory McEwan, Francesca Anderson and Margaret Mee.

Paul Delvaux
*Street of the Trams,*
*1938-39*
*in the exhibition 'The*
*Gabrielle Keiller*
*Bequest'*
© *Scottish National*
*Gallery of Modern*
*Art*

05·07·97-14·09·97    **The Gabrielle Keiller Bequest**   *Dada, Surrealism and their Inheritors*
Gabrielle Keiller, who died in 1995, was one of Britain's last great
collectors of Surrealist art. The bequest includes major works by
Bacon, Burra, Dali, Delvaux, Duchamp, Ernst, Magritte, Picabia,
Tanguy and Man Ray.

Oct 97-Nov 97    **New Works by Calum Colvin**   This exhibition of specially-
commissioned photographs by the Glasgow-born artist Calum
Colvin is one of the highlights of the Fotofeis '97 programme. The
new work reflects this year's Fotofeis theme of sexuality.

## Glasgow

**ART GALLERY AND MUSEUM**
Kelvingrove  Glasgow G3 8AG  Director: Julian Spalding
☎ +44 141 3573929  🖷 +44 141 3574537
Open: Monday-Saturday 10.00-17.00  Sunday 11.00-17.00
Closed: 1 Jan, 25 Dec

COLLECTION    The Art Gallery and Museum is housed in a red sandstone building
completed in 1902. The collection includes paintings by Botticelli,
Giorgione, Rembrandt, Millet, Monet, Van Gogh, Derain, Picasso
and Dufy, as well as works by contemporary artists. There are also
displays of historic and modern silver, jewellery, glass and ceramics;
European armour, swords and firearms; and clothing, weapons and
tools from prehistoric times. The museum conducts an extensive
programme of temporary exhibitions.

EXHIBITIONS
09·05·97-Dec 97    **Open Sesame**   An exhibition of previously unseen Islamic artefacts
from Glasgow Museum's own collection, assembled in a sumptuous
setting and arranged thematically to reflect the most important
aspects of Islamic life, religion and culture.

27·06·97-05·09·97    **Pilgrim of the Pen: Ghani al-Ani**   *Master Calligraper*   An exhibition
of traditional and contemporary from this famous Islamic artist,
now based in Paris. Fifty paintings are featured depicting the
superb skill of one of the last masters of the craft.

## Glasgow

**THE BURRELL COLLECTION**
2060 Pollokshaws Road  Glasgow G41 1AT  Director: Julian Spalding
☎ +44 141 6497151  🖷 +44 141 6360086
Open: Wednesday-Monday 10.00-17.00  Sunday 11.00-17.00
Closed: Tuesday and 1 Jan, 25 Dec

COLLECTION    The Burrell Collection, housed in a building of red sandstone,

Portland limestone and timber, three miles south of Glasgow's centre, was assembled by a wealthy shipowner from Glasgow, Sir William Burrell, and contains more than 8000 items. In the Hutton Castle rooms, a reconstruction of rooms in Burrell's home, works from ancient civilisations and decorative arts of Northern Europe are displayed. The Oriental Collection includes Chinese ceramics, jades, bronzes, Japanese prints and a collection of Middle Eastern carpets and rugs. There is also a collection of European paintings, including many fine works by Degas.

**EXHIBITION**
16·05·97-31·08·97

***Europe in India*** *Moghul Paintings and Their European Prototypes*
Part of an Islamic Festival to take place in four Glasgow museums, this exhibition explores the ways in which European art influenced Indian art, at first through illustrated bibles and later through British and Dutch traders.

## Glasgow

**MCLELLAN GALLERIES**
270 Sauchiehall Street  Glasgow G2 3EH  Director: Julian Spalding
☎ +44 141 3311854  📠 +44 141 3329957
Open: Monday-Saturday 10.00-17.00  Sunday 11.00-17.00
Closed: 1 Jan, 25 Dec and between exhibitions

**COLLECTION**

No permanent collection.

**EXHIBITIONS**
22·05·97-07·09·97

***The Birth of Impressionism***   This exhibition gives the public a vivid insight into the story of Impressionism's evolution, beginning with the Salon painters, the early pioneers of painting 'en plein air', the view photographers, and influential foreign artists.

Nov 97-Dec 97

***The Royal Glasgow Institute's 136th Annual Exhibition***   This annual exhibition is open to professional artists and others and aims to display the best of contemporary painting and sculpture in Scotland.

## Glasgow

**GALLERY OF MODERN ART**
Queen Street  Glasgow G1 3AZ  Director: Julian Spalding
☎ +44 141 3311854  📠 +44 141 3329957
Open: Wednesday-Monday 10.00-17.00  Sunday 11.00-17.00
Closed: Tuesday and 1 Jan, 25 Dec

**COLLECTION**

Glasgow's Gallery of Modern Art, which opened in March 1996, is housed in a refurbished neo-classical Georgian building in the heart of the city. The museum collection consists of post-war art and design, including a great many works acquired since 1990 through a specially created modern art fund.
The Gallery is spread over four floors of exhibition space, with each floor linked thematically to one of the four natural elements of fire, earth, water or air. The world-class works on display include pieces by innovators with international reputations, such as Niki de Saint Phalle, David Hockney, Sebastiao Salgado and Eduard Bersudsky, and a diverse cross-section of other international artists from countries as far afield as Papua New Guinea, Ethiopia, Australia and Mexico.
Some of Scotland's best-known artists are also represented in the museum's collection, including Peter Howson, John Bellany, Alan Davie, Adrian Wiszniewski, Steven Campbell and Alison Watt.

Both in exhibitions and in the building itself, contemporary craft and design play an important role, with commissions awarded for the design of public seating, tiling and window recesses as part of the renovation of the building.

**EXHIBITIONS**

until end May 97

***The Lord Provost's Prize*** *Shortlist of Artists* One recent work from each of six shortlisted artists is displayed, with the public voting to determine the prizewinner.

20·06·97-21·09·97

***Contemporary Muslim Art*** This exhibition features the work of three artists from different Muslim backgrounds, all currently working in Britain. As part of the programme, the artists will also work with local communities.

## Grasmere

**THE WORDSWORTH MUSEUM**
**Dove Cottage  Grasmere Cumbria LA22 9SH  Director: Robert Woof**
**☎ +44 15394 35544  📠 +44 15394 35748**
**Internet http://www.dovecott.demon.co.uk.**
**Open: Daily 09.30-17.30**
**Closed: 24-26 Dec and 4 weeks in Jan-Feb**

**COLLECTION**

Dove Cottage was the home of the poet William Wordsworth (1770-1850) from December 1799 until May 1808. It was here that he wrote 'Michael', 'Resolution and Independence', 'Ode: Intimations of Immortality', and 'The Prelude (1805)' in its entirety. The award-winning museum opened to the public in 1935.
The Wordsworth Collection contains primary verse and letter manuscripts of Wordsworth, his family and circle of friends. There is a collection of portraits and printed early editions of these figures including Wordsworth himself, Samuel Taylor Coleridge, Lord Byron, Robert Southey and Thomas De Quincey. The Trust has a fine art collection centring on landscape drawings, paintings and prints emerging from the developing culture surrounding the Lake District, 1750-1850.

**EXHIBITIONS**

Apr 97 - mid Jul 97

***Fay Godwin*** *A Perfect Republic of Shepherds*

end Jul 97-Oct 97

***The Ancient Mariner / Mary Wollstonecraft***

Winter 97 - 98

***Fay Godwin*** *A Perfect Republic of Shepherds*

## Hull

**FERENS ART GALLERY**
**Queen Victoria Square  Hull HU1 3RA  Director: Michael Stanley**
**☎ +44 1482 593902  📠 +44 1482 593710**
**Open: Monday-Saturday 10.00-17.00  Sunday 13.30-16.30**

**COLLECTION**

The Ferens Art Gallery possesses a collection of European and British works of art dating from the 15th century to the present. Chronological displays in the museum begin with Dutch and European Old Masters. Refined 18th-century portraiture, moralising and narrative Victorian images and the radical artistic developments of the early 1900s carry the story into the 20th century, with Post-War art and a varied selection of contemporary works. In addition to these chronological displays, there are marine paintings and local scenes offering insights into Hull's thriving maritime past.

The museum also possesses a Live Art Space and auditorium, where traditional art forms can mix freely with film, video, computers and installations to produce new works, the latest in 'crossover' performance and time-based art.

**EXHIBITIONS**
until 18·05·97

**Jonathan Allen**   *The Float in the Sight of Things*   Using this extraordinary collection as a catalyst, Allen explores our relationship to the material world of objects.

until-01·06·97

**Steve Dilworth**   *Earthing Memories*   Using materials from Hull Museums' natural history collections, Dilworth creates evocative, enigmatic and disturbing sculptures.

17·05·97-15·06·97

**From the Interior**   *Female Perspective on Figuration*
Contemporary women artists from China & Britain.

31·05·97-29·06·97

**Contemporaries**   Contemporary works from the permanent collection.

05·07·97-02·11·97

**Ferens Collection**   Major exhibition of works on paper from the Ferens permanent collection.

11·10·97-25·10·97

**Root 97**   Annual festival of live art, installation and new media.

15·11·97-Jan 98

**The Mag Collection**   Unique exhibition of contemporary British art from the last 20 years from a collection assembled by a private collector. Includes many key figures in British art.

## Kirkcaldy

### KIRKCALDY MUSEUM AND ART GALLERY
**War Memorial Gardens  Kirkcaldy Fife KY1 1YG  Curator: Dallas M. Mechan**
☎ +44 1592 412860  🖷 +44 1592 412870
**Open: Monday-Saturday 10.30-17.00 Sunday 14.00-17.00**

**COLLECTION**

The Kirkcaldy Museum and Art Gallery, set in the attractive garden grounds of the town's War Memorial Gardens, houses a collection of fine and decorative arts of local and national importance. The museum owns what is probably the largest public collection of the works of William McTaggart and Scottish colourist S.J. Peploe existing outside the National Galleries of Scotland.  The collection also includes works by Sickert, Lowry and Cadell, and features an award-winning permanent local history exhibition. A lively changing exhibition programme of art, craft, history and photography runs throughout the year. Tbe museum café features a fine display of Wemyss Ware pottery, the colourful local ceramic ware which was produced in the town between the 1890s and 1930.

**EXHIBITION**
03·05·97-01·06·97

**Reckoning with the Past**   *Contemporary Chinese Painting*   The fractured history of Chinese culture is felt through the mixture of nostalgia, melancholy, political cynicism, and troubled identity expressed in the paintings of 15 contemporary artists. 'Reckoning With the Past' gives a rare opportunity to assess leading artists from the Chinese art world.

# Leeds

**LEEDS CITY ART GALLERY**
The Headrow  Leeds LSl 3AA  Director: Evelyn Silber
☎ +44 113 2478248  📠 +44 113 2449689
Open: Monday-Friday 10.00-17.30  Wednesday 10.00-21.00
Saturday 10.00-16.00
Closed: Sunday and Bank Holiday Mondays and following Tuesdays

**COLLECTION**

The collection includes Old Masters, a representative collection of 19th-century art, including Victorian academic paintings, landscapes by Constable, Turner and Crome, Barbizon paintings and paintings by Sisley, Renoir, Signac and Fantin-Latour. There are works by Derain, Bonnard and others from the early 20th century.

20th-century art is the main focus of the Gallery's collection and covers all the main movements this century from Camden Town through Vorticism to the present day. There are works from the inter-war years by Wadsworth, Spencer and others and the post-war artists include, among others, Francis Bacon, John Walker and Leon Kossoff.

Among the prints and drawings are a collection of Dürer prints and Rembrandt etchings. The English watercolours are strongly represented.

The sculpture collection contains work by Jacob Epstein, Henry Moore, Barbara Hepworth and Eduardo Paolozzi, with some earlier pieces by Canova and Rodin. More recent trends are represented by Richard Long, Bill Woodrow and others.

Interior view of Silver Gallery shows Tony Cragg and Richard Long
© Leeds City Art Gallery, Leeds

**EXHIBITIONS**

until 15·06·97

**Small Truths**  *Repetition and the Obsessional in Contemporary Art*
This exhibition brings together the work of 13 contemporary international artists. In view of the relationship that has long existed between art and madness, the theme of obsession is explored.

Jul 97-Sep 97

**John Tunnard (1900-1971) & Francis Butterfield (1905-?)**  Tunnard's early work was influenced by Surrealism. His later works display clear landscape motifs. Butterfield was an enigmatic figure whose abstract paintings, like those of Tunnard, were derived from the landscape and the figure.

02·10·97-11·01·98

**Francis Towne (1739/40-1816)**  Francis Towne was one of the most remarkable watercolour painters of the late 18th century. This major exhibition of 88 watercolours shows Towne's idiosyncratic approach to landscapes.

07·11·97-Apr 98

**A Sense of Place**  Watercolours from the gallery's collection are juxtaposed with texts from contemporary guidebooks, painting manuals, and artists' letters from the late 18th and early 19th centuries.

# GREAT BRITAIN

## Leicester

**LEICESTERSHIRE MUSEUM AND ART GALLERY**
New Walk  Leicester LE1 7EA  Director: Tim Schadla-Hall
☎ +44 116 2554100  🖷 +44 116 2473011
Open: Daily 10.00-17.30  Sunday 14.00-17.30
Closed: Good Friday, 25, 26 Dec

| | |
|---|---|
| COLLECTION | A major regional venue with local and national collections. New galleries include Variety of Life (natural history), Leicestershire's Rocks (geology), Ancient Egyptians and Discovering Art. The displays range from beautiful decorative arts, including ceramics, silver and glass and the internationally famous German Expressionist collection; to the Rutland Dinosaur, stunning minerals, and hundreds of butterflies. |
| EXHIBITIONS | No details available. |

## Liverpool

**LIVERPOOL MUSEUM**
William Brown Street  Liverpool L3 8EN  Curator: Eric Greenwood
☎ +44 151 4784747  🖷 +44 151 4784390
Open: Monday-Saturday 10.00-17.00  Sunday 12.00-17.00
Closed: 1 Jan, 23-26 Dec

| | |
|---|---|
| COLLECTION | The Liverpool Museum houses a collection with subjects ranging from the wonders of the rain forest to the mysteries of outer space. Permanent displays include a vivarium and an aquarium, historic transport, archaeology, ethnology, the award-winning Natural History Centre, the Time and Space Gallery and a planetarium. |
| EXHIBITION 23·05·97-03·11·97 | *Missing Links Alive*  Displayed in realistic prehistoric settings, a range of lifelike moving models, featuring Australo-pithecines, Homo erectus, Neanderthals and Cro-Magnon cave painters, convey the story of human evolution in an accessible, fun way. |

## Liverpool

**MERSEYSIDE MARITIME MUSEUM**
Albert Dock  Liverpool L3 4AQ  Curator: Mike Stammers
☎ +44 151 2070001  🖷 +44 151 4784590
Open: Daily 10.30-17.00

| | |
|---|---|
| COLLECTION | Merseyside Maritime Museum is one of Europe's largest maritime museums, covering seven acres at the prestigious Albert Dock, Liverpool. It includes full-size, historic vessels, quaysides and two docks. The open-air section of the site, Ships and Quaysides, is open during the summer. The displays reflect the history of the merchant navy, the transatlantic slave trade, emigration, shipping from the 13th century, and the development of the port of Liverpool and its international links. |
| EXHIBITIONS | No exhibitions planned. |

## Liverpool

**TATE GALLERY LIVERPOOL**
Albert Dock  Liverpool L3 4BB  Curator: Lewis Biggs
☎ +44 151 7093223  🖷 +44 151 7093122
Closed: The museum is closed for renovation.  *Reopening May 1998*

ol L3 8EL  Curator: Julian Treuherz
4784190
17.00  Sunday 12.00-17.00

allery houses an outstanding collection of
n 1300 to the present day. It is especially rich in
European Old Masters, Victorian and Pre-Raphaelite paintings and
modern British art. It also houses an award-winning sculpture
gallery.

**EXHIBITIONS**

until 08·06·97 | *Sir Lawrence Alma-Tadema*   Victorian artist Alma-Tadema specialised in paintings of life in classical times and was especially noted for his exquisite rendering of fine detail, exotic flowers, rich fabrics, precious objects and the sheen of marble.

18·07·97-18·09·97 | *Nicholas Horsfield*   Celebrating the artist's 80th birthday, this retrospective exhibition includes some 60 paintings and 40 drawings and watercolours which reflect the style and personality of a individual artist who never abandoned his roots in the north west.

Nov 97-Feb 98 | *John Moores Liverpool Exhibition 20*   Viewed as a barometer of the state of British painting for the last 40 years, the John Moores Liverpool Exhibition will be held for the 20th time.

# London

**ROYAL ACADEMY OF ARTS**
**Burlington House  Piccadilly London W1V 0DS  Director: Pears Rodgers**
☎ +44 171 4397438  📠 +44 171 4340837
**Open: Daily 10.00-18.00**

**COLLECTION** | Founded in 1768 by King George III, the Royal Academy of Arts was the first British institution devoted to the promotion of the visual arts. Famous for its annual Summer Exhibition and for its unrivalled programme of international loan exhibitions, today it welcomes up to one million visitors each year. The Academy also has a permanent art collection which includes one of only four sculptures by Michelangelo outside Italy. Michelangelo's 'Tondo' is on permanent display outside the award-winning Sackler Galleries (1991) designed bij Sir Norman Foster.

**EXHIBITIONS** | [SACKLER GALLERIES]

until 08·06·97 | *The Berlin of George Grosz*   *Drawings, Watercolours and Prints 1912-1930*   Grosz was a merciless satirist and an astute social commentator whose graphic work describes life in Germany from the end of the First World War, through economic and political crisis, to the rise of Fascism.

03·07·97-28·09·97 | *Hiroshige*   *Images of Mist, Rain, Moon and Snow*   Hiroshige (1797-1858) was one of the greatest Japanese masters of the coloured woodcut. He explored the possibilities of atmospheric landscape, and his prints give a vivid picture of Japanese society in the 19th century.

13·11·97-08·02·98 | *Victorian Fairy Painting (Working Title)*   This exhibition examines the phenomenon, from the mid-19th century until the outbreak of

## Leicester

### LEICESTERSHIRE MUSEUM AND ART GALLERY
New Walk  Leicester LE1 7EA  Director: Tim Schadla-Hall
☎ +44 116 2554100  📠 +44 116 2473011
Open: Daily 10.00-17.30  Sunday 14.00-17.30
Closed: Good Friday, 25, 26 Dec

| | |
|---|---|
| COLLECTION | A major regional venue with local and national collections. New galleries include Variety of Life (natural history), Leicestershire's Rocks (geology), Ancient Egyptians and Discovering Art. The displays range from beautiful decorative arts, including ceramics, silver and glass and the internationally famous German Expressionist collection; to the Rutland Dinosaur, stunning minerals, and hundreds of butterflies. |
| EXHIBITIONS | No details available. |

## Liverpool

### LIVERPOOL MUSEUM
William Brown Street  Liverpool L3 8EN  Curator: Eric Greenwood
☎ +44 151 4784747  📠 +44 151 4784390
Open: Monday-Saturday 10.00-17.00  Sunday 12.00-17.00
Closed: 1 Jan, 23-26 Dec

| | |
|---|---|
| COLLECTION | The Liverpool Museum houses a collection with subjects ranging from the wonders of the rain forest to the mysteries of outer space. Permanent displays include a vivarium and an aquarium, historic transport, archaeology, ethnology, the award-winning Natural History Centre, the Time and Space Gallery and a planetarium. |
| EXHIBITION 23·05·97-03·11·97 | *Missing Links Alive*   Displayed in realistic prehistoric settings, a range of lifelike moving models, featuring Australo-pithecines, Homo erectus, Neanderthals and Cro-Magnon cave painters, convey the story of human evolution in an accessible, fun way. |

## Liverpool

### MERSEYSIDE MARITIME MUSEUM
Albert Dock  Liverpool L3 4AQ  Curator: Mike Stammers
☎ +44 151 2070001  📠 +44 151 4784590
Open: Daily 10.30-17.00

| | |
|---|---|
| COLLECTION | Merseyside Maritime Museum is one of Europe's largest maritime museums, covering seven acres at the prestigious Albert Dock, Liverpool. It includes full-size, historic vessels, quaysides and two docks. The open-air section of the site, Ships and Quaysides, is open during the summer. The displays reflect the history of the merchant navy, the transatlantic slave trade, emigration, shipping from the 13th century, and the development of the port of Liverpool and its international links. |
| EXHIBITIONS | No exhibitions planned. |

## Liverpool

### TATE GALLERY LIVERPOOL
Albert Dock  Liverpool L3 4BB  Curator: Lewis Biggs
☎ +44 151 7093223  📠 +44 151 7093122
Closed: The museum is closed for renovation. *Reopening May 1998*

## Liverpool

**WALKER ART GALLERY**
William Brown Street  Liverpool L3 8EL  Curator: Julian Treuherz
☎ +44 151 2070001  ⊒ +44 151 4784190
Open: Monday-Saturday 10.00-17.00  Sunday 12.00-17.00
Closed: 1 Jan, 23-26 Dec

COLLECTION

The Walker Art Gallery houses an outstanding collection of European art from 1300 to the present day. It is especially rich in European Old Masters, Victorian and Pre-Raphaelite paintings and modern British art. It also houses an award-winning sculpture gallery.

EXHIBITIONS

until 08·06·97

*Sir Lawrence Alma-Tadema*   Victorian artist Alma-Tadema specialised in paintings of life in classical times and was especially noted for his exquisite rendering of fine detail, exotic flowers, rich fabrics, precious objects and the sheen of marble.

18·07·97-18·09·97

*Nicholas Horsfield*   Celebrating the artist's 80th birthday, this retrospective exhibition includes some 60 paintings and 40 drawings and watercolours which reflect the style and personality of a individual artist who never abandoned his roots in the north west.

Nov 97-Feb 98

*John Moores Liverpool Exhibition 20*   Viewed as a barometer of the state of British painting for the last 40 years, the John Moores Liverpool Exhibition will be held for the 20th time.

## London

**ROYAL ACADEMY OF ARTS**
Burlington House  Piccadilly London W1V 0DS  Director: Pears Rodgers
☎ +44 171 4397438  ⊒ +44 171 4340837
Open: Daily 10.00-18.00

COLLECTION

Founded in 1768 by King George III, the Royal Academy of Arts was the first British institution devoted to the promotion of the visual arts. Famous for its annual Summer Exhibition and for its unrivalled programme of international loan exhibitions, today it welcomes up to one million visitors each year. The Academy also has a permanent art collection which includes one of only four sculptures by Michelangelo outside Italy. Michelangelo's 'Tondo' is on permanent display outside the award-winning Sackler Galleries (1991) designed bij Sir Norman Foster.

EXHIBITIONS

[SACKLER GALLERIES]

until 08·06·97

*The Berlin of George Grosz*   *Drawings, Watercolours and Prints 1912-1930*   Grosz was a merciless satirist and an astute social commentator whose graphic work describes life in Germany from the end of the First World War, through economic and political crisis, to the rise of Fascism.

03·07·97-28·09·97

*Hiroshige*   *Images of Mist, Rain, Moon and Snow*   Hiroshige (1797-1858) was one of the greatest Japanese masters of the coloured woodcut. He explored the possibilities of atmospheric landscape, and his prints give a vivid picture of Japanese society in the 19th century.

13·11·97-08·02·98

*Victorian Fairy Painting (Working Title)*   This exhibition examines the phenomenon, from the mid-19th century until the outbreak of the First World War, whereby painters frequently chose fairy subjects for their works.

[MAIN GALLERIES]

01·06·97-10·08·97 **229th Summer Exhibition**   The Royal Academy's annual Summer Exhibition brings together paintings, sculptures, drawings and models by many of Britain's most distinguished artists and architects.

22·01·98-12·04·98 **English Public Collections (Working Title)**   This major exhibition celebrates the artistic treasures of England's regional museums. It includes works by artists such as Canaletto, Titian, Hogarth, Burne-Jones, Canova, Giacometti, Stanley Spencer and Francis Bacon.

[SCHOOLS STUDIOS]

Jul 97 **Royal Academy Schools Final Year Show**   Work by some of Britain's most promising young artists who have completed their three-year postgraduate course at the Royal Academy Schools.

## London

**THE EUROPEAN ACADEMY & THE ACCADEMIA ITALIANA**
8 Grosvenor Place  London SW1X 7SH   Director: Rosa Maria Letts
☎ +44 171 2350303  ☷ +44 171 2350404
Open: Tuesday-Saturday 10.00-17.20  Sunday 12.00-17.30
Closed: Monday

COLLECTION  |  No permanent collection.

EXHIBITION
13·05·97-20·07·97 **Serenissima, The Arts of Fashion in Venice from the 13th to the 18th Century**   A first major study of a remarkable era in the history of fashion in which Venice was 'La Serenissima', the exhibition includes over 180 works from both private and public collections ranging from costumes, prints and paintings to tools of the trade.

## London

**BARBICAN ART GALLERY**
Level 3 Barbican Centre  London EC2Y 8DS  Director: Melvyn Barnes
☎ +44 171 6384141  ☷ +44 171 6280364
Open: Monday-Saturday 10.00-18.45  Tuesday 10.00-17.45
Closed: Sunday

COLLECTION  |  No permanent collection.

EXHIBITIONS
until 26·05·97 **Modern Art in Britain**   The exhibition conveys the enormous impact which Modernism had on artistic life in Britain, and demonstrates how British critics and selectors strongly influenced what is now the accepted canon of European Modernist artists.

until 26·05·97 **Lucie Rie & Hans Coper**  *Potters in Parallel*   One of the exhibition's main features is the tableware produced through the artists' joint efforts between 1949 and 1958; it then studies both careers in the 60s and 70s, focusing on Rie's and Coper's interpretations of vessels.

19·06·97-17·08·97 **Serious Games**   'Serious Games' features artists who challenge our preconceptions of what is to exist in a world where human interaction is often mediated by the computer.

19·06·97-17·08·97 **Marc Riboud in China**  *Forty Years of Photography*

11·09·97-14·12·97    *James Ensor (1860-1949)*    The exhibition provides a rare opportunity to see paintings, drawings and etchings spanning the entire career of this highly individual and influential artist.

11·09·97-14·12·97    *Don McCullin*    The exhibition tells the compelling story of this photojournalist from 1959 to the present day. It features 250 prints covering McCullin's war work and the photographer's more recent atmospheric still-life and landscape photographs.

## London

**THE BRITISH MUSEUM**
**Great Russell Street  London WC1B 3DG  Director: R.G.W. Anderson**
☎ **+44 171 6361555**   **+44 171 3238118**
**Internet http://www.british-museum.ac.uk**
**Open: Monday-Saturday 10.00-17.00  Sunday 14.30-18.00**
**Closed: 1 Jan, 28 Mar, 5 May, 24-26 Dec**

COLLECTION

Founded in 1753, the British Museum has a large collection of works of man stemming from Prehistoric times until the present day. There are permanent displays of antiquities from Egypt, Western Asia, Greece, Rome and the Orient, as well as collections of works from the Prehistoric, Romano-British, Medieval, Renaissance and Modern periods. The museum's collections of prints and drawings, coins and medals and Japanese antiquities are displayed in a series of temporary exhibitions, while the Ethnographic collections are housed at the Museum of Mankind.

Upper part of a colossal statue of Ramesses II. From Thebes, 19th Dynasty, c. 1250 BC © The British Museum , London

Examples of the artefacts which can be viewed at the British Museum include the following: The Rosetta Stone and Egyptian mummies (Egyptian antiquities), sculptures from the Parthenon, the Mausoleum of Halicarnassus and the Temple of Artemis at Ephesus, and the Portland Vase (Greek and Roman antiquities), the Sutton Hoo Treasure, Lewis Chessmen, and the 'Nef' Ships Clock (Medieval and Later antiquities), Indian sculptures from Amaravati and Chinese porcelain (Oriental antiquities), the Lindow Man and the Mildenhall Treasure (Prehistoric and Romano-British antiquities), and Assyrian lionhunt reliefs and the Oxus Treasure (Western Asiatic antiquities).
Recently the museum opened a new gallery 'The Hellenistic World' and more galleries are planned for the next year.

EXHIBITIONS
until 20·07·97

*Ancient Faces*   *Mummy Portraits from Roman Egypt*

03·05·97-13·07·97   *Far Eastern and Near Eastern Greenwares*

| 15·05·97-07·9·97 | *The Ceramic Art of Sawada Chitojin* |
|---|---|
| 15·05·97-07·09·97 | *Styles of Japanese Pottery and Porcelain* |
| 20·05·97-14·09·97 | *Coin Jewellery* |
| 23·05·97-14·09·97 | *Printmaking in Paris*  Picasso and his Contemporaries |
| 23·05·97-14·09·97 | *Modernism in French Medal Design* |
| 11·0·97-2000 | *Arts of Korea* |
| 16·09·97-07·12·98 | *From Persepolis to the Punjab*  Coins and the Exploration of the East |
| 25·09·97-04·01·98 | *Ogawa Toshu*  Modern Japanese Calligraphy |
| 03·10·97-Jan 98 | *Cartier 1900-1939* |
| Oct 97-begin Jan 98 | *Hogarth and his Times* |
| Oct 97-begin Jan 98 | *The Schilling Bequest of German Renaissance Drawings* |
| 06·12·97-Feb 98 | *Modern Chinese Calligraphy* |
| 09·12·97-01·03·98 | *Writing Arabic* |
| 23·01·98-12·04·97 | *Islamic and Indian Paintings and Drawings from the Collection of Prince Sadruddin Aga Khan* |
| Apr 98-Sep 98 | *Maori* |

## London

**COURTAULD GALLERY**
**Somerset House  Strand  London WC2  Director: John Murdoch**
☎ **+44 171 8732526** 📠 **+44 171 8732589**
**Internet http://www.kcl.ac.uk/inst/courtauld/int.htm**
**Open: Daily 10.00-18.00  Sunday 14.00-18.00**
**Due to renovation the Gallery will be closed from 31-08-97 until 01-07-1998**

COLLECTION | A fine collection of Impressionist paintings in Britain, as well as masterpieces by Botticelli, Tiepolo, Rubens, and Goya, housed in Somerset House, one of the most beautiful 18th-century buildings in London.

EXHIBITIONS | No details available

## London

**DESIGN MUSEUM**
**28 Shad Thames  London SE12 2YD  Director: Paul Thompson**
☎ **+44 171 4036933** 📠 **+44 171 3786540**
**Open: Monday-Friday 11.30-18.00  Saturday, Sunday 12.00-18.00**
**Closed: 25, 26 Dec**

COLLECTION | The Design Museum offers visitors a readily accessible insight into the role that design plays in our everyday lives, from the origins of mass production to the present day. The Collection Gallery on the top floor of the museum provides examples of the development of design in mass production. It is organised into a series of thematic displays showing changes in use and meaning, and the origins of mass production. Many displayed items and methods are still in use today. The Review Gallery examines contemporary design in an international context. On display are concepts, prototypes and finished products from furniture to cameras and cars to computers, providing visitors with an unparalleled opportunity in this country to see some of the most innovative products produced by designers from all over the world. Both these galleries host exciting programmes of regularly changing displays which profile a single product, designer or company in greater depth. Graphic and photographic displays are held in the foyer of the museum.

**EXHIBITION**

Oct 97-Apr 98

*Bicycle*    This exhibition will trace the historical development of the bicycle since the early 1800s to the present day.

# London

**DULWICH PICTURE GALLERY**
**College Road  London SE21 7AD   Director: Desmond Shawe-Taylor**
☎ **+44 181 6935254   ⓕ +44 181 6930923**
**Open: Tuesday-Friday 10.00-17.00  Saturday 11.00-17.00  Sunday 14.00-17.00**
**Closed: Monday and public holidays**

**COLLECTION**

Dulwich Picture Gallery has an outstanding collection of Old Master paintings, primarily from 17th-century artists, as well as many well-known 18th-century artists.
The collection came into existence as a result of political events in 17th-century Europe. A London art dealer named Noel Desenfans was commissioned by the King of Poland to acquire paintings for a Polish national collection, but the king was forced to abdicate his throne and the pictures were left without a home. An heir of Desenfans, Sir Francis Bourgeois, established the gallery in Dulwich. The building was designed for the collection in 1811 by Sir John Soane and was Britain's first public art gallery. The founders of the Gallery lie in the mausoleum which Soane designed for them in the centre of the Gallery.

Francesco Zuccarelli
*Landscape with a*
*fountain, figures &*
*cattle*
© Dulwich Picture
Gallery, London

**EXHIBITIONS**

until 01·06·97

*The Inner Eye   Art Beyond the Visible*    This exhibition looks at artistic representations of the invisible, inner world in art and popular culture since the Middle Ages. Dreams, fantasies, visions, the supernatural, witchcraft, fairies, devils and angels, ecstasy and miracles are all explored.

25·06·97-Sep 97

*Stehpen Cox at Dulwich Picture Gallery*    A retrospective of the work of sculptor Stephen Cox.

Mar 98-May 98

*Italy and British Art in the Age of Turner*

## London

### HAYWARD GALLERY
Belvedere Road  London SE1 8XZ  Director: Susan Ferleger Brades
☎ +44 171 9283144  📠 +44 171 4012664
Open: Daily 10.00-18.00  Tuesday, Wednesday 10.00-20.00

| | |
|---|---|
| **COLLECTION** | No permanent collection. |

**EXHIBITIONS**

19·06·97-17·08·97 — ***The Harlem Renaissance (Working Title)***  This multi-media presentation focuses on the cultural revolution of the 1920s known as the Harlem Renaissance, and includes photos, paintings, and rare archive sound and film footage of the great jazz musicians, and of singer and activist Paul Robeson.

19·06·97-17·08·97 — ***Tatsuo Miyajima***  *Big Time*  The first major UK exhibition of one of Japan's most dynamic young artists. Using the universal language of numbers, Miyajima investigates the nature of time, space and infinity.

Oct 97-Jan 98 — ***Objects of Desire***  *The Modern Still Life*  Exploring the traditional genre of the still life, this major exhibition draws together 150 of the most significant 20th-century still life paintings and sculptures, by more than 60 leading artists.

## London

### ICA INSTITUTE OF CONTEMPORARY ARTS
The Mall  London SW1Y 5AH  Director: Philip Dodd
☎ +44 171 9300493  📠 +44 171 8730051
Open: Daily 12.00-19.30  Friday 12.00-21.00

| | |
|---|---|
| **COLLECTION** | No permanent collection. |

**EXHIBITIONS**

until 15·06·97 — ***Billy Name***  *Factory \*\*Fotos\*\* 1964-1968*  Known as Factory \*\*Fotographer\*\*, this artist created over 1500 photographs which record the legendary events, milieu and atmosphere of the 60s' most famous Underground phenomenon.

12·07·97-28·09·97 — ***Assuming Positions***  An exhibition concerning the multifarious positions assumed by artists in contemporary culture.

22·10·97-Dec 97 — ***Made in Italy***  Including the work of Vanessa Beecroft, Grazia Toderi, Miltos Manetas, Vedova Mazzei, Mario Airo, Maurizio Cattelan, Franco Silvestro and Margerita Manzelli.

Spring 98-Summer 98 — ***Future Systems***  The designs of Future Systems testify to the potential of 'advanced technology architecture at a time when most architects have fled from the leading edge into the imagined safety of the past' (Martin Pawley).

## London

### LEIGHTON HOUSE MUSEUM & ART GALLERY
12 Holland Park Road  London W14 8LZ  Director: Julia Findlater
☎ +44 171 6023316  📠 +44 171 3712467
Open: Monday-Saturday 11.00-17.30
Closed: Sunday and public holidays

| | |
|---|---|
| **COLLECTION** | Leighton House was the home of Frederic, Lord of Leighton (1830-1896), the great Classical painter and President of the Royal Academy. The house was built between 1864 and 1879 to designs |

by George Aitchison, and is the expression of Leighton's vision of a private palace devoted to art.

The Arab Hall is the centrepiece of Leighton House. The gilt mosaic frieze, depicting birds and scenes of mythology, the sound of the fountain in the centre of the Arab Hall, and the intricate designs of the Isnik tiles all create an extraordinary oriental ambiance. This atmosphere extends throughout the other rooms of the house, culminating in Leighton's Studio, which is the heart of the house and the reason for its existence. Leighton House contains a fine collection of Victorian art. Paintings by Leighton, Burne-Jones, Millais and their contemporaries are displayed throughout the House. There is also an extensive exhibition programme in the adjacent art galleries.

**EXHIBITIONS**

19·05·97-31·05·97   *Piers De Laszlo*   *Travel Paintings*

09·06·97-21·06·97   *Suad al Attar*   Paintings inspired by Iraqi myths and legends.

14·07·97-02·08·97   *The Kensington and Chelsea Artists' Exhibition*   Open exhibition for local artists, young and old.

22·09·97-04·10·97   *Charles and Patricia Lester*   An exhibition of interior textiles by the internationally renowned fashion designers.

13·10·97-15·11·97   *Iniva*   Specially commissioned work by artist-in-residence.

24·11·97-06·12·97   *Marian Wenzel*   Paintings inspired by the conflict in Bosnia.

15·12·97-10·01·98   *Tales from the Arabian Nights: A Victorian Fantasy*   Book illustrations, pantomime designs and toy theatres. Special events for children.

# London

**MUSEUM OF MANKIND -**
**THE ETHNOGRAPHY DEPT. OF THE BRITISH MUSEUM**
6 Burlington Gardens   London W1X 2EX   Director: J. Mack
☎ +44 171 6361555   🖪 +44 171 3238013
Open: Monday-Saturday 10.00-17.00   Sunday 14.30-18.00
Closed: 1 Jan, 28 Mar, 5 May, 24-26 Dec

**COLLECTION**

**Ethnography**   The Museum of Mankind is the British Museum's Department of Ethnography. Its main concern is studying and collecting items from recent and contemporary Indigenous societies in Africa, the Americas, Asia, Oceania and parts of Europe. The archaeology of sub-Saharan Africa is also a subject of one of the museum's collections.

Examples of items on display include Benin bronzes and ivories from West Africa, textiles and wood sculpture from West and Central Africa, stone and mosaic work from pre-Columbian times and Meso-America, collections made in the Pacific and on the north-west coast of America during the voyage of Captain Cook and Vancouver, and the Raffles collection from the early 19th century.

**EXHIBITIONS**

until 31·12·97   *Stairways to the Sky*   *Rice and Life in the Philippines*

until 31·12·97   *Great Benin*   *A West African Kingdom*

until 31·12·97   *Treasures from the Ethnographic Collection*

until 31·12·97   *The Gilded Image*   *Pre-Columbian Gold from Central and South America*

| until 31·12·97 | *Tent Felts from Kyrgyzstan* |
| Jun 97-31·12·97 | *Patagonia*   *The Uttermost End of the Earth* |
| 03·07·97-31·12·97 | *Pottery in the Making*   *World Ceramic Traditions* |

## London

**THE NATIONAL GALLERY**
Trafalgar Square  London WC2N 5DN  Director: Neil MacGregor
☎ +44 171 7472885  📠 +44 171 9304764
Open: Monday-Saturday 10.00-18.00  Wednesday 10.00-20.00
Sunday 12.00-18.00
Closed: 1 Jan, Good Friday, 24-26 Dec

**COLLECTION**

The National Gallery houses the national collection of Western European painting, comprising more than 2 000 pictures dating from the late 13th to the early 20th century: in other words, from Giotto to Picasso. The pictures belong to the public and access to them is free, as it has been since the Gallery was founded in 1824. All pictures are normally on show.

The Gallery's unique strength lies in the balance of the collection across all European schools. Virtually all the great artists are represented by masterpieces and the collection is hung to emphasise the international nature of European painting at all periods since the Renaissance.

The Sainsbury Wing (Painting from 1260 to 1510) exhibits works by Van Eyck, Piero della Francesca, Botticelli, Leonardo da Vinci, Bellini, Raphael and others. Paintings by artists such as Cranach, Michelangelo, Holbein, Titian, Veronese and El Greco are on display in the West Wing (Painting from 1510 to 1600), while in the North Wing (Painting from 1600 to 1700) works by Rubens, Poussin, Velázquez, Van Dyck, Claude, Rembrandt and Vermeer can be viewed. Canvasses by Gainsborough, Turner, Constable, Cézanne, Monet, Van Gogh, Seurat and Picasso are exhibited in the East Wing (Painting from 1700 to 1920).

**EXHIBITIONS**

[SAINSBURY WING]

until 18·05·97

***Discovering the Italian Baroque***  *The Denis Mahon Collection*   An outstanding collection of 17th and 18th-century Italian paintings including works by Guercino, Guido Reni, Domenichino and Annibale Carracci.

Seurat
***Bathers at Asnières***
*in the exhibition*
*Seurat and The*
*Bathers*
© *The National*
*Gallery, London*

02·07·97-28·09·97

***Seurat and The Bathers***   This exhibition brings together Seurat's great masterpiece 'Bathers at Asnières' with virtually all its preparatory drawings and oil sketches. It also shows the diversity of his sources, from Poussin to Pissarro.

| | |
|---|---|
| 05·11·97-01·02·98 | **Making & Meaning   Holbein's 'Ambassadors'**   Holbein's newly conserved painting of the two ambassadors to the Court of Henry VIII is the centrepiece of this exhibition. The artist's technique and the political and religious background of the work are examined.<br><br>[SUNLEY ROOM] |
| until 22·06·97 | **Back to the Future**   *Student Interpretations of National Gallery Paintings* |
| 16·07·97-14·09·97 | **Themes and Variations   Sleep**   An exploration of the manner in which artists have portrayed the sleeping figure and the variety of meanings they have ascribed to sleep. |
| 15·10·97-18·01·98 | **Hogarth's 'Marriage A-la-Mode'**   This exhibition examines the artist's 'modern moral subject' — the six paintings comprising 'Marriage A-la-Mode'.<br><br>[ROOM 1] |
| until 08·06·97 | **Dürer's 'Saint Jerome'**   Dürer's 'Saint Jerome', recently acquired by the Gallery, is on display, along with prints and watercolours reflecting his preoccupations as he painted this small double-sided picture. |
| 18·06·97-07·09·97 | **Cranach**   *A Closer Look*   The National Gallery's Cranachs are exhibited, along with three of his works on loan from the Statens Museum for Kunst in Copenhagen. |

## London

**NATURAL HISTORY MUSEUM**
Cromwell Road  London SW7 5BD  Director: Neil Chalmers
☎ +44 171 9389123  ⊞ +44 171 9389267
Open: Monday-Saturday 10.00-17.50  Sunday 11.00-17.50
Closed: 23-26 Dec

| | |
|---|---|
| COLLECTION | The museum is home of national collections of living and fossil animals and plants, rocks and meteorites and the finest dinosaur exhibition for 65 million years. In addition, there are various interactive exhibitions, including Ecology, Creepy Crawlies, Human Biology, Discovering Mammals and the Origin of Species. |
| EXHIBITIONS<br>18·05·97-31·08·97 | **Gobi Desert Dinosaurs**   The exhibition focuses on the dinosaur specimens found in the Mongolian desert from the 1920s to the present day and includes skeletons and eggs which have never been seen before in the UK. |
| Winter 97 onwards | **From the Beginning**   This new permanent exhibition explores the formation of the Earth, from the condensation of matter and the solar system's formation to the beginning of life and the migration of the continental plates. |
| Winter 97 onwards | **Earth's Treasury**   A new permanent display of minerals and gemstones, in which the basics of mineral and crystal structure are also explained. |

## London

**NATIONAL MARITIME MUSEUM**
Romney Road, Greenwich  London SE10 9NF  Director: Richard Ormond
☎ +44 181 8584422  ⊞ +44 181 3126632
Open: Daily 10.00-17.00
Closed: 24-26 Dec

**COLLECTION**

Accommodated in historical buildings, the museum rotates displays of its extensive international holdings of marine art, ship models, globes, plans, navigational and astronomical instruments and historic manuscripts. A reconstruction project (1996-1999) has reduced the permanent gallery displays.

The 20th-century Seapower Gallery uses videos and reconstructions to illustrate advances in both military and merchant shipping.

The Old Royal Observatory delineates the Greenwich Meridian, Longitude 0, and contains Harrison's marine chronometers and many of the other clocks that helped to make Greenwich famous as the reference for international time zones. The Queen's House, designed by Inigo Jones, was built for the wives of Stuart monarchs and is decorated in the vivid colours favoured by the flamboyant Henrietta Maria. The marine art collection is also noteworthy. Library, book publishing, education, and photo library and research facilities are available.

**EXHIBITION**

onwards

*Nelson*   Using Nelson's possessions, this exhibition sets the scene of conflict between Britain and France, in which Nelson achieved fame. Illustrated with impressive tableaux, oil paintings and artefacts, the displays depict major naval actions and the popular acclaim for a man who died at the moment of his greatest victory.

## London

### NATIONAL PORTRAIT GALLERY
Saint Martin's Place  London WC2H OHE  Director: Charles Saumarez Smith
☎ +44 171 3060055  📠 +44 171 3060058
Open: Daily 10.00-18.00  Sunday 12.00-18.00

**COLLECTION:**

The National Portrait Gallery was founded in 1856 to collect the likenesses of famous British men and women. Today the collection is the most comprehensive of its kind in the world and constitutes a unique record of the men and women who created (and are still creating) the history and culture of the nation. The Gallery houses a primary collection of over nine thousand works, as well as an immense archive. There is no restriction on medium - there are oil paintings, watercolours, drawings, miniatures, sculptures, caricatures, silhouettes and photographs.

View of the Victorian
Galleries
© *National Portrait
Gallery, London*

The collection, arranged chronologically, begins on the top floor (level 5) with the Tudors and their predecessors. Each room has a particular historical theme. The collection includes: Holbein's Cartoon of Henry VIII, the 'Ditchley' portrait of Queen Elizabeth I and the 'Chandos' portrait of Shakespeare. Among the Victorians (level 3) are the portraits of Queen Victoria, Prince Albert, politicians, scientists, artists, writers and explorers of the era. The early 20th-century Galleries (level 2) cover the period from 1914 to 1945. The display includes First World War portraits and a fine collection of the War Poets. Politicians, scientists, sportsmen and major figures from all sections of the arts are displayed alongside a superb collection of Bloomsbury portraits. The late 20th-century Galleries (level 1) feature contemporary portraits from 1945 to the present day. The collection includes works by Andy Warhol, David Hockney, Allen Jones and Lucian Freud.

**EXHIBITIONS**

until 26·05·97

*Variations on a Theme*   *150 Years of Photographs of British Composers*   A celebration of the extraordinary diversity (and occasional eccentricity) of musical creativity in Britain over the last 150 years.

until 08·06·97

*August Sander*   *In Photography there are no Unexplained Shadows* This exhibition covers all aspects of Sander's work, including the series of uncompromisingly direct photographs in which he recorded rural and urban society in Germany, both before and after the First World War.

30·05·97-07·09·97

*Pursuit of Beauty*   *Five Centuries of Body Adornment in Britain* Interactive elements explore the persistent quest for beauty by both sexes. The visitor can also try on wigs, ruffs, farthingales, top hats, corsets and doublets.

13·06·97-28·09·97

*Clifford Coffin*   Coffin is known to admirers as the greatest of Vogue's 'lost' photographers. For over a decade, in London, Paris and New York, Coffin produced some of Vogue's most impeccable fashion photographs.

26·06·97-05·10·97

*BP Portrait Award and BP Travel Award 1997*

19·09·97-11·01·98

*Glenys Barton*   Barton's ceramic heads and portraits exploit her use of an unusual medium in a way that is unique among sculptors. This exhibition traces the development in her work and includes recent portraits of friends and family.

17·10·97-11·01·98

*John Kobal Photographic Portrait Award 1997*

24·10·97-01·02·98

*Sir Henry Raeburn (1756-1823)*   A major loan exhibition of Raeburn's portraits, shown to illuminate a whole society - that of Edinburgh and Scotland in the era of the late 'Enlightenment' - in a way that is unparalleled.

20·11·97-end Feb 98

*Bruce Weber*   *Retrospective*

## London

### THE SERPENTINE GALLERY
Kensington Gardens  London WC2 3XA  Director: Julia Peyton-Jones
☎ +44 171 4026075  🖷 +44 171 4024103
Open: Daily 10.00-18.00  Oct 97-Feb 98 10.00-16.00

**COLLECTION**

No permanent collection.

**EXHIBITIONS**

until Sep 97

*Inside Out*   *Artists' Commissions on the Gallery Lawn*
During the year-long renovation of the Serpentine, the Gallery is exhibiting five major sculptural commissions on the lawn outside the building.

21·05·97-22·06·97   **Anya Gallaccio**   An outdoor installation which the artist describes as 'monumentally invisible'. Recent works have involved the use of materials which are perceptibly corrupted by the passage of time, such as ice blocks, salt pillars and flowers.

01·07·97-07·09·97   **Tadashi Kawamata**   Kawamata's project consists of materials retrieved from the demolition of the Gallery building prior to its renovation. The artist will use internal and external doors, windows and staircases to create a structural framework reflecting the Serpentine's architecture.

## London

**SIR JOHN SOANE'S MUSEUM**
13 Lincoln's Inn Fields  London WC2A 3BP  Director: P.K. Thornton
☎ +44 171 4052107  ▤ +44 171 8313957
Open: Tuesday-Saturday 10.00-17.00 and on first Tuesday of each month
18.00-21.00
Closed: Sunday, Monday and public holidays

COLLECTION

**Architecture**   Sir John Soane (1753-1837), one of the leading British architects of his time, designed and built No. 13 Lincoln's Inn Fields both as his private residence and to house his collection of paintings, drawings, sculpture and antiquities.
The architecture reflects his own personal style with shallow vaulted ceilings, mirrors to reflect and suggest extensions of space, planes opening to reveal more pictures hung behind, openings between rooms and in floors to give unusual views, and many overhead skylights often incorporating coloured glass which provide dramatic and picturesque lighting. The collection contains architectural models of classical buildings and Soane's own architectural works.
**Old Masters**   The painting include two series by Hogarth, 'The Rake's Progress' and 'An Election', and works by Canaletto, Watteau, Reynolds, Lawrence, Turner and Piranesi.
**Sculpture**   Original marbles and plasters by Bandini, Quellin, Flaxman, Westmacott, Chantry, Banks, and others are on display.
**Antiquities**   Works on display include the alabaster sarcophagus of Seti I of Egypt (c. 1300 B.C.), fragments from the Erectheum, the Pantheon, originals and casts of architectural and sculptural fragments, and Greek fragments.
**Drawings**   The Research Library houses an important collection of 30 000 architectural drawings by Thorpe, Wren, Kent, Chambers, Adam, both Dances, and Soane, as well as others Italian drawings from the 16th to 18th century.

EXHIBITIONS
until-31·08·97

**Hogarth's Rake's Progress**   *A Tercentenary Exhibition.*

Oct 97-Mar 98

**The Soane's at Home**   *Domestic Life at 13 Lincoln's Inn Fields.*

## London

**TATE GALLERY**
Millbank  London SW1P 4RG  Director: Nicholas Serota
☎ +44 171 8878000  ▤ +44 171 8878007
Open: Daily 10.00-17.50

COLLECTION

The Tate Gallery houses the national collection of British painting from the 16th century to the present day. It is also the national gallery for Modern art, encompassing painting and sculpture made in Britain, Europe, America, and other countries associated with the

European tradition in this century. The collection also includes substantial holdings of drawings and watercolours after 1945. The Clore Gallery, added in 1987, houses the paintings, watercolours, drawings and sketchbooks of J.M.W. Turner, left to the nation on his death.

Exterior Tate Gallery, London
Photocredit:
© Marcus Leith
*Tate Gallery, London*

**EXHIBITIONS**

until 15·06·97

*Luciano Fabro   Supported by Coutts Contemporary Arts Foundation and the Friends of the Tate Gallery*   For the annual sculpture exhibition, celebrated Italian artist Luciano Fabro has created a spectacular new work consisting of two great columns, representing the sun and moon, which form a dramatic link with the classical architecture and columns of the Duveen Galleries.

until 08·06·97

*Hogarth the Painter   An Exhibition Marking the 300th Anniversary of the Birth of William Hogarth*   An unrivalled collection of paintings to be displayed in its entirety together with more than a dozen significant loans. The works either mark peaks in the artist's career or are new works which have been recently discovered.

12·06·97-07·09·97

*Ellsworth Kelly*   Some 50 works and several sculptures dating from 1949 to the present will display how this American abstract artist succeeded in combining post-war American art with the European tradition.

16·10·97-05·01·98

*Symbolism in Britain   The Age of Rossetti, Burne-Jones and Watts 1860-1910*   The exhibition focuses on the interrelationship of British and Continental Symbolist art in the late 19th century, arguing that the works of Rossetti, Burne-Jones and Watts can only be understood as part of the post-European movement of Symbolism.

## London

**VICTORIA AND ALBERT MUSEUM**
Cromwell Road  South Kensington  London SW7 2RL  Director: Alan Borg
☎ +44 171 9388500  🖷 +44 171 9388341  Internet http://www.vam.ac.uk
Open: Tuesday-Sunday 10.00-17.50  Monday 12.00-17.50
Closed: Good Friday, May Day Bank Holiday, 24-26 Dec

**COLLECTION**

The museum's collections comprise sculpture, furniture, fashion and textiles, paintings, silver, glass, ceramics, jewellery, books, prints and photographs from Britain and all over the world. Highlights include the world's greatest collection of Constables and the national collection of watercolours; the famous 15th-century Devonshire Hunting Tapestries; the Dress Court showing fashion from 1500 to the present day; a superb Asian collection, including the much-loved Tippoo's Tiger; Medieval treasures; magnificent collections of Renaissance and Victorian sculpture; the Jewellery Gallery including the Russian Crown Jewels; and the 20th-Century Gallery, devoted to contemporary art and design. There are also magnificent new galleries devoted to European art and design, glass, ceramics, ironwork and English silver, Chinese, European and Indian art, 20th-century design and the architect Frank Lloyd Wright.

## EXHIBITIONS

until 26·07·98

***The Power of the Poster***   This exhibition focuses on the nature and dynamics of the poster, looking at the special qualities that have enabled it to survive and flourish as an art form.

until 27·07·97

***The Cutting Edge***   *50 Years of British Fashion*   This exhibition explores the diverse achievements of Britain's post-war fashion industry and considers its tailoring tradition, penchant for romantic dress, love of bohemian styles and renowned classic country clothes.

23·10·97-18·01·98

***Carl and Karin Larsson***   *Creators of the Swedish Style*   At the end of the last century, Swedish artist Carl Larsson and his wife Karin were responsible for creating the Swedish interior design style which continues to be a potent influence on modern design.

# London

## THE WALLACE COLLECTION
Hertford House Manchester Square  London W1M 6BN  Director: R. Savill
☎ +44 171 9350687  📠 +44 171 2242155
Open: Monday-Saturday 10.00-17.00  Sunday 14.00-17.00
Closed: 1 Jan, Good Friday, 1 May, 24-26 Dec

## COLLECTION

The Wallace Collection displays superb works of art against the sumptuous backdrop of Hertford House.
In the richly decorated rooms are fine Old Master paintings by Titian, Canaletto, Rembrandt, Hals, Rubens, Velasquez and Gainsborough, among others, and excellent collections of French 18th-century painting, furniture and Sevre porcelain. There are also four impressive galleries for the display of an outstanding collection of arms and armour, miniatures, gold boxes, French and Italian sculpture, and Renaissance works of art, including Limoges enamels, majolica, glass, silver, cuttings from illuminated manuscripts and carvings in ivory, rock crystal and boxwood.
Under the terms of Lady Wallace's bequest, the collection may not be enlarged, nor may items be loaned from it. It thus remains a testament to the tastes and interests of a single wealthy family over a period of four generations.

## EXHIBITIONS

[GALLERY 21]

sep 97- Dec 97

***Paul Delaroche***

[CENTRED ON THE LANDING]

Feb 98-May 98

***Madame de Pompadour***

# London

## WHITECHAPEL ART GALLERY
Whitechapel High Street  London E1 7QX  Director: Catherine Lampert
☎ +44 171 5227888  📠 +44 171 3771685
Open: Tuesday-Sunday 11.00-17.00  Wednesday 11.00-20.00
Closed: Monday

## COLLECTION

No permanent collection.

## EXHIBITIONS

until 18·05·97

***Antechamber***   Five younger artists, from Britain and abroad, will create their own spaces in the gallery. Each artist's space will include their own work but also material chosen by them which has a relationship to their working practice - including TV broadcasts, philosophical and literary texts, sign paintings and Egyptian antiquities.

30·05·97-20·07·97　　**Cathy de Monchaux**　Young British sculptor Cathy de Monchaux (born 1960) makes fetishistic and highly-crafted objects in materials such as iron and brass. For this show she will transform the lower gallery with a dramatic installation of her work. The upper galleries will feature a separate exhibition.

## Manchester

**MANCHESTER CITY ART GALLERIES**
Mosley Street  Manchester M2 3JL  Director: Richard Gray
☎ +44 161 2365244  🖷 +44 61 2367369
Open: Daily 10.00-17.45  Sunday 14.00-17.45
Closed: 25, 26 Dec, 1 Jan, Good Friday

COLLECTION　　Manchester City Art Galleries' collection of fine art is particularly rich in the field of 19th-century British paintings, including work by Turner and the Pre-Raphaelites as well as important 18th-century works by Gainsborough and Stubbs. The galleries' collection of 20th-century art is also very strong, with works by Henry Moore, Ben Nicholson, Augustus John, Francis Bacon and Lucian Freud.

Exhibition room
© Manchester City
Art Galleries,
Manchester

The decorative arts collection includes Greek vases from the 4th century and more contemporary pieces by the best artists in Britain and abroad. The decorative arts in the upper galleries are shown in the context of the paintings with which they are displayed. Downstairs, in the collection 'A New Look at Decorative Arts', ceramics, glass and silver are displayed thematically. Visitors are encouraged, for example, to compare a rare 17th-century slipware dish with a plate designed and decorated by Picasso.

EXHIBITIONS
until-01·06·97　　**Tony Oursler**　Video Works

until-26·05·97　　**Likeness**　Reflecting Sexuality

07·06·97-13·07·97　　**Sean Scully**　Paintings 1982-1996

13·09·97-26·10·97　　**Glenys Barton**　Ceramic Sculpture

15·11·97-25·01·98　　**Pre-Raphaelite Women Artists**

Nov 97-Feb 98　　**Keiko Mukaide**　Glass

Feb 98-Mar 98　　**Manchester Academy of Fine Art**　139th Annual Open Exhibition.

## Middlesbrough

**MIDDLESBROUGH ART GALLERY**
320 Linthorpe Road  Middlesbrough TS1 4AW  Assistant Curator: Alison Lloyd
☎ +44 1642 247445  📠 +44 1642 813781
Open: Tuesday-Saturday 10.00-17.30
Closed: Sunday and Monday

**COLLECTION**

The Middlesbrough Art Gallery's collection of 20th-century art includes work by Frank Auerbach, David Bomberg, Gaudier Brzeska, Gwen John, Stanley Spencer and Paula Rego. The museum's most recent acquisition is a crayon and pencil work on paper by Claes Oldenburg, entitled 'Bottle of Notes'.
The Middlesbrough Art Gallery presents an exciting and varied programme of contemporary art and related events.

Marina Abramovic
*The House - 5 Rooms and Storage*
Installation: shot of Bathroom at ©
Middlesbrough Art Gallery

**EXHIBITIONS**

until 31·05·97

***Cornelia Hesse Honegger***   Paintings and drawings of mutating insects collected from the perimeters of nuclear power stations.

17·06·97-28·06·97

***Cleveland College of Art***   *Fine Art Degree Show*

04·07·97-16·08·97

***Cleveland Art Society***   *Annual Exhibition*

30·08·97-25·10·97

***Stephen Willats: Between Me and You***   *Between Buildings and People*   An interactive conceptual art work for Middlesbrough

01·11·97-10·01·98

***Independent Thoughts***   *Rasheed Araeen, Freda Rana*   New Art commissions to mark the 50th anniversary of Indian Independence and the creation of Pakistan as a separate Nation State.

## New Bridge

**SCOTTISH AGRICULTURAL MUSEUM**
**(NATIONAL MUSEUMS OF SCOTLAND)**
Rhas Showground  New Bridge Midlothian EH28 8NB  Director: Mark Jones
☎ +44 131 3332674  📠 +44 131 333 2674  Internet: http://www.nms.ac.uk
Open: Apr-Sep Daily 10.00-17.00  Oct-Mar Monday-Friday 10.00-17.00
Closed: Oct-Mar Saturday, Sunday and Christmas-New Year

**COLLECTION**

**Historical items**   The collections trace the history of rural life in Scotland and the progress from hand skills to mechanisation in farming and crofting communities. The main themes of the permanent displays are: The Agricultural Revolution to the coming of the tractor and combine harvester; the social and economic life of the countryside; the traditional use of materials in the countryside; and the changing relationship between people and animals. Objects include tools, implements, photographs and folk art.

Jun-Aug 97

***Pictures by William Robbie***   An exhibition of paintings of horses by the naïve artist William Robbie (1887-1967) who was born in Aberdeenshire, Scotland, and worked all his life as a farm servant in the area. He was particularly noted for his depiction of the Clydesdale horse. His work included watercolours, collages and plywood cut-outs.

19·06·97-22·06·97

***Combine Harvesters***   During the Royal Highland Show, a spectacular display of combine harvesters will take place outside the museum, including the newly-restored Claas Columbus, dating from the early 1960s, and the self-propelled Jones baler built in the early 1950s.

## Newcastle upon Tyne

**THE HATTON GALLERY**
**Newcastle University  Newcastle upon Tyne NE1 7RU  Director: Gavin Robson**
**☎ +44 191 2226057  📠 +44 191 2611182**
**Open: Monday-Friday 10.00-17.30**
**Saturday (University term time only) 10.00-16.30**
**Closed: Sunday and public holidays**

COLLECTION

The Hatton Gallery collection was founded in the 1920s when Professor Hatton of the King Edward VII School of Art in Newcastle donated a small collection of Indian miniatures and an edition of Burgkmair's 'Triumphal Procession'. Paintings ranging through the Renaissance to Modern periods were acquired in the 1940s and 1950s, and these now form the core of the collection. Further expansion followed from the 1950s to the 1980s. A large body of contemporary British art was donated by the Contemporary Art Society, including works by Patrick Herron, Francis Bacon and Prunella Clough. Among important bequests made to the Gallery are the Bosanquet collection of textiles, the Hall Bequest of Baxter and Victorian prints, and the Charlton Bequest, comprising watercolours, drawings, prints and oils by the Charlton brothers and other artists from their circle, such as Crawhall. Recent bequests include Kurt Schwitter's 'Merzbarn' donated by Harry Pierce in 1965, and the Uhlman Collection of African Sculpture donated in 1985.

Anthony Whishaw
exhibition
© *Hatton Gallery,*
*Newcastle upon Tyne*

EXHIBITIONS
01·05·97-31·05·97

***Masterpieces***   Paintings, sculptures and prints from the Hatton Gallery's own extensive collection of 17th-20th century art.

14·06·97-12·07·97

***The BA Fine Art Degree Show***   An exhibition of work presented for Degree examination by students of the Fine Art Department at Newcastle University.

28·07·97-22·08·97

***The Friends of the Hatton Summer Exhibition***   Landscapes, still-lifes, portraits, and abstracts in all media by members of The Friends of the Hatton Gallery association.

03·09·97-19·09·97 **MFA Degree Show** An exhibition of work presented for Degree examination by post-graduate students of the Fine Art Department at Newcastle University.

04·10·97-01·11·97 **Roger de Grey** Retrospective

# Newcastle upon Tyne

**LAING ART GALLERY**
New Bridge Street Newcastle upon Tyne NE1 8AG Director: John Millard
☎ +44 191 2327734 ☏ +44 191 2220952
Open: Daily 10.00-17.00 Sunday 14.00-17.00
Closed: Good Friday

COLLECTION

The Laing Art Gallery is the North East's principal gallery with a collection of paintings, watercolours, costumes, silver, glass, pottery and sculpture as well as a permanent programme of temporary exhibitions, talks and activities. Among the highlights of the permanent collection are works by Gauguin, William Holman Hunt, Burne-Jones and the Northumberland-born Victorian painter John Martin. Modern art is also represented with works by Stanley Spencer and Henry Moore. The Laing Art Gallery has the award-winning 'Art On Tyneside' exhibition on permanent display. This explores the region's art from the Middle Ages to the present. Games, videos and reconstructions make this journey through history particularly enjoyable.

EXHIBITIONS

until 18·05·97 **Victorian Dreams** Water-Colours from the Laing Art Gallery
A wonderful exhibition of water-colours from the Laing's collection including a series of paintings specially conserved and not seen for more than 50 years.

until 08·06·97 **Eastern Edge** Contemporary art by women artists from Pakistan and India.

07·06·97-07·09·97 **Jan Niedojadlo** A large scale contemporary exhibition, featuring interactive sculptures made from recycled materials, foam and used tyres.

20·06·97-17·08·97 **The Young Gainsborough** A national gallery touring exhibition that includes several well known works from the artist's earlier years.

# Northampton

**CENTRAL MUSEUM AND ART GALLERY**
Guildhall Road Northampton NN1 1DP Director: Sheila Stone
☎ +44 1604 233500 ☏ +44 1604 238720
Open: Daily 10.00-17.00 Sunday 14.00-17.00

COLLECTION

Northampton possesses the largest collection of footwear in Britain and one of the most important collections of this kind in the world. **Footwear on display** ranges from Roman and Medieval examples to present-day boots and shoes. There are even unusual specimens such as the boots worn by 'Jumbo' the elephant in a re-creation of Hannibal's trek across the Alps.
A number of specially commissioned works, such as a depiction of

Saint Crispin, the patron saint of shoemakers, illustrate subjects associated with the footwear industry. There is also a number of paintings and other illustrations of shoemakers and shoemaking as well as two indexes, one of shoemakers and shoemaking companies and another of 'concealed shoes' (shoes hidden in buildings for good luck).

**The Fine Arts Gallery** possesses a small but important collection of Italian works. Although focusing on late Venetian artists, all the most important artistic centres of Italy are represented. Other pieces in the collection are displayed on a rotating basis.

**The Decorative Arts Gallery** displays a selection from its fine collection of British ceramics and its comprehensive collection of Oriental ceramics. British and Irish glass dating from the mid-17th century to the late 20th century is displayed along with one of the earliest complete dated bottles in existence (1657).

**The archaeological and social history** displays focus on the development of Northampton and range from prehistoric worked flint to furniture designed by the Scottish architect Charles Rennie Mackintosh for the home of local model-maker W.J. Bassett Lowke.

**EXHIBITIONS**

until-15·06·97 | ***Through Celtic Mists*** *Life and Ritual in the Iron Age*

28·06·97-27·07·97 | ***Victorian Visions*** *Image and Reality in Victorian Paintings*

09·08·97-31·08·97 | ***Flying Around Town*** *Paintings by Julie Rose Bills.*

13·09·97-05·10·97 | ***Northamptonshire Portraits and Sculptures*** *The Work of Bob Dawson.*

11·10·97-16·11·97 | ***Moment in Time*** *The History of College Street Baptist Church 1697 - 1997*

18·10·97-16·11·97 | ***A Boy Named Sioux*** *Traditional and Contemporary Images of the Plains Indians. Paintings on muslin in the Plains Indian Style by Peter Bowles.*

29·11·97-04·01·98 | ***The Northampton Town and County Art Society*** *84th Annual Exhibition*

# Norwich

**CASTLE MUSEUM**
Norwich NR1 3JU  Curator: Andrew Moore
☎ +44 1603 223624  ⊠ +44 1603 765651
Internet http://Paston.Co.UK/Users/NCM/NMS-Home.HTML
Open: Monday-Saturday 10.00-17.00  Sunday 14.00-17.00
Closed: 24 - 26 Dec

**COLLECTION**

This regional museum houses a collection of watercolours and oils by John Sell Cotman and the Norwich School of Artists, together with displays of Norwich silver, Lowestoft porcelain, English ceramics and the Twining Teapot Gallery. Dutch oils by Hobbema and Jan van Goyen are also featured, as well as etchings by Rembrandt. The Castle Museum also cares for a public collection of contemporary craft and the museum shop sells selected work. The Modern Art collection is diverse and includes work by Ernst, Nolde and Warhol in the Adeane Bequest.

The Castle Keep, designed as a royal palace before 1100, was built partly from Caen stone and houses some of the large archaeological collections which tell the story of the people of Norfolk. Egyptian mummies are also displayed along with material from other ancient civilisations. Gold and silver found at Snettisham includes the largest

John Crome
(1768-1821)
*Norwich River:
Afternoon c.1819*
© Castle Museum,
Norwich

collection of Iron Age gold neck rings anywhere in Europe, and many examples of Roman craftsmanship found in the region are also shown in the Archaeology Gallery.

The Natural History galleries house specimens of unique animals and plants from the wildlife areas in Norfolk. There are also Ice Age fossils found in Norfolk and the 600 000 year-old elephant remains discovered on the Cromer coast.

## EXHIBITIONS

| | |
|---|---|
| until 15·06·97 | ***Young Gainsborough***   On tour from the National Gallery London |
| until 15·06·97 | ***Edvard Munch***   *A Picture in Focus*   Supported by the Tate in East Anglia Foundation and the Royal Norwegian Embassy, London. |
| until 16·11·97 | ***Big Pictures from the Castle Museum's Collection*** |
| until Mar 98 | ***Joseph Stannard***   *Watercolours* |
| 05·07·97-23·11·97 | ***Sensations!***   Come to your senses in a hands-on experience for all ages |
| 13·12·97-25·01·98 | ***The Castle Art Show***   Recent work by Norfolk artists |
| 14·02·98-26·04·98 | ***Tate Gallery Collection*** |

# Norwich

**SAINSBURY CENTRE FOR VISUAL ARTS**
University of East Anglia  Norwich NR4 7TJ  Director: Nicola Johnson
☎ +44 1603 456060  ⅸ +44 1603 259401
Open: Tuesday-Sunday 11.00-17.00
Closed: Monday and throughout University Christmas vacation

## COLLECTION

The museum and gallery of the University of East Anglia was designed by the world-famous architect Sir Norman Foster to house the Robert and Lisa Sainsbury Collection, which was given to the University in the 1970s. Modern European sculpture and painting, including works by Bacon, Degas, Epstein, Giacometti, Moore and Picasso are displayed alongside one of the finest British collections of non-Western art outside London.

## EXHIBITIONS

| | |
|---|---|
| until 11·05·97 | ***Collections and Reflections***   *New Works by 5 Artists* |
| 03·06·97-06·07·97 | ***Disembodied***   *The 1997 Museology MA Exhibition*   The 4th annual exhibition curated by the students on UEA's highly successful Museology MA course this year takes the fascinating subject of the Body as its theme. |

© Sainsbury centre
for visual arts at
dusk,
Norwich

| | |
|---|---|
| 17·06·97-14·09·97 | **Contemporary Japanese Photography by Sugimoto** |
| 13·07·97-30·08·97 | **EAST 97**   The Sainsbury Centre once again joins forces with the Norwich Gallery and Norwich School of Art and Design to present the 1997 EAST International selection. |
| 07·10·97-14·12·97 | **Drawings by Federico Garcia Lorca**   An exhibition of drawings by Lorca, the Spanish author, poet, playwright and artist who died tragically young during the Spanish Civil War. |
| 07·10·97-14·12·97 | **The Age of Dürer**   *German Renaissance Prints*   A national touring exhibition of the very best of German Renaissance Art in the age of Dürer. |
| Mid Feb 98-May 98 | **The Crafts in Britain Since World War II**   An overview of the crafts in Britain from 1939 till the mid 1990s with a strong emphasis on social context. Display will include textiles, silversmithing, blacksmithing, jewellery, ceramics, stained glass, glass, furniture, letter cutting, calligraphy, bookbinding. |

## Oxford

**ASHMOLEAN MUSEUM AND UNIVERSITY GALLERIES**
Beaumont Street  Oxford OX1 2PH  Director: Christopher White
☎ +44 1865 278000  📠 +44 1865 278018
Internet: http://www.ashmol.ox.ac.uk/
Open: Tuesday-Saturday 10.00-16.00  Sunday 14.00-16.00
Closed: Monday and during St. Giles's Fair, Christmas and Easter

COLLECTION

Britain's oldest public museum (founded 1683) now housed in C.R. Cockerell's classical building of the 1840's.

© Ashmolean
Museum
Oxford

On display are the University's rich and diverse collections of British, European, Egyptian and Near Eastern antiquities; European paintings and drawings, sculpture, silver, ceramics and musical instruments; coins and medals in the Heberden Coin Room; Oriental art - Chinese, Japanese, Islamic and Indian metalwork, ceramics, paintings, textiles and sculpture.

**EXHIBITIONS**

until 13·07·97   **Life Drawings**   A selection from the permanent collection of British and European drawings, ranging from the 11th to the 20th century - Michelangelo to Cezanne.

20·05·97-13·07·97   **Museum Acquisitions 1985-1997**

22·07·97-28·09·97   **Indian Block-Printed Textiles in Egypt**   *From the Newberry Collection*   This unique collection of block-printed cotton textiles, many of them traded to Egypt as part of the pre-European Indian Ocean trade, was donated to the Ashmolean in 1946 and is of outstanding historical importance.

Mid Jul 97-Mid Sep 97   **15th Century Netherlandish Engravings**

30·09·97-late Dec   **Prints from the Hope Collection of Engraved Portraits**

30·09·97-08·12·97   **Forrest Reid Collection**

09·12·97-late Jan 98   **Samuel Palmer**

# Oxford

**MUSEUM OF MODERN ART**
30 Pembroke Street   Oxford OX1 1BP   Director: David Elliott
☎ +44 1865 722733   🖷 +44 1865 722573
Open: Tuesday-Saturday 10.00-18.00   Thursday 10.00-21.00
Sunday 14.00-18.00
Closed: Monday

**COLLECTION**   No permanent collection.

**EXHIBITIONS**

until 06·07·97   **In Visible Light**   *Photography and Classification in Art, Science and the Everyday*   Inspired by various themes, among which the museum, crime and degeneracy, disease and madness, origins, myths and narratives, mortality, the culture of nature, the everyday and beauty and desire, the exhibition explores how photography has been used to order, classify, record and measure.

20·07·97-28·09·97   **In Place (Out of Time)**   *Contemporary Art in Australia*   The first exhibition outside Australia to include both Aboriginal and non-Aboriginal Australian artists on an equal basis, it includes works by Tracy Moffatt, Narelle Jubelin, Juan Davila, Rosalie Gascoigne, Mike Parr and Gordon Bennet.

# Southampton

**SOUTHAMPTON CITY ART GALLERY**
Civic Centre   Southampton SO14 7LP   Director: Stephen Snoddy
☎ +44 1703 832277   🖷 +44 1703 832153
Open: Tuesday-Saturday 10.00-17.00   Thursday 10.00-19.00
Sunday 13.00-16.00
Closed: Monday

**COLLECTION**   The Southampton City Art Gallery, opened in 1939 and housed in a beautiful Portland stone listed building, has a permanent collection which spans 6 centuries of European art, from a 14th century altarpiece by Allegretto Nuzi to a film installation by 1996 Turner Prize winner Douglas Gordon, including 17th century Dutch landscapes, 18th century portraiture and a small number of French Impressionist works, Edward Burne-Jones' Perseus Series and an installation by Daniel Buren in the impressive vaulted Main Hall. 20th century Britisch works are particularly well-represented, including many fine works by artists such as Stanley Spencer, Gilbert and George, Helen Chadwick, Barry Flanagan, Anthony Gormley and Rachel Whiteread.

Douglas Gordon
*Hysterical, 1995*
*edition 1 of 3*
© Southhampton City
Art Gallery,
Southampton

## EXHIBITIONS

**until 15·06·97**

***Art in Boxes***   *Open Exhibition*   Artists in the region will be exhibiting work produced in response to this specific brief.

**until 15·06·97**

***Moore & Blatch Student Exhibition***   The very best work produced by Fine Art students of the region's major art colleges.

**27·06·97-14·09·97**

***Turner's Watercolours Explorations***   This exceptional exhibition of 70 J.M.W. Turner watercolours, mainly drawn from the Turner bequest now held at the Tate Gallery, London, explores every aspect of the artist's passionate examination of the power and significance of colour.

**03·10·97-07·12·97**

***Basque Art c. 1890-1950***   Works from the Bilbao Museum of Fine Art demonstrating art from Basque region c. 1890-1950 which has strong historical and cultural links with southern England.

**03·10·97-07·12·97**

***Jan Hackaert***   *A Painter Illuminated*   The extraordinary story of 'The Avenue', a painting by this Dutch 17th Century landscape painter, painstakingly restored by Gallery Conservators using new technologies and with historical research of the work and the artist to accompany the display.

**16·01·98-22·03·98**

***Stephen Willats***   In this project, Willats will be executing one of his characteristic interventions into the local community.

**16·01·98-22·03·98**

***Joseph Wright of Derby***   This exhibition brings together a recently discovered collection of graphic work by this important 18th century British painter.

**27·03·98-24·05·98**

***Chris Ofili***   This will be the first major solo exhibition by one of the most exciting of young British painters. Ofili's work investigates the fusing of different cultural expressions through the innovative use of collage and painting techniques.

## St. Ives

**TATE GALLERY ST. IVES**
Porthmeor Beach  St Ives TR26 1TG  Director: Michael Tooby
☎ +44 1736 796226  📠 +44 736 794480
Open: Apr-Oct Sunday and public holidays 11.00-17.00
Monday-Saturday 11.00-19.00 Tuesday and Thursday 11.00-21.00;
Nov-Mar Tuesday-Sunday 11.00-17.00
Closed: Nov-Mar Monday and 24, 25 Dec

**COLLECTION**

The Tate Gallery St. Ives opened in 1993 in a stunning new building overlooking the spectacular Cornish coastline. The gallery offers a unique introduction to modern art, where over 200 works can be seen at any one time in an environment which has inspired artistic development in the area for over a hundred years.

The Tate Gallery St. Ives presents changing displays of 20th-century art from the Tate Gallery's collections, focusing on the post-war modern movement St. Ives is so famous for. Key artists represented in the collection include Alfred Wallis, Ben Nicholson, Barbara Hepworth, Naum Gabo, John Wells, Patrick Heron, Terry Frost and Wilhelmina Barns-Graham. The displays are complemented by a serie of exhibitions where works are loaned from other public and private collections.

Exterior Tate Gallery
St.Ives
Photocredit:
© Marcus Leith
*Tate Gallery, St.Ives*

The Barbara Hepworth Museum and Sculpture Garden have been run by the Tate Gallery since 1980 and are now an integral part of the Tate Gallery St. Ives. The Museum offers a remarkable insight into the work and outlook of one of Britain's most important 20th-century sculptors, who lived and worked in St. Ives from 1939-1975.

**EXHIBITIONS**

until 02·11·97

***Clive Bowen***  *Ceramics*  Each year Tate Gallery St. Ives invites a contemporary potter to display his or her work. Clive Bowen is this year's participant.

10·05·97-02·11·97

***St. Ives International***  *A Quality of Light*  Six artists participate in this collaborative visual arts project, working in a wide range of media around the theme of light.

15·11·97-Nov 98

***Displays 1997-98***  *Fifth Annual Displays*  Tate Gallery St. Ives presents the annual renewal of the gallery's core displays, drawn from its collections of British and modern art.

15·11·97-Apr 98

***Roger Hilton***  Roger Hilton (1911-1975) was one of the few British abstract painters in the early 1950s. His later work was characterised by humour and erotic connotations.

## Truro

**ROYAL CORNWALL MUSEUM**
River Street  Truro Cornwall TR1 2SJ  Director: Caroline Dudley
☎ +44 1872 72205  🖷 +44 1872 40514
Open: Monday-Saturday 10.00-17.00
Closed: Sunday and Bank Holidays

**COLLECTION**

The Royal Cornwall Museum is one of the largest and most diverse regional museums in the UK with collections of minerals, human history, art, applied art, natural history, toys, numismatics and a large archive of photographs dating from the 1840s to the present day.

**Minerals**  The Rashleigh collection of minerals is particularly rich in copper ores, collected when copper mining in Cornwall was at its height. A highlight in the collection is the world's largest specimen of liroconite. A new gallery is devoted to the history of Cornish mining and minerals.

**Human History**  The museum is the primary repository for all officially excavated archaeological material from Cornwall and includes three of the only four known Bronze Age gold collars found in England.

**Art**  The Fine Art collection centres on a collection of more than 300 Old Master drawings from the 14th to the 20th century and includes important drawings by Turner, Constable, Rossetti, Blake, Rubens, Claude and Gericault. There are also collections of European prints and 19th and 20th-century oil paintings.

**Applied Art**  The museum has collections of ceramics ranging from the Medieval period to the 20th-century studio potters such as Bernard Leach and Michael Cardew. Smaller but high-quality collections include Japanese and Chinese applied art, West Country silver, British pewter, textiles and European ceramics.

**EXHIBITIONS**

02·05·97-31·05·97　　*Cornwall Photographic Alliance*

02·05·97-31·05·97　　*The Imagery of Light*

14·06·97-12·07·97　　*Arts in Trust*  Work by local schools in collaboration with artists and The National Trust.

09·08·97-30·08·97　　*Truro Art Society*　　Annual exhibition of paintings, watercolours, drawings, engravings, ceramics and sculpture.

06·09·97-24·09·97　　*Cornwall Heritage Trust*　　An exhibition on the work of the Cornwall Heritage Trust to co-incide with the European Heritage weekend.

04·10·97-29·11·97　　*The Hall for Cornwall*　　An exhibition to celebrate the opening of the Hall for Cornwall including archaeological finds and the history of the project.

24·10·97-19·12·97　　*Teapotmania*　　The story of the British craft teapot and teacosy from the mid 19th century to the present day.

30·01·98-14·03·98　　*Travelling Discovery Centre*　　The Natural History Museum's touring exhibition

21·03·98-19·04·98　　*Six Fairy Tales from the Brothers Grimm*　　An exhibition of 39 etchings by David Hockney.

## Wakefield

**WAKEFIELD ART GALLERY**
Wentworth Terrace  Wakefield WF1 3QW  Director: Gordon Watson
☎ +44 1924 305796  ▥ +44 1924 305770
Open: Daily 10.30-17.30  Sunday 14.30-17.00
Closed: 1 Jan, 25, 26 Dec

COLLECTION

Two of the most outstanding British sculptors of the 20th century, Henry Moore and Barbara Hepworth, were born within a few miles of Wakefield Art Gallery and, not surprisingly, the Gallery has acquired some significant early sculpture and drawings by these now internationally celebrated artists. These and important work from other major British modern artists form the core of the collection. Works from other periods and European schools are also on display.

Displays at nearby Wakefield Museum include the Waterton Collection - exotic birds and animals collected in South America and elsewhere by Charles Waterton, the remarkable 19th-century traveller and naturalist.

EXHIBITIONS

10·05·97-06·07·97  **Wakefield Art Club**   An annual exhibition of work by local art club members.

01·08·97-14·09·97  **Zoo**   A photographic exhibition by the German artist Britta Jaschinski questioning the validity of animal confinement in modern day zoos.

20·09·97-02·11·97  **Janet Beckwith**   Glass encased mixed media sculptures investigating both personal memories and shared experiences. Janet is a Wakefield based artist.

08·11·97-07·12·97  **Networking**   *Art by Post, fl and Phone*   This exhibition presents around 25 international artists who attempt, in different ways, to transmit visual images across the globe.

## York

**YORK CITY ART GALLERY**
Exhibition Square  York Y01 2EW  Curator: Richard Green
☎ +44 1904 551861  ▥ +44 1904 551866
Open: Daily  Good Friday-2 Nov 10.00-16.30  Winter 10.00-16.00
Closed: 25 Dec

COLLECTION

Six hundred years of European painting from early Italian gold-ground panels to the art of the twentieth-century. Exceptional in its range and interest, the collection includes pictures by Parmigianino and Bellotto, Lely and Reynolds, Frith and Boudin, Lowry and Nash, and nudes by Yorkborn William Etty. There is also an outstanding collection of pioneer studio pottery.

EXHIBITIONS

until 24·05·97  **Teapotmania**   *The Story of the British Craft Teapot and Teacosy*   Teapotmania provides a survey of contemporary craft teapots and teacosies set in a context of the 19th and earlier 20th century tradition.

14·06·97-03·08·97  **Vikings and Gods in European Art**   York provides the perfect venue for this internatonal exhibition which explores the ways Viking gods and heroes have been depicted by European artists from the mid-16th century onwards. It shows how their representations have shaped modern understanding of the Viking era.

Fungai
*The martyrdom of*
*St.Clement, 1355*
© *York City Art*
*Gallery, York*

16·08·97-14·09·97 | ***In the Mind's Eye***  *Surrealist Works on Paper*   Works by Salvador Dali, Roland Penrose, Man Ray and other figures in the surrealist movement, lent from a private collector.

27·09·97-26·10·97 | ***Contemporary Textiles from North Yorkshire***   A selected exhibition of textiles from the local region.

08·11·97-06·12·97 | ***Art from York Primary Schools***   The first exhibition of work selected from primary schools in the City of York area.

13·12·97-20·01·98 | ***The Room in View***   Oil paintings, drawings and photographs from the 18th century to the 1950s depicting famous people in their own surroundings.

## York

**YORKSHIRE MUSEUM**
**Museum Gardens  York YO1 2DR  Director: Paul Howard**
☎ +44 1904 629745  ⌕ +44 1904 651221
**Open: Daily 10.00-17.00; Nov-Mar 10.00-17.00 Sunday 13.00-17.00**
**Opening hours are subject to change. Please call to check.**

COLLECTION | **Archaeology**  The Yorkshire Museum houses one of the finest archaeological collections in Europe, ranging from prehistoric times through the Roman, Anglo-Saxon, Viking and Medieval periods. There is a large and outstanding collection of Roman sculptures, mosaics, jewellery and other objects. Anglo-Saxon artefacts include the fine 8th-century silver gilt bowl from Ormside and the Gilling sword as well as sculptures and personal ornaments. The renowned Viking collection comprises decorated metalwork, stone carvings and a variety of organic objects. The Medieval section is particularly known for its sculpture, including the life-size Romanesque figures of the Apostles from St. Mary's Abbey.
**Numismatics**  The Yorkshire Museum has one of the country's most important collections of coins, comprising about 35 000 specimens. Particular areas of strength include the coinages of Roman Britain and of Anglo-Saxon and Medieval England.
**Decorative Art**  The museum's collection of ceramics is of national importance, including comprehensive assortments of tin-glazed Delftware, Leeds creamware and Rockingham porcelain as well as pieces from most Yorkshire potteries, examples of county pottery and late-Victorian art pottery production and work by York silversmiths. Selected items from the collection are on view in the pottery gallery on the first floor of the museum.
**Geology**  The museum has an extensive geological collection comprising more than 100 000 specimens, as well as the Tempest Anderson Collection of some 5000 negatives of vulcanological topics from around the world (1880-1913).

EXHIBITIONS

until-07·09·97

***Fangs*** Fangs gives you the chance to become a jungle explorer and find out more about some of the world's deadliest creatures. Fangs includes live tarantulas, frogs and snakes.

until-31·10·97

***Carnosaur!*** Carnosaur is the greatest gathering of flesh eating dinosaurs for 65 million years. Animated dinosaurs will re-create the sights and sounds of the pre-historic world.

05·05·97-02·11·97

***Megafun with Computers*** In the Hospitium in the Museum Gardens is a dynamic show of interactive computer exhibits from the Edinburgh Science Festival.

## Dublin

**IRISH MUSEUM OF MODERN ART**
Royal Hospital Kilmainham  Dublin 8  Director: Declan McGonagle
☎ +353 1 6718666  ☎ +353 1 6718695
Open: Tuesday-Saturday 10.00-17.30  Sunday and public holidays 12.00-17.30
Closed: Monday and Good Friday, 24-26 Dec

**COLLECTION**

Founded in 1991, the Irish Museum of Modern Art presents a wide cross-section of Irish and international art of the 20th century, including pivotal figures such as Picasso, Giacometti and Joseph Beuys, and leading contemporary artists.
Displays from the Collection  will run continuously with works being rotated, including Work in Focus and New Acquisistion strands.
Associated Education/Community projects integrated into the displays.

**EXHIBITIONS**

Mar - onwards

*Damien Hirst*   A sculptural installation from the IMMA Collection

until 11·06·97

*Joseph Kosuth*    Conceptual artist, new projects and selected works over 20 years

01·05·97-13·07·97

*IMMA Glen Dimplex Artists Award 1997*

26·06·97-02·11·97

*A Case for Painting*   An exhibition about European painting in the 20th century selected by Stephen Mc Kenna. Balthus, Bonnarc, Leger, Derain, De Chirico, Gris, Helion, John, Malevich, Morandi, Yeats, Picabia, Gorman, Rego, McComb.

Jun-Aug 97

*IMMA/Nissan Project*   New work for the public domain

24·07·97-mid Oct 97

*New Artists / New Work*   A large group show looking at new works by young Irish and non-Irish artists

| | |
|---|---|
| Oct-Dec 97 | ***Once is Too Much***   A collaborative project between five Irish artists and Women's groups to address issues of violence against women - in association with the Rowntree Trust and the Arts Council |
| mid Oct-Jan 98 | ***Kiki Smith - Sculpture and Drawings*** |
| mid Nov-Feb 98 | ***Andy Warhol***   Last works and selected pieces including drawings from the 1950s onwards |

## Dublin

**NATIONAL GALLERY OF IRELAND**
**Merrion Square (West)  Dublin 2  Director: Raymond Keaveney**
☎ +353 1 6615133  ⊞ +353 1 6615372
**Open: Daily 10.00-17.30  Thursday 10.00-20.30  Sunday 14.00-17.00**
**Closed: 24-26 Dec, Good Friday**

COLLECTION

**Italian School**   The collection of Italian art includes a number of acknowledged masterpieces, most notably Fra Angelico's 'Attempted Martyrdom of Saints Cosmas and Damian'.
Works from the sixteenth century North Italian school include Titian's 'Ecco Uomo' and Tiepolo's 'Allegory of Immaculate Conception'.
The Gallery has an impressive collection of Florentine seventeenth-century art.
Caravaggio's highly dramatic painting, 'The Taking of Christ' is one of the highlights.
**German and Early Netherlandish Schools**   The German collection represents works dating from the fifteenth and sixteenth centuries. Highlights include: Portraits by Conrad Faber, Wolf Huber, George Pencz and Bernard Strigel.
Also in this collection is 'The Peasant Wedding' by Pieter Brueghel the Younger.

*Front façade*
*National Gallery of*
*Ireland, Dublin*
*© NGI*

**Dutch school**   The Dutch School is one of the strongest in the Gallery's collection. Among them, Rembrandt's 'Landscape with the Rest on the Flight into Egypt', Jan Steen's 'Village School', Ferdinand Bol's 'David's Dying Charge to Solomon', Hobbema's Wooded Landscape-'The Path on the Dyke' and Jacob van Ruisdael's 'The Castle of Bentheim'.
Other important paintings include 'Marriage Feast at Cana' by Jan Steen, 'Lute-Playe'r by Frans Hals and 'Lady writing a Letter' by Johannes Vermeer.

**Later Flemish School**   Flemish paintings date from the seventeenth to the nineteenth century. Highlights of this collection include works by Jordaens, Rubens and Van Dyck.

**Spanish School**   The Gallery's holding of Spanish paintings comprises works by Nicolás Francés and a number of works by Murillo including the complete set of six paintings on the theme of the prodigal son.Other important works include 'The Immaculate Conception' by Zurbarán, 'St. Francis receiving the Stigmata' by El Greco, Goya's 'Lady in a Black Mantilla', 'The Kitchen Maid with the Supper at Emmaus' by Velázquez and 'Still-live with Mandolin' by Picasso.

**French School**   The French collection includes masterpieces from the seventeenth to the nineteenth century. Worth noting are works by Nicolas Poussin, Jaques-Louis David and Eugène Delacroix. The collection of French Impressionist and early twentieth century paintings include 'A River Scene' by Claude Monet, 'Bords du Canal du Loing à St-Mammes' by Alfred Sisley and 'Ballet Dancers' by Edgar Degas.

**British School**   The British collection is strong in eighteenth century portraiture with works by William Hogarth, Thomas Gainsborough, Joshua Reynolds and George Romney. The nineteenth century is highlighted by a collection of 35 Turner Watercolours. Among the modern works are four Augustus John portraits.

**Irish School**   The Irish School spans works from the seventeenth century to the present day. Among the most notable Irish landscape artists are Thomas Roberts, Robert Carver, George Barret and William Ashford. Portraiture include works by John Michael Wright, James Latham, Thomas Frye and Nathaniel Hone the Elder. A major exponent of the nineteenth century history painting was Daniel Maclise.

One of the greatest Irish artists of the twentieth century is Jack B. Yeats, whose work reveals his fascination with the people, places and legends encountered in his youth in Sligo.

**EXHIBITIONS**
22·05·97-27·07·97

***The Art of the Book***   *500 Years of the Art of the Book in Ireland* This exhibition, drawing on material from collections in Ireland and abroad, shows for the first time the extraordinary richness and variety of the art of the book in Ireland during the past 500 years. The decoration of both manuscript and printed book, including calligraphy, illustration, typography and in particular, binding, will be explored.

05·09·97-07·12·97

***200 Years of Watercolours***   *Watercolours by Irish, English and European artists from the permanent collection.*

# Dublin

**NATIONAL MUSEUM OF IRELAND**
Kildare Street  Dublin 2  Director: Patrick F. Wallace
☎ +353 1 6777444  📠 +353 1 6766116
Open: Tuesday-Saturday 10.00-17.00  Sunday 14.00-17.00
Closed: Monday and 25 Dec

**COLLECTION**

The National Museum houses collections consisting of antiquities, historical objects and works of decorative art tracing the development of Irish civilisation from the Mesolithic period, ca. 7000 B.C., to the 20th century.
Permanent exhibitions include 'Prehistoric Ireland', which covers the period from the Mesolithic to the Iron Age and complements the metalwork on display in the other exhibitions, as well as 'Ireland's Gold' which focuses on the museum's collection of Bronze Age gold; one of the most comprehensive of its kind in Western Europe.

'The Treasury' traces the history of Irish art from the Celtic Iron Age, ca. 300 B.C., to the late Middle Ages. An audio-visual presentation lasting ten minutes and available with English, French or German commentary provides an introduction to this exhibition.

The exhibition 'Ireland - the Viking Age' deals with the Viking invasions during the late Middle Ages and the impact of these on Irish society.

The historical display includes such exhibits as 'The Road to Independence', tracing the events which led to the foundation of the modern Irish State.

A new permanent exhibition 'Ancient Egypt' is on display.

**EXHIBITIONS**

No exhibitions planned.

## Ancona

**MUSEO ARCHEOLOGICO NAZIONALE DELLE MARCHE**
Via Ferretti 1  Ancona  Director: Rita Virzí
☎ +39 71 202602
Open: Daily 09.00-13.30

COLLECTION

The museum is housed in the 15th-century Palazzo Ferretti and contains all the archaeological material from excavations carried out in Le Marche, as well as objects from private collections that were presented to the state.

The Protohistoric and Prehistoric sections are open to the public, the Roman and Early Medieval sections are in preparation.

The exhibited material also includes a decorated ostrich egg, which was found in a grave in oriental style in Pitino di S. Severino, a youth's head in bronze from Cagli and splendid gold objects found in the Gallic graves of S. Paolina di Filottrano and Montefortino di Arcevia.

**Protohistoric Section**   There is extensive documentation on the two principal civilisations that developed in Le Marche during the Iron Age: the Picena and Gallic civilisations. The two civilisations are illustrated mainly by funerary objects.

**Prehistoric Section**   Five rooms are dedicated to the Palaeolithic and the Neolithic periods in Le Marche.

Prom the Palaeolithic period there are some double-faced statues and several stone tools, as well as artistic objects, such as the engraved stone from Tolentino.

The Neolithic period is represented by clay household products, some decorated, articles made of stone, such as hatchets of polished stone and millstones for grain, obsidian blades, spindles and pieces of weaving looms.

EXHIBITIONS

No details available.

## Bari

**PINACOTECA PROVINCIALE DI BARI**
Via Spalato 19  70121 Bari  Director: Clara Gelao
☎ +39 80 5412421   +39 80 5588147
Open: Tuesday-Saturday 09.30-13.00 / 16.00-19.00, Sunday 09.00-13.00
Closed: Monday

COLLECTION

Founded in 1928, the Pinacoteca Provinciale di Bari is located in the Palazzo della Provincia, a building constructed in the 1930s. The museum focuses primarily on works of art originating in the region. The collections include a Medieval section of capitals and sculptures from the 11th to the 14th century; icons and frescoes from the 13th and 14th century; 15th and 16th-century paintings of the Venetian School produced for churches and convents by such artists as Antonio and Bartolomeo Vivarini, Giovanni Bellini, Paris Bordon, Paolo Veronese and Tintoretto; and 17th and 18th-century paintings of the Neopolitan School including works by Massimo Stanzione, Paolo Finoglio, Maestro degli Annunci, Luca Giordano, Giuseppe Bonito, Francesco De Mura, Paolo De Matteis, Lorenzo De Caro and Andrea Miglionico. There is also a collection of valuable paintings by Corrado Giaquinto, a section of paintings from 19th-century painters such as Giuseppe De Nittis, Francesco Netti, Domenico Morelli, Francesco S. Altamura and Teofilo Patini, and a group of ceramics and statues from the 17th and 18th century. The museum also possesses a collection of plaster pieces from the 19th and 20th century by the Apulian sculptor Filippo Cifariello and a collection of contemporary works of art, including paintings, installations and sculpture, by artists such as P. Dorazio and P. Pascali.

In 1987, the Grieco Collection, consisting of fifty 19th and 20th-century paintings, was donated to the museum. This important addition to the museum collection includes works by Giovanni Fattori, Silvestro Lega, Giuseppe Abbati, Giovanni Boldini, Telemaco Signorini, Mario Sironi, Giorgio Morandi and Filippo De Pisis.

**EXHIBITIONS**

Jun 97-Jul 97    ***Society, Culture and Sport in Puglia***    An exhibition organised on the occasion of the 13th Mediterranean Games

Oct 97    ***Vincenzo Simone (1892-1968)***    An exhibition on the work of this Puglia photographer.

Nov 97    ***Wim Wenders***   *Photographs*

# Bergamo

**ACCADEMIA CARRARA**
Piazza G. Carrara 82a  24121 Bergamo  Director: Francesco Rossi
☎ +39 35 399640  🖷 +39 35 224510
Open: Wednesday - Monday 9.30-12.30 / 14.30-17.30
Closed: Tuesday and public holidays

**COLLECTION**

The Accademia Carrara, comprising the Picture Gallery and the School of Painting, was founded in 1796 by Count Giacomo Carrara, who bequeathed his personal collection to the new institution. It was taken over by the Municipality of Bergamo in 1958. Much of its collection is from bequests and legacies. The neoclassical building (1810), which has maintained its original façade, houses more than 1600 paintings as well as collections of drawings, prints, coins, bronzes, sculptures, china and miniatures. The entrance hall contains work by the Bergamo sculptor Giacomo Manzù. The School of Painting, with frescoes by Achille Funi and his school, was built between 1912 and 1930.

© Accademia Carrara,
Bergamo

**EXHIBITIONS**

Spring 97    ***Academies in Europe***   *Continuity and Innovation in the Visual Arts* This is an international exhibition in connection with art education, containing works from several European countries.

Jun 97    ***The Lochis Collection in Accademia Carrara***    The 250 paintings were collected by Guglielmo Lochis between 1820 and 1858. There are works by Raphael, Titian, Lotto, Fra Galgario, Dürer, Canaletto and Guardi.

Autumn 97    ***Monographs on Lorenzo Lotto***

## Bologna

**MUSEO CIVICO ARCHEOLOGICO**
Via dell'Archiginnasio 2  40124 Bologna  Director: Cristiana Morigi Govi
☎ +39 51 233849  📠 +39 51 266516
Internet: http://www.comune.bologna.it/bologna/Musei/Archeologico
Open: Tuesday-Friday 09.00-14.00, Saturday, Sunday
and public holidays 09.00-13.00 / 15.30-19.00
Closed: Monday + 25 Dec, 1 Jan

COLLECTION

The museum is one of the most important archaeological museums in Italy, rich in exhibits with local origins and antique collections which document the prehistoric civilisations. Exhibits from the Villanova and the 9th to the middle of the 6th century B.C. include the famous Benacci 'Askos' the 'Tomb of Gold' with its bronze tintinnabulum and gold fibula. Notable objects from the Etruscan period include the 'Situla della Certosa', a bronze vase with relief decoration of scenes from military, religious and civil life during mid-6th century B.C.; funerary stelae; the votive statuettes from the Monteguragazza Santuario; and the Tomb of Panathenaic Amphorae. The collection also includes Greek and Magna Graecia ceramics, the head of Atena Lemnia, a marble Roman copy of the bronze statue by Fidia, Roman glassware, bronze statuettes, ivories, gravestones from Bologna and a statue of Emperor Nero. The Egyptian civilisations are represented by a new exhibition (1994) with reliefs from the Tomb of Horemheb, funerary stelae, coffins, shabti and statues of Pharaoh.

EXHIBITION
until mid Jun 97

*Roman Oil-Lamps*  *Lighting in Ancient Rome*  Consisting of over 100 clay and bronze oil-lamps from the museum's Archaeological collection, including oil-lamps from Pompeii and Hercolaneum, this exhibition will allow the visitor to reconstruct the history of lighting during the Roman age.

## Bologna

**PINACOTECA NAZIONALE**
Via Belle Arti 56  40126  Bologna  Director: Andrea Emiliani
☎ +39 51 243222  📠 +39 51 251368
Open: Tuesday-Saturday 09.00-14.00 Sunday 09.00-13.00
Closed: Monday

COLLECTION

The picture gallery, housed in a former Jesuit college, contains a major collection of 14th to 18th-century paintings from Emilia-Romagna, in particular from Bologna. There are also works by Giotto, Raphael and Perugino, all of whom worked in Bologna. The works include 'St. George and the Dragon' by Vitale da Bologna, detached frescoes done by Vitale da Bologna and pupils, 'Crucifixion' by Giovanni da Modena, a polyptych by Giotto, three Byzantine panels of the Life of Christ, Venetian paintings by Vivarini and Cima da Conegliano, 'Madonna Enthroned' by Franceso del Cossa and 'St. Michael Archangel' by Ercole de'Roberti, from the Ferrara school, Bolognese works by Francesco Francia, including 'Annunciation and Saints', 'Ecstasy of St Cecilia' by Raphael, and 'Madonna and Saints' by Perugino. Foreign paintings include 'Esther and Ahasuerus' by De Bles, 'Last Supper' by El Greco and a fragment of the 'Crucifixion' by Titian. Among the Mannerist paintings are Giorgio Vasari's 'Dinner of St. Gregory the Great', frescoes by Agostino and Annibale Carracci, and the 'Madonna Bargellini' by Ludovico Carracci. There is a large painting by Guido Reni, 'Pietà dei Mendicanti' and a portrait of his mother. Other Bolognese artists include Francesco Albani, Guercino ('St. Bruno'), Domenichino (altar pieces and 'Martyrdom of St. Agnes'), Giuseppe Maria Crespi, Donato Creti, the Gandolfi, Carlo Cignani ('Madonna and Child with Saints'), and Niccolò dell'Abate.

EXHIBITIONS | No details available.

## Bolzano

**MUSEO CIVICO**
**Cassa di Risparmio 14  39100 Bolzano  Director: Reimo Lunz**
☎ +39 471 974625  📠 +39 471 980144
**Open: Tuesday-Friday 09.00-12.00 / 14.30-17.30  Sunday 10.00-13.00**
**Closed: Monday**

COLLECTION | The Museo Civico (Municipal Museum) of Bolzano houses an eclectic collection of archaeological artifacts, artistic works and folk art from the South Tyrol.
The archaeological section includes an extensive assortment of Mesolithic stone tools as well as Early to Late Iron Age artefacts from the burial ground at Vadena and a milestone from the time of the Emperor Claudius. Artistic works of historical value include a collection of wooden sculpture dating from the Romanesque to the Late Gothic and a magnificent selection of 8th-century paintings. The Folk Arts section exhibits a splendid collection of 19th-century costumes, farming tools and objects of daily use, as well as a few 'Stuben' from the Gothic period.

EXHIBITIONS | No details available.

## Bolzano

**MUSEION - MUSEUM FOR MODERN ART**
**Via Sernesi 1  39100  Bolzano  Director: Pier Luigi Siena**
☎ +39 471 977116  📠 +39 471 980001
**Open: Tuesday-Sunday 10.00-12.00 / 15.00-19.00**
**Closed: Monday**

COLLECTION | The Bolzano Museum of Modern Art was founded in 1987 and focuses on the artistic relation between German and Italian art, but also on mixed-media phenomena (for example image and word, image and sound). The museum's collection, consisting of works by modern Italian, German and Austrian artists and a special section dealing with 'language and art', is expected to be opened to the public in the summer of 1997.

EXHIBITIONS
until 18·05·97 | *Antonia Corpora*  *90 Paintings*

30·05·97-31·08·97 | *Sebastian Matta*  *Sculptures, Drawings and Ceramics*

12·09·97-09·01·98 | *Abstracta*  *Austria, Italy, Germany 1919-1939*

21·11·97-10·02·98 | *Prospettive 2000*  *Araki, Fogliati, Ontani, Serrano, Tillmans, Viola, Zumthor a.o.*

20.02.98-10.05.98 | *Marzona Collection*  *Conceptual Works*
[PARC SHOW]

Summer 97 | *Robert Schad*  *Metal Sculptures*

Summer 97 | *Italo Antico*  *Metal Sculptures*

## Città di Castello

---

**FONDAZIONE PALAZZO ALBIZZINI 'COLLEZIONE BURRI'**
Via Albizzini 1  06012 Città di Castello (Perugia)  Director: Nemo Sarteanesi
☎ +39 75 8554649/8559848  🖷 +39 75 8554649
Open: Tuesday-Saturday 10.00-12.00 / 15.00-18.00,
Sunday and public holidays 09.00-13.00
Closed: Monday

---

COLLECTION

The museum's collection of works by Alberto Burri is housed in two buildings: in the 15th-century Palazzo Albizzini and in the Ex Seccatoi del Tabacco. The works on the first floor of the Palazzo date from 1948 to 1967 and include tar, burlap, wood, iron and plastic paintings. The ground floor is occupied by works from the period 1967-1982. This display features 'Cretti' and 'Cellotex' works, models of theatre scenery and graphic works dating from the 1970s to 1989. The Palazzo also houses the archives and library of the Foundation which are open to the public by appointment only. The Ex Seccatoi Del Tobacco opened to the public in 1990 and houses work by Burri from the period 1974-1993. The huge sheds of this former tobacco curing plant contain a permanent exhibition of 128 works ranging from the 'Cretti' and large sculptures to the extensive 'Cellotex' cycles.

EXHIBITION
05·06·97-17·08·97

*Palais des Beaux Arts, Brussels*

## Firenze - Florence

---

**GALLERIA DELL'ACCADEMIA**
Via Ricasoli 60  50123 Firenze  Director: Franca Falletti
☎ +39 55 2388609/2388612  🖷 +39 55 2388609/2388699
Open: daily 09.00-19.00

---

COLLECTION

The Galleria was started in 1874 with paintings donated by Grand Duke Pietro Leopoldo I, intended to familiarise students with representative art from all periods. It displays a collection of primarily Florentine paintings in the rooms of the 'Pinacoteca' (picture gallery) but is most famous for its sculptures by Michelangelo, in particular the 'David', displayed in the Tribune. Michelangelo sculpted the 'David' between 1501 and 1504 from a high but shallow block of marble which was first offered to other sculptors who included Leonardo da Vinci and Andrea Sansovino. This statue established Michelangelo's reputation as the leading sculptor of his time. His other sculptures exhibited in the Galleria are the four 'Slaves' or Prisoners and the 'St. Matthew', both of which are unfinished (non-finito), and the 'Pietà di Palestrina'.

Mannerist paintings by contemporaries of Michelangelo hang on the walls of the Tribune. The picture gallery begins with works from the 15th and 16th century. Other rooms contain early Tuscan works from the 13th to 14th century and Byzantine paintings. One hall serves as a gallery for 19th-century sculptures and paintings by members of the Accademia, among which are plaster models by Lorenzo Bartolini. On the first floor there are Florentine paintings from the 14th and 15th century, as well as a collection of Russian paintings and icons from the 16th to the 18th century.

EXHIBITIONS

No details available.

## Firenze-Florence

**MUSEO ARCHEOLOGICO**
Via della Colonna 38  50100  Firenze  Director: Francesca Nicosia
☎ +39 55 247864  📠 +39 55 242213
Open: Tuesday-Saturday 09.00-14.00  Sunday 09.00-13.00
Closed: Monday

COLLECTION

The museum occupies the Palazzo della Crocetta, built for Grand Duchess Maria Maddalena of Austria in 1620. The collection originated with the Medici, who were especially interested in Etruscan antiquities. The exhibit begins with the 'François Vase', a Greek krater made in Athens (c. 570 B.C.), found in an Etruscan tomb. Among the Etruscan antiquities from the 5th century B.C. are cinerary urns and the tomb statue 'Mater Matuta' of an Etruscan woman seated on a throne and holding a baby. There are two kourai from the 6th century B.C.
The extensive Egyptian collection contains prehistoric objects, statues of female servants preparing beer and kneading dough from 2625-2475 B.C., part of the granite statue of a Pharaoh from the 19th century B.C., bas reliefs from tombs, a wooden Hittite chariot, sarcophagi, mummies, stelae, Coptic fabrics, scarabs and other objects.
The upper floors contain Etruscan sculpture, urns with Greek mythological scenes, an urn in the form of an Etruscan house, an alabaster sarcophagus from Tarquinia from the 4th century B.C., Etruscan small bronzes and mirrors with inscriptions, the 'Idolino', thought to be a Roman copy of a Greek statue by Polykleitos from 420 B.C., the 'Chimera', a 5th-century B.C. Etruscan work and the 'Orator', a late Hellenistic Etruscan bronze. There are vases and terracottas from Crete, Cyprus and Asia Minor, prehistoric objects and a collection of coins and precious stones.

EXHIBITIONS

No details available.

## Firenze-Florence

**GALLERIA D'ARTE MODERNA**
Piazza Pitti 1  50125  Firenze  Director: Ettore Spaletti
☎ +39 55 287096  📠 +39 55 215655
Open: daily 09.00-19.00

COLLECTION

The Pitti Palace was bought by Cosimo I and used as the Medici residence from c. 1540 to the 19th century. Most likely designed by Brunelleschi, it was originally built by the wealthy banker Luca Pitti in 1457. The Pitti Palace now houses eight museums. The Galleria, located on the second floor, has a collection of Tuscan works from the 18th century through to the Second World War. Of particular interest are paintings by the 'Macchiaioli' (Abbati, Fattori, Lega, Signorini, Boldini, Zandomeneghi, etc). These artists, who could be considered Tuscan Impressionists, were inspired by nature and used spots of colour (macchie) in their work. There are landscapes by Camille Pisarro, Neo-Classical paintings by Batoni, Tofanelli and Landi, and Romantic works by Hayez and Sabatelli as well as the head of Napoleon by Canova. The last Grand Dukes, Ferdinand III and Leopold II, decorated the rooms during the 19th century. The collection includes their portraits, a large Sèvres vase, bronze statues of Cain and Abel by Giovanni Dupré, portraits by Giovanni Boldini and genre paintings. A room devoted to the Risorgimento contains the bust of Mazzini by Cecioni and paintings of battle scenes by Fattori and Lega. There are paintings by Böcklin, Hildebrand and other German artists who worked in Florence during the 19th century. The 20th-century collection includes works by Tosi, Colacicchi, Conti, Soffici, De Pisis, Severini, De Chirico and others.

EXHIBITIONS No details available.

## Firenze - Florence

**MUSEO NAZIONALE DEL BARGELLO**
Via del Proconsolo 4  50122 Firenze  Director: Giovanna Gaeta Bertelà
☎ +39 55 2388606  📠 +39 55 2388699
Open: Tuesday-Saturday 08.30-13.50 2nd, 4th Sunday, 1st, 3rd,
4th Monday every month
Closed: 1st, 3rd, 5th Sunday, 2nd, 4th Monday every month and 25 Dec, 1 Jan,
1 May

COLLECTION **Renaissance Sculpture, Applied Art**  The museum is housed in the Bargello Palace, one of the oldest Florentine public monuments, built in 1250 after a design by Lapo Tedesco. In the 14th century the palace served as the residence of the Podestà (civil city authority). In 1574 it became the seat of the Chief of Police and municipal prison, and finally, in 1865, after restoration, it became the National Museum. The building now has Neo-Medieval features and includes a wide inner court and the Maddalena Chapel on the first floor with frescoes by pupils of Giotto. The palace contains Renaissance sculpture (mostly from Medici collections) and a large collection of applied art (gifts from private collectors).
A spacious hall on the first floor contains marbles, bronzes, terracotta objects of the early 15th century, several masterpieces by Ghiberti and Brunelleschi, as well as famous works by Donatello. The second floor accommodates sculptures by Andrea Verrocchio and other masters.
Michelangelo Buonarroti's marbles, together with works by such masters as Benvenuto Cellini and Jacopo Sansovino, are located on the ground floor.
The museum's wide-ranging applied art collection includes Gothic and Renaissance ivories, Limoges enamels, furniture, cameos, carpets, medallions, seals, coins and arms and other items.

EXHIBITIONS

Spring 97  **Baroque Cloth**  Exhibits donated by the Association of Friends of the Bargello.

Autumn 97  **Renaissance Majolica**  An exhibition of a gift from the Pilletteri family.

## Firenze - Florence

**CASA BUONARROTI**
Via Ghibellina 70  50122 Firenze  Director: Pina Ragionieri
☎ +39 55 241752  📠 +39 55 241698
Open: Wednesday-Monday 08.30-13.30
Closed: Tuesday

COLLECTION The Casa Buonarroti Museum is both a museum and an artistic monument to the genius of Michelangelo and the splendour of the Baroque era. Its extensive collection, making it one of Florence's most stimulating museums, was donated by the artist's family and includes two of the young Michelangelo's celebrated marbles, 'Madonna of the Steps' and the 'Battle of the Centaurs'. Other works of the great master are the 'Crucifixion' from Santo Spirito, the 'Wooden Model for the Facade of San Lorenzo' and the 'River

God'. An important collection of signed drawings is displayed in small groups on a rotating basis.

The museum is located in the townhouse of the artist's great nephew, Michelangelo Buonarroti the Younger (1568-1647) and still has the appearance of that era. Four sumptuously decorated period rooms display how Michelangelo the Younger recounted the history of his family and his famous ancestor through the works of the most important Florentine artists from the mid-17th century. Here, too, is where Michelangelo the Younger kept the most precious pieces in his collection which are still displayed today in their original locations. These pieces include the portraits commissioned by Cristofano Allori and Giuliano Finelli, and an early Renaissance masterpiece by Giovanni di Francesco, 'The Stories of San Nicola'.

**EXHIBITION**
Spring 97 - onwards

*Archaeological Collections*   The archaeological collections of the Buonarotti family, returning to the museum after more than a century, will be housed in a new permanent room.

# Firenze - Florence

**MUSEO DI PALAZZO VECCHIO**
Piazza della Signoria  50122  Firenze  Director: Fiorenza Scalia
☎ +39 55 27681  ⓕ +39 55 288049
Open: Friday-Wednesday 09.00-19.00  Public holidays 08.00-13.00
Closed: Thursday

**COLLECTION**

The Palace, built in the form of a trapezoid, is thought to have been designed by Arnolfo di Cambio around 1300. The courtyard was redone by Michelozzo in the 15th century, and later stuccos and frescoes were added by Giorgio Vasari. It was a medieval palace, fortress and seat of city government.
The museum is housed in several public rooms and the apartments of Duke Cosimo I. The Salone dei Cinquecento was built in 1495 by Cronaca for the Consiglio Maggiore of the Republic. There were unsuccessful attempts by both Leonardo da Vinci and Michelangelo to fresco the walls, which were finally carried out by Vasari, Borghini, Stradano, Zucchi and Naldini. The raised Udienza contains the 'Victory' by Michelangelo and two other statues by Bandinelli and de' Rossi. The study of Francesco I (Studiolo) was executed by Vasari and Borghini in Florentine Mannerist style and now displays bronze statuettes and paintings on the theme of alchemy and science. The original 'Putto with a Dolphin' by Verrocchio is in the enclosed Terazzo di Giunone. There is a fresco by Domenico Ghirlandaio in the Sala dei Gigli, where the bronze statue of 'Judith and Holofernes' by Donatello is displayed. The museum also houses

the Cherubini collection of antique musical instruments and the
Loeser Collection with works by Rustici, Sansovino, da Camaino and
others, and a bust of Machiavelli.

EXHIBITIONS No details available.

## Firenze - Florence

### MUSEO DI SAN MARCO
Piazza San Marco 3  50121 Firenze  Director: Magnolia Scudieri
☎ +39 55 2388608  📠 +39 55 2388699
Open: daily 09.00-19.00

COLLECTION

The San Marco Museum is housed in an ancient convent of medieval
origin; Cosimo de'Medici commissioned the architect Michelozzo
Michelozzi to rebuild it entirely to accomodate Dominican friars.
The reconstruction took place between 1437 and 1450, during
which years Beato Angelico (Fra' Giovanni da Fiesole, 1400-1445)
and his assistants frescoed many of the rooms, including the 43 cells
on the first floor with the History of Christ. There is an
'Annunciation' by Fra' Angelico at the top of the stairs leading to
the cells and scenes of the Crucifixion in the corridor. Cosimo
De'Medici used one of the cells from time to time and the Prior's
cell once housed Savonarola. The library, built by Michelozzi in
1441, was the first public library in Europe and contains illuminated
choir books and psalters. At the end of the 15th century Domenico
Ghirlandaio painted a 'Last Supper' on the wall of the Small
Refectory. At the beginning of the 16th century Fra' Bartolomeo
painted five frescoes above the doors in the old Pilgrim's Hospice,
which now serves as a gallery for the paintings of Fra' Angelico. In
addition, Giovanni Antonio Sogliani painted the 'Miraculous Supper
of Saint Dominic' in the Great Refectory, which also contains altar
pieces, altar steps and polyptychs by Fra' Angelico. The fresco
'Crucifixion and Saints' was painted by Fra' Angelico in the Chapter
House. The Cloister of St Dominic contains 18th-century frescoes by,
among others, Alessandro Gherardini and Cosimo Ulivelli.
Today the museum has a collection of almost all Fra' Angelico's
panel paintings from Florentine churches and monasteries, panel
paintings by Fra' Bartolomeo and his school, illuminated books from
the 13th to 15th century, and sculptures, carved stones and
detached frescoes from buildings destroyed at the end of the last
century in the old centre of Florence.

EXHIBITIONS No details available.

## Firenze - Florence

### MUSEO DI SANTA MARIA NOVELLA
Piazza S. Maria Novella  50129 Firenze  Director: Fiorenza Scalia
☎ +39 55 282187  📠 +39 55 288049
Open: Saturday-Thursday 09.00-14.00  Public holidays 08.00-13.00
Closed: Friday

COLLECTION

The museum is located in part of the Dominican Basilica of
Santa Maria Novella. The Convent of Santa Maria Novella was one
of the most prominent in Florence, and Pope Eugenius IV held
meetings of the Council of Florence there in 1439. The Cloisters,
now property of the city, are the site of further excavation. In the
15th century Paolo Uccello painted frescoes depicting stories from
the Book of Genesis. These have since been restored and returned
to the Chiostro Verde, which is decorated in green tints. There are

also 15th-century frescoes by Dello Delli, 14th-century frescoes by Stefano Fiorentino and Andrea di Bonaiuto, a fresco ascribed to Bernardino Poccetti (c.1592) and others by unknown Florentine Renaissance artists, and a Sienese lunette from c. 1330. The vaults contain roundels of Dominican Saints. The refectory has a display of church silver and vestments.

**EXHIBITIONS** No details available.

# Firenze - Florence

## MUSEO STEFANO BARDINI
**Piazza de' Mozzi 1  50125  Firenze  Director: Fiorenza Scalia**
☎ +39 55 2342427  📠 +39 55 288049
**Open: Thursday-Tuesday 09.00-14.00  Public holidays 08.00-13.00**
**Closed: Wednesday**

**COLLECTION** The collection is housed in the Palazzo Bardini, built by the collector and antiquarian Stefano Bardini in 1883. His collection, bequeathed to the city in 1922, comprises Etruscan, Roman, Romanesque and Gothic architectural fragments, Medieval and Renaissance sculpture, paintings, sarcophagi, decorative arts, arms and armour, furniture and musical instruments.
The collection includes a carved 16th-century window from Sassari, an early 16th-century bust of St. John the Baptist, a classical sarcophagus with Medusa's head, a statue of 'Charity' attributed to Tino da Camaino, a well-head of red Veronese marble and an effigy by Paolo di Gualdo Cattaneo. Tomb slabs and wall-tombs are displayed in a large room built in the form of a crypt. There is a sculpted sarcophagus attributed to Michelozzo and an Altarpiece by Andrea della Robbia. The collection of arms and armour includes 16th-century swords, crossbows and other infantry weapons, a helmet from the 6th century B.C., halberds, pikes, spears, painted shields, tournament weapons and firearms. In a room with a marble doorway from 1548 there are two works attributed to Donatello, one in polychrome terra cotta and the other in polychrome stucco, glass and mosaic. Another room contains carpets, portraits and furniture, as well as cases of bronze medals, plaques and statuettes and frescoes by Giovanni di San Giovanni, detached from Palazzo Pucci. Among the instruments is a spinet made in Rome in 1577.

**EXHIBITIONS** No details available.

# Firenze-Florence

## OPERA DI S. MARIA DEL FIORE OR OPERA DEL DUOMO
**Piazza del Duomo 9  50122  Firenze  Director: Patrizio Osticresi**
☎ +39 55 2302885  📠 +39 55 2302898
**Open: Daily Apr-Oct 09.00-19.30; Nov-Mar 09.00-18.00**

**COLLECTION** The collection comprises works of art gathered from the major and most ambitious religious monuments of Florence (the Baptistery, the Cathedral and its Cupola and Bell Tower). These include sculptures from the Cathedral's ancient Gothic facade by sethe great Arnolfo di Cambio, and works by 14th-century sculptors and by early-15th-century masters such as Nanni di Banco and Donatello. Masterpieces by other 15th-century artists include two marble choirs from the Cathedral; the first one by Luca della Robbia and the second one by Donatello.
There are also the large statues originating from the niches of the Bell Tower (substituted by copies on location), the work of Andrea Pisano (14th century) and Donatello (15th century), as well as panels

in bas relief depicting Biblical Stories and the Labours of Man by Andrea Pisano, the Sciences by Luca della Robbia, the Planets, the Virtues and the Liberal Arts by followers of Andrea Pisano and the Sacraments by Alberto Arnoldi.

Luca Della Robbia
*Marble Choir (detail)*
© Opera di. S. Maria
del Fiore or Opera
del Duomo,
Firenze

Recent acquisitions include the tormented Mary Magdalene by Donatello and the unfinished marble Pietà that Michelangelo had destined for his own tomb, as well as four restored panels from the 'Gate of Paradise' by Lorenzo Ghiberti.
The collection includes paintings, mosaics, terracotta pieces, Roman sarcophagi and silver liturgical objects, corals, reliquaries and several simple 'machines' used by Brunelleschi to raise the Cupola.

**EXHIBITIONS** No details available.

# Firenze - Florence

**OPERA MUSEO STIBBERT**
**Via Stibbert 26  50134 Firenze  Director: Kirsten Aschengreen-Placenti**
☎ +39 55 486049   📠 +39 55 486049
**Open: Friday-Wednesday 09.00-14.00, Sunday 09.00-13.00**
**Closed: Thursday**

**COLLECTION** The Stibbert Museum originated in the collection of Frederick Stibbert (1838-1906), a wealthy collector and traveller who fought with Garibaldi and knew Queen Victoria. With the help of the architect Cesare Fortini, Stibbert expanded the 14th- century house left to him by his mother, connecting it to another house and making a park.
Some rooms were designed for his collections, which include porcelain, leatherwork, sculptures, bronze statuettes, tapestries, paintings, costumes, clocks, furnishings and embroidery. Stibbert's main passion was collecting armour from all over the world. There are cases with Etruscan, Roman and Lombard armour, and a series of fully arrayed mannequins, including six dressed in 16th-century oriental armour standing in a room hung with Belgian tapestries which depict the Labours of Hercules. The Sale Japonese contain a collection of Japanese arms and armour from the Edo period, and Turkish armour used by Sultan Selim I at the end of the 15th century. There are also Persian and Indian arms, armour and costumes. The mantle Napoleon Bonaparte wore at his coronation as King of Italy in 1805 can be seen in the Sala Imperio, and another room contains English and German armour.
The richly furnished part of the house used as Stibbert's residence

contains Art Nouveau tiles and stained glass, Murano chandeliers, a collection of oriental and other porcelain and paintings by Italian, Dutch and Flemish artists, as well as some by Stibbert himself.

**EXHIBITIONS**     No details available.

# Firenze - Florence

## MUSEO STORICO TOPOGRAFICO FIRENZE COM'ERA
Via dell'Oriuolo 24  50122 Firenze  Director: Fiorenza Scalia
☎ +39 55 2398483  ☒ +39 55 288049
Open: Friday-Wednesday 09.00-14.00 public holidays 08.00-13.00
Closed: Thursday

**COLLECTION**     Situated in the former Convento delle Oblate, the museum contains maps, drawings, engravings, paintings and records illustrating the life, history and urban transformation of the city since the 15th century. The 'Veduta della Catena' depicts Florence c. 1470. Bonsignori's topographical plan of 1594 was the first scientifically drawn plan of the city. There is a series of lunettes by the Flemish painter Giusto Utens (1599) of the Medici villas; Giovanni Battista Nelli (1661-1725) made the first measured survey of the Cathedral, Baptistry and Campanile for the Opera del Duomo. The cartographical collection also contains works by Valerio Spada (1650), F.B. Werner (1705) and Federigo Fantozzi (1843 and 1866). Also featured are paintings of Florence by Thomas Patch and Guiseppe Maria Terreni, engravings by Telemaco Signorini of the Mercato Vecchio in 1874, engravings by Giuseppe Zocchi of the city and surrounding villas (1754) and lithographs by A. Durand (1863). There is a permanent exhibition of 58 works by Ottone Rosai (1895-1957).

**EXHIBITIONS**     No details available.

# Firenze - Florence

## GALLERIA DEGLI UFFIZI - UFFIZI ART GALLERY
Piazzale degli Uffizi 6  50122 Firenze  Director: Anna Maria Petrioli Tofani
☎ +39 55 2388651  ☒ +39 55 2388699
Open: Tuesaday-Sunday 08.30-18.50  public holidays 08.30-13.50
Closed: Monday

**COLLECTION**     The Medici originally commissioned Vasari to construct the massive Palazzo degli Uffizi to serve as government offices in 1560. The building now houses the Uffizi Art Gallery and contains the most important collection of paintings in Italy and one of the finest in the world. The collection is particularly rich in Renaissance and Manneristic works. To enable the visitors to gain an overview of the various schools of Italian art the paintings are arranged in chronological order.
Works are included in the exhibition by the masters of the Early Renaissance: Giotto, Fra. Angelico, Masaccio and Dominico Veneziano. The students of perspective are represented primarily by Pierro della Francesca, but Paolo Uccello, Ghirlandaio Perugino and Filippo Lippi with their Romantic Madonnas are also present. Lippi taught Botticelli, his student, the art of creating enchanting madonnas. Botticelli is best known for his sublime mythological allegories, all of which were painted for the Medici family. Paintings by both Leonardo da Vinci and his master Verrocchio are present in the collection, as are Mantegna, Raphael as a representative of the High Renaissance, Pontormo and Michelangelo. Dutch, Flemish, German, Spanish, Bolognese and Venetian artists are also exhibited.

The Uffizi Gallery also houses a fine collection of ancient sculpture collected by the Medici cardinals in Rome.

The beautiful 'Tribuna' with its mother-of-pearl dome and 'pietra dura' floor was built by Buontalenti (1584) and was designed to display the most valuable objects in the Medici collection. The best known is 'The Venus de Medici', a Greek sculpture and the most erotic ancient sculpture.

**EXHIBITIONS**        No details available.

## Genova-Genoa

**MUSEO CIVICO DI ARCHEOLOGIA LIGURE DE GENOVA**
Via Pallavicini 11  16155 Genova-Pegli  Director: A.M. Pastorino
☎ +39 10 680204  🖷 +39 10 206022
Open: Winter  Tuesday-Saturday 09.00-17.00  Sunday 09.00-12.30;
Summer  Tuesday-Saturday 09.00-19.00  Sunday 09.00-13.00
Closed: Monday

**COLLECTION**

The museum documents the prehistoric and historic period of Liguria from the Paleolithic Age to Roman times.

The first part of the museum's collection comprises finds from the Paleolithic Age. These remains include Pleistocenic fauna, pottery and polished stone tools from Western Liguria and the Ligurian and Piedmontese Apennines.

A considerable number of metal remains documents the beginning of metallurgy in this region.

The Luigi Bernabo Brea excavation produced exceptional finds from one of Europe's most significant archaeological deposits: the Arene Candide Cave with its spectacular Paleolithic burials. The oldest of these is dated at around 20 000 B.C. and is rich in materials (pottery, stone and fauna) from the Neolithic Age to the Late Prehistoric Age.

The Iron Age is represented by single burials and by remains from settlements in the inland region, in particular from a necropolis in Genoa: a rich source of Greek pottery, Etruscan bronzes and Middle Eastern products that document the importance of the town's first port in the 6th century B.C.

From a 1993 excavation comes a display from the 'Tavola di Polcevera' collection: the first written juridical documents of Roman times in Liguria.

The exhibition is completed with a display of Greek and Roman materials belonging to the 'Principe Oddone di Savoia Collection' and a collection of antique, especially Roman, glass.

**EXHIBITIONS**
until Sep 97

***Echoes of the past.*** *Ancient Tyrrhenian Civilization*   [IN THE AQUARIUM OF GENOA]   This exhibition, covering a period of 20 000 years, begins with Upper Palaeolithic objects from the Ligurian caves and traces the development of Etruscan, Sardinian and Roman seafaring cultures.

until Jun 97

***The Marvels of the First Ligurians***   [IN THE DUCAL PALACE - GENOA]
The exhibition presents original engravings, designs, rubbings and rock engravings from the Valley of Marvels in the Department of the Maritime Alps (France).

## Genova · Genoa

**GALLERIA DI PALAZZO BIANCO**
Via Garibaldi 11  Genova  Director: Clario Di Fabio
☎ +39 10 291803  📠 +39 10 206022
Open: Tuesday, Thursday, Friday, Sunday 09.00-13.00
Wednesday, Saturday  09.00-19.00
Closed: Monday

COLLECTION

The collections present a review of Genoese and Ligurian paintings between the 14th and the 18th century. The collections include works by L. Cambiaso, G.B. Castello ('il Bergamasco'), B. Strozzi, G.Assereto, Gregorio de Ferrari, Domenico Piola and Alessandro Magnasco, whose famous 'Entertainment in a Garden of Albaro' is on view. Three rooms are dedicated to Italian painting, where works by Filippino Lippi, Veronese, Procaccini, Cerano and Morazzone are the main pieces on display, topped by Caravaggio's 'Ecce Homo'.  The collections of Flemish and Dutch art are very comprehensive, ranging from the end of the 15th century up to the 18th century. The collections include works by Hans Memling ('Christ's Blessing'), Gerard David ('Polyptych of Cervara'), Jean Provost and Jan Matsys. Also on display are masterpieces by Rubens ('Venus and Mars') and by Van Dyck ('Monetary Tribute' and 'Vertuno and Pomona') as well as by other Flemish artists who were active in Genoa (J. Roos, C. De Wael, J. Wildens).
The palace, which is situated on the magnificent 16th-century 'Strada Nuova' road (now via Garibaldi) dates back to the beginning of the 18th century and was presented to the city in 1889 by Maria Brignole Sale de Ferrari, Duchess of Galliera, together with the rich art collections, which were later enlarged through gifts and legacies.

EXHIBITIONS

No exhibitions planned.

## Genova · Genoa

**GALLERIA DI PALAZZO ROSSO**
Via Garibaldi 18  16124 Genova  Director: Piero Boccardo
☎ +39 10 282641  📠 +39 10 206022
Open: Tuesday, Thursday, Friday, Sunday 09.00-13.00
Wednesday, Saturday 09.00-19.00
Closed: Monday

COLLECTION

Palazzo Rosso was designed and constructed between 1671 and 1677 by the architect Pietro Antonio Corradi on behalf of Ridolfo and Gio. Francesco Brignole-Sale, and remained the residence of the Brignole-Sale family for about two centuries. The palace and its collection of paintings, sculpture and furniture were donated to the municipality of Genoa in 1874. The collection includes works from Venice (Veronese, Paris Bordon), the Bologna School (Ludovico Carracci, Reni, Guercino) and the Rome School (Maratta). There is also an assemblage of works by Genoese masters, including Luca Cambiaso, Pellegro Piola, Strozzi, Scorza, Castiglione and Guidobono.
During the Second World War, the fresco in the upper-floor vault by Gregorio De Ferrari was destroyed, but in adjoining rooms other fine frescoes by De Ferrari and his father-in-law Domenico Piola and others remain. The upper floors also exhibit paintings by foreign masters, including three portraits of members of the Brignole-Sale family by Van Dyck and other family portraits by Yacinthe Rigaud. Throughout the palace are pieces of fine furniture as well as important examples of oriental pottery.

EXHIBITIONS

No exhibitions planned.

## Genova - Genoa

**GALLERIA NAZIONALE DI PALAZZO SPINOLA**
Piazza Pellicceria 1  16126 Genova   Director: Farida Simonetti
☎ +39 10 294661  📠 +39 10 294661
Open: Tuesday-Saturday 09.00-19.00  Sunday 14.00-19.00  Monday 09.00-13.00

**COLLECTION**

Palazzo Spinola retains its original residential qualities and gives visitors the opportunity to relive the atmosphere of a 17th and 18th-century abode. This is possible thanks to the completeness of the furnishings, which not only include furniture but also curtains, porcelain and silver objects that have been collected in the palace over the centuries by its various owners: the Grimaldis, Ansaldo Pallavicino, Maddalena Doria, the Spinolas. In addition, works by Da Messina, Van Cleve, Van Dyck or of Genoese artists such as Parodi, Castello, Il Grechetto and De Ferrari can be viewed in mural paintings in the salons and in the picture gallery, which is also arranged according to 18th-century taste.

The 3rd and 4th floors focus on Genoese artists such as Pisano and Giambola, and on Rubens. Local and European majolica and porcelain are also on display here, around an outstanding collection of Oriental porcelain.

Great hall, second
noble floor
© Galleria Nazionale
di Palazzo Spinola,
Genova

The Workroom of Didactic Games is of special interest to visitors with children: adults and children can colour and cut out models of furniture, put on a doge's costume, invent stories and have them performed in the puppet theatre.

**EXHIBITIONS**
until Jun 97

***Music from the Books***   *From Liturgical Opera to Opera Librettos*
In this exhibition, from the collection of the University of Genoa Library, three themes of this exhibition (Music and Liturgy; Theory and Practice of Music; Music on Stage) are illustrated by books from the original Jesuit library and from suppressed religious groups.

Sep 97-Jan 98

***Antique Dreams***  *The Bedrooms of the Genovese Residences*
Continuing the series on the Genovese aristocracy, this exhibition shows the manner of sleeping and the furniture and ornaments of the 18th and 19th centuries. The bedroom of the last Marquis of Spinola has been reconstructed.

# Genova - Genoa

## MUSEO DI ARCHITETTURA E SCULTURA LIGURE DI SANT'AGOSTINO
Piazza Sarzano 35 r.  16124 Genova  Director: Clario Di Fabio
☎ +39 10 2511263  📠 +39 10 206022
Open: Tuesday-Saturday 09.00-19.00  Sunday 09.00-12.30
Closed: Monday

COLLECTION

The monastic complex of St. Augustine consists of a 13th-century church, irregular triangular cloisters of the same period and rectangular cloisters from the 17th century. In Napoleonic times the church was desecrated and the entire complex fulfilled various functions. Recently, however, the two cloisters have been converted into a museum and the church is now used for all kinds of cultural purposes. The two cloisters contain architectural fragments, sculptures and loose fresco pieces (originating from Classical Roman frescoes, which were employed for reasons of prestige in Genoese aristocratic residences and in religious buildings up to the Middle Ages and the 18th century).
Main works: fragments of the tomb of Margaret of Brabant by Giovanni Pisano; sculptures by Gaggini, Filippo Parodi, Pierre Puget, Francesco Schiaffino, Antonio Canova; frescoes by Luca Cambiaso, Valerio Castello, Domenico Piola and Gregorio De Ferrari.
The museum also houses a didactical section and the Topographic Collection of the Genoa Municipality, a collection of designs and engravings (more than 5 000 pieces) which document the urban, architectonic and territorial evolution of the city of Genoa and its surrounding areas.

EXHIBITIONS

No details available.

# Lucca

## MUSEO E PINACOTECA NAZIONALE DI PALAZZO MANSI
Via Galli Tassi 43  55100  Lucca  Director: Maria Teresa Filieri
☎ +39 583 55570  📠 +39 6 58432180
Open: Tuesday-Wednesday 09.00-19.00 (winter 14.00)
Closed: Monday

COLLECTION

The museum displays a collection of Italian and Flemish works from the 15th to 17th century. The paintings include 'Tobias and the Angel' by Jacopo Vignali, 'Annunciation' by Morazzone and 'Holy Family and St. Anne' attributed to Van Dyck. The ballroom contains 17th-century frescoes, one of which depicts the 'Judgement of Paris', by Gian Gioseffo dal Sole and paintings by Rosa da Tivoli and Niccolò Cassana, 'Crucifixion and Two Saints' by Guido Reni, 'Sacrifice of Isaac' by Fernando Bol and 'St. John the Baptist' by Carlo Dolci. 17th-century Flemish tapestries hang in the drawing rooms, and the bedroom has 18th-century hangings from Lucca. The museum also contains portraits of the Medici by Sustermans, Cosimo I and the young Fernando de'Medici by Bronzini, 'Prayer in the Garden' by Bassano, 'Portrait of a Boy' by Sweerts and paintings by Paul Brill.

EXHIBITIONS

No details available

# Milano - Milan

## GALLERIA D'ARTE MODERNA
Via Palestro 16  20121  Milano  Director: Maria Teresa Fiorio
☎ +39 2 86463054/76002819  📠 +39 2 86463054
Open: Tuesday-Sunday 09.30-17.30
Closed: Monday

**COLLECTION**

The Gallery of Modern Art is housed in the Neo-Classical Villa Reale or Villa Belgiojoso, built for the Belgiojoso family in 1790 and Napoleon's Milan residence. The collection of 19th-century art from Lombardy reflects international styles as well as its own 'Scapigliati' ('wild-haired') movement. It includes 'Quarto Stato' by Giuseppe Pellizza da Volpeda, paintings by Appiani, Carnovali and Hayez, a section of paintings by Marino Marini, and sculptures by Medardo Rosso and Enrico Butti. The Carlo Grassi bequest of 19th-century French and Italian paintings is shown on the second floor. French paintings by Corot, Millet, Boudin, Sisley, Manet, Gauguin and Cézanne are displayed together with work by Van Gogh. There are also graphics by Corot and Toulouse-Lautrec. Works by Matisse, Picasso and Renoir have recently been added. The Italian paintings are by Morelli, Ciardi, Cabianca, Fattore, Lega, Signorini, de Nittis and Boldini. The last rooms contain 19th and 20th-century Italian paintings by Spadini, Segantini, Mancini, Giorgio de Chirico, Umberto Boccioni and others. Contemporary work and temporary exhibitions are shown in the Pavilion. Some of the works were stolen twice, in 1975 and 1976. While the majority were later recovered, a Renoir and a Corot are still missing.

**EXHIBITIONS**

No details available.

## Milano

**MUSEI DI CASTELLO SFORZESCO**
Piazza Castello  20121 Milan  Director: Maria Teresa Fiorio
☎ +39 2 62083931  🖷 +39 2 86463054
Open: Tuesday-Wednesday 09.30-17.30
Closed: Monday

**COLLECTION**

[MUSEO D'ARTE ANTICA DEL CASTELLO SFORZESCO]
The sculpture collections are deeply associated with the city and its surrounding countryside. Indeed they consist of works originating from Milanese or Lombard churches and palazzi no longer in existence, from locally conducted excavations, and from a very homogeneous tissue, offering the richest record of sculpture in the Po Valley from palaeo-Christian times to the 16th century.

Francesco Hayez
*Portrait of Signora*
*Matilde Juva Branca*
© Musei di Castello
Sforzesco, Milano

The few, but superb exceptions include: a bas-relief by the Tuscan Agostino di Duccio, purchased at the beginning of the 19th century, and Michelangelo's Pietà Rondanini, another outstanding and relatively recent aquisition (1952).
Highlights of the sulpture collection are the very rare head known as the Teodora (6th century), the remains of the Longobard

monastery of Santa Maria d'Aurona; the Telamone from Cremona, recently attributed to Wiligelmo; the grandiose tomb-monument to Bernabò Visconti, which still bears traces of precious gildings; and the sculptures by Giovanni di Balduccio for Santa Maria di Brera and for a Visconti tomb formerly in Santa Tecla. Extraneous to the specific character of these collections is the exquisite bas-relief by Agostino di Duccio which was carved for a chapel in the Tempio Malatestiano at Rimini (c. 1450).

A work of outstanding interest and superb quality is the sculptural complex formed by the Tomb of Gaston de Foix by Agostino Busti, called il Bambaia. But dominating the entire collection with dramatic impact is Michelangelo's Pietà Rondanini, which was the artist's last great masterpiece.

**EXHIBITIONS**

No details available.

[PINACOTECA DEL CASTELLO SFORZESCO]

**COLLECTION**

Lombard and Venetian artists are the best represented in the collections. And among the latter, the monumental altarpiece painted by Mantegna in 1497 for the church of S. Maria in Organo at Verona, and the haunting Madonna with Child, and early work by Giovanni Bellini can be admired.

By Foppa should be mentioned the Madonna with Book, while Bramantino is present with a dramatic Deposition and Cesare da Sesto with the polyptich of S. Rocco, his last masterpiece.

Not to be neglected is the exquisite Madonna by Correggio.

Among the portraits are some of the most important works in the whole Picture Gallery: the enigmatic Poet Laureate, the attribution of which is disputed between Giovanni Bellini and Antonello da Messina, The Reader by Correggio, the Young Man by Lotto, the aristocratic portrait by Bronzino and another, of extraordinary vitality, by Tintoretto.

And again, among the 17th-century Lombards, the St Rocco by Morazzone, a St Sebastian by Giulio Cesare Procaccini, St Michael the Archangel by Cerano, up to the threshold of the 18th-century with Magnasco's The Market and then, with Tiepolo and Guardi, to the peaks of 18th-century Venetian art.

**EXHIBITIONS**

No exhibitions planned

# Milano - Milan

## PINACOTECA DI BRERA
Via Brera 28  20121 Milano  Director: Pietro Petranoie
☎ +39 2 722631  🖷 +39 2 72001140
Open: Tuesday-Saturday 09.00-17.30  Sunday 09.00-12.30
Closed: Monday

**COLLECTION**

The Picture Gallery is located in the 17th-century Palazzo di Brera with a statue of Napoleon by Canova in the courtyard. Founded in the 18th century by the Accademia di Belle Arti, it houses an important collection of North Italian art which was begun when Napoleon 'collected' art from churches and monasteries in Northern Italy and placed them in Milan, his Cisalpine capital. It has been expanded over the years through acquisitions and donations.

The Gallery's highlights include the 'Marriage of the Virgin' by Raphael and the 'Pala di Urbino', the last painting by Piero della Francesca. There is a collection of portraits by Palma Giovane, Daniele Crespi, Francesco Hayez and Sir Thomas Lawrence. Among the Venetian paintings are 'The Last Supper' by Veronese, 'St. Helena with Saints and Donors' and 'Pietà' by Tintoretto, a Polyptych by Antonio Vivarini and Giovanni d'Alemagna, 'Scenes from the Life of the Virgin' and others by Carpaccio, 'Madonna and

Child' and 'Pietà' by Giovanni Bellini. Other North Italian works include 'St. Ursula and her Maidens' by Martino da Udine, 'Madonna and Child with Saints' and 'St. Peter Martyr' by Cima da Conegliano, 'Madonna and Child' attributed to Giovanni Battista Martini da Udine and 'Pietà' by Girolamo da Treviso il Vecchio. There are frescoes by Donato Bramante taken from the Casa Panigarola and paintings and frescoes by Bernardino Luini from the church of Santa Maria della Pace in Milan. Coreggio is represented by his 'Adoration of the Magi' and 'Nativity', Caravaggio by 'Supper at Emaus' and Tiepolo by 'Madonna del Carmelo' and a sketch for a battle scene.

The works of foreign artists include 'Portrait of the Princess of Orange' by Van Dyck, 'The Last Supper' by Rubens, a Triptych by Jan de Beer, El Greco's 'St. Francis', Rembrandt's 'Portrait of his Sister' and other Dutch works, and 'Lord Donoughmore' by Sir Joshua Reynolds.

**EXHIBITIONS** | No exhibitions planned

## Milano

**MUSEO POLDI PEZZOLI**
Via Manzoni 12  20121  Milano  Director: Alessandra Mottola Molfino
☎ +39 2 796334  🖷 +39 2 8690788
Open: Tuesday-Sunday 09.30-12.30 / 14.30-18.00
Saturday 09.30-12.30 / 14.30-19.30
Closed: Monday and Sunday afternoon (Apr-Sept)

**COLLECTION** | The Poldi Pezzoli Museum was first opened in 1881 as part of Gian Giacomo Poldi Pezzoli's legacy. Rebuilt and rearranged in 1951, the museum has retained the atmosphere of a private house. Its collection is a good example of 19th-century trends in collecting. The collection of paintings includes masterpieces dating from the 14th to the 19th century, the highlights of which are the 'Portrait of a Woman' attributed to Piero del Pollaiolo, the 'Mourning over the Death of Christ' and the 'Madonna and Child' by Sandro Botticelli. Other works of interest in the collection are those by such Lombard painters as Solario, Luini, Boltraffio, Cesare da Sesto and works by the 18th-century Venetian painters Canaletto, Tiepolo and Guardi. The museum also has a collection of decorative art which features arms and armour, jewellery and enamels, watches, clocks and sundials, Venetian glass, European and Oriental ceramics, Islamic bronzes, textiles, lace, tapestries and carpets. The collection includes a Persian carpet dating back to 1542/43.

**EXHIBITIONS** | No details available.

## Modena

**GALLERIA ESTENSE**
Piazza S. Agostino 336  Palazzo dei Musei  41100 Modena  Director: J. Bentini
☎ +39 59 222145  🖷 +39 59 230196
Open: Tuesday, Friday, Saturday 09.00-19.00,
Wednesday, Thursday, 09.00-14.00, Sunday 09.00-13.00
Closed: Monday

**COLLECTION** | The gallery's paintings come from the collection started by the Este family, former rulers of Modena, in the 16th century. It contains a selection of 15th to 17th-century paintings from Emilia-Romagna, as well as small Etruscan, Italic and Greek bronzes, Romanesque sculpture, Venetian enamel work and Islamic ceramics. There are 14th-century portable altars by Tommaso and Barnaba da Modena,

'St. Anthony of Padua' by Cosmè Tura, panels by Bartolomeo Erri, Lombard, French, Spanish and Byzantine sculptures in marble and ivory, and works by Joos van Cleve, Albrecht Bouts, Cima da Conegliano, Apollonio di Giovanni, Correggio, Lendinara, Ferrari, Botticini, Bonascia, Catena, Romano, Maineri, Panetti and Pieter Brueghel the Younger. The collection also contains a 16th-century decorated Estense harp, bronzes by Il Riccio, a bust of Francesco I d'Este by Bernini, busts by L'Antico and Tullio Lombardo, sculptures by Mazzoni, dell'Arca and Begarelli and ceramics from Urbino. The gallery also has portraits of Alfonso I and Hercules I d'Este' by Dosso Dossi, a bust of a woman by Francesco Duquesnoy and bronzes by Tacca, Sansovino and Giambologna, a portrait of Francesco I d'Este by Velásquez, 'Adoration of the Magi' from Rubens' workshop and 'Rape of Europa' by Tintoretto.
The museum contains coins, medals and other artefacts, the archaeological section has prehistoric, Etruscan and Roman objects, and the Este Library possesses illuminated codices.

**EXHIBITIONS** | No details available.

## Napoli - Naples

### MUSEO ARCHEOLOGICO NAZIONALE DI NAPOLI
Piazza Museo 19  80135 Napoli  Director: Maria Rosario Borriello
☎ +39 81 440166  📠 +39 81 440013
Open: Wednesday-Monday 09.00-14.00
Closed: Tuesday and 1 Jan, 1 May, 25 Dec

**COLLECTION** | Since 1777 the archaeological finds from excavations in Herculaneum and Pompeii have been arranged in the late 16th-century building. Among the original Greek statues and Roman copies are the Tyrannicides and a relief showing Orpheus, Eurydice and Hermes. Also displayed are the 'Farnese Cup' and 'Farnese Bull', mosaics from Pompeii, mural paintings, bronze statuettes and the bronze 'Dancers' from Herculaneum, as well as musical instruments and scales and surgical instruments.

**EXHIBITIONS**
Spring 97 | *Finds from Illegal Excavations in Puglia, Origins Unknown*

Spring 97 | *Opening of the new rooms devoted to the topography of Pithecusa (Ischia)*

Spring 97 | *Ancient Cloth from Pompeii*

## Napoli - Naples

### NATIONAL MUSEUM OF CERAMICS 'DUCA DI MARTINA'
Via Cimarosa 77  80100  Napoli  Director: Paola Giusti
☎ +39 81 5788418  📠 +39 81 5781776
Open: Tuesday-Sunday 09.00-14.00
Closed: Monday

**COLLECTION** | A large part of the museum's collection is made up of European and Oriental porcelain. Works from such European centres as Meissen, Real Fabbrica di Capodimonte, Ginori, Rouen Chantilly, Saint Cloud, Mennecy and Sevrès are on display. The collection of Oriental porcelain includes white and blue Chinese porcelain and Japanese porcelain in Kakiemon and Imari style. Gubbio, Deruta, Faenza and Palermo are represented in the collection of Renaissance earthenware (majolica). Glassworks, tapestries and enamel and ivory objects are also exhibited.

The collection also includes some 126 paintings, among which 18th-century sketches from the Neapolitan School.

No details available.

## Parma

### MUSEO ARCHEOLOGICO NAZIONALE DI PARMA
Via della Pilotta 4  43100 Parma  Director: Maria Bernabò Brea
☎ +39 521 233718  📠 +39 521 282787
Open: Daily 09.00-14.00

COLLECTION

The museum is housed at the Palazzo della Pilotta of the Farnese family. It was founded in 1760 by Philip of Bourbon to contain all objects dug up during excavations in the Roman town of Veleia. Now it holds all the archaeological material of Parma province. The museum is divided into various sections:
**The Veleia section,** featuring the 'tabula alimentaria', the biggest bronze inscription from antiquity; twelve marble statues of the imperial family and Calpurnio Pisone; two bronze portraits and numerous small bronzes.
**Collection material** mainly obtained under the dukedom of Maria Luigia.
**The Prehistoric and Protohistoric section** with objects from the Bronze and Iron Ages.
**The Roman section** with objects from Roman times found in the town and province of Parma.
**The collection of medals,** consisting of a collection of Greek, Roman, Medieval and modern coins. At the moment this collection is only open to researchers.

EXHIBITIONS  No details available.

## Parma

### FONDAZIONE MAGNANI ROCCA
Via Vecchia di Sala 18  43030 Mamiano di Traversetolo (Parma)
Director: Simona Tosini Pizzetti
☎ +39 521 848327/848148  📠 +39 521 848337
Open: daily Mar-Nov 10.00-17.00
Closed: Monday and Dec-Feb

COLLECTION

The Museum of the Magnani Rocca Foundation is located in the Mamiano di Traversetolo Villa near Parma. The Luigi Magnani collection is housed there and includes works from Gentile da Fabriano, Filippo Lippi, Dürer, Titian, Rubens, Van Dyck, Goya and the contemporaries Monet, Renoir, Cézanne up to De Pisis, Morandi and Burri. The sculptures include a major work by Canova and two works by Lorenzo Bartolini. The original arrangement of the furniture has been respected in the Villa to preserve a lived-in atmosphere, also enabling one to view important pieces of furniture from the Empire period including a Thomire malachite bathtub, a gift from Czar Alexander I to Napoleon, and Jacob furniture. In addition to its cultural attractions the Villa is surrounded by a centuries-old park which makes it a very pleasant destination.

EXHIBITION
07·09·97-07·12·97

*Füssli and Shakespeare*  *Painting and Theatre 1775-1825*
Paintings and drawings dating from the late 18th century to early 19th century by Johann Heinrich Füssli and his contemporaries, depicting Shakespearean themes.

# Pavia

## MUSEI CIVICI DI PAVIA - CASTELLO VISCONTEO
Piazza Castello  27100 Pavia  Director: Donata Vicini
☎ +39 382 33853  🖷 +39 382 303028
Open: Tuesday-Friday 08.30-13.30  Saturday, Sunday 08.30-13.00;
Spring and autumn Tuesday-Friday 08.30-13.30
Saturday, Sunday 09.00-12.30 / 15.00-17.30

COLLECTION

The Museum Castello Visconteo in Pavia has archaeological, historical and art exhibitions. The archaeological section contains displays of artefacts from local excavations and an important collection of Roman glasses. The Early Medieval and Romanesque sections have exhibits of materials such as bas-reliefs, portals and mosaics taken from the ruins of old churches in the town. The Renaissance section displays terracotta panels and marble works. Paintings from the 13th through to the 18th century, including works by Antonello de Messina, B. Luini, Bergognone, D. Crespi, G. Bellini, C Procaccini, P.and C.F. Nuvolone, G.D. Tiepolo, and P. Magatti are on display in the Pinacotheca Malaspina. The Modern Pinacotheca houses paintings from the 19th and 20th century, including works by Appiani, Hayez, Piccio, Kienerk, and others. There is also a modern sculpture section and a gallery of plaster casts. Noteworthy is the 'Sala del Modello del Duomo', one of the greatest wooden models produced during the Renaissance.

EXHIBITIONS

May 97

*Giorgio Kienerk*    A 'post-macchiaiolo' and symbolist painter.

Summer 97

*Ambrogio*    Exhibition of Ambrogio of Fossano, known as Bergognone, who painted the Certosa Monastery.

Autumn 97

*Inauguration of the Historical and Ethnographical Museum*

end 97

*Paintings from the 17th and 18th Centuries*

# Perugia

## GALLERIA NAZIONALE DELL'UMBRIA
Palazzo dei Priori -Corso Vannucci  06100 Perugia  Director: Vittoria Garibaldi
☎ +39 75 5720316  🖷 +39 75 5720316
Open: Daily 09.00-13.30 / 15.00-109.00 Sunday 09.00-13.00
Closed: 1 Jan, 1 May, 25 Dec

COLLECTION

The Galleria Nazionale dell'Umbria houses the greatest existing collection of Umbrian art, with works from the 13th to the 19th century. The Romantic period is represented by the wooden sculpture of the Deposed Christ from Roncione. The 13th-century is highlighted by five fragments of a fountain by Arnolfo di Cambio, by works by Maestro di San Francisco and Maestro del Trittico di Perugia. The Gothic period is represented by exhibits of works by Sienese artists such as Vigoroso da Siena, Duccio da Buoninsegna and Meo da Siena. Within the international Gothic tradition are works by Gentile da Fabriano and a monochrome fresco by Lorenzo Salimbeni. Notable among Renaissance masters are works by Beato Angelico, Piero della Francesca and Pinturicchio. From the same period is the Cappella dei Priori with frescoes by Benedetto Bonfigli. The Galleria houses numerous paintings by Perugino and members of his school such as Bartolomeo Caporali, Fiorenzo di Lorenzo and Berto Giovanni. Works by Domenico Alfani, Raffaellino dal Colle and Arrigo Fiammingo are representative of Mannerism, while Orazio Gentileschi shows the influence of Caravaggio. The 17th-century section includes works by Pietro da Cortona.

Sebastiano Conca and Pierre Subleyras are among the 18th-century masters in the collection. Collections of 14th-century jewellery, 15th and 16th-century Umbrian fabrics, and ceramics from Deruta and Castelli are also noteworthy.

**EXHIBITIONS** No details available.

## Ravenna

**MUSEO NAZIONALE DI RAVENNA**
Via Fiandrini 17  48100 Ravenna  Director: Luciana Martini
☎ +39 544 34424  📠 +39 544 37391
Open: Tuesday-Sunday 08.30-19.30
Closed: Monday

**COLLECTION** Accommodated in three cloisters of a former Benedictine convent, the museum has a collection of Roman and early Christian artefacts. There are funerary stelae from 100 B.C. to 100 A.D., a collection of arms and armour, a 5th-century sarcophagus, 6th-century capitals and a Byzantine capital, as well as prehistoric Etruscan and Roman objects, Roman herms, portraits and glass, and medieval fabrics including the embroidered 'Veil of Classis'. Ivories include a Murano diptych from the 6th century and a relief of Apollo and Daphne. There is a sinopia from Sant'Apollinare in Classe and a collection of Cretan-Venetian icons from the 14th to 18th century which combine local and Byzantine styles. The museum also contains a collection of ceramics, a numismatic collection extending back to the Roman period and Roman epigraphy, funerary stelae and reliefs excavated in the Ravenna area.

**EXHIBITIONS**

1997 *14th-Century Frescoes from Santa Chiara in Ravenna*  An exhibition of frescoes from the pictorial cycle of Pietro da Rimini for the church of Santa Chiara in Ravenna, removed and shown on a support which reproduces the original setting.

Spring 97 *The Hoard of Via Luca Longhi in Ravenna*  An exhibition of 662 medieval coins minted in Italy which were discovered in Ravenna in 1957.

## Roma - Rome

**GALLERIA NAZIONALE D'ARTE MODERNA E CONTEMPORANEA**
Via delle Belle Arti 131  00197 Roma  Director: Augusta Monferini
☎ +39 6 3224152  📠 +39 6 3221579
Open: Tuesday-Saturday 09.00-14.00  Sunday 09.00-13.00
Closed: Monday

**COLLECTION** The collection, housed in the Palazzo delle Belle Arti built in 1911 by Cesare Bazzani, contains works from the 19th and 20th century, including Italian Art Nouveau and works by Giacomo Balla from 1902 to 1942. There are Futurist paintings by Umberto Boccioni, Gino Severini, Enrico Prampolini and Alberto Magnelli, and work from the 20s by Piet Mondrian, Laszlo Moholy-Nagy, Marcel Duchamp, Giorgio de Chirico and others. The Veranda has a selection of sculptures, including 'The Pardon' by Libero Andreotti, 'Bust of Arturo Toscanini' by Adolfo Wildt and works by Bruno Innocenti. Other rooms display works by Guidi, Soffici, Morandi, Fausto Pirandello, Vassily Kandinsky (Angular Line, 1930), Dante Gabriele Rossetti ('Mrs William Morris'), Gustav Klimt ('The Three Ages of Man'), Rodin (bust of the sculptor Dalou, 'Bronze Age' and a bozzetto (sketch) for a ballerina), and works by Modigliani, Degas,

Van Gogh, Klee, Mirò, Moore, Utrillo, Braque, Picasso, Pollock and Giacometti. From the 19th century there are works by the Tuscan 'Macchiaioli' (Fattori, Lega, Abbati and Signorini, among others), Giovanni Boldoni (Portrait of Guiseppe Verdi) and prints and drawings by Hogarth, Blake, several German artists and the Japanese artists Hiroshige, Utamaro and Hokusai. There are also prints and drawings by Prud'hon, Ingres, Corot, Millet, Courbet, Fantin-Latour, Rodin, Manet, Sisley, Degas, Renoir, Pissarro, Toulouse-Lautrec, Gauguin, Edvard Munch, Egon Schiele and Whistler.

**EXHIBITIONS** | No details available.

## Roma - Rome

**MUSEO BARRACCO**
Corso Vittorio Emanuele II 166A  00186 Roma  Director: Maresita Nota
☎ +39 6 68806848/48899200  🖷 +39 6 68806848
Open: daily 09.00-19.00

**COLLECTION** | The museum's ancient sculpture was collected by Senator Giovanni Barracco (1829-1914) and given to the city in 1902. It is housed in the Renaissance palace 'Farnesina ai Baullari'. There is an exhibit of Egyptian sculpture from 3000 B.C. to Roman times, comprising reliefs of a 4th Dynasty court official and the milking of cows, statuettes of a woman kneading dough and a scribe, the Sphinx of Queen Hatshepsut, lions' heads, head of the young Ramses II, and the head of a priest wearing a diadem from Roman times. There are gilded Egyptian funeral masks, Sumerian and Assyrian works in alabaster, bronze and terracotta, and Assyrian reliefs.
Etruscan works include funerary cippi from the 5th century B.C. and statues of the Phoenician god Bes. There are also statuettes from Cyprus of musicians playing instruments, a Phoenician alabaster lion mask and frescoes detached from the Roman building beneath the museum. Original Greek statues from the 5th century B.C. are shown together with the fragment of a funerary stele, the heads of Athena, Apollo, Marsyas, an athlete and an ephebus and copies of works by Polykleitos. The Greek collection also includes 5th-century B.C. amphoras, statuettes, funerary artefacts and a votive relief. Among the Hellenistic art are ceramics, sculptures, portraits of Demosthenes and Epicurus, a relief of the cave of Pan, a statuette of Neptune, a head of Mars and sepulchral reliefs.

**EXHIBITIONS**
until 31·05·97 | ***Gutenberg and Rome***  *The Origin of Printing in the City of Popes 1467-1477*

10·06·97-31·07·97 | ***Corso Vittorio Emanuele II***  *Places and Persons of Rome at the Time of Umberto I*

## Roma - Rome

**GALLERIA BORGHESE**
Piazzale Scipione Borghese 5  00197 Roma  Director: Alba Costamagna
☎ +39 6 8548577  🖷 +39 6 8840756
Open: daily 09.00-19.00

**COLLECTION** | The Museo and Galleria Borghese is housed in the Villa de Borghese, built in the early 15th century by F. Ponzio and G. Vasanzio for Cardinal Scipione Borghese. With the help of his uncle, Paul V, the cardinal acquired numerous works of art, while other members of the family continued to add works to the family collection. Part of the former sculpture collection, however, now resides in the Louvre.

The gallery is surrounded by a beautiful park and the halls are decorated with frescoes, marbles and stuccoes. As the villa is undergoing structural repairs, currently only the ground floor is open.

Caravaggio
*Giovane with a basket of fruit*
© Galleria Borghese, Roma

The collection includes ancient works of sculpture containing such masterpieces as 'The Rape of Proserpine', 'Apollo and Daphne', 'Aeneas and Anchises' and the widely celebrated 'Victorious Venus' (Pauline Borghese sculpted by Canova).

A selection from among the paintings is currently being exhibited in Travestevere at the Ex instituto de San Michele a Ripa. Masterpieces not on view at present include: 'The Deposition' (also known as 'Christ Carried to the Sepulchre') by Raphael (1507), the restored 'Sacred and Profane Love' by Titian, 'Portrait of a Man' by Antonello da Messina and 'Madonna and Child' by Giovanni Bellini. Nevertheless about 200 paintings are being displayed including works by Perugino, Raphael, Bronzino, Lucas Cranach, Rubens, Gian Lorenzo Bernini, Paole Veronese, Corregio, Lorenzo Lotto, Titian, Vittore, Carpaccio, Dosso Dossi and Palma Vecchio.

**EXHIBITIONS** | No details available.

## Roma - Rome

**MUSEI CAPITOLINI**
Piazza del Campidoglio 1  00186 Roma  Director: Anna Mura Sommella
☎ +39 6 67102071  📠 +39 6 67103118
Open: Tuesday-Saturday 09.00-13.30  Tuesday, Saturday 17.00-20.00
Sunday 09.00-13.00
Closed: Monday

**COLLECTION** | The collection of the Musei Capitolini is one of the oldest in the world. It was started in 1471 by Pope Sixtus IV who presented the city with a number of bronze statues. It now houses a collection of Roman sculptures, such as the famous 'Lupa Capitolina', inscriptions, coins, mosaics, and objects connected with everyday life. The collection also contains Greek, Etruscan and Egyptian works of art. The museum's collection of marble sculptures and inscriptions was greatly enlarged in the 17th and 18th centuries by gifts from private collections. After Rome became Italy's capital in the 19th century, a great number of artefacts, found whilst digging the foundations for the city's new quarters, joined the collection. The collection is exhibited in two palaces: the 17th-century Museo Capitolino and the 15th-century Palazzo dei Conservatori, which also houses the famous Conservatori Apartment well known for its large frescoes. The Palazzo dei Conservatori has been enlarged twice this century, once in 1925 and again in 1950. An underground gallery, excavated in the 1940s, houses a collection of Latin and Greek inscriptions. The painting gallery or Pinacoteca is famous for its Italian and foreign masterpieces by such artists as Titian, Veronese, Tintoretto, Caravaggio and Rubens.

EXHIBITIONS    No details available.

## Roma - Rome

### GALLERIA NAZIONALE D'ARTE ANTICA, PALAZZO BARBERINI
Via Quattro Fontane 13  00184 Roma  Director: Lorenza Mochi-Ouori
☎ +39 6 4824184   ☳ +39 6 4880560
Open: Tuesday-Saturday 09.00-14.00, Sunday 09.00-13.00
Closed: Monday

COLLECTION    The Baroque Palazzo Barberini, the home of the National Gallery of Antique Art, was designed by Maderno, Borromini and Bernini for Urban VIII and has been owned by the State since 1949. The Gallery contains over 200 works, beginning with a 12th-century 'Madonna Avvocata' from the Roman school and including Nicolò di Pietro's 'Coronation of Mary', Filippo Lippi's, 'Madonna and Child', Perugin's, Raphael's portrait 'La Fornarina', Lorenzo Lotto's 'Mystical Marriage of St. Catherine', El Greco's 'Adoration of the Shepherds' and 'Baptism of Christ', Titian's 'Venus and Adonis' and Tintoretto's 'Christ and the Adulteress', Caravaggio's 'Narcissus' and 'Judith and Holofernes', and Bernini's 'Portrait of Urban VIII' and 'David with the Head of Goliath'. In the Chapel, with a ceiling by Andrea Sacco and frescoes by Pietro da Cortona and Giovanni Francesco Romanelli, there are two portraits of Henry VIII by Holbein. Pietro da Cortona frescoed the ceiling of the Salone, which contains works dedicated to the Barberini family and the Papacy of Urban VIII.
The second floor houses the Barberini apartments and 18th- century works by Tiepolo, Canaletto, Boucher, Fragonard and others, as well as the Dusmet collection of paintings and oriental works.

EXHIBITIONS    No details available.

## Roma - Rome

### MUSEO DI PALAZZO VENEZIA
Via del Plebiscito 118  00186  Roma  Director: Maria Letitia Casanovy Uccella
☎ +39 6 6798865   ☳ +39 6 58432180
Open: Daily 09.00-13.00

COLLECTION    The Palace, simultaneously a fortress, was built in 1455 for Cardinal Pietro Barbo (later Pope Paul III). It was the residence of the Ambassadors of the Republic of Venice between 1564 and 1797, and Mussolini's residence during the Fascist period. The museum contains paintings, wood sculptures, bronze statuettes, Romanesque and 14th-century ivories, majolica, church silver and terracotta works. There is a collection of arms and armour and Italian, German and Flemish tapestries from the 15th to 17th century and Oriental porcelain and ceramics.
The Cardinals' apartments on the first floor contain the first part of the collection, among which are architectural and sculptural fragments, a 10th-century triptych of the Deesis and Saints, a marble transenna from the 14th century, a Byzantine work in metal

and enamel, Byzantine crosses and a German lunette from the 13th century, 14th-century ceramics from Orvieto and a series of dower chests. One ceiling is decorated with the signs of the zodiac, and another with grotteschi. Other rooms have Tuscan 'fondi oro' paintings, a reliquary by Jacopo Tondi, wood statues and 12th to 13th-century seals. The applied arts include 4th-century Coptic fabrics. Italian ceramics and European porcelain are displayed in the corridor between the apartments and the Palazzetto di Venezia. The rooms in the Palazzetto contain furniture, bronze statuettes, Medieval sculptures, busts, terracotta bozzetti by Bernini, and paintings by Veneziano, Gozzoli, Guercino, Cranach and others.

**EXHIBITIONS**    No details available.

## Roma - Rome

### MUSEO NAZIONALE ROMANO
**Piazza della Finanza 1  00185  Roma  Director: Maria Rita Di Mino**
☎ +39 6 4880530   🖷 +39 6 58432180
**Open: Daily 09.00-19.00**

**COLLECTION**    The collections of the National Museum of Rome include archaeological finds since 1870 from excavations in Rome, and the Kircherian and Ludovisi collections, bought by the State in 1901 from the Prince of Piombino, Rodolfo Boncompagn-Ludovisi. The present museum contains mosaics, busts and herms, the Ludovisi Throne, decorated with reliefs of the birth of Aphrodite and thought to be an original work from the 5th century B.C., and a replica of 'The Discus-Thrower' by Myron. The Great Cloister, built in 1565 and attributed to Michelangelo, has gardens and a fountain dating from 1695. It contains statues of Roman generals, groups of seated people, statues of women, inscribed pilasters, a Nilotic mosaic, statues of Jupiter and Hercules and ancient landmarks from the Tiber area.

The classical sculptures are due to be moved to the former Collegio Massimo, built in 1883-87 by Camillo Pistrucci. The ground floor will have art, including some original Greek works, from the time of Sulla to Augustus. The first floor will display sculptures found in the Imperial villas of Hadrian, Nero and others. The second floor will house wall paintings and mosaics and a reproduction of the room of Livia, wife of Augustus, and the basement will contain a collection of coins, medals and jewellery. Many other works from the 5th century B.C. to the 4th century A.D. will be exhibited, including a head of Hypnos attributed to Praxiteles.

**EXHIBITIONS**    No details available

## Roma - Rome

### GALLERIA DELL'ACCADEMIA NAZIONALE DI SAN LUCA
**Piazza dell'Academia di S. Luca 77  00187  Roma**
☎ +39 6 6798850   🖷 +39 6 58432180
**Open: Monday, Wednesday, Friday and last Sunday of the month 10.00-13.00**
**Closed: Tuesday, Thursday and Saturday**

**COLLECTION**    The collection is housed in the 16th-century Palazzo Carpegna and comprises works from the 16th to 19th century. The 20th-century works are no longer on view and the Sale Accademiche are closed to the public except on St Luke's Day (18 October).
The collection starts with 'Portrait of Clement IX' by Baciccia; 'Shepherds and Sheep' by Girolamo and Giovanni Battista Bassano; 'Spinster' by Francesco Mola; 'St. Jerome' and 'Portrait of Marino Cornaro', attributed to Titian; Putto, fragment of a fresco (1512) by

**ITALY**

Raphael and a mask attributed to Michelangelo; a 'Madonna and Child' from the 15th-century Florentine school and 'Portrait of a Woman' from the 17th-century Flemish school. Works from the 18th and 19th century include Domenico Pellegrini's 'Augustus Frederick, Duke of Sussex' and 'Self-Portrait'; Giuseppe Grassi's portraits of the architect Henry Wood and of Vincenzo Camuccini; 'Niobe' by Mme Brossard de Beaulieu; 'Hope' by Angelica Kaufman; a bust of Canova by Allessandro d'Este; and a bust of Piranesi by Joseph Nollekens. Other works include 'Jacob's Dream' by Aniello Falcone, works by Giovanni van Bloemen and the Master of the St. Lucy Legend, 'Nymphs rowning Abundance' by Rubens and Van Dyck's 'Madonna and Angels'. The collection is rounded off with terracotta reliefs resulting from 18th-century competitions. There are also portraits of academicians.

EXHIBITIONS No details available.

## Roma - Rome

**MUSEO NAZIONALE DI VIA GIULIA**
Piazzale di Villa Giulia 9  00196  Roma  Curator: Giovanni Scichilone
☎ +39 6 3201500  📠 +39 6 3201993
Open: Tuesday-Sunday Oct-May 09.00-14.00  Sunday 09.00-13.00;
Jun-Sep  09.00-19.30  Sunday 09.00-13.00
Closed: Monday

COLLECTION Occupying a 16th-century palace built for Pope Julius III, the museum mostly contains pre-Roman exhibits. The first rooms contain 9th to 5th-century B.C. finds from the some of the 15 000 tombs unearthed in the necropolis of Vulci, including a stone sculpture of a man on a seahorse, bronze armour, a Sardinian statuette of a praying warrior, Greek or Ionian red and black vases, an urn in the form of a hut, an Etruscan-Corinthian amphora found in the area, votive terracotta models, heads and figurines. There is 8th-century B.C. geometric pottery from Bisenzio-Vesentium and 5th and 6th-century B.C. Etruscan sculpture. Finds from the necropolis in the Etruscan port of Cerveteri include inscribed gold-leaf plaques and a sarcophagus with figures of a husband and wife, skyphoi, kylixes, amphorae and kraters. The collection includes alabaster vases from Greece and Cyprus, Etruscan vases revealing oriental influence, and Faliscan, Campanian and Apulian artefacts and jewellery from the Minoan period. Material from the Ager Faliscus includes a dish depicting a war elephant with its baby, bronze shields, mirrors and vases. There is a coffin in the form of an oak tree from Gabii and sculptures from the 6th-century B.C. temple of Mater Matuta. Gold and silver works from the 7th century B.C. constitute a mixture of Assyrian, Egyptian and Greek art.

EXHIBITIONS No details available.

## Roma, Vatican City

**MONUMENTI, MUSEI E GALLERIE PONTIFICIE**
00120 Vatican City  Director: Carlo Pietrangeli
☎ +39 6 69883333  📠 +39 6 69885061
Open: Monday-Saturday and last Sunday of each month 08.45-13.45;
17 Mar - 13 jun and Sep, Oct 08.45 - 16.45
Closed: Sunday (except last Sunday of each month)

COLLECTION The Monumenti, Musei e Gallerie Pontificie (the Vatican Museums) are comprised of a variety of collections established over the years. The first developments in the long history of the Vatican Museums occurred in the court of Innocent VIII's Belvedere Palace, which Julius II laid out in gardens and embellished with masterpieces of classical sculpture such as the 'Apollo Belvedere' and 'Laocoön'. The responsibility for preserving a patrimony threatened by the ever-increasing exportation of antiquities, among other factors, led the popes Clement XIV, Pius VI and Pius VII to set up the Pio Clementine Museum (1771-1793), the Chiaramonti Museum, the Lapidary Gallery (1807-1810) and the Braccio Nuovo (1822).

As a consequence of the intensive excavations carried out in Southern Etruria in the early 19th century, the Gregorian Etruscan Museum was opened by Gregory XVI in 1837. The deciphering of hieroglyphics (by Jean-François Champollion, 1822) stimulated a similar interest in Egyptian antiquities, resulting in the opening of the Gregorian Egyptian Museum in 1839.

The Gregorian Profane Museum was founded by Gregory XVI in 1844. In 1854, a significant collection of Christian antiquities was established by Pius IX. Pius XI founded the Missionary-Ethnological Museum in 1926 and the Pinacoteca in 1932, in which paintings which had been seized from Napoleon under the terms of the Treaty of Tolentino (1797) and returned to the Vatican in 1815 were put on display, along with others already in the Vatican. The Gregorian Profane and the Pio Christian museums (1970) and the Missionary Ethnological Museum (1973) were transferred from the Lateran Palace to the Vatican.

In 1973, Paul VI founded the Collection of Modern Religious Art, located in the Borgia Apartment, and the Vatican Historical Museum. The latter is divided into the two parts. One, called the Vatican Historical Museum, is located in the Lateran Palace. The other, the Carriage Pavillon, is located in the Vatican.

You may also include a visit in the Vatican Apostolic Palace to the Cappella Niccolina, the Cappella Sistina, the Stanze di Raffaello, the Galleria dell Carte Geografiche, the Sale di S. Pio V and on request, the Loggia di Raffaello. Several areas of the Biblioteca Apostolica Vaticana are also open to the public, including the Museo Sacro, the Museo Profano, the Sala delle Nozze Aldobrandine, and the Salone Sistino and Gallerie.

**EXHIBITIONS** No details available.

## Siena

**MUSEO DELL'OPERA DEL DUOMO**
Piazza Duomo 8  53100 Siena  Director: Enzo Carli
☎ +39 577 283048   +39 577 280626
Open: 15 Mar-31 Oct  09.00-19.30  1 Nov-14 Mar: 09.00-13.30
Closed: 25 Dec, 1 Jan

**COLLECTION** The collection contains sculpture, paintings, goldwork, illuminated manuscripts and tapestries. The ground floor houses a collection of marble sculpture including twelve statues sculpted by Giovanni Pisano between 1285 and 1297, and later works of his disciples. The transenna of the ancient presbytery enclosure is attributed to the school of Nicola Pisano, father of Giovanni. A lunette in the centre of the room contains the last work of Jacopo della Quercia (1438) and there are several 13th and 15th-century bas reliefs and the front of a Roman sarcophagus on the wall.

The museum's most treasured exhibit is the 'Maestà' by Duccio di Boninsegna, a masterpiece of the Siena school painted between 1308 and 1311 which combines Byzantine iconographic tradition with Gothic style. The same room contains the 'Madonna di Crevole', an early painting by Duccio, and the 'Nativity of Mary' (1342) by Pietro Lorenzetti. Other important paintings of the Siena school are to be found on the third floor. The numerous illuminated manuscripts include a group of seven late 13th-century anthem

books and three anthem books illustrated by Lippo Vanni (1340-45). Among the museum's treasures are the gilt reliquary made to contain the head of St. Galgano, a silver Renaissance-style urn for the arm of St. John the Baptist, wooden statues and other religious artefacts dating from the 13th to the 18th century. The last room contains many hangings ranging from the 16th to the 19th century. Also part of the cathedral complex are the Piccolomini library inside the Cathedral, with a fresco cycle (1502-1507) by Pinturicchio, and the Baptistery of St. John, housing a monumental baptismal font decorated in bronze relief by Donatello, Lorenzo Ghiberti, Jacopo della Quercia and Giovanni Turino, and walls and ceiling frescoed by Sienese Quattrocento painters.
The Oratory of San Bernardino (Piazza San Francesco 9) contains works by Sienese artists of the 15th and 16th century.

**EXHIBITIONS**  No exhibitions planned.

## Siracusa

**MUSEO ARCHEOLOGICO REGIONALE 'PAOLO ORSI'**
Viale Teocrito 66/A  96100 Siracusa  Director: Giuseppe Voza
☎ +39 931 464022  🖷 +39 931 462347
Open: Tuesday-Saturday 09.00-14.00  Sunday 09.00-13.00
Closed: Monday

**COLLECTION**  The Paolo Orsi Archaeological Museum houses a vast archaeological collection representative of the ancient history of the eastern half of Sicily. The museum has two floors with a total of 9 000 m$^2$ of exhibition space, plus an auditorium and storage areas. The ground floor includes a large circular room, surrounded by three exhibition halls. The first floor houses collections of Hellenistic, Roman, Early Christian, and Byzantine artefacts. The collections are divided into sections depicting Prehistory, Greek colonies, and sub-colonies and Hellenized centres.
**Prehistory**  This section includes a geological illustration of Sicily, a description of its quaternary fauna, and chronological and thematic displays of Stone Age, Bronze Age, and Iron Age cultures.
**Greek colonies**  Finds are displayed from the earliest Greek colonies in Sicily. A section is devoted to the local pottery of Megara Hyblaea (7th to 6th century B.C.). There are extensive displays on Syracuse, including 'Venus Anadiomene', a Roman copy of a Hellenistic statue; thematic displays of artefacts from Ortygia; displays of diverse materials discovered in necropoli and in recent excavations; and models of the temples of Apollo and Athena.
**Sub-colonies and Hellenized centres**  This section includes displays of materials originating from Heleros, Akrai, Kasmeni, Kamarina and from Hellenized centres such as Gela and Arigento. Among the artefacts on display are examples of Attic pottery, terracotta votive reliefs, the Ephebus of Mendolito (a bronze from the 5th century B.C.), architectural terracottas, and wooden statuettes dating back to the 7th century B.C.

**EXHIBITIONS**  No exhibitions planned.

## Torino - Turin

**CASTELLO DI RIVOLI MUSEO D'ARTE CONTEMPORANEA**
Piazza del Castello  10098  Rivoli (Torino)  Director: Ida Gianelli
☎ +39 11 9581547  🖷 +39 11 9561141
Internet http://csi2000.csi-it/~laval/Rivoli:html.piemonte cultura musei
Open: Tuesday-Friday 10.00-17.00  Saturday-Sunday 10.00-19.00
3rd Thursday every month 10.00-22.00
Closed: Monday

COLLECTION

The first floor of the castle `Castello di Rivoli' houses the collection of this museum of contemporary art. The ancient structure of the building and various frescoes create a special contrast to the contemporary art works on display. The collection covers the period after the Second World War until the present day and includes paintings, sculptures, photographs and installations. The following artists are represented: Accardi, Anselmo, Bagnoli, Baumgarten, Bianchi, Birnbaum, Lee Byars, Calzolari, Castellani, Cattelan, Charlton, Cucchi, Delvoye, Dibbets, Fabro, Fontana, Förg, Gilbert & George Kirkeby, Lemieux, LeWitt, Long, Mainolfi, Melotti, Mario Merz, Marisa Merz, Moro, Mullican, Nordman, Oldenburg, Paolini, Penck, Penone, Pistoletto, Salvadori, Sieverding, Spalletti, Toroni, Vedova, Vercruysse, Verhoef and Zorio. Works by the photographers Mario Giacomelli and Mimmo Jodice are also displayed.

*© Castello di Rivoli Museo d'Arte Contemporanea, Torino*

EXHIBITIONS

until 25·05·97

***Stage Curtain***   The exhibition presents a selection of stage curtains, sketches and drawings produced for the theatre by Giacomo Balla, Giorgio de Chirico, Alberto Savinio, Pablo Picasso, Giolio Paolini and Enzo Cucchi

until 25·05·97

***Andy Warhol***   *Paintings for Children*   Warhol's work for children, small canvases depicting animals and clowns in different colour variations, is on display in this exhibition, organized by the education department.

until 08·06·97

***Anteprima***   *Maurizio Cattelan*

Summer 97

***Collections and Collectionism***

Oct 97

***Twenty Years of American Art (1975-1995)***

## Torino - Turin

**GALLERIA CIVICA D'ARTE MODERNA E CONTEMPORANEA**
Via Magenta 31  10128 Torino  Director: Riccardo Passoni
☎ +39 11 5629911   📠 +39 11 5628637
**Open: Tuesday-Sunday 09.00-19.00**
**Closed: Monday**

COLLECTION

The gallery's collections consist of some 5 000 paintings, 400 sculptures and a rich collection of drawings and engravings spanning the period from the 18th century to the present. The gallery also possesses photographs, artist's photographic plates and installations. The focus of these collections is primarily on Italian art, but there are importants examples of foreign art as well. The 19th-century section features works by Massimo d'Azeglio, landscape painters Fontanesi and Deleani. The 20th-century collection includes works by Casorati, Martini, Morandi, De Pisis, Manzú, Melotti, Burri, Colla, Fontana and Mastroianni. The international Avant-Garde movements are represented by a small but highly selective collection of paintings including works by Modigliani, Balla, Severini, Boccioni, De Chirico, Dix, Itten, Gonrcharova, Puni, Ernst, Klee and Picabia. Contemporary art is represented on an international scale by Arman, Nevelson, Calder, Tilson, Soto, Warhol, Vedova, Novelli, Dorazio, Twombly, Pascali, Manzoni, Paolini, Gilardi, Anselmo, Penone, Zorio and others.

**EXHIBITIONS**

until 01·06·97

*A Different Art*   *The Informal Style of Michel Tapié in Turin*
The exhibition recalls the activities of Michel Tapié (1909-1987), critic of French art, theoretician and promoter of the informal style, through the works of international artists who came in contact with him in Turin, his home from 1956 to 1977.

24·06·97-28·09·97

*Antonio Fontanesi in the 18th-Century Landscape*   Fontanesi's work is compared with that of the artists he came to know in the large European cities where he lived. The gallery's collection is supplemented by works from several European museums.

## Torino - Turin

**MUSEO EGIZIO**
Via Accademia Delle Scienze 6  10123  Torino  Director: A.M. Donadoni Roveri
☎ +39 11 5617776  ⌕ +39 11 5623157
Open: Tuesday-Saturday 09.00-19.00  Sunday 09.00-14.00
Closed: Monday

**COLLECTION**

The museum's original collection of Egyptian antiquities dates back to 1824 and first belonged to the Consul B. Drovetti. It consisted of more than· 8 000 objects, ranging from the New Kingdom to the Late Era. These included large statues, among which the seated Ramses II and the Sethi II 'colossus' from Karnak, papyri, among which Books of the Dead, stelae, coffins, mummies and amulets. Thanks to E. Schiaparelli and his expeditions during the Royal Italian Archaeological Mission in Egypt at the beginning of the 20th century, this collection was increased by more than 17 000 objects originating from the prehistoric to the Coptic Era. Reliefs from Heliopolis (III Dyn.), funerary objects from private tombs at Asjut (VI-XII Dyn.) and paintings from a funerary chapel at Gebelein (XI Dyn.) are a few examples of these acquisitions. Furthermore, the museum features the intact tomb, complete with furnishings, of the architect Kha and his wife Mirit (Deir el Medina, 14th century B.C.): gilded coffins, flower garlands, food and beverage offerings, dresses, linen, pottery, furniture, etc. In addition, the rock temple of Ellesija, carved in Nubia by Thutmosis III (1450 B.C.), can also be viewed.

**EXHIBITIONS**

No details available.

## Torino - Turin

**FONDAZIONE ITALIANA PER LA FOTOGRAFIA**
**MUSEO DELLA FOTOGRAFIA STORICA E CONTEMPORANEA**
Via Avogadro 4  10121 Torino  Director: Luisella d'Allessandro
☎ +39 11 546594  📠 +39 11 544132
Open: Tuesday-Sunday 10.00-19.00
Closed: Monday

COLLECTION | **Historical and Contemporary Photography**   The foundation was founded in 1992 for the purpose of promoting photography by means of exhibitions (production and distribution), a study centre and library, acquisition of historical and contemporary photographs, financing projects, publishing activities and photography classes.

EXHIBITIONS
09·05·97-01·06·97 | ***Family Album***  Vintage prints from the private archives of noble families living in Turin between the end of the 19th century and the 1940s.

12·06·97-24·08·97 | ***Sunday Is Always Sunday***   100 photographs from the RAI collection covering the first 20 years of the Italian Broadcasting Company.

04·09·97-12·10·97 | ***7th International Biennial of Photography***   More than 40 exhibitions on the main theme: Romance, images from the heart and pictures of guilt.

05·09·97-17·10·97 | ***A Collection of Italian Photography***   A selection from the Sandretto Rebaudengo contemporary collection.

23·10·97-14·12·97 | ***Dorothea Lange***   Images of the Depression and the New Deal, giving dignity to the suffering of millions of countrymen.

## Torino - Turin

**GALLERIA SABAUDA**
Via Accademia delle Scienze 6  10123 Torino  Director: Paola Astrua
☎ +39 11 547440/530501  📠 +39 11 549547
Open: Tuesday-Sunday 09.00-14.00 Thursday 10.00-19.00
Closed: Monday

COLLECTION | The Galleria Sabauda, located in the 17th-century Palazzo dell'Accademia delle Scienze, houses an outstanding and broad-ranging collection of fine art. It is particularly noted for its Italian (especially Piedmontese and Venetian), Flemish, Dutch, German and French paintings from the 15th century to the present. The collection also includes works from ancient Rome, Byzantium, and China (Gualino Collection).
Beyond the superb and in many cases rather rare examples of the Piedmont School (Barnaba da Modena, Macrino d'Alba, Gaudenzio Ferrari, Defendente Ferrari, Gerolamo Giovenone, Bernardino Lanino, etc.) and the Venetian and Bolognese collection (Veronese, Tintoretto, Bassano, Albani, Reni, Guercino, etc.), Italian masterpieces include works by Fra Angelico, Desiderio da Settignano, Antonio and Piero Pollaiolo, Botticini, Botticelli, Moretto, and Bellini, among others.
Highlights of the Dutch and Flemish collection include works by Van der Weyden, Van Eyck, Rembrandt, Van Ruisdael, Jan Brueghel, Memling, Van Dyck and Van Huysum. Recent additions to the Dutch and Flemish collection include works by Rubens and David Teniers the Younger.
The origins of the collection date back to the House of Savoy, and

quite a number of the works in the collection were either commissioned or acquired by the princes of the House of Savoy or have as their subject members of the House.

**EXHIBITIONS**  No exhibitions planned.

# Trento

## CASTELLO DEL BUONCONSIGLIO
Via B. Clesio 5  38100 Trento  Director: Franco Marzatico
☎ +39 461 233770  📠 +39 461 239497
Open: Tuesday-Sunday Oct-Mar 09.00-12.00 / 14.00-17.00;
Apr-Sep 09.00-12.00 / 14.00-17.30
Closed: Monday

**COLLECTION**  Castello del Buonconsiglio houses many collections, the first of which was formed in the mid-19th century in the Civic Museum of Trento. Ever since their move to the castle in the 1920s the collections have continued to grow.
The Medieval and Modern art collections are extremely valuable. They contain a considerable number of manuscripts, including famous 15th-century music codices and the Feininger collection. The museum conserves a large collection of paintings, sculptures from the Carolingian to the Rococo period, furnishings, detached frescoes, majolica tiles, chinaware, prints, drawings and many other objects including those of ethnographic interest.
The Archaeology section of the museum is also significant, with relics of particular interest, including materials and wood of the Bronze Age and objects of the Iron Age and Roman and Lombard times. The collection of Egyptian and Far Eastern art is also important.

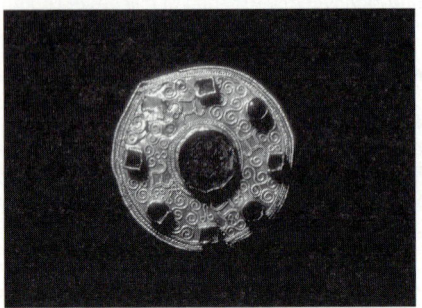

*Disk-shaped fibula in gold and stone, from Brez (Non Valley), 7th century AD*
*© Castello del Buonconsiglio, Trento*

Monuments and provincial collections are on display in various places throughout the province. Since 1973, Castello di Stenico in the Giudicarie has also been included. Castel Beseno, near Rovereto, and Castel Thun have been included since 1988.

**EXHIBITION**
20·06·97-09·11·97

***Jewels from the Alps.*** *Ornamental objects from prehistoric times and the early Middle Ages*

# Trento

## MUSEO DI ARTE MODERNA E CONTEMPORANEA DI TRENTO E ROVERETO
Palazzo delle Albere, Via R. da Sanseverino 45  38100 Trento  Director: G. Belli
☎ +39 461 234860  📠 +39 461 234007
Open: Tuesday-Sunday 16 Sep-14 Jun 09.00-12.30 / 14.30-18.00
15 Jun-15 Sep 10.00-12.30 / 14.30-19.00
Closed: Monday

| COLLECTION | The museum's permanent collection consists of over 2 000 works of art covering the era of Romanticism to the Modern period. Both locally and nationally known artists are featured here and include Bezzi, Bonazza, Cangiullo, B. Disertori, T. Garbari, R. Iras Baldessari, Marinetti, U. Moggioli, L. Ratini and Vallorz. |

**EXHIBITIONS**

23·05·97-20·08·97    ***The British Art of the 90s***    An exhibition of works by some 20 artists, who together symbolise the vivacity of English contemporary art, including Damien Hirst, Rachel Whiteread, Sarah Lukas, Jake and Dino Chapman, Steve McQuinn, Elisabeth Wright and Angela Bullock.

11·09·97-11·01·98    ***Trash***   *Expressing the Tragedy of Our World*    An exhibition of works by artists, such as Duchamp, Schwitters and Manzoni, who use trash as a metaphor in their representation of today's world.

22·01·98-10·03·98    ***Abstracts***    The exhibition presents works of international interest which refer to the abstract experiences between the two World Wars in Austria, Germany and Italy.

13·04·98-31·08·98    ***Carlo Fornara***   *A Master of Divisionism*    The result of research and studies which the museum has conducted on Italian Divisionism since 1987, the exhibition presents paintings and graphic works by Fornara dating from 1890 to 1940.

# Trieste

**CIVICO MUSEO DI STORIA ED ARTE E ORTO LAPIDARIO**
Via Cattedrale 15   34121 Trieste   Director: Adriano Dugulin
☎ +39 40 310500/308686   📠 +39 40 311301
Open: Tuesday-Sunday 09.00-13.00
Closed: Monday

| COLLECTION | The Orto Lapidario hosts Roman epigraphs from the city and the surroundings and a small building, reproducing a classical temple, that preserves the cenotaph of J.J. Winckelmann by A. Bosa. The Museum is arranged in a fine building with simple neoclassical lines. On the ground floor roman sculptures are on display in the entrance hall. The roman period is also explained by a series of daily life objects and by some small masterpieces in amber, glass, gold and bronze. The Egypt room shows an interesting collection including a mummy, a richly painted sarcophagus and some other objects. The Gandhara room contains several reliefs from the Swat Valley of Pakistan. On the first floor stone and bone tools and potsherds testify the human frequentation of the Karst's caves in prehistoric times. A wide section is devoted to local protohistory; it features pottery from castellieri (a kind of elevated fortified settlement) and finds from necropolis. A room exhibits the rich material of Santa Lucia di Tolmino, where more than 8 000 Iron age tombs were excavated. The Museum owns an important collection of Greek vases (both black and red figures painted) from Magna Graecia and the Taranto collection including a superb silver rhyton. The numismatic cabinet and the archive of prints, drawings and photographs can be consulted on request. The library, (specialised on archaeology, history, applied arts and local history) is open Monday-Saturday 09.00-13.00. |

| EXHIBITIONS | No exhibitions planned. |

## Venezia - Venice

### GALLERIE DELL'ACCADEMIA
Campo della Carità 1059a  30121  Venezia  Director: Giovanna Nepi Sciré
☎ +39 41 22247
Open: Daily 09.00-19.00

COLLECTION

Former religious buildings now house the Gallerie dell'Accademia, which contain the world's foremost collection of Venetian paintings from the 14th to 18th century. The works are displayed chronologically, starting with primitive gilt-background paintings shown in a room with a gilt wooden ceiling made by Marco Cozzi (1461-1484). Among the many paintings in this room are 'Justice between Two Archangels' by Jacobello del Fiore 'Coronation of the Virgin' by Paolo Veneziano, the 'Polyptych of St. Helen and the Cross' by Michele di Matteo and 'Coronation of the Virgin' by Michele Giambono. The next room contains large Renaissance altarpieces including Carpaccio's 'The Ten Thousand Martyrs on Mount Ararat', Giovanni Bellini's 'Sacred Conversation' and Marco Basaiti's 'Calling of the Sons of Zebedee'. One room is entirely devoted to Carpaccio's 'Legend of St. Ursula' series. A group of small 15th-century paintings, including 'St. Jerome in the Desert' by Piero della Francesca, 'Portrait of a Youth' by Hans Memling and paintings by Giovanni Bellini, Vivarini, Cima da Conegliano and others, are followed by 'The Tempest' and 'Col tempo' by Giorgione.

The following rooms contain works from the Italian High Renaissance, including Paolo Veronese's 'Tondo of San Nicolò' and 'St Francis receiving the Stigmata', both taken from ceilings. Further works representing the High Renaissance are Paolo Veronese's 'Crucifixion' and 'Christ in the House of Levi'(1573), originally titled 'The Last Supper' but considered too secular to bear that title, Tintoretto's 'Transport of the Body of St. Mark', 'Madonna in Glory with Saints' and Titian's 'La Pietà'. The corridor contains 17th-century landscapes, bacchanals and hunting scenes by Giuseppe Zais, Marco Ricci and Francesco Zuccarelli, and there are also 17th-century paintings by foreigners living in Venice. 18th-century works include 'Rape of Europa' by Giambattista Tiepolo, 'Fortune Teller' by Giambattista Piazzetta, a number of Venetian scenes by Canaletto and Guardi and portraits by Rosalba Carriera. Another room contains architectural scenes by Moretti, Gaspari and Joli and statuettes by Canova.

EXHIBITIONS

No details available.

## Venezia-Venice

### MUSEO CORRER
Piazza San Marco 52  30124  Venezia  Director: Giandomenico Romanelli
☎ +39 41 25625  ⛶ +39 41 5208297
Open: Wednesday-Monday 10.00-18.00
Closed: Tuesday

COLLECTION

Museo Correr, which occupies the Procuratie Nuove facing the Doges' Palace on the Piazza San Marco, is the city museum of art and history.  First opened to the public in the house of Teodoro Correr in 1836, it was moved to this location in 1922. The collection contains a wood engraving by Jacopo de'Barbari, shown with the six original blocks, which presents a bird's-eye view of Venice in 1500. There is a collection of prints of Venice from the 16th to the 18th century. The Ballroom contains marble and plaster statues and bas reliefs by Canova, along with some of his bozzetti for funerary monuments, including one for Titian. The Throne Room displays frescoes by Giovanni Carlo Bevilacqua from the rooms of the Procuratie Nuove (the Procurators were officials elected permanently and only second to the Doges in status - their residence became a palace in the period of Napoleon) and panels by Francesco Hayez from 1817.

The historical collection contains a painting of the arrival of the Queen of Cyprus in Venice in 1489, apparel worn by the Doges and platform shoes worn by Venetian women, documents, medals and commemorative paintings. There is also a coin collection ranging from the 9th century to the fall of the Venetian Republic, as well as weaponry, Italian and oriental china and bronze and a prayer book with a hidden dagger.

The upstairs picture gallery shows paintings by Carpaccio, Antonello da Messina, Giovanni Bellini, Cosmé Tura and Daniele Manin.

**EXHIBITIONS** No details available.

# Venezia - Venice

## PALAZZO DUCALE
**Piazza San Marco 1  30124 Venezia  Director: Umberto Franzoi**
☎ +39 41 5224951  📠 +39 41 5285028
**Open: daily Nov-Mar 08.30-17.00; Apr-Oct 08.30-19.00**
**Closed: 25 Dec, 1 Jan**

**COLLECTION** The Doges' Palace, originally founded in the 9th century when Venice was consolidated, was destroyed by fire on several occasions. It was redecorated with paintings by Veronese and Tintoretto and restored in the old Gothic style during the 17th century. The outside of the building is decorated with groups of sculptures including the 'Judgement of Solomon' by Jacopo della Quercia, and beautifully carved façades with balconied windows. The Porta della Carta is a Gothic gateway by Giovanni and Bartolomeo Bon, with groups of statues including a figure of Venice as Justice. Visitors enter the Palace by way of the Scala d'Oro, a stairway built by Sansovino in the 1580s and decorated with gilded stuccoes by Vittoria which leads to the Primo Piano Nobile (first floor), the former Doges' apartments where exhibitions are now held. Rooms on this floor contain chimney pieces, a bas-relief by Pietro Lombardi of Doge Leonardo Laredan at the feet of the Virgin, a stucco Madonna attributed to Antonio Rizzo, gilded and otherwise decorated ceilings, maps and charts, paintings of philosophers by Tintoretto and Veronese and a fresco painted by Titian.

Venice was governed from the Secondo Piano Nobile. One of the waiting rooms for ambassadors, the Anticollegio, contains paintings by Tintoretto, Veronese and Jacopo Bassano. The Sala del Collegio, where council meetings were held, has a ceiling made by Francesco Bello and painted by Veronese. Paintings by Tintoretto are also situated there and in the Sala del Senato  The huge Sala del Maggior Consiglio features Tintoretto's correspondingly large 'Paradise', the biggest oil painting in the world. The Sala del Consiglio dei Dieci, where the Council of Ten originally met to try political crimes, contains 'Juno Offering Gifts to Venice' by Veronese and paintings by Francesco and Leandro Bassano, Aliense, and Marco Vecellio.

The main ceiling panel was taken to Paris and never returned. In the waiting room there is a Bocca del Leone, one of many boxes spread throughout the city in which accusations were placed. Weaponry can be seen in the Armoury, and the dungeons may also be visited.

**EXHIBITIONS** No details available.

## Venezia-Venice

### PALAZZO GRASSI
San Samuele 3231  30124 Venezia  Director: Pasquale Bonagura
☎ +39 41 5231680  ☳ +39 41 5286218
Open: Daily 09.00-19.00

| | |
|---|---|
| COLLECTION | No permanent collection. |
| EXHIBITIONS<br>until 13·07·97 | *Art of the XX Century*  *The Dutch and Flemish Painting*  From Van Gogh, Ensor, Magritte and Mondrian to the contemporaries. |
| Sep 97-Jan 98 | *German Expressionism* |

## Venezia - Venice

### PEGGY GUGGENHEIM COLLECTION PALAZZO VENIER DEI LEONI
Dorsoduro 701  30123 Venezia  Deputy Director: Philip Rylands
☎ +39 41 5206288  ☳ +39 41 5206885
Open: Wednesday-Monday 11.00-18.00
Closed: Tuesday and 25 Dec

COLLECTION

The Peggy Guggenheim Collection is a museum of Modern art created by the American heiress Peggy Guggenheim. The collection was largely assembled in London, Paris and New York between 1938 and 1947. One of this century's most inspired and important art patrons, Peggy Guggenheim was an influential supporter and collector of European Cubist, Surrealist and Abstract art. In particular, her patronage of a group of then unknown American artists was instrumental in the development of American Abstract Expressionism in the 1940s.

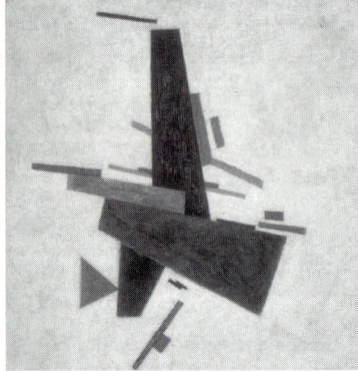

Kazimir Malevich
*Untitled, c.1916*
*Peggy Guggenheim*
*Collection, Venezia*
© 1995 The Solomon
R. Guggenheim
Foundation

In 1948, Peggy Guggenheim's collection was exhibited for the first time in Europe at the Venice Biennale. A year later she bought Palazzo Venier dei Leoni, an unfinished 18th-century palace on the Grand Canal. She lived there for 30 years and opened the palace to the public as a museum. In 1976, before her death, Peggy Guggenheim gave the palace and the collection to the Solomon R. Guggenheim Foundation, New York. The foundation has assumed the management of the museum since her death in 1979. The collection holds a large number of masterworks by Picasso, Mondrian, de Chirico, Kandinsky, Mirò, Magritte and Max Ernst; sculptures by Brancusi, Giacometti and Calder; and superb examples from the New York school including works by Pollock, Rothko and Motherwell. The Peggy Guggenheim Collection is the most comprehensive and impressive collection of early 20th-century Modernist art in Italy.

## EXHIBITIONS

| | |
|---|---|
| until 18·05·97 | **George Grosz** *The Berlin Years* |
| 07·06·97-05·10·97 | **Stuart Davis** |
| Summer 97 | **Robert Colescott** USA exhibition at the 1997 Venice Biennale at the US Pavillion. |
| 18·10·97-10·01·98 | **Eduardo Chillida** |

## Luxembourg

**CASINO LUXEMBOURG FORUM D'ART CONTEMPORAIN**
41, Rue Notre Dame  L-2013 Luxembourg  Director: J. Kox
☎ +352 225045  📠 +352 229595
Internet http://www.men.lu/casino/casino.html
Open: Tuesday-Sunday 10.00-18.00  Thursday 10.00-20.00
Closed: Monday

**COLLECTION**　　No permanent collection.

© Aquarium of the
Casino Luxembourg
*Luxembourg*

**EXHIBITIONS**

15·05·97-29·06·97　　*Perspectives*　Acquisitions for a new museum: Becher, Cragg, Deacon, Federle, Frize, Lasker, Ruff, Sherman, Usle, Struth, etc.
*Inviter: Sherrie Levine*　Since the 1980s, this American artist has been demystifying art history, systematically questioning the notions of 'work of art', 'artistic property' and 'original work' by reproducing and representing well-known works of great masters.

10·07·97-21·09·97　　*A Beautiful Summer*　Paintings, photographs, videos and installations by some thirty modern and contemporary artists question the strange familiarity of 'everyday life'.

02·10·97-30·11·97 | **The Nineties, A Family of Man?** This perspective on modern mankind presents Visions of Man in contemporary art. Drawn from themes of the famous exhibition The Family of Man, which was organised by Edward Steichen in 1955, this exhibition includes works by Beat Streuli, Patrick Raynaud, Fabrizio Plessi, Hans Haacke, Andres Serrano, Thomas Struth, Cindy Sherman and Araki.
*Inviter: Michel Aubry* Many of Michel Aubry's 'sculptures' are based on sounds, without being sound-producing themselves. Through his works he conveys the history of popular music, while managing to avoid nostalgia.

11·12·97-15·02·98 | This exhibition is being curated by Rudi Fuchs (no further details available).
*Inviter: Robert Adams* Robert Adams presents black & white landscape photographs.

## Luxembourg

**MUSÉE D'HISTOIRE DE LA VILLE DE LUXEMBOURG**
**14, Rue du Saint-Esprit 1475 Luxembourg Conservator: Danièle Wagener**
☎ +352 47962766 🖷 +352 471707
**Open: Tuesday-Sunday 10.00-18.00 Thursday 10.00-20.00**
**Closed: Monday**

COLLECTION | Luxembourg City's new historical museum offers an opportunity to discover the city's more than 1000 years of history from different perspectives. One of the main tasks of the city has been the preservation and enhancement of its architectural heritage. For this reason, the new museum has been installed in a group of four restored houses in the heart of the old part of Luxembourg. One of the main features is the panoramic elevator which virtually travels through time by passing though the museum's six exhibition levels. Both the building and the museum's collections reflect Luxembourg's history within an architectural, military, social and cultural context. Ancient views of the city, portraits of some of the

A guide explaining a
17th-century mortar-
piece to a group of
students
Photo: Imedia
© *Musée d'Histoire
de la ville de
Luxembourg*

great figures of local history, items of the citizens' daily life,
weapons, furniture, costumes and dresses, as well as liturgical
objects are on display.

**EXHIBITIONS**
04·07·97-05·10·97

*From Middle Ages to Modern Times*   *Luxembourg in 16th-century
Europe*

07·02·98-10·05·98

*Luxembourg, Metz, Trèves*   *Three Medieval Towns in the Mosel
Region*

## Luxembourg

**MUSÉE NATIONAL D'HISTOIRE ET D'ART**
3,Rue Wiltheim, Marché-aux-Poissons  2345 Luxembourg  Director: Paul Reiles
☎ +352 4793301  ⌗ +352 223760
Open: Tuesday-Friday 10.00-16.45  Saturday 14.00-17.45
Sunday 10.00-11.45 / 14.00-17.45
Closed: Monday

**COLLECTION**

The museum is housed in a former governor's mansion which has
been completely restored. Its collection, ranging from prehistoric to
modern times, includes Celtic numismatics and Celto-Roman finds
from excavations in the area. The Romans had settlements,
mansions and farms in Luxembourg; models of the 18th and 19th
century archaeological sites are on display. There are medieval
sculptures, a medieval retable, folk art and folklore, ceramics, a
collection of arms and armour and a 16th-century travellers'
currency guidebook. The Natural History section covers the fields of
palaeontology, geography, geology, mineralogy, ornithology and
botany, and the museum also has a small planetarium. The Fine Art
section has works by Pieter Brueghel the Younger ('Calvary'),
Pieter Brueghel III ('Village Wedding'), Lucas Cranach, Van Dyck,
Jacob Jordaens, David Teniers, Adriaan Brouwer ('The Foot
Operation'), David Rijckaert ('Smokers in the Tavern') and others.
There is also an exhibit of contemporary Luxembourg art.

**EXHIBITIONS**
until 11·05·97

*Cecil Beaton*   *Portraits of an Aesthete*

03·07·97-18·08·97

*Paul Strand*   *The World On My Doorstep, 1950-1976*

20·06·97-end Aug 97

*The Golden Age of Danish Painting*

Sep 97-Oct 97

*Les Kutter*   *Photographs*

## Luxembourg

**MUSÉE JEAN- PIERRE PESCATORE**
Parc municipal   Avenue Emile Reuter  2090 Luxembourg
Curator: Daniëlle Wagener
☎. +352 47962766  Fax. +352 471707
Open:Tuesday-Sunday 10.00-18.00  Thursday 10.00-20.00
Closed:Monday (except holidays)
Note: The permanent collection is only on display from 24 Jun-31 Aug 1997

**COLLECTION**

The permanent collection of the Jean-Pierre Pescatore Museum features some 120 paintings by 17-th and 18th-century Flemish and Dutch masters such as Teniers the Younger, Van Dyck, Jan Steen, Canaletto, Dou, Van de Capelle, Wouwerman, Delacroix and Courbet as well as works by important French, Belgian, German and Swiss artists of the 19th century.

**EXHIBITIONS**

30·05·97-16·06·97
*Jan Steen*   *Documentary*

25·09·97-26·10·97
*Eugenio Carmi*   *Abstract Paintings*

14·11·97-11·01·98
*Ben Heyart*   *Retrospective of the works of a Luxembourg painter*

## Amstelveen

### COBRA MUSEUM OF MODERN ART AMSTELVEEN
Sandbergplein 1-3 1181 ZX Amstelveen  Director Leo Duppen
☎ +31 20 5475050 🖷 +31 20 5475025
Open: Tuesday-Sunday 11.00-17.00
Closed: Monday, 25 Dec, 1 Jan and 30 Apr

**COLLECTION**

The museum's collection comprises some 500 works belonging to the CoBrA movement (Copenhagen, Brussels, Amsterdam), including works by such artists as Karel Appel, Constant, Asger Jorn and Pierre Alechinsky. Despite its brief existence (1948-1951), this international experimental movement was of great significance to modern art in the Netherlands in the latter part of the 20th century. In 1998, the museum will organise a number of special exhibitions celebrating '50 years of CoBrA'. As the Cobra Museum also has important works from the Dutch artists' groups 'Vrij Beelden' and 'Creatie' (1945-1955), it offers a broad perspective of the first post-war decade in which Dutch artists battled for freedom for the visual arts.

**EXHIBITIONS**
until 25·05·97

*Corneille  Retrospective (1947-1997)*  One of the pioneers of

CoBrA, this Dutch painter has gained great popularity with his lithographs and screen prints of simple, colourful subjects. The exhibition emphasises the historical importance of Corneille's work.

13·06·97-03·08·97 | *Tajiri* *Motionless Dynamic and Unity in Pluriformity* Shinkichi Tajiri's work does not look static, nor does it suggest movement. The exhibition comprises four Japanese themes in Tajiri's recent works, the Koan, the Ronin, 'new technologies' and 'decorative pluriformity'.

08·08·97-05·10·97 | *Eugène Brands* *Assemblages and Collages*

03·10·97-18·01·98 | *CoBrA Collection* *A Broad Perspective*

## Amsterdam

### ALLARD PIERSON MUSEUM
Archaeological Collection of the University of Amsterdam
Oude Turfmarkt 127  1012 GC Amsterdam  Director: H.A.G. Brijder
☎ +31 20 5252556  🖷 +31 20 5252561  Internet http://www.let.uva.nl/~apm
Open: Tuesday-Friday 10.00-17.00  Saturday, Sunday 13.00-17.00
Closed: Monday

COLLECTION | The collection contains three sections: Egypt; the Near East, Cyprus and Prehistoric Greece; and the Greek World, Etruria, and the Roman Empire.
The Egyptian civilisation is displayed by means of mummies and sarcophagi, images of gods and Egyptians, and objects relating to everyday life. Scale models of the pyramids of Giza and the temple of Edfu help to unlock the secrets of the Egyptian pharaohs, Greek kings and Roman emperors who ruled here from 5 000 B.C. to 700 A.D.
Jewellery, weapons, statuettes, vases and cuneiform tablets offer a glimpse into religious and daily life of Iran, Mesopotamia, Syria, Palestine and Anatolia between 5000 B.C. and 800 A.D. Pottery and marble idols display early civilisations on the Cycladic Islands, Crete and the Greek mainland.
Greek colonists took their culture to Italy where elements of it were adopted by the Etruscans and then by the Romans.
This Graeco-Roman civilisation then spread throughout the Roman Empire, greatly influencing Western ideas. Stone statues and

# Willem Lenssinck

*sculptor*

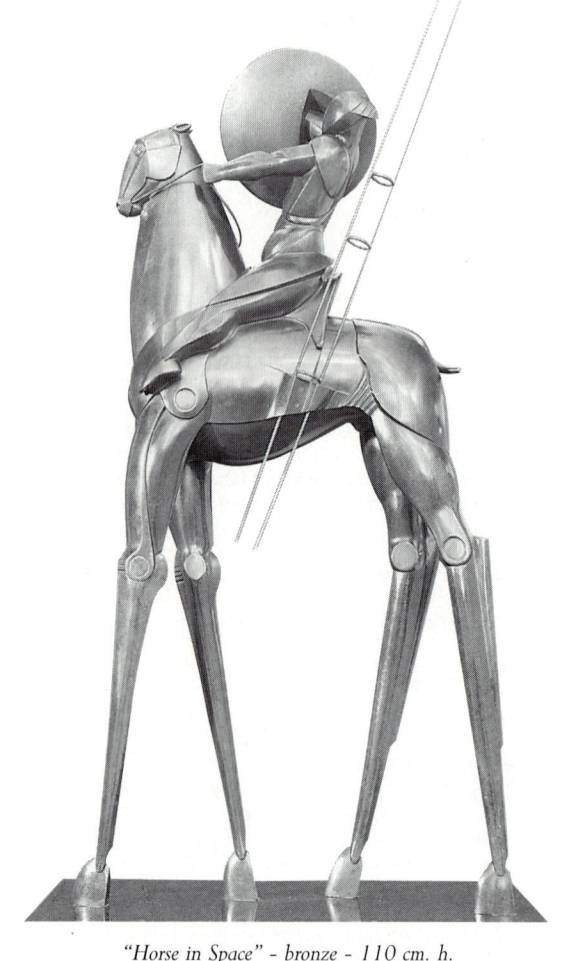

*"Horse in Space" - bronze - 110 cm. h.*

# Gallery Laimböck

other artists:

| | | |
|---|---|---|
| Fons Bemelmans | Pieter d'Hont | Gerhard Lentink |
| Federico Carasso | Guus Hellegers | Juan Ripolles |
| Paul Grégoire | Lia Laimböck | Francisca Zijlstra |

Daily open by appointment:
Doornseweg 10, 3947 ME, Langbroek, The Netherlands
tel / fax: +31 343 561699

portraits, bronzes and glass, pottery, jewellery and household items give an impression of how these people lived.

**EXHIBITIONS**

until -21·09·97

***Fabulous!*** *Greek Monsters and Fabled Creatures* An entertaining exhibition with sirens, satyrs, centaurs and many other fabled creatures.

Autumn 97

***Transportation in Antiquity (Working Title)***

Winter 97-98

***Bloomington Goldcollection (Working Title)***

## Amsterdam

**VAN GOGH MUSEUM**
Paulus Potterstraat 7  1007 CX Amsterdam  Director: J. Leighton
☎ +31 20 5705200  ⊠ +31 20 6735053
Open: Daily 10.00-17.00
Closed: 1 Jan

**COLLECTION**

With more than 200 paintings and some 500 drawings, the museum maintains the largest and most varied Van Gogh collection in the world. Many of the paintings are on permanent exhibition in chronological order, from the sombre canvasses of Brabant to the brightly coloured works of his late period, providing a fine survey of Van Gogh's development as an artist. Highlights include 'The Potato Eaters', 'Self-Portrait with Felt Hat', 'Still Life with Sunflowers', 'Wheat Field with Crows', etc.

Vincent van Gogh
(1853-1890)
*Self-portrait with straw hat, 1887*
© Van Gogh Museum, Amsterdam

The collection of contemporary works, also largely on permanent exhibition, comprises paintings by Toulouse-Lautrec, Gauguin, Fantin-Latour, Monet, Isaac Israëls and many other artists known to Van Gogh. The museum is striving to expand the collection with paintings, drawings, pastels and sculpture from the 1840-1920 period.

**EXHIBITIONS**

until 15·06·97

***Art in Vienna 1870-1920*** *Paintings, Sculpture, Graphic and Decorative Art*

20·06·97-12·10·97

***Vincent van Gogh: The Drawings of the Van Gogh Museum***
*Part 2: Brabant 1883-1885* Because of the vulnerability of the work there will be a complete change of the drawings on August 18.

17·10·97-11·01·98

***Auguste Préault (1810-1879)*** *Romanticism in bronze*

## Amsterdam

**AMSTERDAM HISTORICAL MUSEUM**
Kalverstraat 92  1012 RM Amsterdam  Director: P.W. Kruseman
☎ +31 20 5231822   ☎ +31 20 6207789
Open: Monday-Friday 10.00-17.00  Saturday, Sunday 11.00-17.00
Closed: 30 Apr, 25 Dec, 1 Jan

COLLECTION

The Amsterdam Historical Museum is the custodian of the older Fine and Applied art collection of the city of Amsterdam. This collection has been augmented by bequests, legacies, loans and acquisitions. The paintings, furniture, art objects and everyday artefacts in the museum relate the story of the city of Amsterdam and its inhabitants.

One of the highlights of the collection is formed by the group portraits of civic guards and regents from the 16th, 17th and 18th century. Many of these are on permanent display in the museum's 'Civic Guard Gallery'. The anatomical lessons form a separate category within this collection, an important piece among the museum's holdings being Rembrandt's 'Dr. Deijman's Anatomy Lesson'. The silver showpieces of the 16th and 17th-century civic guard guilds are an interesting feature of the museum's decorative art collection. In addition, the museum possesses some good examples of carved wooden furniture as well as a large collection of everyday artefacts. There are also collections of silver, china, pewter and decorated glassware.

The Print Room houses a large number of drawings and prints. These include drawings by Rembrandt, Rubens, Ruysdael and Van Ostade. The museum is renowned for its large collection of prints and drawings by Jan and Caspar Luiken.

EXHIBITIONS
until 24·05·97

*I've Got An Auntie in Morocco*   *Photographs by Kadir van Lohuizen*
Photographer Kadir van Lohuizen was commissioned by the city of Amsterdam to chart the life of a Moroccan family in Amsterdam. He photographed them at home and during a visit to relatives in Morocco.

16·05·97-28·09·97

*Herman Gordijn's Amsterdam*   Especially for the Amsterdam Historical Museum, artist Herman Gordijn (born 1932) has produced eleven large paintings and a triptych featuring the city of Amsterdam. These and other earlier works are included in the exhibition.

26·09·97-Jan 98

*Prints and Drawings by Jan Luyken*   Jan Luyken's prints and drawings depict everyday life and occupations during the period in which he lived (1649-1712). Other objects which illustrate life in the 17th century are also included in the exhibition.

## Amsterdam

**JOODS HISTORISCH MUSEUM - JEWISH HISTORICAL MUSEUM**
Jonas Daniël Meijerplein 2-4  1011 RH Amsterdam  Director: J. Belinfante
☎ +31 20 6269945   ☎ +31 20 6241721
Open: Daily 11.00 - 17.00
Closed: Yom Kippur, the Day of Atonement (11 Oct 97)

COLLECTION

The permanent collection illustrates the many aspects, both of the past and present, of Judaism in the Netherlands; the religion, culture and history of Jews in this country form the central theme. At the start of this tour, in the New Synagogue, five elements are presented which play a part in the Dutch-Jewish identity today: religion, the bond with Israel, the experiences of the Shoah, personal history (including the story of Charlotte Salomon), and the influence of Dutch culture on Jewish culture. The presentation in the Great Synagogue explains the Jewish life cycle, festivals and the differences between the various Jewish religious communities in the Netherlands. The story of the Jewish socio-economic history in this country is told in the presentations which can be viewed in the galleries of the synagogue.

Charlotte Salomon
*Gouache from 'Life or Theatre? An Autobiography 1940-1942'*
© Joods Historisch Museum, Amsterdam

**EXHIBITIONS**

until 31·08·97 | *Jewish Women Worldwide*   *Photographs by Joan Roth*

until 19·10·97 | *Gold Thread and Silver Braid*   *Anniversary Exhibition*   17th and 18th-century covers for the Torah scroll, curtains hanging in front of the Ark, and prayer shawls are all on display. This exhibition provides a rich and varied picture of the Sephardi and Ashkenazi communities in the Netherlands.

Dec 97 onwards | *Michal Shabtay*   *Video Presentation*

[GALLERIES OF THE NEW SYNAGOGUE]

07·11·97-08·02·98 | *Jews / America / A Representation*   *Photographs by Fréderic Brenner*

# Amsterdam

**DE NIEUWE KERK**
Gravenstraat 17  1012 NL Amsterdam  Director : E.W. Veen
☎ +31 20 6268168  ✇ +31 20 6226649
Open: Opening times vary

**COLLECTION** | No permanent collection.

**EXHIBITIONS**

until 15·06·97 | *World Press Photo Exhibition*

01·10·97-02·02·98 | *Kingdoms on the Nile (Working Title)*

# Amsterdam

**MUSEUM HET REMBRANDTHUIS**
Jodenbreestraat 4-6  1011 NK Amsterdam  Director: A.R.E. de Heer
☎ +31 20 6249486  ✇ +31 20 6232246
Open: Daily 10.00-17.00  Sunday and public holidays 13.00-17.00

**COLLECTION** | Once Rembrandt van Rijn's residence, the museum houses a virtually complete collection of the master's etchings. Of the 280 prints

Rembrandt made, 250 are on display, together with paintings by his teachers and pupils.

When Rembrandt moved into this three-story house in 1639, he was already a well-established and wealthy artist. However, the cost of buying and furnishing the house eventually led to his financial downfall in 1656. When Rembrandt was declared insolvent, an inventory of the contents of the house was drawn up, which listed more than 300 paintings by Rembrandt himself and some by his teacher, Pieter Lastman, and his friends, Peter Paul Rubens and Jan Lievens. To meet his debts, Rembrandt was forced to sell most of his possessions. He ultimately moved out in 1660.

The museum is now home to his graphic art. Rembrandt's prints reveal his eye for detail and his skill in creating dramatic effects of light and dark. He depicted a varied range of subjects, including landscapes, patriarchs, emaciated beggars, children at play, and himself in numerous self-portraits.

**EXHIBITIONS**    No details available.

## Amsterdam

**RIJKSMUSEUM**
Stadhouderskade 42  1071 ZD Amsterdam  Director: R. de Leeuw
☎ +31 20 6732121   ⊞ +31 20 6798146
Open: Daily 10.00-17.00
Closed: 1 Jan

**COLLECTION**    The Rijksmuseum is Holland's principal museum and houses a large and wide-ranging collection of objects.

**Paintings**   The core of the collection is made up of Dutch paintings from the 17th century. Rembrandt is well represented with 19 works, of which 'The Nightwatch' has a central place in the museum. This period is also represented with paintings by such artists as Hals, Vermeer, Steen and Ter Borch. Artists from the 15th and 16th centuries are also on display, including Jan Scorel, Maerten van Heemskerck, Lucas van Leyden and Hendrick Goltzius. A small collection of paintings of Foreign Schools, among which Rubens, Murillo and Tintoretto, is also on display.

**Sculpture and Decorative Arts**   Sculpture and decorative arts stemming from the Middle Ages to Jugendstil and Art Nouveau can be viewed. The museum focuses on its collections of Medieval sculpture, 16th and 17th-century silver and its Delftware and Meissen collections.

**Dutch History**   The display consists of all kinds of memorabilia (ship models, flags, objects of gold and silver, documents, etc.) relating mainly to the political and military history of the Netherlands.

**Asiatic Art**   A large part of this collection of art objects from South and South-East Asia and the Far East is on loan from the Society of Friends of Asiatic Art.

**Print Room**   The collection covers Dutch Drawing from the 15th to the 20th century, including drawings by Rembrandt and his pupils and Dutch graphic artists of the 16th and 17th century. International schools, among which Japanese Art, are also well represented.

**EXHIBITIONS**

until 22·06·97      *Decorative Arts Acquisitions*

until 14·09·97      *Paintings by Italian Masters*

until 14·09·97      *Exotic Textiles in the Netherlands*

10.05.97-03.08.97   *The Nude*    *Prints, Drawings and Photographs*      Nude figures have appeared in scenes from the Bible and mythology for hundreds of years. In this exhibition, artists spanning five centuries give their individual interpretations of these figures: Adam and Eve, gods such as Mars and Venus, and many other heroes and saints. As the nude has traditionally been the object of study par excellence for budding artists, the exhibition includes many nude studies as well.

21·06·97-23·06·97    **Chinese Porcelain**    *400 pieces from the Ming and Ching dynasties.*

05·07·97-19·10·97    **Decorative Arts Acquisitions**

16.08.97-09.11.97    **Whistler and Holland**    The famous artist James McNeill Whistler paid several visits to the Netherlands between 1863 and 1903. His 'Dutch period' resulted in many works, including etchings of Amsterdam and watercolours of Zeeland and Dordrecht. Moreover, Whistler had his Dutch followers in the shape of painters such as Witsen and Breitner. This exhibition displays etchings and watercolours by Whistler and works by his Dutch confrères.

04·10·97-29·03·98    **Chapeau Chapeaux!**    *150 Hats (1750-1950)*

01·11·97-28·01·98    **Window-Panes from the 15th and 16th Centuries**    *Presentation related to restoration.*

22.11.97-11.01.98    **The Hausbach of the Master of the Amsterdam Cabinet**    The Hausbach is a book of works by the Master of the Amsterdam Cabinet, one of the greatest European engravers during the late Middle Ages. The Hausbach contains 64 folios with brilliant drawings illustrating court life of that period. As the Hausbach has temporarily been taken apart, this exhibition is the chance of a lifetime to view all of the drawings in the book.

Anton Mauve
(1838-1888)
*Riders in the snow in the woods of The Hague*
in the exhibition 'On country roads and fields' - aquarelle
© *Rijksmuseum, Amsterdam*

29.11.97-03.03.98    **On Country Roads and Fields**    *The Depiction of the 18th and 19th Century Landscape*    19th-century Dutch landscape painting, including the work of the Romantic and the Hague Schools, has enjoyed a good deal of public interest in recent years. 18th-century landscape art, on the other hand, is not nearly as well-known. This large winter exhibition provides a coherent survey of two centuries of landscape art, in paintings, watercolours and drawings. Major works by such artists as De Wit, Koekkoek, Schelfhout, Bilders and Mauve illustrate the development of Dutch landscape painting.

# Amsterdam

**NEDERLANDS SCHEEPVAARTMUSEUM AMSTERDAM**
Kattenburgerplein 1  1018 KK Amsterdam  Director: W. Bijleveld
☎ +31 20 5232222  📠 +31 20 5232213
Internet http://www.generali.nl/scheepvaartmuseum
Open: Tuesday-Saturday 10.00-17.00  Sunday and public holidays
12.00-17.00; 16 Jun-8 Sep  Monday 10.00-17.00
Closed: Monday (8 Sep-15 Jun) and 1 Jan, 30 Apr

**COLLECTION**

The large storehouse, now home to the Netherlands Maritime
Museum, once contained munitions, ropes and sails for the Dutch
Navy. Today, the building houses a permanent exhibition displayed
on two floors on which the entire Dutch seafaring history comes to
life.  There are ships models, modern and historical paintings,
nautical instruments, sea charts, weapons and an attic full of yachts.
There is also a radar hut with an interactive computer programme,
a periscope with a view of the entire city and the Royal Barge.
The towering masts of the Dutch Eastindiaman 'Amsterdam' can be
seen from the Central Station. It is a replica of the ill-fated
Eastindiaman 'Amsterdam' that went down on its maiden voyage to
Asia in 1749. The Dutch Eastindiaman is open to the public all year
round. On board from March to November the crew takes the
visitors back to the world of 1749. The first mate sets course, the
cook prepares an authentic seaman's meal, the sailors swab the
deck, the guns are fired and the cargo is loaded.

*© Nederlands
Scheepvaartmuseum
Amsterdam,
Amsterdam*

You can experience the long and dangerous voyage to the East
Indies in the Philips Multi Media Theatre. The film realistically shows
the visitor what it is like to be on board and bound for Batavia

**EXHIBITIONS**

*until 30-06-97*

***Maritime Masters***   *Drawings of Ships and the Sea 1600-1800*
Rare drawings give a fascinating image of maritime life at the time
of the Dutch Republic. Because of their vulnerability, the drawings
are seldom on show. This exhibition contains about a hundred
drawings of maritime history of the Netherlands. There are works
on parchment or paper made by artists, cartographs, marine
architects or seamen. Drawings by masters like father and son
Van de Velde, Ludolf Backhuysen and Abraham Storck can be seen.

*04·10·97-02·03·98*

***Photgraphs & Memories***   An exhibition to celebrate the 75th
anniversary of the Maritime Museum. A nostalgic view on maritime
Holland with original photographs from the museum's collection.

## Amsterdam

**STEDELIJK MUSEUM  MUSEUM OF MODERN ART**
Paulus Potterstraat 13  1071 CX Amsterdam  Director: Rudi Fuchs
☎ +31 20 5732737  🖷 +31 20 5732789
Internet: http://art.cwi.nl/stedelijk
Open: Daily Apr-Sep 10.00-18.00  Oct-Mar 11.00-17.00
Closed: 1 Jan

COLLECTION

The Stedelijk Museum is an important museum of modern and contemporary art in The Netherlands. It is a dynamic museum that presents developments in the visual arts. A number of works is permanently on view from the Stedelijk Museum's renowned collection of paintings and sculpture, drawings, prints, photographs, graphic design, applied art and design.
Highlights of the collection are some fifty paintings, watercolours and drawings by the Russian artist Malevich and works by Kandinsky, Chagall, Picasso, Monet, Cézanne, Matisse and Dubuffet. German Expressionism is represented by Kirchner and Campendonck, and Dutch art by Van Gogh, Breitner, 'De Stijl' painters Mondrian and Doesburg, the 'Cobra' painters Appel, Constant and Corneille, as well as others such as Willink, Jan Toorop and Charley Toorop.
Other styles include Pop Art by Rauschenberg, Liechtenstein and Warhol, Hard Edge paintings, Minimal Art and Nouveau Réalisme. The collection also contains furniture by Gerrit Rietveld, industrial design, audio-visual art, kinetic art and installations.

# Aschenbach Gallery Amsterdam

Tel. +31 20 6853580    Fax +31 20 6890009

© by Désirée Dolron

Can men with human speech be here - close by?
But i must try, must see it with my own eyes. (Odyssey VI 125-126)

K. Malevich
*An Englishman in
Moscow, 1913-14*
© Stedelijk Museum,
Amsterdam

**EXHIBITIONS**

| | |
|---|---|
| until 19·05·97 | ***Ulrich Ruckriem***   *Sculptures* |
| until 01·06·97 | ***Catharina Sieverding***   *Photography.* |
| 31·05·97-17·08·97 | ***Nan Goldin***   *Photography.* |
| 14·06·97-end Jul | ***Theme Exhibition Europe***   Special exhibition in view of the European summit. |
| 28·06·97-31·08·97 | ***Scandinavian Design*** |
| Sep 97-Oct 97 | ***Partenheimer***   *Paintings* |
| mid Sep 97-end Oct 97 | ***Theme Exhibition 1960***   European photography and paintings prior to the introduction of American Pop Art. |
| 12·09·97-05·10·97 | ***World Wide Media Festival*** |
| 15·10·97-30·11·97 | ***One Hundred Languages***   An exhibition of many forms of art created by Italian children within the scope of a special teaching method. A number of young Dutch artists will also supervise workshops for children. |
| Nov 97-Dec 97 | ***Pichler***   *Paintings* |
| Nov 97-Dec 97 | ***Rodchenko and Others***   *Photography.* |
| Nov 97-Dec 97 | ***Oehlen***   *Paintings* |
| Nov 97-Dec 97 | ***Municipality Acquisitions***   Works by young artists from Amsterdam which are included in the works of art acquired by the municipality in 1997. |

## Amsterdam

**TROPENMUSEUM**
Linnaeusstraat 2  1092 CK Amsterdam  Director: H.J. Gortzak
☎ +31 20 5688200   ⛫ +31 20 5688331
Open: Monday-Friday 10.00-17.00 Tuesday evening 17.00-21.30
Saturday, Sunday and public holidays 12.00-17.00
Closed: 1 Jan, 30 Apr, 5 May, 25 Dec

**COLLECTION**   The Tropenmuseum houses about ten permanent collections which offer a many-sided picture of human life in the tropics and subtropics. There are a number of lifelike exhibits in which one can imagine oneself in a different world. A few examples include: walking through an Arab street to the sound of buyers, sellers and donkey-drivers, hearing the monotonous singing of the monks at a Buddhist temple, and finding one's way through shelters similar to those found in the cities of Bombay and Calcutta. Furthermore, objects reflecting the history and culture of the peoples in the tropics are on display in showcases. A special exhibition for children aged 6-12 can be visited in the Children's Museum (different opening hours).

Entrance Tropenmuseum
© Tropenmuseum, Amsterdam

**EXHIBITIONS**

until 1 Jun 97

***Modern Art from Ethiopia***   Everyday scenes painted by Oromo Qanna Sambata (1945-1991).

until 31·08·97

***Amazonia***   This exhibition highlights the cultural wealth of the Amazon Indians, but also examines the consequences of deforestation and mercury poisoning.

until 20·10·97

***Irian Jaya***   Unique historical photographic material and artifacts from the Tropenmuseum's own extensive collection give an impression of the cultural wealth of the population of Irian Jaya (Western New Guinea).

6 Mar-onwards

***Man and Environment***   This new permanent exhibition focuses on four mayor ecosystems: the tropical rainforest (Amazon region), the savannah (Mali), the sea and the coast (Thailand/Philippines) and the metropolis (Manilla)

27·11·97-01·08·98

***Messenger between Heaven and Earth.*** *What possesses the Shaman?*   Large exhibition about the mythological role, origins, dissemination and development of shamanism in various cultures.

## Apeldoorn

### PALEIS HET LOO - NATIONAAL MUSEUM
Koninklijk Park 1  7315 JA Apeldoorn  Director: A.W. Vliegenthart
☎ +31 55 5772400  ⮻ +31 55 5219983
Open: Tuesday-Sunday 10.00-17.00
Closed: Monday (except public holidays) and 25 Dec

**COLLECTION**

Het Loo Palace, in the woodland setting of Apeldoorn in the heart of the Netherlands, was the favourite summer residence of the Viceregents and the Royal Family of the Netherlands from 1686 to 1975. Since 1984 the palace has served as a museum following a significant restoration of the buildings and the gardens which returned them to their original 17th-century state. The palace, with its interiors dating from William and Mary up to the reign of Queen Wilhelmina, reflects the lifestyles of the members of the family of the Dutch House of Orange-Nassau over three centuries. The wings, with their permanent and visiting exhibitions of historical objects, documents, paintings, china, silver, royal garments and court costumes, present a picture of the historical ties of the House of Orange-Nassau with the Netherlands.

A large collection of national and international orders and decorations is housed in the Museum of the Chancery of the Netherlands Orders of Knighthood.

The spring and summer planting of the Baroque garden parterres, surrounded by terraces, pergolas, statues and vases, is in exactly the same fashion as in the 17th century.

The Royal Stables house royal carriages, hunting carriages, sleighs and vintage court cars, including the 'wagon' in which Queen Wilhelmina went out on painting excursions.

The entire complex is surrounded by extensive woodland, dotted with lakes, and is fully open to the public.

**EXHIBITIONS**

until 29·06·97

***The Emperor's Table***   *Treasures from the Silver Room of the Viennese Court*   This exhibition features the customary imperial 19th-century Viennese court table laid with authentic gilt and porcelain tableware, candelabra, bowls, plates, cutlery, glass and damask table cloths and napkins.

04·07·97-13·07·97

***National Sweet Pea Competition***   Het Loo will be exhibiting a range of new varieties of sweet pea which will also be incorporated into flower arrangements in the palace.

15·07·97-15·08·97

***In the King's Attic***

15·07·97-15·08·97

***Riding Out with the King***

15·07·97-15·08·97

***The House of Orange on Coins***

18·10·97-18·01·98

***Charles Rochussen (1814-1894)***   *A Versatile Artist*   Rochussen was famous for the accuracy with which he drew and painted historical scenes and was a regular guest of King Willem III at Het Loo.

# Apeldoorn

**VAN REEKUM MUSEUM**
Churchillplein 2  7314 BZ Apeldoorn  Director: Frits Bless
☎ +31 55 5219155  🖷 +31 55 5225456
Open: Tuesday-Friday 10.00-17.00  Saturday, Sunday 13.00-17.00
Closed: Monday and 1 Jan, 30 Mar, 8, 18 May, 25 Dec

**COLLECTION**

The emphasis of the museum is on Dutch art since 1960. There are works by Cesar Domela, Carel Visser, Jan Schoonhoven, Johan Claassen, Cees Andriessen, Waldo Bien, Frank van Hemert, Berend Hoekstra, Sjoerd Buisman, Mark Brusse and many others. Artists from other countries are also featured, and include Joseph Beuys, François Morellet, Franz Eggenschwiler, Leon Tarasewicz, KCHO, Belkis Ayon, Marcos Lora Read, Romuald, Hazoumé, Michael Bethé, Selassié, Joseph Semah.

The Van Reekum Museum also houses a photography collection with work by, among others, Bernard Faucon, Teun Hocks, Anja de Jong, Paul de Nooyer, Duane Michals, Lydia Schouten and David Ward.

There is also an interesting collection of modern art jewellery by designers such as Emmy van Leersum, Marion Herbst, Coen Mulder, Birgit Laken, Susanna Heron and Caroline Broadhead.

On permanent display in the Van Reekum Museum is also the reconstruction of the Neoplastic Room by Wladislaw Strzeminski (1893-1952). Strzeminski designed this room in 1948 for the Museum Sztuki in Lódz (Poland). The Van Reekum Museum acquired the replica in 1989.

EXHIBITIONS

Jun 97-Aug 97    **Nicholas Dings**   *Drawings*

Autumn 97    **Ed Kienholz**   *Works from the period 1955-1965*

Spring/Summer 98    **Fruits from South-Africa**   About 15 artists who show in their work a strong engagement with the socio-cultural developments in their country.

## Arnhem

**MUSEUM VOOR MODERNE KUNST ARNHEM -
MUSEUM OF MODERN ART ARNHEM**
Utrechtseweg 87  6812 AA Arnhem  Director: L. Brandt Corstius
☎ +31 26 3512431  🖷 +31 26 4435148
Open: Tuesday-Saturday 10.00-17.00  Sunday and public holidays 11.00-17.00
Closed: Monday

COLLECTION    The permanent collection of Contemporary Fine Art includes paintings by the Magical Realists and their contemporaries, such as Carel Willink, Pyke Koch, Dick Ket and Charley Toorop. The museum's acquisitions place the accent on contemporary art, in particular figurative works by Dutch artists. The museum also possesses an important collection of modern Dutch jewellery.

EXHIBITIONS

until 08·06·97    **Andrea Fisher**   An important starting point in Fisher's work is memory and its distortion. This also applies to the concept of 'time' because, in the artist's view, it stands for the immaterialisation of what was once reality.

until 15·06·97    **Archetypes**   Photographs by Michèle Talens of non-Western men and women who live in the Netherlands while maintaining their own cultural and religious traditions.

31·05·97-Aug 97    **Faience Factory in Arnhem**   The 'Arnhemse Fayencefabriek' (1907-1935) manufactured both ornamental china, such as 'Arnhems Wit', and earthenware for everyday use.

15·06·97-31·08·97    **New Acquisitions**

22·06·97-17·08·97    **Karl Illjitsj ('Karl') Pelgrom (1927-1994)**   The massive oeuvre of this artist from Rotterdam is illustrated here by sculptures, installations, paintings, drawings and photographs.

07·09·97-23·11·97    **Paul de Reus**   *Sculptures*

14·09·97-16·11·97    **Meret Oppenheim (1913-1985)**   Noted for 'Fur Cup' (cup, saucer and spoon made of fur) and 'My Nanny' (a pair of stiletto heels on a serving tray), this exhibition focuses on other works by this Swiss surrealistic artist.

20·09·97-09·11·97    **Cosmopolitan**   An installation by Ilya and Soheila Najand which allows children to get acquainted with the similarities and differences between Western and non-Western cultures.

23·11·97-Jan 98    **Honorary Members Visual Artists Community**   An exhibition to celebrate the 50th anniversary of the Visual Artists Community (including Berend Hendriks, Marius van Beek, Fred Sieger, Henk Peeters).

Dec 97-Jan 98    **Female Power Stations**   An art project by Jacqueline Hassink in which the artist observes and records the worlds of the ten most prominent female top-managers in the world.

## Assen

**DRENTS MUSEUM**
Brink 1 - 5  9401 HS Assen  Director: G.G. Horstmann
☎ +31 592 312741  📠 +31 592 317119
Open: Tuesday-Sunday 11.00-17.00
Closed: Monday and 25 Dec, 1 Jan

**COLLECTION**

The archaeological department of the museum presents treasures from Drenthe's distant past, including flint axes and a 10 000 year-old dugout canoe, made from the trunk of a fir tree, which is the oldest known vessel in the world. In addition, the famous bog body known as the 'Girl from Yde' is on display.

The Art Nouveau and Art Deco department includes a collection of art and products of applied and industrial design from the first decades of the 20th century.

There is also a tax collector's house with period rooms displaying furniture, wall coverings and decoration, lighting, china and a fully equipped kitchen typical of a prosperous family in Drenthe in the 17th or 18th century. The exhibition 'Drenthe 1920-1940' shows how dramatically Drenthe changed between the two world wars. The textile and costume departments concentrate on 'urban' and traditional costumes from 1750 up to the present. The applied art department focusses on furniture, glass and ceramics, base metals, gold and silver, folklore, and coins and pennies from Drenthe. The museum's collection of paintings from Drenthe extending from the 18th to the 20th century is displayed in the halls and stairways. Highlights are paintings from the Hague School.

J.J. van de Sande
Bakhuyzen
(1835-1925)
*Landscape in Drente
with cows on a
country lane*
© Drents Museum,
Assen

**EXHIBITIONS**

| | |
|---|---|
| until 30·11·97 | *A Selection from the Museum's Collection* |
| 25·05·97-27·07·97 | *Gouda Delftware* |
| 31·05·97-31·08·97 | *Textiles 1880-1930* |
| 10·08·97-12·10·97 | *Frans Molenaar* |
| 12·09·97-23·11·97 | *Suze Robertson* |
| 18·10·97-16·11·97 | *Moluccan Artist* |
| 29·11·97-Mar 98 | *Church Silver* |
| 06·12·97-01·02·98 | *Project Contemporary Art* |
| 13·12·97-Mar 98 | *W.O.J. Nieuwenkamp* |

## Den Haag - The Hague

**HAAGS GEMEENTEMUSEUM**
Stadhouderslaan 41  2517 HV Den Haag   Director: J.L. Locher
☎ +31 70 3381111  ⌕ +31 70 3557360
Internet http://www.hgm.denhaag.nl
Closed:  The museum is closed for renovation
Reopening October 1998

## Den Haag - The Hague

**HAAGS HISTORISCH MUSEUM**
Korte Vijverberg 7  2513 AB Den Haag  Director: M.C. van der Sman
☎ +31 70 3646940  ⌕ +31 70 3646942
Open: Tuesday-Friday 11.00-17.00  Saturday-Sunday 12.00-17.00
Closed: Monday and 25 Dec, 1 Jan

COLLECTION

The museum shows the development of the Hague from village to city and the life of its inhabitants. History is displayed by means of guild silver, Rozenburg porcelain, antique furniture, a doll's house, photographs (also in stereo), models and numerous paintings. There is also a nearly five-metre wide 'View of the Hague' by the famous painter Jan van Goyen as well as other cityscapes by Jan Steen, the La Fargue family, Jan ten Compe and Floris Arntzenius.

EXHIBITIONS

until·01·06·97   *Brahms in the Netherlands*

24·05·97·31·08·97   *Portraits*   *From the Museum's Own Collection 1600-1900*

13·09·97·23·11·97   *Van de Sande-Bakhuyzen*   *A Painters Family from the Hague (19th Century)*

15·12·97·15·02·98   *Frederick Hendrik and Courtly Art*   *Cultural Life at the Hague Court in the Golden Age*

## Den Haag - The Hague

**MAURITSHUIS**
Korte Vijverberg 8  2513 AB Den Haag  Director: F.J. Duparc
☎ +31 70 3023456  ⌕ +31 70 3653819
Open: Tuesday-Saturday 10.00-17.00  Sunday 11.00-17.00
Closed: Monday

COLLECTION

The Mauritshuis, a 17th-century palace, is uniquely situated in the centre of The Hague, at a corner of the Hofvijver, directly adjacent to the seat of the Dutch government. It was built between 1634 and 1644 for Johan Maurits van Nassau Siegen, who was a nephew of Viceregent Frederik Hendrik.

The Mauritshuis was designed by Jacob van Campen and, in collaboration with Pieter Post, constructed in the Dutch Classicist style. In 1822 the Mauritshuis became a museum. The museum houses a collection of world-famous paintings from the Dutch Golden Age, with works such as 'The Anatomy Lesson' by Rembrandt, Vermeer's 'View of Delft' and paintings by Jan Steen, Frans Hals, Paulus Potter and others. In 1994 the collection was enriched with a magnificent landscape by Meindert Hobbema. The collection of works by Flemish and Dutch masters of the 15th and 16th century includes works by Rogier van der Weyden, Rubens and Van Dyck.

Vermeer Johannes
(1632-1675)
*Girl with the pearl
earring*
© Mauritshuis,
Den Haag

**EXHIBITIONS**

until 22·06·97

***Art On Wings***　*Celebrating the Reunification of a Triptych by Gerard David*　An exhibition of diptychs and triptychs with special emphasis on the original form and function of these late Medieval works of art. On display will be paintings from the Mauritshuis' permanent collection supplemented with loans. The focus of the presentation will be the temporarily reassembled 'Triptych with the Adoration' by Gerard David (1460-1523), parts of which are owned by the Mauritshuis and by the Metropolitan Museum of Art in New York.

Dec 97-Mar 98

***Frederik Hendrik and Courtly Art***　*Cultural Life at the Hague Court in the Golden Age*　A representative selection of works from the collection of Stadtholder Frederik Hendrik will be on view. Frederik Hendrik (1584-1647) and Amalia van Solms introduced a truly grand courtly style in The Hague between 1620 and 1650. They spent lavishly, building palaces and country manors and assembling a magnificent collection of paintings. They commissioned numerous works from eminent artists such as Rembrandt, Rubens, Jordaens, Honthorst and Anthony van Dyck to grace the walls of their various stately residences.

## Den Haag - The Hague

**MUSEUM MESDAG**
**Laan van Meerdervoort 7f 2517 AB Den Haag　Director: J. Leighton**
**☎ +31 70 3621434　🖷 +31 70 3614026**
**Open: Tuesday-Sunday 12.00-17.00**
**Closed: Monday**

**COLLECTION**

The Mesdag Museum houses a collection of works by the famous maritime painter Hendrik Willem Mesdag (1831-1915). As the extent of his collection had increased significantly by 1887, he built a special museum next to his house.
This museum - together with the artist's former residence and supplemented with a beautiful garden - was recently restored to the state it was in around 1900. The collection includes not only paintings from The Hague School and the Barbizon School, but also Mesdag's extensive collection of applied art, ranging from Colenbrander's Rozenburg ceramics to Chinese and Japanese bronzes.

**EXHIBITIONS**

No exhibitions planned.

Jules Bastien-Lepage
*Sketch for `The
mowing grass', 1876*
© Museum Mesdag,
Den Haag

## Den Haag - The Hague

**HET PALEIS**
Lange Voorhout 74  2514 EH Den Haag   Director: J.L. Locher
☎ +31 70 3381111  🖷 +31 70 3557360
Internet http://www.hgm.denhaag.nl
Open: Tuesday-Sunday 11.00-17.00
Closed: Monday

**COLLECTION**            No permanent collection.

**EXHIBITIONS**
until 19·05·97            ***The Golden Age of Denmark, 1800-1850***

07·06·97-31·08·97         ***The Dandy***  *Attire, Art and Literature*   An exhibition on the
'dandy', a figure which dictated men's fashions, personified the true
artist and played leading roles in fashionable novels during the 19th
century.

13·09·97-16·11·97         ***Venetian Glass***  *Secrets of Murano*   Throughout the years, the
traditional craft skills of the glassblowers of Venice have been
preserved on the island of Murano, their home for centuries and a
state secret in the past.

13·09·97-16·11·97         ***Steltman 1917-1997***  *Jewels, Silver and Haute Couture*
Masterpieces of the jeweller's art produced by the renowned
Steltman business are displayed in part on appropriate examples of
haute couture, and accompanied by original design sketches and
other documentation.

© Het Paleis,
Den Haag

29·11·97-22·02·98         ***Auke de Vries***  *Sculpture*   Known principally for his large-scale
sculptures, this exhibition reveals a less familiar aspect of the artist's
oeuvre: small sculptures created in his studio and serving as
prototypes for the major works.

07·03·98-15·06·98    **The Hague Around 1900**   *Painting, Ceramic, Textile and Furniture Design in The Hague*   This exhibition examines various high points of the Hague School, ideas about 'Gesammtkunstwerk' and the work of Piet Mondrian and focuses both on painting and applied arts, such as furniture, ceramics and fashion.

# Dordrecht

**DORDRECHTS MUSEUM**
Museumstraat 40   3311 XP Dordrecht   Director: J.M. de Groot
☎ +31 78 6134100   ⊠ +31 78 6141766
Open: Tuesday-Saturday 10.00-17.00   Sunday and public holidays 13.00-17.00
Closed: Monday and 25 Dec, 1 Jan

COLLECTION    The museum has an interesting collection of paintings, prints and drawings, with the emphasis on Dutch painting from the 17th century up to the present day.
**The Golden Age**   The collection includes works from famous Dutch Masters of the Golden Age with prize pieces from the Cuyp family and Rembrandt's local students. Dordrecht's past prominence is reflected in the museum's masterpieces by Albert Cuyp, Nicolaes Maes and Samuel van Hoogstraten. Work by Jan van Goyen and less famous masters such as Cornelis Bisschop and Jacob van Geel are also well represented.
**From Romanticism to Impressionism**   Paintings from the 18th, 19th and early 20th century occupy a special place in the museum. Highlights include the landscapes by Jacob van Strij and Romantic masterpieces from B.C. Koekkoek and A. Schelfhout. Work by Ary Scheffer, the 19th-century Franco-Dutch painter, is permanently displayed. The collection of works from the Hague and the Amsterdam schools is impressive with paintings by Mauve, Breitner and the Maris brothers.
**Old and New Developments**   The collection of 20th-century paintings, prints and drawings includes work by important pre-war masters such as Jan Toorop and Jan Sluyters. More recent developments are well represented with work from the Cobra group including Appel, Constant and Wolvecamp and important contemporary masters such as J.C.J. van der Heyden, Lataster and Armando.

B.C.Koekkoek
*Hilly landscape, 1840*
© Museum Hans
Koekoek, Kleef

EXHIBITIONS
18·05·97-14·09·97   **Barend Cornells Koekkoek (1803-1862)**   Koekkoek was one of the most talented and famous painters of the Romantic period. He painted landscapes of trees and woods. He also produced watercolours and lithographs. One of Koekkoek's most influential pupils was P.J.C. Gabriël.

20·08·97-23·11·97   **The Brothers De Witt**   325 years ago, the brothers Johan en Cornelis de Witt were murdered. This politically important moment in Dutch history is commemorated with a presentation of paintings, documents and objects.

12·10·97-11·01·98 **Philip Kouwen** *Landscapes, Still Lifes and Figure Studies* This exhibition presents Philip Kouwen's drawings in the Print Gallery.

## Eindhoven

**STEDELIJK VAN ABBEMUSEUM**
Vonderweg 1 5611 BK Eindhoven Director: J. Debbaut
☎ +31 40 2755275 ⓕ +31 40 2460680
Open: Tuesday-Sunday 11.00-17.00
Closed: Monday (except public holidays) and 16 Jun-4 Jul, 1-13 Sep

COLLECTION

The Van Abbemuseum has always geared its acquisition policy to its exhibition policy and vice versa. As a result, its permanent collection charts, to a large extent, the history of its exhibitions. Major works such as Richard Serra's 'T-junction', Joseph Beuy's installation 'Voglio vedere i miei montagne' occupying an entire room, and Mario Merz's 'Igloo Nero' were made especially for exhibitions at the museum. Through its adventurous exhibition policy, relatively early works by such artists as Christo, Frank Stella, Anselm Kiefer and Donald Judd have come into the museum's collection. To provide a context for these contemporary, post-war works, the museum also possesses examples of the historic avant-garde including important works by Picasso, Chagall, Braque, Léger, Mondrian, Delaunay, Kandinsky, Kokoschka, Van Doesburgh and Moholy-Nagy, among others. In addition, the Van Abbemuseum has a large collection of major works by the Russian Constructivist El Lissitzky. In recent years the museum has built up significant ensembles of the work of a new generation of sculptors including Thomas Schütte, Jan Vercruysse, Jean-Marc Bustamante, Juan Muñoz, Miroslaw Balka and Rachel Whiteread.

*As of 1 January 1995 the Van Abbemuseum on the Bilderdijklaan is closed for expansion and renovation. All museum departments have been temporarily relocated to Vonderweg 1 in Eindhoven (opposite the PSV football grounds).*

EXHIBITIONS

until 15·06·97 **Ulay/Marina Abramovic - Marina Abramovic/Ulay** *Film and Video Installations 1976-1988*

until 15·06·97 **Steve McQueen** *Film Installations*

until 15·06·97 **Mart Mullican, Lawrence Welner** Exhibition to mark the completion of the art route 'The Red Carpet' on the Stadhuisplein in Eindhoven.

until 15·06·97 **Book Works** A selection from the Lawrence Welner collection in the library.

06·07·97-31·08·97 **Mike Kelly** *Works from 1985*

06·07·97-31·08·97 **Atonietta Peeters**

14·09·97-09·11·97 **Just Installations....** Presentation of installation art from the museum's collection.

23·11·97-11·01·98 **Jan Vercruysse** *Selfportraits and Related Works 1977-1984*

Spring 1998 **René Daniëls**

# Enschede

## RIJKSMUSEUM TWENTHE
Lasondersingel 129-131  7514 BP Enschede  Director: D.A.S. Cannegieter
☎ +31 53 4358675  🖷 +31 53 4359002
Open: Tuesday-Sunday 11.00-17.00
Closed: Monday and 1 Jan

COLLECTION

The museum's collection comprises fine art and applied art from the 13th to the 19th century, as well as modern and contemporary art. The fine art collection emphasises on Dutch art and includes Late Medieval painting (Van Cleve, Cranach and Holbein), 16th and 17th-century artists (Brueghel the Younger, Van Goyen, Ruisdael, Avercamp, Van Beyeren and Van Kessel), Romantics (with Koekkoek, Schelfhout and Leickert), the Barbizon School (with Daubigny and Troyon), the Den Haag and Amsterdam Schools (with the Maris brothers, Mauve, Israels and Breitner) and Impressionism (Monet, Sisley and Jongkind).
The collection also includes manuscripts and incunabula, sculptures, Delft earthenware, furniture, tapestries, glassware and silver.
A collection devoted to Dutch art and applied arts of the 18th century, with works by De Wit and Troost, forms a separate component within this collection.

Breitner, George
Hendrik
*Girl in white kimono,*
*1893*
© *Rijksmuseum*
*Twenthe, Enschede*

The collection of modern and contemporary art includes works by CoBrA members (Appel, Brands, Constant, Corneille, Lucebert, Rooskens and Wolvecamp) and by experimental artists (Ouborg, Hussem, Sinemus and Nanninga), systematic, serial and fundamental art from the 60s and 70s, and works by the contemporary artists Akkerman, Buisman, Colton, Dings, Van den Dobbelsteen, Dumas, Van Dijk, Geurts, Van Hemert, Hendriks, Van Hoek, Van Koningsbruggen, Kramer, Loerakker, Van der Mark, Müller, Van Oostende, Van de Pavert, Roeland, Rogge, Ruygrok, Sanders, Schuil, Semah, De Vaal, Verhoef, Verkerk, Visch and Visser.

EXHIBITIONS

No details available.

# Gouda

## CATHARINA GASTHUIS
Oosthaven 9  2801 PB Gouda  Director: N.C. Sluijter-Seijffert
☎ +31 182 588440  🖷 +31 182 588671
Open: Daily 10.00-17.00  Sunday and public holidays 12.00-17.00
Closed: 25 Dec, 1 Jan

COLLECTION

The Catharina Gasthuis was originally established as a hospital at

the beginning of the 14th century and remained a hospital until 1910. The adjoining chapel dates from 1474. In 1939 the building was made into a museum with a very varied collection consisting of old art, modern art, applied art and a medical collection.
A highlight in the collection are the 16th-century altarpieces, especially because they survived the Iconoclasm in that century. You will also find some very interesting church-silver. The Catharina Gasthuis also houses antique toys, an old city dispensary, a surgeon's guild room, an 18th-century kitchen, an isolation cell, torture instruments as well as 17th-century paintings and work of the 'Barbizon' and 'Hague Schools' (19th/20th century). The applied arts collection houses furniture, glass, silver, tin and objet d'arts dating from the late 16th to the early 20th century.

*Silver-gilt chalice, 1425*
*© Photographer: T.Haartsen*
*Catharina Gasthuis, Gouda*

**EXHIBITIONS**

until-20·07·97

***Miniature Fair 1920***   With moving parts such as a merry-go-round, a steam carousel, a ferris wheel with gondola's and two caravans.

03·05·97-21·06·97

***Chess and Art***   Exhibition planned to honour the 150th-birthday of the oldest chess-club in The Netherlands: The Messemaker. Twenty contemporary artists of Gouda and its surroundings show works inspired by the game of chess.

14·06·97-19·10·97

***Crockery made by Gouda Earthenware Factories 1900-1970***   The Gouda earthenware factories were world famous during a period of more than 80 years, from 1898 onwards. This exhibition gives an overview of the vast amount of crockery that was made between 1900 and 1970.

## Groningen

**GRONINGER MUSEUM**
**Museumeiland 1  Groningen  Director: Reyn van der Lugt**
☎ +31 50 3666555   ⌨ +31 50 3120815
Open: Tuesday-Sunday 10.00-17.00
Closed: Monday and 1 Jan, 28 Aug, 25 Dec

**COLLECTION**

**Archaeology**   The Archaeology display contains objects from the Bronze Age, urns found in urnfields in Westerwolde, Iron Age objects, and Roman urns and artefacts discovered during archaeological excavations of the city up to 1993.
**History**   Maces, guild silver, city seals and a coin and medal collection form the core of this department's collection.

Topographical material, including city portraits by Cornelis Pronk, Johannes Bulthuis and A.J. van Prooijen, 16th and 17th-century church treasures and textiles, and portraits by Herman Collenius, Philips van Dijk and Janszoon de Stomme can also be viewed here.

**Decorative Art**    The core of the collection is formed by Chinese and Japanese export porcelain shipped to the Netherlands by the VOC (Dutch East India Company) in the 17th and 18th century. The collection also features porcelain, stoneware and earthenware from Korea, Vietnam and Thailand.

**Art after 1950**    This department aims to acknowledge, collect and preserve new trends in art, starting at the earliest stages of their development. Examples on display here include Figuration Libre, German Neo-Expressionism, Mülheimer Freiheit, graffiti artists, Pattern & Decoration, staged photography, work which can be described as `between art, architecture and design' and Art Business, in which visual artists include business elements in their artistic concepts.

**Old Art (1500-1950)**    The collection gives a picture of the history of art in the Netherlands from 1600-1950. It includes works by members of the De Ploeg group, the society of Expressionist artists in Groningen, the R.J. Veendorp collection, works by the Hague School and the collection of Dr. C. Hofstede de Groot, among which Fabritius, Heda and Rubens and drawings by Rembrandt.

**EXHIBITIONS**

| | |
|---|---|
| until 08·06·97 | ***Old Visual Arts*** |
| until 18·06·97 | ***In Context 2***    *Acquisitions visual arts.* |
| until 31·08·97 | ***'90 000 Packets of Margarine, 100 Meters Ahead!'***   *West 8 on Landscape in Acceleration*    Passion and optimism, acceleration and progress... Featuring models and photos by the Rotterdam landscape architecture bureau West 8, the exhibition reveals Adriaan Geuze's critical vision of Dutch Urban Planning. |
| 17·05·97-17·08·97 | ***The American Interior 1930-1960*** |
| 08·06·97-14·09·97 | ***The Golden Age in Groningen***    The museum presents paintings by Hermannus Collenius, beautiful wooden carvings, silver plates and cups, Chinese porcelain, all of which were made and collected during Groningen's so called 'Golden Age', during the late 17th century and early 18th century. |
| 23·08·97-16·11·97 | ***Marten Klompien***    The museum presents paintings by Marten Klompien, a post-war member of the De Ploeg. |
| 23·08·97-16·11·97 | ***Lellens and the Wijchgel Family***    Presentation centred the Wijchgel family and their mansion Lellens. |
| 14·09·97-07·12·97 | ***Mutant Materials in Contemporary Design*** |
| 28·09·97-23·11·97 | ***Job Hansen & Groninger Silver*** |
| 15·11·97 - Apr 1998 | ***Accents***    Acquisitions policies of three directors: Jos de Guyter, Bram Westers and Frans Haks |
| 23·11·97 - Feb 98 | ***Onno Boekhoudt***    *Jewellery* |
| 07·12·97 - mid Feb 98 | ***Azzedine Alaïa***    *Fashion by top designer Azzedine Alaïa.* |

## Haarlem

**FRANS HALSMUSEUM-DE HALLEN**
Groot Heiligland 62  2011 ES Haarlem  Director: D.P. Snoep
Vleeshal Verweyhal  Grote Markt 16  2011 RD Haarlem
☎ +31 23 5164200  📠 +31 23 5311200
Open: Monday-Saturday 11.00-17.00  Sunday and public holidays 13.00-17.00
Closed: 25 Dec, 1 Jan

**COLLECTION**

Apart from the Frans Halsmuseum itself, there are two branch museums in Haarlem: the Vleeshal and the Verweyhal, both located on the old marketplace (Grote Markt).

*Entrance of the main building*
*© The Frans Hals Museum, Haarlem*

The museum's permanent display of 17th-century portraits, landscapes, genre paintings and still-lifes includes works by the likes of Hendrick Goltzius, Judith Leyster, Johannes Verspronck, Pieter Claesz, Willem Heda, Adriaen van Ostade and Jacob van Ruisdael. Frans Hals' eight group portraits of militia companies and regents form the high point of the collection. The museum also houses a large collection of period furniture, Haarlem silver and ceramics. The collection of Modern and Contemporary art includes paintings, sculptures, the graphic arts, objects and ceramics. It features work by the Dutch Impressionists and Expressionists, the Cobra group, contemporary art and work by artists from the Haarlem area. Artists such as Isaac Israëls, Herman Kruyder, Jan Sluyters, Corneille, Constant, Karel Appel, Reinier Lucassen, Armando, Mari Boeyen and Ger Dekkers alternate in the permanent display. The museum's two other buildings on the Grote Markt are devoted to temporary exhibitions and Classic Modern art respectively.

**EXHIBITIONS**

[MUSEUM]

until 19·05·97

***Hans van Benthem***  Designs and ceramic objects of this artist on display in the showcase at the department of Modern Art

until 19·05·97

***The Bouquet***  A selection of paintings, prints, books and ceramic and glass objects connected with, or depicting flowers.

20·12·97-15·02·98

***The Haarlem Lottery of 1607***  The great campaign to fund the building of the almshouse for old men which is now the Frans Halsmuseum.

[VERWEYHAL]

14·06·97-31·08·97

***Kees Verwey (1900-1995)***  A selection of work by this Haarlem artist

| | |
|---|---|
| 31·08·97-19·10·97 | **40 Years Galerie Espace**   Works by artists exhibited at some stage in the past of one of the eldest and most influential galleries in the Netherlands |
| 20·09·97-30·11·97 | **Children Choose Art**   Children select work of arts from the museum's depot. |
| 13·12·97-08·02·98 | **Sigurdur Gudmundson**   Ceramic objects, sculpture and drawings |

[VLEESHAL]

| | |
|---|---|
| until 19·05·97 | **Twintig in de Hallen : A Visual Feast**   An exhibition composed by Haarlem artists of work by guest artists |
| until 19·05·97 | **De Groep**   An exhibition of the work of members of the Haarlem artists' association De Groep |
| 31·05·97-17·08·97 | **Cornelis Pronk**   An exhibition of drawings by 18th century Cornelis Pronk, draughtsman from North Holland. |
| 21·11·97-15·02·98 | **Majolica**   An overview of the development om majolica between 1580 - 1640 with a selection of Haarlem majolica of that period |
| 01·12·97-04·01·98 | **Kunst Zij Ons Doel**   A presentation of the work of members of the Haarlem artists' association Kunst Zij Ons Doel (May Art Be Our Aim) |

## Haarlem

**TEYLERS MUSEUM**
Spaarne 16  2011 CH Haarlem  Director: E. Ebbinge
☎ +31 23 5319010   🖷 +31 23 5342004
Internet http://www.nedpunt.nl/teylersm
Open: Tuesday-Saturday 10.00-17.00  Sunday and public holidays 12.00-17.00
Closed: Monday, 25 Dec and 1 Jan

COLLECTION

The Teylers Museum was established by Pieter Teyler van der Hulst, a prosperous merchant born in Haarlem in 1702. In his last will and testament, he provided for its establishment by endowing the Teyler Foundation, part of whose task would be to further progress in the arts and sciences.
Ever since his death in 1778, his ideals have been given concrete expression through the museum. For example, the Neo-Classical Oval Hall was built in 1784 for the display of the collection and demonstrations of physics. The museum's first curator, Wybrand Hendriks, acquired a portion of the Queen of Sweden's collection of 16th and 17th-century drawings by Italian masters. Subsequent curators have continued to add to the collection, which now includes five centuries of Dutch draughtsmanship, works produced by the Romantic and The Hague Schools, and Impressionist prints. The museum's first director, Martinus van Marum, encouraged scientific research and laid the foundations for the scientific collections belonging to the Teyler Museum, including fossils and mineral specimens. There is also an important collection of coins and medals.
A new wing provides space for a gallery for temporary exhibitions, a smaller space to exhibit books from the Library and a pavilion for didactic programmes.
Selections from the international renowned collection of drawings, will be on display in the new Printroom.

EXHIBITIONS

[NEW WING]

| | |
|---|---|
| until 25·05·97 | **Master Drawings of the Golden Age**   This exhibition comprises over 100 17th-century drawings from the museum's collection. It coincides with the publication of the first volume of a catalogue of |

Rembrandt
*The return of the
Prodigal Son*
© Teylers Museum,
Haarlem

Old Master drawings, including examples by Nicolaas Berchem, Albert Cuyp, Jan van Goyen, the Van Ostade brothers, Jacob van Ruysdael, Rembrandt van Rijn and Philips Wouwerman.

| | |
|---|---|
| 07·06·97-07·09·97 | **Circus Posters** *Friedlander Posters of the 'Best Collection'* |
| 20·09·97-23·11·97 | **Ad Cadavrum** *The Death Portrait in the Netherlands* |
| Dec 97-Feb 98 | **Rembrandt and His Circle** *Drawings from the Foundation Custodia, Paris* A loan exhibition of 100 drawings from the Lugt collection. |
| | [PRINT ROOM] |
| until end May | **Geer van Velde (1898-1977)** *Works on Paper* |
| Jun 97-Aug 97 | **Master Drawings** *Highlights from the Collection* |
| Dec 97-14·02·98 | **Rembrandt Etchings** |
| 21·02·98-23·05·98 | **Stanley Roseman** |
| | [BOOK CABINET] |
| until Jul 97 | **The Tattooed Human Being** |

## Heerlen

**STADSGALERIJ HEERLEN**
**Raadhuisplein 19  6411 HK  Heerlen  Director: A van der Laan**
**☎ +33 45 5604449  🖷 +33 45 5717475**
**Open: Tuesday-Friday 11.00-17.00  Saturday, Sunday and public holidays 14.00-17.00**
**Closed: Monday and 25 Dec, 1 Jan, Carnival**

**COLLECTION**
In addition to offering quality, diversity and an international perspective in its exhibition programme, the collection of this municipal museum includes an important part of the artistic legacy of Aad de Haas, the non-conformist painter who played a unique role on the Limburg art scene following the Second World War. Furthermore, the town of Heerlen began collecting work by contemporary artists in the 50s. A selection of these works, including CoBrA and post-CoBrA painters, Amsterdam-based artists of Limburg origin and works from the youngest generation of Dutch painters, is on permanent display in the monumental lobby of Heerlen's town hall, adjoining the Stadsgalerij (City gallery).

**EXHIBITIONS**
until 08·06·97

**Kurt Schwitters in the Netherlands**

19·06·97-31·08·97

**Aad de Haas (Rotterdam, 1920 - Schaesberg 1972)**

© Stadsgalerij
Heerlen
Heerlen

| 07·09·97-09·11·97 | *Kurt Schwitters As Inspiration* |
| 16·11·97-18·01·98 | *Surinamese Artists* |
| 24·01·98-29·03·98 | *Attitudes III* |
| 04·04·98-07·06·98 | *Four Young Artists of Limburg Origin* |

# 's-Hertogenbosch

**NOORDBRABANTS MUSEUM**
Verwersstraat 41  5211 HT 's-Hertogenbosch  Director: Margriet van Boven
☎ +31 73 6877800  🖷 +31 73 6877899
Open: Tuesday-Friday 10.00-17.00  Saturday-Sunday 12.00-17.00
Closed: Monday

**COLLECTION**

The North Brabant Museum is located in the former residence of the Governors of Noord-Brabant. Two modern wings haven been added in 1987. The museum's permanent collection is founded on the rich past of the Roman Period and the Duchy of Brabant. The archeological objects, paintings and sculpture attest to the region's leading cultural position during the Roman Period and the late Middle Ages, Renaissance and Baroque periods. Keeping up-to-date with recent developments, the museum frequently organizes extensive exhibitions on an international art level.

**EXHIBITIONS**

until 06·07·97

*Children of All Time*   The exhibition offers a broad view of the world as it is seen through the eyes of children and emphasises the specific role which children have occupied in society through the centuries.

18·07·97-31·08·97   *Contemporary Art from North Brabant*

13·09·97-30·11·97   *La Gare*   *The New Railway Station of 's-Hertogenbosch*

13·09·97-30·11·97   *19th-Century Brabantine Photography*

13·12·97-08·03·98   *Hendrik Wiegersma*   A special exhibition featuring the works of Hendrik Wiegersma (1891-1969), a late exponent of Dutch Expressionism.

28·03·98-28·06·98   *Pop Culture, Sound and Vision*   An international exhibition on the visual aspects of pop music, ranging from the 60s up to the present.

## Laren

**SINGER MUSEUM**
Oude Drift 1  1251 BS Laren  Director: E.J.C. Raassen-Kruimel
☎ +31 35 5315656  🖷 +31 35 5317751
Open: Tuesday-Saturday 11.00-17.00  Sunday and public holidays 12.00-17.00
Closed: Monday and 1 Jan, 30 Apr, 25 Dec

**COLLECTION**

The museum started with the private collection of the American painter W.H. Singer and his wife. Singer lived and worked in Laren at the beginning of the 20th century. It was here that he built a house that nowadays forms part of the museum. The museum was built in 1956 and renovated in 1994. In 1996 the 40th anniversary will be celebrated.

H.E. le Sidaner
(1862-1939)
*Table with fruit in a
sunny square*
© *Singer Museum,
Laren*

The collection mainly consists of paintings, watercolours and drawings of Laren painters, French artists from the School of Barbizon, works of a few American painters and of French and Dutch sculptors from the 19th and 20th century. The French painter Henri Le Sidaner, who was a friend of William Singer, is represented with twelve paintings. A great number of works by William Singer has been added to this collection. The Foundation of Friends of the private Singer Museum has enabled the acquisition of more important works from the School of The Hague and of Amsterdam Impressionists. Through the years, numerous gifts and legacies have completed the collection, such as the Hart Nibbrig endowment and in 1995 the gift of the Groeneveld Collection.

**EXHIBITIONS**

until 11·05·97    *Maria van Kesteren & Marian Plug*   Objects, Paintings

until 22·06·97    *Henri le Sidaner*   From Symbolism to Neo-Impressionism   Paintings

18·05·97-22·06·97    *Winnie Teschmacher*   Glass-objects

07·09·97-05·10·97    *Painters-Society Laren-Blaricum*   Paintings

12·10·97-30·11·97    *Boncompain*   Paintings, Pastels and Ceramics

18·10·97-18·01·98    *The Art Collection of the American Company, Sara Lee Corporation, Chigago*   The collection is known as one of America's finest and most varied, containing artwork by Renoir, Monet, Picasso, Chagall, Moore, Giacometti and others.

## Leeuwarden

**FRIES MUSEUM**
Turfmarkt 11  8911 KS Leeuwarden  Director: R.H.C. Vos
☎ +31 58 2123001  ☱ +31 58 2132271
Open: Daily 11.00-17.00  Sunday and public holidays 13.00-17.00
Closed: 25 Dec, 1 Jan

COLLECTION

The first part of an entirely renovated Fries Museum opened on 15 April, 1995. The museum has been expanded with the addition of the facing 16th-century 'kanselarij' (Chancellery). The collections of the Fries Museum include paintings from the 16th century through to the 20th century, a large collection of drawings and graphics, a significant costume collection, a famous collection of Frisian silver and many archaeological objects. There is also a section devoted to the Second World War, and various period rooms open to the public.

EXHIBITIONS

until 11·05·97

*A Journey of the Heart along the 11 Cities*

until 11·05·97

*Show off at Table*    Small exhibition of modern Frisian Silver.

until 01·06·97

*Liberation in Pictures*    *Drawings by Inge Krassenburg*

until 15·06·97

*Leeuwarden 1750-1850*    Drawings and water-colours of the city of Leeuwarden.

28·06·97-31·08·97

*Marleen Felius  Cows*    More than 700 cattle breeds in water-colour and a number of oilpaintings by Marleen Felius, expert on cattle breeds.

13·09·97-09·11·97

*Bouke van der Sloot*    Retrospective of the Frisian painter Bouke van der Sloot (1908-1995).

29·11·97-14·02·98

*Dolls*    *Everything There is to Know about Dolls.*

Apr 98-Jun 98

*Our Indies? Our Indies!*    *The Dutch Colonial Period in Indonesia*

## Leeuwarden

**KERAMIEKMUSEUM HET PRINCESSEHOF**
Grote Kerkstraat 11  8911 DZ Leeuwarden  Director: J.A. Mulder
☎ +31 58 2127438  ☱ +31 58 2122281
Open: Daily 10.00-17.00  Sunday and public holidays 14.00-17.00
Closed: 25 Dec, 1 Jan

COLLECTION

Once the official residence of Princess Maria-Louise of Hessen-Kassel, widow of the Frisian Viceregent John William Friso, Prince of Orange, the palace now houses the National Museum of Ceramics (since 1917). The dining-room on the ground floor is decorated with stucco ceiling, gold curtains, various portraits and Chinese porcelain. There are a total of thirty rooms containing collections of porcelain, pottery and stoneware pieces. The museum's extensive collections can be divided into four main categories: Oriental ceramics, European ceramics, the Tile department and Modern and contemporary ceramics.
The Princessehof's main collection consists of Asian ceramics, including works from Japan, China, Vietnam and Thailand. In its entirety, the collection of Chinese ceramics illustrates the development of this industry: starting with terracotta pieces made in the 3rd millenium B.C. and leading up to objects manufactured during the Ching dynasty (1644-1912). There are also objects belonging to the famous Famille Verte, Noire and Rose.

The European ceramics include Italian Renaissance earthenware (majolica), delftware, Wedgwood, porcelain and Art-Nouveau and Art-Deco ceramics. The museum also houses an extensive collection of tiles from the Middle-East, Spain, Portugal, France and the Netherlands. Finally, contemporary ceramics from several European countries, particularly the Netherlands, are also on display.

**EXHIBITIONS**

02·05·97-18·08·97    *Persian Ceramics*

06·09·97-31·11·97    *Jan van der Vaart & the Multiples*

19·12·97-09·03·98    *Raku*   *Japanese Ceramics*

## Leiden

**RIJKSMUSEUM VAN OUDHEDEN**
**NATIONAL MUSEUM OF ANTIQUITIES**
Rapenburg 28  2301 EC Leiden  Director: P.J.Th. Schoots
☎ +31 71 5163163  📠 +31 71 5149941
Open: Tuesday-Saturday 10.00-17.00  Sunday and public holidays 12.00-17.00
Closed: Monday and 1 Jan, 3 Oct, 25 Dec

**COLLECTION**

The National Museum of Antiquities, set up at the behest of King William I in 1818, exhibits artefacts that were long considered miracles due to their age and unique histories. The display of works from Classical Greek antiquity includes distinctive square-bearded sculptured heads, intimate sculptured funeral scenes and tragic theatre masks. The Near East comes alive through ritual statuettes, figurines of priests and inscriptions. The collection includes an inscription relating the story of King Nebuchadnezzar II's hanging gardens of Babylon. The Egyptian collection of mummies, funeral requisites, temple statues and utensils evoke this wondrous civilisation. Highlight of this section is the Isis Sanctuary, the temple of Taffeh.

The Netherlands has often been 'flooded'; not just by water but also by foreign peoples and their cultures. These events have left telltale clues in the Dutch soil, ranging from fishing tackle and snares (c. 1000 years B.C.), the flint implements of reindeer hunters and Roman altars from the coast of Zeeland, to Frankish and Saxon treasures. The display 'Archaeology in the Netherlands' offers a survey of national history from Prehistory to Medieval times. Most of the exhibits were recovered by archaeologists from the National Museum.

**EXHIBITIONS**

until end 98    *Mummies!*   Among other things, this exhibition explores why the Egyptians were moved to mummify their dead. It deals with the Egyptian underworld, the techniques used for mummification and the religious and social aspects of this custom.

27·06·97-end 98    *Action Roman*   An exhibition for children that allows them to get acquainted with various aspects of the Romans in the Netherlands, such as city life and school, using puzzles, games and music.

29·08·97-end 98    *Antique Tourism*   *A Trip along the Most Beautiful Objects of the National Museum of Antiquities*   A trip around the Mediterranean allows the visitor to get acquainted with the numerous aspects of Near-East and Egyptian cultures, the Graeco-Roman world and the Romans in the Netherlands.

29·08·97-end 98    *Who's Afraid of Ancient Blue?*   Egyptian memorial statuettes, Roman torsos and other monumental sculptures are presented in an attractive, scenic setting situated around the Egyptian temple of Taffeh.

# Leiden

## STEDELIJK MUSEUM DE LAKENHAL
Oude Singel 28-32  2312 RA Leiden  Director: H. Bolten-Rempt
☎ +31 71 5165360  ⛬ +31 71 5134489
Internet http://www.leiden.nl./lakenhal
Open: Tuesday-Friday 10.00-17.00  Saturday, Sunday and public holidays
12.00-17.00
Closed: Monday

COLLECTION

The Municipal Museum of Leiden is a museum of typical Dutch urban culture from the 16th century to the present. Since 1874 it has been housed in the Lakenhal, the former clothmakers' hall built in 1640 by Arent van 's Gravensande. A series of 16th-century paintings by Isaac van Swanenburgh depicting the various stages of the wool production process is supplemented by a loom, sample books, scissors, stamps, etc. Events from Leiden's history are also depicted, such as the siege of the city and its relief on 3 October 1574. The collection contains Leiden silver, engraved glass, pewter, tiles and paintings by 16th-century Leiden artists. The 17th century is represented by the young Rembrandt, Lievens, David Bailly, Jan Steen, Gerard Dou and the Leiden 'Precise School'. The 18th century is presented in rooms furnished in the style of the period. The 19th- and 20th-century collection contains work by Bakker, Korff, Jan Toorop, H.P. Bremmer, Floris Vester, Kamerlingh Onnes, Hendrik Valk, Theo van Doesburg and early examples of 'De Stijl'. Works from the contemporary collection are exhibited every summer.

EXHIBITIONS

until 28·07·97

*Leiden's Passion*   Twenty people born in Leiden, both famous and unknown, present their personal choices from the museum collection, in combination with the favourite items from their own private collections.

14·06·97-11·08·97

*Hendrik Valk   Drawings in Chalk*   Hendrik Valk (1897-1986) was one of the pioneers of abstract art in Holland. On exhibition are drawings made in the years 1918 to 1926, during his stay in Leiden.

20·12·97-23·03·98

*Isaac van Swanenburgh (1537-1614)*   An exhibition about this painter and scientist, who was governor of Leiden during the Golden Age.

# Leiden

## RIJKSMUSEUM VOOR VOLKENKUNDE
Steenstraat 1  2312 BS Leiden  Director: S.B. Engelsman
☎ +31 71 5168800  ⛬ +31 71 5128437
Open: Tuesday-Friday 10.00-17.00  Saturday, Sunday and public holidays
12.00-17.00
Closed: Monday and 1 Jan, 3 Oct

COLLECTION

The National Museum of Ethnology in Leiden is one of the oldest scientific ethnological museums in the world. It has grown out of an ethnological museum established in 1837 by Dr. Ph. F. von Siebold, who had served as a physician to a Dutch trading post near Nagasaki, Japan, and who opened his well-documented Japanese collection to the public a few years after his return to the Netherlands.
The museum's collections have been greatly expanded over the years, and now include items from many non-Western cultures, including Sub-Saharan Africa, the Arctic, China, the islands of Southeast Asia, Japan and Korea, Southwest and Central Asia, Latin America, North America, Oceania, and the mainland of Southeast Asia.

The museum is currently undergoing extensive renovations, and the exhibitions are restricted to special temporary exhibitions, guided tours, films, lectures and demonstrations.

**EXHIBITIONS**

until end Aug 97

***Veils Unveiled***    The subject of veils and veiling is currently one of the most emotive subjects within costume history, both for the participants and the observers. This exhibition is intended to show that the development and use of veiling has ancient antecedents, which are spread throughout Europe, the Meditterranean and the Middle East.

Oct 97

***To Tibet with TinTin***    This exhibition focuses on Tibeten culture and is introduced by the popular comic-strip character TinTin.

## Maastricht

**BONNEFANTENMUSEUM**
**Avenue Ceramique 250  6221 KX Maastricht  Director: A. van Grevenstein**
☎ **+31 43 3290190  📠 +31 43 3290199**
**Open: Tuesday-Sunday 11.00-17.00**
**Closed: Monday (except public holidays) and Carnival week**
**(Saturday-Tuesday), 25 Dec, 1 Jan**

**COLLECTION**

The Bonnefantenmuseum is the Province of Limburg's museum for fine arts and archaeology.
Archaeology   The archaeology collection consists of finds from Limburg dating from approximately 250 000 B.C. to the Modern Era. At the heart of the collection are important archaeological assemblages from the Stone Age, the Roman period, and the early Middle Ages.

© Bonnefanten-
museum, Maastricht

Medieval to 18th Century   The collection of Medieval to 18th century art is divided into three main categories: Medieval sculpture, early Italian painting (1325-1525) and painting of the Southern Netherlands from the 16th and 17th centuries. Pieter Brueghel the Younger highlights this collection.
Contemporary   The collection of contemporary art covers a select number of artists. At its core is the Seminal Collection, which includes Beuys, Broodthaers, Dibbets, Fabro, Kounellis, LeWitt, Mangold, Merz, Ryman, and Serra. The museum also houses a number of smaller collections, including Maastricht earthenware and silver.

**EXHIBITION**
28-09-97-04-01-98

***Exile on Main Street***    Wesley, Copley, Westermann, Guston, Saul, Gianakos.

## Middelburg

**ZEEUWS MUSEUM**
Abdij  4331 BK Middelburg  Director: J.V.T. van Spaander
☎ +31 118 626655  📠 +31 118 638998
Open: Monday-Saturday 10.00-17.00  Sunday and public holidays 12.00-17.00
Closed: 24 and 30 Dec after 15.00 and 25 Dec, 1 Jan

COLLECTION

The Zealand Museum is housed in a centuries-old Norbertine Abbey in Middelburg. The collections recount thousands of years of Zealand's history and include archaeological finds such as the votive stones dedicated to the goddess Nehalennia, 18th-century rarity cabinets, 17th and 18th-century porcelain and silver from the society collections, and an overview of Zealand's regional costumes.
**Classic and Modern Art**  The collection includes works by the 17th-century painters François Rijckhals and Adriaen van de Venne. Among the 20th-century artists inspired by Zealand's landscape are Jan Toorop, Jacoba van Heemskerck, the Hungarian painter Maurice Goth and his daughter Sarika Goth, Charley Toorop and Reimond Kimpe, Jan van Munster, Paul de Nooijer, Marinus Boezem and Piet Dieleman.
**16th-Century Tapestries**  The series of 16th-century tapestries illustrating the battle between Zealand's 'geuzen' (Protestant fighters) and the Spanish on the Schelde rivers during the Eighty Years' War (1568-1648) was commissioned by the Provincial Council of Zealand and woven in Delft and Middelburg.

EXHIBITIONS

until 15·06·97

*Reimond Kimpe (1885-1970)*  The Golden Mean - Paintings and Drawings

05·07·97-31·08·97

*Locations*  Photographs by Wim Riemens

12·07·97-end Jan 98

*Nehalennia  350 Years*  350 years ago the first Nehalennia stones were found on the beach of Domburg. As part of this exhibition, the museum will rearrange its permanent archaeology presentation.

13·09·97-02·11·97

(subject to confirmation) *Contemporary Art*  A Selection from the Museum's Collection by a Guest Curator

15·11·97-Feb 98

*Saudara*  Installation with Photographic Works by Jan Malawauw
An exhibition of photographs by the first and later generations of Moluccans in the Netherlands, and of objects from the Society.

Feb 98-end May 98

*Contemporary Art*  A Selection from the Museum's Collection by a Guest Curator

## Nijmegen

**NIJMEEGS MUSEUM COMMANDERIE VAN SINT-JAN**
Franse Plaats 3  6511 VS Nijmegen  Director: G.Th.M. Lemmens
☎ +31 24 3229193  📠 +31 24 3605073 Internet http://www.nijmegen.nl
Open: Monday-Saturday 10.00-17.00  Sunday and public holidays 13.00-17.00
Closed: 25 Dec

COLLECTION

The municipal museum of the city of Nijmegen derives its name from the cloister/hospital Commanderie van St. Jan, dating from 1296 and originally belonging to the order of the Knights of St. John. The museum houses a cultural-historical collection, comprising the town's collection in the field of history, art and applied art from the 11th until the 19th century, as well as a collection of modern art.
The 'Kanis Family Triptych', the monumental view of the Valkhof

citadel by Jan van Goyen, and the painting of the Peace of Nijmegen by Henry Gascard are highlights of the collection. The museum also has a unique collection of Nijmegen silver. The modern art collection consists of more than 500 paintings and over 2000 works on paper, mainly focusing on a number of movements in Dutch art since the 60s, including Pop Art, Fundamental Art, Reliefs/Assemblies, and especially Contemporary Expressionism.

**EXHIBITIONS**

10·05·97-29·06·97

*A Useful and Elegant Attribute*   *The Schnitzler Umbrella Factory in Nijmegen*   Umbrellas played an important role in turn-of-the-century fashion. This exhibition of various elements of old umbrellas shows the craftsmanship and the fantasy intrinsic to this vital accessory.

14·05·97-29·06·97

*Above Ground Level*   *Contemporary Hat Design*   25 Dutch hat designers are represented with various 'sculptures for wearing', some of which were designed especially for this occasion. Hat designing is shown to be a discipline of almost unlimited potential.

05·07·97-31·08·97

*A Trip Along the Lower Rhine*   Topographic Drawings and Etchings from the Collection Robert Angerhausen and the Kleve Museum (Germany)This exhibition includes a selection of topographic drawings and etchings, primarily by Dutch artists, of towns, villages, castles and landscapes in the area of the German Lower Rhine adjacent to the Dutch province of Gelderland.

13·09·97-02·11·97

*Decayed Past*   *Ruins in Dutch Drawing and Painting*   This exhibition of works from the 16th to the 20th century focuses on the presentation of ruins in pictorial art, both as a topical reproduction and a romanticised element in painted landscapes.

08·11·97-14·12·97

*50 Years of the GBK (Society of Pictorial Artists)* In commemoration of its 50th anniversary, the GBK presents this exhibition celebrating the pleasures and passion of buying and collecting pictorial art.

08·11·97-14·12·97

*Gerard Noodt 1647-1997*   A celebration of the 350th anniversary of the birth of the jurist Gerard Noodt, son of a Nijmegan silversmith, who achieved prominence for his writings concerning freedom of religion and the sovereignty of the people.

## Nijmegen

**PROVINCIAAL MUSEUM G.M. KAM**
**Museum Kamstraat 45  6522 GB Nijmegen  Director: A.M. Gerhartl-Witteveen**
☎ +31 24 3220619  📠 +31 24 3604799
**Open: Tuesday-Friday 10.00-17.00  Saturday, Sunday and public holidays 13.00-17.00**
**Closed: Monday and 25 Dec**
**From October 1997 the Museum Kam will be closed for the public.**

**COLLECTION**

In the Provinciaal Museum G.M. Kam, the archaeology of the province of Gelderland, from prehistory to the Middle Ages, comes to life. With both its permanent collection and temporary exhibitions the Museum gives a picture of the earliest history of the province, and in particular of Roman Nijmegen.
In recent decades, extensive excavations have taken place, adding many interesting finds to the Museum collection. New, unexpected things are still being brought to light. The museum is the archaeological depository for the province, which means that the greater part of what is excavated in Gelderland is stored here.

**EXHIBITION**
18·05·97-Oct 97

**Museum Kam 75 Years Old/Young**    The archaeological museum was opened 75 years ago in 1922. The exhibition, at the same time the last one in the current building, will give an impression of the history of the museum.

## Otterlo

### KRÖLLER-MÜLLER MUSEUM
Houtkampweg 6  6731 AW Otterlo  Director: Evert J. van Straaten
☎ +31 318 591241  ☷ +31 318 591515
Open: Tuesday-Sunday and public holidays 10.00-17.00
Closed: Monday except public holidays and 1 Jan

**COLLECTION**

The Kröller-Müller Museum houses a world-famous collection of fine art, mainly from the 19th and 20th century, incorporating paintings, sculptures, drawings, graphic and applied arts. A focal point of the museum's collection is the wide collection of works by Vincent van Gogh, representing one of the most comprehensive collections of this artist's work to be found anywhere in the world. The museum also boasts important paintings by many other great artists including Georges Seurat, Pablo Picasso, Fernand Léger and Piet Mondrian, to name but a few.

Vincent van Gogh
(1853-1890)
*Café terrace at night,*
*'Place du Forum',*
Arles 1888
© Kröller-Müller
Museum, Otterlo

Sculpture of the late 19th and 20th century also occupies an important place in the Kröller-Müller Museum. The sculpture garden, covering 21 hectares, is one of the largest in Europe. Accomodating a unique collection of works in the setting of a varied landscape, the sculpture garden offers the visitor a fascinating survey of the manner in which sculptural art has developed from the end of the 19th century up to the present. Among the sculptors represented are August Rodin, Henry Moore, Barbara Hepworth, Richard Serra, Mario Merz, Jean Dubuffet and Claes Oldenburg.

**EXHIBITIONS**

until 22·06·97

**Overholland at the Kröller-Müller Museum**

06·07·97-26·10·97

**Acquisitions and Panamarenko**

15·11·97-18·01·98

**Sculptures by Picasso, Gonzalez, Miró and Chillida**

# NRC ✠ HANDELSBLAD

## Rotterdam

**MUSEUM BOIJMANS VAN BEUNINGEN**
Museumpark 18-20  3015 CX Rotterdam  Director: Chris Dercon
☎ +31 10 4419400  📠 +31 10 4360500
Internet: http://www.boijmans.rotterdam.nl
Open: Tuesday-Saturday 10.00-17.00  Sunday and public holidays 11.00-17.00
Closed: Monday and 1 Jan, 30 Apr, 25 Dec

**COLLECTION**

The collection of Old Masters provides a fine survey of Western European art dating from the 14th to the mid-19th century. Particularly well represented is Northern and Southern Netherlandish art from the 15th and 16th century and Dutch painting from the 17th century. Highlights of the collection include 'The Vagabond' by Hieronymus Bosch, Brueghel's 'Tower of Babel', Rembrandt's 'Portrait of Titus' and works by Van Eyck, Rubens, Titian and Saenredam.

Covering the period from 1850 to the present, the collection contains famous works by the Surrealists Magritte and Dali.

The Modern Classics Department boasts superb paintings by Monet, Van Gogh, Kandinsky and Van Dongen. There are also important examples of recent German and American art and contemporary sculpture.

*© Museum Boijmans Van Beuningen Rotterdam*

The Department of Applied Art and Design houses precious objects and everyday utensils dating from the Middle Ages to the present. There are important collections of majolica, pewter, silver, glass, pre-industrial utensils and modern decorative art. In recent years work from the field of industrial design has come to occupy a prominent place in the museum.

As well as having a large number of prints, the Print Room has custody of one of the world's biggest and most important collections of drawings. Numerous schools from the Middle Ages to the present are represented, as well as masters such as Dürer, Rembrandt, Goya, Giorgione, Watteau, Manet, Cézanne and Picasso.

**EXHIBITIONS**

until 25·05·97

*Christopher Williams*   As a follow-up to Albert Renger-Patzsch's book 'Die Welt ist schön', Christopher Williams has compiled a contemporary vademecum of commonplace, time-defining objects.

17·05·97-03·08·97

*Martin Margiela: Fashion Designs*   Martin Margiela is one of the most controversial Belgian fashion designers on the international scene. His designs include reproduced items of clothing made of second-hand materials such as plastic bags, fragments of porcelain, panty hose and papier-maché.

12·06·97-18·08·97

*Hubert Damisch, Guest Curator — Moves*   French philosopher Hubert Damisch, renowned for his daring art history texts, selects objects from the museum collection for his own show.

30·08·97-16·11·97

*17th-Century Genre Paintings*   This exhibition presents works from the museum's collection.

17·09·97-17·12·97

*Eternal Youth (Part of the R-97 Festival): Furniture for Children* This display of furniture is designed by an architect.

17·09·97-17·12·97

*Daan van Golden*   This photo project revolves around the photographer's daughter.

17·09·97-17·12·97

*Children Choose Art*   In this exhibition, children choose and comment on works from the museum collection.

17·09·97-17·12·97

*Mike Kelley/Sharon Lockhart/Nan Goldin/Rineke Dijkstra* Mike Kelly's photographs of children's drawings, accompanied by a false analysis suggesting that the drawings show that the children have been subject to sexual abuse.

06·12·97-Mar 98

*Max Ernst*

# Rotterdam

**KUNSTHAL ROTTERDAM**
**Museumpark, Westzeedijk 341  3015 AA Rotterdam  Director: W. van Krimpen**
☎ +31 10 4400300  ▣ +31 10 4367152
 Internet http://mediaport.org/~kunsthal/agenda.htnl
**Open: Tuesday-Saturday 10.00-17.00  Sunday and public holidays 11.00-17.00**
**Closed: Monday**

**COLLECTION**   No permanent collection.

**EXHIBITIONS**

until 04·05·97

*Komar & Melamid/Trademark*   *The People's Choice: The Most Desired and Least Desired Painting in the Netherlands*   After a poll of Dutch taste concerning opinions on a beautiful or ugly painting, the New York duo Komar & Melamid produce paintings based on the findings.

until 18·05·97

*Undressed*   *Body Fashion and Lingerie by Marlies Dekkers*   Marlies Dekkers' collections of swimwear, luxury lingerie and stylish erotic underwear for men and women have attracted the attention of the international design world

until 08·06·97

*The Early Mondrian*   *Paintings, Watercolours and Drawings from the Haags Gemeentemuseum* The early work of Piet Mondrian (1872-1944) is presented, showing the manner in which visible reality gradually gave way to abstract compositions.

10·05·97-29·06·97 **Colin Gray (Photography)** *The Parents* British photographer Colin Gray presents the results of a project in which he took photographs of his parents over a period of 15 years.

24·05·97-15·08·97 **The World of Charles Burki** *Inventions and Designs from the Future of Yesterday* It is no exaggeration to say that designer/ illustrator/ filmmaker/artist Charles Burki (1909-1994), determined the look of the 50s and 60s with his designs.

31·05·97-03·08·97 **Robert Longo** *The 365 Magellan Drawings* Inspired by the 'metropolitan culture' of the United States, Robert Longo produced one drawing a day for twelve months.

21·06·97-05·10·97 **Highlights from the Painting Collection of the Haags Gemeentemuseum** Selections from one of the most important painting collections in the Netherlands, the Haags Gemeentemuseum collection, include works by Picasso, Braque, Kokaschka, Schiele, Morandi and Delvaux.

28·06·97-28·09·97 **My First Chair** *Children's Furniture from All over the World* The Kunsthal Rotterdam presents the first exhibition on the development of children's furniture throughout the world.

05·07·97-14·09·97 **Meret Oppenheim Meets Man Ray** This exhibition consists of over 150 objects and photos by both artists, who met in Paris in 1933.

23·08·97-02·11·97 **Brancusi, Tzara and the Romanian Avant-Garde** This exhibition is the first to deal with the forgotten Modernist movement in Romania and consists of photographs, graphic design and artworks.

20·09·97-30·11·97 **Inge Morath (Photography)** *Europa!* Morath was among the first generation to work for the famous Magnum agency in the 1950s. In this exhibit, photos made in Europe are featured.

13·09·97-30·11·97 **Edward Steichen** *Retrospective* Steichen had enormous influence on every genre of photography from portrait, landscape and still-life to social photography, advertising and celebrity photography.

11·10·97-18·01·98 **Masters of the Hague School** *Haags Gemeentemuseum Collection* The Kunsthal Rotterdam presents a major overview of the leading Dutch art movement of the 19th century. It includes works by the Maris brothers, Mauve and Weissenbruch.

06·12·97-30·01·98 **W.O.J. Nieuwenkamp** The exhibition of work by Nieuwenkamp forms part of a series featuring Dutch artists who worked in the former Dutch East Indies. Many of these works have never been exhibited before.

# Rotterdam

**MARITIEM MUSEUM 'PRINS HENDRIK'**
Leuvehaven 1 3011 EA Rotterdam Director: ad interim
☎ +31 10 4132680 ☳ +31 10 4137342
Open: Tuesday-Saturday 10.00-17.00 Sunday and public holidays 11.00-17.00
Closed: Monday and 1 Jan, 30 Apr, 25 Dec

COLLECTION **Vademecum** A shipping manual in the form of an exhibition offers an introduction to shipping.
**'Professor Splash'** The children's activity centre at the Maritime

Museum 'Prins Hendrik' 'Professor Splash' allows children aged 4-12 to experiment, experience and discover for themselves, making it fun to find out about ships, shipping and basic maritime principles.
**Men Aboard, Life at Sea in the 17th-18th Century** The collection focuses on the sailors who worked and lived on the Dutch sailing ships during the time of the Republic. It includes handwritten ship's logs, rare nautical charts and atlases, engravings of disasters at sea, pictures of sea battles and navigational instruments.
**Open Storeroom** A look behind the scenes: showcases, shelves and cupboards containing clothing, coins, crockery and various other items.
**Museumship 'Buffel'** Built in 1868 and largely restored to its original state, this former armourclad turret-ram of the Royal Dutch Navy features a fully-equipped upper deck and furnished officers' quarters. Within the ship are a number of displays on such subjects as life on board, navigation, and artillery.

**EXHIBITIONS**

until-25·05·97

*The City according to Sirks* *Etchings from Rotterdam*

until-22·06·97

*The Dutch Shallows: Clouds, Wind and Water* Twenty Dutch artists explore the world of tides, streams, harbours, dikes and ancient polders. Forty works are shown in this special exhibition.

until-14·09·97

*Something Kept, Something Had* *Private Maritime Collections* Fifty private maritime collections confront the visitor with an enormous variety of objects: stamps, playing cards, buttons, light houses and so forth.

31·05·97-07·09·97

*Eye and Ear of the Waterweg* *125 years Dirkzwager*

28·06·97-05·10·97

*Records of Travel* Presentation of log-books and other records of travel from the collection from the 17th century to the present.

13·09·97-07·12·97

*Anna Kool* *Three-dimensional Paintings* Anna Kool is inspired by what she finds on beaches. She uses these pieces of driftwood and other objects in her often colourful paintings. Consequently, almost all her work is somehow connected to sea and water.

27·09·97-30·11·97

*Tetsuo Mizu* The japanese artist Tetsuo Mizu is fascinated by marine signal-flags. In his paintings he combines the flags to form words related to the world of shipping.

20·12·97-08·03·98

*Shipowners of the Century* Starting from the museum's extensive photocollection of shipowner Nedlloyd, visitors are introduced to various aspects of the shipping-trade.

28·03·98-20·09·98

*125 Years Dutch-American Steamship Company*

# Rotterdam

**NATUURMUSEUM ROTTERDAM**
Westzeedijk 345  Museumpark 3015 AA Rotterdam  Director: J.W.F. Reumer
☎ +31 10 4364222  📠 +31 10 4364399
Open: Tuesday-Saturday 10.00-17.00  Sunday and public holidays 11.00-17.00
Closed: Monday and 30 Apr, 25 Dec, 1 Jan

**COLLECTION**

The Natuurmuseum Rotterdam was established in 1927. It is the only museum in the region with exhibitions, activities, information and collections concerning natural history and environmental issues. The museum possesses an important collection of stuffed birds, fossilised remains of mammals, skulls and skeletons, insects, shells, minerals, and a collection of preserved organisms.

The Natuurmuseum, along with the four other museums which surround it, is an antique mansion flanked by a modern pavilion and is situated in the new cultural heart of Rotterdam called the Museumpark.

**EXHIBITIONS**

until 22·06·97

*Flip de Nooyer  Photographer of Birds*    Portraits of european birds.

01·06·97 onwards

*Along the Border of the River Rotte*    Natural history of the Rotterdam regio.

## Rotterdam

**NAI NEDERLANDS ARCHITECTUURINSTITUUT**
**Netherlands Architecture Institute**
**Museumpark 25  3015 CB Rotterdam  Director: H. van Haaren**
**☎ +31 10 4401200  🖷 +31 10 4366975  Internet http://www.nai.nl**
**Open: Tuesday-Saturday 10.00-17.00  Sunday and public holidays 11.00-17.00**
**Closed: Monday**

**COLLECTION**

The Institute's Collection Department manages some 300 archives, 100 collections of the most prominent Dutch architects and urbanists of the 19th and 20th century, and various partial collections containing models, furniture, posters and a large number of glass negatives and slides.

**EXHIBITIONS**

until 11·05·97

*As Good As New   Five Plans for Buildings of the Post-War Reconstruction Period in Rotterdam*    Architects and historians have investigated how characteristic buildings from the reconstruction period could be imbued with new life in such a way that justice would be done to both their historical value and future use.

until 11·05·97

*Coast Wise Europe*    Some 22 countries are participating in this project, which runs from 1995 to 1998 and focuses on various aspects of the European coast. These include coastal architecture, urban development, landscape architecture and tourism.

until 01·10·97

*Nine Plus One  10 Young Dutch Architect Offices*    The exhibition aims to provide an insight into the latest developments in contemporary Dutch architecture.

03·05·97-03·08·97

*Michel de Klerk  Master Builder and Draughtsman of the Amsterdam School*    The Netherlands Architecture Institute has a large and valuable collection of archives, one of the most impressive being the collection of drawings, watercolours and sketches by the architect Michel de Klerk (1884-1923).

27·05·97-20·07·97

*Americanism, Dutch Architecture and the Transatlantic Model*
50 years ago this summer the Marshall Aid programme started, now forming the occasion for an exhibition on American influences on post-war Dutch architecture. Many Dutch architects were inspired by developments in American architecture.

30·08·97-23·11·97

*Daniel Libeskind*    Born in Poland in 1946, David Libeskind, with his highly complex designs, has been an international trend-setter in the roles of designer, theorist and teacher for more than a decade.

# Rotterdam

## WITTE DE WITH CENTER FOR CONTEMPORARY ART
Witte de Withstraat 50  3012 BR Rotterdam  Director: Bartomeu Marí
☎ +31 10 4110144  ✉ +31 10 4117924  Internet http://www.wdw.nl
Open: Tuesday-Sunday 11.00-18.00
Closed: Monday

**COLLECTION**

No permanent collection.

**EXHIBITIONS**

until 25·05·97

*David Lamelas, A New Refutation of Time*   By making the connection between interpretation and context visible in his works, this Argentinean artist entices the observer to analyse his own way of dealing with visual information.

07·06·97-27·07·97

*Michel François*   Exploring the unexpected sculptural possibilities of everyday objects, this Belgian artist's work is characterised by an exceptional sensitivity for touch, scent and space.

06·09·97-26·10·97

*Words and Images*   Inspired by poet and publicist Michaël Zeeman, the museum put together this exhibition in which images created by poetry are confronted with the visual arts.

08·11·97-11·01·98

*Rita McBride*   In addition to existing work, this American artist will present two new installations created specifically for the spaces of the museum.

# Schiedam

## STEDELIJK MUSEUM SCHIEDAM
Hoogstraat 112  3111 HL Schiedam  Director: D. Wind
☎ +31 10 2463666  ✉ +31 10 2463664
Open: Tuesday-Saturday 11.00-17.00  Sunday 12.30-17.00
Closed: Monday

**COLLECTION**

The Stedelijk Museum Schiedam is primarily a museum of modern and contemporary art. The museum has a collection consisting primarily of paintings from the post-war period. Works from the 'Cobra' movement, Abstract Expressionism, radical painting and systematic art are included. The 'Unisono' series features recent works by artists who have garnered attention early in their careers, and also highlights new developments in the careers of more established artists.
The Cobra collection is the best known and most popular part of the museum collection and includes works by Karel Appel, Corneille, Eugène Brands, Constant, Lucebert and Anton Rooskens. In the basement of the building a semi-permanent display of the historical collection focuses on the history of the city of Schiedam.

**EXHIBITIONS**

until 11·05·97

*L'Homme Sucré*   *Drawings from the Cees van der Geer Collection*
Art critic Cees van der Geer is also an avid collector of works on paper, with a preference for 'pure' drawings which are still very close to handwriting.

17·05·97-29·06·97

*Unisono 3 — Dianne Hagen*   Dianne Hagen's objects, composed from mundane materials, are balanced in a fragile equilibrium on the borders of the wall, floor and exhibition space.

28·06·97-07·09·97

*Summer Exhibition from the Museum Collection*   This exhibiton features a selection of works from the museum collection, organized around recent acquisitions, including Marinus Boezem's 'Portrait of the Artist as a Young Man.'

| 13·09·97-16·11·97 | ***Radical Image/Object***   In pursuing its long held interest in 'fundamental' painting, the museum highlights contemporary 'fundamental' or 'radical' paintings, where emphasis is placed on paintings with characteristics of objects, and objects with characteristics of paintings. |
| 15·11·97-1998 | ***Basement Installation*** |
| 05·12·97-1998 | ***From the Museum Collection*** |
| 13·12·97-1998 | ***Constant — View of the Dove*** |
| 13·12·97-1998 | ***Unisono 4*** |

## Tilburg

**DE PONT  FOUNDATION FOR CONTEMPORARY ART**
**Wilhelminapark 1  5041 EA  Tilburg  Director: Hendrik Driessen**
☎ +31 13 5438300   🖷 +31 13 5420952
**Open: Tuesday-Sunday 11.00-17.00**
**Closed: Monday**

**COLLECTION**

One of the primary aims of De Pont is the forming of a collection of contemporary art from within the Netherlands and abroad. Its policy focuses on bringing together the work of personalities who reflect the diversity of expressive forms that characterizes the art of our time. In addition to painting and sculpture, consideration is given to the realization of works and installations that require unusual spatial accomodations. De Pont's collection includes important works by such artists as Richard Serra, Roni Horn, Gerhard Merz, James Turrell, Marlene Dumas, Jan Dibbets, Guido Geelen, Rob Birza, Gerhard Richter, Jeff Wall, Thierry De Cordier, Marien Schouten, Thomas Schütte, Toon Verhoef, Anish Kapoor, Marc Mulders, Wolfgang Laib, Richard Long, Bill Viola and Luc Tuymans.

Thomas Schütte
*Awestruck 1994;*
*steel, bronze*
© De Pont
Foundation for
Contemporary Art,
Tilburg

**EXHIBITIONS**

| 17·05·97-Sep 97 | ***Summer Exhibition***   Special attention for recent acquisitions |
| Autumn 97 | ***Robert Zandvliet***  *Recent Paintings*   Presentations at the end of his working period in De Pont's studio |
| 11·10·97-08·02·98 | ***Giuseppe Penone***   *Recent Sculptures and Drawings* |

## Utrecht

**MUSEUM CATHARIJNECONVENT**
Nieuwegracht 63  3512 LG Utrecht  Director: H.L.M. Defoer
☎ +31 30 2313835   ⊨ +31 30 2317896
Open: Tuesday-Friday 10.00-17.00  Saturday, Sunday and public holidays
11.00-17.00
Closed: Monday and 1 Jan

**COLLECTION**

Museum Catherijneconvent, the cloisters of Utrecht, is housed in a 15th-century convent in the centre of Utrecht. It contains a collection of paintings, sculpture, textiles, manuscripts and gold and silver illustrating the evolution of Christianity in the Netherlands from its beginnings to the present. The medieval art section is the most important in the Netherlands.
The evolution of Catholic and Protestant churches is shown in their historical context. Various themes are addressed: construction, style and decorative elements of churches, the religious universe and the works of art it inspired, the different ceremonies, the role of faith in daily life and the relationship between Church and State.
The museum also contains works by 17th-century Dutch masters such as Rembrandt, Frans Hals and Pieter Saenredam.

**EXHIBITIONS**

until 17·08·97

*Four Hundred Years of Dutch Protestantism*   A survey of the preacher's vocation from the 16th century to the present, from the simple, uneducated minister through the dignified 19th-century parson to the modern 'pastor'. The aspects treated in this presentation include education, the performance of duties, political and social activities, the preacher-poet and pastoral work.

11·10·97-11·01·98

*Pilgrimages in the Netherlands*   An exhibition about the most popular places of pilgrimage in the Netherlands, from the Middle Ages to present times.

01·11·97-04·01·98

*Saint Martin*   A presentation in commemoration of Saint Martin, who died 1600 years ago. Saint Martin is the patron saint of the city and province of Utrecht.

13·12·97-07·01·98

*The Napolitan Crib*   This crib, dating from the 18th century, was made in Naples. It features 56 figures arranged within a realistic landscape.

## Utrecht

**CENTRAAL MUSEUM UTRECHT**
Agnietenstraat 1  3512 XA Utrecht  Director: Sjarel Ex
☎ +31 30 2362362   ⊨ +31 30 2332006
Rietveld Schröderhuis
Prins Hendriklaan 50a  3583 EP Utrecht
Open: Tuesday-Saturday 10.00-17.00  Sunday and public holidays 12.00-17.00
Closed: Monday and 25 Dec, 1 Jan

**COLLECTION**

The Centraal Museum, the oldest municipal museum in the Netherlands, has developed from modest beginnings to become one of the most important museums in the Netherlands. The large and varied collection of works of art is spread over a complex of buildings around a beautiful enclosed garden.
The main building houses the collection of art from before 1900, including fashion and dress, period rooms, arts and crafts, and paintings by Utrecht masters. The entire top floor is devoted to the history of the city of Utrecht. The building also houses a coin and medal collection, a print collection, and in the basement, an extremely rare Utrecht ship dating from the 12th century. Other

highlights of the museum include a 17th-century doll's house, the paintings of Jan van Scorel and the so-called Utrecht Caravaggists (Bloemaert, Ter Brugghen, Van Honthorst) and the silver produced by the Van Vianen family of silversmiths. A very unusual double chapel, built around 1514 as part of the former Agnieten-klooster (Convent of St. Agnes) is also located in this section of the museum. The former artillery stables, converted into an exhibition room in 1986, now generally house a collection of modern art providing a comprehensive survey of 20th century Dutch art. The stables are sometimes used for temporary exhibitions. The Nicolaikerk (Nicholas Church), a Gothic church dating from the middle of the 15th century, serves as an unusual exhibition room, and is accessible via the museum during the summer months.

**The Rietveld Schröder House**    The Rietveld Schröder house, an outstanding example of the 'De Stijl' architectural style, is an integral and important part of the Centraal Museum. The house was designed in 1924 by architect Gerrit Rietveld in close cooperation with Truus Schröder-Schräder, and was restored in 1987. The primary colours, the styling and use of space make the house entirely unique. It also possesses some of the functionalist characteristics which Rietveld was to elaborate on further during the 1930s. It is a 15-minute walk from the Centraal Museum.

**EXHIBITIONS**

03·05·97-29·06·97    *Collection of Contemporary Drawings from the Province of Utrecht*
A presentation of the collection of contemporary drawing which have been collected in cooperation with the Province of Utrecht

31·05·97-29·06·97    *Futuro   Finnish Design*    Featuring Finnish design of the 1960s.

12·07·97-31·08·97    *Around the Dinner Table with Friends (Working Title)*    This exhibition features the painting 'Around the Dinner Table with Friends' (1935) by Charley Toorop, in which Pyke Koch and Gerrit Rietveld appear.

19·07·97-31·08·97    *Scratches and Stripes   Ancient Drawings from the Collection*
This is a presentation of ancient drawings from the collections of the Centraal Museum

13·09·97-26·10·97    *Narcisse Tordoir*    A display of contemporary art.

25·10·97-04·01·98    *Archaeological Findings from the Archaeological Centre of the City of Utrecht*    The history of the City of Utrecht is presented, based on archaeological and architectural research.

08·11·97-04·01·98    *Saucy Fashion (Working Title)*    The Centraal Museum Utrecht presents the designs of more than 100 fashion designers.

# Zwolle

**STEDELIJK MUSEUM ZWOLLE**
Melkmarkt 41  8011 ML Zwolle  Director: H.J. Aarts
☎ +31 38 4214650  ⅏ +31 38 4219248
Open: Tuesday-Saturday 10.00-17.00  Sunday and public holidays 13.00-17.00
Closed: Monday, 1 Jan, 30 Mar, 18 May, 8 Aug-20 Sep and 25 Dec

**COLLECTION**    The collection contains paintings, prints and drawings, silver, furniture and textiles concerning the province of Overijssel and in particular the city of Zwolle. Several of these objects are presented in a historical context. Highlights of the collection are the paintings by Gerard Ter Borch and the Zwolle city council's silver.

**EXHIBITION**
end Sep 97-end Nov 97    *Painters in Zwolle in the 17th Century and Today*

## Cascais

### MUSEU CONDES DE CASTRO GUIMARÃES
Av. Rei Humberto II Itália  2750 Cascais  Director: José Rego de Sousa
☎ +351 1 4840861
Open: Daily 10.00-17.00

| | |
|---|---|
| COLLECTION | The permanent collection of the Museu Condes de Castro Guimarães includes a 16th-century illuminated codex on parchment which chronicles the kings of the first dynasty of Duarte Galvão; 17th-century Indo-Portuguese counting frames; prehistoric ceramics; furniture from the 16th, 17th and 18th century; and silverware from the 17th and 18th century. |
| EXHIBITIONS | No details available. |

## Coimbra

### MUSEU NACIONAL DE MACHADO DE CASTRO
Largo Dr. José Rodrigues  3000 Coimbra  Director: Maria José Sampaio
☎ +351 39 23727  ⓕ +351 39 22706
Open: Tuesday-Sunday 09.30-17.30
Closed: Monday

**COLLECTION**

The Museu Nacional de Machado de Castro, which was established in 1911, occupies the former Palace of the Bishop, a centuries-old building whose present-day appearance reflects alterations effected in Romanesque, Manueline, and Renaissance architectural styles. The building occupies the site of the Roman Cryptoportic, architecturally the most impressive feature of the building, which was built to provide a larger platform for the Forum of the ancient Roman city of Aeminium. The museum's collection of Portuguese sculpture is one of the largest and most important in the world. Medieval and Renaissance masters are represented in the collection, including works by Master Pero, João de Ruão and Chanterenne.

The painting collection, covering the period from the middle of the 15th century to the 19th century, includes famous works by Portuguese artists, such as Cristóvão de Figueiredo and Garcia Fernandes, as well as paintings by foreign artists such as Quinten Metsys and Adrian Isenbrandt.

The collection of works in gold, which includes more than 700 objects from the 10th to the 19th century, is especially notable. Among the most important examples are the Cup of Gueda Mendes, from 1152, and the Treasure of Queen Saint Isabel, from the 14th century.

**EXHIBITIONS**

No exhibitions planned.

## Lisboa-Lisbon

### MUSEU NACIONAL DE ARQUEOLOGIA
Praça do Império - Belém  1400 Lisboa  Director: H. Luís Raposo
☎ +351 1 3620000  ⓕ +351 1 3620016
Open: Tuesday 14.00-18.00  Wednesday-Sunday 10.00-18.00
Closed: Monday and Tuesday morning

**COLLECTION**

The National Museum of Archaeology, founded in 1893, has built up a wide-ranging collection comprising archaeology, ethnography, gold jewellery, coins and medals, epigraphy, sculpture, mosaics and physical anthropology. There are additional noteworthy archaeoloical and ethnographic comparative collections featuring items from different countries, with particular emphasis on Ancient Egypt.

The majority of the museum's collection consists, however, of Portuguese archaeological artefacts collected during field work undertaken during the museum's activities throughout the country.

**Treasures of Portuguese Archaeology**  The collection of ancient gold jewellery, one of the most important collections of its kind in Europe, consists of 1500 pieces (600 of which are on display). The most impressive pieces in the jewellery collection date back to pre-Roman times. Through this collection, the evolution of decorative art, styles, and manufacturing techniques, as well as commercial links among the peoples of Western Iberia, can be traced from the Calcolithic Age to the Late Middle Ages.

**Egyptian Antiquities**  This collection comprises more than 500 pieces, 300 of which are on display. It is the largest Egyptian collection in Portugal. The pieces on display are exhibited according to both thematic and chronological criteria and range from prehistoric times to the Coptic Age. Each theme is accompanied by a short informative introductory text. The first section is devoted to prehistoric items, with stone containers (especially alabaster), everyday objects, stone carvings and engravings, sculptures, chauabtis, amulets and scarabs. Another section is devoted to ritual mummification and includes two sarcophagi, a human mummy, several animal mummies, funeral masks, entrail jars and a funeral boat. Also on exhibit are funeral cones, bronzes and later materials from the Graeco-Roman and Coptic periods.

**EXHIBITIONS**

until Apr 98    **Roman Portugal**   *An Exploration of Natural Resources*

May 97-Aug 97    **Roman Glass from Croatia**

17-05-96-1997    **From Ulysses to Viriatus**   *The First Millennium BC*   This exhibition depicts Portugal as Ulysses actually would have found it. There are archaeological remains from the Late Bronze Age, the Phoenician colonists, the Celts and the conquering Roman legions.

## Lisboa-Lisbon

**MUSEU NACIONAL DE ARTE ANTIGA**
Rua das Janelas Verdes   1293   Lisboa
☎ +351 1 3976001/2   🖷 +351 1 3973703   Director: Ana Maria Brandão
Open: Tuesday 14.00-18.00   Wednesday, Friday, Sunday 10.00-18.00
Thursday, Saturday 10.00-20.00
Closed: Monday

**COLLECTION**

The painting collection covers the 14th to the mid-19th century, including works by Piero della Francesca, Memling, Cranach, Holbein, Zurbáran, Tiepolo and Courbet, as well as Hieronymus Bosch's triptych 'The Temptation of St. Anthony' and Albrecht Dürer's 'St. Jerome'. The Portuguese collection ranges from the 15th-century 'St. Vincent's Panels' to Sequeira's Pre-Romantic works and from 16th-century conventional retables to 17th-century portraits. A vast collection of Portuguese religious sculpture from the Middle Ages to the Baroque period is on display.
**Decorative Arts**   There are precious objects from wealthy houses, convents and churches, such as furniture, Oriental and Arraiolo rugs, ceramics and textiles, Portuguese gold and silverwork from the Middle Ages, 18th-century Baroque works from the age of Brazilian gold, and silverplate by the French goldsmiths Germain, father and son.

Master of Saint Auta
*The martyrdom of the 11.000 virgins, c. 1520*
© Museu Nacional de Arte Antiga, Lisboa

**Oriental Art**   The collection contains precious and decorative objects from the Age of Discovery, ivories from Sierra Leone and

Benin, furniture, embroidery and silver objects from India, porcelain, silk, embroidery and ivories from China and screens and lacquers from Japan (Namban Art).

May 97-Nov 97

***Jewels for Alexander of Medicis***   This exhibition presents jewels by contemporary jeweller Teresa Seabra. She takes her inspiration from Renaissance jewellery, and especially from the mood created by Pontormo's 'Portrait of Alexander of Medicis'.

Jul 97-Nov 97

***The Image and the Sculpture***   Religious Portuguese sculpture from the 15th century is presented. The exhibition is comprised of approximately 400 sculptures belonging to the museum but not usually on display.

Autumn 97-Winter 98

***The Rau Donation***   This show presents both foreign prints and humorous prints about Portugal from the 17th and 18th centuries.

## Lisboa · Lisbon

### MUSEU NACIONAL DO AZULEJO
**Rua Madre de Deus, 4  Lisboa  Director: João Castel-Branco Pereira**
☎ +351 1 8147747  🖷 +351 1 8149534
**Open: Wednesday-Sunday 10.00-18.00  Tuesday 14.00-18.00**
**Closed: Monday and 1 Jan, 1 May, Easter Sunday, 25 Dec**

COLLECTION

The Museu Nacional do Azulejo is housed in a former monastery founded in 1509 and redecorated in the 18th century, with tiles, carved gilt wood, paintings and sculptures.
The museum features a collection of tiles covering the period from the 15th century to the present, primarily from Portugal, with additional examples from Spain, Antwerp and the Netherlands. All the tiles were made for the Portuguese market. Portuguese production is presented from the earliest items (c. 1565) to panels designed and painted by contemporary artists.
Highlights of the collection are the panel of 'Our Lady of Life' (c.1580), the altar frontals with oriental influence (17th century) and the 23 metre-long 'Panorama of Lisbon' from the beginning of the 18th century.

EXHIBITIONS

No details available.

## Lisboa · Lisbon

### MUSEU CALOUSTE GULBENKIAN
**Av. de Berna 45a  1093  Lisboa  Director: Maria Teresa Gomes Ferreira**
☎ +351 1 7935131  🖷 +351 1 7955249
**Open: Tuesday-Sunday Jun-Sep 10.00-17.00**
**Wednesday, Saturday 14.00-19.30; Oct-May 10.00-17.00**
**Closed: Monday and public holidays**

COLLECTION

Calouste Gulbenkian was a wealthy Armenian, born in Turkey and educated in England, who spent the last 13 years of his life in Portugal. He left his collection, and his estate to Portugal in the form of a foundation for charitable, artistic, scientific and educational purposes.
The collection is divided into an Oriental & Classical Art section and a European Art section. The former section includes an Egyptian 18th Dynasty statue of Lady Henut Taoul, an alabaster funerary bowl, bronze cats and an early Ptolemaic study for the portrait of a Pharaoh, an Assyrian alabaster bas relief of Spring (9th century B.C.) and Persian artefacts and miniatures. The Graeco-Roman collection

consists mainly of Greek coins and Roman glass. Chinese works include porcelain, carved jade and rock crystal and a screen. From Japan there are lacquer boxes, netsukes and prints by Utamaro, Hiroshige and others. Gulbenkian also collected glass, ceramics, lamps and illuminated manuscripts from the Islamic world.
The European section begins with French 14th-century ivories. The illuminated manuscripts include the Book of Hours of Margaret of Cleves. Among the early paintings are 'Annunciation' by Diereck Bout, 'St. Catherine' by Van der Weyden, 'Holy Conversation' by Cima da Conegliano, 'Young Woman' by Domenico Ghirlandaio, 'Virgin and Child, with Donors' by Carpaccio, 'Alexander the Great' and 'Portrait of an Old Man' by Rembrandt, 'Portrait of Hélène Fourment' by Rubens, Van Dyck's 'Portrait of a Man' and 'Portrait of Sara Andriesdr. Hessix' by Frans Hals. There is a section with French furniture, Belgian and Italian tapestries and other decorative arts from the 18th century, including French bindings, goldwork and silverwork. Gulbenkian was able to purchase Marie Antoinette's writing table and a desk from Versailles made by Riesener. The sculptures include the terracotta 'Nymph and Satyr' by Clodion and the marble 'Diana' by Houdon, as well as bronzes by Rodin, Barrye and others. Among the English paintings are Gainsborough's 'Portrait of Mrs Lowndes-Stone', Turner's 'Quilleboeuf, Mouth of the Seine' and 'Shipwreck' and works by Romney, Lawrence and Hoppner.

**EXHIBITIONS** No details available.

## Lisboa - Lisbon

**MUSEU DO CHIADO**
Rua Serpa Piuto 6  1200  Lisboa  Director: Raquel Heuriques da Silva
☎ +351 1 343 2148  ⊞ +351 1 3432151
Open: Daily 10.00-18.00

**COLLECTION** The permanent collection was derived from the 19th-century Fine Arts Museum, following its division in 1911 into the Ancient Art Museum and the Contemporary Art Museum, and expanded with donations from private individuals such as Columbano Bordalo Pinheiro and Adriano de Sousa Lopes, the Valmour Legacy and purchases made by the directors of the museum over the years.
It presents the history of Portuguese visual art 1850-1950 through emblematic works, following a diachronic sequence from Romanticism to Realism, the eclecticism of the turn of the century, especially the Symbolists, opposing late Naturalist tendencies of the 19th century to Modernist cycles, from the Orpheu generation to the upheavals of the 1940s and 1950s.
Although international art is not the museum's main focus, a small but significant series of drawings by Rodin and some French sculpture of the 1900s have been included to place Portugal's national art in the context of its contemporaries.

**EXHIBITIONS** No details available.

## Lisboa - Lisbon

**CENTRO DE ARTE MODERNA JOSÉ DE AZEREDO PERDIGÃO**
Rua Dr. Nicolau Bettencourt  1093  Lisboa Codex  Director: Jorge Molder
☎ +351 1 7935131   📠 +351 1 7939294
Open: Tuesday-Sunday 10.00-17.00
Closed: Monday and public holidays

**COLLECTION**

**Modern and Contemporary Art**   The Modern Art Centre's collection reflects the visual arts in Portugal during the 20th century and includes paintings, sculptures, installations, drawings, photographs and graphic works. A comprehensive view of each artist is presented with works from different periods of their career. There is a unique representation of Modernist painters, notably Amadeo de Souza-Cardoso.

**International Art**   Artists that have a strong connection with Portuguese art are represented, including important pieces by Sonia and Robert Delaunay, Vieira da Silva, Arpad Szenes, Candido Portinari and Torres Garcia.

**British Art**   The collection encompasses British art from the 60s to the present day and includes work from Peter Blake, Howard Hodgkin, Hamish Fulton, Julian Opie and Rachel Whiteread.

**Armenian Art**   Arshile Gorky is especially well represented in this selection of Armenian artists.

Selections from the main collection are shown for periods of one to two years. There are also three temporary exhibitions of Portuguese and international Contemporary art at all times, and the Gulbenkian Park has a number of sculptures including works by Henry Moore and Ruben Nakian.

**EXHIBITIONS**

May 97-Jun 97

*Pedro Casqueiro*   This exhibition reviews the work of Portuguese painter Pedro Casqueiro, who came to prominence in the early 1980s.

Sep 97-Dec 97

*From Here to There*   'From Here to There' presents the work of artists who use photography. Artists represented include Cindy Sherman, Bustamante, Helena de Almeida, Jeff Wall, Geneviéve Cadieux, Marin Kasimir, Lorna Simpson and Marc Luyten.

May 97-Jul 97

*Sculpture of Alberto Carneiro*   This exhibition-project presents works reflecting Portuguese sculptor Alberto Carneiro's voyages to the Orient.

03·07·97-31·08·97

*Betty Woodman*   Exhibition of this American ceramic artist.

Sep 97

*Robert Schad*   Presentation of a site-specific work by this German sculptor at the Modern Art Centre.

[MAIN BUILDING OF THE GULBENKIAN FOUNDATION]

until Jun 97

*Arpad Szenes*   This retrospective exhibition presents the work of Arpad Szenes on the occasion of the centennial anniversary of his birth.

until 15·06·97

*Portuguese Comics Between the Two World Wars*

Oct 97-Nov 97

*Eduardo Neri*   *Retrospective of his Public Art Works.*

## Porto

**FUNDAÇÃO DE SERRALVES**
**Rua de Serralves 977 4150 Porto Director: Vicente Todolí**
**☎ +351 2 6180057 📠 +351 2 6173862**
**Open: Tuesday-Friday 14.00-20.00 Saturday, Sunday and public holidays 10.00-20.00**
**Closed: Monday**

**COLLECTION**

The collection includes 1 600 works of art from Portuguese and foreign artists. These works have either been purchased by the Foundation or have been presented by private collectors, artists and the National Government. Of particular interest is the government's long loan of its collection of international photography, both historic and contemporary.

*© Fundaçao de Serralves Porto*

The core of the Serralves Foundation is composed of works from the 60s up to the present day, through which the Foundation hopes to offer an interplay between national and international art. Work of the following national artists of international renown is on display: Paula Rego, Julião Sarmento, Cabrita Reis and António Dacosta. Foreign artists include Muntadas, Juan Munõz, Cristina Iglésias, Garcia Sevilla, Canogar, Saura and Tàpies. Also represented are G. Richter, Jesus Raphael Soto, Dennis Oppenheim, Gilberto Zorio, Donald Judd, Dan Flavin, Robert Gober, Cindy Sherman, Clegg & Guttman, Tony Cragg, Fischli and Weiss, Hanne Darboven, On Kawara and Joseph Kosuth.

**EXHIBITIONS**

08·05·97-22·06·97 ***Robert Schad***

03·07·97-09·07·97 ***A Decade of Rupture*** *The Seventies in Portugal*

09·10·97-07·12·97 ***James Lee Byars***

18·12·97-15·02·98 ***Franz West***

La Coruña

OVIEDO

Gijon

SANTANDER

SANTIAGO DE
COMPOSTELA

Leon

Burgos

Pontevedra

Vigo

Orense

Palencia

Zamora

VALLADOLID

Salamanca

MADRID

San Lorenzo

TOLEDO

Caceres

MERIDA

Badajoz

Ciudad Real

Cordoba

Jaén

Huelva

SEVILLA

Jerez de la Frontera

Cadiz

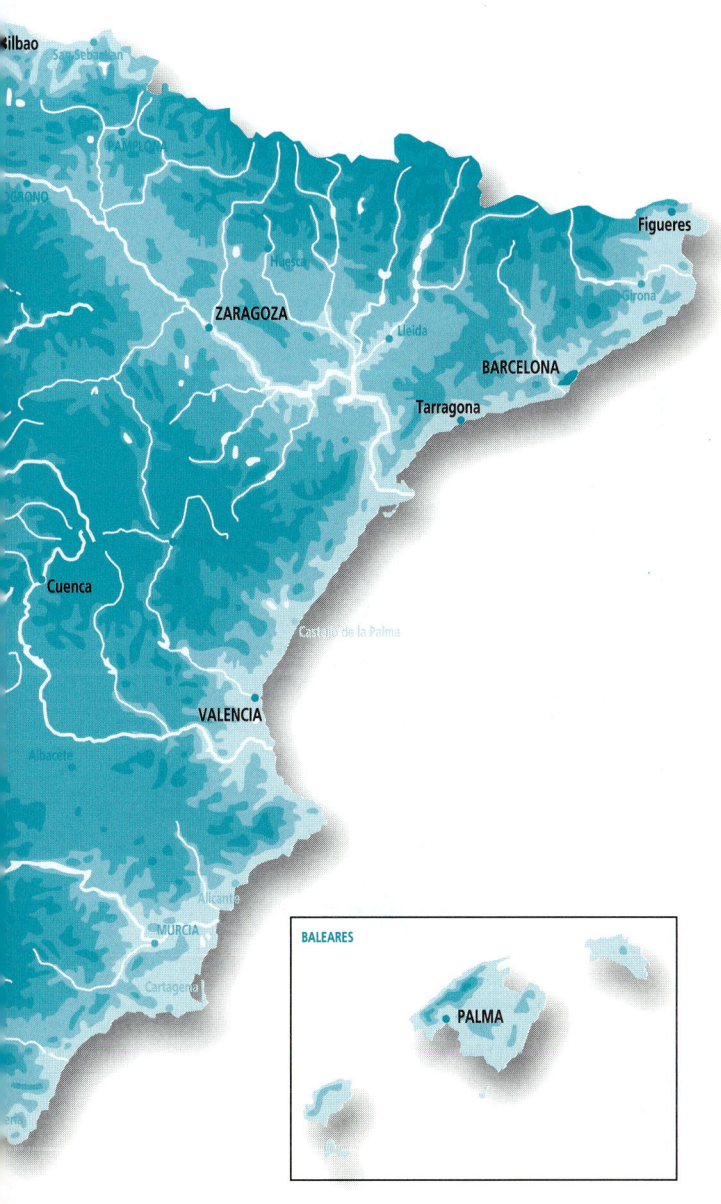

Bilbao
San Sebastian
PAMPLONA
OGROÑO
Huesca
ZARAGOZA
Lleida
Figueres
Girona
BARCELONA
Tarragona
Cuenca
Castelló de la Palma
VALENCIA
Albacete
Alicante
MURCIA
Cartagena

BALEARES

PALMA

## Barcelona

### FUNDACIÓ ANTONI TÀPIES
Aragó 255  08007  Barcelona  Director: Miquel Tàpies
☎ +34 3 4870315  🖷 +34 3 4870009
Open: Tuesday-Friday 11.00-20.00
Closed: Monday, Saturday and Sunday

COLLECTION

Established in 1984 by the Catalan painter Antoni Tàpies, the foundation's goal is to promote the study and understanding of modern art and culture. The museum displays works of modern and contemporary art from all over the world, among which the most complete collection of works by Antoni Tàpies. There is a library (admission by appointment only) which contains extensive literature and documentation on Western and non-Western art and artists of this century. The museum is housed in a building created by the architect Lluís Domènech i Montaner. Built between 1880 and 1885, its structure represents the urban and architectural renewal of Barcelona during the Modernista period.

Marcel Broodthaers
© Fundació Antoni
Tàpies, Barcelona

EXHIBITIONS
until 15·06·97

***Marcel Broodthaers*** *Cinema*  This exhibition is an opportunity to get acquainted with the filmmaking of Belgian artist Marcel Broodthaers. Broodthaers used film, as he used other media, to question the very nature of art.

10·07·97-28·09·97

***László Moholy-Nagy*** *Photograms 1922-1943*  186 of Moholy-Nagy's photograms — photographic images obtained without using a camera — are on display. These photograms permit the viewer to follow the different phases of his work as he progressed in the use of this technique.

07·10·97-14·12·97

***Lygia Clark***  This retrospective exhibition of Brazilian artist Lygia Clark (1920-1988) analyses her perception of communication between artist and spectator. Clark draws the spectator into her work as a fellow creator-spectator.

## Barcelona

### MUSEU D'ART DE CATALUNYA
Palau Nacional, Parc de Montjuïc  08038 Barcelona  Director: Eduard Carbonell
☎ +34 3 4237199  🖷 +34 3 3255773
Open: Tuesday-Saturday 10.00-19.00  Sunday 10.00-14.30
Closed: Monday

**COLLECTION** The collection features 12th and 13th-century Romanesque mural paintings, the majority of which stem from the Pyrenees area. In addition to Romanesque apses with their wall paintings, the collection also includes altar frontals and sculpture, as well as an assortment of metalwork. Works representing the Catalan Gothic period (14th-15th century), among which paintings by Arnau Bassa, the Serra brothers and Jaume Huguet, are also displayed here, along with works from other areas of the peninsula, mainly Aragon and Valencia. Joan Gascó and Pere Mates are examples of artists from the early Renaissance period in Catalonia whose works are displayed here. The museum's Baroque collection includes Francesc Ribalta, Rubens, Ribera, Zurbarán and Velasquez. Finally, a range of typical Rococo and Neo-Classical works are on display, by such artists as Giambattista and Giandomenico Tiepolo, Fragonard Goya and others.

**EXHIBITIONS**

30-04-97 onwards ***The Legacy of Francesc Cambó*** This exhibition will form part of the museum's permanent collection.

May 97-Nov 97 ***Drawings and Engravings by the Sculptor Clarà***

Nov 97 ***The Image of Power*** *Numismatics Exhibition*

## Barcelona

**MUSEU DE CERÀMICA**
**Palau Reial de Pedralbes-Diagonal 686  08034  Barcelona**
**Director: M. Dolors Giral**
☎ +34 3 2801621  🖷 +34 3 2054518
**Open: Tuesday-Sunday 10.00-15.00**
**Closed: Monday**

**COLLECTION** The Museum of Ceramics is located on the first floor of the Royal Palace of Pedralbes in Barcelona. The historical collections include decorated pieces from various centres of Spanish ceramics, Islamic objects from the 10th century, and other pieces dating up to the 19th century. Contemporary Spanish and foreign ceramics are displayed on the second floor. Of special note are Catalan ceramics, the 18th-century pottery of Alcora, and pieces by Miró and Picasso.

La Chocolatada
*Barcelona 1710*
© *Museu de Ceràmica, Barcelona*

**EXHIBITION**

Oct 97 ***Between Cultures*** *Contemporary Ceramics by Rosa Vila Abadal and Jordi Marcet*

# Barcelona

## FREDERIC MARÈS MUSEUM
Pl. de Sant Iu 5-6  08002 Barcelona  Director: Pilar Vélez
☎ +34 3 3105800  ✉ +34 3 3194116
Open: Tuesday-Saturday 10.00-17.00  Sunday and public holidays 10.00-14.00
Closed: Monday

COLLECTION

This museum was created and donated to the city by the sculptor Frederic Marès i Deulovol (1893-1991). It is essentially a collector's museum, the personality, variety of artistic interest and tastes of its creator being obvious to the visitor.

The museum consists of two distinct sections. One of these is the sculpture collection, consisting of pieces from Spain which date from the Pre-Roman age up to the 19th century, including interesting pieces from the Middle Ages. The relief of the apparition of Jesus before his disciples from the Sant Pere de Rodes Monastery is a true masterpiece. Renaissance sculpture and the Castilian Baroque is well represented. The sculpture section also includes pieces of very high quality: religious apparel, passementerie, needlework, lace and other textiles, and Medieval tables.

The Sentimental Department consists of a collection of works by artisans. These items attest to the daily life of our ancestors in the 15th to 19th century. The women's room (fans, parasols, jewels), smokers' room, creche figures room, watches, and photography, etc. contain a surprising diversity of objects. The entertainment room contains theatres, toys, and automatons that evoke the amusements of times past.

The museum's collection contains a wealth of items, all of which provide an ambience of the kind of abundance which is so characteristic of private collections. The viewer's visit ends with a look at Frederic Marès' study.

EXHIBITIONS

No details available

# Barcelona

## JOAN MIRÓ FOUNDATION
Parc De Montjuic  08038  Barcelona  Director: Rosa Maria Malet
☎ +34 3 3291908  ✉ +34 3 3298609  Internet http://www.bcn.fjmiro.es
Open: Tuesday-Saturday 11.00-19.00  Friday 11.00-21.30  Sunday 10.30-14.30
Closed: Monday

COLLECTION

The Foundation's collection of Joan Miró's works, the majority of which was donated bij Miró himself, includes paintings, textiles, his complete graphic works, drawings, sketches and studies. In addition, a series of canvases donated by Miró's wife on establishment of the foundation is also on display. The canvases cover different periods and give an overall view of the development of his art.

The graphic works include the complete Barcelona series, consisting of fifty lithographs in black and white, which can be considered as Miró's artistic comment on the Spanish Civil War.

The collection of drawings, sketches and notes, designated by Alexandre Cirici as the `Miró papers', allows one to follow the development of Miró's forms of expression, his reasons for exploring new paths and his own ideas on his work.

The museum also has a small collection in which other artists are represented. This collection was formed as a tribute to Miró and includes paintings, sculptures, photographs and objects from such artists as Alechinsky, Balthus, Bissier, Brossa, Calder, Caro, Chillida, Duchamp, Ernst, Francis, González, Guston, Lam, Matisse, Millares, Moore, Motherwell, Saura, Serra, Tanguy and Torres-Garcia.

**EXHIBITION**
22·05·97-14·09·97

***Lightmade*** *Frederic Montomés, Curator*   This is a group exhibition that considers how light can alter and/or change people's behaviour and state of mind when they enter a space illuminated in colour.

## Barcelona

**MUSEU D'ART MODERN (MNAC)**
Parc de la Ciutadella  08003  Barcelona  Director: Cristina Mendoza
☎ +34 3 3195728  🖷 +34 3 3195965
Open: Wednesday-Monday 09.00-21.00
Closed: Tuesday

**COLLECTION**

One part of the museum's collection consists of 19th and 20th century works of art stemming from the Realist movement; these include Martí Alsina, the artist who introduced Courbet's ideas into Spain, and Joaquim Vayreda, an important representative of Olot's landscape school. Modernism was an important artistic movement in Catalonia, of which the museum offers a good overview: paintings by Rusiñol and Casas and sculptures by Blay, Arnau, Clarassó and Llimona. In the same period, the development of other arts and crafts progressed strongly: furniture by Busquets and Homar forms a relevant example on display here. Noucentism (1901-1931) was an artistic movement which can mainly be characterised as being based on a global conception of art and as the return to Classicism. Works by Sunyer, Obiols and other painters are examples of this school shown here. The avant-garde movement and the resurgence of the art of sculpture are represented by works from Juli González and Pau Gargallo.

**EXHIBITIONS**
May 97 onwards

***The Cultures of Clarà***   This exhibition will form part of the museum's permanent collection.

Autumn 97

***Santiago Rusiñol***

## Barcelona

**MUSEU PICASSO**
Montcada 15-19  08003 Barcelona  Director: Teresa Ocaña
☎ +34 3 3196310  🖷 +34 3 3150102
Open: Tuesday-Saturday 10.00-20.00  Sunday 10.00-15.00
Closed: Monday and 1 Jan, 1 May, 24 Jun, 25, 26 Dec, Good Friday

**COLLECTION**

The Museu Picasso in Barcelona, opened in 1963, is witness to Picasso's connection with Barcelona, the city where he completed his artistic apprenticeship and where he produced his early works. The museum itself is located in the Berenguer d'Aguilar Palace, built in medieval times and an exceptional example of a Catalan bourgeois dwelling.
The museum has the world's largest and most complete collection of the young Picasso's works. The permanent collection contains more than 3 600 works which are divided into three sections: paintings and drawings, engravings, and ceramics.
The dates of paintings range from the period 1890-1897 ('The First Communion', 1896 and 'Science and Charity' 1897), through to 1900 when he started visiting Paris ('Margot' and 'The Midget', both from 1901), on through the Blue Period (1901-1904) and the Pink Period, and on into 1917 when he produced 'Harlequin' and 'The Gored Horse'. His interpretative series of Velázquez's 'Las Meninas' from 1957 is remarkable.
The collection of the artist's engravings (1904-1972) displays his

total mastery of this medium. 41 pieces of ceramics (1947-1965) were donated by Jacqueline Picasso in 1982.

**EXHIBITION**
until 29·06·97

*André Derain 1904-1912*   The exhibition focuses on works Derain produced during the period in which he was closely connected with Pablo Picasso. It covers the artist's Expressionist period and reveals his ties with Cubism.

## Barcelona

**CENTRE D'ART SANTA MÒNICA**
Rambla de Santa Mònica 7  08002 Barcelona  Director: Josep Miquel Garcia
☎ +34 3 4122279   📠 +34 3 4122288
Open: Monday-Saturday 11.00-14.00 / 17.00-20.00  Sunday 11.00-15.00

**COLLECTION**

No permanent collection.

**EXHIBITIONS**
until May 97

*Video in Germany*

until Jun 97

*Philipe Stark & André Ricard*   Spring Design

until Jun 97

*Roma Vallés*

Jun 97

*Joan Furriol*

Jun 97-Sep 97

*Artists from Argentina*   Antonio Berni, Jorge de la Vega, Juan Carlos Distefano, Pablo Suarez, Luis Felipe Noé, Norberto Gómez, Roberto Elia, Marcia Schwartz, Roberto Paez, Luis Fernando Benedit and Marcos López.

## Bilbao

**MUSEO DE BELLAS ARTES DE BILBAO**
Plaza del Museo 2  48011  Bilbao  Director: Miguel Zugaza
☎ +34 94 4419536   📠 +34 94 4273846
Open: Tuesday-Saturday 10.00-13.30 / 16.00-19.30  Sunday 10.00-14.00
Closed: Monday and public holidays

**COLLECTION**

The Museum of Fine Arts of Bilbao is the result of a merger of the original Museum of Fine Arts, founded in 1914, and the Museum of Modern Art, inaugurated eight years later. The present-day museum is housed in a Neo-Classical building dating from 1945, to which a modern wing was added in 1972.
The museum's collections were originally based on a number of donations and legacies from individuals, private businesses and public institutions. They have been built up gradually through later acquisitions and new donations.
The Museum of Fine Arts of Bilbao has four main sections. They are devoted to Medieval, contemporary, Basque and applied arts. The collection as a whole shows a large range of artistic styles from the 12th century to the present day.
There is a noteworthy collection of antique Spanish panels, the work of 16th-century masters such as Morales, El Greco and Antonio Moro and the masterpieces of Spanish Baroque, including works by Velázquez, Zurbaran, Ribera and Murillo. Three Goyas head the collection of 18th and 19th-century art, which also includes works by Meléndez, Vicente López and Paret y Alcázar. The museum also has an extensive collection of works by Flemish painters, including Van Dyck, Jordaens, Ruisdael and Brueghel, an Italian room and a French room, all on the ground floor of the old building.

A complete collection of Basque Classical artists, with separate rooms for Regoyos, Echevarría, Zuloaga, Iturrino, Arteta and Ucelay, is housed on the first floor of the old building. Finally, there is a collection of contemporary art ranging from Gauguin and Picasso to Tàpies, Chillida and Bacon in the main room of the modern wing.

© Museo de Belles
Artes de Bilbao
Bilbao

## EXHIBITIONS

| | |
|---|---|
| 06·05·97-29·06·97 | **Maeztu**   Lithographs |
| Summer 97 | **The Thyssen Baroness Collection** |
| 15·07·97-21·09·97 | **Old and Modern Masters from the Jado Legacy** |
| 04·09·97-26·10·97 | **Alberto Sanchez** |
| 30·09·97-07·12·97 | **The Modern Tradition of British Painting, from Gainsborough to Nicholson**   The Southamptom Art Gallery Collection |
| 06·11·97-28·12·97 | **Manet**   Graphic Work |
| 16·12·97-22·02·98 | **Sorolla-Zuloaga**   Two Views for the Turn of a Century |

## Burgos

**MUSEO DE BURGOS**
Calle Calera 25  09003 Burgos  Director: Juan Carlos Elorza Guinea
☎ +34 47 265875  ☷ +34 47 276792
Open: Tuesday-Friday 10.45-14.00 / 16.15-19.00  Saturday, Sunday 10.00-14.00
Closed: Monday and public holidays

COLLECTION

The purpose of the Burgos Museum is to present the historical and cultural evolution of the city and province of Burgos from prehistoric times up to the 20th century. The museum, which was established in 1873, consists of the Department of Prehistory and Archaeology and the Department of Fine Arts.
**Prehistory and Archaeology**   The museum's collection includes human fossils from the Paleolithic Age, classified as Pre-Neanderthal, dating back about 250 000 years. These represent the oldest evidence of humans in Europe. There are also articles discovered in prehistoric dolmens, and the Iron Age necropolis at Bureba, as well as noteworthy Celtibéric goldsmith work. A variety of additional articles date from the Roman, Paleo-Christian and Visogothic periods.
**Fine Arts**   The fine art collection includes paintings, sculpture and architectural works from the 9th to the 20th century. Most noteworthy is the 'Urna de Santo Domingo' (also known as Frontal de Silos). Richly decorated with enamelled and gilded copper, this masterpiece, produced in the workshops of the Santo Domingo monastery in Silos between 1165 and 1179, depicts Christ with the

Apostles. Also in the collection are Moorish works from the 9th and
10th century, Medieval coins, and painting and sculpture from
Renaissance and contemporary artists.

EXHIBITIONS | No details available.

## Cádiz

**MUSEO DE CÁDIZ**
Plaza de Mina, s/n  Cádiz  11004  Director: Antonio Alvarez Rojas
☎ +34 56 212281  🖷 +34 56 226215
Open: Tuesday-Sunday 09.30-14.00
Closed: Monday and public holidays

COLLECTION | A number of remains from the very first inhabitants of the Province
of Cádiz are on display, including objects from the Palaeolithic,
Neolithic and Bronze Age. There is a reproduction of cave paintings
from the site of 'La Laja Alta' depicting the arrival of Phoenician
vessels (c. 1000 B.C.). The oldest Phoenician architectonic element
known in Cádiz, 'El Capitel Protoeolico' is shown here, as well as
two anthropomorphic sarcophagi, burial finds including gold
jewellery and semiprecious stones, amphoras, ritual objects and
offerings to Phoenician divinities. There are reconstructions of
Roman cremation and inhumation tombs found in the local
necropolis, a collection of incinerating urns and a display of
sepulchral tombstones. Other exhibits reflect everyday life during
the Roman period.
Objects from the Moorish period, from the 8th to the 15th century,
include vessels, oil lamps and coins. There are also exhibits
illustrating the history of Cádiz coinage.
The painting collection includes 17th-century works by Zurbarán,
Murillo and others as well as Flemish and Italian Baroque paintings.
A series of panels and canvases from the Carthusian Monastery in
Jerez and an Altarpiece from the Capuchin Convent in Cádiz are on
display. There are also works by painters from Cádiz and Seville. The
oldest paintings are from the 16th century and include works by
Flemish painters living in Spain. The traditional crafts of Cádiz are
also displayed.

EXHIBITIONS | No details available.

## Cordoba

**MUSEO ARQUEOLÓGICO**
Plaza Jerónimo Paez  14003  Córdoba  Director: F. Godoy Delgado
☎ + 34 57 471076
Open: Daily 10.00-14.00 / 15.30-17.30  Sunday 10.00-14.00

COLLECTION | The Archaeological Museum contains prehistoric objects such as
figurines, weapons, pottery and Iberian stone lions, as well as
images of the two-faced Janus and the Persian god Mithras. There
are also Roman mosaics, silver from Pozoblanco, a 2nd-century
figure of a bull, Roman sarcophagi, funerary artefacts including
stelae with inscriptions and examples of terra sigillata, bronzes,
tiles, glass and early Christian art. The first floor houses an
important collection of Moorish art, such as sculpted bases, capitals
and well-heads from the time of the Caliphate and pottery
excavated from Medina Azahara.

EXHIBITIONS | No details available.

## Cordoba

**MUSEO DE BELLAS ARTES**
Plaza del Potro 1  14002  Córdoba  Director: Fuensanta García de la Torre
☎ +34 57 473345  🖷 +34 57 292724
Open: 15 Jun-15 Sep Tuesday-Saturday 10.00-14.00 / 18.00-20.00;
16 Sep-14 Jun Tuesday-Saturday 10.00-14.00 / 17.00-19.00
Sunday and public holidays 10.00-13.30
Closed: Monday

COLLECTION

The Museum of Fine Arts of Córdoba originated in the Secularisation of 1835 when works from secularised convents were moved to several other places before coming to rest in the old hospital that became a museum in 1862. Today, the old Chapel is all that remains of the hospital.

The museum's collections contain works from many periods of the history of painting in Córdoba. The oldest paintings are fragments of 14th-century murals from the Mezquita Cathedral, which are displayed together with late Medieval and Renaissance works by Luis Fernández, Pedro de Córdoba and others. The Mannerists and Pre-Baroque painters who worked in Córdoba include Pablo de Céspedes, Juan de Peñalosa and Juan Luis Zambrano. The most important Baroque painters from Córdoba and Andalusia are, among others, José Ruiz de Sarabia, Francisco de Zurbarán and Antonio del Castillo. Other Baroque paintings include Spanish and foreign works, the majority of which are anonymous.

The museum has a large collection of drawings, mainly from the late 19th and early 20th century. There are also engravings by Carnicero and Francisco de Goya, among others. There are sculptures from the Baroque period, the 18th century, and the period of Spanish Realism from the end of the 19th century.

EXHIBITIONS

No details available.

## Cuenca

**MUSEO DE ARTE ABSTRACTO ESPAÑOL**
Casas Colgadas  16001 Cuenca  Director: José Luis Yuste Grijalba
☎ +34 69 212983  🖷 +34 69 212285
Open: Tuesday-Friday 11.00-14.00 / 16.00-18.00
Saturday 11.00-14.00 / 16.00-20.00  Sunday and public holidays 11.00-14.30
Closed: Monday

COLLECTION

Between 1950 and 1960 there emerged in Spain a group of artists known as the 'Abstract Generation'. Although their works were exhibited in museums and galleries in Europe and America, there was no public collection representing this important trend in Spanish art. Their works are now shown in the Museum of Spanish Abstract Art, which was established by the painter Fernando Zóbel. The museum is housed in the famous 'Hanging Houses' owned by the Municipality of Cuenca. These houses, which are a unique example of local Gothic architecture, were originally built in the 15th century and have been restored many times over the years. The museum itself is privately operated. Its main collection, donated by Fernando Zóbel to the Juan March Foundation, consists of the works of Abstract Generation painters, including Canogar, Feito, Guerrero, Lorenzo, Lucio Muñoz, Millares, Mompó, Palazuelo, Rivera, Rueda, Saura, Sempere, Tàpies, Torner and Zóbel, and the sculptors Chillida, Chirino, Oteiza and Serrano.

EXHIBITION
until 15·06·97

*Frank Stella   26 Works from the Collection of Kenneth Tyler*

# Figueres

## DALI THEATRE-MUSEUM
Plaça Gala-Salvador Dali 5  17600  Figueres  Director: Luis Peñuelas
☎ +34 72 511800  📠 +34 72 501666
Open: Tuesday-Sunday Jul-Sep 09.00-20.00; Oct-Jun 10.00-17.15
Closed: Monday

COLLECTION

**The Museum Building and Area**  The Dali Theatre-Museum, the largest Surrealistic object in the world, was created by Salvador Dali from the ruins of the former Municipal Theatre, which was destroyed at the end of the Spanish Civil War. As he explained: "Where, if not in my own city, should the most extravagant and solid examples of my art remain? The Municipal Theatre, or what was left of it, seemed to me to be very appropriate for three reasons. First of all, because I am an eminently theatrical painter. Secondly, because the Theatre faces the church where I was baptised. And thirdly, because my first exhibition of paintings was held precisely in the lobby of the Theatre."
**The Dali Theatre-Museum**  incorporates two exhibition areas. The first is the old burnt-out theatre itself (rooms 1 to 16), which was transformed according to Salvador Dali's own criteria and designs into a single unique art object, in which each separate element forms an intrinsic part of the whole.
The second area is the complex created as the Theatre-Museum gradually expanded (rooms 19 to 24).
**Works of Art on Display**  Surrounded by the ambience created by Dali according to his own aesthetic parameters, the broad panorama of works on display at the Theatre-Museum traces the artistic development of the painter from the Empordan from his initial experiments with Impressionism, Futurism, Cubism and other movements through his own Surrealistic creations to the work of his final years.
While the museum is primarily devoted to a permanent display of paintings, drawings, sculptures, stage settings and other works by Salvador Dali, other artists are represented as well. Works by Antoni Pitxot and Evarist Vallès can be viewed in rooms 12 and 8 respectively, while Salvador Dali's private collection, including works by Greco, Fortuny, Urgell, Meissonier, Duchamp, Bou and Bouguerau, is on display in room 14.In addition, works by Bouguerau, John de Andrea, Meifren, Ernst Fuchs, Silvère Godere, Olivier Brice and others can be seen in various rooms in the Theatre-Museum.

EXHIBITIONS

No details available.

# Madrid

## MUSEO DE AMÉRICA
Avenida De Los Reyes Católicos 6  28040  Madrid  Director: Paz Cabello Carro
☎ +34 1 5492641  📠 +34 1 5446742
Open: Tuesday-Saturday 10.00-15.00  Sunday and public holidays 10.00-14.30
Closed: Monday

COLLECTION

The origins of the Museum of America go back to 1941, but it took until 1962 for the museum to be moved to where it is presently housed. The museum's collections are made up of the collections of the former Royal Natural History Museum, donations and items either left to the museum or bought on the open market. The contents of the collection cover the period from American prehistory up to the present day, with an emphasis on Pre-Columbian archaeology, ethnography and Colonial Art. The museum is divided into 5 sections, covering various aspects of the Americas.

**The Instruments of Knowledge** is a display which examines how notions of America, from allegorical ideas and myths to the accounts of reality, spread through Europe. The emphasis is on the Spanish chroniclers who provided first-hand knowledge of the new world. An additional room is dedicated to the evolution of geographical knowledge.

**The American Reality section** is designed to give insight into the geography of the continent and the peoples who have inhabited it, starting with the Palaeolithic migrations. This section also gives an overview of the evolution of the principal cultures of the continent.

**The Society section** provides us with insight into the complex social structure of American societies. Starting with the life cycle of the individual, birth, death and related ceremonies, the exhibition covers the organisation of man into social groups and explores their structure by examining their artefacts and lifestyles.

**The fourth section is devoted to Religion** and features representations of the god-kings and the pantheons of the various American religions. In another room it deals with the sacred aspects of these religions and special emphasis is placed on ceremonies and the adornment of the dead.

**The Communication section** houses samples of the various American methods of communication, from primitive pictorial forms to Colonial iconography, mesoamerican writing, native languages and the influence of the Spanish language on the Continent.

EXHIBITIONS | No details available.

# Madrid

**MUSEO ARQUEOLÓGICO NACIONAL**
Calle Serrano 13  28001 Madrid  Director: Eduardo Ripoll Perello
☎ +34 1 4314003  📠 +34 1 4036607
Open: daily 09.15-13.45

COLLECTION | The collection of the museum, founded in 1867 and housed since 1895 in the Palace of Libraries and Museums, ranges from the prehistoric age to the 19th century and consists of archaeological finds and decorative art from Spain and other Mediterranean countries.

There are skulls and tusks from early elephants found in Toledo and other areas, Palaeolithic artefacts from the Cerro de S. Isidro, finds from caves on the coast including incised bones, Neolithic ceramics, knives and an alabaster idol. Bronze and Iron Age objects include goddess figures from Los Millares, necklaces made of shells, bone and bronze, weapons, glass from Ciempozuelos, a golden diadem from El Argar, gold torques, spiral bracelets and vases from Axtroki, Celto-Iberian silver from Cuenca.

Megalithic finds from the Balearics include three bronze heads of bulls. One room is devoted to the culture of the Canary Islands before Spanish colonisation in the 15th century. Several rooms contain articles from the Sahara, Egypt, Nubia and Cyprus, as well as Etruscan, Greek and Roman ceramics, armour and other antiquities. Iberian sculptures showing Phoenician and Greek influence include the 'Dama de Baza' (4th century B.C.), the 'Dama de Elche' and an Iberian funerary monument from Pozo Moro. There are Celto-Iberian female figures from Cerro de los Santos (Albacete). Other rooms are devoted to the Roman era, displaying bronze plaques, mosaics, inscriptions, a statue of Tiberius, glass, jewellery and early Christian sarcophagi.

From the time of the Visigoths (6th-8th century) there are the Guarrazar votive crowns of crafted precious metals, the ivory and silver 'Bote de Zamora' with Cufic inscriptions, a bronze statue of a deer, an ivory crucifix and several pendant crosses. Two rooms

display artesonado ceilings from Toledo and Seville.
Other rooms contain Moorish artefacts, Romanesque and Gothic sculptures, arms and armour, scientific instruments, glass, porcelain and a numismatic collection. A model of the caves of Altamira has been constructed below ground in the gardens.

**EXHIBITIONS**   No details available.

## Madrid

**MUSEO CERRALBO**
Calle Ventura Rodriguez 17  28008  Madrid
Director: Pilar de Navascues Benlloch
☎ +34 1 5473647  🖷 +34 1 5591171
Open: Tuesday-Saturday 09.30-14.30  Sunday 10.00-14.00
Closed: Monday

**COLLECTION**   Enrique de Aguilera y Gamboa (1845-1922), the 17th Marquis of Gamboa, was the founder and major contributor of the museum. Doña Amelia del Valle, Marchioness of Villa-Huerta also donated her collections and provided the site for the museum building. Two rooms for temporary exhibits and cultural activities are situated on the ground floor. From there the monumental main staircase with its hand-wrought iron balustrade in Louis XV-style leads up to the first and second floors of the palace where the permanent collections are exhibited.
The Armoury contains an interesting collection of European weapons and armour from the Modern Age, including the battle armour of the 2nd Marquis of Cerralbo. The Oriental Room has an exhibition of Japanese armour and various weapons and items from the East.
The walls of the sumptuous Gala Dining Room, with its central mahogany table, are decorated with still lifes from the Spanish School, many works by B. de Ledesma and also a splendid painting 'Porcupines and Vipers' by Snyders. Many more rooms house collections of paintings, drawings, prints, furniture, sculpture, ceramics and porcelain, silverware and jewellery. The visit finishes in the palace ballroom, richly adorned with mirrors and marble and presided over by Barbedienne's impressive 'mysterious clock'.

**EXHIBITION**
until Jun 97

***The Collection of Clocks and Watches of the Cerralbo Palace***
This exhibition focuses on one of the more attractive collections of this Palace Museum. The Marquis of Cerralbo gathered over 50 clocks and watches which come from different countries: France, Great Britain, Switzerland, Austria, Spain, etc. and are dated from the 17th century throughout the 20th century.

## Madrid

**FUNDACION JUAN MARCH**
Castelló 77  28006 Madrid  Director: José Luis Yuste Grijalba
☎ +34 1 4354240  🖷 +34 1 5763420
Open: Daily 10.00-14.00 / 17.30-21.00  Sunday 10.00-14.00
Closed: Public holidays

**COLLECTION**   The Juan March Foundation, established in 1955, is an institution with cultural, scientific and funding aims. In terms of both assets and breadth of activities, it is among the largest in Europe.
In the field of art it has organised over 300 exhibitions in Spain and abroad, and has awarded over 500 scholarships for study or work in the creative arts.

In addition to its own collection at the Museum of Spanish Abstract Art at Cuenca and the Museo d'Art Espanyol Contemporani, displayed in Palma on the island of Mallorca, the Juan March Foundation has a collection of paintings and sculptures exhibited at its head offices in Madrid, and elsewhere on a travelling basis. In 1980, the Foundation was awarded a Gold Medal for merit in the Fine Arts.

Max Beckmann
*Double picture of*
*Carnival, 1925*
© *Fundación Juan*
*March, Madrid*

**EXHIBITION**
until 08·06·97

***Max Beckmann*** *Retrospective*  Having abandoned Impressionism for New Realism, Beckmann's paintings manifest his interest for the 'common and vulgar' and 'the gross banality of life' with their intense and concentrated images, and strong, violent lines.

## Madrid

**MONASTERIO DE SAN LORENZO DEL ESCORIAL**
Avenida Juan de Borbon y B. s/n  28200 San Lorenzo del Escorial  Madrid
Director: D. Pedro Criado Juarez
☎ +34 1 8905902  🖷 + 34 1 8907818
Open: Daily Apr-Sep 10.00-18.00; Oct-Mar 10.00-17.00

**COLLECTION**  The granite, slate-roofed 'El Escorial' was constructed in Tuscan style and measures 207 metres from north to south and 161 metres from east to west. Admirers call it the 8th wonder of the world. King Philip II commissioned architect Juan Bautista de Toledo and later Juan Herrera to build the Escorial, and construction took place from 1563-1584. El Escorial includes the basilica, a monastery, a library, the Royal Pantheon (an octagonal vault c. 9 metres in diameter), and the palaces of the Austrians and Bourbons.
Philip II was a great lover of art and assembled more than 1 150 works of art including a substantial number of works by Titian. Important artists who decorated the Escorial include Navarette, Cambiasco, Zucarro, Tibaldi and Leoni.
Most works are found in the Church, the 'Templo'. The Templo also houses gold and silver vessels and 515 reliquaries with 7421 relics. Housed in the sacristy, with its arabesque ceiling, are paintings by Fabricio Castello, Ribera, Titian and others. The lecture halls, main stairway ('La escalera principal') and palaces are decorated with beautiful tapestries, some of which come from Brussels.
The Bourbon Palace and the Hall of Battle are richly ornamented. ElEscorial houses a pinacotheca (located in the convent), a library and a museum of architecture. The Flemish and German schools (15th and 16th century) are represented by works of Hieronymus Bosch, Dürer and M. Coxcie. Special halls are dedicated to certain

masters: Titian, Ribera and El Greco. Other halls display works by Tintoretto, Veronés, Velasquez, Rubens, El Greco and Van der Weyden.

The library, a long vaulted room with a marble floor, has ceiling frescoes painted by Tibaldi and contains 40 000 printed volumes. Printed works include the missals of Charles V̇ and Fernando and Isabel, and the golden manuscript 'Codex Aureus' of Philip II. Exhibited in the Biblioteca de los Manuscritos (opened only with special permission) are 2000 Arabic and Islamic manuscripts. The museum of architecture displays numerous designs, models, plans, tools and financial budgets used in the construction of the Escorial.

**EXHIBITIONS**    No details available.

## Madrid

**MUSEO NACIONAL CENTRO DE ARTE REINA SOFIA**
Santa Isabel, 52  28012 Madrid  Director: José Guirao Cabrera
☎ +34 1 4675062  ⚒ +34 1 4673163
Open: Monday-Saturday 10.00-21.00  Sunday 10.00-14.30
Closed: Tuesday

**COLLECTION**    The Reina Sofia Art Centre is the National Museum of 20th- Century Art. The museum focuses on Spanish painting and sculpture of the 20th century. It boasts work by Picasso (e.g. 'Guernica'), Juan Gris, Miró, Dalí, Julio González, Garcallo, Solana. The museum also displays work from artists who have become internationally famous since 1950, including Tàpies, Chillida, Oteiza, and the El-Paso Group: Millares, Saura, Eduardo Arrovo, Gordillo, Antonio López, Miguel Navarro, Sicilia. Foreign artists are also represented, including Yves Tanguy, Magritte, Calder, Sutherland, Max Ernst, Masson and Barnet Newman. The rooms are arranged according to the various styles: Cubism, Surrealism, Avant-Garde Art, Realism, Spanish Art after 1940, Informalism and the latest trends. The museum aims at interpreting the art of the 20th century, and while exhibiting its permanent collection it also features exhibitions of international movements in the 20th century. The National Museum and Art Centre also has a comprehensive library with over 50 000 volumes, all on contemporary art, more than 7 000 slides of famous paintings, 4 000 sound recordings, as well as videos, magazines and exhibition catalogues.

© Museo Nacional
Centro de Arte Reina
Sofia, Madrid

The National Museum and Art Centre Reina Sofia is housed in the old San-Carlos Hospital, which was designed by Sabatini in the 18th century and built in a Neo-Classical style. Two glass towers give the museum a special external appearance and provide a beautiful view over a characteristic part of Madrid.

**EXHIBITIONS**
until 16·06·97    *Rivera*

| | |
|---|---|
| until end Jun 97 | *Gerardo Rueda* |
| until 15·09·97 | *Biennial Hispano-Americana* [Biblioteca] |
| until 30·09·97 | *Eugenio d'Ors* [Palacio Velázquez] |
| 08·05·97-08·09·97 | *Piel de Toro* |
| 03·06·97-09·09·97 | *Lipchitz* |
| 17·06·97-27·10·97 | *Art Madi* |
| 08·07·97-20·10·97 | *Fraile* |
| 16·09·97-17·11·97 | *Moholy Nagy* |
| 07·10·97-09·01·98 | *Revista Artes* [Biblioteca] |
| 14·10·97-19·01·98 | *Sicilia* [Palacio Velazquez] |
| 21·10·97-13·01·98 | *Drawings of Pablo Gargallo* |
| 28·10·97-12·01·98 | *Léger* |
| 11·11·97-12·01·98 | *Tobey* |
| 25·11·97-19·01·98 | *Togores* |
| 02·12·97-12·01·98 | *Literature and Photography* |

## Madrid

**PALACIO REAL**
**Calle Bailén s/n 28071 Madrid Director: Gerente del Patrimonio Nacional**
☎ +34 1 5420059 📠 +34 1 5597697
**Open: Daily Apr-Sep 09.00-18.00 Sunday and public holidays 09.00-15.00;
Oct-Mar 09.30-17.00 Sunday and public holidays 09.00-15.00**
**Closed: ceremonial days**

COLLECTION

In 1738 Philip V commissioned the architect Juan Bautista Sachetti to build the New Palacio Real on the former site of the Alcázar. Carlos III (1764) was the first monarch to reside in the palace.
The Palacio is constructed in Neo-Classical style with white stone from Colmenar and granite from the Sierra de Guadarrama.
The four wings, built around a central courtyard, are adorned with Ionic columns and Doric pilasters.
The staircase is by Sabatini, who was the architect of the modifications the building underwent later.
The dining-room, The 'Gran Comedor', also known as the 'Salón de Columnas, was decorated by Corrado Giaquinto. It contains unique tapestries from Brussels which are part of the 'Apostle Story', created by Raphael as tapestry designs. There are also busts of emperors from the Heraculaneum and bronzes from the 16th century.
The 'Gasparini Salón' was decorated in Rococo style by the Neapolitan artist Gasparini. The floor is made of marble. A small Rococo-Pastor by Jaquet Droz from the Royal Clock Collection is exhibited in the salon.
The antechamber contains the four portraits of Carlos IV and Maria Luisa by Goya.
The 'Salón de Carlos III', in which he died, is decorated with portraits by such artists as Vincente López (1828).
The Hall of the Porcelain, the 'Salón de Porcelanas' is one of the finest European palace collections of this type.

The 'Salón del Trono' features bronze lions, sculptures and clocks and a composition by Triopolo.

Also a large collection of gold, silver and bronze commemorative medals from the 18th century onwards as well as medals from abroad (15th-20th century) are on display.

Furthermore a large number of musical instruments, including some made by Stradivarius.

In the Pharmacy Museum, the 'Museo real de Farmacia', the pharmacy of Carlos V with its Talavera ware and glass from the Royal Factory 'La Granja' is well preserved.

**EXHIBITIONS** | No details available.

# Madrid

**MUSEO DEL PRADO**
Paseo del Prado s/n 28014 Madrid Director: Fernando Checa Cremades
☎ +34 1 3302800 📠 +34 1 3302856
Open: Tuesday-Saturday 09.00-19.00 Sunday and public holidays 09.00-14.00
Closed: Monday and Good Friday, 1 Jan, 1 May, 25 Dec

**COLLECTION** | Monarchs such as Philip II, Philip IV and Isabel of Farnese assembled many of the great masterpieces of Spanish, Italian, Flemish and French painting on display in the museum today. This core collection was subsequently enlarged through acquisitions resulting from the appropriation of convents and churches during the past century, as well as bequests and gifts during the 19th and 20th centuries.

© Museo del Prado, Madrid
Main entrance: the Velasquéz gate and main façade

**Spanish Painting** All periods of Spanish painting, from the Middles Ages to the 19th century, are amply represented in the museum's collection. It includes works by El Greco, Zurbarán, Ribera, Murillo, Alonso Cano and Goya.

**Italian Painting** This section includes works by Raphael, Fra Angelico, Botticelli and Mantegna, 16th-century Venetian painting and a fine assemblage of works by Titian.

**Flemish Painting** A rich assortment of works by such masters as Bosch, Patinir and Rubens, as well as an extensive sampling of Flemish Baroque.

**The Prado's holdings of Renaissance and classical sculpture,** together with selected paintings from the French and German Schools, complete the collection. Room 51c, on the ground floor, houses the oldest pictorial works of the Prado Museum: murals originally found in the medieval churches of Casillas de Berlanga (Soria) and Maderuelo (Segovia). Rooms 100, 101 and 102 house the so-called Dauphin's treasure: a rich set of tableware made of semi-precious stones and rock crystal dating from the Middle Ages to the 17th century.

**EXHIBITION**
Oct 97 | *El Greco's Portrait*

## Madrid

### MUSEO DE LA REAL ACADEMIA DE BELLAS ARTES DE SAN FERNANDO
Calle Alcalá 13  28014  Madrid  Director: J. María de Azcarate y Risetori
☎ +34 1 5221491
Open: Tuesday-Saturday 09.00-19.00  Sunday, Monday 09.00-14.00

**COLLECTION**

Bequests and donations from former students have made this museum, located in the Baroque Goyenche Palace built by Churriguera and restored by Villanueva, the second largest picture gallery in Madrid. The most notable paintings from the Spanish school are 'Self-Portrait', 'Burial of the Sardine', 'Bullfight' 'Fernando VII on Horseback' and 'Penitents' by Goya, as well as his portrait of the architect Juan de Villanueva, 'San Jerónimo' by ElGreco, 'Pietà' by Morales and portraits by Velásquez of Felipe IV and Mariana of Austria. There is an extensive collection of works by Zurbarán, including six portraits of monks, and Murillo, including 'S.Diego de Alcalá', 'Magdalen', 'Resurrection' and 'Ecstasy of St.Francis of Assisi'.

Among the other works are 'Susanna and the Elders', 'St. Augustin between Christ and the Virgin' and 'Hercules and Omphale' by Rubens, 'Christ' by Bellini, 'Spring' by Eschimboldo, Lucan Jordan's 'Adoration of the Shepherds', Ribera's 'Burial of Christ' and Ribalta's 'S. Juan de Ribera'. There are also paintings by members of the Academy, prints by Picasso and drawings from the Renaissance and early Baroque. The sculpture collection has works by Pedro de Mena and polychrome sculptures by José Gines. The museum also contains the National Collection of Engravings (Calcografía Nacional), including a series by Goya.

**EXHIBITIONS**

No details available.

## Madrid

### MUSEO ROMÁNTICO
Calle San Mateo 13  28004  Madrid  Director: Rosa Donoso Guerrero
☎ +34 1 4481071  🖷 +34 1 5942893
Open: Monday-Saturday 09.00-15.00  Sunday and public holidays 10.00-14.00
Closed: Tuesday and August

**COLLECTION**

The museum was founded in 1924 by the second Marquis de la Vega-Inclán, who installed it in a typical Madrid palace built in 1779 by the architect Manuel Rodriguez Martín. The interior recreates the atmosphere of a 19th-century residence, more specifically of the Age of Romanticism.

**Paintings**  The collection of paintings comprises the most representative 19th-century Spanish artists: Vicente López, Federico de Madrazo, Eugenio Lucas, Alenza Esquivel, Pérez-Villaamil, José Aparicio, Gutiérrez de la Vega, Lacoma, etc.

**Sculpture**  There are sculptures by José Gragera, Gayrad, José Piquer, Pérez del Valle, Ponciano Ponzano, Antonio Solá, etc.

**Prints**  The museum has a large collection of engravings and lithographs.

**Decorative Arts**  The collection includes porcelain, fans, watches, miniatures, etc.

The furniture in the rooms is varied, with emphasis on the style of Ferdinand and Isabella.

**EXHIBITIONS**

No details available.

# Madrid

**THYSSEN-BORNEMISZA MUSEUM**
Paseo del Prado 8  28014 Madrid  Curator: Tomàs Llorens Serro
☎ +34 1 4203944  🖷 +34 1 4202780
Open: Tuesday-Sunday 10.00-19.00
Closed: Monday

COLLECTION

Built between the end of the 18th century and the beginning of the 19th century, the Palace of Villahermosa is a fine example of Madrid's neo-classical architecture. The collection is laid out in historical sequence, beginning on the second floor where the Renaissance and Classicism eras are located. Important side rooms are dedicated to Flemish and German painting, and to French and Spanish works. The second floor ends with the first two rooms dedicated to Dutch art, seen here in its more Italian aspect. The remaining Dutch art can be found on the first floor, from the 17th-century Frans Hals to the 20th-century Max Beckmann. Here the visitor can also contemplate Impressionist and post-Impressionist paintings, as well as two of the most significant parts of the collection, North American painting and German Expressionism. The ground floor is dedicated to 20th-century painting, from Cubism and the first decades of the Avant-garde movements through Pop Art.

El Greco
*The Annunciation,*
*c.1596-1600*
© *Fundación*
*coleccion Thyssen-*
*Bornemisza, Madrid*

EXHIBITIONS

until 29·06·97

**The Annunciation by El Greco**  *The Cycle of the Colegio de Maria de Aragon*  Together with different paintings by El Greco on the subject of the Annunciation, the exhibition includes the X-rays, pigment analyses, photographs etc. used for the restoration of the museum's copy of 'The Annunciation'.

28·05·97-14·09·97

**George Grosz**  *The Berlin Years 1894-1932*  The exhibition consists of some 20 oil paintings, 100 works on paper and various sketch books, illustrated books and portfolios both from other museums and from the Grosz Legacy.

30·09·97-11·01·98

**Joan Miro**  *Catalan Peasant with a Guitar, 1924*  The selected work of art will be shown surrounded by other paintings related to it, such as other oil paintings by Miro on the subject of the Catalan peasant and preparatory drawings.

Nov 97-Feb 98

**The Triumph of Venus**  *Images of Women in 18th-Century Venetian Painting*  An exhibition of works on different themes, such as allegorical compositions related to the idea of Beauty, historical scenes linked to feminine virtue and courage, portraits and scenes from everyday life.

## Mérida

**MUSEO NACIONAL DE ARTE ROMANO**
José Ramón Melida s/n  06800 Mérida  Director: José Maria Alvarez Martinez
☎ +34 24 311690  ☒ +34 24 302006
Open: Tuesday-Saturday 10.00-14.00 / 17.00-19.00
Sunday and public holidays 10.00-14.00
Closed: Monday

COLLECTION

Merida was founded by Emperor Augustus in 25 B.C. and was the most important city of Roman Spain, itself one of the major Roman provinces. The current archaeological park, which contains the remains of a theatre, amphitheatre and circus, also includes the Museum of Roman Art. This is a modern building in a 'Roman' style constructed over archaeological excavations of thermae and other facilities.

The ground floor features a large collection of sculptures from the 1st century A.D., including representations of Venus, Pluto, Ceres, Proserpina, Oceanus, a bust of Augustus, Chronos, Isis and Mercury, together with cippi, stelae, well-heads, lamps, bronzes, mosaics and murals. Many of these exhibits come from the nearby theatre and circus. The first floor features glass, ceramics, jewellery and coins. The display on the second floor is more heterogeneous, with mosaics, reliefs, collections of epigraphs, stelae and several busts. The collections provide an insight into many aspects of Roman life and culture such as religion and funerary rites, social structures, politics and administration, industry, the performing arts, and the household.

The museum also possesses a specialist library and a photographic archive.

EXHIBITIONS

No details available

## Palma de Mallorca

**MUSEU D'ART ESPANYOL CONTEMPORANI**
San Miguel 11  07002  Palma de Mallorca  Director: José Luis Yuste
☎ +34 71 713515  ☒ +34 71 712601
Open: Monday-Friday 10.00-18.30  Saturday 10.00-13.30
Closed: Sunday and public holidays

COLLECTION

The Col. Lecció March Art Espanyol Contemporani is exhibited in a Mallorcan style building in the centre of Palma de Mallorca. The museum contains 36 works of art, representing some of the most important Spanish artists of the 20th century. The oldest piece is a Picasso from 1907, part of his series 'Les Demoiselles d'Avignon'. The exhibit also includes paintings and sculptures by Juan Gris, Joan Miró, Salvador Dalí, Julio González, Antoni Tàpies, Miguel Barceló, Eduardo Chillida, Antonio López and others.

The collection originates mainly from funds of the Juan March Foundation, an institution that promotes numerous cultural activities, devoting special interest to the Fine Arts. The Foundation also owns the collection exhibited in the Museum of Spanish Abstract Art in Cuenca.

EXHIBITION

until 10·05·97

*Millares*

## Sevilla

### MUSEO ARQUEOLÓGICO DE SEVILLA
Plaza de América s/n  Sevilla  Director: Fernando Fernandez Gomez
☎ +34 5 4232401
Open: Tuesday-Sunday 09.00-14.30
Closed: Monday

COLLECTION | The Archaeological Museum is housed in the Renaissance palace on the Plaza de América. The objects are on display to the public in 27 exhibition rooms. The first ten rooms house the Prehistoric and Historic collections from the Phoenician, Greek and Punic colonisation periods. The other rooms contain Iberian and Roman sculptures and objects from the Palaeo-Christian, Visigothic, Arabic and Hispanic-Muslim cultures.

EXHIBITIONS | No details available.

## Sevilla

### MUSEO DE ARTE CONTEMPORANEO DE SEVILLA
Santo Tomás 5  41004  Sevilla  Director: Luisa López Moreno
☎ +34 5 4215830  🖷 +34 5 4210417
Open: Tuesday-Friday 10.00-20.00  Saturday, Sunday 10.00-14.00
Closed: Monday and public holidays

COLLECTION | Acquired in the first years after the museum's foundation in 1970, the original collection consists mainly of Spanish contemporary works from the 60s and 70s. Abstraction, Pop Art, Constructivism and Abstract Expressionism are the styles represented here by such artists as Alcain, Rafols Casamada, Equipo Crónica, Gordillo, Tapies, Millares, Mompó, Lucio Muñoz, Saura, Sempere, Zóbel and others. A small part of the permanent collection dates back to the earlier years of this century, including works by Bacarisas, Gargallo, Iturrino, Homero de Torres and Zuloaga.
The museum also has an extensive collection of Andalusian contemporary art. An initiative of the regional government, Junta de Andalucia, this collection aims to preserve earlier Andalusian works which make up the cultural heritage. The museum recently acquired the collections of Manuel Angeles Ortiz (Jaen 1895 Paris 1984) and Antonio Rodriguez Luna (born in Córdoba, 1910). Secondly, the collection aims to recognise and secure new trends in present-day artistic activity. Three generations of artists are represented here, among which Burguillos, Meana, Soto, Sierra, Delgado, Tovar, Chema Cobo, Pérez Villalta o Bermejo, Paneque, Cabrera, Isidro, Agredano, P.G. Romero, Báez and López Cuenca. A collection of international art, featuring such artists as Schulze, Dokoupil and Kosuth, is also on display.

EXHIBITIONS | No details available.

## Sevilla

### MUSEO DE BELLAS ARTES DE SEVILLA
Plaza Del Museo 9  41001  Sevilla  Director: Enrique Pareja Lopez
☎ +34 5 4220790  🖷 +34 5 4224324
Open: Tuesday-Sunday 09.00-15.00
Closed: Monday

COLLECTION | The Seville Museum of Fine Arts occupies a former convent, most of which was built in the 17th century to a design attributed to Juan de Oviedo y la Bandera. A number of additions and renovations were made in the following centuries, including the decoration of the church interior by Domingo Martínez and the Great Cloister by Leonardo de Figueroa. The most recent building work was completed in 1992, allowing the museum to be reopened. The permanent exhibition provides an overview of the Seville School of painting and sculpture from its origins in the Middle Ages right up to the 20th century. It houses famous works by Murillo, Zurbarán and Valdés Leal which were painted for the main convents of Seville in the 17th century and acquired by the museum during the secularisation of 1835. The collection includes sculptures by Pietro Torrigiano, Seville sculptor Juan Martínez Montañez and his pupil Juan Mesa. The display of decorative arts features furniture, silverwork and a large collection of ceramics including Renaissance and Baroque glazed Seville tiles. The latter are on show in the museum's courtyards.

**EXHIBITIONS** No details available

## Tarragona

**MUSEU ARQUEOLÓGICO PROVINCIAL DE TARRAGONA**
Plaça del Rei 5  43003  Tarragona  Director: Francesc Tarrats Bou
☎ +34 77 236211  🖷 +34 77 245393
Open: 16 Sep-15 Jun Tuesday-Sunday 10.00-13.00 / 16.00-19.00; 16 Jun-15 Sep Daily 10.00-13.00 / 16.30-20.00  Sunday and public holidays 10.00-14.00
Closed: Monday (16 Sep-15 Jun)

**COLLECTION** The museum is built at the site of a Roman wall. The collection consists of antiquities from ancient Tarraco taken from temples, palaces and homes. There are mosaics, including one depicting the head of Medusa, friezes, sculptures, tiles, terra sigillata and a sarcophagus. The foundations of the wall are visible in the basement.

**EXHIBITIONS** No details available.

## Toledo

**MUSEO DE EL GRECO**
Calle Levi 3  Toledo
☎ +34 25 224046
Open: Tuesday-Saturday 10.00-14.00 / 16.00-18.30  Sunday 10.00-14.00
Closed: Monday

**COLLECTION** As the name suggests, the core of this museum's collection consists of works by the Spanish artist El Greco. With the exception of 'Las lágrimas de San Pedro', which dates from the 1580s, the majority of the collection is made up of works of art from the period 1600-1614. A few examples include: 'El Apostolado', 'La Vista y Plano de Toledo' and the portraits 'Covarrubias'. The museum also houses important collections of 17th-century paintings, among which 'La Escuela Madrileña', 'La Escuela Sevillana' and 'La Escuela Toledana'. The latter includes works by Luis Tristán, who was closely connected to El Greco and his son Jorge Manuel Theotokopoulous. A separate gallery houses a variety of works from different periods and styles, which were acquired by the Marquis of Vega-Inclán.

**EXHIBITIONS** No details available.

## Toledo

**MUSEO DE SANTA CRUZ**
**(MUSEO PROVINCIAL DE BELLAS ARTES Y ARQUEOLÓGICO)**
Calle Cervante 3  45001  Toledo  Director: García Serrano
☎ +34 25 221402
Open: Daily 10.00-18.30  Sunday 10.00-14.00  Monday 10.00-14.00 /
16.00-18.30

**COLLECTION**

The collection is housed in the Hospital de Santa Cruz, built for
Cardinal Pedro Mendoza in 1514. The provincial archaeological
section contains Roman mosaics, well-heads, and Visigothic and
Mudéjar objects including storage jars, carved beams and capitals.
In addition to a large collection of 15th to 17th-century Brussels
tapestries, there are pennants, furniture and religious art from the
San Vincente Parish Museum on display.
The paintings on display include Morales, 'Christ at the Column';
Moro, 'Calvary'; a 16th-century Hispano-Flemish triptych;
22paintings by El Greco, including 'The Assumption', 'La Veronica',
'La Inmaculada', 'St. John the Baptist', St. Joseph with the Christ
Child' and 'Santiago'; Goya, 'Crucifixion' and 'Charles V'; an
anonymous Flemish diptych; Ribera, 'Descent from the Cross' and
'Holy Family'; and Pedro de Mena, 'Virgin of the Fishes'. The
sculptures include a wooden image of Christ by Iacopo d'Indaco, a
16th-century polychrome wooden statue of St. Martin and a marble
bust of a Cardinal by Nicolás de Busi.

**EXHIBITIONS**

No details available.

## Toledo

**MUSEO SEFARDI - THE SEPHARDIC MUSEUM**
Calle Samuel Levi s.n.  45002 Toledo  Director: Ana Maria López Álvarez
☎ +34 25 223665  📠 +34 25 215831
Open: Tuesday-Saturday 10.00-13.45 / 16.00-17.45
Sunday and public holidays 10.00-13.45
Closed: Monday and 1 Jan, 1 May, 24, 25, 31 Dec

**COLLECTION**

The museum, created in 1964, has recently been restored and
enlarged. It is located in the Samuel Levi Synagogue ('El Transito'
Synagogue) and in rooms of the ancient Archive of the Calatrava
and Alcantara Orders. The synagogue, with its wooden beamed
ceiling and rich stucco decoration, is one of the most beautiful and
characteristic buildings of the 14th-century Mudejar style of
architecture.
The museum aims to preserve the Sephardic cultural legacy as part
of the Spanish heritage and to display the art, history and culture of
the Jews from Spain (Sepharad) since their earliest arrival in Spain
up to 1492 when the Jews were driven out of the country and then
established communities all over the world.
The collection includes archaeological objects from the Israel
Antiquities Authority which display geographical, historical and
cultural ties with the ancient Near East. Also included are objects
reflecting Jewish culture during the time that the Jews lived in
Spain: the Roman and Visigothic times and the Middle Ages. The
northern yard contains gravestones with Hebraic inscriptions from
various Jewish necropolises in Spain. The eastern yard displays
archaeological excavations revealing a vaulted building which
probably belonged to ancient Jewish quarter's public baths. The
Women's Gallery displays cultural evidence of the various Sephardic
communities all over the world.

**EXHIBITION**
Sep 97

| | |
|---|---|
| | ***Great-Grandparents of the Orchestra*** *Musical Instruments of the Middle Ages* |

## Valencia

### MUSEO DE BELLAS ARTES SAN PÍO V
Calle de San Pío V 9  46010  Valencia  Director: Fernando Benito Doménech
☎ +34 6 3605793  📠 +34 6 3697125
Open: Tuesday-Saturday 10.00-14.00 / 16.00-18.00
Sunday and public holidays 10.00-14.00
Closed: Monday and Good Friday, 25 Dec, 1 Jan

COLLECTION

The Museum of Fine Arts shows the evolution of the arts in Valencia and surroundings between the 14th and the 20th centuries.
The Valencian Primitive School is particularly well represented, with well-known religious paintings and altar pieces from Valencian churches and monasteries: 'Retable of Bonifacio Ferrer' (c. 1400), 'Retable of the Holy Cross' by Miguel Alcanyis, 'Retable of the Virgin' by Pere Nicolau, 'Retable of Saint Martin' by Gonzalo Peris, 'Retable of the Epiphany' by Mater of Perea, etc.
Among the 16th century artists are Vicente Macip (St. Sebastian), Joan de Joanes (Mystical Wedding of the Venerable Agnesio), Yañez de la Almedina, Luis de Morales (Calvary) and El Greca (St. John the Baptist). The collection includes also works by baroque local artists, such as Francisco and Juan Ribalta, Sariñena, March, Espinosa, Yepes. The major painters of the Spanish School are represented, including Orrente, Alonso Cano, Pereda, Valdés Leal, Murillo, Ribera and Velázquez (Self-Portrait). The route through the museum continues with the works of Maella, Vicente Lopez and Goya (including three portraits: Doña Joaquina Candado, Grabador Esteve, Bayeu). The 19th century is represented by Muñoz Degrain, Pinazo and Sorolla.
Other European Schools are represented by Pinturicchio, a follower of Jerome Bosch (Triptich with Christ Crowned with Thorns), Alessandro Allori, Onofrio Loth, PellegrinoTibaldi, Daniel Seghers, Luca Giordano, among others. The Museum also possesses a fine collection of sculptures, including works by Damian Forment, Ignacio Vergara and Mariano Benlliure. In addition, the department of prints and drawings contains a rich collection of works by artists such as Berruguete, Machuca, Goya, Vergara, Polidoro da Caravaggio, Zuccaro, Piranesi and others.

EXHIBITIONS
until May 97

***Vicente Macip*** *Retrospective* This painter's works are important contributions to Spanish Art Renaissance

Oct 97-Nov 97

***Yañez de la Almedina*** For the first time a comprehensive exhibition of drawings and paintings of this 16th century painter.

Dec 97

***The Vergara*** *Paintings, Sculptures and Drawings.*

## Valladolid

### MUSEO NACIONAL DE ESCULTURA
Cadenas de San Gregorio 1  47011 Valladolid  Director: Jesús Urrea
☎ +34 83 250916  📠 +34 83 259300
Open: Tuesday-Saturday 10.00-14.00 / 16.00-18.00  Sunday 10.00-14.00
Closed: Monday and 1 Jan, 1, 13 May, 24, 25, 31 Dec

COLLECTION

The collection includes a splendid assortment of religious sculptures from the 13th to the 18th century. The material is wood, a material traditionally used in Spain for this kind of work. The altarpieces, choir stalls, sepulchres, processional floats ('pasos') etc. which make up this collection illustrate the evolution of Spanish imagery as it continued to change parallel to shifts in belief.

*© Museo Nacional de Escultura Valladolid*

The three artists who represent the most perfect examples of Mannerist expression and Baroque naturalism in Castile - Alonso Berruguete, Juan de Juni and Gregorio Fernández - are well represented by some of their most significant works. Other important works include a selection of sculpture pieces from the 13th and 14th century, remarkable examples of Flemish and Spanish-Flemish Gothic art, Renaissance ensembles, and a broad representation of Baroque sculpture evolving from the sober spirituality of the 17th century to the informality and ornamental nature of the 18th century. The viewer travels through time with artists such as Felipe Bigarny, Diego de Siloe, Alonso Cano and Pedro de Mena.

The volume and quality of this collection is due largely to pieces originating from churches and monasteries in Valladolid that were deconsecrated during the 19th century. Works from other Iberian schools were gradually added, thus making this sculpture museum truly national in nature. In addition to the high quality of its collection, the museum is located in St. Gregory College, one of Spain's most beautiful buildings of the Late Gothic style.

**EXHIBITIONS** | No details available

## Zaragoza

**MUSEO DE ZARAGOZA**
Plaza de los Sitios 6  50001  Zaragoza  Director: Miguel Beltran Lloris
☎ +34 76 222181 📠 +34 76 222378
Open: Daily 9.00-14.00 / 17.00-21.00  Sunday 9.00-14.00

**COLLECTION** | The museum has an archaeological collection including Iberian scripts on bronze, a Visigothic exhibit, Roman mosaics and Moorish stucco from the Aljaferia. It also has Primitive paintings by artists from Aragon and Catalonia, Renaissance sculpture and works by Goya and others.
On the first floor there are panels from the retables, Magdalenas from the 17th century and a statue of Saint Onofre by Damián Froment. Works by Goya include portraits of the Duke of SanCarlos, Carlos IV, Fernando VIII and Maria Luisa. There are also works by Francisco Bayeu, Vicente Lopez, Sorolla, Rusiñol and David Wilkie.

**EXHIBITIONS** | No details available.

## Aarau

**AARGAUER KUNSTHAUS AARAU**
Aargauerplatz  5001 Aarau  Director: Beat Wismer
☎ +41 62 8352330  🖷 +41 62 8352329
Open: Tuesday-Sunday 10.00-17.00  Thursday 10.00-20.00
Closed: Monday

**COLLECTION**

The museum's collection gives a picture of the development of art in Switzerland from the late 18th century until the present day. Some 18th-century artists whose works are displayed here include Johann Heinrich Füssli and Caspar Wolf. Swiss art in the 19th century is represented by numerous landscape paintings, as well as works by Albert Anker and Arnold Böcklin. Finally, the Modern age of Swiss art is illustrated by works of such artists as Ferdinand Hodler, Cuno Amiet and Giovanni Giacometti. The collection also includes Swiss contemporary artists. Due to a lack of adequate space, it is often only possible to view parts of the permanent collection.

**EXHIBITIONS**

until 01-06-97  **Mountains - Views - Belvedere**   A panorama of art in Switzerland from the Enlightenment to the Modern.

until 01-06-97  **Pia Fries, Kiki Lamers, Renee Levi**

until 01-06-97  **Dirk Reinartz   Deathly Still**

15-06-97-24-08-97  **I Want To See My Mountains**

13-09-97-09-11-97  **Guido Nussbaum**

13-09-97-09-11-97  **Annelies Strba**

29-11-97-04-01-98  **Annual Exhibition of Aargau Artists**   This year's guest is Barbara Müller.

## Basel - Basle

**ANTIKENMUSEUM BASEL UND SAMMLUNG LUDWIG**
**BASLE MUSEUM OF ANCIENT ART AND LUDWIG COLLECTION**
St. Albangraben 5  4010 Basel  Director: Peter Blome
☎ +41 61 2712202  📠 +41 61 2721861
Internet http://www.unibas.ch/museum/amb/
Open: Tuesday-Friday 10.00-17.00 Wednesday 10.00-21.00
Closed: Monday

**COLLECTION**

The Basle Museum of Ancient Art is the only Swiss museum devoted exclusively to Classical Antiquity. The exhibits housed by the museum date from the 3rd millennium B.C. to 300 A.D. and are mostly Greek, but there are also objects of Ancient Italian, Etruscan and Roman origin. Sculptures and ceramics form the core of the permanent exhibition, but bronze statuettes, clay figurines, gold jewellery and coins are represented as well. The majority of the pieces are gifts from private collectors of our time, such as Robert Käppeli and Giovanni Züst. In 1980 Peter and Irene Ludwig donated their collection to the museum, an event that led to the enlargement of the premises.

*Vessel shaped like a*
*squatting Gorgon*
Late 7th century B.C.
H. 21.5 cm
© *The Basle museum*
*of Ancien Art and*
*Ludwig Collection,*
*Basle*

An interesting feature of the museum is the diversity of its architecture. Two connected classical townhouses contain the vases and smaller objects, while the sculptures can be found in the skylight gallery of the modern annex and in the vaulted cellar (Roman sarcophagi and portraits). A courtyard with trees and flowers forms the heart of this block of buildings.
The Educational department of the museum runs instructive exhibitions and workshops in an adjacent building (Luftgässlein 5).
The collection of plaster casts is located on the Mittlere Strasse 17 and provides the first comprehensive survey of the Parthenon.

**EXHIBITION**

until 13·07·97

*Moments of Eternity*    *Egyptian Art in Swiss Private Collections*
This exhibition comprises selected works of Ancient Egyptian art from Swiss private collections. Some 350 items, including decorative art, sculptures, reliefs and paintings, give a unique impression of the wealth of Egypt's artistic creativity from the 4th millennium B.C. to the 4th century A.D.

## Basel · Basle

### MUSEUM FÜR GEGENWARTSKUNST
St. Alban-Rheinweg 60  4010 Basel  Curator: Theodora Vischer
☎ +41 61 2728183  📠 +41 61 2710536
Open: Tuesday-Sunday 10.00-17.00 and Easter Monday, Whit Monday
Closed: Monday and Carnival, Good Friday, 1 May, 1 Aug, 24, 25, 31 Dec

**COLLECTION**
The Museum of Contemporary Art is a joint project of the Emanuel Hoffmann Foundation, the Christoph Merian Foundation and the canton of Basle-Stadt. The architects Wilfried and Katharina Steib linked a 19th-century factory to a new structure to create an appealing complex that blends harmoniously into the surrounding old part of the city. The works on display date from the 1960s to the present, starting with Minimal Art, Conceptual Art and 'Wild Painting' and continuing up to the latest in installation art. Focal points are works by Frank Stella, Bruce Nauman, A.R. Penck. Joseph Beuys and Rosemarie Trockel.

*Works of the collection*
© *Museum für Gegenwartskunst, Basel*

**EXHIBITIONS**
until 31·08·97

***Katharina Fritsch***   Katharina Fritsch's sculptures take banal objects and figures from everyday life, alienating them and evoking the atmosphere of a dream.

04·10·97-early 1998

***Check-in!***   In 'Check-in!', the museum draws on works from its two collections as well as loans and contributions from artists to show the diversity of styles and contradictory approaches to contemporary art.

## Basel · Basle

### KUNSTHALLE BASEL
Steinenberg 7  4051 Basel  Director: Peter Pakesch
☎ +41 61 2724833  📠 +41 61 2724826
Open: Tuesday-Sunday 11.00-17.00  Wednesday 11.00-20.30
Guided tours on Sunday 11.00
Closed: Monday

**COLLECTION**
No permanent collection.

**EXHIBITIONS**

until 25·05·97
***Albert Oehlen***

04·05·97-18·06·97
***Zoe Leonard***

08·06·97-24·08·97
***Liz Larner***

27·06·97-07·09·97
***Clegg and Guttmann***   *100 Years of Zionism*

21·09·97-09·11·97
***Claudia and Julia Müller***

30·11·97-04·01·98
***Annual Exhibition of Basle Artists***

# Basel - Basle

**COLLECTION**

The Museum of Fine Arts houses the collections of the Departments of Painting and of Prints and Drawings. The emphasis is on Upper Rhenish paintings and drawings from 1400 to 1600 and on 19th and 20th-century art. The Öffentliche Kunstsammlung Basle has the world's largest collection of works by the Holbein family. The Renaissance is also represented by numerous major works. These old masterpieces largely originate from the collection, purchased in 1661, of Basilius Amerbach. Paintings by the Basle artist Arnold Böcklin form one highlight of the 19th-century exhibits.
20th-century art focuses on Cubism, German Expressionism, Abstract Expressionism and Pop Art.

Hans Holbein d.J.
(1497/98-1543)
*Laïs of Corinth, 1526*
© *Kunstmuseum,*
*Basel*

**EXHIBITIONS**

14·05·97-24·08·97

***Dürer, Holbein, Grünewald***  *Old Master Drawings of the German Renaissance from Berlin and Basel*    170 drawings offer unique insight into German draftsmanship of the 13th and 16th centuries. The works of Dürer, Holbein and Grünewald, along with examples from their contemporaries, are placed in contexts of their respective ages.

14·05·97-07·09·97

***The Prints of Hans Holbein the Younger***  *Exhibition of all Prints in the Basel Kupferstichkabinett*    To commemorate the quincentenary of Hans Holbein the Younger, the museum presents an exhibition of his prints. Holbein, like Albrecht Dürer and Ambrosius, came to Basel to produce illustrations for books.

26·06·97-07·09·97

***Put into Light III***  *Holbein's Contribution to Early Genre Painting*
An unusual 'advertisement', intended to be hung from a pole in front of a schoolmaster's house to attract the attention of passersby, is on display.

20·09·97-04·01·98

***111 Drawings by 111 Artists***    This is an unconventional exhibition of drawings and watercolours in which the works will be exchanged and rearranged periodically.

27·09·97-11·01·98

***Peter and Samuel Birmann***  *Artists, Collectors, Dealers and Patrons*

On the 150th anniversary of his death, this exhibition celebrates the art of Samuel Birmann (1793-1847) and his father Peter Birmann (1758-1844). Their art marks an important chapter in the development of landscape painting.

27·09·97-11·01·98    ***Collecting and Donating for the Öffentliche Kunstsammlung Basel Emilie Linder and Jacob Burckhardt***    This exhibition focuses on two individuals who made substantial contributions to the museum's collection during the 19th century.

Nov 97-Jan 98    ***A Special Guest***    This exhibition features Cézanne's 'Still Life with Apples and Peaches', on loan from the National Gallery of Art, Washington.

## Bern

**BERNISCHES HISTORISCHES MUSEUM**
Helvetiaplatz 5   3000 Bern 6   Director: Peter Jezler
☎ +41 31 3507711   🖷 +41 31 3507799
Open: Tuesday-Sunday 10.00-17.00
Closed: Monday

**COLLECTION**

**History**   A wide variety of exhibits focus on different aspects of Berne's history from the Middle Ages to the present.
Large Flemish tapestries once belonging to the dukes of Burgundy and the bishops of Lausanne exemplify the sumptuous courtly style of the Late Middle Ages in Burgundy and the Republic of Berne. The 'Pourtalès Salon' offers a faithful representation of upper class life during the 18th century, 'the Golden Age of Berne'. A portrait gallery, together with displays of luxurious silver, glass and porcelain objects, and furniture pieces help to illustrate the way of life during this period. Additional exhibits, including a scale-model of Berne constructed in the 1850s, document the town's subsequent development.

*Traian and Herkinbald carpet, Tournai c. 1450*
*Detail with the entourage of Emperor Traian*
© *Bernisches Historisches Museum, Bern*

Guild silver pieces, a portrait gallery of various Lord Mayors of the City of Berne, and their chairs of state illustrate the life of the ranking classes of old Berne. Other contrasting exhibits depict the new political order that began with the French invasion in 1798. A cycle of portraits by the painter Josef Reinhart provides a realistic and undistorted picture of 18th-century Swiss peasantry.
**Prehistory and early history**   A wealth of artefacts document several thousand years of human occupation, beginning with life among Stone Age hunter groups, and extending through early agrarian life, metal crafting, the development of Celtic culture, the subsequent Roman conquest, and the arrival of the Alemanni.
**Ethnography**   The department consists of the Oriental-Islamic Henry Moser Charlottenfels's collection and a collection which was built up by the Bernese painter Johan Wäber, who accompanied Captain Cook to the South Seas, Alaska and Siberia.

**Numismatics**   The core of the museum's coin collection includes coins from the Roman Empire, Bernese and Swiss coins and medals, and an assortment of coins from Central Asia.

# Bern

**KUNSTMUSEUM BERN**
Hodlerstrasse 8-12  3000 Bern 7  Director: Toni Stooss
☎ +41 31 3110944  ☷ +41 31 3117263
Open: Wednesday-Sunday 10.00-17.00 Tuesday 10.00-21.00
Closed: Monday

**COLLECTION**   The Museum of Fine Arts Bern has an outstanding collection of national and international art ranging from the 14th to 20th centuries.
In the lower rooms of the Old Building, the visitor is presented with Italian paintings from the 14th to 16th centuries as well as works by Swiss artists from Niklaus Manuel Deutsch to Albert Anker. On the upper stories, works by later Swiss artists are presented, from Arnold Böcklin and Ferdinand Hodler and continuing up to the 20th century.
Important collections of works by Paul Klee are shown on the ground floor in the New Building.
Artists represented on the top floor include Pierre Bonnard, Georges Braque, Paul Cézanne, Gustave Courbet, Salvador Dali, Edgar Degas, Robert Delaunay, Vincent van Gogh, Juan Gris, Vassily Kandinsky, Ludwig Kirchner, Eduard Manet, Franz Marc, Henri Matisse, Joan Miró, Amedeo Modigliani, Pablo Picasso, Camille Pissarro, Auguste Renoir, Chaim Soutine and many more.

Cuno Amiet
(1868-1961)
*Portrait of Anna Amiet in yellow with hat adorned with flowers, 1906*
© *Kunstmuseum Bern, Bern*

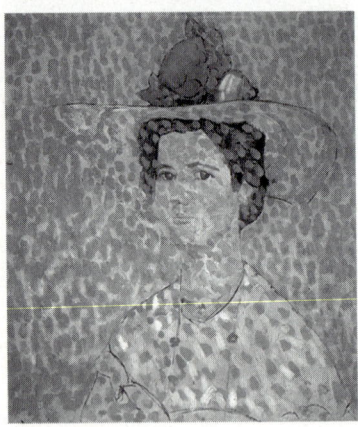

| Sep 97-Nov 97 | **Rebecca Horn**  *Drawings and Boxes 1965-1996* |
| 05·12·97-01·03·98 | **The Blue Four Feininger-Jawlensky-Kandinsky-Klee in the New World**  This will be the first exhibition in Europe on Galka Scheyer's activities is the U.S. and on the highly productive artistic relationship between the four artists. |

## La Chaux-de-Fonds

### MUSÉE DES BEAUX-ARTS
33, Rue des Musées   2300 La Chaux-de-Fonds  Director: Edmond Charrière
☎ +41 32 9130444  📠 +41 32 9136193
Open: Tuesday-Sunday 10.00-12.00 / 14.00-17.00
Wednesday 10.00-12.00 / 14.00-20.00
Closed: Monday

**COLLECTION**

The museum houses a permanent collection of paintings, sculptures, engravings, drawings, photographs and tapestries from the 19th and 20th century.
Art from La Chaux-de-Fonds, Neuchâtel and other parts of Switzerland is represented with works by Kaiser, L'Eplattenier, Le Corbusier, Anker, Vallotton and Baily.
A special exhibition is devoted to the Romantic painter and native of La Chaux-de-Fonds, Leopold Robert (1794-1835), celebrated for his portrayals of Italian brigands.

Interior view of the extension, 1993
© Musée des Beaux-Arts, La Chaud-de-Fonds

Works by Lieland, Constable, Delacroix, Van Gogh, Matisse, Deran, Rouault and Soutine form part of a prestigious legacy, the René and Madeleine Junod Collection.
The contemporary abstract tradition is represented with works by Buchet, Bissière, Manessier, Winter, Jacobsen, Poraodoro, Morellet and others.

**EXHIBITIONS**

| until 15·06·97 | **Sides of the Modernity in Tessin**  Adriana Beretta, Luisa Figini, Ingeborg Lüscher, Filippo Broggini, Rolando Raggenbass |
| 08·08·97-21·09·97 | **The Caves in Swiss Art from 17th to 20th Century** |
| 11·10·97-02·11·97 | **Le Musée des Beaux-Arts de La Chaux-de Fonds on Display** Exhibition organized by the School of decorative arts from Geneva. |
| 30·11·97-11·01·98 | **63th Biennial Exhibition of the Artsfriends' Society**  Artists from La Chaux-de-Fonds and Neuchâtel. |

## Davos

**KIRCHNER MUSEUM DAVOS**
Ernst Ludwig Kirchner Platz  7270 Davos  Curator: Roland Scotti
☎ +41 81 4132202  📠 +41 81 4132210
Internet http://www.museums.ch/guide/indexd.htm
Open: Tuesday-Sunday 15 Jul-30 Sep / Christmas-Easter 10.00 - 12.00 /
14.00 - 18.00 1 Oct - Christmas / Easter - 14 Jul 14.00 - 18.00
Closed: Monday

COLLECTION
The Kirchner Museum Davos gives visitors the opportunity to see the works of the Expressionist painter Ernst Ludwig Kirchner in the place where they were created. Davos and the surrounding area were a source of inspiration for many of the artist's important paintings.
The museum collection includes more than 1200 drawings, prints, paintings and pieces of sculpture, as well as photographs, documents and an extensive library relating to Kirchner's life.
The graphic works offer insights into Kirchner's broader work, and show many of his favourite motifs. The paintings reveal his mastery of the Alpine landscape and his affinity for the region's inhabitants.

EXHIBITION
Dec 97-Mar 97

***Karl Schmidt-Rottluff**   Exhibition from the Brücke Museum, Berlin*

## Genève - Geneva

**MUSÉE ARIANA**
10, Avenue de la Paix  1202 Genève  Director: Cäsar Menz
☎ +41 22 4185450  📠 +41 22 4185451
Internet  http://www.geneva-online.ch/tourisme-culture/arts-spectacles/
expositions/geneve.htm
Open: Wednesday-Monday 10.00-17.00
Closed: Tuesday

COLLECTION
The Musée Ariana is the Swiss glass and ceramics museum. Built by Gustave Revilliod (1817-1890) for his private collections of glass and ceramics and completed in 1884, this Italianate palace is situated in the quarter of the international organisations. At his death Revilliod left his museum, its collections and the surrounding park to the city of Geneva. In 1934 it became part of the Musée d'art et d'histoire. The collections reflect seven centuries of creation - from the Middle Ages to the present - in Europe, the Middle East and Asia. All the main techniques of glass and ceramic-making are represented, and the contemporary scene is given special attention.
In addition to the permanent collection and research/teaching facilities, space has been allotted for temporary exhibitions.

© Musée Ariana,
Genève

until 19·05·97

**Exchanged Looks at Contemporary Ceramics** *Two Private Collections and a Museum* This exhibition includes 120 pieces chosen from the private collections of Charles Roth and Csaba Gaspar, displayed together with their donations to the museum.

12·06·97-22·09·97

**Paul Bonifas** *Ceramist of Purism* Paul Bonifas (1893-1967) was one of the rare European ceramists of the day to reconcile industrial techniques, aesthetics and functionalism. This exhibition focuses on work between 1922 and 1940.

23·10·97-14·01·98

**Bernard Dejonghe** *Ceramics and Glass* For some ten years, ceramist Bernard Dejonghe has also pursued glass making. Whatever the medium, the artist remains resolutely sculptural in his approach, with simple, massive forms.

20·11·97-04·01·98

**Brunschwig Prize** This prize honouring original work in all fields of the applied arts is the only one of its kind in Switzerland and is awarded every other year since 1987.

## Genève · Geneva

**MUSÉE D'ART ET D'HISTOIRE**
2, Rue Charles-Galland  1206 Genève 3  Director: Cäsar Menz
☎ +41 22 4182600  ⅢⅢ +41 22 4182601
Internet  http://www.geneva-online.ch/tourisme-culture/arts-spectacles/expositions/geneve.htm
Open: Tuesday-Sunday 10.00-17.00
Closed: Monday

COLLECTION

The Musée d'art et d'histoire is one of the largest museums in Switzerland. It brings together archaeological, applied art and fine art collections.
Ancient Egyptian and Greco-Roman art is represented by an important group of sculptures, decorated vases, coins, engraved stones and metalwork (the Missorium, a Roman silver plate). The Orient has long fascinated Geneva, and is present in both the archaeological and applied art collections (Byzantine metalwork, Coptic textiles, Ottoman embroidery) and a fine collection of icons.
Medieval sculpture and stained glass are exhibited in the Historic Rooms, as well as Genevan interiors of the 16th to the 18th centuries.
The altarpiece of Konrad Witz (1444), a precursor of realistic landscape painting in the Western world, portrays a biblical scene against the backdrop of Lake Geneva and its mountains. French and Italian painting from the 16th to the 18th centuries and a charming Avercamp attest to the high quality of Genevan collections of this period. The Genevese artist Jean-Etienne Liotard is represented by one of the largest collections of his pastels and oils, featuring scenes from oriental life.
Genevan Romantic and Impressionist landscape painting (Töpffer, Agasse, Calame) is displayed next to oils by Corot, Renoir, Monet and Cézanne. Works by the prominent artists Vallotton and Hodier mark the beginnings of modern art. The 20th-century collection, which includes works by Giacometti and Bram van Velde among other contemporary artists, is constantly growing, and is the source of frequent exhibitions.

EXHIBITIONS

until 08·06·97

**Museum Music** *Listening to Antiquity* This exhibition shows numerous objects bearing some relation to instrumental music, including sculptures, vases, terracotta ware, bronzes and coins.

until 31·08·97    **The Bishopric of Geneva**   *Money in the 11th Century*   The Numismatic Collection of the Musée d'Art et d'Histoire presents an exhibition devoted to the beginnings of coinage in the Bishopric of Geneva.

until 07·09·97    **Ceramics from Magna Graecia: Selected Pieces**   *The Herbert A. Cahn Collection of Fragments*   The museum attempts a novel experiment by presenting ancient Greek ceramics exclusively in the form of a series of pieces or fragments.

until 28·09·97    **The Art of Imitation**   *Falsifications, Manipulations, Pastiches: Images of the Italian Renaissance at the Musée d'Art et d'Histoire* When the museum's Italian collection was catalogued in 1979, a number of falsifications were recognised. This exhibition, resulting from research into the falsifications, provides, ironically, important information about interest in Italian art around 1900.

until 28·09·97    **Regards II**   *Daniel Berset*   Daniel Berset deals with the fundamental questions of sculpture; his sculptures permit a heightened awareness of problems of perspective and viewpoint.

26·03·97 onwards    **A Display Bias**   *New Presentation of the Museum's Collections* This new display of the Beaux-Arts presents an itinerary composed of ensembles and strong points of the collection.

29·05·97-30·11·97    **The Musical Box**   *A Genevan Industry*   This exhibition focuses on both the technical and musical evolution of the musical box, which was a Genevan invention.

18·09·97-Winter 97    **The Great Shrine of Sion Cathedral**   *Conservation and Laboratory Study*   This exhibition focuses on the conservation methods and sophisticated research techniques employed in study and conservation of the 11th-century Great Shrine of Sion Cathedral.

09·10·97-Spring 98    **The Spirit of India in the Collections of the Musée d'Art et d'Histoire**   This exhibition brings together a selection of works from the museum's collections of applied arts and miniatures.

Dec 97 onwards    **The Banque Cantonale de Genève Prize for Contemporary Art 1997** **Bernard Voïta**   In the works of prizewinner Bernard Voïta, the reality of a photograph is disturbed by reworking the real — the subject of the photograph — as a geometrical composition.

## Genève - Geneva

### COLLECTIONS BAUR
8, Rue Munier-Romilly  1206 Genève  Director: Frank Dunand
☎ +33 22 3461729  📠 +33 22 7891845
Open: From Sep 97  Tuesday-Sunday 14.00-18.00
Closed: Until Sep 1997 and Monday

**COLLECTION**

In a former private home near the Russian church and the Museum of Art and History, you will find a private foundation exhibiting a collection of Chinese and Japanese Art.

Chinese Porcelain.
*Flask painted in underglaze blue and yellow enamel. Mark and reign of Yongzheng 1723-1735.*
© Collections Baur, Genève

The collection displays more than 1000 years of Chinese ceramics as well as beautiful jade pieces of the 18th century. The monochrome porcelains of the Qing dynasty are perhaps the most remarkable set of the Chinese ceramics collection. A wide variety of materials and decoration techniques are found in the Chinese snuff-bottles which were bought by Alfred Baur over a period of some thirty years. Japanese sword-fittings, lacquer boxes, ceramics, netsuke and objects linked to the tea ceremony are also on display.

**EXHIBITIONS**

No details available.

## Genève - Geneva

### CENTRE D'ART CONTEMPORAIN DE GENÈVE
10, Rue des Vieux-Grenadiers  1211 Genève  Director: Paolo Colombo
☎ +41 22 3291842  📠 +41 22 3291886
Open: Tuesday-Sunday 11.00-18.00
Closed: Monday

**COLLECTION**

No permanent collection.

**EXHIBITIONS**

until end Feb 98 — *Jane and Louise Wilson*   Video installations and photographs

24-06-97-12-10-97 — *Fatto in Italia*   An exhibition of young Italian artists

Sep 97-Dec 97 — *Projects Room*   Devoted to young artists from Geneva

23-10-97-end Jan 98 — *Sue Williams*   Paintings and Drawings

## Genève - Geneva

**CENTRE GENEVOIS DE GRAVURE CONTEMPORAINE**
17, Route de Malagnou  1208 Genève  Director: Véronique Bacchetta
☎ +41 22 7351260  🖷 +41 22 7352897
Open: Monday-Friday 11.00-13.00 / 14.00-18.00
Saturday (during exhibitions) 14.00-17.00
Closed: Sunday

COLLECTION

The stated goal of the Centre Genevois de Gravure Contemporaine is to promote an appreciation of engraving in the context of contemporary art. Established in 1966, the Centre Genevois de Gravure Contemporaine is open to international artists as well as artists from Geneva and the rest of Switzerland. Since 1986 it has been actively involved in the publication of engravings, artists' books and photographic prints, and the production of videos. It endeavours to focus attention on the problems intrinsic to reproducible pictures and objects. Artists are provided with an environment conducive to experimentation and to reflection on the possible links between contemporary art and the techniques of reproduction. Their work is presented in editions which the Centre produces and shows.

Among the works which have been exhibited are large monotypes by John Armleder, metal points by Philippe Favier, monochrome engravings by Olivier Mosset, lithographs by Jean-Michel Othoniel, Karen Kilimnik, Kristin Oppenheim, Luc Tuymans, Heimo Zobernig, engravings by Ian Anüll, Alex Hanimann and Rosemarie Trockel, artists' books by Emmett Williams and Claude Closky, a publication by Thomas Hirschhorn, and a video by Roman Signer. The Centre has also held a retrospective of the graphic work of Marcel Broodthaers. The works on exhibit are illustrative of the diversity of attitudes and approaches to the printing process and, more generally, to the reproduction of objects.

EXHIBITIONS

until May 97

*Hinrich Sachs (D) and B.T. Tamokoué (CAM)*   Exhibition of the winners of the C.G.G.C.'s Scholarship for 1996

Summer-Autumn

*Collective Manifestation*   About 20 swiss and foreign artists will present performances, installations, sonor pieces and videos.

## Genève - Geneva

**CABINET DES ESTAMPES DU MUSÉE D'ART ET D'HISTOIRE**
5, Promenade du Pin  1204 Genève  Director: Cäsar Menz
☎ +41 22 4182770  🖷 +41 22 4182771
Internet http://www.geneva-online.ch/tourisme-culture/arts-spectacles/expositions/geneve.htm
Open: Tuesday-Sunday 10.00-12.00 / 14.00-18.00
Closed: Monday

COLLECTION

The Cabinet des estampes owns an estimated 300 000 examples of engraving dating back over 500 years, and offers an overview of the evolution of the art of engraving from its origins. Highlights of the collection include works by Piranesi, Callot, Hogarth, Carrière, Redon and Meryon. Particularly distinctive is a rare ensemble of glass plate prints by Camille Corot.
In its acquisitions policy regarding modern works, the Cabinet des estampes has chosen to focus on specific currents and artists. Avant-garde Russian and Hungarian prints from the period between 1913 and 1925 are represented in one of the best collections in Europe. Also notable is the collection of works by Giorgio de Chirico,

Jean Fautrier, Antonio Saura, Bram van Velde, Markus Raetz, Georg Baselitz, Urs Lüthi and John M. Armleder.

The engravings of the Lausanne artist Felix Valloton provide a complement to the collection of his paintings in the Musée d'art et d'histoire.

Prominent in the collection is a group of artists' books, ranging from sumptuous collectors' editions from the beginning of the century to booklets produced during the 1960s.

While the collections are not on permanent display, specific works can be viewed by appointment.

**EXHIBITIONS**

until 15·06·97

*Geneviève Asse   The Focused Flood, Prints and Engraved Books*
The work of Geneviève Asse is built on the paring down of object and landscape, and on her ability to concentrate space in a flood of colour (blue) on the surface.

25·06·97-07·09·97

*Admirable Engravings and Drawings from the Kupferstichkabinett of Basle*

01·10·97-30·11·97

*The Ecart Group*

## Genève - Geneva

**MUSÉE DE L'HORLOGERIE**
15, Route de Malagnou  1208 Genève  Director: Cäsar Menz
☎ +41 22 4186470  📠 +41 22 4186471
Internet  http://www.geneva-online.ch/tourisme-culture/arts-spectacles/
expositions/geneve.htm
Open: Wednesday-Monday 10.00-17.00
Closed: Tuesday

**COLLECTION**

Renewed presentation of the permanent collections covering the 16th - 20th centuries: watches, mantel clocks, jewellery, snuff boxes, handiwork items, watchmaker's and enameller's tools, watch dials, educational hall on time as phenomenon.

© Musée de
l'Horlogerie, Genève

**EXHIBITIONS**

No exhibitions planned.

## Genève - Geneva

**PETIT PALAIS, MUSÉE D'ART MODERNE**
2, Terrasse Saint Victor  1206 Genève  President: Oscar Ghez
☎ +41 22 3461433  🖷 +41 22 3465315
Open: Daily 10.00-12.00 / 14.00-18.00
Saturday, Sunday 10.30-13.00 / 14.00-17.00

COLLECTION

The Petit Palais contains modern art from the period 1880-1930 by both famous and lesser-known artists. The collection illustrates the transitions and interconnections of the various movements. Beginning with Courbet, it includes works by Impressionists such as Manet, Monet, Sisley, Pissarro, Renoir, Degas, Cézanne, Berthe Morisot, Marie Bracquemond, Guillaumin, Whistler, Lebourg, Fantin-Latour, Caillebotte and Thaulow; the Post-Impressionists Albert André, Georges d'Espagnat, Moret, Montezin, Louis Carrand and Charreton; painters of the Nabi movement such as Gauguin, Sérusier, Maurice Denis, Bonnard, Vuillard, Meyer de Haan and others; Pointillists such as Seurat and his followers Luce, Cross, Angrand and Théo van Rysselberghe; the Fauvists Louis Valtat, Dufy, Friesz, Van Dongen, Matisse, Manguin, Puy, Camoin and August Chabaud, Larionov and Gontcharova; Montmartre artists such as Steinlen, Bottini, the engraver Galanis, Picasso, Edmond Heuzé, Suzanne Valadon and her son Maurice Utrillo, and Quizet. The Paris School is represented by the Cubists Braque, Fernand Léger, Juan Gris, La Fesnaye, Le Fauconnier, Henry Hayden, Kisling, Maria Blanchard and Marie Laurencin. 20th-century Primitives, or Naïfs, are exhibited ex-voto style in the crypt.

EXHIBITION

until mid Jun 97

*The Customs Official Rousseau and the French Naïve Painters of the 20th Century*

## Genève - Geneva

**MUSÉE RATH**
Place Neuve  1204 Genève  Director: Cäsar Menz
☎ +41 22 3105270  🖷 +41 22 3121858
Internet http://www.geneva-online.ch/tourisme-culture/arts-spectacles/expositions/geneve.htm
Open: Tuesday-Sunday 10.00-17.00  Wednesday 12.00-21.00
Closed: Monday

COLLECTION

Opened in 1828, the Musée Rath was the first Swiss museum devoted to the fine arts. Its mission was to exhibit and house original works of art and plaster casts used for the study of art. Since the inception of the Musée d'art et d'histoire, the Musée Rath, under its auspices, has been used exclusively for major exhibitions.

EXHIBITIONS

until 25·05·97

*Pierre Tal Coat*  This exhibition shows the diverse facets of the art of Tal-Coat (born 1905), from realism in the 1930s to his later expressionist works, with nearly 150 paintings, drawings and sculptures.

06·06·97-07·09·97

*Balthasar Burkhard*  The Bern photographer Balthasar Burkhard, working in black and white, has developed seemingly paradoxical parameters for his work: monumental treatment of intimate subjects, fragmentation of the oversized, and a tension between sensuality and objectivity.

25·09·97-11·01·98

*Moments from Eternity*  *Egyptian Objects in Private Collections in Switzerland*  More than 200 objects from ancient Egypt are on display, tracing the history of Egyptian civilisation from prehistoric times to the Roman period.

## Genève - Geneva

**MUSÉE D'HISTOIRE DES SCIENCES  VILLA BARTHOLONI**
**128, Rue de Lausanne  1202 Genève  Director: Cäsar Menz**
☎ **+41 22 7316985**  📠 **+41 22 7411308**
**Internet  http://www.geneva-online.ch/tourisme-culture/arts-spectacles/**
**expositions/geneve.htm**
**Open: Wednesday-Monday 13.00-17.00**
**Closed: Tuesday**

**COLLECTION**

Geneva boasts a collection of scientific instruments sufficiently important to merit its own museum. Historically, 18th-century Geneva was home to scholars, many from families of substantial means, whose keen interest in science led them to acquire scientific instruments from the finest manufacturers of the time in Europe. Over the years the collection has been steadily increased through acquisitions, and provides a broad picture of the evolution of science.

**EXHIBITION**
01·05·97-Spring 1998

*Genevan Scientific Instruments in the 19th Century*   After the Musée Académique was established in 1818, the production of scientific instruments in Geneva increased considerably, culminating with the establishment of the SIP (Societé Genevoise d'Instruments de Physique) at the end of the 19th century.

## Genève - Geneva

**MAISON TAVEL**
**6, Rue du Puits-Saint-Pierre  1204 Genève  Director: Cäsar Menz**
☎ **+41 22 3102900  Internet  http://www.geneva-online.ch/**
**tourisme-culture/arts-spectacles/expositions/geneve.htm**
**Open: Tuesday-Sunday 10.00-17.00**
**Closed: Monday**

**COLLECTION**

The oldest private residence in Geneva (13th-14th century), built by the patrician Tavel family and occupied over the centuries by a number of prominent Genevans, the Maison Tavel was acquired by the city in 1963 and, following extensive restoration, opened to the public in 1986.
This historic monument of national importance houses a museum devoted to the history of Geneva as a city, and to its domestic traditions. Objects, drawings, engravings and photographs, coins, furniture and silver illustrate Geneva's past from the Middle Ages to the beginning of the 20th century. An impressive historic model of the city shows it as it was in the times of Calvin and Rousseau.

**EXHIBITION**
19·06·97-04·01·98

*Francois d'Albert-Durade (1804-1886) and Henri Silvestre (1842-1900)* *Painters and Photographers of Old Geneva*   This exhibition presents paintings and drawings representing the old town and compares them to photographs taken by the same artists. The influence and the use of photography are revealed in their pictorial works, which are of a historical and documentary character.

## Lausanne

**MUSÉE CANTONAL DES BEAUX-ARTS**
Place de la Riponne 6  1014 Lausanne  Director: Jörg Zutter
☎ +41 21 3128332  🖷 +41 21 3209946
Open: Tuesday, Wednesday 11.00-18.00  Thursday 11.00-20.00
Friday-Sunday 11.00-17.00
Closed: Monday

COLLECTION

The Museum of Fine Arts houses the collections of the cantonal departments of painting, prints, drawings and sculpture. The emphasis is on Swiss paintings from 1750 through to 20th-century art. These works are permanently exhibited in the first three galleries. The Museum of Fine Arts has the world's largest collections of works by the famous watercolourist Louis Ducros (1748-1810), the academic painter Charles Gleyre (1806-1874), the highly respected wood engraver and painter Félix Valloton (1865-1925) and the 'art brut' artist Louis Sourter (1871-1942).

EXHIBITIONS

until 01·06·97

*Giovanni Giacometti*　Born in 1868, Giovanni Giacometti, the father of Alberto, was a major artist in his own right. His subjects are drawn from the mountain landscapes of Maloja, from his family and the village people.

15·06·97-14·09·97

*COBRA - Experimental Art 1948-1951*　*Painting, Sculpture and Drawing from the Post-War Period in Denmark, Belgium and the Netherlands*　This is the first exhibition in Switzerland dedicated to the COBRA group, consisting of Karel Appel, Asger Jorn, Carl-Henning Pedersen and Pierre Alechinsky.

28·09·97-11·01·98

*Contemporary Expression in Europe and the Unites States*
*Drawings and Prints from the Collection*　An exhibition featuring works by G. Brus, A. Rainer, F. Clemente, M. Raetz, T. Huber, Chuck Close, R. Tuttle, L. Weiner, B. Nauman and D. Oppenheim.

## Lugano

**MUSEO CANTONALE D'ARTE**
Via Canova 10  6900 Lugano  Director: Manuela Kahn-Rossi
☎ +41 91 9104780  🖷 +41 91 9104789
Open: Tuesday 14.00-17.00  Wednesday-Sunday 10.00-17.00
Closed: Monday

COLLECTION

In addition to several Renaissance works, the permanent collection of the museum consists of paintings, sculptures and graphic works of the 19th and 20th century and photographs of the 20th century. It aims to give an overview of the various art movements of the last two centuries, especially in relation to the Ticino Canton, which is situated strategically on one of the main routes between Northern and Southern Europe. The Ticinese artists of the 19th century include C.A. Meletta, V. Vela, A. Ciseri, F. Feragutti-Visconti, L. Rossi, E. Berta, F. Franzoni, L. Chialiva and F. Agnelli. The earlier part of the 20th century is represented by F. Boldini, C. Cotti, G. Gonzato, F. Filippini, S. Brignoni, R. Rossi and E. Dobrzansky, while contemporary artists include M. Cavalli, L. Bernasconi, R. Ferrari, F. Paolucci, N. Toroni and N. Snozzi.
There are also works from the internationally known 19th-century artists E. Degas, A. Renoir C. Pissarro and M. Rosso and turn-of-the-century works by the Swiss artists F. Hodler, C. Amiet and S. Righini. The present century is mainly represented by Avant-Garde artists who lived in Ticino for varying lengths of time. Besides O. Schlemmer, J. Arp, S. Taeuber-Arp, A. von Jawlenski, P. Klee,

M. von Werefkin, H. Richter, W. Varlin and J. Bissier, there are works by artists of the Swiss Expressionist group from the 1920s which was known as Rot-Blau.

The collection is completed by a number of works by artists belonging to two Italian movements: Novecento Italiano (C. Carrà, A. Funi and F. Casorati) and Corrente (R. Birolli and I. Valenti).

**EXHIBITIONS**

until 08·06·97

***Bruno Monguzzi*** *The Graphic Designer of the Museum*   This exhibition is dedicated to the graphic designer Bruno Monguzzi. Over the last ten years the design which he developed for the museum gained international recognition.

06·06·97-26·07·97

***A View of Contemporary Art***   *Unedited Works from the Panza di Biumo Donation*   The unedited portion of a gift of 200 works of art from Count Giuseppe Panza di Biumo to the Cantonal Museum of Art will be exhibited.

06·09·97-16·11·97

***Rabisch***   *The Grotesque and Profane in Art, 1550-1600*   The theme of the arabesque is treated in this exhibition, featuring works by Leonardo and his contemporaries, armours, and objects such as crystals, hard stones, clothing and tapestry.

29·11·97-02·02·98

***Fragile***   *18 Artists from Three Regions of Europe*   This exhibition presents works by artists from Ticino, Nord-Pas de Calais and Liverpool and shows a great diversity of attitudes and techniques.

## Lugano

**FONDAZIONE THYSSEN-BORNEMISZA**
**Villa Favorita  6976 Lugano-Castagnola  Director: Maria De Peverelli**
☎ **+41 91 9721741**  ⮌ **+41 91 9716151**
**Open: Apr - Oct  Friday-Sunday 10.00-17.00**
**Closed: Monday-Thursday and Nov - Mar**

**COLLECTION**

The Gallery of the Villa Favorita has been presenting an exhibit of about 150 European and American 19th and 20th-century paintings and watercolours from the Thyssen-Bornemisza Collection since 1992. A third of these works are 19th-century American paintings. They include works from 1835 to 1900 by the major exponents of Luminism and the Hudson River School of painting, as well as leading American Impressionists and Western painters such as Cole, Hassam, Hade, Kensett, Robinson, Twatchman and Wittredge. The remaining one hundred paintings illustrate the development of the art of the 20th century on both sides of the Atlantic through representative examples of every major style, including Cubism, German Expressionism, Russian Avant Garde, Dada, Surrealism, American Scene painting and Precessionism, Abstract Expressionism, Pop Art and Photorealism. The works include oil paintings, works on paper and some sculpture. Artists with works in the collection include Chashnik, de Chirico, Ernst, Freud, Itten, Larionov, Macke, Malevich, Marc, Masson, Munch, Nolde, Schiele, Benton, Davis, Demuth, Estes, Henri, Homer, Hopper, Marin, Parrish, Pollock, Shahn, Wesselmann and Wyeth.

**EXHIBITIONS**

No details available.

## Solothurn

**KUNSTMUSEUM SOLOTHURN**
**Werkhofstrasse 30 4500 Solothurn Director: Andre Kamber**
**☎ +41 65 222307 📠 +41 65 225001**
**Open: Thursday-Saturday 10.00-12.00 / 14.00-17.00 Tuesday 10.00-12.00 / 14.00-21.00 Sunday 10.00-17.00**
**Closed: Monday**

**COLLECTION**

The Solothurn Museum of Art unites the collections of the city, the art association and the Dübi-Müller, Josef Müller and Max Gubler foundations. Although the museum's collection is defined as Swiss, its first works were two small Medieval German paintings. A range of 19th-century Swiss art by Buchser, Fröhlicher, Hodler, Amiet, Trachsel, Berger and Gubler characterises the collection, though it also contains more European works of art by the likes of Degas, Van Gogh, Matisse, Braque, Gris and Léger.
Contemporary art is represented by the work of artists such as Roth, Thomkins, Eggenschwiler, Oppenheim, Luginbühl, Tinguely, R. Müller and Wiggli. The Kunstmuseum also houses a section devoted to Primitive art (in cooperation with the Musée Barbier-Müller in Geneva) and a section dedicated to the graphic arts - mainly new Swiss drawing.

**EXHIBITIONS**

until 19·05·97
***Kurt Blum*** *Photo Experiments*

until 01·06·97
***Product: Art!*** *What Happens to the Original?* This exhibition focuses on 'Edition MAT', launched in Paris in 1959 by Daniel Spoerri. 'Edition MAT' was the first exhibition of multiplied three-dimensional objects.

15·06·97-10·08·97
***Selections from the Museum's Recent Acquisitions/Distinction for Martin Disler*** This exhibition highlights trends that play an important role in the most recent acquisitions. One part of the exhibition honours the memory of Martin Disler, who was a friend and patron of the museum.

23·08·97-28·09·97
***4 Hüppi*** Rather than a retrospective of his work, Alfonso Hüppi proposed an exhibition together with his wife Brigitta and his sons Thaddäus and Johannes.

18·10·97-04·01·98
***The Chamber Orchestra*** *An Exhibition Organised by Michael Biberstein, Roberto Medici, Hanspeter Rederlechner and Percy Slanec* This exhibition honours retiring conservator Andre Kamber, whose contact with Swiss artists has had a major impact on the museum.

01·03·98 onwards
***Art of the Steppe*** *Ornaments and Tomb Offerings of the Former Steppe People Living between the Caucasus and China*
The exhibition focuses on the nomads who inhabited the Asiatic steppe beginning in the first half of the first millennium BC.

## Vevey

**SWISS CAMERA MUSEUM**
**6, Ruelle des Anciens-Fosses 1800 Vevey Director: P. & J-M. Bonnard Yersin**
**☎ +41 21 9219460 📠 +41 21 9216458**
**Open: Daily Mar-Oct 10.30-12.00 / 14.00-17.30 Nov-Feb 14.00-17.30**

**COLLECTION**

The museum is housed in a refurbished 18th-century building, combining old and modern architecture. Each floor, with its own theme, has a different colour. The basement, or level 1, is yellow and contains studio cameras, laboratory equipment and other photographic items.

The blue level 0 displays cameras arranged according to country of origin. The red level 1 has a chronological display of stereoscopic cameras. Level 2, grey, houses regularly changing exhibitions, and the attic, level 3, features the exhibition on projection, ranging from magic lanterns to state-of-the-art projectors.

One notable exhibit is the Leica showcase that displays the work of Oscar Barnack: almost inadvertently, he invented the Leica 35mm still camera while trying to develop a prototype for 35mm motion film without wasting too much film. Other notable exhibits include Le Compass, a technical marvel manufactured by the watchmakers Le Coultre, and an amazing panoramic camera with a 360 degree image produced by Alpa.

**EXHIBITIONS**

until 19·05·97    ***The Cameras of the Pioneers***    The cameras of the Swiss cinematography pioneers François-Henri Lavanchy-Clarke and Casimir Sivan, accompanied by a video presentation of the first projections in Switzerland.

until 19·05·97    ***The Swiss Photography Foundation***    This exhibition of works from the Foundation, housed in the Zurich Kunsthaus, contains photographs by Swiss and foreign artists.

29·05·97-26·10·97    ***Hans Knuchel***    This Zurich artist produces unique photographs by means of specially constructed cameras, called 'Loch Cameras' (hole cameras), which accompany the exhibition.

06·11·97 onwards    ***Dance***   *Serge Borner, Photographer*    Fascinated by the posters of the dance company 'Les Nomades', the museum introduces the photographer who made them. Dance carte blanche with Serge Borner!

## Winterthur

**MUSEUM OSKAR REINHART AM STADTGARTEN**
Stadthausstraße 6   8400 Winterthur   Director: Peter Wegmann
☎ +41 52 2675172   📠 +41 52 2676228
Open: Tuesday-Sunday 10.00-17.00
Closed: Monday

**COLLECTION**    The collection is housed in the Old Gymnasium, built by Leonhard Zeugheer between 1838 and 1842, and includes around 600 works by German, Swiss and Austrian artists from the 18th to the 20th century. Swiss painting is especially well represented with work from Liotard to Füssli, Graff, Wolf, Agasse, Töpffer, Calame, Menn, Böcklin and Anker up to Hodler, Segantini and Amiet. The art of German Romanticism (Friedrich, Runge, Kersting, Blechen, Schwind, Spitzweg), Realism and Idealism (Waldmüller, Menzel, Thoma, Leibl, Trübner, Feuerbach, Marées) as well as Impressionism (Uhde, Liebermann, Slevogt) also form focal points.

**EXHIBITION**

until-Nov 98    ***The Oskar Reinhart Collection Am Römerholz***    Due to the renovation of the building, the fabulous French holdings of the Oskar Reinhart Collection Am Römerholz will be on display in this house. A unique opportunity to see all of Oskar Reinhart's works reassembled.

# Zug

**KUNSTHAUS ZUG**
Dorfstrasse 27  6301 Zug  Director: Matthias Haldemann
☎ +41 41 7111150  📠 +41 41 7104465
Open: Tuesday-Friday 12.00-18.00  Saturday-Sunday 10.00-17.00
Closed: Monday

COLLECTION | The focus of the collection is on objects belonging to the realms of Surrealism and Fantastic art, and includes the works of such artists as Moeschlin, Seligmann, Von Moos, Ballmer, Jacob, Kuhn, Weber, Wipf and Wölffli. In addition, the collection contains various works from the Viennese sculptor Fritz Wotruba (1907-1975), figurative Swiss sculptures, concrete art and art from central Switzerland. The various parts of the collection are alternatingly on display and can be viewed at regular intervals.

EXHIBITIONS

until 25·05·97 | **Fantastically Surreal**   *The Collection*

until 25·05·97 | **Tadashi Kawamata**   *Work in Progress in Zug*

08·06·97-31·08·97 | **Richard Tuttle**   *Replace the Abstract Picture Plane*

14·09·97-09·11·97 | **Peter Stein**   *Works 1957-1997*

26·09·97-09·11·97 | **Grant and Scholarship Contributions of the Canton of Zug 1997**

23·11·97-31·01·98 | **Kurt Seligmann**   *Retrospective*

# Zürich

**FOUNDATION E.G. BÜHRLE COLLECTION**
Zollikerstrasse 172  8008 Zürich  Director: Christian Bührle
☎ +41 1 4220086  📠 +41 1 4220347
Open: Tuesday and Friday 14.00-17.00  Wednesday 17.00-20.00
Closed: Monday, Thursday, Saturday, Sunday

COLLECTION | The Emil G. Bührle Collection is a private art collection exhibited in a 19th-century villa. It comprises Medieval wood carvings and paintings by the old masters, but above all works by French artists of the 19th and 20th century.

Vincent van Gogh
*The sower, Arles*
*1888*
© Foundation E.G.
Bührle Collection,
Zürich

The French Impressionists form a nucleus embracing eight works by Manet, seven each by Cézanne and Van Gogh and five by Gauguin. The collection includes the trio of portraits by Cézanne consisting of 'The Artist's Wife in an Armchair', the 'Self-Portrait with Palette' and 'The Boy in the Red Waistcoat'. In addition, there are works of Monet, Renoir, Pissarro, Sisely, Degas and Toulouse-Lautrec as well as works by the Nabis, the Fauves and the Cubists.

The 18th-century Venetian school is represented by Canaletto, Guardi and Tiepolo. The Dutch Baroque paintings include the 'Portrait of a Man' by Frans Hals.
Thirty sculptures from the 12th to the 16th century are also on display.

**EXHIBITIONS**    No exhibitions planned

## Zürich

**HAUS FÜR KONSTRUKTIVE UND KONKRETE KUNST**
Seefeldstrasse 317  8008 Zürich  Curator: Elisabeth Grossmann
☎ +41 1 3813808  📠 +41 1 3820592
Open: Tuesday-Friday 10.00-12.00 / 14.00-17.00  Saturday, Sunday 10.00-17.00
Closed: Monday

**COLLECTION**    The heart of the display is the long-term presentation of an 'imaginary collection' of the Zürich Concrete artists, in particular Bill, Glarner, Graeser, Hinterreiter, Loewensberg and Lohse. All of them participated to a large extent in the development of Constructivist art in Zürich; their influence can still be felt in contemporary art.
The exhibition is changed once a year; it is created through the collaboration with collectors and museums and the relevant curators.
Besides works by Graeser and Lohse, young swiss and foreign artists are also represented.

**EXHIBITIONS**

| | |
|---|---|
| until 18·05·97 | *Paul Talman*   Painter, Sculptor, Designer |
| until 05·10·97 | *Bill-Glarner-Graeser-Hinterreiter-Loewensberg-Lohse* |
| 30·05·97-27·07·97 | *Mary Heilman*   American Abstract Paintings |
| 08·08·97-05·10·97 | *Gottfried Honegger*   Retrospective |
| 24·10·97-11·01·98 | *Schweiz Konstruktiv 1960-1997* |
| 23·01·98-29·03·98 | *Richard Anuszkiewicz*   A Representative of Op Art |
| 23·01·98 onwards | *Bill-Glarner-Graeser-Hinterreiter-Loewensberg-Lohse* |
| 10·04·98-07·06·98 | *Tadaaki Kuwayama* |

## Zürich

**KUNSTHAUS ZÜRICH**
Helmplatz 1  8024 Zürich  Director: Felix Baumann
☎ +41 1 2516765  📠 +41 1 2512464
Open: Tuesday-Thursday 10.00-21.00  Friday-Sunday 10.00-17.00
Closed: Monday and 1 Aug

**COLLECTION**    **Old Masters**   A selection of sculptures and paintings, mainly by the Masters of Carnation, represents Medieval art. Pictures from the Ruzicka and Koetser Foundations highlight the Baroque period. A comprehensive department is devoted to Zürich painting after the Reformation, culminating in the work of Saloman Gessner and Henry Fuseli.
**Swiss Artists**   This representative collection includes works by Koller, Zünd, Böcklin, Welti, Segantini, Hodler, Augusto Giacometti,

Vallotton, Amiet and Giovanni Giacometti. It also covers the realistic and surrealistic figuration of the inter-war period, Zürich 'concrete art' and post-1945 sculpture.

**Classical Moderns**   Works by Edvard Munch, Kokoschka, Beckmann, Corinth, Matisse (mainly sculpture), Picasso, Max Ernst and Miró are on display in this collection.

**New Tendencies**   Examples on display include works by Baselitz, Penck and Kiefer, Bacon, Disler and Cucchi.

**Graphic Art Collection**   A collection of approx. 80 000 prints and drawings, including Old Master drawings, Swiss landscape drawing, 20th-century art, works of Zero movements and Minimal and Conceptual art.

**Swiss Foundation of Photography**   The works of Swiss and foreign photographers, both past and present, can be admired in this display, as well as a collection of original photographic prints and publications.

Hans Arp (1886-1966)
*The entombment of the birds and butterflies*
*Portrait of Tristan Tzara, 1916-17*
© Kunsthaus Zürich, Zürich

**EXHIBITIONS**

until 01·06·97   ***The Caprice as Artistic Principle***   *The Pre-history of Modernism from Arcimboldo to Callot, Tiepolo to Goya*   The caprice as artistic principle blossomed during Mannerism; a product of the inherent tension between fabrication and naturalistic representation. A variation of whimsical fantasy and a combination of real and fictitious elements, the caprice remains an elusive tradition.

16·05·97-29·06·97   ***I. Simon Patterson***   *Drawings*

06·06·97-24·08·97   ***Zürich 97, A Photograph Portrait***

18·06·97-07·09·97   ***Birth of the Cool***   *American Painting from Georgia O'Keeffe to Christopher Wool*   The works of art presented in this exhibition emphasise the currency, richness and refinement of the American 'tradition in painting' - a tradition that is both sensual and severe and open to the emotionality of modern society.

18·07·97-31·08·97   ***Maria Eichhorn***   *Drawings*

22·08·97-09·11·97   ***Christian Schad (1894-1982)***   The term 'Neue Sachlichkeit' (New Objectivity) is used to describe the intensely neo-realistic artistic style which emerged in Germany in the 1920s. Today, Christian Schad is considered the absolute master of this style.

05·09·97-26·10·97   ***Christian Marclay***   *Preis für junge Kunst der Zürcher Kunstgesellschaft 1997*

19·09·97-02·11·97   ***Gary Simmons***   *Drawings*

03·10·97-18·01·98   ***Arnold Böcklin - Giorgio de Chirico - Max Ernst***   *A Journey into the Unknown*   Böcklin - de Chirico - Ernst, these three highly poetic painters find common ground through the creative exploration of their archetypal dreams, fantasies and visions. The major works of the three artists have been collected here for our post-modern, post surrealistic eyes to examine and contemplate.

07·11·97-04·01·98 | **Walter Bosshard**  *A Pioneer of International Press Photography*

## Zürich

**SCHWEIZERISCHES LANDESMUSEUM**
**THE SWISS NATIONAL MUSEUM**
Museumstrasse 2  8023 Zürich  Director: Mr. Furger
☎ +41 1 2186511  📠 +41 1 2112949
Open: Tuesday-Sunday 10.00-17.00
Closed: Monday

**COLLECTION**

The Swiss National Museum, which was opened in 1898 and housed in a building designed by Gustav Gull, displays the cultural diversity of Switzerland with exhibits dating from the Stone Age to the 19th century. The museum's collections cover prehistoric and early history, weapons, gold, silver, copper and brass work, pewter and ceramic artefacts, textiles and costumes, jewellery, coins, medallions and seals.

View of the entrance
of the SLM from the
station side
© *Schweizerisches
Landesmuseum,
Zürich*

The museum also features glass painting, painting and sculpture, furniture and interiors, watches and musical instruments. The National Museum houses Ferdinand Hodler's famous 'Retreat of the Swiss Confederates at Marignano' (1899-1900). A number of special collections such as catalogues and photographs can be viewed by appointment only. The museum's library has restricted lending facilities.

**EXHIBITIONS**
until 29·06·97

*Swiss Modedesign 1972-1997*

24·10·97-25·01·98

*The Alamans*

# Zürich

**MUSEUM RIETBERG ZÜRICH - VILLA WESENDONCK - PARK-VILLA RIETER**
Gablerstraße 15  8002 Zürich  Director: Eberhard Fischer
☎ +41 1 2024528  ⊠ +41 1 2025201
Open: Tuesday-Sunday 10.00-17.00
Closed: Monday
Branch: Haus zum Kiel  Hirschengraben 20  8001 Zürich
☎ +41 1 2619652  ⊠ +41 1 2025201
Open: Tuesday-Saturday 13.00-17.00  Sunday 10.00-17.00
Closed:Monday

**COLLECTION**

The Museum Rietberg, located in Rieter Park, is a small museum with important works of art from Asia, Africa, the Americas and Oceania. Built in 1857, the Villa Wesendonck was the social and cultural centre of Zürich for many years. The internationally recognised sculptures bequeathed to the City of Zürich by Baron Eduard von der Heydt constitute the core of the permanent collection. Two to three special exhibitions of international significance are presented each year.

The Museum Rietberg presents its collection of Asian painting in the Park-Villa Rieter, which is also located in Rieter Park. The associated 'Haus zum Kiel', a small gallery located in the heart of Zürich, is used by the museum for temporary exhibitions.

**EXHIBITIONS**

[MUSEUM RIETBERG: VILLA WESENDONCK]

04·05·97-14·09·97

*Mexico    The Precolumbian Cultures on the Gulf of Mexico*

23·11·97-08·02·98

*Indian Painting from Rajasthan    The Royal Collection of the Maharaja of Kota*

[HAUS ZUM KIEL]

until 08·06·97

*India Observed    Three Swiss Artists in India: Juliet Brown, Alice Boner, Georgette Boner*

11·07·97-05·10·97

*The Artist as Collector    African Masks from the Charles Hug's Collection*

24·10·97-08·02·98

*Nainsukh    A Great Indian Painter of the 18th Century*

# INDEX
## Cities

MUSEUM MEDIA PUBLISHERS

Cities in alphabetical order by country.

Cities in alphabetical order by country.

Cities in alphabetical order by country.

Cities in alphabetical order by country.

Cities in alphabetical order by country.

Cities in alphabetical order by country.

Cities in alphabetical order by country.

Cities in alphabetical order by country.

| THE NETHERLANDS | | | |
|---|---|---|---|
| CITY | MUSEUM | PICTURE | PAGE |
| Eindhoven | Stedelijk Van Abbemuseum | | 313 |
| Enschede | Rijksmuseum Twenthe | ▣ | 314 |
| Gouda | Catharina Gasthuis | ▣ | 314 |
| Groningen | Groninger Museum | | 315 |
| Haarlem | Frans Halsmuseum | ▣ | 317 |
| Haarlem | Teylers Museum | ▣ | 318 |
| Heerlen | Stadsgalerij Heerlen | ▣ | 319 |
| 's-Hertogenbosch | Noordbrabants Museum | | 320 |
| Laren | Singer Museum | ▣ | 321 |
| Leeuwarden | Fries Museum | | 322 |
| Leeuwarden | Princessehof (Keramiekmuseum het) | | 322 |
| Leiden | De Lakenhal (Stedelijk Museum) | | 324 |
| Leiden | Oudheden (Rijksmuseum van) Museum of Antiquities | | 323 |
| Leiden | Volkenkunde (Rijksmuseum voor) | | 324 |
| Maastricht | Bonnefantenmuseum | ▣ | 325 |
| Middelburg | Zeeuws Museum | | 326 |
| Nijmegen | Commanderie Sint-Jan (Nijmeegs Museum) | | 326 |
| Nijmegen | Provinciaal Museum G.M. Kam | | 327 |
| Otterlo | Kröller-Müller Museum | ▣ | 328 |
| Rotterdam | Boijmans-Van Beuningen (Museum) | ▣ | 329 |
| Rotterdam | Kunsthal Rotterdam | | 330 |
| Rotterdam | Maritiem Museum 'Prins Hendrik' | | 331 |
| Rotterdam | NAI Nederlands Architectuurinstituut Architecture | | 333 |
| Rotterdam | Natuurmuseum Rotterdam | | 332 |
| Rotterdam | Witte de With Center for Contemporary Art | | 334 |
| Schiedam | Stedelijk Museum Schiedam | | 334 |
| Tilburg | De Pont Foundation for Contemporary Art | ▣ | 335 |
| Utrecht | Catharijneconvent (Museum) | | 336 |
| Utrecht | Centraal Museum Utrecht | | 336 |
| Zwolle | Stedelijk Museum Zwolle | | 337 |

| PORTUGAL | | | |
|---|---|---|---|
| CITY | MUSEUM | PICTURE | PAGE |
| Cascais | Condes de Castro Guimarães (Museu) | | 338 |
| Coimbra | Nacional de Machado de Castro (Museu) | | 339 |
| Lisboa - Lisbon | Calouste Gulbenkian (Museu) | | 341 |
| Lisboa - Lisbon | Do Chiado (Museu) | | 342 |
| Lisboa - Lisbon | Centro de Arte Moderna J. de Azeredo Perdigão | | 343 |
| Lisboa - Lisbon | Nacional de Arqueologia (Museu) | | 339 |
| Lisboa - Lisbon | Nacional de Arte Antiga (Museu) | ▣ | 340 |
| Lisboa - Lisbon | Nacional do Azulejo (Museu) | | 341 |
| Porto | Fundação de Serralves | ▣ | 344 |

| SPAIN | | | |
|---|---|---|---|
| CITY | MUSEUM | PICTURE | PAGE |
| Barcelona | Centre d'Art Santa Monica | | 352 |
| Barcelona | Frederic Marès Museum | | 350 |
| Barcelona | Fundació Antoni Tàpies | ▣ | 348 |
| Barcelona | Joan Miró Foundation | | 350 |
| Barcelona | Museo de Cerámica | ▣ | 349 |
| Barcelona | Museu d'Art de Catalunya | | 348 |
| Barcelona | Museu d'Art Modern (MNAC) | | 351 |
| Barcelona | Museu Picasso | | 351 |
| Bilbao | Museo de Bellas Artes de Bilbao | ▣ | 352 |
| Burgos | Museo de Burgos | | 353 |
| Cádiz | Museo de Cádiz | | 354 |
| Cordoba | Museo Arqueológico | | 354 |
| Cordoba | Museo de Bellas Artes | | 355 |
| Cuenca | Museo de Arte Abstracto Español | | 355 |
| Figueres | Dali Theatre-Museum | | 356 |

Cities in alphabetical order by country.

# INDEX

# Museums

MUSEUM MEDIA PUBLISHERS

**Museums in alphabetical order by country.**

## AUSTRIA

| MUSEUM | CITY | PICTURE | PAGE |
|---|---|---|---|
| Akademie der Bildenden Künste (Gemäldegalerie der) | Wien - Vienna | ● | 8 |
| Belvedere (Österreichische Galerie) | Wien - Vienna | ● | 9 |
| Graphische Sammlung Albertina | Wien - Vienna | ● | 9 |
| Joanneum (Alte Galerie des Steiermärkischen Landesm.) | Graz | ● | 4 |
| Joanneum, Bild- und Tonarchiv (Landesmuseum) | Graz | | 5 |
| Kunstforum Bank Austria | Wien - Vienna | ● | 10 |
| KunstHausWien | Wien - Vienna | ● | 11 |
| Kunsthistorisches Museum | Wien - Vienna | | 11 |
| Ludwig Wien (Museum moderner Kunst Stiftung) | Wien - Vienna | ● | 12 |
| Neue Galerie der Stadt Linz (Wolfgang-Gurlitt-Museum) | Linz | ● | 6 |
| Residenzgalerie Salzburg | Salzburg | | 6 |
| Rupertinum | Salzburg | | 7 |
| Tiroler Volkskunstmuseum | Innsbruck | | 5 |
| Völkerkunde (Museum für) | Wien - Vienna | ● | 14 |
| Volkskunde (Österreichisches Museum für) | Wien - Vienna | ● | 15 |
| Wiener Secession | Wien - Vienna | | 16 |

## BELGIUM

| MUSEUM | CITY | PICTURE | PAGE |
|---|---|---|---|
| Ansembourg (Musée d') | Liège - Luik | | 33 |
| Arentshuis (The Brangwyn Museum) | Brugge - Bruges | | 23 |
| Arts Anciens du Namurois (Musée des) | Namur | | 34 |
| Beaux-Arts (Musée des) | Charleroi | | 28 |
| Beaux-Arts (Palais des) | Bruxelles - Brussels | | 25 |
| Beeldhouwkunst Middelheim (Openluchtmuseum voor) | Antwerpen - Antwerp | | 20 |
| Dhondt-Dhaenens (Museum) | Deurle | | 30 |
| Etnografisch Museum | Antwerpen - Antwerp | ● | 17 |
| Groeninge Museum | Brugge - Bruges | ● | 23 |
| Gruuthuse Museum | Brugge - Bruges | | 24 |
| Hedendaagse Kunst (Museum van) | Gent - Ghent | | 30 |
| Mariemont (Musée Royal de) | Morlanwelz | ● | 33 |
| Mayer van den Bergh (Museum) | Antwerpen - Antwerp | ● | 19 |
| Memling Museum | Brugge - Bruges | | 24 |
| MIAT (Museum for Industrial Archaeology and Textiles) | Gent - Ghent | | 31 |
| Midden-Afrika (Koninklijk Museum voor) | Tervuren | ● | 36 |
| Musical Instruments (Brussels Museum of) | Bruxelles - Brussels | | 25 |
| Natuurwetenschappen (Museum Kon. Belg. Inst. voor) | Bruxelles - Brussels | | 26 |
| Photographie (Musée de la) | Charleroi | | 29 |
| Plantin-Moretus (Museum) | Antwerpen - Antwerp | ● | 21 |
| PMMK - Museum voor Moderne Kunst | Oostende - Ostend | ● | 35 |
| Royaux des Beaux Arts de Belgique (Musée) | Bruxelles - Brussels | ● | 27 |
| Royaux d'Art et d'Histoire (Musée) | Bruxelles - Brussels | ● | 26 |
| Rubenshuis | Antwerpen - Antwerp | | 22 |
| Scheepvaartmuseum (Nationaal) | Antwerpen - Antwerp | | 19 |
| Schone Kunsten (Koninklijk Museum voor) | Antwerpen - Antwerp | ● | 18 |
| Schone Kunsten (Museum voor) | Gent - Ghent | ● | 31 |
| Sierkunst en Vormgeving (Museum voor) | Gent - Ghent | ● | 32 |
| Stedelijk Prentenkabinet | Antwerpen - Antwerp | | 22 |

## FRANCE

| MUSEUM | CITY | PICTURE | PAGE |
|---|---|---|---|
| Abbaye Saint Germain | Auxerre | | 47 |
| Adrien Dubouché (Musée National) | Limoges | ● | 68 |
| Alsacien (Musée) | Strasbourg | ● | 103 |
| Ancienne Abbaye Saint-Vaast (Musée d'Arras) | Arras | | 46 |
| Antiquités Nationales (Musée des) | Saint-Germain-en-Laye | ● | 100 |
| ARC-Musée d'Art Moderne de la Ville de Paris | Paris | | 79 |
| Archeologique de Cimiez (Musée) | Nice | | 75 |
| Archéologique de Dijon (Musée) | Dijon | ● | 59 |
| Archéologique (Musée) | Strasbourg | ● | 104 |
| Art Moderne (Musée d') | Céret | | 54 |

Museums in alphabetical order by country.

### FRANCE

| MUSEUM | CITY | PICTURE | PAGE |
|---|---|---|---|
| Art Moderne (Musée d') | Saint-Etienne | | 100 |
| Art Moderne (Musée d') | Villeneuve d'Ascq | | 110 |
| Arts Asiatiques - Guimet (Musée National des) | Paris | ▣ | 81 |
| Arts Décoratifs (Musée des) | Bordeaux | ▣ | 51 |
| Arts Décoratifs (Musée des) | Lyon | | 70 |
| Arts Décoratifs (Musée des) | Paris | ▣ | 80 |
| Arts Décoratifs (Musée des) | Strasbourg | ▣ | 104 |
| Arts et Traditions Populaires (Musée National des) | Paris | | 80 |
| Augustins (Musée des) | Toulouse | | 106 |
| Beaux Arts et de la Dentelle (Musée des) | Calais | | 53 |
| Beaux Arts (Musée des) | Nantes | | 74 |
| Beaux-Arts et d'Archéologie (Musée des) | Besançon | ▣ | 48 |
| Beaux-Arts et de la Dentelle (Musée des) | Alençon | ▣ | 42 |
| Beaux-Arts (Musée des) | Agen | | 40 |
| Beaux-Arts (Musée des) | Angers | | 43 |
| Beaux-Arts (Musée des) | Angoulême | | 44 |
| Beaux-Arts (Musée des) | Bordeaux | | 50 |
| Beaux-Arts (Musée des) | Caen | | 52 |
| Beaux-Arts (Musée des) | Chambéry | | 56 |
| Beaux-Arts (Musée des) | Chartres | | 57 |
| Beaux-Arts (Musée des) | Dijon | ▣ | 59 |
| Beaux-Arts (Musée des) | Lille | | 67 |
| Beaux-Arts (Musée des) | Lyon | | 69 |
| Beaux-Arts (Musée des) | Marseille | | 71 |
| Beaux-Arts (Musée des) | Nancy | | 73 |
| Beaux-Arts (Musée des) | Nice | | 75 |
| Beaux-Arts (Musée des) | Orléans | | 79 |
| Beaux-Arts (Musée des) | Reims | | 98 |
| Beaux-Arts (Musée des) | Rennes | | 98 |
| Beaux-Arts (Musée des) | Rouen | | 99 |
| Beaux-Arts (Musée des) | Strasbourg | ▣ | 105 |
| Beaux-Arts (Musée des) | Tours | | 107 |
| Beaux-Arts (Musée des) | Valenciennes | | 108 |
| Bonnat (Musée) | Bayonne | | 48 |
| Cantini/Art Moderne et Contemporain | Marseille | | 71 |
| capcMusée d'Art Contemporain | Bordeaux | | 50 |
| Carnavalet (Musée) | Paris | | 82 |
| Carré d'Art-Musée d'Art Contemporain | Nîmes | | 78 |
| Céramique (Musée National de) | Sèvres | | 103 |
| Chartreuse (Musée de la) | Douai | ▣ | 62 |
| Château de Pau (Musée National du) | Pau | | 96 |
| Cognacq-Jay Museum | Paris | | 82 |
| Condé (Musée) | Chantilly | | 56 |
| Consortium (Le) | Dijon | | 61 |
| Départemental d'Art Ancien et Contemporain (Musée) | Épinal | | 64 |
| Dupuy (Musée Paul) | Toulouse | | 107 |
| Eugène Boudin (Musée) | Honfleur | | 67 |
| Fabre (Musée) | Montpellier | | 73 |
| Faure (Musée) | Aix-les-Bains | | 41 |
| Fernand Léger (Musée National) | Biot | | 49 |
| Fontainebleau (Musee National du Château de) | Fontainebleau | ▣ | 65 |
| FRAC Limousin | Limoges | | 69 |
| Goya (Musée) | Castres | | 54 |
| Grand Palais (Galeries Nationales du) | Paris | | 83 |
| Granet (Musée) | Aix-en-Provence | | 40 |
| Grenoble (Musée de) | Grenoble | | 66 |
| Histoire Naturelle (Muséum National d') | Paris | | 89 |
| Ile de France (Musée de l') | Sceaux | ▣ | 102 |
| Ingres (Musée) | Montauban | | 72 |
| Jacquemart-André (Musée) | Paris | ▣ | 83 |
| Jeu de Paume (Galerie Nationale du) | Paris | | 84 |
| Louvre (Musée du) | Paris | ▣ | 85 |
| Maeght (Fondation) | Saint-Paul | | 101 |

Museums in alphabetical order by country.

## FRANCE

| MUSEUM | CITY | PICTURE | PAGE |
|---|---|---|---|
| Magnin (Musée) | Dijon | | 62 |
| Marine (Musée de la) | Paris | | 86 |
| Marmottan (Musée) | Paris | | 87 |
| Matisse (Musée) | Nice | ▣ | 76 |
| Mode et du Textile (Musée de la) | Paris | | 87 |
| Modern and Contemporary Art (Museum of) | Nice | ▣ | 77 |
| Moyen Age (Musée National du)/Thermes de Cluny | Paris | ▣ | 88 |
| Nicéphore Niépce (Musée) | Chalon-sur-Saône | ▣ | 55 |
| Normandie (Musée de) | Caen | | 52 |
| Oeuvre Notre-Dame (Musée de l') | Strasbourg | ▣ | 105 |
| Orangerie (Musée National de l') | Paris | ▣ | 89 |
| Orsay (Musée d') | Paris | ▣ | 90 |
| Périgord (Musée du) | Périgueux | | 97 |
| Petit Palais (Musée du) | Avignon | ▣ | 47 |
| Petit Palais (Musée du) | Paris | | 91 |
| Photographie (Centre National de la) | Paris | ▣ | 92 |
| Picardie (Musée de) | Amiens | ▣ | 42 |
| Picasso (Musée) | Antibes | | 45 |
| Picasso (Musée) | Paris | ▣ | 93 |
| Pompidou (Centre National d'Art et Culture Georges) | Paris | | 94 |
| Réattu (Musée) | Arles | | 45 |
| Renaissance (Musée National de la) | Écouen | ▣ | 63 |
| Rigaud (Musée Hyacinthe) | Perpignan | | 97 |
| Rodin (Musée) | Paris | | 95 |
| Sciences et de l'Industrie (La Cité des) | Paris | ▣ | 95 |
| Thomas Henry (Musée) | Cherbourg | ▣ | 58 |
| Tissus (Musée des) | Lyon | | 70 |
| Toulouse-Lautrec (Musée) | Albi | | 41 |
| Unterlinden (Musée d') | Colmar | | 58 |
| Versailles et de Trianon (Château de) | Versailles | | 109 |

## GERMANY

| MUSEUM | CITY | PICTURE | PAGE |
|---|---|---|---|
| Abteiberg (Städtisches Museum) | Mönchengladbach | | 172 |
| Alte Meister (Gemäldegalerie) | Dresden | ▣ | 139 |
| Alte Nationalgalerie | Berlin | ▣ | 116 |
| Alte Pinakothek | München - Munich | ▣ | 172 |
| Angewandte Kunst (Museum für) | Köln - Cologne | | 161 |
| Antikensammlung | Berlin | | 117 |
| Antikensammlungen und Glyptothek (Staatliche) | München - Munich | | 173 |
| Archäologie/M. Kaiserpfalz (Westfälisches Museum für) | Paderborn | ▣ | 182 |
| Architektur-Museum (Deutsches) | Frankfurt am Main | | 146 |
| Augustinermuseum | Freiburg im Breisgau | | 149 |
| Badisches Landesmuseum | Karlsruhe | ▣ | 157 |
| Bauhaus-Archiv / M. für Gestaltung | Berlin | ▣ | 118 |
| Berlinische Galerie/M. Kunst Photographie und Arch. | Berlin | | 119 |
| Brücke-Museum | Berlin | | 119 |
| Die Neue Sammlung | München - Munich | | 177 |
| Ehrenhof (Kunstmuseum Düsseldorf im) | Düsseldorf | | 142 |
| Focke-Museum M. für Kunst und Kulturgeschichte | Bremen | | 133 |
| Folkwang Essen (Museum) | Essen | | 144 |
| Galerie der Stadt Esslingen | Esslingen | | 145 |
| Galerie der Stadt Stuttgart | Stuttgart | | 186 |
| Gemäldegalerie | Berlin | ▣ | 121 |
| Gemäldegalerie Alte Meister | Kassel | | 159 |
| Germanisches Nationalmuseum | Nürnberg - Nuremberg | ▣ | 180 |
| Gutenberg-Museum Mainz | Mainz | ▣ | 168 |
| Hamburger Kunsthalle | Hamburg | | 151 |
| Haus der Kunst | München - Munich | | 174 |
| Herzog Anton Ulrich Museum | Braunschweig | | 133 |
| Hessisches Landesmuseum | Darmstadt | | 135 |
| Hessisches Landesmuseum | Kassel | | 159 |

Museums in alphabetical order by country.

Museums in alphabetical order by country.

Museums in alphabetical order by country.

### GREAT BRITAIN

| MUSEUM | CITY | PICTURE | PAGE |
|---|---|---|---|
| Portrait Gallery (National) | London | ▣ | 227 |
| Royal Cornwall Museum | Truro | | 242 |
| Royal Museum of Scotland (National M. of Scotland) | Edinburgh | ▣ | 209 |
| Russell-Cotes Art Gallery and Museum | Bournemouth | ▣ | 199 |
| Sainsbury Centre for Visual Arts | Norwich | ▣ | 237 |
| Scottish National Gallery of Modern Art | Edinburgh | ▣ | 211 |
| Scottish National Portrait Gallery | Edinburgh | | 210 |
| Serpentine Gallery (The) | London | | 228 |
| Sir John Soane's Museum | London | | 229 |
| Southampton City Art Gallery | Southampton | ▣ | 239 |
| Tate Gallery | London | ▣ | 229 |
| Tate Gallery Liverpool | Liverpool | | 217 |
| Tate Gallery St. Ives | St. Ives | ▣ | 241 |
| Ulster Museum | Belfast | | 196 |
| Victoria and Albert Museum | London | | 230 |
| Wakefield Art Gallery | Wakefield | | 243 |
| Walker Art Gallery | Liverpool | | 218 |
| Wallace Collection (The) | London | | 231 |
| Whitechapel Art Gallery | London | | 231 |
| Wordsworth Museum (The) | Grasmere | | 214 |
| York City Art Gallery | York | ▣ | 243 |
| Yorkshire Museum | York | | 244 |

### IRELAND

| MUSEUM | CITY | PICTURE | PAGE |
|---|---|---|---|
| Modern Art (Irish Museum of) | Dublin | | 246 |
| National Gallery of Ireland | Dublin | ▣ | 247 |
| National Museum of Ireland | Dublin | | 248 |

### ITALY

| MUSEUM | CITY | PICTURE | PAGE |
|---|---|---|---|
| Accademia Carrara | Bergamo | ▣ | 252 |
| Casa Buonarroti | Firenze - Florence | ▣ | 257 |
| Castello del Buonconsiglio | Trento | ▣ | 284 |
| Castello Di Rivoli M. D'Arte Cont. | Torino - Turin | ▣ | 280 |
| Civico M. di Storia ed Arte e Orto Lapidario | Trieste | | 285 |
| Fondazione Italiana per La Fotografia | Torino - Turin | | 283 |
| Fondazione Magnani Rocca | Parma | | 271 |
| Fondazione Palazzo Albizzini | Città di Castello | | 255 |
| Gal. dell'Accademia Nazionale di San Luca | Roma - Rome | | 277 |
| Gal. Naz. d'Arte Moderna e Contemporanea | Roma - Rome | | 273 |
| Gall. Naz. d'Arte Antica, Palazzo Barberini | Roma - Rome | | 276 |
| Galleria Borghese | Roma - Rome | ▣ | 274 |
| Galleria Civica d'Arte Moderna e Cont. | Torino - Turin | | 281 |
| Galleria d'Arte Moderna | Firenze - Florence | | 256 |
| Galleria d'Arte Moderna | Milano - Milan | | 266 |
| Galleria degli Uffizi - Uffizi Art Gallery | Firenze - Florence | | 262 |
| Galleria dell'Accademia | Firenze - Florence | | 255 |
| Galleria di Palazzo Bianco | Genova - Genoa | | 264 |
| Galleria di Palazzo Rosso | Genova - Genoa | | 264 |
| Galleria Estense | Modena | | 269 |
| Galleria Nazionale dell'Umbria | Perugia | | 272 |
| Galleria Nazionale di Palazzo Spinola | Genova - Genoa | ▣ | 265 |
| Galleria Sabauda | Torino - Turin | | 283 |
| Gallerie dell'Accademia | Venezia - Venice | | 286 |
| M. Arch. Nazionale Delle Marche | Ancona | | 251 |
| M. Arch. Nazionale di Parma | Parma | | 271 |
| M. Civico di Archeologia Ligure de Genova | Genova - Genoa | | 263 |
| M. di Architettura e Scultura Ligure | Genova - Genoa | | 266 |
| M. e Pinacoteca Naz. di Palazzo Mansi | Lucca | | 266 |
| Monumenti, Musei e Gallerie Pontificie | Roma, Vatican City | | 278 |

Museums in alphabetical order by country.

Museums in alphabetical order by country.

Museums in alphabetical order by country.

# INDEX

## Exhibitions

MUSEUM MEDIA PUBLISHERS

Exhibitions in chronological order.

## AUSTRIA

| DATE | CITY | MUSEUM | ARTIST/THEME |
|------|------|--------|--------------|
| until 18·05·97 | Linz | N. Gal. Linz/ Wolfgang-Gurlitt-M. | Markus Prachensky |
| until 25·05·97 | Linz | N. Gal. Linz/ Wolfgang-Gurlitt-M. | Maconde and MapicoMasks |
| until 25·05·97 | Wien - Vienna | Kunsthistorisches Museum | Vittoria Colonna  Michelangelo's Muse |
| until 25·05·97 | Wien - Vienna | Wiener Secession | James Coleman |
| until 25·05·97 | Wien - Vienna | Wiener Secession | Thomas Reinhold |
| until 01·06·97 | Wien - Vienna | Kunstforum Bank Austria | William Turner |
| until 01·06·97 | Wien - Vienna | Museum für Völkerkunde | Shining South Seas |
| until 08·06·97 | Wien - Vienna | M. Mod. Kunst Ludwig Wien | Nahum Tevet |
| until 15·06·97 | Wien - Vienna | Österreichische Gal. Belvedere | Rudolf Hoflehner |
| until 15·06·97 | Wien - Vienna | M. Mod. Kunst Ludwig Wien | Valie Export: Split: Reality |
| until 22·06·97 | Wien - Vienna | Österreichische Gal. Belvedere | Georg Eisler |
| until 29·06·97 | Wien - Vienna | Österreichisches M. für Volkskunde | Pictures from Galicia |
| until 02·07·97 | Salzburg | Residenzgalerie Salzburg | Copper Rust and Shield Louse |
| until 24·08·97 | Wien - Vienna | KunstHausWien | Schmidt-Rottluff |
| 04·05·97 - 14·09·97 | Wien - Vienna | Österreichisches M. für Volkskunde | The Bagpipes in Europe |
| 06·05·97 - 15·07·97 | Wien - Vienna | Graphische Sammlung Albertina | Ludwig Attersee |
| 06·05·97 - 15·07·97 | Wien - Vienna | Graphische Sammlung Albertina | Hildegard Joos |
| 06·05·97 - 15·07·97 | Wien - Vienna | Graphische Sammlung Albertina | Masterpieces of the Albertina Museum |
| 06·05·97 - 27·05·97 | Wien - Vienna | Kunsthistorisches Museum | Orient & Occident |
| 08·05·97 - 06·07·97 | Salzburg | Rupertinum | Christo & Jeanne Claude |
| 15·05·97 - 15·06·97 | Salzburg | Rupertinum | Rössing Prize 1997 |
| 22·05·97 - 29·05·97 | Linz | N. Gal. Linz/ Wolfgang-Gurlitt-M. | Association of Friends |
| 26·05·97 - 29·09·97 | Wien - Vienna | Kunsthistorisches Museum | Henry Moore |
| 04·06·97 - 13·07·97 | Wien - Vienna | Wiener Secession | It's a Better World |
| 05·06·97 - 14·09·97 | Linz | N. Gal. Linz/ Wolfgang-Gurlitt-M. | Hermann Nitsch  Retrospective |
| 06·06·97 - Sep 97 | Innsbruck | Tiroler Volkskunstmuseum | Gardens and Parks |
| 12·06·97 - 24·08·97 | Wien - Vienna | Kunstforum Bank Austria | The Froehlich Collection |
| 20·06·97 - 14·09·97 | Wien - Vienna | Österreichisches M. für Volkskunde | Tool Transformations |
| 25·06·97 - 31·08·97 | Wien - Vienna | Österreichische Gal. Belvedere | Henry Koerner 1915-1991 |
| 27·06·97 - 31·08·97 | Wien - Vienna | M. Mod. Kunst Ludwig Wien | Jiri Georg Dokoupil |
| 29·06·97 - 21·09·97 | Wien - Vienna | Kunsthistorisches Museum | Capriccio |
| 04·07·97 - 31·08·97 | Wien - Vienna | M. Mod. Kunst Ludwig Wien | East-Middle-West |
| 18·07·97 - 19·10·97 | Salzburg | Rupertinum | Wilhelm Thöny |
| 23·07·97 - 14·09·97 | Wien - Vienna | Wiener Secession | Zoe Leonard |
| 23·07·97 - 14·09·97 | Wien - Vienna | Wiener Secession | X2 |
| Aug 97-Oct 97 | Wien - Vienna | Kunsthistorisches Museum | Gold from Mexico |
| Sep 97-Jan 98 | Wien - Vienna | Kunsthistorisches Museum | Treasures from the Land of the Bible |
| 04·09·97 - 19·10·97 | Salzburg | Rupertinum | Peter Krawagna  New Works |
| 05·09·97 - 07·12·97 | Wien - Vienna | Kunstforum Bank Austria | Art and Madness |
| 07·09·97 - 19·10·97 | Wien - Vienna | Kunsthistorisches Museum | Violin Construction |
| 11·09·97 - 02·11·97 | Wien - Vienna | M. Mod. Kunst Ludwig Wien | Alois Mosbacher |
| 11·09·97 - 25·01·98 | Wien - Vienna | KunstHausWien | Herb Ritts |
| 12·09·97 - 02·11·97 | Wien - Vienna | M. Mod. Kunst Ludwig Wien | Manfred Wakolbinger |
| 16·09·97 - Nov 97 | Wien - Vienna | Graphische Sammlung Albertina | German Drawings |
| 19·09·97 - 26·10·97 | Wien - Vienna | Österreichische Gal. Belvedere | Conrad Laib |
| Autumn 97 | Wien - Vienna | Kunsthistorisches Museum | The Pharaohs' Gold |
| 24·09·97 - 09·11·97 | Wien - Vienna | Wiener Secession | Nobuyoshi Araki |
| 25·09·97 - 02·11·97 | Linz | N. Gal. Linz/ Wolfgang-Gurlitt-M. | O. Nakajima & J. Yanaguihara |
| Oct 97- onwards | Wien - Vienna | Kunsthistorisches Museum | Karl Rössing |
| 09·10·97 - 23·11·97 | Salzburg | Rupertinum | The Hellmut Czerny Donation |
| 11·10·97 - 11·11·97 | Graz | Landesmuseum Joanneum | Berique & Sebastianutti |
| 20·10·97 - 30·11·97 | Salzburg | Rupertinum | Still-life Today |
| 26·10·97 - 29·03·98 | Wien - Vienna | Österreichisches M. für Volkskunde | With Baggage and Bags |
| 30·10·97 - Jan 98 | Salzburg | Rupertinum | John Heartfield |
| Nov 97-Feb 98 | Wien - Vienna | Kunsthistorisches Museum | Jan Brueghel |
| Nov 97-Mar 98 | Wien - Vienna | Museum für Völkerkunde | Bhutan - A Kingdom in Balance |
| 15·11·97 - 13·01·98 | Wien - Vienna | M. Mod. Kunst Ludwig Wien | Haim Steinbach |
| 19·11·97-Jan 98 | Wien - Vienna | Wiener Secession | Group Exhibition |
| Dec 97-Jan 98 | Wien - Vienna | Graphische Sammlung Albertina | Acquisitions, Part II |
| Dec 97-Jan 98 | Wien - Vienna | Graphische Sammlung Albertina | Expressionist Graphics in the Albertina |
| 11·12·97 - Feb 98 | Salzburg | Rupertinum | Christian Rohlfs |
| 30·12·97 - 01·02·98 | Wien - Vienna | Österreichisches M. für Volkskunde | Christmas Exhibition 97/98 |

Exhibitions in chronological order.

## BELGIUM

| DATE | CITY | MUSEUM | ARTIST/THEME |
|---|---|---|---|
| onwards | Antwerpen-Antwerp | M. Beeldhouwk. Middelheim | Wide White Space Gallery |
| until 18·05·97 | Bruxelles - Brussels | Musées Royaux d'Art et d'Histoire | Yemen |
| until 19·05·97 | Deurle | Museum Dhondt-Dhaenens | Jacques Charlier & Ray Grayson |
| until 24·05·97 | Gent - Ghent | M. voor Sierkunst en Vormgeving | Design and Identity |
| until 24·05·97 | Gent - Ghent | M. voor Sierkunst en Vormgeving | The Other Vessel |
| until 25·05·97 | Bruxelles - Brussels | Palais des Beaux-Arts | The Art of Collecting |
| until 25·05·97 | Bruxelles - Brussels | Palais des Beaux-Arts | Esko Männikkö |
| until 01·06·97 | Oostende - Ostend | PMMK - M. voor Moderne Kunst | Riera i Arago |
| until 01·06·97 | Oostende - Ostend | PMMK - M. voor Moderne Kunst | Barcello |
| until 07·06·97 | Charleroi | Musée des Beaux-Arts | International Triennial of Young Talent |
| until 22·06·97 | Antwerpen-Antwerp | Koninklijk M. voor Schone Kunsten | Flemish Miniatures |
| until 28·06·97 | Bruxelles - Brussels | M. Royaux des Beaux-Arts de B. | René Magritte (1898-1967) |
| until 29·06·97 | Antwerpen-Antwerp | Museum Plantin-Moretus | Abraham Ortelius |
| until 27·07·97 | Bruxelles - Brussels | M. Royaux des Beaux-Arts de B. | Paul Delvaux |
| until 31·08·97 | Charleroi | Musée de la Photographie | Derision and Reason |
| until 28·09·97 | Morlanwelz | Musée Royal de Mariemont | Egyptian Coptic Textiles of the the Nile |
| until 30·09·97 | Antwerpen-Antwerp | Nationaal Scheepvaartmuseum | Rika Loyens & Leon Ost |
| until 26·10·97 | Bruxelles - Brussels | Musées Royaux d'Art et d'Histoire | The Gallo-Romans in Belgium |
| 01·05·97 - May 97 | Antwerpen-Antwerp | Stedelijk Prentenkabinet | Acquisitions |
| 24·05·97 - 17·08·97 | Antwerpen-Antwerp | M. Beeldhouwk. Middelheim | Anthony Caro (1924, New Malden) |
| 24·05·97 - 14·09·97 | Namur - Namen | Musée des Arts Anciens du Namurois | The Namur Glassmaking Heritage |
| 25·05·97 - 29·06·97 | Deurle | Museum Dhondt-Dhaenens | K. Kloosterboer, P. Zimmermann a.o. |
| 05·06·97 - 17·08·97 | Bruxelles - Brussels | Palais des Beaux-Arts | Alberto Burri |
| 14·06·97 - 05·10·97 | Oostende - Ostend | PMMK - M. voor Moderne Kunst | Emiel Claus |
| 14·06·97 - 05·10·97 | Oostende - Ostend | PMMK - M. voor Moderne Kunst | Antoon De Clerck |
| 17·06·97 - 16·08·97 | Charleroi | Musée des Beaux-Arts | New Acquisitions |
| 17·06·97 - 16·08·97 | Charleroi | Musée des Beaux-Arts | New Acquisitions |
| 20·06·97 - 17·08·97 | Gent - Ghent | M. voor Sierkunst en Vormgeving | Lacquerwork from East Asia |
| Summer 97 | Tervuren | Koninklijk M. voor Midden-Afrika | Tervuren and the World Exhibition |
| 06·07·97 - 05·10·97 | Deurle | Museum Dhondt-Dhaenens | Exhibition of Architects |
| 07·08·97 - 09·11·97 | Antwerpen-Antwerp | Koninklijk M. voor Schone Kunsten | Trance Dance |
| 05·09·97 - 28·09·97 | Bruxelles - Brussels | Palais des Beaux-Arts | Prix de la Jeune Peinture Belge |
| 05·09·97 - 21·11·97 | Charleroi | Musée de la Photographie | Gustave Marissiaux |
| 05·09·97 - 21·11·97 | Charleroi | Musée de la Photographie | Paul Den Hollander   Botanical Voyage |
| 05·09·97 - 21·11·97 | Charleroi | Musée de la Photographie | Cameras from the Collection |
| 06·09·97 - 16·11·97 | Antwerpen-Antwerp | M. Beeldhouwk. Middelheim | Wim Delvoye |
| 06·09·97 - 14·12·97 | Gent - Ghent | Museum voor Schone Kunsten | Paris-Brussels / Brussels-Paris |
| 10·09·97 - 16·11·97 | Brugge - Bruges | Arentshuis (The Brangwyn Museum) | Lace in Europe |
| 12·09·97 - Feb 98 | Bruxelles - Brussels | Musées Royaux d'Art et d'Histoire | The Belgian Excavations in Jordan |
| 12·09·97 - 23·11·97 | Gent - Ghent | M. voor Sierkunst en Vormgeving | Art Nouveau |
| 12·09·97 - 28·12·97 | Gent - Ghent | MIAT | Worker or Matron, Domestic Slave... |
| 18·09·97 - 30·03·98 | Tervuren | Koninklijk M. voor Midden-Afrika | Zimbabwe |
| 19·09·97 - 21·12·97 | Antwerpen-Antwerp | Museum Plantin-Moretus | Justus Lipsius and the Plantin House |
| 20·09·97 - 08·11·97 | Charleroi | Musée des Beaux-Arts | The Painter Arsène Detry (1897-1981) |
| 10·10·97 - 16·11·97 | Antwerpen-Antwerp | Stedelijk Prentenkabinet | Frans Dille Award 1997 |
| 12·10·97 - 07·12·97 | Deurle | Museum Dhondt-Dhaenens | Günter Umberg (D) |
| 18·10·97 - 30·11·97 | Oostende - Ostend | PMMK - M. voor Moderne Kunst | Mc Dermott &  McGough |
| 18·10·97 - 30·11·97 | Oostende - Ostend | PMMK - M. voor Moderne Kunst | Wouter Deruytter |
| 18·10·97 - 30·11·97 | Oostende - Ostend | PMMK - M. voor Moderne Kunst | Angh Duong |
| 24·10·97 - 04·01·98 | Bruxelles - Brussels | Palais des Beaux-Arts | Paribas Bank Collection |
| 09·11·97 - 31·12·97 | Namur - Namen | Musée des Arts Anciens du Namurois | Aegedius Gaspard Pierard |
| 21·11·97 - 29·03·98 | Antwerpen-Antwerp | Etnografisch Museum | Shamanism |
| 28·11·97 - onwards | Charleroi | Musée de la Photographie | National Outdoor Photography Prize |
| 12·12·97 - Jan 98 | Gent - Ghent | M. voor Sierkunst en Vormgeving | The Henry van de Velde / Vizo Awards |
| 20·12·97 - 01·03·98 | Oostende - Ostend | PMMK - M. voor Moderne Kunst | The Collection Stephane Janssen |
| 21·03·98 - Spring 98 | Antwerpen-Antwerp | M. Beeldhouwk. Middelheim | Franz West |
| | | | |
| | | | |
| | | | |
| | | | |
| | | | |

Exhibitions in chronological order.

| FRANCE | | | |
|---|---|---|---|
| **DATE** | **CITY** | **MUSEUM** | **ARTIST/THEME** |
| until 05·05·97 | Paris | Centre National de la Photographie | Hannah Collins  Hotel of Being |
| until 12·05·97 | Paris | Centre Nat. d'Art&Culture Pompidou | Prints |
| until 18·05·97 | Paris | Galerie Nationale du Jeu de Paume | Jaume Plensa |
| until 18·05·97 | Paris | Galerie Nationale du Jeu de Paume | Bernard Moninot |
| until 18·05·97 | Paris | Musée d'Orsay | Auguste Préault  Romantic Sculptor |
| until 18·05·97 | Paris | Musée d'Orsay | Théophile Gautier  Liberated Critic |
| until 19·05·97 | Besançon | M. Beaux-Arts et d'Archéologie | Landscapes French Artists 17th Century |
| until 19·05·97 | Chalon-sur-Saône | Musée Nicéphore Niépce | Shaken But Not Stirred |
| until 19·05·97 | Nantes | Musée des Beaux Arts | Sarkisend |
| until 19·05·97 | Paris | Centre Nat. d'Art&Culture Pompidou | The Seven Deadly Sins: Gluttony |
| until 23·05·97 | Aix-les-Bains | Musée Faure | Joël Negr |
| until 25·05·97 | Bordeaux | capcMusée d'Art Contemporain | The Collection Unveiled |
| until 25·05·97 | Grenoble | Musée de Grenoble | Signac and the Liberation of Colour |
| until 25·05·97 | Nice | M. d'Art Moderne et Contemporain | Collection of the Business Foundation |
| until 25·05·97 | Nîmes | Carré d'Art-Musée d'Art Cont. | Alan Charlton |
| until 26·05·97 | Caen | Musée des Beaux-Arts | Engravings |
| until 26·05·97 | Paris | Galeries Nationales du Grand Palais | Angkor and 10 Centuries of Khmer Art |
| until 29·05·97 | Chantilly | Musée Condé | Raphaël and his Circle |
| until 31·05·97 | Perpignan | Musée Hyacinthe Rigaud | Pierre Daura |
| until 01·06·97 | Amiens | Musée de Picardie | Homages |
| until 01·06·97 | Colmar | Musée d'Unterlinden | The Carnation Period |
| until 08·06·97 | Angers | Musée des Beaux-Arts | The Painter Alexis Mérodack-Jeaneau |
| until 08·06·97 | Angers | Musée des Beaux-Arts | Sébastien Leysner |
| until 08·06·97 | Calais | M. des Beaux Arts et de la Dentelle | State of Places, State of Things |
| until 09·06·97 | Besançon | M. Beaux-Arts et d'Archéologie | The Ainus, Japanese Natives |
| until 09·06·97 | Nice | M. of Modern and Contemporary Art | Man Ray  Retrospective |
| until 09·06·97 | Paris | Centre Nat. d'Art&Culture Pompidou | Martial Raysse |
| until 09·06·97 | Paris | Musée Picasso | The Black Mirror |
| until 15·06·97 | Aix-en-Provence | Musée Granet | Devotion |
| until 15·06·97 | Antibes | Musée Picasso | Pierrick Sorin |
| until 15·06·97 | Paris | Centre Nat. d'Art&Culture Pompidou | Identical, Not Identical |
| until 15·06·97 | Paris | Musée Rodin | Towards The Bronze Age |
| until 15·06·97 | Pau | Musée National du Château de Pau | At the Palace Tables |
| until 15·06·97 | Strasbourg | Musée de l'Oeuvre Notre-Dame | Sebastien Stoskopff |
| until 16·06·97 | Périgueux | Musée du Périgord | Marcel Loth |
| until 21·06·97 | Dijon | Le Consortium | Pierre Huyghe |
| until 21·06·97 | Dijon | Le Consortium, Usine | Angela Bulloch |
| until 22·06·97 | Paris | Musée du Petit Palais | Forerunners of Europe |
| until 23·06·97 | Paris | Musée du Louvre [Richelieu Wing] | A Challenge to Good Taste |
| until 27·06·97 | Biot | Musée National Fernand Léger | Fernand Léger |
| until 27·06·97 | Biot | Musée National Fernand Léger | The City |
| until 29·06·97 | St-Germain-en-Laye | Musée des Antiquités nationales | Merovingian Treasures |
| until 29·06·97 | St-Germain-en-Laye | Musée des Antiquités nationales | Gregory of Tours (538-594) |
| until 29·09·97 | Paris | Centre Nat. d'Art&Culture Pompidou | Made in France 1947-1997 |
| until 30·06·97 | Douai | Musée de la Chartreuse | Douai and Its Fortifications |
| until Jun 97 | Pau | Musée National du Château de Pau | Restoration of the Château Park |
| until 07·07·97 | Toulouse | Musée Paul Dupuy | Portraits of François de Troy |
| until 07·07·97 | Toulouse | Musée Paul Dupuy | François de Troy |
| until12·07·97 | Paris | Galeries Nationales du Grand Palais | Paris-Brussels / BrusselsParis |
| until13·07·97 | Paris | Musée d'Orsay | Emile Verhaeren |
| until13·07·97 | Versailles | Château de Versailles et de Trianon | From J. Vivien to J.-E. Blanche |
| until 14·07·97 | Villeneuve d'Ascq | Musée d'Art Moderne | Outsider Art  Aracine Collection |
| until 21·07·97 | Paris | Musée du Louvre [Hall Napoléon] | Sponsors by the Thousands |
| until 21·07·97 | Paris | Musée du Louvre [Sully Wing] | The Dezallier d'Argenville Collection |
| until 27·07·97 | Marseille | Musée des Beaux-Arts | Rodin  The Inner Voice |
| until 28·07·97 | Nice | Musée des Beaux-Arts | Nicaise de Keyser |
| until Jul 97 | Montauban | Musée Ingres | The Apotheosis of Homer |
| until 31·08·97 | Angoulême | Musée des Beaux-Arts | Armand Vergeaud |
| until 31·08·97 | Paris | Musée des Arts Décoratifs | Saint Cloud Porcelain |
| until Aug 97 | Orléans | Musée des Beaux-Arts | Collection of Architectural Models |
| until Sep 97 | Angoulême | Musée des Beaux-Arts | In André Juillard's Footsteps |
| until 02·11·97 | Strasbourg | Musée Archéologique | Niedernai |
| until 20·11·97 | Rouen | Musée des Beaux-Arts | Joan Mitchell |
| until 05·01·98 | Paris | M. National d'Histoire Naturelle | Life between the Sky and the Sea |

Exhibitions in chronological order.

## FRANCE

| DATE | CITY | MUSEUM | ARTIST/THEME |
|---|---|---|---|
| 30-04-97 - 27-07-97 | Paris | Musée Carnavalet | Nureyev |
| May 97 | Céret | Musée d'Art Moderne | 25 Years of Contemporary Art |
| May 97 | Montpellier | Musée Fabre | Claude Viallat |
| May 97-Jun 97 | Orléans | Musée des Beaux-Arts | Aignan-Thomas Desfriches |
| May 97-Jul 97 | Marseille | M. Cantini d'Art Mod. et Cont. | Oskar Schlemmer |
| May 97-mid Sep 97 | Nantes | Musée des Beaux-Arts | James Reilly |
| May 97-Sep 97 | Rennes | Musée des Beaux-Arts | Caravaggio in Rennes |
| 09-05-97 - 20-06-97 | Epinal | M. Dép. d'Art Ancien et Cont. | Ephemeral Sanctuary |
| 10-05-97 - 30-06-97 | Honfleur | Musée Eugène Boudin | Louis Garneray   A Painter and Sailor |
| 13-05-97 - 14-06-97 | Limoges | FRAC Limousin | Collection, Part II |
| 14-05-97 - 11-08-97 | Paris | Centre National de la Photographie | Anthony Hernandez |
| 14-05-97 - 11-08-97 | Paris | Centre National de la Photographie | Carl de Keyzer   Historical Pictures |
| 14-05-97 - 11-08-97 | Paris | Centre National de la Photographie | Pascal Convert   'Live' |
| 14-05-97 - 01-09-97 | Écouen | Musée National de la Renaissance | From the Légion d'Honneur to the NRM |
| mid May 97-mid Sep 97 | Strasbourg | Musée des Beaux-Arts | Kaufman/Sclageter Donation |
| 16-05-97 - 31-08-97 | Tours | Musée des Beaux-Arts | Freemasonry |
| 16-05-97 - 19-10-97 | Valenciennes | Musée des Beaux-Arts | Archaeological Treasures |
| 17-05-97 - 22-06-97 | Castres | Musée Goya | Luis Penaranda   Poetic Illustration |
| 23-05-97 - 29-08-97 | Bordeaux | Musée des Beaux-Arts | Rosa Bonheur |
| 23-05-97 - 31-08-97 | Lyon | Musée des Tissus | Lyon Silk |
| 23-05-97 - 07-09-97 | Saint-Etienne | Musée d'Art Moderne | Pivovarov |
| 28-05-97 - 30-06-97 | Paris | Centre Nat. d'Art&Culture Pompidou | The Seven Deadly Sins: Greed |
| 28-05-97 - 17-08-97 | Lyon | Musée des Beaux-Arts | Campaigning for Modern Art |
| 28-05-97 - 25-08-97 | Besançon | M. Beaux-Arts et d'Archéologie | Landscapes French Artists18th Century |
| 28-05-97 - 08-09-97 | Paris | M. Nat. du Moyen Age/Thermes Cluny | Insignia and Souvenirs |
| 29-05-97 - 29-09-97 | Paris | Centre Nat. d'Art&Culture Pompidou | Fernand Léger |
| 30-05-97 - 30-06-97 | Aix-les-Bains | Musée Faure | Joe Downing |
| 30-05-97 - 01-09-97 | Caen | Musée de Normandie | Archaeology of the Black Sea |
| 30-05-97 - 29-09-97 | Chartres | Musée des Beaux-Arts | Restoration of the Chartres Museum |
| 31-05-97 - 30-06-97 | Agen | Musée des Beaux-Arts | A Poet and a Traveller |
| Jun 97-Aug 97 | Lille | Musée des Beaux-Arts | From Raphael to Guardi |
| Jun 97-Sep 97 | Bordeaux | capcMusée d'Art Contemporain | Richard Baquié |
| Jun 97-Sep 97 | Bordeaux | capcMusée d'Art Contemporain | Jack Pierson |
| Jun 97-Sep 97 | Nîmes | Carré d'Art-Musée d'Art Cont. | Giuseppe Pencee |
| Jun 97-Sep 97 | Orléans | Musée des Beaux-Arts | The Time of Passion |
| Jun 97-end Sep 97 | Montauban | Musée Ingres | From Heaven to Earth |
| Jun 97-Oct 97 | Caen | Musée de Normandie | Cows and People |
| Summer 97 | Nantes | Musée des Beaux-Arts | Claude Parmiggianni |
| 04-06-97 - 01-09-97 | Toulouse | Musée des Augustins | Henri Rousseau |
| 06-06-97 - 12-10-97 | Cherbourg | Musée Thomas Henry | Henri Hayden (1883-1970) |
| 10-06-97 - 31-08-97 | Paris | Musée d'Orsay | Eugène Cuvelier |
| 10-06-97 - 31-08-97 | Paris | Musée d'Orsay | Photography in Sèvres |
| 10-06-97 - 31-08-97 | Paris | Musée d'Orsay | Scenes of the Polish Ghetto |
| 10-06-97 - 19-10-97 | Paris | Galerie Nationale du Jeu de Paume | César   Restrospective |
| 13-06-97 - Autumn 97 | Chalon-sur-Saône | Musée Nicéphore Niépce | The Red Eye   Dominique Pasqualini |
| 13-06-97 - Nov 97 | Agen | Musée des Beaux-Arts | A rediscovery of Goya |
| 14-06-97 - 27-07-97 | Perpignan | Musée Hyacinthe Rigaud | The sculptor Gabriel Farail |
| 14-06-97 - 14-09-97 | Colmar | Musée d'Unterlinden | Tal-Coat |
| 14-06-97 - 13-10-97 | Dijon | Musée des Beaux-Arts | Prague 1900-1938 |
| mid Jun 97-mid Nov 97 | Paris | Musée de la Marine | Antarctica  Winter in Spitzberg |
| 15-06-97 - 21-09-97 | Alençon | M. Beaux-Arts et de la Dentelle | Jean-Jacques François Monanteuil |
| 18-06-97 - 25-06-97 | Dijon | Musée Archéologique de Dijon | The Children's Workshop |
| 18-06-97 - 04-08-97 | Paris | Centre Nat. d'Art&Culture Pompidou | Jean-Jacques Rullier |
| 20-06-97 - 15-09-97 | Nantes | Musée des Beaux-Arts | Faces of the 17th Century |
| 21-06-97 - Summer 97 | Bayonne | Musée Bonnat | Henri Zo (1873-1933)  The Bullfights |
| 21-06-97 - Summer 97 | Grenoble | Musée de Grenoble | Presentation on the reorganisation |
| 21-06-97 - Summer 97 | Limoges | Musée National Adrien Dubouché | Jean Jaques Prolongeau |
| 21-06-97 - Summer 97 | Montpellier | Musée Fabre | Geer van Velde |
| 21-06-97 - Summer 97 | Nantes | Musée des Beaux-Arts | Ricardo Lanzarini |
| 21-06-97 - 08-09-97 | Besançon | M. Beaux-Arts et d'Archéologie | Sonia Delaunay |
| 21-06-97 - 20-09-97 | Chambéry | Musée des Beaux-Arts | From Landscape to Landscape |
| 21-06-97 - 20-09-97 | Chambéry | Musée des Beaux-Arts | Marcel Giraud |
| 25-06-97 - 29-09-97 | Paris | Centre Nat. d'Art&Culture Pompidou | The Art of the Engineer |
| 26-06-97 - 31-10-97 | Limoges | FRAC Limousin | William Wegman |

Exhibitions in chronological order.

## FRANCE

| DATE | CITY | MUSEUM | ARTIST/THEME |
|---|---|---|---|
| 27·06·97 - 07·09·97 | Saint-Etienne | Musée d'Art Moderne | Erik Dietman |
| 27·06·97 - 15·09·97 | Epinal | M. Dép. d'Art Ancien et Cont. | Centenary of the Painter Louis Français |
| 27·06·97 - 20·10·97 | Nice | Musée Matisse | TheCôte d'Azur and Modern Times |
| 27·06·97 - 30·10·97 | Biot | Musée National Fernand Léger | The New Spirit |
| 28·06·97 - 28·09·97 | Calais | M. des Beaux Arts et de la Dentelle | Carmen Perrin  Sculpture |
| 28·06·97 - 30·09·97 | Antibes | Musée Picasso | Black Sun |
| 28·06·97 - 26·10·97 | Nice | Musée des Beaux-Arts | Dufy |
| 28·06·97 - 27·10·97 | Nice | M. d'Art Moderne et Contemporain | The Côte d'Azur and Modern Art |
| 28·06·97 - 27·10·97 | Nice | M. d'Art Moderne et Contemporain | Edward Quinn |
| 28·06·97 - 02·11·97 | Amiens | Musée de Picardie | Antique Glass |
| 29·06·97 - 31·08·97 | Céret | Musée d'Art Moderne | Picasso  Drawings and Collages |
| 29·06·97 - 29·09·97 | Albi | Musée Toulouse-Lautrec | Paul Belmondo (1898-1982) |
| Jul 97 onwards | Aix-en-Provence | Musée Granet | Regards from Cézanne |
| Jul 97-Aug 97 | Arles | Musée Réattu | International Encounters |
| Jul 97-Sep 97 | Nice | M.  Arch. de Cimiez et Sité Arch. | Photographies of archaelogical sites |
| Jul 97-Nov 97 | Périgueux | Musée du Périgord | 19th-Century Physics Collection |
| 02·07·97 - 19·10·97 | Saint-Paul | Fondation Maeght | Sculpture by Painters |
| 04·07·97 - Sep 97 | Dijon | Le Consortium | Liam Gillick |
| 04·07·97 - Sep 97 | Dijon | Le Consortium, Usine | Peter Halley |
| 04·07·97 - 19·10·97 | Angers | Musée des Beaux-Arts | François Morellet |
| 05·07·97 - 05·10·97 | Castres | Musée Goya | French and Spanish Painters |
| 05·07·97 - 06·10·97 | Honfleur | Musée Eugène Boudin | The Cow |
| 07·07·97 - 28·09·97 | Aix-les-Bains | Musée Faure | Paintings of Lake Bourget |
| 09·07·97 - 11·08·97 | Paris | Centre Nat. d'Art&Culture Pompidou | The Seven Deadly Sins: Lust |
| mid Jul 97- Nov 97 | Montauban | Musée Ingres | The Golden Age (Third Stage) |
| 15·07·97 - 15·11·97 | Reims | Musée des Beaux-Arts | Le Legs Lundy |
| Aug 97-05·10·97 | Marseille | M. Cantini d'Art Mod. et Cont. | Collective Antifascist Painting, 1961 |
| 01·08·97 - end 97 | Perpignan | Musée Hyacinthe Rigaud | Daura and the Rousillon Painters |
| 04·08·97 - 29·09·97 | Paris | Centre Nat. d'Art&Culture Pompidou | The Seven Deadly Sins: Pride |
| 20·08·97 - 29·09·97 | Paris | Centre Nat. d'Art&Culture Pompidou | Didier Trenet |
| Sep 97-Nov 97 | Toulouse | Musée Paul Dupuy | Alexandre Roubtzoff |
| Sep 97-Jan 98 | Chantilly | Musée Condé | Pierre-Paul Prud'hon |
| Sep 97-Jan 98 | Chantilly | Musée Condé | A Prince and His Architects |
| 03·09·97 - 01·12·97 | Besançon | M. Beaux-Arts et d'Archéologie | Charles Lapicque's Lithographs |
| 10·09·97 - 14·11·97 | Paris | Centre National de la Photographie | Thomas Ruff  Works 1979-1996 |
| 15·09·97 - 15·12·97 | Arles | Musée Réattu | Jacques Réattu |
| 17·09·97 - 15·11·97 | Rouen | Musée des Beaux-Arts | Romanian Icons |
| 17·09·97 - 15·12·97 | Rouen | Musée des Beaux-Arts | The Dufy Collection |
| 19·09·97 - 23·11·97 | Saint-Etienne | Musée d'Art Moderne | Jochen Gerz |
| Autumn 97 | Marseille | Musée des Beaux-Arts | New Acquisitions |
| Autumn 97 | Bayonne | Musée Bonnat | Auguste Durst (1842-1930) |
| Autumn 97 | Chambéry | Musée des Beaux-Arts | 10th Anniversary of the 'Artothèque' |
| Autumn 97 | Fontainebleau | M. National Château Fontainebleau | Books for Exile |
| Autumn 97 | Nantes | Musée des Beaux-Arts | Camille Bryen |
| Autumn 97 | Nantes | Musée des Beaux-Arts | The Museum Factory |
| Autumn 97-Winter 97 | Nîmes | Carré d'Art-Musée d'Art Cont. | The Forms of Colour |
| end Sep 97- Jan 98 | Besançon | M. Beaux-Arts et d'Archéologie | Northern Paintings of Free-County  M. |
| 24·09·97 - 12·01·98 | Écouen | Musée National de la Renaissance | Bernard Palissy |
| 25·09·97 - 05·01·98 | Sèvres | Musée National de Céramique | Japanese Stoneware |
| 26·09·97 - 12·01·98 | Paris | Galeries Nationales du Grand Palais | Prud'hon |
| Oct 97 | Versailles | Château de Versailles et de Trianon | Louis de Silvestra |
| Oct 97-Dec 97 | Bordeaux | capcMusée d'Art Contemporain | Niele Toroni |
| Oct 97-Dec 97 | Bordeaux | capcMusée d'Art Contemporain | Tony Oursler |
| 01·10·97 - 15·12·97 | Tours | Musée des Beaux-Arts | The legend of St. Martin |
| 01·10·97 - 05·01·98 | Angoulême | Musée des Beaux-Arts | When Charente was under the Sea |
| 03·10·97 - 05·01·98 | Paris | Musée du Louvre [Richelieu Wing] | A Mission in Persia |
| 03·10·97 - 05·01·98 | Paris | Musée du Louvre [Sully Wing] | Engravers from the Netherlands |
| 06·10·97 - 04·01·98 | Paris | Musée d'Orsay | Jean-Paul Laurens |
| 07·10·97 - 28·12·97 | Paris | Musée des Arts Décoratifs | Chinese Cloisonné Enamel |
| 08·10·97 - 05·01·98 | Paris | Galeries Nationales du Grand Palais | Georges de la Tour |
| 08·10·97 - 05·01·98 | Toulouse | Musée des Augustins | Faces of the 17th Century |
| 10·10·97 - 14·12·97 | Aix-les-Bains | Musée Faure | Alfred Boucher |
| 10·10·97 - 12·01·98 | Dijon | Musée Archéologique de Dijon | The Birth of Art in Europe |
| 15·10·97  mid Oct 97 | Paris | Musée de la Marine | Books about the Sea |

Exhibitions in chronological order.

## FRANCE

| DATE | CITY | MUSEUM | ARTIST/THEME |
|---|---|---|---|
| 15·10·97 - end Dec 97 | Epinal | M. Dép. d'Art Ancien et Cont. | Works by Women Plastic Artists |
| 15·10·97 - 05·01·98 | Paris | Galeries Nationales du Grand Palais | The Iberians |
| 15·10·97 - 15·01·98 | Rouen | Musée des Beaux-Arts | Jacques-Emile Blanche |
| 15·10·97 - mid Feb 98 | Pau | Musée National du Château de Pau | Jacques-Charles Derrey |
| 16·10·97 - 05·01·98 | Chartres | Musée des Beaux-Arts | Remembrances of Madeleine Castaing |
| 16·10·97 - 11·01·98 | Lyon | Musée des Beaux-Arts | Barye  Claws and Teeth |
| 18·10·97 - end Dec 97 | Calais | M. des Beaux Arts et de la Dentelle | Lace and Lingerie |
| 18·10·97 - 04·01·98 | Strasbourg | Musée des Arts Décoratifs | Olympe Aguado, photographer |
| 18·10·97 - 18·01·98 | Alençon | M. Beaux-Arts et de la Dentelle | Goya - Lacombe |
| 18·10·97 - 15·02·98 | Colmar | Musée d'Unterlinden | Outside the Walls  The Fifties |
| 24·10·97 - 18·01·98 | Marseille | M. Cantini d'Art Mod. et Cont. | Charles Camoin |
| 24·10·97 - 19·01·98 | Paris | Musée du Louvre [Hall Napoléon] | Augustin Pajou, Sculptor of the King |
| 25·10·97 - end Mar 98 | Honfleur | Musée Eugène Boudin | Headdresses, Costumes and Objects |
| 30·10·97 - 04·01·98 | Antibes | Musée Picasso | Tal Coatmid |
| 31·10·97 - 10·01·98 | Nice | Musée Matisse | The Picaron Editions |
| Nov 97-Dec 97 | Arras | Musée des Beaux-Arts | Oceania |
| Nov 97-end Jan 98 | Montauban | Musée Ingres | The Watercolours of Bourdelle |
| Nov 97-end Jan 98 | Nantes | Musée des Beaux-Arts | Jessica Stockholder |
| Nov 97-Jan 98 | Lyon | Musée des Tissus | Olivier Lapidus and the Lyon Silk Ind. |
| Nov 97-Jan 98 | Orléans | Musée des Beaux-Arts | Michel Leiris  Friendship |
| Nov 97-Mar 98 | Bordeaux | Musée des Arts Décoratifs | 50 Years of Creative Glass Art |
| 04·11·97 - 20·04·98 | Paris | M. Nat. Arts&Traditions Populaires | Street Musicians of Paris |
| 07·11·97 - 03·01·98 | Limoges | FRAC Limousin | Collection, Part III |
| 08·11·97 - 15·02·98 | Paris | Musée du Petit Palais | Marianne and Germania |
| 13·11·97 - 04·01·98 | Paris | Galerie Nationale du Jeu de Paume | Emil Schumacher  Retrospective |
| 15·11·97 - 15·01·98 | Cherbourg | Musée Thomas Henry | Painting in Jersey |
| 15·11·97 - end Mar 98 | Nice | M. d'Art Moderne et Contemporain | The Sixties  Paris-Nice-New York |
| end Autumn 97 | Chalon-sur-Saône | Musée Nicéphore Niépce | The Little Bird of Light |
| end Autumn 97 | Chalon-sur-Saône | Musée Nicéphore Niépce | The 1997 Niépce Prize |
| 26·11·97 - 26·01·98 | Paris | Centre National de la Photographie | Anna and Bernhard Blume |
| 01·12·97 - Dec 97 | Biot | Musée National Fernand Léger | Paintings, Ceramics and Tapestries |
| 01·12·97 - Dec 97 | Biot | Musée National Fernand Léger | Drawings from the Collection |
| Dec 97-Jan 98 | Reims | Musée des Beaux-Arts | Victor &  Dana Roman |
| Dec 97-Feb 98 | Périgueux | Musée du Périgord | Homage to Robert Filliou |
| Dec 97-Mar 98 | Amiens | Musée de Picardie | 100 Drawings |
| Dec 97-Mar 98 | Bayonne | Musée Bonnat | Italian Art 1861-1911 |
| Dec 97-Spring 98 | Besançon | M. Beaux-Arts et d'Archéologie | Recumbent Figure of John of Burgundy |
| 04·12·97 - 01·03·98 | Douai | Musée de la Chartreuse | St. Barbara |
| 06·12·97 - 08·03·98 | Strasbourg | Musé Alsacien | Shawls from Alsace |
| 10·12·97 - 09·03·98 | Paris | Centre Nat. d'Art&Culture Pompidou | Bruce Nauman |
| Winter 97 | Chambéry | Musée des Beaux-Arts | Nicole Lombard |
| early 1998 | Calais | M. des Beaux Arts et de la Dentelle | English 19th-Century Watercolours |
| Jan 98-Mar 98 | Antibes | Musée Picasso | Jessica Stockholder |
| Jan 98-Mar 98 | Epinal | M. Dép. d'Art Ancien et Cont. | Archaeologist and Watercolourist |
| end Jan 98-May 98 | Nantes | Musée des Beaux-Arts | Kandinsky |
| 03·02·98 - 02·05·98 | Toulouse | Musée des Augustins | Jean-Paul Laurens |
| 04·02·98 - 13·04·98 | Paris | Centre National de la Photographie | Eugene Richards  Retrospective |
| Mar 98-May 98 | Lyon | Musée des Beaux-Arts | Renovation Phase V |
| Mar 98-Jun 98 | Périgueux | Musée du Périgord | Emile Vergeaud |
| mid Mar 98- Jun 98 | Paris | Galeries Nationales du Grand Palais | The Arts under Philippe Le Bel |
| Spring 98 | Douai | Musée de la Chartreuse | The Tradition of Beer |
| Apr 98-Jun 98 | Epinal | M. Dép. d'Art Ancien et Cont. | Pictures of Epinal |
| 09·04·98 - 20·07·98 | Paris | Galeries Nationales du Grand Palais | Delacroix  The Final Years |
| 16·04·98 - 30·06·98 | Bordeaux | Musée des Beaux-Arts | Goya |

## GERMANY

| DATE | CITY | MUSEUM | ARTIST/THEME |
|---|---|---|---|
| onwards | Berlin | Antikensammlung | The Telephos Frieze |
| onwards | Berlin | Museum für Völkerkunde | Pre-Columbian Stone Sculptures |
| onwards | Hamburg | Hamburger Kunsthalle | International Art since 1960 |
| onwards | Hamburg | Museum für Kunst und Gewerbe | Original - Photography - History |
| onwards | Kassel | Neue Galerie | Rubens - Rembrandt - Hals |

Exhibitions in chronological order.

| GERMANY | | | |
|---|---|---|---|
| **DATE** | **CITY** | **MUSEUM** | **ARTIST/THEME** |
| onwards | Trier | Rheinisches Landesmuseum Trier | Roman Viticulture |
| onwards | Trier | Rheinisches Landesmuseum Trier | Carolingian Coins |
| until 11·05·97 | Berlin | Alte Nationalgalerie | Adolph Menzel |
| until 11·05·97 | Mainz | Landesmuseum Mainz | Peter Vogel Cybernetic Objects |
| until 15·05·97 | Berlin | Deutsches Technikmuseum Berlin | The History of the Berlin Gas Service |
| until 18·05·97 | Hannover | Sprengel Museum Hannover | Bogomir Ecker |
| until 19·05·97 | Bonn | Kunstmuseum Bonn | Giuseppe Penone |
| until 19·05·97 | Schwerin | Staatliches Museum Schwerin | Sonja Rolfs |
| until 19·05·97 | Weimar | Kunstsammlungen zu Weimar | The Other Bauhaus |
| until 19·05·97 | Wolfsburg | Kunstmuseum Wolfsburg | Pietro Donzelli The Light of Solitude |
| until 20·05·97 | Berlin | Alte Nationalgalerie | Christen Koebke |
| until 25·05·97 | Baden-Baden | St. Kunsthalle Baden-Baden | Urban Legends 'London' |
| until 25·05·97 | Berlin | Gemäldegalerie | Masters of the Sea, Masters of Art |
| until 25·05·97 | Berlin | Museum für Ostasiatische Kunst | Masterpieces of Japanese Woodcut |
| until 25·05·97 | Bonn | Bonner Kunstverein | Graw Böckler |
| until 25·05·97 | Bonn | Bonner Kunstverein | Tamara Gri |
| until 25·05·97 | Duisburg | Wilhelm Lehmbruck Museum | Max Couper  The Plot |
| until 25·05·97 | Frankfurt am Main | Deutsches Architektur-Museum | Architecture in the 20th C.: Ireland |
| until 25·05·97 | Frankfurt am Main | Deutsches Architektur-Museum | Urban Planning Discourse |
| until 25·05·97 | Hamburg | Museum für Kunst und Gewerbe | René Lalique  Perfume Bottles |
| until 25·05·97 | Hannover | Sprengel Museum Hannover | Peter Brüning Works on Paper |
| until 25·05·97 | Kassel | Gemäldegal Alte Meister & Antik. | Carthage |
| until 25·05·97 | Köln - Cologne | Josef-Haubrich-Kunsthalle | Keith Haring  The Graphic Work |
| until 25·09·97 | Weil am Rhein | Vitra Design Museum | Castiglioni! |
| until 25·05·97 | Stuttgart | Staatsgalerie Stuttgart | Eugène Cuvelier |
| until 26·05·97 | Münster | Westfälisches Landesmuseum | The Unconditional Look/View |
| until.31·05·97 | Berlin | Bauhaus-Archiv/M. Gestaltung | Ulrich Bauss  Sculptures in Concrete |
| until 01·06·97 | Aachen | Suermondt Ludwig M. | Lotte Jacobi |
| until 01·06·97 | Berlin | Neue Gesellschaft für Bildende Kunst | The Work Factor |
| until 01·06·97 | Darmstadt | Hessisches Landes.Darmstadt | L'Art Gourmand |
| until 01·06·97 | Düsseldorf | Kunstm. Düsseldorf im Ehrenhof | 23 Years of the Rinke Class |
| until 01·06·97 | Frankfurt am Main | Schirn Kunsthalle | Collection of the Aargauer Kunsthaus |
| until 01·06·97 | Karlsruhe | Badisches Landesmuseum Karlsruhe | Paul Speck |
| until 01·06·97 | Karlsruhe | St. Kunsthalle Karlsruhe | Edda Renouf  Retrospective |
| until 01·06·97 | Köln - Cologne | Museum Ludwig | Jasper Johns |
| until 01·06·97 | München - Munich | Die Neue Sammlung | Jan Eisenloeffel |
| until 01·06·97 | Saarbrücken | Saarland Museum | Oskar Holweck |
| until 01·06·97 | Schwerin | Staatliches Museum Schwerin | Rainer Splitt |
| until 08·06·97 | Bonn | Kunstmuseum Bonn | Drawing Today I |
| until 08·06·97 | Bonn | Rheinisches Landesmuseum Bonn | Glass Painting of the 20th Century |
| until 08·06·97 | Frankfurt am Main | Portikus Frankfurt am Main | Steve McQueen |
| until 08·06·97 | Mannheim | Reiß-Museum | The Hats of Adele List |
| until 08·06·97 | Nürnberg | Germanisches Nationalmuseum | 800 Years of European Cutlery |
| until 08·06·97 | Aachen | Suermondt Ludwig M. | Enzo Cucchi |
| until 15·06·97 | Aachen | Ludwig Forum für Int. Kunst | Art in Rumania Today |
| until 15·06·97 | Dortmund | Museum am Ostwall | Heinze-Günter Prager |
| until 15·06·97 | Duisburg | Wilhelm Lehmbruck Museum | INTER ACT! |
| until 15·06·97 | Frankfurt am Main | Museum für Kunsthandwerk | Brave Old World |
| until 15·06·97 | Kiel | Kunsthalle zu Kiel | Max Pechstein  Paintings |
| until 15·06·97 | Ulm | Ulmer Museum | William N. Copley (1919-1996) |
| until 15·06·97 | Mönchengladbach | Schloß Rheydt | Pomp and Splendous from China |
| until 16·06·97 | Hannover | Historisches Museum | Old Hannoverian Security Papers |
| until 22·06·97 | Aachen | Suermondt Ludwig M. | Franz-Josef Weidenhaupt |
| until 22·06·97 | Dortmund | Museum am Ostwall | Otto Mueller |
| until 22·06·97 | Hannover | Sprengel Museum Hannover | Albert Renger-Patzsch |
| until 22·06·97 | Mannheim | Reiß-Museum | Noah's Ark |
| until 29·06·97 | Bonn | Bonner Kunstverein | Jochen Lempert |
| until 29·06·97 | Frankfurt am Main | Schirn Kunsthalle | Zoran Music |
| until 29·06·97 | Leverkusen | St. Leverkusen Schloß Morsbroich | Dieter Goltzsche |
| until 29·06·97 | Ludwigshafen | Wilhelm-Hack-Museum | Auguste Herbin |
| until 29·06·97 | München - Munich | Kunsth. der Hypo-Kulturstiftung | Alberto Giacometti (1901-1966) |
| until 29·06·97 | München - Munich | Städtische Galerie im Lenbachhaus | Albert Bloch (1882-1961) |
| until 29·06·97 | München - Munich | Städtische Galerie im Lenbachhaus | Hans Hofmann (1880-1966) |
| until 29·06·97 | Dresden | Albertinum St. Kunstsammlungen | Ernst Ferdinand Oehme |

Exhibitions in chronological order.

## GERMANY

| DATE | CITY | MUSEUM | ARTIST/THEME |
|------|------|--------|--------------|
| until 29·06·97 | Mönchengladbach | Schloß Rheydt | Anatolian Kelims |
| until 29·06·97 | München - Munich | Villa Stuck | Pippilotti Rist & Samir |
| until Jun 97 | Darmstadt | Hessisches Landes.Darmstadt | Antonio Canaletto |
| until Jun 97 | Köln - Cologne | Römisch-Germanisches Museum | Medieval Household Goods |
| until mid 97 | Düsseldorf | Kunstm. Düsseldorf im Ehrenhof | The 7th Year Children's Pictures |
| until 06·07·97 | Chemnitz | Städtische Kunstsammlungen | Wolfgang Mattheuer |
| until 06·07·97 | München - Munich | Neue Pinakothek | Claude-Joseph Vernet (1714-1789) |
| until 06·07·97 | Weimar | Kunstsammlungen zu Weimar | New Discoveries |
| until 13·07·97 | Bremen | Übersee-Museum Bremen | Huichun - Chinese Medicine |
| until 20·07·97 | Hamburg | Hamburger Kunsthalle | Menzel |
| until 20·07·97 | München - Munich | Haus der Kunst | Carl Philipp Fohr |
| until 20·07·97 | Düsseldorf | Kunsthalle Düsseldorf | Ich Narr des Glücks |
| until 27·07·97 | Köln - Cologne | Rautenstrauch-Joest-Museum | African Art |
| until 03·08·97 | Düsseldorf | Kunstm. Düsseldorf im Ehrenhof | Eye-Witnesses |
| until 06·08·97 | Hamburg | Museum für Kunst und Gewerbe | From South to North |
| until 17·08·97 | Frankfurt am Main | Museum für Moderne Kunst | Rei Nato Spatial Installation |
| until 24·08·97 | Düsseldorf | Kunstsamml. Nordrhein-Westfalen | Moved Unmoved |
| until 31·08·97 | Hamburg | Hamburg. M. Völkerkunde | Indians of the Plains and Prairies |
| until 31·08·97 | Hamburg | Hamburg. M. Völkerkunde | Red Cloud, Blue Horse |
| until Autumn 97 | Bonn | Kunst- und Ausstellungsh. BRD | Future Garden Part 1 |
| until Autumn 97 | Karlsruhe | St. Kunsthalle Karlsruhe | Paper Art |
| until 14·09·97 | Berlin | Brücke-Museum | Painters of 'Die Brücke' |
| until 28·09·97 | Bonn | Kunstmuseum Bonn | François Morellet |
| until 19·10·97 | Köln - Cologne | Rautenstrauch-Joest-Museum | Art-icles from South-East Asia |
| until 16·11·97 | Trier | Rheinisches Landesmuseum Trier | Roman Mosaics |
| until Nov 97 | Berlin | Museum für Völkerkunde | Masks and Disguises |
| until Dec 97 | Berlin | Bauhaus-Archiv/M. Gestaltung | The Bauhaus Weimar Dessau Berlin |
| until Feb 98 | Dresden | Albertinum Staatliche Kunsts. | The Medals of the Saxon States |
| May 97 onwards | Kassel | Hessisches Landesmuseum | Dürer - Tizian - Poussin |
| May 97 onwards | Kassel | Hessisches Landesmuseum | Small Renaissance |
| May 97-29·06·97 | Berlin | Kunstgewerbemuseum | Shellfish and Snails |
| 01·05·97 - 30·04·98 | Bonn | Kunstmuseum Bonn | P.O. Box |
| 03·05·97 - 07·09·97 | Goslar | Mönchehaus-M. für moderne Kunst | Heinz Mack |
| 04·05·97 - 29·06·97 | Hamburg | Museum für Kunst und Gewerbe | Uwe Loesch Graphic Design |
| 04·05·97 - 27·07·97 | Mönchengladbach | Städtisches Museum Abteiberg | Lucio Fontana Il Disegno |
| 07·05·97 - 13·07·97 | Dresden | Albertinum Staatliche Kunsts. | Early Meissener Porcelain |
| 07·05·97 - 27·07·97 | Frankfurt am Main | St. Kunstinstitut & Städt. Galerie | Pablo Picasso Suite Vollard |
| 08·05·97 - 22·06·97 | Nürnberg | Kunsthalle Nürnberg | Rémy Zaugg |
| 08·05·97 - 13·07·97 | Leipzig | M. der Bildenden Künste Leipzig | Paul Klee Southern Journeys |
| 08·05·97 - 20·07·97 | München - Munich | Haus der Kunst | Michail Wrubel The Russian Symbolist |
| 08·05·97 - 20·07·97 | München - Munich | Haus der Kunst | Frantisek Kupka and Otto Gutfreund |
| 08·05·97 - 24·08·97 | Bonn | Kunst- und Ausstellungsh. BRD | German Photography |
| 09·05·97 - 29·06·97 | Mainz | Gutenberg-Museum Mainz | Miniature Books |
| 09·05·97 - 27·07·97 | Hamburg | Hamburger Kunsthalle | Johann Christoph Erhard |
| 09·05·97 - 7·09·97 | Karlsruhe | Badisches Landesmuseum Karlsruhe | New Building in the 20s |
| 10·05·97 - 06·07·97 | Leverkusen | St. Leverkusen Schloß Morsbroich | Location Germany |
| 11·05·97 - 15·06·97 | Lübeck | Overbeck-Gesellschaft | Aldo Rossi |
| 11·05·97 - 06·07·97 | Essen | Museum Folkwang Essen | Ansgar Nierhoff |
| 13·05·97 - 20·07·97 | Berlin | Bauhaus-Archiv/M. Gestaltung | Home and Workspace |
| 14·05·97 - 13·07·97 | Frankfurt am Main | St. Kunstinstitut & Städt. Galerie | Johannes Vermeer |
| 14·05·97 - 19·10·97 | Hannover | Historisches Museum | At 17 Youth in Hannover |
| 15·05·97 - 15·06·97 | Essen | Museum Folkwang Essen | Karl Heinz Adler |
| 15·05·97 - 20·07·97 | Ludwigshafen | Wilhelm-Hack-Museum | Rolf Nolden |
| 15·05·97 - 03·08·97 | Bielefeld | Kunsthalle Bielefeld | Not Vital Totem and Taboo |
| 15·05·97 - 03·08·97 | Bielefeld | Kunsthalle Bielefeld | African Masks |
| 15·05·97 - 24·08·97 | Bonn | Rheinisches Landesmuseum Bonn | ..and they left Germany |
| 15·05·97 - 07·09·97 | Nürnberg | Germanisches Nationalmuseum | Art in Leipzig since 1945 |
| 15·05·97 - 21·09·97 | München - Munich | Prähistorische Staatssammlung | Mappot |
| 16·05·97 - 13·07·97 | Hamburg | Museum für Kunst und Gewerbe | Japanese Lacquer Art of the Present |
| 16·05·97 - 27·07·97 | Hamburg | Museum für Kunst und Gewerbe | Alphonse Mucha |
| 16·05·97 - 03·08·97 | Köln - Cologne | Museum für Angewandte Kunst | Rudolf Schwarz Inhabited Images |
| 16·05·97 - 12·08·97 | Berlin | Deutsches Historisches M. GmbH | Wolfsburg/Eisenhüttenstadt |
| 17·05·97 - 20·07·97 | Berlin | Brücke-Museum | Ernst Ludwig Kirchner Photographs |
| 17·05·97 - 10·08·97 | Düsseldorf | Kunstsamml. Nordrhein-Westfalen | Barnett Newman |

Exhibitions in chronological order.

## GERMANY

| DATE | CITY | MUSEUM | ARTIST/THEME |
|------|------|--------|--------------|
| 17·05·97 - 14·09·97 | Stuttgart | Staatsgalerie Stuttgart | Tension |
| 21·05·97 - 03·08·97 | Mainz | Gutenberg-Museum Mainz | Bülent Erkmen |
| 23·05·97 - 13·07·97 | Hamburg | Museum für Kunst und Gewerbe | The Secrets of the Pharaohs |
| 23·05·97 - 14·09·97 | Köln - Cologne | Römisch-Germanisches Museum | Death on the Rhine Burials |
| 24·05·97 - 14·09·97 | Wolfsburg | Kunstmuseum Wolfsburg | Bruce Nauman |
| 25·05·97 - 29·06·97 | Esslingen | Galerie der Stadt Esslingen | Beate Jacob and Tamara Khundadze |
| 25·05·97 - 06·07·97 | Göttingen | Städtische Museum Göttingen | Compassion and Rebirth in Tibetan Art |
| 25·05·97 - 20·07·97 | Esslingen | Galerie der Stadt Esslingen | Heimo Zobernig (Vienna) |
| 27·05·97 - Aug 97 | Dresden | Albertinum Staatliche Kunsts. | Gerda Lepke |
| 29·05·97 - 01·06·97 | Nürnberg | Germanisches Nationalmuseum | Blackwhiteblack |
| 30·05·97 - 20·07·97 | Berlin | Museum für Ostasiatische Kunst | Haiga and Haiku |
| 31·05·97 - 24·08·97 | Bonn | Kunstmuseum Bonn | Body and Soul |
| 31·05·97 - 07·09·97 | Stuttgart | Staatsgalerie Stuttgart | Mapplethorpe |
| 31·05·97 - 14·09·97 | Karlsruhe | Badisches Landesmuseum Karlsruhe | Germany's Longing For Italy |
| Jun 97-Aug 97 | Bonn | Kunstmuseum Bonn | Art in Nature: Holland |
| Jun 97-Oct 97 | Kassel | Neue Galerie | Joseph Beuys 7000 Oaks |
| 01·06·97 - 13·07·97 | Regensburg | Museum Ostdeutsche Galerie | Lotte Jacobi  Berlin-New York |
| 01·06·97 - 13·07·97 | Schwerin | St. M. Schwerin-Kunstsammlungen | Georges Vantongerloo |
| 01·06·97 - 24·08·97 | Hannover | Sprengel Museum Hannover | Felix Gonzalez-Torres |
| 03·06·97 - 06·07·97 | Bonn | Bonner Kunstverein | Nana Petzet |
| 05·06·97 - 31·07·97 | Freiburg im Breisgau | Augustinermuseum | Crystal Polishing |
| 05·06·97 - 17·08·97 | Braunschweig | Herzog Anton Ulrich Museum | Dialogue with the Old Masters |
| 05·06·97 - 24·08·97 | Stuttgart | Galerie der Stadt Stuttgart | Peter Chevalier |
| 06·06·97 - 17·08·97 | Hamburg | Museum für Kunst und Gewerbe | The Anne Wolf Class |
| 06·06·97 - 07·09·97 | Bonn | Kunstmuseum Bonn | Multiple Identity |
| 06·06·97 - 30·11·97 | Berlin | Museum für Völkerkunde | The Treasure in the Sea |
| 07·06·97 - 13·07·97 | Berlin | Neue Gesellschaft für Bildende Kunst | Dorothy Iannone |
| 07·06·97 - mid Aug 97 | Karlsruhe | Staatliche Kunsthalle Karlsruhe | Paco Knöller |
| 07·06·97 - 05·10·97 | Kassel | Neue Galerie | Olav Christopher Jenssen |
| 08·06·97 - 17·08·97 | Münster | Westfälisches Landesmuseum | Artists in the Mirror of a Collection |
| 10·06·97 - 06·07·97 | Frankfurt am Main | Schirn Kunsthalle | Georg Heck |
| 10·06·97 - 06·07·97 | Frankfurt am Main | Schirn Kunsthalle | Pietro Donzelli |
| 13·06·97 - 19·10·97 | Bonn | Kunst- und Ausstellungsh. BRD | Sigmar Polke |
| 14·06·97 - 10·08·97 | Aachen | Suermondt Ludwig M. | Ralf Kreuels |
| 14·06·97 - 24·08·97 | Frankfurt am Main | Deutsches Architektur-Museum | FORUM in the German Architecture M. |
| 14·06·97 - 14·09·97 | Baden-Baden | Staatliche Kunsthalle Baden-Baden | Im Kunstlicht |
| 14·06·97 - 14·09·97 | Baden-Baden | Staatliche Kunsthalle Baden-Baden | ...Just Below My Skin... |
| 15·06·97 - 17·08·97 | Mainz | Landesmuseum Mainz | Hans Arp |
| 15·06·97 - 31·08·97 | Weimar | Kunstsammlungen zu Weimar | Colours of the Light |
| 15·06·97 - 14·09·97 | Mannheim | Reiß-Museum | Correspondences |
| 17·06·97 - 24·08·97 | Stuttgart | Galerie der Stadt Stuttgart | Les Levine |
| 19·06·97 - 03·08·97 | Leipzig | M. der Bildenden Künste Leipzig | Cranach Rediscovered |
| 19·06·97 - 10·08·97 | Frankfurt am Main | Portikus Frankfurt am Main | Matthew Barney |
| 20·06·97 - onwards | Hannover | Niedersächsisches Landesmuseum | M. Liebermann, M. Slevogt, L. Corinth |
| 20·06·97 - 14·09·97 | Köln - Cologne | Wallraf-Richartz-Museum | L'Art Gourmand |
| 20·06·97 - end 97 | Berlin | Deutsches Technikmuseum Berlin | Arbours on Wheelsend |
| 21·06·97 - Summer 97 | Hamburg | Museum für Kunst und Gewerbe | Viewing a Century  Martin Haller |
| 21·06·97 - Summer 97 | Hamburg | Museum für Kunst und Gewerbe | Ten Years of Painting |
| 21·06·97 - Summer 97 | Stuttgart | Staatsgalerie Stuttgart | Art Games |
| 22·06·97 - 03·08·97 | Essen | Museum Folkwang Essen | "World Art Grows ....." |
| 22·06·97 - 03·08·97 | Kiel | Kunsthalle zu Kiel | Olav Christopher Jenssen  Radio |
| 22·06·97 - 31·08·97 | Saarbrücken | Saarland Museum | Monika von Boch |
| 22·06·97 - 31·08·97 | Weimar | Kunstsammlungen zu Weimar | Focus on the Time of Goethe I |
| 22·06·97 - 14·09·97 | Karlsruhe | Badisches Landesmuseum Karlsruhe | Stefan Szczesny  Ceramics |
| 22·06·97 - 28·09·97 | Münster | Westfälisches Landesmuseum | Sculpture Projects in Münster 1997 |
| 26·06·97 - 10·08·97 | Bonn | Rheinishes Landesmuseum Bonn | Sitting |
| 26·06·97 - 24·08·97 | Nürnberg | Germanisches Nationalmuseum | Valuables |
| 27·06·97 - 07·09·97 | Aachen | Ludwig Forum für Int. Kunst | Günther Grass |
| 27·06·97 - 07·09·97 | München - Munich | Die Neue Sammlung | Photographing Architecture |
| 27·06·97 - 14·09·97 | Köln - Cologne | Museum für Angewandte Kunst | From the Tables |
| 27·06·97 - 25·11·97 | Berlin | Deutsches Historisches M. GmbH | Bohemia And Dictatorship in the GDR |
| 27·06·97 - 15·01·98 | Frankfurt am Main | Museum für Moderne Kunst | Change of Scene XII |
| 28·06·97 - 14·09·97 | Mannheim | Reiß-Museum | Garden-Furniture from the Art Nouveau |
| 29·06·97 - onwards | Dortmund | Museum am Ostwall | Masterpieces from the Collection |

Exhibitions in chronological order.

| GERMANY | | | |
|---|---|---|---|
| **DATE** | **CITY** | **MUSEUM** | **ARTIST/THEME** |
| 29·06·97 - 27·07·97 | Duisburg | Wilhelm Lehmbruck Museum | Constantin Brancusi |
| 29·06·97 - 24·08·97 | Mainz | Landesmuseum Mainz | Johann Peter Melchior |
| 29·06·97 - 07·09·97 | Ulm | Ulmer Museum | Schopper-Schiffer-Donaufisher |
| Jul 97 onwards | Nürnberg | Germanisches Nationalmuseum | Art and Culture |
| Jul 97-Aug 97 | Chemnitz | Städtische Kunstsammlungen | Richard Anuszkiewicz |
| Jul 97-Aug 97 | Mainz | Landesmuseum Mainz | Ludwig Wilding |
| Jul 97-Sep 97 | Berlin | Kunstgewerbemuseum | Porcelain Brands |
| 03·07·97 - 31·08·97 | Frankfurt am Main | Museum für Kunsthandwerk | A Leased Inheritance |
| 04·07·97 - 24·08·97 | Esslingen | Galerie der Stadt Esslingen | Hauke Harder and Stephan Ullmann |
| 05·07·97 - 05·10·97 | Aachen | Suermondt Ludwig M. | Sebastian Stoskopff |
| 10·07·97 - 24·08·97 | Nürnberg | Kunsthalle Nürnberg | Unlimited |
| 11·07·97 - 14·09·97 | München - Munich | Kunsth. der Hypo-Kulturstiftung | Markus Lüpertz |
| 12·07·97 - 17·08·97 | Ludwigshafen | Wilhelm-Hack-Museum | 'The Anchor' Artists Group |
| 12·07·97 - 28·09·97 | Stuttgart | Staatsgalerie Stuttgart | Hanne Darboven |
| 13·07·97 - 17·08·97 | Lübeck | Overbeck-Gesellschaft | Young Art International '97 |
| 13·07·97 - 31·08·97 | Göttingen | Städtische Museum Göttingen | In memoriam Kurt Manni |
| 13·07·97 - 28·09·97 | Dresden | Albertinum Staatliche Kunsts. | Conrad Felixmüller |
| 15·07·97 - 07·09·97 | Bonn | Bonner Kunstverein | Bon Direct 3 |
| 16·07·97 - 26·10·97 | München - Munich | Städtische Galerie im Lenbachhaus | Paula Modersohn-Becker (1876-1907) |
| 17·07·97 - 02·09·97 | Berlin | Deutsches Historisches M. GmbH | Photographs by Orgel-Köhne |
| 17·07·97 - 19·10·97 | München - Munich | Villa Stuck | Villa Stuck Anniversary exhibition |
| 19·07·97 - 24·08·97 | Berlin | Neue Gesellschaft für Bildende Kunst | Art and the Computer |
| 19·07·97 - 26·10·97 | Weimar | Kunstsammlungen zu Weimar | The Karl-Peter Röhl Foundation Weimar |
| 20·07·97 - 31·08·97 | Schwerin | St. M. Schwerin-Kunstsammlungen | Positions |
| 20·07·97 - 07·09·97 | Regensburg | Museum Ostdeutsche Galerie | Gudrun Wassermann |
| 23·07·97 - 05·10·97 | München - Munich | Städtische Galerie im Lenbachhaus | Harald Klingelhöller |
| 24·07·97 - 21·09·97 | Berlin | Museum für Ostasiatische Kunst | Andô Hiroshige |
| end Jul 97-Oct 97 | München - Munich | Haus der Kunst | München 1997 |
| 25·07·97 - 07·09·97 | Esslingen | Galerie der Stadt Esslingen | Esslingen Artists' Society |
| 25·07·97 - 14·09·97 | Aachen | Ludwig Forum für Int. Kunst | Art in Aachen |
| 26·07·97 - 14·09·97 | Berlin | Brücke-Museum | Max Klaus Graphic Reproductions |
| 26·07·97 - 19·10·97 | Mannheim | Reiß-Museum | Confidants of the Gods |
| 27·07·97 - 31·08·97 | Göttingen | Städtische Museum Göttingen | Jutta Keul Paintings and Sculptures |
| 31·07·97 - 28·09·97 | Ludwigshafen | Wilhelm-Hack-Museum | Jean-Michel Frouin |
| 31·07·97 - 26·10·97 | München - Munich | Villa Stuck | Grete Stern Photographs |
| 01·08·97 - 05·10·97 | Köln - Cologne | Museum für Angewandte Kunst | Ernst Riegel |
| 01·08·97 - 12·10·97 | München - Munich | Haus der Kunst | Deep Storage |
| 03·08·97 - 05·10·97 | Essen | Museum Folkwang Essen | Patrick Tosani Colour Photographs |
| 05·08·97 - 05·10·97 | Berlin | Bauhaus-Archiv/M. Gestaltung | Velten Articles |
| 09·08·97 - 21·09·97 | Düsseldorf | Kunsthalle Düsseldorf | Imi Knoebel |
| 09·08·97 - 21·09·97 | Kiel | Kunsthalle zu Kiel | Gustav Kluge |
| 10·08·97 - 21·09·97 | Essen | Museum Folkwang Essen | Antique Art from the 13th to 18th Cent. |
| 10·08·97 - 12·10·97 | Schwerin | Staatliches Museum Schwerin | Triennale of Arts and Crafts |
| 15·08·97 - 26·10·97 | Berlin | Museum für Ostasiatische Kunst | Nurimono |
| 16·08·97 - 19·10·97 | Dresden | Albertinum Staatliche Kunsts. | Van Eyck, Brueghel, Rembrandt |
| 17·08·97 - 16·10·97 | Duisburg | Wilhelm Lehmbruck Museum | Photography Collection of the Museum |
| 17·08·97 - 05·10·97 | Bielefeld | Kunsthalle Bielefeld | Robert Longo The Magellan Project |
| 17·08·97 - 16·11·97 | Bielefeld | Kunsthalle Bielefeld | New Collection III |
| 20·08·97 - 12·10·97 | Bonn | Rheinisches Landesmuseum Bonn | The Total Healing Method |
| 22·08·97 - 05·10·97 | Berlin | Kunstgewerbemuseum | Walked All Over |
| 22·08·97 - 19·10·97 | Hamburg | Hamburger Kunsthalle | The Hamburg Artists Club of 1897 |
| 24·08·97 - 24·10·97 | Aachen | Suermondt Ludwig M. | Heiner Hoffman |
| 27·08·97 - 16·11·97 | Hannover | Sprengel Museum Hannover | Art in Context Artist's Museum (3) |
| 28·08·97 - 31·12·97 | Mainz | Gutenberg-Museum Mainz | 'Look, there he is...' |
| 30·08·97 - 12·10·97 | Berlin | Neue Gesellschaft für Bildende Kunst | Timm Ulrichs The Detecting Glance |
| 30·08·97 - 26·10·97 | Ludwigshafen | Wilhelm-Hack-Museum | Hans Arp |
| Sep 97 | Bremen | Übersee-Museum Bremen | Manus |
| Sep 97 - Oct 97 | Hamburg | Museum für Kunst und Gewerbe | Frauke Hänke & Klaus Kienle |
| Sep 97 - Nov 97 | Chemnitz | Städtische Kunstsammlungen | 20 Years of Clara Mosch |
| Sep 97 - Nov 97 | Essen | Museum Folkwang Essen | Norske Profiler |
| Sep 97 - Nov 97 | Hamburg | Museum für Kunst und Gewerbe | Seven German Goldsmiths |
| Sep 97 - Jan 98 | Weil am Rhein | Vitra Design Museum | The World of Charles & Ray Eames |
| 01·09·97 - 20·12·97 | Berlin | Kunstgewerbemuseum | Contemporary Jewellery |
| 02·09·97 - 02·11·97 | Leverkusen | St. Leverkusen Schloß Morsbroich | On the Path to Natural Perception |

Exhibitions in chronological order.

## GERMANY

| DATE | CITY | MUSEUM | ARTIST/THEME |
|------|------|--------|--------------|
| 04·09·97 - 23·09·97 | Berlin | Deutsches Historisches M. GmbH | Clicks  Simone Kornfeld |
| 04·09·97 - 03·11·97 | Berlin | Berlinische Galerie | Correspondences Berlin-Edinburgh |
| 04·09·97 - 30·12·97 | Stuttgart | Galerie der Stadt Stuttgart | Man Ray |
| 05·09·97 - 02·11·97 | Hamburg | Museum für Kunst und Gewerbe | On the 100th Anniversary J. Brahms |
| 05·09·97 - 09·11·97 | Bonn | Kunstmuseum Bonn | August Macke |
| 06·09·97 - 30·11·97 | Düsseldorf | Kunstsamml. Nordrhein-Westfalen | Max Beckmann  'The Night' |
| 06·09·97 - 30·11·97 | Köln - Cologne | Wallraf-Richartz-Museum | Pointillism A Theory Becomes Art |
| 07·09·97 - 19·10·97 | Lübeck | Overbeck-Gesellschaft | Georg Baselitz |
| 07·09·97 - 16·11·97 | Ulm | Ulmer Museum | Hans Multscher |
| 07·09·97 - 23·11·97 | Mönchengladbach | Städtisches Museum Abteiberg | In the Realm of Phantoms |
| 07·09·97 - 23·11·97 | Schwerin | St. M. Schwerin-Kunstsammlungen | Paul Holz (1883-1938) |
| 07·09·97 - 30·11·97 | Hannover | Sprengel Museum Hannover | Conrad Felixmüller  The Dresden Years |
| 08·09·97 - 09·11·97 | München - Munich | Haus der Kunst | From Füsli to Menzel |
| 13·09·97 - 02·11·97 | Frankfurt am Main | Schirn Kunsthalle | Hans Hofmann |
| 13·09·97 - 23·11·97 | Frankfurt am Main | Deutsches Architektur-Museum | Architecture in the 20th C.: Portugal |
| 14·09·97 - 09·11·97 | Dortmund | Museum am Ostwall | Ian Hamilton Finlay |
| 14·09·97 - end Jan 98 | Goslar | Mönchehaus-M. für moderne Kunst | Art for Goslar |
| 15·09·97 - 23·09·97 | Köln - Cologne | Josef-Haubrich-Kunsthalle | Antiquarian Days |
| 15·09·97 - 14·11·97 | Saarbrücken | Saarland Museum | Till Neu  The St. Donat Project |
| 16·09·97 - 23·11·97 | Berlin | Berlinische Galerie | Jeanne Mammen  Retrospective |
| 18·09·97 - 21·09·97 | Baden-Baden | Staatliche Kunsthalle Baden-Baden | New Pop Festival |
| 18·09·97 - 09·11·97 | Mainz | Gutenberg-Museum Mainz | Finnland - 500 Years on Map of Europe |
| 18·09·97 - 16·11·97 | Aachen | Suermondt Ludwig M. | Luisa Schatzmann |
| 18·09·97 - 18·01·98 | Braunschweig | Herzog Anton Ulrich Museum | Fürstenberg Chinaware |
| 20·09·97 - 07·12·97 | Köln | Museum für Ostasiatische Kunst | Masterpieces of Japanese Woodcuts |
| Autumn 97 | Aachen | Ludwig Forum für Int. Kunst | Music Box |
| Autumn 97 | Berlin | Kunstgewerbemuseum | The Dowry of Princesses |
| Autumn -Winter 97 | Frankfurt am Main | St. Kunstinstitut & Städt. Galerie | The Adoration of the Kings |
| 21·09·97 - 09·11·97 | Göttingen | Städtische Museum Göttingen | 250 Years Freemasonry in Göttingen |
| 21·09·97 - 09·11·97 | Ulm | Ulmer Museum | The Deschler Collection |
| 21·09·97 - 30·11·97 | Esslingen | Galerie der Stadt Esslingen | ZERO in Paris 1960. And Today |
| 21·09·97 - 30·11·97 | Esslingen | Galerie der Stadt Esslingen | Martin Gostner (Innsbruck) |
| 23·09·97 - 02·11·97 | Bonn | Bonner Kunstverein | Böttcherstrasse Kunstpreis 1997 |
| 23·09·97 - 02·11·97 | Bonn | Bonner Kunstverein | Peter Mertes Stipendium '97 |
| 24·09·97 - 26·10·97 | Bonn | Kunstmuseum Bonn | Tinka Von Hasselbach |
| 25·09·97 - 16·11·97 | Bonn | Kunstmuseum Bonn | Oswaldo Romber  Bypass |
| 26·09·97 - 16·11·97 | Aachen | Ludwig Forum für Int. Kunst | Johannes Gruetzke |
| 26·09·97 - 30·11·97 | Berlin | Museum für Ostasiatische Kunst | Inrô  Japanese Medicine Boxes |
| 26·09·97 - 30·11·97 | Berlin | Museum für Ostasiatische Kunst | Robes in Japanese Woodcuts |
| 26·09·97 - 11·01·98 | München - Munich | Kunsth. der Hypo-Kulturstiftung | Cobra |
| 27·09·97 - 26·10·97 | Duisburg | Wilhelm Lehmbruck Museum | Heinz-Günter Prager  Borobodur |
| 27·09·97 - 23·11·97 | Karlsruhe | Badisches Landesmuseum Karlsruhe | Janna Syvänoja  Working in Paper |
| 27·09·97 - 30·11·97 | Frankfurt am Main | Schirn Kunsthalle | Fernando Pessoa |
| 27·09·97 - 11·01·98 | Stuttgart | Staatsgalerie Stuttgart | Johann Heinrich Füssli |
| 28·09·97 - 16·11·97 | Essen | Museum Folkwang Essen | Lotte Errell  Journalist of the 1930s |
| 28·09·97 - 23·11·97 | Saarbrücken | Saarland Museum | Drawings from Tuscany |
| 28·09·97 - 04·01·98 | Berlin | Brücke-Museum | The Blue Rider |
| Oct 97-Nov 97 | Berlin | Berlinische Galerie | Henry Ries  On His 80th Birthday |
| Oct 97-Dec 97 | Berlin | Kunstgewerbemuseum | Prussian Portraits |
| Oct 97-Dec 97 | Frankfurt am Main | St. Kunstinstitut & Städt. Galerie | Germans Drawings of the 17th Century |
| Oct 97-Dec 97 | Mönchengladbach | Schloß Rheydt | Giottos Message |
| Oct 97-Jan 98 | München - Munich | Die Neue Sammlung | Plastics & Design |
| Oct 97-Jan 98 | München - Munich | Prähistorische Staatssammlung | Culinaria Romana |
| 01·10·97 - 18·01·98 | Hannover | Sprengel Museum Hannover | Henri Toulouse-Lautrec |
| 02·10·97 - 07·12·97 | Nürnberg | Kunsthalle Nürnberg | Arte Povera |
| 02·10·97 - 31·12·97 | Leipzig | M. der bildenden Künste Leipzig | Art and Artists in Leipzig 1945-95 |
| 03·10·97 - 10·11·97 | Düsseldorf | Kunsthalle Düsseldorf | Marcel Broodthaers  Cinema |
| 03·10·97 - 09·12·97 | Berlin | Deutsches Historisches M. GmbH | Klaus Fußmann |
| 04·10·97 - 16·11·97 | Baden-Baden | Staatliche Kunsthalle Baden-Baden | Water Colours Romantic Movement |
| 04·10·97 - 16·11·97 | Baden-Baden | Staatliche Kunsthalle Baden-Baden | Sol LeWitt  '100 cubes' |
| 08·10·97 - 09·11·97 | Weimar | Kunstsammlungen zu Weimar | Norbert W. Hinterberger |
| 09·10·97 - 23·11·97 | Stuttgart | Staatsgalerie Stuttgart | Ars Viva 97/98 - New Media |
| 09·10·97 - 07·12·97 | Ludwigshafen | Wilhelm-Hack-Museum | Günther Meck |
| 09·10·97 - 31·12·97 | Bonn | Rheinisches Landesmuseum Bonn | The House Laughs for Silver |

Exhibitions in chronological order.

Exhibitions in chronological order.

| GERMANY | | | |
|---|---|---|---|
| **DATE** | **CITY** | **MUSEUM** | **ARTIST/THEME** |
| 29·11·97 - 07·12·97 | Karlsruhe | Badisches Landesmuseum Karlsruhe | Arts and Crafts Christmas Market |
| 29·11·97 - 14·01·98 | Duisburg | Wilhelm Lehmbruck Museum | Homage to Erwin Heerich |
| 29·11·97 - Jan 98 | Berlin | Neue Gesellschaft für Bildende Kunst | Interrupted Career |
| 30·11·97 - 11·08·98 | Kiel | Kunsthalle zu Kiel | David Lynch |
| 30·11·97 - 25·01·99 | Bielefeld | Kunsthalle Bielefeld | Jonathan Lasker |
| Dec 97-Jan 98 | Freiburg im Breisgau | Augustinermuseum | Johann Christian Wentzinger |
| Dec 97-Feb 98 | Aachen | Ludwig Forum für Int. Kunst | Love, Sadness and Time |
| Dec 97-Easter 98 | Mannheim | Reiß-Museum | The Big `Winter-Exhibition' |
| 04·12·97 - Feb 98 | Bonn | Kunstmuseum Bonn | Andy Warhol Last Supper |
| 05·12·97 - 18·01·98 | Esslingen | Galerie der Stadt Esslingen | Esslingen Artists' Society |
| 06·12·97 - Jan 98 | Mönchengladbach | Schloß Rheydt | Santa Claus likes polished shoes |
| 06·12·97 - 01·02·98 | Düsseldorf | Kunstm. Düsseldorf im Ehrenhof | The Alpha and Omega |
| 06·12·97 - 06·02·98 | Düsseldorf | Kunsthalle Düsseldorf | Andreas & Oswald Aschenbach |
| 06·12·97 - 01·03·98 | Baden-Baden | Staatliche Kunsthalle Baden-Baden | Impresionism & Symbolism from Poland |
| 07·12·97 - 15·01·98 | Schwerin | Staatliches Museum Schwerin | Georg Friedrich Kersting |
| 07·12·97 - 18·01·98 | Esslingen | Galerie der Stadt Esslingen | Eva Maria Reiner (Stuttgart) |
| 07·12·97 - 18·01·98 | Ulm | Ulmer Museum | Ulmer Art |
| 07·12·97 - 01·02·98 | Mönchengladbach | Städtisches Museum Abteiberg | Ars Viva  Art and New Media |
| 07·12·97 - Feb 98 | Saarbrücken | Saarland Museum | Thomas Wojciechowicz |
| 12·12·97 - 15·02·98 | Hamburg | Museum für Kunst und Gewerbe | Porcelain of the 18th Century |
| 13·12·97 - 22·02·98 | Frankfurt am Main | Deutsches Architektur-Museum | Power and Monument |
| 14·12·97 - Feb 98 | Dresden | Albertinum Staatliche Kunsts. | 4 * 1 in Albertinum |
| 14·12·97 - 22·02·98 | Hannover | Sprengel Museum Hannover | International Prize for Photography |
| 14·12·97 - 22·02·98 | Ulm | Ulmer Museum | Historical Tin-Plate Toys |
| 15·12·97 - 13·02·98 | Saarbrücken | Saarland Museum | Heinrich Zille  Berlin Milieu |
| 16·12·97 - 17·05·98 | Köln - Cologne | Rautenstrauch-Joest-Museum | Treasures from the Golden Age |
| 18·12·97 - 25·01·98 | Nürnberg | Kunsthalle Nürnberg | Der Kreis |
| 18·12·97 - 20·02·98 | Ludwigshafen | Wilhelm-Hack-Museum | Siegfried Assfalg |
| 18·12·97 - Feb 98 | Aachen | Suermondt Ludwig M. | Friedrich Gräsel |
| 18·12·97 - 03·03·98 | Berlin | Deutsches Historisches M. GmbH | The Lion And The Cock or .... |
| 19·12·97 - 19·04·98 | Bonn | Kunst- und Ausstellungsh. BRD | Arctic - Antarctic |
| Winter 97/98 | Aachen | Ludwig Forum für Int. Kunst | Cuba & North-Rhine Westphalia |
| Jan 98- Feb 98 | Regensburg | Museum Ostdeutsche Galerie | Janosch |
| Jan 98- mid Apr 98 | Stuttgart | Galerie der Stadt Stuttgart | Alessandro Mendini |
| Jan 98- Jun 98 | Weil am Rhein | Vitra Design Museum | Childrens Furniture |
| mid Jan 98-Mar 98 | Köln - Cologne | Wallraf-Richartz-Museum | Caspar Scheuren  Rhine Series |
| 23·01·98 - 05·04·98 | Hamburg | Hamburger Kunsthalle | Lyonel Feininger |
| 29·01·98 - 12·04·98 | München - Munich | Kunsth. der Hypo-Kulturstiftung | Carl Rottman (1797-1850) |
| 01·02·98 - 29·03·98 | Bremen | Übersee-Museum Bremen | Images of Power |
| 01·02·98 - 13·04·98 | Schwerin | Staatliches Museum Schwerin | Dutch Graphic Art |
| 07·02·98 - 26·04·98 | Wolfsburg | Kunstmuseum Wolfsburg | Peter Fischli & David Weiss |
| 11·02·98 - 12·04·98 | Frankfurt am Main | St. Kunstinstitut & Städt. Galerie | Max Liebermann as Realist |
| 27·02·98 - May 98 | Mannheim | Reiß-Museum | With Fury and Eagerness` |
| 28·02·98 - Jul 98 | Karlsruhe | Badisches Landesmuseum Karlsruhe | Revolution of the German Democrats |
| Mar 98-Apr 98 | Regensburg | Museum Ostdeutsche Galerie | Rolf Cavael Retrospective |
| Mar 98-May 98 | Mönchengladbach | Schloß Rheydt | Collection Köster |
| 01·03·98 - 19·04·98 | Saarbrücken | Saarland Museum | Young Art |
| 05·03·98 - 30·07·98 | Hannover | Historisches Museum | Jewish Culture, Jewish Destiny |
| 20·03·98 - onwards | Berlin | Deutsches Historisches M. GmbH | Myths of the Nations |
| 21·03·98 - 14·06·98 | Düsseldorf | Kunstsamml. Nordrhein-Westfalen | The Blue Four |
| Spring 98 | Berlin | Brücke-Museum | Ernst Ludwig Kirchner |
| 27·03·98 - 25·01·99 | Bonn | Kunst- und Ausstellungsh. BRD | Gene Worlds |
| end Mar 98-Summer 98 | Berlin | Deutsches Technikmuseum Berlin | Peter Behrens |
| 29·03·98 -03·05·98 | Göttingen | Städtische Museum Göttingen | Torun |
| 15·04·98 - 26·05·98 | Berlin | Deutsches Historisches M. GmbH | Tsingtau |
| Apr 98 - Jun 98 | Braunschweig | Herzog Anton Ulrich Museum | Duke Heinrich Julius and Prague |
| 01·05·98 - 23·08·98 | Bonn | Kunst- und Ausstellungsh. BRD | The Iberians |
| 18·05·98 - 18·09·98 | Frankfurt am Main | Schirn Kunsthalle | 1848 En Route to Freedom |
| | | | |
| | | | |
| | | | |
| | | | |
| | | | |

Exhibitions in chronological order.

| GREAT BRITAIN | | | |
|---|---|---|---|
| DATE | CITY | MUSEUM | ARTIST/THEME |
| onwards | London | National Maritime Museum | Nelson |
| until 11·05·97 | Norwich | Sainsbury Centre for Visual Arts | Collections and Reflections |
| until 18·05·97 | Hull | Ferens Art Gallery | Jonathan Allen |
| until 18·05·97 | London | The National Gallery | Discovering the Italian Baroque |
| until 18·05·97 | London | Whitechapel Art Gallery | Antechamber |
| until 18·05·97 | Newcastle u. Tyne | Laing Art Gallery | Victorian Dreams |
| until 24·05·97 | York | York City Art Gallery | Teapotmania |
| until 25·05·97 | Derby | Derby Museum & Art Gallery | Denby Stonewares |
| until 25·05·97 | Derby | Derby Museum & Art Gallery | Derby Sketching Club  110 Years |
| until 25·05·97 | Derby | Derby Museum & Art Gallery | Emmanuel Cooper |
| until 26·05·97 | Cambridge | Fitzwilliam Museum | Gerhart Frankl |
| until 26·05·97 | London | Barbican Art Gallery | Modern Art in Britain |
| until 26·05·97 | London | Barbican Art Gallery | Lucie Rie & Hans Coper |
| until 26·05·97 | London | National Portrait Gallery | Variations on a Theme |
| until 26·05·97 | Manchester | Manchester City Art Galleries | Likeness |
| until 31·05·97 | Middlesbrough | Middlesbrough Art Gallery | Cornelia Hesse Honegger |
| until 31·05·97 | Cheltenham | Cheltenham Art Gallery & Museum | Tsuguni Ota, Woodcuts and Carvings |
| until end May 97 | Glasgow | Gallery of Modern Art | The Lord Provost's Prize |
| until 01·06·97 | Coventry | Herbert Art Gallery & Museum | Heart of England Biennial 2 |
| until 01·06·97 | London | Dulwich Picture Gallery | The Inner Eye  Art Beyond the Visible |
| until 01·06·97 | Edinburgh | Scottish National Portrait Gallery | Signs and Wonders   Owen Logan |
| until 01·06·97 | Edinburgh | Scottish National Portrait Gallery | John Kobal |
| until 01·06·97 | Hull | Ferens Art Gallery | Steve Dilworth |
| until 01·06·97 | Manchester | Manchester City Art Galleries | Tony Oursler |
| until 02·06·97 | Birmingham | M. and Art Gal. / The Gas Hall | Star Trek, The Exhibition |
| until 08·06·97 | Bournemouth | Russell-Cotes Art Gal. and M. | Evelyn De Morgan |
| until 08·06·97 | Edinburgh | National Gallery of Scotland | Cassiano dal Pozzo's Paper Museum |
| until 08·06·97 | Edinburgh | Royal Museum of Scotland | Objects of OUr Time - Crafts in the 90's |
| until 08·06·97 | Liverpool | Walker Art Gallery | Sir Lawrence Alma-Tadema |
| until 08·06·97 | London | National Portrait Gallery | August Sander |
| until 08·06·97 | London | The National Gallery | Dürer's 'Saint Jerome' |
| until 08·06·97 | London | Royal Academy of Arts | The Berlin of George Grosz |
| until 08·06·97 | London | Tate Gallery | Hogarth the Painter |
| until 08·06·97 | Newcastle u. Tyne | Laing Art Gallery | Eastern Edge |
| until 13·06·97 | Bath | Holburne M. and Crafts Study Centre | Lady in Waiting, Watercolours |
| until 13·06·97 | Bath | Holburne M. and Crafts Study Centre | Dancing at Almack's |
| until 15·06·97 | Cambridge | Fitzwilliam Museum | Masterpieces of Japanese Printmaking |
| until 15·06·97 | Leeds | Leeds City Art Gallery | Small Truths |
| until 15·06·97 | London | ICA Institute of Contemporary Arts | Billy Name |
| until 15·06·97 | London | Tate Gallery | Luciano Fabro   Supported by Coutts |
| until 15·06·97 | Northampton | Central Museum and Art Gallery | Through Celtic Mists |
| until 15·06·97 | Norwich | Castle Museum | Young Gainsborough |
| until 15·06·97 | Norwich | Castle Museum | Edvard Munch |
| until 15·06·97 | Southampton | Southampton City Art Gallery | Art in Boxes |
| until 15·06·97 | Southampton | Southampton City Art Gallery | Moore & Blatch Student Exhibition |
| until 21·06·97 | Chichester | Pallant House Gallery | The Art of Drawing |
| until 22·06·97 | London | The National Gallery | Back to the Future |
| until 22·06·97 | Belfast | Ulster Museum | W.J. Leech Retrospective |
| until 29·06·97 | Brighton | Brighton Museum & Art Gallery | Les Sixties |
| until 29·06·97 | Cambridge | Fitzwilliam Museum | Shakespeare and the 18th Century |
| until 06·07·97 | Oxford | Museum of Modern Art | In Visible Light |
| until 13·07·97 | Oxford | Ashmolean M. and Univ. Galleries | Life Drawings |
| until 20·07·97 | London | The British Museum | Ancient Faces |
| until 20·07·97 | Edinburgh | Royal Museum of Scotland | Khalili Collection |
| until 27·07·97 | London | Victoria and Albert Museum | The Cutting Edge |
| until Jul 97 | Grasmere | The Wordsworth Museum | Fay Godwin |
| until 31·08·97 | London | Sir John Soane's Museum | Hogarth's Rake's Progress |
| until 01·09·97 | Cambridge | Fitzwilliam Museum | Samplers |
| until 07·09·97 | York | Yorkshire Museum | Fangs |
| until 11·09·98 | Belfast | Ulster Museum | The 18th Century on Paper |
| until 21·09·97 | Belfast | Ulster Museum | Traveling through Time |
| until Sep 97 | London | The Serpentine Gallery | Inside Out |
| until 26·10·97 | Bristol | City Museum and Art Gallery | Cabot 500 From Bristol to the Sea |
| until 31·10·97 | York | Yorkshire Museum | Carnosaur! |

## GREAT BRITAIN

| DATE | CITY | MUSEUM | ARTIST/THEME |
|------|------|--------|--------------|
| until 02·11·97 | St. Ives | Tate Gallery St. Ives | Clive Bowen  Ceramics |
| until 16·11·97 | Norwich | Castle Museum | Big Pictures from the Collection |
| until 16·11·97 | Belfast | Ulster Museum | British and Irish Paintings |
| until 31·12·97 | London | Museum of Mankind | Stairways to the Sky |
| until 31·12·97 | London | Museum of Mankind | Great Benin |
| until 31·12·97 | London | Museum of Mankind | Treasures |
| until 31·12·97 | London | Museum of Mankind | The Gilded Image |
| until 31·12·97 | London | Museum of Mankind | Tent Felts from Kyrgyzstan |
| until 04·01·98 | Derby | Pickford's House Museum | The Art of 18th-Century Dress |
| until 22·02·98 | Cardiff | National Museum of Wales | Images of Botany |
| until Mar 98 | Norwich | Castle Museum | Joseph Stannard  Watercolour |
| until Spring 98 | Cambridge | Cambridge Univ. M. of  Arch & Anthr. | Metal in Africa |
| May 97-Jul 97 | Edinburgh | Scottish Nat. Gallery of Modern Art | Picasso |
| 01·05·97 - 31·05·97 | Newcastle u. Tyne | The Hatton Gallery | Masterpieces |
| 02·05·97 - 31·05·97 | Truro | Royal Cornwall Museum | Cornwall Photographic Alliance |
| 02·05·97 - 31·05·97 | Truro | Royal Cornwall Museum | The Imagery of Light |
| 02·05·97 - 19·06·97 | Dorchester | Dorset County Museum | Sandra Spencer |
| 03·05·97 - 25·05·97 | Aberdeen | Aberdeen Art Gallery | Aberdeen Artists' Society |
| 03·05·97 - 01·06·97 | Kirkcaldy | Kirkcaldy Museum and Art Gallery | Reckoning with the Past |
| 03·05·97 - 29·06·97 | Edinburgh | Royal Museum of Scotland | Beauty and the Banknote |
| 03·05·97 - 13·07·97 | Derby | Pickford's House Museum | Silent Companions |
| 03·05·97 - 13·07·97 | London | The British Museum | Far and Near Eastern Greenwares |
| 05·05·97 - 02·11·97 | York | Yorkshire Museum | Megafun with Computers |
| 06·05·97 - 31·08·97 | Cambridge | Fitzwilliam Museum | Mexican Prints |
| 09·05·97 - 31·08·97 | Belfast | Ulster Museum | Dinosaurs: A New Generation |
| 09·05·97 - Dec 97 | Glasgow | Art Gallery and Museum | Open Sesam |
| 10·05·97 - 06·07·97 | Wakefield | Wakefield Art Gallery | Wakefield Art Club |
| 10·05·97 - 02·11·97 | St. Ives | Tate Gallery St. Ives | St. Ives International |
| 12·05·97 - 23·06·97 | Dorchester | Dorset County Museum | George Dannatt |
| 13·05·97 - 20·07·97 | London | Academy & the Accademia Italiana | Serenissima |
| 15·05·97 - 27·05·97 | Bristol | City Museum and Art Gallery | Cabot 500  Schools Fashion Show |
| 15·05·97 - 07·9·97 | London | The British Museum | The Ceramic Art of Sawada Chitojin |
| 15·05·97 - 07·09·97 | London | The British Museum | Japanese Pottery and Porcelain |
| 16·05·97 - 31·08·97 | Belfast | Ulster Museum | The Narrow Road to the Deep North |
| 16·05·97 - 31·08·97 | Glasgow | The Burrell Collection | Europe in India |
| 17·05·97 - 14·06·97 | Coventry | Herbert Art Gallery & Museum | Free to Move |
| 17·05·97 - 15·06·97 | Hull | Ferens Art Gallery | From the Interior |
| 18·05·97 - 13·07·97 | Edinburgh | Royal Museum of Scotland | Scottish Potters Association |
| 18·05·97 - 31·08·97 | London | Natural History Museum | Gobi Desert Dinosaurs |
| 19·05·97 - 31·05·97 | London | Leighton House M. & Art Gallery | Piers De Laszlo |
| 20·05·97 - 13·07·97 | Oxford | Ashmolean M. and Univ. Galleries | Museum Acquisitions 1985-1997 |
| 20·05·97 - 14·09·97 | London | The British Museum | Coin Jewellery |
| 21·05·97 - 22·06·97 | London | The Serpentine Gallery | Anya Gallaccio |
| 22·05·97 - 07·09·97 | Glasgow | McLellan Galleries | The Birth of Impressionism |
| 23·05·97 - 14·09·97 | London | The British Museum | Printmaking in Paris |
| 23·05·97 - 14·09·97 | London | The British Museum | Modernism in French Medal Design |
| 23·05·97 - 03·11·97 | Liverpool | Liverpool Museum | Missing Links Alive |
| end May 97-mid Jul 97 | Durham | The Bowes Museum | Royal Shakespeare Company Exhibition |
| end May 97-mid Jul 97 | Edinburgh | Scottish Nat. Gallery of Modern Art | Botanical Paintings |
| 30·05·97 - 29·06·97 | Bristol | City Museum and Art Gallery | Cabot 500  The Italian Community |
| 30·05·97 - 20·07·97 | London | Whitechapel Art Gallery | Cathy de Monchaux |
| 30·05·97 - 07·09·97 | London | National Portrait Gallery | Pursuit of Beauty |
| 31·05·97 - 29·06·97 | Hull | Ferens Art Gallery | Contemporaries |
| 31·05·97 - 26·07·97 | Aberdeen | Aberdeen Art Gallery | Fishing and Farming |
| Jun-Aug 97 | New Bridge | Scottish Agricultural Museum | Pictures by William Robbie |
| Jun 97   - 31·12·97 | London | Museum of Mankind | Patagonia |
| 01·06·97 - 10·08·97 | London | Royal Academy of Arts | 229th Summer Exhibition |
| 03·06·97 - 06·07·97 | Norwich | Sainsbury Centre for Visual Arts | Disembodied |
| 05·06·97 - 11·07·97 | Birmingham | M. and Art Gal. / The Gas Hall | Roots of the Future |
| 07·06·97 - 13·07·97 | Manchester | Manchester City Art Galleries | Sean Scully |
| 07·06·97 - 02·08·97 | Aberdeen | Aberdeen Art Gallery | Hats, Headwear and Millinery |
| 07·06·97 - 30·08·97 | Cheltenham | Cheltenham Art Gallery & Museum | Sophie Ryder |
| 07·06·97 - 07·09·97 | Newcastle u. Tyne | Laing Art Gallery | Jan Niedojadlo |
| 09·06·97 - 21·06·97 | London | Leighton House M. & Art Gallery | Suad al Attar |

Exhibitions in chronological order.

| GREAT BRITAIN | | | |
|---|---|---|---|
| **DATE** | **CITY** | **MUSEUM** | **ARTIST/THEME** |
| 12·06·97 - 07·09·97 | London | Tate Gallery | Ellsworth Kelly |
| 13·06·97 - 21·09·97 | Edinburgh | National Gallery of Scotland | Sir Denis Mahon Collection |
| 13·06·97 - 28·09·97 | London | National Portrait Gallery | Clifford Coffin |
| 14·06·97 - 12·07·97 | Newcastle u. Tyne | The Hatton Gallery | The BA Fine Art Degree Show |
| 14·06·97 - 12·07·97 | Truro | Royal Cornwall Museum | Arts in Trust |
| 14·06·97 - 03·08·97 | York | York City Art Gallery | Vikings and Gods in European Art |
| 14·06·97 - 31·08·97 | Coventry | Herbert Art Gallery & Museum | Kaleidoscope |
| 17·06·97 - 28·06·97 | Middlesbrough | Middlesbrough Art Gallery | Cleveland College of Art |
| 17·06·97 - 14·09·97 | Norwich | Sainsbury Centre for Visual Arts | Photography by Sugimoto |
| 18·06·97 - 07·09·97 | London | The National Gallery | Cranach  A Closer Look |
| 19·06·97 - 22·06·97 | New Bridge | Scottish Agricultural Museum | Combine Harvesters |
| 19·06·97 - 17·08·97 | London | Barbican Art Gallery | Serious Games |
| 19·06·97 - 17·08·97 | London | Barbican Art Gallery | Marc Riboud in China |
| 19·06·97 - 17·08·97 | London | Hayward Gallery | The Harlem Renaissance |
| 19·06·97 - 17·08·97 | London | Hayward Gallery | Tatsuo Miyajima  Big Time |
| 19·06·97 - 31·08·97 | Edinburgh | Scottish National Portrait Gallery | The Face of Denmark |
| 20·06·97 - 17·08·97 | Newcastle u. Tyne | Laing Art Gallery | The Young Gainsborough |
| 20·06·97 - 21·09·97 | Glasgow | Gallery of Modern Art | Contemporary Muslim Art |
| 21·06·97 - 08·09·97 | Coventry | Herbert Art Gallery & Museum | Kaleidoscope |
| 21·06·97 - 28·09·97 | Derby | Derby Museum & Art Gallery | Joseph Wright Bicentenary Exhibition |
| 24·06·97 - 28·09·97 | Cambridge | Fitzwilliam Museum | A Gardener's Roses |
| 25·06·97 - Sep 97 | London | Dulwich Picture Gallery | Stephen Cox |
| 26·06·97 - 05·10·97 | London | National Portrait Gallery | BP Portrait Award and BP Travel Award |
| 27·06·97 - 05·09·97 | Glasgow | Art Gallery and Museum | Pilgrim of the Pen: Ghani al-Ani |
| 27·06·97 - 14·09·97 | Southampton | Southampton City Art Gallery | Turner's Watercolour Explorations |
| 27·06·97 - 15·03·98 | Belfast | Ulster Museum | A Century of Applied Art 1850-1950 |
| 28·06·97 - 27·07·97 | Northampton | Central Museum and Art Gallery | Victorian Visions |
| 28·06·97 - 31·08·97 | Birmingham | M. and Art Gal. / The Gas Hall | Favourite Things! |
| 28·06·97 - end 97 | Bournemouth | Russell-Cotes Art Gal. and M. | Martyn Brewster |
| 30·06·97 - 25·08·97 | Dorchester | Dorset County Museum | Elisabeth Frink |
| Jul 97 | London | Royal Academy of Arts | Schools Final Year Show |
| Jul 97-Aug 97 | Durham | The Bowes Museum | Birds and Plants |
| Jul 97-Mid Sep 97 | Oxford | Ashmolean M. and Univ. Galleries | 15th Century  Engravings |
| Jul 97-Sep 97 | Leeds | Leeds City Art Gallery | John Tunnard & Francis Butterfield |
| 01·07·97 - 19·07·97 | Chichester | Pallant House Gallery | Artist in Residence |
| 01·07·97 - 07·09·97 | London | The Serpentine Gallery | Tadashi Kawamata |
| 02·07·97 - 28·09·97 | London | The National Gallery | Seurat and The Bathers |
| 03·07·97 - 28·09·97 | London | Royal Academy of Arts | Hiroshige |
| 03·07·97 - 31·12·97 | London | Museum of Mankind | Pottery in the Making |
| 04·07·97 - 16·08·97 | Middlesbrough | Middlesbrough Art Gallery | Cleveland Art Society |
| 05·07·97 - 14·09·97 | Edinburgh | Scottish Nat. Gallery of Modern Art | The Gabrielle Keiller Bequest |
| 05·07·97 - 28·09·97 | Bath | Holburne M. and Crafts Study Centre | John Downton |
| 05·07·97 - 02·11·97 | Hull | Ferens Art Gallery | Ferens Collection |
| 05·07·97 - 23·11·97 | Norwich | Castle Museum | Sensations  Come to your Senses |
| 10·07·97 - 28·09·97 | Birmingham | M. and Art Gal. / The Gas Hall | Home from Home |
| 11·07·97 - 17·08·97 | Bristol | City Museum and Art Gallery | Cabot 500  Avon Crafts Guild |
| 11·07·97 - until 2000 | London | The British Museum | Arts of Korea |
| 12·07·97 - 24·08·97 | Brighton | Brighton Museum & Art Gallery | Regency Cartoons |
| 12·07·97 - 24·08·97 | Brighton | Brighton Museum & Art Gallery | Private Eye Times |
| 12·07·97 - 28·09·97 | London | ICA Institute of Contemporary Arts | Assuming Positions |
| 13·07·97  30·08·97 | Norwich | Sainsbury Centre for Visual Arts | EAST 97 |
| 14·07·97 - 02·08·97 | London | Leighton House M. & Art Gallery | The Kensington and Chelsea Artists' |
| 16·07·97 - 14·09·97 | London | The National Gallery | Themes and Variations  Sleep |
| 18·07·97 - 18·09·97 | Liverpool | Walker Art Gallery | Nicholas Horsfield |
| 20·07·97 - 28·09·97 | Oxford | Museum of Modern Art | In Place (Out of Time) |
| 22·07·97 - 28·09·97 | Oxford | Ashmolean M. and Univ. Galleries | Indian block printed Textiles in Egypt |
| end Jul 97-Oct 97 | Grasmere | The Wordsworth Museum | The Ancient Mariner |
| 26·07·97 - 19·10·97 | Edinburgh | Royal Museum of Scotland | Colours of Africa |
| 28·07·97 - 28·09·97 | Newcastle u. Tyne | The Hatton Gallery | The Friends of the Hatton |
| 01·08·97 - 14·09·97 | Wakefield | Wakefield Art Gallery | Zoo |
| 01·08·97 - 05·10·97 | Edinburgh | National Gallery of Scotland | Raeburn |
| 05·08·97 - 11·10·97 | Chichester | Pallant House Gallery | The Sidney Burney 1934 Collection |
| 08·08·97 - 19·10·97 | Edinburgh | National Gallery of Scotland | A Lady  Sargeant and Lady Agnew |
| 08·08·97 - 02·11·97 | Edinburgh | Royal Museum of Scotland | Precious Cargo |

# INDEX OF EXHIBITIONS

Exhibitions in chronological order.

| GREAT BRITAIN | | | |
|---|---|---|---|
| **DATE** | **CITY** | **MUSEUM** | **ARTIST/THEME** |
| 09·08·97 - 30·08·97 | Truro | Royal Cornwall Museum | Truro Art Society |
| 09·08·97 - 31·08·97 | Northampton | Central Museum and Art Gallery | Flying Around Town |
| 16·08·97 - 14·09·97 | York | York City Art Gallery | In the Mind's Eye |
| 25·08·97 - 14·09·97 | Bristol | City Museum and Art Gallery | 50 Years of Twinning |
| 30·08·97 - 25·10·97 | Middlesbrough | Middlesbrough Art Gallery | Stephen Willats |
| Sep 97 | Durham | The Bowes Museum | Tom McGuinness |
| Sep 97- Dec 97 | London | The Wallace Collection | Paul Delaroche |
| 01·09·97 - 22·09·97 | Dorchester | Dorset County Museum | Dorset Craft Guild |
| 03·09·97 - 19·09·97 | Newcastle u. Tyne | The Hatton Gallery | MFA Degree Show |
| 03·09·97 - 19·10·97 | Coventry | Herbert Art Gallery & Museum | TBC |
| 06·09·97 - 24·09·97 | Truro | Royal Cornwall Museum | Cornwall Heritage Trust |
| 06·09·97 - 18·10·97 | Cheltenham | Cheltenham Art Gallery & Museum | Cheltenham Fellows |
| 06·09·97 - 19·10·97 | Brighton | Brighton Museum & Art Gallery | Animals in Art |
| 11·09·97 - 16·11·97 | Edinburgh | Scottish National Portrait Gallery | Women in White |
| 11·09·97 - 16·11·97 | Edinburgh | Scottish National Portrait Gallery | Eve Arnold  In Retrospect |
| 11·09·97 - 14·12·97 | London | Barbican Art Gallery | James Ensor |
| 11·09·97 - 14·12·97 | London | Barbican Art Gallery | Don McCullin |
| 13·09·97 - 04·10·97 | Aberdeen | Aberdeen Art Gallery | Sara Radstone |
| 13·09·97 - 05·10·97 | Northampton | Central Museum and Art Gallery | The work of Bob Dawson |
| 13·09·97 - 26·10·97 | Manchester | Manchester City Art Galleries | Glenys Barton |
| 13·09·97 - 30·11·97 | Birmingham | M. and Art Gal. / The Gas Hall | Print in Focus, Part 1 |
| 16·09·97 - 07·12·98 | London | The British Museum | From Persepolis to the Punjab |
| 19·09·97 - 26·10·97 | Bristol | City Museum and Art Gallery | Cabot 500  Schools Displays |
| 19·09·97 - 11·01·98 | London | National Portrait Gallery | Glenys Barton |
| 20·09·97 - 02·11·97 | Wakefield | Wakefield Art Gallery | Janet Beckwith |
| 22·09·97 - 04·10·97 | London | Leighton House M. & Art Gallery | Charles and Patricia Lester |
| 25·09·97 - 04·01·98 | London | The British Museum | Ogawa Toshu |
| 27·09·97 - 26·10·97 | York | York City Art Gallery | Contemporary Textiles |
| 29·09·97 - 17·11·97 | Dorchester | Dorset County Museum | Work of the Dorchester Camera Club |
| 30·09·97 - 08·12·97 | Oxford | Ashmolean M. and Univ. Galleries | Forrest Reid Collection |
| 30·09·97 - late Dec | Oxford | Ashmolean M. and Univ. Galleries | Prints from the Hope Collection |
| Oct 97- begin Jan 98 | London | The British Museum | Hogarth and his Times |
| Oct 97- begin Jan 98 | London | The British Museum | The Schilling Bequest |
| Oct 97-Jan 98 | London | Hayward Gallery | Objects of Desire  The Modern Still Life |
| Oct 97-Mar 98 | London | Design Museum | Bicycle |
| Oct 97-Mar 98 | London | Sir John Soane's Museum | The Soane's at Home |
| Oct 97-Nov 97 | Edinburgh | Scottish Nat. Gallery of Modern Art | New Works by Calum Colvin |
| 02·10·97 - 11·01·98 | Leeds | Leeds City Art Gallery | Francis Towne |
| 03·10·97 - 07·12·97 | Southampton | Southampton City Art Gallery | Basque Art c. 1890-1950 |
| 03·10·97 - 07·12·97 | Southampton | Southampton City Art Gallery | Jan Hackaert |
| 03·10·97-Jan 98 | London | The British Museum | Cartier 1900-1939 |
| 04·10·97 - 01·11·97 | Newcastle u. Tyne | The Hatton Gallery | Roger de Grey |
| 04·10·97 - 08·11·97 | Aberdeen | Aberdeen Art Gallery | Fotofeis |
| 04·10·97 - 29·11·97 | Truro | Royal Cornwall Museum | The Hall for Cornwall |
| 07·10·97 - 04·12·97 | Norwich | Sainsbury Centre for Visual Arts | The Age of Dürer |
| 07·10·97 - 14·12·97 | Norwich | Sainsbury Centre for Visual Arts | Federico Garcia Lorca |
| 10·10·97 - 16·11·97 | Belfast | Ulster Museum | RUA Exhibition |
| 11·10·97 - 25·10·97 | Hull | Ferens Art Gallery | Root 97 |
| 11·10·97 - 16·11·97 | Northampton | Central Museum and Art Gallery | Moment in Time |
| 11·10·97 - 14·12·97 | Bath | Holburne M. and Crafts Study Centre | British Folk Art Collection |
| 13·10·97 - 15·11·97 | London | Leighton House M. & Art Gallery | Iniva |
| 15·10·97 - 18·01·98 | London | The National Gallery | Hogarth's 'Marriage A-la-Mode' |
| 16·10·97 - 05·01·98 | London | Tate Gallery | Symbolism in Britain |
| 17·10·97 - 11·01·98 | London | National Portrait Gallery | John Kobal Photographic Award 1997 |
| 18·10·97 - 16·11·97 | Northampton | Central Museum and Art Gallery | A Boy Named Sioux |
| 22·10·97 - Dec 97 | London | ICA Institute of Contemporary Arts | Made in Italy |
| 23·10·97 - 18·01·98 | London | Victoria and Albert Museum | Carl and Karin Larsson |
| 24·10·97 - 19·12·97 | Truro | Royal Cornwall Museum | Teapotmania |
| 24·10·97 - 01·02·98 | London | National Portrait Gallery | Sir Henry Raeburn (1756-1823) |
| 25·10·97 - 07·12·97 | Coventry | Herbert Art Gallery & Museum | Animals in Art |
| 28·10·97 - 03·01·98 | Chichester | Pallant House Gallery | The Shell Art Collection |
| 29·10·97 - 14·12·97 | Coventry | Herbert Art Gallery & Museum | Frank Bowling |
| 29·10·97 - 11·01·98 | Birmingham | M. and Art Gal. / The Gas Hall | Walter Langley |
| Nov 97-Dec 97 | Glasgow | McLellan Galleries | The Royal Glasgow Annual Exhibition |

Exhibitions in chronological order.

| GREAT BRITAIN | | | |
|---|---|---|---|
| **DATE** | **CITY** | **MUSEUM** | **ARTIST/THEME** |
| Nov 97-Jan 98 | Bristol | City Museum and Art Gallery | A Respectable Trade |
| Nov 97-Feb 98 | Liverpool | Walker Art Gallery | John Moores Liverpool Exhibition 20 |
| Nov 97-Feb 98 | Manchester | Manchester City Art Galleries | Keiko Mukaide |
| 01·11·97 - 30·11·97 | Brighton | Brighton Museum & Art Gallery | Lure |
| 01·11·97 - 10·01·98 | Middlesbrough | Middlesbrough Art Gallery | Independent Thoughts |
| 01·11·97 - 11·01·98 | Coventry | Herbert Art Gallery & Museum | Chinese Children's Art |
| 05·11·97 - 01·02·98 | London | The National Gallery | Making & Meaning |
| 07·11·97 - Apr 98 | Leeds | Leeds City Art Gallery | A Sense of Place |
| 08·11·97 - 06·12·97 | York | York City Art Gallery | Art from York Primary Schools |
| 08·11·97 - 07·12·97 | Wakefield | Wakefield Art Gallery | Networking |
| 12·11·97 - 01·02·98 | Birmingham | M. and Art Gal. / The Gas Hall | Anwar Shemza (1928-1985) |
| 13·11·97 - 08·02·98 | London | Royal Academy of Arts | Victorian Fairy Painting |
| 15·11·97 - 10·01·98 | Aberdeen | Aberdeen Art Gallery | Camden Town |
| 15·11·97 - 11·01·98 | Derby | Pickford's House Museum | Nature's Rich Tapestry |
| 15·11·97 - 25·01·98 | Manchester | Manchester City Art Galleries | Pre-Raphaelite Women Artists |
| 15·11·97 - Jan 98 | Hull | Ferens Art Gallery | The Mag Collection |
| 15·11·97 - Apr 98 | St. Ives | Tate Gallery St. Ives | Roger Hilton |
| 15·11·97 - Nov 98 | St. Ives | Tate Gallery St. Ives | Displays 1997-98 |
| 20·11·97 - end Feb 98 | London | National Portrait Gallery | Bruce Weber   Retrospective |
| 22·11·97 - 13·12·97 | Aberdeen | Aberdeen Art Gallery | Gray's Former Students |
| 22·11·97 - 10·01·98 | Cheltenham | Cheltenham Art Gallery & Museum | Art Pottery |
| 24·11·97 - 06·12·97 | London | Leighton House M. & Art Gallery | Marian Wenzel |
| 24·11·97 - Jan 98 | Dorchester | Dorset County Museum | Howard Phipps |
| 28·11·97 - 19·04·98 | Belfast | Ulster Museum | Paul Henry |
| 29·11·97 - 04·01·98 | Northampton | Central Museum and Art Gallery | 84th Annual Exhibition |
| Dec 97-Jun 98 | Edinburgh | Royal Museum of Scotland | Art and Empire |
| 05·12·97 - 22·02·98 | Edinburgh | Scottish National Portrait Gallery | Stanley Cursiter |
| 06·12·97 - Feb 98 | London | The British Museum | Modern Chinese Calligraphy |
| 09·12·97 - end Jan 98 | Oxford | Ashmolean M. and Univ. Galleries | Samuel Palmer |
| 09·12·97 - 01·03·98 | London | The British Museum | Writing Arabic |
| 13·12·97 - 20·01·98 | York | York City Art Gallery | The Room in View |
| 13·12·97 - 25·01·98 | Brighton | Brighton Museum & Art Gallery | Krishna The Divine Lover |
| 13·12·97 - 25·01·98 | Norwich | Castle Museum | The Castle Art Show |
| 14·12·97 - 01·03·98 | Birmingham | M. and Art Gal. / The Gas Hall | Print in Focus, Part 2 |
| Winter 97 - 98 | Grasmere | The Wordsworth Museum | Fay Godwin |
| 15·12·97 - 10·01·98 | London | Leighton House M. & Art Gallery | Tales from the Arabian Nights |
| Winter 97 onwards | London | Natural History Museum | From the Beginning |
| Winter 97 onwards | London | Natural History Museum | Earth's Treasury |
| 16·01·98 - 22·03·98 | Southampton | Southampton City Art Gallery | Stephen Willats |
| 16·01·98 - 22·03·98 | Southampton | Southampton City Art Gallery | Joseph Wright of Derby |
| 17·01·98 - 01·03·98 | Cheltenham | Cheltenham Art Gallery & Museum | Nigel Temple |
| 22·01·98 - 12·04·98 | London | Royal Academy of Arts | English Public Collections |
| 23·01·98 - 12·04·97 | London | The British Museum | Islamic and Indian Paintings&Drawings |
| 30·01·98 - 14·03·98 | Truro | Royal Cornwall Museum | Travelling Discovery Centre |
| Feb 98-Mar 98 | Bristol | City Museum and Art Gallery | Robert Lenkiewicz |
| Feb 98-Mar 98 | Manchester | Manchester City Art Galleries | Manchester Academy of Fine Art |
| Feb 98-May 98 | London | The Wallace Collection | Madame de Pompadour |
| 14·02·98 - 26·04·98 | Norwich | Castle Museum | Tate Gallery Collection |
| Mid Feb 98-May 98 | Norwich | Sainsbury Centre for Visual Arts | The Crafts in Britain Since World War II |
| 21·02·98 - 22·03·98 | Brighton | Brighton Museum & Art Gallery | The Sussex Open |
| Mar 98 May 98 | London | Dulwich Picture Gallery | Italy and British Art |
| Spring 98 onwards | Cambridge | Cambridge Univ. M. of Arch & Anthr. | The Torres Strait |
| Spring 98-Summer 98 | London | ICA Institute of Contemporary Arts | Future Systems |
| 21·03·98 - 19·04·98 | Truro | Royal Cornwall Museum | Six Fairy Tales |
| 27·03·98 - 24·05·98 | Southampton | Southampton City Art Gallery | Chris Ofili |
| Apr 98-Sep 98 | London | The British Museum | Maori |
| 03·04·98 - 30·08·98 | Belfast | Ulster Museum | Up in Arms! |
| 09·04·98 - 26·07·98 | London | Victoria and Albert Museum | The Power of the Poster |

Exhibitions in chronological order.

## IRELAND

| DATE | CITY | MUSEUM | ARTIST/THEME |
|---|---|---|---|
| onwards | Dublin | Irish Museum of Modern Art | Damien Hirst A sculptural installation |
| until 11·06·97 | Dublin | Irish Museum of Modern Art | Joseph Kosuth |
| 01·05·97 - 13·07·97 | Dublin | Irish Museum of Modern Art | IMMA Glen Dimplex Artists Award 1997 |
| 22·05·97 27·07·97 | Dublin | National Gallery of Ireland | The Art of the Book |
| Jun-Aug 97 | Dublin | Irish Museum of Modern Art | IMMA/Nissan Project |
| 26·06·97 - 02·11·97 | Dublin | Irish Museum of Modern Art | A Case for Painting |
| 24·07·97 - mid Oct 97 | Dublin | Irish Museum of Modern Art | New Artists / New Work |
| 05·09·97 07·12·97 | Dublin | National Gallery of Ireland | 200 Years of Watercolours |
| Oct-Dec 97 | Dublin | Irish Museum of Modern Art | Once is Too Much |
| mid Oct-Jan 98 | Dublin | Irish Museum of Modern Art | Kiki Smith - Sculpture and Drawings |
| mid Nov-Feb 98 | Dublin | Irish Museum of Modern Art | Andy Warhol |

## ITALY

| DATE | CITY | MUSEUM | ARTIST/THEME |
|---|---|---|---|
| until 18·05·97 | Bolzano | Museion - M. d'Arte Moderna | Antonio Corpora (1947-1994) |
| until 18·05·97 | Venezia - Venice | Peggy Guggenheim Collection | George Grosz |
| until 25·05·97 | Torino - Turin | Castello Di Rivoli M. D'Arte Cont. | Stage Curtain |
| until 25·05·97 | Torino - Turin | Castello Di Rivoli M. D'Arte Cont. | Andy Warhol |
| until 31·05·97 | Roma - Rome | Museo Barracco | Gutenberg and Rome |
| until 01·06·97 | Torino - Turin | Gall. Civica d'Arte Moderna e Cont. | A Different Art |
| until 08·06·97 | Torino - Turin | Castello Di Rivoli M. D'Arte Cont. | Anteprima |
| until mid Jun 97 | Bologna | Museo Civico Archeologico | Roman Oil-Lamps |
| until Jun 97 | Genova - Genoa | M. Civico Archeologia Ligure | The Marvels of the First Ligurians |
| until Jun 97 | Genova - Genoa | Gall. Nazionale di Palazzo Spinola | Music from the Books |
| until 13·07·97 | Venezia - Venice | Palazzo Grassi | Art of the XX Century |
| until Sep 97 | Genova - Genoa | M. Civico Archeologia Ligure | Echoes of the past |
| 1997 | Ravenna | Museo Nazionale di Ravenna | 14th-Century Frescoes |
| Spring 97 | Bergamo | Accademia Carrara | Academies in Europe |
| Spring 97 | Firenze - Florence | Museo Nazionale del Bargello | Baroque Cloth |
| Spring 97 | Ravenna | Museo Nazionale di Ravenna | The Hoard of Via Luca Longhi |
| Spring 97 - onwards | Firenze - Florence | Casa Buonarroti | Archaeological Collections |
| May 97 | Pavia | M. Civici Pavia-Cast. Visconteo | Giorgio Kienerk |
| 09·05·97 - 01·06·97 | Torino - Turin | Fondazione It. per La Fotografia | Album di Famiglia (Family Album) |
| 23·05·97 - 20·08·97 | Trento | Museo di Arte Moderna e Cont. | The British Art of the 90s |
| 30·05·97 - 31·08·97 | Bolzano | Museion - M. d'Arte Moderna | Robert Sebastian Matta |
| Jun 97 | Bergamo | Accademia Carrara | The Lochis Collection |
| Jun 97-Jul 97 | Bari | Pinacoteca Provinciale di Bari | Society, Culture and Sport in Puglia |
| 05·06·97 - 17·08·97 | Città di Castello | Fondazione Palazzo Albizzini | Palais des Beaux Arts, Brussels |
| 07·06·97 - 05·10·97 | Venezia - Venice | Peggy Guggenheim Collection | Stuart Davis |
| 10·06·97 - 31·07·97 | Roma - Rome | Museo Barracco | Corso Vittorio Emanuele II |
| 12·06·97 - 24·08·97 | Torino - Turin | Fondazione It. per La Fotografia | Sunday is always Sunday |
| 20·06·97 - 09·11·97 | Trento | Castello del Buonconsiglio | Jewels from the Alps |
| Summer 97 | Bolzano | Museion - Museum for Modern Art | Robert Schad |
| Summer 97 | Bolzano | Museion - Museum for Modern Art | Italo Antico |
| Summer 97 | Pavia | M. Civici Pavia-Cast. Visconteo | Ambrogio |
| Summer 97 | Torino - Turin | Castello Di Rivoli M. D'Arte Cont. | Collections and Collectionism |
| Summer 97 | Venezia - Venice | Peggy Guggenheim Collection | Robert Colescott |
| 24·06·97 - 28·09·97 | Torino - Turin | Gall. Civica d'Arte Moderna e Cont. | Antonio Fontanesi |
| Sep 97-Jan 98 | Genova - Genoa | Gall. Nazionale di Palazzo Spinola | Antique Dreams |
| Sep 97-Jan 98 | Venezia - Venice | Palazzo Grassi | German Expressionism |
| 04·09·97 - 12·10·97 | Torino - Turin | Fondazione It. per La Fotografia | 7th International Biennial |
| 05·09·97 - 17·10·97 | Torino - Turin | Fondazione It. per La Fotografia | A Collection of Italian Photography |
| 07·09·97 - 07·12·97 | Parma | Fondazione Magnani Rocca | Füssli and Shakespeare |
| 11·09·97 - 11·01·98 | Trento | Museo di Arte Moderna e Cont. | Trash |
| 12·09·97 - 09·01·98 | Bolzano | Museion - Museum for Modern Art | Abstracta |
| Autumn 97 | Bergamo | Accademia Carrara | Monographs on Lorenzo Lotto |
| Autumn 97 | Firenze - Florence | Museo Nazionale del Bargello | Renaissance Majolica |
| Autumn 97 | Pavia | M. Civici Pavia-Cast. Visconteo | Inauguration |
| 01·10·97 - Oct 97 | Bari | Pinacoteca Provinciale di Bari | Vincenzo Simone (1892-1968) |
| 01·10·97 - Oct 97 | Torino - Turin | Castello Di Rivoli M. D'Arte Cont. | Twenty Years of American Art |
| 18·10·97 - 10·01·98 | Venezia - Venice | Peggy Guggenheim Collection | Eduardo Chillida |
| 23·10·97 - 14·12·97 | Torino - Turin | Fondazione It. per La Fotografia | Dorothea Lange |

Exhibitions in chronological order.

### ITALY

| DATE | CITY | MUSEUM | ARTIST/THEME |
|---|---|---|---|
| Nov 97 | Bari | Pinacoteca Provinciale di Bari | Wim Wenders   Photographs |
| 15·11·97 - end 97 | Pavia | M. Civici Pavia-Cast. Visconteo | Paintings from the 17th and 18th C |
| 21·11·97 - 10·02·98 | Bolzano | Museion - Museum for Modern Art | Prospettive 2000 |
| 22·01·98 - 10·03·98 | Trento | Museo di Arte Moderna e Cont. | Abstracts |
| 20.02.98 - 10.05.98 | Bolzano | Museion - Museum for Modern Art | Marzona CollectionConceptual Works |
| 13·04·98 - 31·08·98 | Trento | Museo di Arte Moderna e Cont. | Carlo Fornara |

### LUXEMBOURG

| DATE | CITY | MUSEUM | ARTIST/THEME |
|---|---|---|---|
| until 11·05·97 | Luxembourg | Musée National d'Histoire et d'Art | Cecil Beaton   Portraits of an Aesthete |
| 15·05·97 - 29·06·97 | Luxembourg | Casino Lux. Forum d'Art Cont. | Perspectives |
| 30·05·97 - 16·06·97 | Luxembourg | Musée Jean- Pierre Pescatore | Jan Steen   Documentary |
| 20·06·97 - end Aug 97 | Luxembourg | Musée National d'Histoire et d'Art | The Golden Age of Danish Painting |
| 03·07·97 - 18·08·97 | Luxembourg | Musée National d'Histoire et d'Art | Paul Strand |
| 04·07·97 - 05·10·97 | Luxembourg | M.d'Histoire de la Ville de Lux. | From Middle Ages to Modern Times |
| 10·07·97 - 21·09·97 | Luxembourg | Casino Lux. Forum d'Art Cont. | A Beautiful Summer |
| Sep 97-Oct 97 | Luxembourg | Musée National d'Histoire et d'Art | Les Kutter   Photographs |
| 25·09·97 - 26·10·97 | Luxembourg | Musée Jean- Pierre Pescatore | Eugenio Carmi  Abstract Paintings |
| 02·10·97 - 30·11·97 | Luxembourg | Casino Lux. Forum d'Art Cont. | The Nineties, A Family Of Man? |
| 14·11·97 - 11·01·98 | Luxembourg | Musée Jean- Pierre Pescatore | Ben Heyart   Retrospective |
| 11·12·97 - 15·02·98 | Luxembourg | Casino Lux. Forum d'Art Cont. | No title (inviter) |
| 07·02·98 - 10·05·98 | Luxembourg | M. d'Histoire de la Ville de Lux. | Luxembourg, Metz, Trèves |

### THE NETHERLANDS

| DATE | CITY | MUSEUM | ARTIST/THEME |
|---|---|---|---|
| onwards | Amsterdam | Tropenmuseum | Mad and Environment |
| until 04·05·97 | Rotterdam | Kunsthal Rotterdam | Komar & Melamid/Trademark |
| until 11·05·97 | Laren | Singer Museum | Maria van Kesteren, Marian Plug |
| until 11·05·97 | Leeuwarden | Fries Museum | A Journey of the Heart |
| until 11·05·97 | Leeuwarden | Fries Museum | Show off at Table |
| until 11·05·97 | Rotterdam | NAI Nederlands Architectuurinstituut | As Good As New |
| until 11·05·97 | Rotterdam | NAI Nederlands Architectuurinstituut | Coast Wise Europe |
| until 11·05·97 | Schiedam | Stedelijk Museum Schiedam | L'Homme Sucré |
| until 18·05·97 | Rotterdam | Kunsthal Rotterdam | Undressed |
| until 19·05·97 | Amsterdam | Stedelijk Museum of Modern Art | Ulrich Ruckriem |
| until 19·05·97 | Den Haag-The Hague | Het Paleis | The Golden Age ofDenmark |
| until 19·05·97 | Haarlem | Frans Halsmuseum-De Hallen | Hans van Benthem |
| until 19·05·97 | Haarlem | Frans Halsmuseum-De Hallen | The Bouquet |
| until 19·05·97 | Haarlem | Frans Halsmuseum-De Hallen | Twintig in de Hallen : A Visual Feast |
| until 19·05·97 | Haarlem | Frans Halsmuseum-De Hallen | De Groep |
| until 24·05·97 | Amsterdam | Amsterdam Historical Museum | I've Got An Auntie In Morocco |
| until 25·05·97 | Haarlem | Teylers Museum | Master Drawings of the Golden Age |
| until 25·05·97 | Amstelveen | Cobra Museum of Modern Art | Corneille   Retrospective |
| until 25·05·97 | Rotterdam | Maritiem Museum 'Prins Hendrik' | The City according to Sirks |
| until 25·05·97 | Rotterdam | Museum Boijmans-van Beuningen | Christopher Williams |
| until 25·05·97 | Rotterdam | Witte de With  Center for Cont. Art | David Lamelas |
| until 01·06·97 | Amsterdam | Tropenmuseum[Park Hall] | Modern Art from Ethiopia |
| until 01·06·97 | Amsterdam | Stedelijk Museum of Modern Art | Catharina Sieverding |
| until 01·06·97 | Den Haag-The Hague | Haags Historisch Museum | Brahms in the Netherlands |
| until 01·06·97 | Leeuwarden | Fries Museum | Liberation in Pictures |
| until 08·06·97 | Arnhem | Museum voor Moderne Kunst | Andrea Fisher |
| until 08·06·97 | Groningen | Groninger Museum | Old Visual Arts |
| until 08·06·97 | Rotterdam | Kunsthal Rotterdam | The Early Mondrian |
| until 08·06·97 | Heerlen | Stadsgalerij Heerlen | Kurt Schwitters in the Netherlands |
| until 15·06·97 | Amsterdam | De Nieuwe Kerk | World Press Photo Exhibition |
| until 15·06·97 | Arnhem | Museum voor Moderne Kunst | Archetypes |
| until 15·06·97 | Eindhoven | Stedelijk Van Abbemuseum | Ulay/Marina Abramovic |
| until 15·06·97 | Eindhoven | Stedelijk Van Abbemuseum | Steve McQueen Film Installations |
| until 15·06·97 | Eindhoven | Stedelijk Van Abbemuseum | Mart Mullican, Lawrence Welner |
| until 15·06·97 | Eindhoven | Stedelijk Van Abbemuseum | Book Works |

Exhibitions in chronological order.

## THE NETHERLANDS

| DATE | CITY | MUSEUM | ARTIST/THEME |
|---|---|---|---|
| until 15·06·97 | Leeuwarden | Fries Museum | Leeuwarden 1750-1850 |
| until 15·06·97 | Middelburg | Zeeuws Museum | Reimond Kimpe |
| until 15·06·97 | Amsterdam | Van Gogh Museum | Art in Vienna 1870-1920 |
| until 18·06·97 | Groningen | Groninger Museum | In Context 2   Acquisitions visual arts. |
| until  22·06·97 | Rotterdam | Maritiem Museum 'Prins Hendrik' | The Dutch Shallows |
| until 22·06·97 | Rotterdam | Natuurmuseum Rotterdam | Flip de Nooyer |
| until 22·06·97 | Den Haag-The Hague | Mauritshuis | Art On Wings |
| until 22·06·97 | Laren | Singer Museum | Henri le Sidaner |
| until 22·06·97 | Otterlo | Kröller-Müller Museum | Overholland |
| until 29·06·97 | Apeldoorn | Paleis Het Loo - Nationaal Museum | The Emperor's Table |
| until 30-06-97 | Amsterdam | Nederlands Scheepvaartmuseum | Maritime Masters |
| until end May | Haarlem | Teylers Museum | Geer van Velde |
| until 06·07·97 | 's-Hertogenbosch | Noordbrabants Museum | Children of All Time |
| until 20·07·97 | Gouda | Catharina Gasthuis | Miniature Fair 1920 |
| until 28·07·97 | Leiden | Stedelijk Museum De Lakenhal | Leiden's Passion |
| until 17·08·97 | Utrecht | Museum Catharijneconvent | 400 Years of Dutch Protestantism |
| until 31·08·97 | Amsterdam | Joods Historisch Museum | Jewish Women Worldwide |
| until 31·08·97 | Groningen | Groninger Museum | 90 000 Packets of Margarine |
| until 31·08·97 | Amsterdam | Tropenmuseum [Light Hall] | Amazonia |
| until end Aug 97 | Leiden | Rijksmuseum voor Volkenkunde | Veils Unveiled |
| until 14·09·97 | Rotterdam | Maritiem Museum 'Prins Hendrik' | Something Kept, Something Had |
| until 21·09·97 | Amsterdam | Allard Pierson Museum | Fabulous! |
| until 01·10·97 | Rotterdam | NAI Nederlands Architectuurinstituut | Nine Plus One |
| until 19·10·97 | Amsterdam | Joods Historisch Museum | Gold Thread and Silver Braid |
| until 20·10·97 | Amsterdam | Tropenmuseum[Side Wing] | Irian Jaya |
| until 30·11·97 | Assen | Drents Museum | Selection from Museum's Collection |
| until end 98 | Leiden | Rijksmuseum van Oudheden | Mummies! |
| 26·04·97 - Jul 97 | Haarlem | Teylers Museum | The Tattooed Human Being |
| 02·05·97 -18·06·97 | Leeuwarden | Keramiekmuseum het Princessehof | Persian Ceramics |
| 03·05·97 - 21·06·97 | Gouda | Catharina Gasthuis | Chess and Art |
| 03·05·97 - 29·06·97 | Utrecht | Centraal Museum Utrecht | Drawings from the Province |
| 03·05·97 - 03·08·97 | Rotterdam | NAI Nederlands Architectuurinstituut | Michel de Klerk |
| 10·05·97 - 29·06·97 | Nijmegen | Nijmeegs Museum Commanderie | A Useful and Elegant Attribute |
| 10·05·97 - 29·06·97 | Rotterdam | Kunsthal Rotterdam | Colin Gray |
| 10·05·97 - 03·08·97 | Amsterdam | Rijksmuseum | The Nude |
| 14·05·97 - 29·06·97 | Nijmegen | Nijmeegs Museum Commanderie | Above Ground Level |
| 16·05·97 - 28·09·97 | Amsterdam | Amsterdam Historical Museum | Herman Gordijn's Amsterdam |
| 17·05·97 - 29·06·97 | Schiedam | Stedelijk Museum Schiedam | Unisono 3 — Dianne Hagen |
| 17·05·97 - 03·08·97 | Rotterdam | Museum Boijmans-van Beuningen | Martin Margiela: Fashion Designs |
| 17·05·97 - 17·08·97 | Groningen | Groninger Museum | The American Interior 1930-1960 |
| 17·05·97 - Sep 97 | Tilburg | De Pont Foundation for Cont. Art | Summer Exhibition |
| 18·05·97 - 22·06·97 | Laren | Singer Museum | Winnie Teschmacher |
| 18·05·97 - 14·09·97 | Dordrecht | Dordrechts Museum | Barend Cornells Koekkoek |
| 18·05·97 - Oct 97 | Nijmegen | Provinciaal Museum G.M. Kam | Museum Kam 75 Years Old/Young |
| 21·05·97 - Spring 98 | Apeldoorn | Van Reekum Museum | Fruits from South-Africa |
| 24·05·97 - 15·08·97 | Rotterdam | Kunsthal Rotterdam | The World of Charles Burki |
| 24·05·97 - 31·08·97 | Den Haag-The Hague | Haags Historisch Museum | Portraits |
| 25·05·97 - 27·07·97 | Assen | Drents Museum | Gouda Delftware |
| 27·05·97 - 20·07·97 | Rotterdam | NAI Nederlands Architectuurinstituut | Americanism |
| 31·05·97 - 29·06·97 | Utrecht | Centraal Museum Utrecht | Futuro  Finnish Design |
| 31·05·97 - 03·08·97 | Rotterdam | Kunsthal Rotterdam | Robert Longo |
| 31·05·97 - 17·08·97 | Amsterdam | Stedelijk Museum of Modern Art | Nan Goldin |
| 31·05·97 - 17·08·97 | Haarlem | Frans Halsmuseum-De Hallen | Cornelis Pronk |
| 31·05·97 - 31·08·97 | Assen | Drents Museum | Textiles 1880-1930 |
| 31·05·97 - 07·09·97 | Rotterdam | Maritiem Museum 'Prins Hendrik' | Eye and Ear of the Waterweg |
| 31·05·97 - end 97 | Arnhem | Museum voor Moderne Kunst | Faience Factory in Arnhem |
| Jun 97-Aug 97 | Apeldoorn | Van Reekum Museum | Nicholas Dings |
| Jun 97-Aug 97 | Haarlem | Teylers Museum | Master Drawings |
| Jun 97-onwards | Rotterdam | Natuurmuseum Rotterdam | Along the Border of the River Rotte ... |
| 07·06·97 - 27·07·97 | Rotterdam | Witte de With Center for Cont. Art | Michel François |
| 07·06·97 - 31·08·97 | Den Haag-The Hague | Het Paleis | The Dandy, Attire, Art and Literature |
| 07·06·97 - 07·09·97 | Haarlem | Teylers Museum | Circus Posters |
| 12·06·97 - 18·08·97 | Rotterdam | Museum Boijmans-van Beuningen | Hubert Damisch |
| 13·06·97 - 03·08·97 | Amstelveen | Cobra Museum of Modern Art | Tajiri |

Exhibitions in chronological order.

## THE NETHERLANDS

| DATE | CITY | MUSEUM | ARTIST/THEME |
|------|------|--------|--------------|
| 14·06·97 - end Jul 97 | Amsterdam | Stedelijk Museum of Modern Art | Theme Exhibition Europe |
| 14·06·97 - 11·08·97 | Leiden | Stedelijk Museum De Lakenhal | Hendrik Valk  Drawings in Chalk |
| 14·06·97 - 31·08·97 | Haarlem | Frans Halsmuseum-De Hallen | Kees Verwey (1900-1995) |
| 14·06·97 - 19·10·97 | Gouda | Catharina Gasthuis | Crockery |
| 15·06·97 - 31·08·97 | Arnhem | Museum voor Moderne Kunst | New Acquisitions |
| 19·06·97 - 31·08·97 | Heerlen | Stadsgalerij Heerlen | Aad de Haas |
| 20·06·97 - 12·10·97 | Amsterdam | Van Gogh Museum | Vincent van Gogh |
| 21·06·97 - 05·10·97 | Rotterdam | Kunsthal Rotterdam | Highlights from the Painting Collection |
| 22·06·97 - 17·08·97 | Arnhem | Museum voor Moderne Kunst | Karl Illjitsj ('Karl') Pelgrom |
| 27·06·97 - end 98 | Leiden | Rijksmuseum van Oudheden | Action Roman |
| 28·06·97 - 31·08·97 | Amsterdam | Stedelijk Museum of Modern Art | Scandinavian Design |
| 28·06·97 - 31·08·97 | Leeuwarden | Fries Museum | Marleen Felius  Cows |
| 28·06·97 - 07·09·97 | Schiedam | Stedelijk Museum Schiedam | From the Museum Collection |
| 28·06·97 - 28·09·97 | Rotterdam | Kunsthal Rotterdam | My First Chair |
| 28·06·97 - 05·10·97 | Rotterdam | Maritiem Museum 'Prins Hendrik' | Records of Travel |
| 04·07·97 - 13·07·97 | Apeldoorn | Paleis Het Loo - Nationaal Museum | National Sweet Pea Competition |
| 05·07·97 - 31·08·97 | Middelburg | Zeeuws Museum | Locations |
| 05·07·97 - 31·08·97 | Nijmegen | Nijmeegs Museum Commanderie | A Trip Along the Lower Rhine |
| 05·07·97 - 14·09·97 | Rotterdam | Kunsthal Rotterdam | Meret Oppenheim Meets Man Ray |
| 06·07·97 - 31·08·97 | Eindhoven | Stedelijk Van Abbemuseum | Mike Kelly Works from 1985 |
| 06·07·97 - 31·08·97 | Eindhoven | Stedelijk Van Abbemuseum | Atonietta Peeters |
| 06·07·97 - 26·10·97 | Otterlo | Kröller-Müller Museum | Aquisitions and Panamarenko |
| 12·07·97 - 31·08·97 | Utrecht | Centraal Museum Utrecht | 'Around the Dinner Table with Friends' |
| 12·07·97 - end Jan 98 | Middelburg | Zeeuws Museum | Nehalennia  350 Years |
| 15·07·97 - 15·08·97 | Apeldoorn | Paleis Het Loo - Nationaal Museum | In the King's Attic |
| 15·07·97 - 15·08·97 | Apeldoorn | Paleis Het Loo - Nationaal Museum | Riding Out with the King |
| 15·07·97 - 15·08·97 | Apeldoorn | Paleis Het Loo - Nationaal Museum | The House of Orange on Coins |
| 18·07·97 - 31·08·97 | 's-Hertogenbosch | Noordbrabants Museum | Contemporary Art from North Brabant |
| 19·07·97 - 31·08·97 | Utrecht | Centraal Museum Utrecht | Scratches and Stripes |
| 08·08·97 - 05·10·97 | Amstelveen | Cobra Museum of Modern Art | Eugène Brands |
| 10·08·97 - 12·10·97 | Assen | Drents Museum | Frans Molenaar |
| 16·08·97 - 09·11·97 | Amsterdam | Rijksmuseum | Whistler and Holland |
| 20·08·97 - 23·11·97 | Dordrecht | Dordrechts Museum | The Brothers De Witt |
| 23·08·97 - 02·11·97 | Rotterdam | Kunsthal Rotterdam | Brancusi, Tzara & Romanian Av.-Garde |
| 23·08·97 - 16·11·97 | Groningen | Groninger Museum | Lellens and the Wijchgel Family |
| 29·08·97 - end 98 | Leiden | Rijksmuseum van Oudheden | Antique Tourism |
| 29·08·97 - end 98 | Leiden | Rijksmuseum van Oudheden | Who's Afraid of Ancient Blue? |
| 30·08·97 - 16·11·97 | Rotterdam | Museum Boijmans-van Beuningen | 17th-Century Genre Paintings |
| 30·08·97 - 23·11·97 | Rotterdam | NAI Nederlands Architectuurinstituut | Daniel Libeskind |
| 31·08·97 - 19·10·97 | Haarlem | Frans Halsmuseum-De Hallen | 40 Years Galerie Espace |
| Sep 97-end Oct 97 | Amsterdam | Stedelijk Museum of Modern Art | Theme Exhibition 1960 |
| Sep 97-Oct 97 | Amsterdam | Stedelijk Museum of Modern Art | Partenheimermid |
| 06·09·97 - 26·10·97 | Rotterdam | Witte de With  Center for Cont. Art | Words and Images |
| 06·09·97 - 30·11·97 | Leeuwarden | Keramiekmuseum het Princessehof | Jan van der Vaart & the Multiples |
| 07·09·97 - 05·10·97 | Laren | Singer Museum | Painters-Society Laren-Blaricum |
| 07·09·97 - 09·11·97 | Heerlen | Stadsgalerij Heerlen | Kurt Schwitters As Inspiration |
| 07·09·97 - 23·11·97 | Arnhem | Museum voor Moderne Kunst | Paul de Reus  Sculptures |
| 12·09·97 - 05·10·97 | Amsterdam | Stedelijk Museum of Modern Art | World Wide Media Festival |
| 12·09·97 - 23·11·97 | Assen | Drents Museum | Suze Robertson |
| 13·09·97 - 26·10·97 | Utrecht | Centraal Museum Utrecht | Narcisse Tordoir |
| 13·09·97 - 02·11·97 | Middelburg | Zeeuws Museum | Contemporary Art |
| 13·09·97 - 02·11·97 | Nijmegen | Nijmeegs Museum Commanderie | Decayed Past |
| 13·09·97 - 09·11·97 | Leeuwarden | Fries Museum | Bouke van der Sloot |
| 13·09·97 - 16·11·97 | Den Haag-The Hague | Het Paleis | Venetian Glass, Secrets of Murano |
| 13·09·97 - 16·11·97 | Den Haag-The Hague | Het Paleis | Steltman 1917-1997 |
| 13·09·97 - 16·11·97 | Schiedam | Stedelijk Museum Schiedam | Radical Image/Object |
| 13·09·97 - 23·11·97 | Den Haag-The Hague | Haags Historisch Museum | Van de Sande-Bakhuyzen |
| 13·09·97 - 30·11·97 | Rotterdam | Kunsthal Rotterdam | Edward Steichen |
| 13·09·97 - 30·11·97 | 's-Hertogenbosch | Noordbrabants Museum | La Gare |
| 13·09·97 - 30·11·97 | 's-Hertogenbosch | Noordbrabants Museum | 19th-Century Brabantine Photography |
| 13·09·97 - 07·12·97 | Rotterdam | Maritiem Museum 'Prins Hendrik' | Anna Kool |
| 14·09·97 - 09·11·97 | Eindhoven | Stedelijk Van Abbemuseum | Just Installations.... |
| 14·09·97 - 16·11·97 | Arnhem | Museum voor Moderne Kunst | Meret Oppenheim |
| 14·09·97 - 07·12·97 | Groningen | Groninger Museum | Mutant Materials in Cont.Design |

Exhibitions in chronological order.

## THE NETHERLANDS

| DATE | CITY | MUSEUM | ARTIST/THEME |
|------|------|--------|--------------|
| 17·09·97 - 17·12·97 | Rotterdam | Museum Boijmans-van Beuningen | Eternal Youth |
| 17·09·97 - 17·12·97 | Rotterdam | Museum Boijmans-van Beuningen | Daan van Golden |
| 17·09·97 - 17·12·97 | Rotterdam | Museum Boijmans-van Beuningen | Children Choose Art |
| 17·09·97 - 17·12·97 | Rotterdam | Museum Boijmans-van Beuningen | M Kelley/S Lockhart/N Goldin a.o. |
| 20·09·97 - 23·11·97 | Haarlem | Teylers Museum | Ad Cadavrum |
| 20·09·97 - 30·11·97 | Haarlem | Frans Halsmuseum-De Hallen | Children Choose Art |
| 20·09·97 - 30·11·97 | Rotterdam | Kunsthal Rotterdam | Inge Morath  Europa! |
| Autumn 97 | Amsterdam | Allard Pierson Museum | Transportation in Antiquity |
| Autumn 97 | Apeldoorn | Van Reekum Museum | Ed Kienholz |
| Autumn 97 | Tilburg | De Pont  Foundation for Cont. Art | Robert Zandvliet |
| end Sep 97-Nov 97 | Zwolle | Stedelijk Museum Zwolle | Painters in Zwolle |
| 26·09·97 - Jan 98 | Amsterdam | Amsterdam Historical Museum | Prints and Drawings by Jan Luyken |
| 27·09·97 - 30·11·97 | Rotterdam | Maritiem Museum 'Prins Hendrik' | Tetsuo Mizu |
| 28·09·97 - 09·11·97 | Arnhem | Museum voor Moderne Kunst | Cosmopolitan |
| 28·09·97 - 23·11·97 | Groningen | Groninger Museum | Job Hansen & Groninger Silver |
| 28·09·97 - 04·01·98 | Maastricht | Bonnefantenmuseum | Exile on Main Street |
| 01·10·97 - Oct 97 | Leiden | Rijksmuseum voor Volkenkunde | To Tibet with TinTin |
| 01·10·97 - 02·02·98 | Amsterdam | De Nieuwe Kerk | Kingdoms on the Nile |
| 03·10·97 - 18·01·98 | Amstelveen | Cobra Museum of Modern Art | CoBrA Collection  A Broad Perspective |
| 04·10·97 - 02·03·98 | Amsterdam | Nederlands Scheepvaartmuseum | Photographs & Memories |
| 11·10·97 - 11·01·98 | Utrecht | Museum Catharijneconvent | Pilgrimages in the Netherlands |
| 11·10·97 - 18·01·98 | Rotterdam | Kunsthal Rotterdam | Masters of the HagueSchool |
| 11·10·97 - 08·02·98 | Tilburg | De Pont  Foundation for Cont. Art | Giuseppe Penone |
| 12·10·97 - 30·11·97 | Laren | Singer Museum | Boncompain |
| 12·10·97 - 11·01·98 | Dordrecht | Dordrechts Museum | Philip Kouwen |
| 15·10·97 - 30·11·97 | Amsterdam | Stedelijk Museum of Modern Art | One Hundred Languages |
| 17·10·97 - 11·01·98 | Amsterdam | Van Gogh Museum | Auguste Préault |
| 18·10·97 - 16·11·97 | Assen | Drents Museum | A Moluccan Artist |
| 18·10·97 - 18·01·98 | Apeldoorn | Paleis Het Loo - Nationaal Museum | Charles Rochussen |
| 18·10·97 - 18·01·98 | Laren | Singer Museum | Sara Lee Corporation |
| 25·10·97 - 04·01·98 | Utrecht | Centraal Museum Utrecht | Archaeological Findings |
| Nov 97-Dec 97 | Amsterdam | Stedelijk Museum of Modern Art | Pichler |
| Nov 97-Dec 97 | Amsterdam | Stedelijk Museum of Modern Art | Rodchenko and Others |
| Nov 97-Dec 97 | Amsterdam | Stedelijk Museum of Modern Art | Oehlen |
| Nov 97-Dec 97 | Amsterdam | Stedelijk Museum of Modern Art | Municipality Acquisitions |
| 01·11·97 - 04·01·98 | Utrecht | Museum Catharijneconvent | Saint Martin |
| 07·11·97 - 08·02·98 | Amsterdam | Joods Historisch Museum | Jews / America / A Representation |
| 08·11·97 - 14·12·97 | Nijmegen | Nijmeegs Museum Commanderie | 50 Years of the GBK |
| 08·11·97 - 14·12·97 | Nijmegen | Nijmeegs Museum Commanderie | Gerard Noodt |
| 08·11·97 - 04·01·98 | Utrecht | Centraal Museum Utrecht | Saucy Fashion |
| 08·11·97 - 11·01·98 | Rotterdam | Witte de With  Center for Cont. Art | Rita McBride |
| 15·11·97 - 18·01·98 | Otterlo | Kröller-Müller Museum | Picasso, Gonzalez, Miró and Chillida |
| 15·11·97 - Feb 98 | Middelburg | Zeeuws Museum | Saudara |
| 15·11·97 - Apr 1998 | Groningen | Groninger Museum | Accents |
| 15·11·97 - 1998 | Schiedam | Stedelijk Museum Schiedam | Basement Installation |
| 16·11·97 - 18·01·98 | Heerlen | Stadsgalerij Heerlen | Surinamese Artists |
| 21·11·97 - 15·02·98 | Haarlem | Frans Halsmuseum-De Hallen | Majolica |
| 22·11·97 - 11·01·98 | Amsterdam | Rijksmuseum | Hausbach of Master |
| 23·11·97 - Jan 98 | Arnhem | Museum voor Moderne Kunst | Honorary Members Visual Community |
| 23·11·97 - 11·01·98 | Eindhoven | Stedelijk Van Abbemuseum | Jan Vercruysse |
| 23·11·97 - Feb 98 | Groningen | Groninger Museum | Onno Boekhoudt  Jewellery |
| 27·11·97 - 01·08·98 | Amsterdam | Tropenmuseum [Side Wing] | Messenger between Heaven and Earth |
| 29·11·97 - 14·02·98 | Leeuwarden | Fries Museum | Dolls |
| 29·11·97 - 22·02·98 | Den Haag-The Hague | Het Paleis | Auke de Vries |
| 29·11·97 - 03·03·98 | Amsterdam | Rijksmuseum | On Country Roads and Fields |
| 29·11·97 - Mar 98 | Assen | Drents Museum | Church Silver |
| Dec 97 onwards | Amsterdam | Joods Historisch Museum | Michal Shabtay |
| Dec 97-Jan 98 | Arnhem | Museum voor Moderne Kunst | Female Power Stations |
| Dec 97-14·02·98 | Haarlem | Teylers Museum | Rembrandt Etchings |
| Dec 97-Feb 98 | Haarlem | Teylers Museum | Rembrandt and his Circle |
| Dec 97-Mar 98 | Den Haag-The Hague | Mauritshuis | Frederik Hendrik and Courtly Art |
| 01·12·97 - 04·01·98 | Haarlem | Frans Halsmuseum-De Hallen | Kunst Zij Ons Doel |
| 05·12·97 - 1998 | Schiedam | Stedelijk Museum Schiedam | From the Museum Collection |
| 06·12·97 - 30·01·98 | Rotterdam | Kunsthal Rotterdam | W.O.J. Nieuwenkamp |

Exhibitions in chronological order.

## THE NETHERLANDS

| DATE | CITY | MUSEUM | ARTIST/THEME |
|---|---|---|---|
| 06-12-97 - 01-02-98 | Assen | Drents Museum | Project Contemporary Art |
| 06-12-97 - Mar 98 | Rotterdam | Museum Boijmans-van Beuningen | Max Ernst |
| 07-12-97 - mid Feb 98 | Groningen | Groninger Museum | Azzedine Alaïa Fashion by designer |
| 13-12-97 - 07-01-98 | Utrecht | Museum Catharijneconvent | The Neapolitan Crib |
| 13-12-97 - 08-02-98 | Haarlem | Frans Halsmuseum-De Hallen | Sigurdur Gudmundson |
| 13-12-97 - 08-03-98 | 's-Hertogenbosch | Noordbrabants Museum | Hendrik Wiegersma |
| 13-12-97 - Mar 98 | Assen | Drents Museum | W.O.J. Nieuwenkamp |
| 13-12-97 - 1998 | Schiedam | Stedelijk Museum Schiedam | Constant — View of the Dove |
| 13-12-97 - 1998 | Schiedam | Stedelijk Museum Schiedam | Unisono 4 |
| 15-12-97 - 15-02-98 | Den Haag-The Hague | Haags Historisch Museum | Frederick Hendrik and Courtly Art |
| 19-12-97 - 09-03-98 | Leeuwarden | Keramiekmuseum het Princessehof | Raku |
| 20-12-97 - 15-02-98 | Haarlem | Frans Halsmuseum-De Hallen | The Haarlem Lottery of 1607 |
| 20-12-97 - 08-03-98 | Rotterdam | Maritiem Museum 'Prins Hendrik' | Shipowners of the Century |
| 20-12-97 - 23-03-98 | Leiden | Stedelijk Museum De Lakenhal | Isaac van Swanenburgh (1537-1614) |
| Winter 97-98 | Amsterdam | Allard Pierson Museum | Bloomington Goldcollection |
| 24-01-98 - 29-03-98 | Heerlen | Stadsgalerij Heerlen | Attitudes III |
| Feb 98-end May 98 | Middelburg | Zeeuws Museum | Contemporary Art |
| 21-02-98 - 23-05-98 | Haarlem | Teylers Museum | Stanley Roseman |
| 07-03-98 - 15-06-98 | Den Haag-The Hague | Het Paleis | The Hague Around 1900 |
| Spring 1998 | Eindhoven | Stedelijk Van Abbemuseum | René Daniëls |
| 28-03-98 - 28-06-98 | 's-Hertogenbosch | Noordbrabants Museum | Pop Culture, Sound and Vision |
| 28-03-98 - 20-09-98 | Rotterdam | Maritiem Museum 'Prins Hendrik' | Dutch-American Steamship Company |
| Apr 98-Jun 98 | Leeuwarden | Fries Museum | Our Indies? Our Indies! |
| 04-04-98 - 07-06-98 | Heerlen | Stadsgalerij Heerlen | Four Young Artists of Limburg Origin |

## PORTUGAL

| DATE | CITY | MUSEUM | ARTIST/THEME |
|---|---|---|---|
| 1997 | Lisboa - Lisbon | Museu Nacional de Arqueologia | From Ulysses to Viriatus |
| until 15-06-97 | Lisboa - Lisbon | Mod. Art C. J. de Azeredo Perdigão | Portuguese Comics |
| until Jun 97 | Lisboa - Lisbon | Mod. Art C. J. de Azeredo Perdigão | Arpad Szenes |
| until Nov 97 | Lisboa - Lisbon | Museu Nacional de Arte Antiga | Jewels for Alexander of Medicis |
| until Apr 98 | Lisboa - Lisbon | Museu Nacional de Arqueologia | Roman Portugal |
| May 97-Jun 97 | Lisboa - Lisbon | Mod. Art C. J. de Azeredo Perdigão | Pedro Casqueiro |
| May 97-Jul 97 | Lisboa - Lisbon | Mod. Art C. J. de Azeredo Perdigão | Sculpture of Alberto Carneiro |
| May 97-Aug 97 | Lisboa - Lisbon | Museu Nacional de Arqueologia | Roman Glass from Croatia |
| 08-05-97 - 22-06-97 | Porto | Fundação de Serralves | Robert Schad |
| Jul 97-Nov 97 | Lisboa - Lisbon | Museu Nacional de Arte Antiga | The Image and the Sculpture |
| 03-07-97 - 09-07-97 | Porto | Fundação de Serralves | A Decade of Rupture |
| 03-07-97 - 31-08-97 | Lisboa - Lisbon | Mod. Art C. J. de Azeredo Perdigão | Betty Woodman |
| Sep 97 | Lisboa - Lisbon | Mod. Art C. J. de Azeredo Perdigão | Robert Schad |
| Sep 97-Dec 97 | Lisboa - Lisbon | Mod. Art C. J. de Azeredo Perdigão | From Here to There |
| Autumn 97-Winter 98 | Lisboa - Lisbon | Museu Nacional de Arte Antiga | The Rau Donation |
| Oct 97 - Nov 97 | Lisboa - Lisbon | Mod. Art C. J. de Azeredo Perdigão | Eduardo Neri Retrospective |
| 09-10-97 - 07-12-97 | Porto | Fundação de Serralves | James Lee Byars |
| 18-12-97 - 15-02-98 | Porto | Fundação de Serralves | Franz West |

## SPAIN

| DATE | CITY | MUSEUM | ARTIST/THEME |
|---|---|---|---|
| until 10-05-97 | Palma de Mallorca | Museo d'Art Espanyol Cont. | Millares |
| until May 97 | Barcelona | Barcelona | Video in Germany |
| until May 97 | Valencia | Museo de Bellas Artes San Pío V | Vicente Macip |
| until 15-06-97 | Barcelona | Fundació Antoni | Marcel Droodthaers Cinema |
| until 15-06-97 | Cuenca | Museo de Arte Abstracto Español | Frank Stella |
| until 16-06-97 | Madrid | M. Nac.Centro de Arte Reina Sofia | Rivera |
| until 29-06-97 | Madrid | Thyssen-Bornemisza Museum | The Annunciation by El Greco |
| until Jun 97 | Barcelona | Barcelona | Spring Design |
| until Jun 97 | Barcelona | Barcelona | Roma Vallés |
| until Jun 97 | Madrid | Museo Cerralbo | Clocks and Watches Cerralbo Palace |
| until end Jun 97 | Madrid | M. Nac.Centro de Arte Reina Sofia | Gerardo Rueda |
| until 15-09-97 | Madrid | M. Nac.Centro de Arte Reina Sofia | Bienal Hispano-Americana [Biblioteca] |

Exhibitions in chronological order.

## SPAIN

| DATE | CITY | MUSEUM | ARTIST/THEME |
|---|---|---|---|
| until 30·09·97 | Madrid | M. Nac.Centro de Arte Reina Sofia | Eugenio d'Ors [Palacio Velázquez] |
| 06·05·97 - 29·06·97 | Bilbao | Museo de Bellas Artes de Bilbao | Maeztu Lithographs |
| 08·05·97 - 08·09·97 | Madrid | M. Nac.Centro de Arte Reina Sofia | Piel de Toro |
| 22·05·97 - 14·09·97 | Barcelona | Joan Miró Foundation | Lightmade |
| 28·05·97 - 14·09·97 | Madrid | Thyssen-Bornemisza Museum | George Grosz |
| 01·06·97 - Jun 97 | Barcelona | Barcelona | Juan Furriol |
| Jun 97-Sep 97 | Barcelona | Barcelona | Artists from Argentina |
| 03·06·97 - 09·09·97 | Madrid | M. Nac.Centro de Arte Reina Sofia | Lipchitz |
| 17·06·97 - 27·10·97 | Madrid | M. Nac.Centro de Arte Reina Sofia | Art Madi |
| Summer 97 | Bilbao | Museo de Bellas Artes de Bilbao | The Thyssen Baroness Collection |
| 08·07·97 - 20·10·97 | Madrid | M. Nac.Centro de Arte Reina Sofia | Fraile |
| 10·07·97 - 28·09·97 | Barcelona | Fundació Antoni | László Moholy-Nagy |
| 15·07·97 - 21·09·97 | Bilbao | Museo de Bellas Artes de Bilbao | Masters from the Jado Legacy |
| Sep 97 | Toledo | Museo Sefardi - The Sephardic M. | Great-Grandparents of the Orchestra |
| 04·09·97 - 26·10·97 | Bilbao | Museo de Bellas Artes de Bilbao | Alberto Sanchez |
| 16·09·97 - 17·11·97 | Madrid | M. Nac.Centro de Arte Reina Sofia | Moholy Nagy |
| 30·09·97 - 07·12·97 | Bilbao | Museo de Bellas Artes de Bilbao | From Gainsborough to Nicholson |
| 30·09·97 - 11·01·98 | Madrid | Thyssen-Bornemisza Museum | Joan Miro |
| Oct 97 | Barcelona | Museo de Cerámica | Between Cultures |
| Oct 97 | Madrid | Museo del Prado | El Greco's Portrait |
| Oct 97-Nov 97 | Valencia | Museo de Bellas Artes San Pio V | Yañez de la Almedina |
| 07·10·97 - 14·12·97 | Barcelona | Fundació Antoni | Lygia Clark |
| 07·10·97 - 09·01·98 | Madrid | M. Nac.Centro de Arte Reina Sofia | Revista Artes [Biblioteca] |
| 14·10·97 - 19·01·98 | Madrid | M. Nac.Centro de Arte Reina Sofia | Sicilis [Palacio Velazquez] |
| 21·10·97 - 13·01·98 | Madrid | M. Nac.Centro de Arte Reina Sofia | Dibujos de Pablo Gargallo |
| 28·10·97 - 12·01·98 | Madrid | M. Nac.Centro de Arte Reina Sofia | Léger |
| Nov 97-Feb 98 | Madrid | Thyssen-Bornemisza Museum | The Triumph of Venus |
| 06·11·97 - 28·12·97 | Bilbao | Museo de Bellas Artes de Bilbao | Manet Graphic Work |
| 11·11·97 - 12·01·98 | Madrid | M. Nac.Centro de Arte Reina Sofia | Tobey |
| 25·11·97 - 19·01·98 | Madrid | M. Nac.Centro de Arte Reina Sofia | Togores |
| 01·12·97 - Dec 97 | Valencia | Museo de Bellas Artes San Pío V | The Vergara |
| 02·12·97 - 12·01·98 | Madrid | M. Nac.Centro de Arte Reina Sofia | Literatura y Fotografia |
| 16·12·97 - 22·02·98 | Bilbao | Museo de Bellas Artes de Bilbao | Sorolla-Zuloaga |

## SWITZERLAND

| DATE | CITY | MUSEUM | ARTIST/THEME |
|---|---|---|---|
| onwards | Genève - Geneva | Musée d'Art et d'Histoire | A Display Bias |
| until 18·05·97 | Zürich | Haus Konstruktive&Konkrete Kunst | Paul Talman |
| until 19·05·97 | Genève - Geneva | Musée Ariana | Exchanged Looks at Cont.Ceramics |
| until 19·05·97 | Solothurn | Kunstmuseum Solothurn | Kurt Blum Photo Experiments |
| until 19·05·97 | Vevey | Swiss Camera Museum | The Cameras of the Pioneers |
| until 19·05·97 | Vevey | Swiss Camera Museum | The Swiss Photography Foundation |
| until 25·05·97 | Basel - Basle | Kunsthalle Basel | Albert Oehlen |
| until 25·05·97 | Genève - Geneva | Musée Rath | Pierre Tal Coat |
| until 25·05·97 | Zug | Kunsthaus Zug | Tadashi Kawamata |
| until 25·05·97 | Zug | Kunsthaus Zug | Fantastically Surreal |
| until May 97 | Genève - Geneva | Centre Genevois de Gravure Cont. | Hinrich Sachs and B.T. Tamokoué |
| until 01·06·97 | Aarau | Aargauer Kunsthaus Aarau | Mountains - Views - Belvedere |
| until 01·06·97 | Aarau | Aargauer Kunsthaus Aarau | Pia Fries, Kiki Lamers, Renee Levi |
| until 01·06·97 | Aarau | Aargauer Kunsthaus Aarau | Dirk Reinartz Deathly Still |
| until 01·06·97 | Bern | Kunstmuseum Bern | Serge Brignoni Berlin-Paris-Bern |
| until 01·06·97 | Lausanne | Musée Cantonal des Beaux-Arts | Giovanni Giacometti |
| until 01·06·97 | Solothurn | Kunstmuseum Solothurn | Product: Art! |
| until 01·06·97 | Zürich | Kunsthaus Zürich | The Caprice as Artistic Principle |
| until 08·06·97 | Genève - Geneva | Musée d'Art et d'Histoire | Museum Music Listening to Antiquity |
| until 08·06·97 | Lugano | Museo Cantonale d'Arte | Bruno Monguzzi |
| until 08·06·97 | Zürich | M. Rietberg - Haus zum Kiel | India Observed |
| until 14·06·97 | Genève - Geneva | M. d'Histoire des Sciences | Anatomical Casts |
| until 15·06·97 | Genève - Geneva | Cabinet des Estampes | Geneviève Asse |
| until 15·06·97 | La Chaux-de-Fonds | Musée des Beaux-Arts | Sides of the Modernity in Tessin |
| until 29·06·97 | Bern | Kunstmuseum Bern | Luc Tuymans Premonition |
| until 29·06·97 | Zürich | Schweizerisches Landesmuseum | Swiss Modedesign 1972-1997 |

Exhibitions in chronological order.

## SWITZERLAND

| DATE | CITY | MUSEUM | ARTIST/THEME |
|------|------|--------|--------------|
| until mid Jun 97 | Genève - Geneva | Petit Palais, Musée d'Art Moderne | The Customs Official Rousseau |
| until 13-07-97 | Basel - Basle | Antikenm. Basel & Sammlung Ludwig | Egypt Moments of Eternity |
| until 31-08-97 | Basel - Basle | Museum für Gegenwartskunst | Katharina Fritsch |
| until 31-08-97 | Genève - Geneva | Musée d'Art et d'Histoire | The Bishopric of Geneva |
| until 07-09-97 | Genève - Geneva | Musée d'Art et d'Histoire | Ceramics from Magna Graecia |
| until 28-09-97 | Genève - Geneva | Musée d'Art et d'Histoire | The Art of Imitation |
| until 28-09-97 | Genève - Geneva | Musée d'Art et d'Histoire | Regards II Daniel Berset |
| until 05-10-97 | Zürich | Haus Konstruktive&Konkrete Kunst | Bill-Glarner-Graeser-Hinterreiter .... |
| until Oct 97 | Bern | Bernisches Historisches Museum | Helvetica |
| until Nov 98 | Winterthur | M. Oskar Reinhart am Stadtgarten | The Oskar Reinhart Collection |
| until end Feb 98 | Genève - Geneva | Centre d'Art Cont. de Genève | Jane and Louise Wilson |
| 01-05-97 - Spring 98 | Genève - Geneva | M. d'Histoire des Sciences | Genevan Scientific Instruments |
| 04-05-97 - 18-06-97 | Basel - Basle | Kunsthalle Basel | Zoe Leonard |
| 04-05-97 - 14-09-97 | Zürich | M. Rietberg - Villa Wesendonk | Mexico The Precolumbian Cultures |
| 14-05-97 - 24-08-97 | Basel - Basle | Kunstmuseum | Dürer, Holbein, Grünewald |
| 14-05-97 - 07-09-97 | Basel - Basle | Kunstmuseum | The Prints of Hans Holbein the Younger |
| 16-05-97 - 29-06-97 | Zürich | Kunsthaus Zürich | I. Simon Patterson |
| 29-05-97 - 26-10-97 | Vevey | Swiss Camera Museum | Hans Knuchel |
| 29-05-97 - 30-11-97 | Genève - Geneva | Musée d'Art et d'Histoire | The Musical Box |
| 30-05-97 - 27-07-97 | Zürich | Haus Konstruktive&Konkrete Kunst | Mary Heilman |
| 06-06-97 - 26-07-97 | Lugano | Museo Cantonale d'Arte | A View of Contemporary Art |
| 06-06-97 - 24-08-97 | Zürich | Kunsthaus Zürich | Zurich 97 |
| 06-06-97 - 07-09-97 | Genève - Geneva | Musée Rath | Balthasar Burkhard |
| 08-06-97 - 24-08-97 | Basel - Basle | Kunsthalle Basel | Liz Larner |
| 08-06-97 - 31-08-97 | Zug | Kunsthaus Zug | Richard Tuttle |
| 12-06-97 - 22-09-97 | Genève - Geneva | Musée Ariana | Paul Bonifas Ceramist of Purism |
| 15-06-97 - 10-08-97 | Solothurn | Kunstmuseum Solothurn | Recent Acquisitions |
| 15-06-97 - 24-08-97 | Aarau | Aargauer Kunsthaus Aarau | I Want To See My Mountains |
| 15-06-97 - 14-09-97 | Lausanne | Musée Cantonal des Beaux-Arts | COBRA - Experimental Art 1948-1951 |
| 18-06-97 - 07-09-97 | Zürich | Kunsthaus Zürich | Birth of the Cool |
| 19-06-97 - 04-01-98 | Genève - Geneva | Maison Tavel | F. d'Albert-Durade and H. Silvestre |
| Summer-Autumn 97 | Genève - Geneva | Centre Genevois de Gravure Cont. | Collective manifestation |
| 24-06-97 - 12-10-97 | Genève - Geneva | Centre d'Art Cont. de Genève | Fatto in Italia |
| 25-06-97 - 07-09-97 | Genève - Geneva | Cabinet des Estampes | Admirable Engravings and Drawings |
| 26-06-97 - 07-09-97 | Basel - Basle | Kunstmuseum | Put into Light III |
| 27-06-97 - 07-09-97 | Basel - Basle | Kunsthalle Basel | Clegg and Guttmann |
| 27-06-97 - 07-09-97 | Bern | Kunstmuseum Bern | Julio González Drawings in Space |
| 11-07-97 - 05-10-97 | Zürich | M. Rietberg - Haus zum Kiel | Artist as Collector African Masks |
| 14-07-97 - 14-09-97 | Bern | Kunstmuseum Bern | Under the Sign of the Carnation |
| 18-07-97 - 31-08-97 | Zürich | Kunsthaus Zürich | Maria Eichhorn |
| 08-08-97 - 21-09-97 | La Chaux-de-Fonds | Musée des Beaux-Arts | Caves Swiss Art 17th to 20th Century |
| 08-08-97 - 05-10-97 | Zürich | Haus Konstruktive&Konkrete Kunst | Gottfried Honegger Retrospective |
| 22-08-97 - 09-11-97 | Zürich | Kunsthaus Zürich | Christian Schad |
| 23-08-97 - 28-09-97 | Solothurn | Kunstmuseum Solothurn | 4 Hüppi |
| Sep 97-Nov 97 | Bern | Kunstmuseum Bern | Rebecca Horn Drawings and Boxes |
| Sep 97-Dec 97 | Genève - Geneva | Centre d'Art Cont. de Genève | Projects Room |
| 05-09-97 - 26-10-97 | Zürich | Kunsthaus Zürich | Christian Marclay |
| 06-09-97 - 16-11-97 | Lugano | Museo Cantonale d'Arte | Rabisch |
| 13-09-97 - 09-11-97 | Aarau | Aargauer Kunsthaus Aarau | Guido Nussbaum |
| 13-09-97 - 09-11-97 | Aarau | Aargauer Kunsthaus Aarau | Annelies Strba |
| 14-09-97 - 09-11-97 | Zug | Kunsthaus Zug | Peter Stein |
| 18-09-97 - Winter 97 | Genève - Geneva | Musée d'Art et d'Histoire | The Great Shrine of Sion Cathedral |
| 19-09-97 - 02-11-97 | Zürich | Kunsthaus Zürich | Gary Simmons |
| 20-09-97 - 04-01-98 | Basel - Basle | Kunstmuseum | 111 Drawings by 111 Artists |
| 21-09-97 - 09-11-97 | Basel - Basle | Kunsthalle Basel | Claudia and Julia Müller |
| 25-09-97 - 11-01-90 | Genève - Geneva | Musée Rath | Moments from Eternity |
| 26-09-97 - 09-11-97 | Zug | Kunsthaus Zug | Grant and Scholarship Contributions |
| 27-09-97 - 11-01-98 | Basel - Basle | Kunstmuseum | Peter and Samuel Birmann |
| 27-09-97 - 11-01-98 | Basel - Basle | Kunstmuseum | Emilie Linder and Jacob Burckhardt |
| 28-09-97 - 11-01-98 | Lausanne | Musée Cantonal des Beaux-Arts | Contemporary Expression |
| 01-10-97 - 30-11-97 | Genève - Geneva | Cabinet des Estampes | The Ecart Group |
| 03-10-97 - 18-01-98 | Zürich | Kunsthaus Zürich | A Journey into the Unknown |
| 04-10-97 - begin 1998 | Basel - Basle | Museum für Gegenwartskunst | Check-in! |
| 09-10-97 - Spring 98 | Genève - Geneva | Musée d'Art et d'Histoire | The Spirit of India |

Exhibitions in chronological order.

| SWITZERLAND | | | |
|---|---|---|---|
| DATE | CITY | MUSEUM | ARTIST/THEME |
| 11·10·97 - 02·11·97 | La Chaux-de-Fonds | Musée des Beaux-Arts | Musée on Display |
| 18·10·97 - 04·01·98 | Solothurn | Kunstmuseum Solothurn | The Chamber Orchestra |
| 23·10·97 - 14·01·98 | Genève - Geneva | Musée Ariana | Bernard Dejonghe  Ceramics and Glass |
| 23·10·97 - end Jan 98 | Genève - Geneva | Centre d'Art Cont. de Genève | Sue Williams  Paintings and Drawings |
| 24·10·97 - 11·01·98 | Zürich | Haus Konstruktive&Konkrete Kunst | Schweiz konstruktiv 1960-1997 |
| 24·10·97 - 25·01·98 | Zürich | Schweizerisches Landesmuseum | The Alamans |
| 24·10·97 - 08·02·98 | Zürich | M. Rietberg  -  Haus zum Kiel | Nainsukh   Indian Painter |
| Nov 97-Jan 98 | Basel - Basle | Kunstmuseum | A Special Guest |
| 06·11·97 - onwards | Vevey | Swiss Camera Museum | Dance  Serge Borner, Photographer |
| 07·11·97 - 04·01·98 | Zürich | Kunsthaus Zürich | Walter Bosshard |
| 20·11·97 - 04·01·98 | Genève - Geneva | Musée Ariana | Brunschwig Prize |
| 23·11·97 - 31·01·98 | Zug | Kunsthaus Zug | Kurt Seligmann |
| 23·11·97 - 08·02·98 | Zürich | M. Rietberg  - Villa Wesendonk | Indian Painting from Rajasthan |
| 29·11·97 - 04·01·98 | Aarau | Aargauer Kunsthaus Aarau | Annual Exhibition of Aargau Artists |
| 29·11·97 - 02·02·98 | Lugano | Museo Cantonale d'Arte | Fragile |
| 30·11·97 - 04·01·98 | Basel - Basle | Kunsthalle Basel | Annual Exhibition of Basle Artists |
| 30·11·97 - 11·01·98 | La Chaux-de-Fonds | Musée des Beaux-Arts | 63th Biennial Exhibition |
| Dec 97 onwards | Genève - Geneva | Musée d'Art et d'Histoire | Bernard Voita |
| Dec 97-Mar 97 | Davos | Kirchner Museum Davos | Karl Schmidt-Rottluff |
| 05·12·97 - 01·03·98 | Bern | Kunstmuseum Bern | The Blue Four |
| 23·01·98 - onwards | Zürich | Haus Konstruktive&Konkrete Kunst | Bill-Glarner-Graeser-Hinterreiter .... |
| 23·01·98 - 29·03·98 | Zürich | Haus Konstruktive&Konkrete Kunst | Richard Anuszkiewicz |
| Feb 98-Jun 98 | Bern | Bernisches Historisches Museum | One Man's Joy another Man's Misery |
| 01·03·98 - onwards | Solothurn | Kunstmuseum Solothurn | Art of the Steppe |
| 10·04·98 - 07·06·98 | Zürich | Haus Konstruktive&Konkrete Kunst | Tadaaki Kuwayama |

## ORDERING THE EUROPEAN MUSEUM GUIDE

**YES!** **I would like to order the European Museum Guide**

Name:.......................................................................................

Address:...................................................................................

Postalcode:..............................................................................

City:.........................................................................................

Country:...................................................................................

**Please indicate as relevant:**

☐  Please send me a copy of the current edition European Museum Guide '97-'98

☐  Please send me in april 1998 a copy of the next edition European Museum Guide '98-'99

**Price: $ 19,95  (including postage & packing)**

Payment by:   American Express / Eurocard / Mastercard / Access / Visa/ Diners

Card N°:...........................................

Expiration date:............................

Signature:......................................

## THE GUIDE AS A UNIQUE PRESENT

**Yes, I would like to give the European Museum Guide to someone as a special present.**

So please send:

☐  the current edition European Museum Guide '97-'98

☐  the following edition European Museum Guide '98-'99 in april 1998

**not to the above mentioned address, but to**

Name:.......................................................................................

Address:...................................................................................

Postalcode:..............................................................................

City:.........................................................................................

Country:...................................................................................

**Send this page in a sealed envelope to:**
Museum Media Publishers
Stationsstraat 28
P.O. Box 154
5260 AD  Vught
The Netherlands

Museum Media Publishers  P.O. Box 154  5260 AD  Vught  The Netherlands  Telephone +31 (0) 73 6840313  Fax +31 (0) 73 6569634
European Museum Guide '97-'98  **ISBN 90-75339-03-8**